D1566091

READINGS IN
THE HISTORY OF
ECONOMIC THEORY

Holt, Rinehart and Winston
SERIES IN ECONOMICS

Clark W. Reynolds, *Advisor*
Stanford University

William Breit and Harold M.
Hochman, *editors*

READINGS IN MICROECONOMICS

Douglas Needham, *editor*

READINGS IN THE ECONOMICS OF
INDUSTRIAL ORGANIZATION

Ingrid H. Rima, *editor*

READINGS IN THE HISTORY OF
ECONOMIC THEORY

READINGS IN
THE HISTORY OF
ECONOMIC THEORY

Edited by INGRID H. RIMA

Temple University

HOLT, RINEHART AND WINSTON, INC.

NEW YORK · CHICAGO · SAN FRANCISCO · ATLANTA · DALLAS
MONTREAL · TORONTO · LONDON · SYDNEY

1 2 3 4 5 6 7 8 9

Preface

Students of the history of economics generally have the opportunity to read at least portions of the great classics of the subject in the original instead of relying entirely on secondary sources. But they seldom have access to the kind of insight which is to be gotten from reinterpretations and commentaries on these works by contemporary contributors to the various journals. This substantial, often more provocative than the original, literature is studied scarcely at all. The assignment of journal articles is generally impractical even where library facilities are otherwise adequate. Needed journals are inevitably missing, in circulation, or being rebound. Photocopies are expensive and cumbersome to keep. This suggests the need for a well-selected collection of contemporary readings in the history of economic theory.

The present collection consists of recent journal articles which explore the development through time of the concepts and analytical tools which comprise the body of economic theory. These have been class-tested with advanced undergraduate and graduate groups in the history of economic theory as supplements to selections from economic classics and various standard texts. The decision to include a particular article was guided by several considerations which experience suggested as being important. Since the primary purpose of such readings is to supplement other materials, only articles whose substance has not largely been incorporated into secondary sources are included. In general, the more recent the article, the more likely it is to present a new controversy or comparison or offer a reinterpretation of a long established doctrine, sometimes utilizing current analytical tools and concepts. Repeated class use has helped to identify selections which are best avoided because they are concerned with details and refinements of interest only to the specialist, or are overly long, or abstruse in style. These are the guidelines which were followed in assembling this collection.

Experience also suggested that successful use of readings requires considerable direction. Well-prepared undergraduates are usually quite capable of reading journal articles if provided with an orientation that will guide them into the selection. This may be less essential for graduate readers, but it seems to facilitate a more rapid comprehension of the material and provide a basis for more sophisticated understanding. While it might be left to each instructor, it seems efficient, both from the standpoint of the teacher and the students, to preface selections with introductions which provide direction (but avoid the negative effect of summarization).

The order in which the articles are presented in this collection generally coincides with the chronology of the development of the subject matter in the history of economic theory. Most would lend themselves to being categorized with respect to subject matter as Pre-Classical, Classical, Marxian, Neoclassical or Marginalist, or Contemporary. However, several articles were selected precisely because they are broader in scope than the work of a particular writer or school. This facilitates examination of both the continuity of ideas and the evolution of concepts in the history of economic theory.

Specifically, the article "Alternative Theories of Distribution" by Nicholas Kaldor provides not only a comparison and overview of the Classical, Marxian, and Marginalist theories of distribution, but also adapts Keynesian macroeconomic concepts to facilitate their use to explain the determination of income shares; a problem with which Keynes concerned himself not at all. Similarly, "Classic and Current Notions of Measurable Utility" examines the von Neuman and Morgenstern technique of measuring utility in situations of risk and compares it conceptually and technically with older notions of cardinal utility. Adolph Lowe's "The Classical Theory of Economic Growth" may be used to round out an inquiry into classical economics or alternatively, if a course is planned to extend as far as modern growth theory, be postponed until students have a familiarity with contemporary growth models. The article "Mr. Keynes and Mr. Marx" by S. S. Alexander is as appropriate in conjunction with an examination of Marxian theory as it is with Keynesian theory.

The two concluding articles, "Economists and the History of Ideas" by Paul Samuelson and "The Influence of Events and Policies on Economic Theory" by George Stigler are general in another sense. Both explore the kinds of factors which have influenced economic theories and the individuals and schools responsible for their evolution from the earliest beginnings of the discipline to the present. As such they are an appropriate capstone to a collection of readings in the history of economic theory.

Philadelphia, Pennsylvania   Ingrid H. Rima

December 1969

Contents

READINGS IN
THE HISTORY OF
ECONOMIC THEORY

1 Aristotle and Hesiod:
The Economic Problem
in Greek Thought
BARRY GORDON

The search for explanation in the realm of economic phenomena and behavior began relatively late in the history of human inquiry. The speculative activities of the thinkers of the ancient world were primarily concerned with ethics, religion, and politics. Natural phenomena were also of interest to them, but there was neither opportunity nor necessity for economic analysis. The nature of institutional arrangements and the physical environment within which material needs were satisfied were among the reasons for the absence of economic analysis. Consuming units—such as the *oikos*, the latifundium, and the manor—were typically self-sustaining. The goods society required were produced according to time-honored methods and distributed for consumption as dictated by custom or the regulations of the ruling authority. While the pattern differed from one ancient society to the next, all shared two characteristics: Decision-making about economic activities was outside the scope of individual action, and society was not yet oriented to thinking in terms of the ever-expanding abundance of physical goods that later technical skills, organization, and capital accumulation were to make possible.

Philosophical attitudes and the *Weltanschauung* of those whose written and spoken words were influential also impeded speculation about economic phenomena. Indeed, there were relatively few economic phenomena requiring explanation, because provision of material goods was not regarded as a high-priority objective for man to pursue. The "good life" was identified with nonmaterial goals rather than personal acquisition. In short, the attitudinal, physical, and institutional environments were not conducive to extending the occurrence of economic phenomena and behavior, or seeking explanations for them. To the extent that ancient and medieval thinkers engaged in economic inquiry at all, they conducted their discussions within the framework of the body politic and the ethical and religious principles which guided it.

Aristotle's concern with distributive and commutative justice is a case in point. He believed that the wellbeing of individual citizens could not be served in the absence of justice. Distributive justice was concerned with the allocation of responsibility to particular persons or classes, and with the criteria by which honors, income, and wealth were

Reprinted from Barry J. Gordon, "Aristotle and Hesiod: The Economic Problem in Greek Thought," from the *Review of Social Economy*, Vol. XXI, No. 2, September 1963, pp. 147–156. Dr. Gordon is Associate Professor of Economics at the University of Newcastle, New South Wales, Australia.

to be distributed. Commutative justice was concerned with equity in transactions among individuals. Its requirements were satisfied by the exchange of equivalents. If the ratio of exchange between goods reflected an exchange of equivalents, it was consistent with the principles of commutative justice, because each party to the exchange then received what was due him. Thus, the exchange of economic goods in the market place was, for Aristotle, merely one aspect of the broader, predominantly ethical problem of achieving the "good life."

While the Aristotelian view of economic activity is generally thought to be universally representative of ancient Greek thought, Barry Gordon's article, "Aristotle and Hesiod: The Economic Problem in Greek Thought," maintains that other less-well-known Greek thinkers, among them Hesiod, had a conception of the economic problem which is essentially consistent with modern statements. The parallel Gordon draws between Hesiod's view and that of contemporary economic writers poses the ever-provocative question of whether the essential concern of economics is to achieve given ends by determining what is the appropriate allocation of resources, or whether it is also to determine the ends toward which the body social ought to strive.

In almost every treatment of the development of economic doctrine, deference is paid to the early contributions of Plato and especially, Aristotle. A standard example of the prevailing view is provided by the following statement from the admirable and widely-read text by Professor Roll,

> If Plato was the first of a long line of reformers, his pupil Aristotle was the first analytical economist; . . . It was he who laid the foundations of science and who first posed the economic problems with which all later thinkers have been concerned.[1]

It is the purpose of this paper to suggest that this prevailing view concerning Aristotle's position is quite misleading. Aristotle's vision of the economic problem differs markedly from certain more recent views of wide currency. Further, there is at least one extant Greek discussion of the economic problem which precedes Aristotle, and which provides a striking anticipation of a predominant modern viewpoint.

These points call for some reassessment of the conventional treatment of the progress of economic thought. It would seem that the continuing dominance of Aristotle after his rediscovery by the West, may have been instrumental in turning the attention of thinkers from insights which provided possible alternate points of departure for economic speculation, even be-

fore the dawn of the modern mercantilist era.

Again, a comparison of the Aristotelian view of economic activity with other Greek views possessing modern parallels, indicates some necessity for a re-examination of the scope of much current economic theorising. Aristotle's approach seeks to emphasize questions which are pushed to the margin by many modern theorists, while the latter's central concerns he de-emphasises as secondary issues of a technological or "engineering" nature.

Perhaps the clearest Greek assessment of the economic problem as it is widely understood by many economists at present, is to be found in the pre-Aristotelian manuscript by Hesiod. . . .

> *The Works and Days.* This relatively short work contains a well-conceived examination of the problems of scarcity, choice and allocation of resources at the micro-economic level, and seeks to emphasize the centrality of these issues for human well-being.[2]

In contrast with the sophistication and urban orientation of Plato and Aristotle, Hesiod emerges in the course of his poem as a toiling farmer, eking out a rough and precarious existence on the rather inhos-

---

[1] E. Roll, *A History of Economic Thought* (London: Faber and Faber, 1961), p. 31.

[2] Cf. K. Singer, "Oikonomia: An inquiry into beginnings of economic thought and language," *Kyklos,* Vol. XI, 1958, p. 33.

pitable slopes of Mount Helicon. His general goal is quite simple. It is to ". . . find a way to pay your debts and avoid hunger."[3] This end is achieved only through persevering manual labour. Thus, against the Philosophers' reservations concerning manual labour especially when undertaken for economic gain, there is Hesiod's dictum, "Work is no disgrace; it is idleness which is a disgrace."[4]

The conception of the economic problem outlined by the Poet is best appreciated with reference to the well-known views of Lord Robbins. In fact Hesiod's version of the essential factors involved must be accredited as a striking anticipation of this later presentation. Hence, at the risk of unwarranted repetition, we recall the statement that,

> Economics is the science which studies human behaviour as a relationship between ends and scarce means which have alternative uses.[5]

and again,

> From the point of view of the economist, the conditions of human existence, exhibit four fundamental characteristics. The ends are various. The time and the means for achieving these ends are limited and capable of alternative application. At the same time the ends have different importance.[6]

For Hesiod, human existence is dominated by ends, which are summarised as the attainment of "ease and peace" such as existed in the Golden Age, when men, ". . . lived like gods without sorrow of heart, remote and free from toil and grief; miserable age rested not on them; but with legs and arms never failing they made merry with feasting beyond the reach of all evils."[7] But these ends are inevitably not

realised in full. The situation is quite the reverse and the present race of men, ". . . is a race of iron, and men never rest from labour and sorrow by day and from perishing by night."[8]

To explain this contradiction Hesiod introduces the notion of scarcity of resources —". . . the gods keep hidden from men the means of life."[9] This is the central phenomenon which he believes requires explanation, and he enters into lengthy accounts of how the limitation of means has arisen. Two specific answers are given. One is in terms of the well-known myth of Pandora's Box. The other is the theory of a regression of the human creations of the gods through five races of mortals.[10]

Having in this fashion outlined the economic problem, stressed its universal urgency, and explained its origins, Hesiod also examines the behaviour it necessitates. Certain choices are to be made, and labour, time and materials need to be allocated efficiently.

In the first place, he disposes of the moral issues involved and argues at some length against unjust methods of solving the ends-means contradiction. He invokes the wrath of the gods as well as demonstrating the worldly wisdom of the just course. Excluding injustice then, the problem is only to be overcome by work. Thus, "If your heart within you desires wealth, do these things and work with work upon work."[11] He does not enter like Plato and Aristotle into the erection of ideal city structures embodying their principles of justice, in order to solve the difficulty. Rather, he turns to concentrate on the ordering of the life of a small isolated farm as an efficient production unit.

The particular set of allocation questions

---

[3] Hesiod, *The Homeric Hymns and the Homerica* (trans. H. G. Evelyn-White) (London: Heinemann, 1954), p. 33.
[4] Op. cit., p. 27.
[5] L. Robbins, *An Essay on the Nature and Significance of Economic Science* (London: Macmillan, 1952), p. 16.
[6] Op. cit., p. 12.
[7] Hesiod, op. cit., p. 11.

[8] Op. cit., p. 15.
[9] Op. cit., p. 5.
[10] Cf. Lord Robbins' illustrative reference to the Eden story. Op. cit., p. 15. "We have been turned out of Paradise. We have neither eternal life nor unlimited means of gratification."
[11] Hesiod, op. cit., p. 15.

which receives a major part of his attention is choice between work and leisure. He believes that there is an innate desire for the god-like state of leisure, but in his analysis he isolates three main factors which induce men to choose work.

The first factor is basic, material need ". . . work . . . that Hunger may hate you, and venerable Demeter richly crowned may love you and fill your barn with food; for Hunger is altogether a meet comrade for the sluggard." [12]

The second is fear of social disapprobation—". . . an evil shame is the needy man's companion, shame which both greatly harms and prospers men; shame is with poverty, but confidence with wealth." [13] A third, associated inducement is the desire to emulate the consumption habits of those in one's immediate social grouping—". . . ; for a man grows eager to work when he considers his neighbour a rich man who hastens to plough and plant and put his house in good order; and neighbour vies with his neighbour as he hurries after wealth." [14]

Further, he notes that emulation leads to the development of the spirit of competition in work (ἀγαθὴ δ' ῎Ερις ἥδε = this is good strife). Competition is viewed as a fundamental drive that helps relieve the scarcity problem. Thus,

> This Strife is wholesome for men, and potter is angry with potter, and craftsman with craftsman, and beggar is jealous of beggar, and minstrel of minstrel." [15]

It would seem that all advocates of laissez-faire are at liberty to trace at least part of their intellectual heritage as far as Hesiod.

While the Poet's analysis of work-leisure choice is carried out in the general terms just described, his lengthy discussion of other allocation problems proceeds at a particular level. This latter holds some interest for the historian, but unfortunately, there is no attempt at significant generalisations of analytical interest. The world of the small subsistence farm is discussed in considerable detail, but of its very nature the examination is essentially technical. However, this section of the manuscript is prefaced by a series of general observations, one of which represents a further important insight relevant to his exposition of scarcity and allocation.

Although he continually stresses the urgency of the economic problem he indicates that he recognises that it is not without limits. One limit is of course, abundance. The other is extreme dearth. Hence, in providing general instructions on how best to use the stock of goods available over time he suggests,

> Take your fill when the cask is first opened, but midways be sparing; it is poor saving when you come to the lees.[16]

It is "midways" then that questions of apportioning the stock are of importance. Economic behavior in the sense of allocative activity is not particularly prominent at the extremes of those groups who regard themselves as having either a great deal or a very little in terms of their wants. It is in those situations where wants and means are more nearly balanced that economic behaviour attains a major significance, and, presumably, economic science flourishes.

In summary then, Hesiod's vision of the economic problem is seen to agree strikingly with certain recent views. Multiplicity of ends in the face of limited means gives rise to allocative behaviour, and it is this latter which is the proper study of the science.

Before turning to examine Aristotle's position, it is important to note at least

[12] Op. cit., p. 25.
[13] Op. cit., p. 27.
[14] Op. cit., p. 5.
[15] Loc. cit.
[16] Op. cit., p. 31.

one additional approach to the economic problem which may have existed in Greek thought.

In a recent provocative work, E. A. Havelock professes to have uncovered a Greek "liberal" tradition which, over time, has been buried beneath the weight of interest and prestige accumulating about the works of Plato and Aristotle. He groups figures like Democritus, Protagoras, Antiphon and "their successors in the fourth century," and suggests that they represent a non-Platonic tradition of social and moral thought which is built on "the anthropologies of the pre-Socratics." Traces of these latter he finds in the works of Aeschylus, Sophocles, Euripides, and the historian Diodorus Siculus.

Havelock ascribes to these figures an attitude to economic processes which would seem to bear a strong affinity with what is understood as the mercantilist view point. He states,

> What is at least clear is that the liberals envisaged the production of material wealth as a proper goal of community, and that they could abstract goods and services as a significant factor in human life and that they traced a parallel between increasing integration in community and increasing production of wealth.
>
> Their firm grasp of the theoretical important of these insights is shown by the fact that they were ready to admit them as the material of a new discipline—that of "wealth-making" or "economy" (crematistike, oikonomike); an applied science historically invented, in the manner of all the technologies, and employing currency as its finite tool.[17]

This is a most interesting departure which endeavours to show that certain central and generally accepted ideas concerning the development of Greek political and economic thought are quite false. Aristotle is painted as the arch-enemy of economic science, and as the possessor of, ". . . a mind that never really understood

what currency was, and what its possibilities and limitations were and what the liberal analysis meant."[18] He disliked ". . . this prospect of indefinite increase of real wealth."[19] His "primitivism and ruralism" is seen as a dead weight which inhibited the thinkers of Rome and the Middle Ages, such that any tendencies for economic analysis to develop were thwarted.

Even if one accepts the existence of a coherent Greek "liberal" tradition, Havelock's strictures concerning Aristotle are too severe. There are two positive errors in Aristotle's economic analysis. The first is his failure to grasp the role of money as capital. Hence he condemns all interest-taking as unjustified. The second is his failure (unlike Plato) to perceive the process of distribution as a distinct function within economic life which involves a certain type of extension of the division of labour. Thus, we find his condemnation of retail trade and his overdrawn distinction between "oikonomia" (household economy) and "chrematismos" (wealth making). Such failures do not, in themselves, make Aristotle an opponent of economic analysis.

The value of Havelock's analysis lies in emphasising the fact that Aristotle and Plato did not understand the economic problem in mercantilist terms. The central problem in mercantilist doctrine is to increase the aggregate product of the nation while welding the nation into "an economy." This is clearly not the dominant concern of the Philosophers. Thus, for example, when Plato examines the extension of division of labour, or advocates an internal currency of a different type from the international trading currency, he is not moved by national economic policy considerations. Rather, he is directly concerned with the effects of these measures, on the well-being of the individuals involved.

---

[17] E. A. Havelock, *The Liberal Temper in Greek Politics* (London: Jonathan Cape, 1957), pp. 386–7.

[18] Op. cit., p. 364.
[19] Loc. cit.

Having examined the existence of one, and possibly two, modern conceptions of the economic problem in Greek thought, it is possible to introduce Aristotle's approach as involving a rather different vision.

Hesiod's concern with the allocation of scarce means, stands at the margin of Aristotle's schema. The mercantilist desire to enquire into the means of increasing the aggregate product of the region is even further from the Philosopher's locus of interest. For Aristotle, economics is chiefly concerned with the ordering of human purpose and function within the two dominant economic units of his day—the household and the state. The economic problem is essentially a problem of the disposition of ends. The predominant study for economic analysis is the examination of certain sets of human aims and attitudes, not the ordering of means.

Hence in the *Politica* we read, "Thus it is clear that household management attends more to men than to the acquisition of inanimate things, and to human excellence more than to the excellence of property which we call wealth. . . ." [20]

Again, he is explicit,

> . . . the art of household management is not identical with the art of getting wealth, for the one uses the material which the other provides.[21]

However, the multiplication and allocation of means is not entirely excluded. As Dr. Kurt Singer has pointed out in a penetrating study, Aristotle had before him the actual example of Pericles who practised, ". . . a rational and systematic ordering of the whole of household affairs following broad principles and ruthlessly applying logic to the details formerly left to tradition, routine and chance." [22] In the face of

this reality, concern with the allocation of resources could not readily be excluded altogether from the economists' range of interests. Hence, Aristotle writes,

> Of the art of acquisition then, there is one kind which by nature is a part of the management of a household, in so far as the art of household management must either find ready to hand, or itself provide, such things necessary to life, and useful for the community of the family or state, as can be stored.[23]

For Aristotle economics is predominantly concerned with the question of selecting the end or aim to be satisfied, given the availability of certain means. A related, though subsidiary problem is the question of selecting the means, given the existence of certain ends.

This view of the scope of economic thought and activity stems from the Philosopher's theories of value and wealth, and from his overriding concern with what he takes to be the central problem of human thought and action, the nature of the happy life. Concerning this latter problem, his view is that the multiplication and efficient allocation of possessions comprise necessary but not sufficient elements in the solution of difficulties imposed by scarcity. He writes,

> A good man may make the best even of poverty and disease, and the other ills of life; but he can only attain happiness, under the opposite conditions (. . .). This makes men fancy that external goods are the cause of happiness, yet we might as well say that a brilliant performance on the lyre was to be attributed to the instrument and not to the skill of the performer.[24]

On this view, it is pointless to examine the means of increasing one's possessions quite independently of the analysis of the appropriate attitudes which enable the individual to direct those possessions to the maintenance of his own happiness. The

[20] W. D. Ross (Ed.) *The Works of Aristotle,* Vol. X, *Politica* (London: Oxford University Press, 1921), p. 1259b20.

[21] Op. cit., p. 1256a10.

[22] K. Singer, op. cit., p. 47.

[23] W. D. Ross (Ed.), op. cit., p. 1256b25.

[24] Op. cit., p. 1332a20.

scarcity problem may be solved as readily by a shift in attitudes and ends, as by a reallocation or multiplication of available means.

On value, it is well recognised that by and large, Aristotle adopts a "utility" approach (despite some overtones which hint at a labour or a cost of production theory). Utility is not seen as a quality or property inhering in goods, but as a reflex of the attitudes of persons. Further, he continues this emphasis on the relativity of economic quantities to ends, in his discussion of wealth. At the commencement of the *Ethica Nicomachea* he states that the object of economics is wealth, in the sense that the object of medicine is health.[25] Then, in the extensive discussion of the *Politica* he adopts the position that wealth is a meaningful term only when defined in the context of a pre-determined set of ends.[26] It is impossible to analyse increasing or decreasing wealth without examining the nature of the ends involved. To take ends as unexamined "givens" is to grossly inhibit economic analysis. If one is to investigate the scarcity problem, the crucial task is to consider the disposition of aims and goals, which render the problem amenable of solution in any given context of social structure and productive organisation. Aristotle does not even contemplate resting in the naive generalisation that ends are unlimited, as do Hesiod and some modern economists.

In seeking to explain the bases of Aristotle's adoption of this particular view of the scope of economics, it may be important to refer to a further factor which is not explicitly involved in the logic of his position. For the Philosopher, the economic problem is essentially a question of the disposition of ends, so that scarcity difficulties are overcome not so much by multiplying or judiciously allocating means, but by reorienting human demands. This emphasis is understandable in terms of certain notions prevailing at the time, and some remarks of Oswald Spengler are relevant. He suggests, "The word that stands in the classical vocabulary where 'personality' stands in our own is 'persona'—namely, role or mask. In late Greek or Roman speech it means 'the public aspect and mien' of man, which for classical man is tantamount to the essence and kernel of him. . . . What is indicated is not the personality (that is, an unfolding of inward possibilities in active striving) but a permanent and self-contained posture strictly adapted to the so-to-say plastic ideal of being. It is only in the Classical ethic that Beauty plays a distinct role. However labeled—as σωφροσύνη, χαλοχἀγαθία or ἀταραξία it always amounts to the well-ordered group of tangible and publicly evident traits, defined for other men rather than specific to one's self. A man was the object and not the subject of outward life." [27]

If he is essentially the object of outward life, it is understandable then that man will be seen as solving the clash of personal ends and limited objective means by adjusting those ends in terms of socially derived goals. The economic problem is solved mainly by accommodating oneself to the objective data provided by the means available, and is largely a matter of personal attitudes and social relationships. The availability and disposition of physical resources are seen as secondary matters which it is a waste of time to discuss in isolation from the central type of adjustment.

---

[25] W. D. Ross, op. cit., Vol. IX, *Ethica Nichomachea* (London: Oxford University Press, 1915), p. 1094a5.

[26] Hence, we find Aristotle referring to ". . . riches of the spurious kind," and he states that ". . . riches may be defined as a number of instruments to be used in a household or in a state." W. D. Ross, op. cit., Vol. X, p. 1265b35. It is clear then, that he sees questions concerning the appropriate institutional and social organisation as the key problems in economic studies.

[27] O. Spengler, *The Decline of the West*, Vol. I (London: Allen and Unwin, 1954), pp. 316–317.

Despite the almost inevitable limitations of a given social setting, Aristotle's approach to economic thought might be considered as a valuable corrective to certain predominant trends of recent decades in the limitation of the range of economists' interests. There has been a tendency to wish to confine economics to the type of technical resource-allocation problems which were predominant for Hesiod. On the other hand, certain influential writers have adopted views similar to those of Aristotle. Hence, there is a striking re-echo of the Philosopher's views in Max Weber's statement that:

Economic action is primarily oriented to the problem of choosing the end to which a thing shall be applied; technology, to the problem, given the end, of choosing the appropriate means.[28]

If the Aristotle-Weber approach is accorded some recognition economics may remain a broadly-based study of human behaviour in certain of its significant aspects. If this vision is rejected, then economics as a discipline may be confined to the role of a competing technology. Even a casual survey of current issues of journals reveals that the investigation of engineering problems is increasingly coming to be construed as providing a comprehensive answer to issues requiring a less exclusive treatment.

[28] M. Weber, *The Theory of Social and Economic Organisation* (Glencoe: The Free Press, 1947), p. 162.

2   The Concept
of the Just Price: Theory
and Economic Policy

RAYMOND DE ROOVER

The similarities between the economics of the scholastics and the economics of Aristotle reflect the extent to which medieval scholars were influenced by Aristotelian ideas which came into Christian Europe through Jewish and Arabic sources, during the latter years of the twelfth century. Though the initial reaction of the Church was one of condemnation, Thomas Aquinas, the greatest of the Mendicant teachers, saw the wisdom of harmonizing and adopting Aristotle's ideas to Christian beliefs. The essence of the Thomist synthesis of philosophy and theology is that society, like the universe, is an integrated system in which God, nature, and man each has its due place. The "good life" requires a society in which there is a mutual exchange of services and functions within a hierarchy in which each class, priest, artisan, and farmer performs its own proper work in accordance with the laws of God and nature.

In Thomas' view, as in Aristotle's, it is essential that human affairs be conducted in consonance with the principle of justice. All interpersonal relationships, among them the exchange of goods and services, raise questions of commutative justice. Since these relationships are contractual, the principal problem which presented itself to the medieval mind, whose legalistic bent reflected the influence of Roman law, was to determine whether or not natural law had been properly applied in civil contracts. Thus, economics was not a separate discipline for the schoolmen, any more than it was for Aristotle, and the economic principles they set forth were part of a larger set of ethical and legal principles.

The principle economic questions to which the scholastics addressed themselves had to do with just price, monopoly, and usury. That their writings on these subjects continue to provide provocative material for study and reinterpretation is evident from articles like the one that follows. In "The Concept of the Just Price: Theory and Economic Policy," Raymond de Roover argues that the prescriptions for ethical economic behavior found in the writings of the scholastics reflect an awareness of the realities of the marketplace that is not generally appreciated. He maintains that many medieval thinkers

Reprinted from Raymond de Roover, "The Concept of Just Price: Theory and Economic Policy," from *The Journal of Economic History,* Vol. XVIII, No. 4, December 1958, pp. 418–434. Dr. de Roover is Professor of History, Brooklyn College, and The Graduate Center at The City University of New York.

conceived of the just price as the competitive marketprice. His evidence casts doubt on the more usual interpretation of the just price as one which will enable a seller to maintain his status in society.

In the view of many economists the just price is a nebulous concept invented by pious monks who knew nothing of business or economics and were blissfully unaware of market mechanisms. It is true that certain writers, Catholics and non-Catholics alike, have done their best to accredit this fairy tale and to propagate the notion that the just price, instead of being set by the allegedly blind and unconscionable forces of the market, was determined by criteria of fairness without regard to the elements of supply and demand or at least with the purpose of eliminating the evils of unrestrained competition.

According to a widespread belief—found in nearly all books dealing with the subject—the just price was linked to the medieval concept of a social hierarchy and corresponded to a reasonable charge which would enable the producer to live and to support his family on a scale suitable to his station in life.[1] This doctrine is generally thought to have found its practical application in the guild system. For this purpose the guilds are presented as welfare agencies which prevented unfair competition, protected consumers against deceit and exploitation, created equal opportunities for their members, and secured for them a modest but decent living in keeping with traditional standards.[2] One of the main champions of this idyllic view is Max Weber (1864–1920), who describes the guilds as at least originally founded on the subsistence principle (*Nahrungsprinzip*) and as following a livelihood policy by regulating output, technique, quality, and prices.[3] Another German economist, Werner Sombart (1863–1941), goes even further: according to him, not only the medieval craftsmen but even the merchants strove only to gain a livelihood befitting their rank in society and did not seek to accumulate wealth or to climb the social ladder. This attitude, he claims, was rooted in the concept of the just price "which dominated the entire period of the Middle Ages." In support of this statement Sombart refers to the writings of Henry of Langenstein, the Elder (1325–1397).[4]

This is a clue. Indeed, Heinrich von Langenstein states that if the public authorities fail to fix a price, the producer may set it himself, but he should not charge more for his labor and expenses than would enable him to maintain his status (. . . *per*

---

[1] William Ashley, *An Introduction to English Economic History and Theory* (4th ed.; 2 vols.; London: Longmans, Green, 1920), I, Part II, 391; John M. Clark, *The Social Control of Business* (2d ed.; New York: McGraw-Hill Book Co., 1939), pp. 23–24; Shepard B. Clough and Charles W. Cole, *Economic History of Europe* (rev. ed.; Boston: D. C. Heath, 1946), pp. 31, 68; George Clune, *The Medieval Gild System* (Dublin: Browne and Nolan, 1943), p. 55; Alfred de Tarde, *L'idée du juste prix* (Paris: Félix Alcan, 1907), pp. 42–43; Joseph Dorfman, *The Economic Mind in American Civilization* (3 vols.; New York: Viking Press, 1946–49), I, 5; N. S. B. Gras, *Business and Capitalism* (New York: Crofts, 1939), pp. 122–23; Herbert Heaton, *Economic History of Europe* (1st ed.; New York: Harper, 1936), p. 204; George O'Brien, *An Essay on Medieval Economic Teaching* (London: Longmans, Green, 1920), pp. 111–12; Leo S. Schumacher, *The Philosophy of the Equitable Distribution of Wealth* (Washington, D.C.: The Catholic University of America, 1949), p. 47; James Westfall Thompson, *An Economic and Social History of the Middle Ages, 300–1300* (New York: Century Co., 1928), p. 697. This list is by no means exhaustive.

[2] For example, Arthur J. Penty, *A Guildman's Interpretation of History* (New York: Sunrise Turn, n.d.), pp. 38–46.

[3] Max Weber, *General Economic History*, translated by Frank H. Knight (London: Allen & Unwin, n.d.), pp. 138–43. The author recognizes that the guilds, in the course of time, tended to become monopolistic organizations.

[4] Werner Sombart, *Der moderne Kapitalismus* (2d rev. ed.; Munich: Duncker & Humblot, 1916), I, 292–93.

quanto res suas vendendo statum suum con-
tinuare possit).[5] And if he does charge more
in order to enrich himself or to improve his
station, he commits the sin of avarice. Sombart is by no means the first to cite this
text. In so far as I have been able to discover, it was first mentioned by Wilhelm
Roscher (1817–1894) in 1874.[6] Since it fitted in so well with prevailing preconceptions, it was regarded as a characteristic
formulation of the scholastic doctrine of the
just price and copied by one author after
another, including Rudolf Kaulla,[7] Sir
William Ashley,[8] R. H. Tawney,[9] and
Amintore Fanfani,[10] to mention only a few
among the most prominent. Thus Langenstein's text exerted enormous influence. It
was used as historical justification for the
theory of the living wage and was given
wide currency by the supporters of guild
socialism, who expected to cure the ills of
modern industrialism by resurrecting the
medieval guilds. In a subtle way Langenstein was even drafted in defense of the
corporate state.

As a matter of fact, Langenstein enjoys
such popularity that economic historians
usually take his statement as typical of the
scholastic doctrine on the just price.[11] I
question very much whether there is the
slightest justification for according him so
much credit and for considering his statement as authoritative and representative.
Langenstein was not one of the giants in
medieval philosophy but a relatively minor
figure. Like his master, Buridan (d. after
1358), he was a nominalist and a follower
of William of Ockham (ca. 1300–1349),
whose doctrines were tainted with heresy
and were opposed both by the Scotists and
the Thomists. As a disciple of Ockham,
Langenstein stood more or less outside the
main current of scholastic thought.[12] What
applies to philosophy applies also to economics. Langenstein's value and price
theory was strongly influenced by Buridan's and also emphasized psychological
and individual factors as price determinants. I have found that Langenstein is
rarely cited by later scholastic authors, a
sure indication that his writings did not
carry much weight. His influence may have
been greater, however, in central and east-
ern Europe, where the leading universities
(Vienna, Prague, and Cracow) around 1400
were strongholds of nominalism. It is quite
possible that Langenstein inspired such
men as Matthew of Cracow (d. 1397) who,
I have been told by Paul Czartoryski, also
wrote on economic questions. In any case,
the prestige which Langenstein enjoys to-

---

[5] Heinrich von Langenstein, also called Henricus
de Hassia (Hesse), *Tractatus bipartitus de contractibus emptionis et venditionis*, Part I, cap. 12,
published in Johannes Gerson, *Opera omnia*, IV
(Cologne, 1484), fol. 191. No more recent edition
is available. Langenstein's treatise was omitted
from later editions of Gerson. The most detailed
study of Langenstein's economic ideas is in Manuel Rocha, *Travail et salaire à travers la scolas-
tique* (2d ed.; Paris: Desclée de Brouwer, 1933),
pp. 21–48, esp. p. 44. Cf. Edmund Schreiber, *Die
volkswirtschaftlichen Anschauungen der Scholastik
seit Thomas v. Aquin* (Jena: Gustav Fischer,
1913), pp. 196–202.

[6] *Geschichte der National-Oekonomik in
Deutschland* (Munich, 1874), pp. 19–20.

[7] "Die Lehre vom gerechten Preis in der Scholastik," *Zeitschrift für die gesamte Staatswissen-
schaft*, LX (1904), 598 ff., and *Theory of the Just
Price* (London: Allen and Unwin, 1940), p. 44.

[8] *English Economic History*, I, Part II, 391 and
474, n. 45. The reference is to Roscher.

[9] *Religion and the Rise of Capitalism* (rev. ed.;
New York: Harcourt, Brace, and Co., 1937), pp.
41–42 and 295, n. 56.

[10] *Le origini dello spirito capitalistico in Italia*
(Milan: Vita e Pensiero, 1933), p. 7. He also
refers to Sombart.

[11] This observation is made by Bernard W.
Dempsey, S.J., "The Economic Philosophy of St.
Thomas," in Robert E. Brennan, ed., *Essays in
Thomism* (New York: Sheed and Ward, 1942),
p. 250.

[12] Maurice De Wulf, *Histoire de la philosophie
médiévale* (5th ed.; 2 vols.; Paris: Félix Alcan,
1924–25), II, 191. Cf. Joseph Höffner, *Statik und
Dynamik in der scholastischen Wirtschaftsethik*
(Cologne: Westdeutscherverlag, 1955), pp. 19–22.
This author points out that the idea of social
status and the subsistence principle was stressed
by the nominalists and not by their opponents,
the Thomists.

day among economic historians is due to the mere chance that his pronouncements on the just price were put into circulation and hailed as oracles by the German economists of the historical school and their English followers.

The purpose of this paper is to demonstrate that the generally accepted definition of the just price is wrong and rests on misinterpretation of the scholastic position on the matter. According to the majority of the doctors, the just price did not correspond to cost of production as determined by the producer's social status, but was simply the current market price, with this important reservation: in cases of collusion or emergency, the public authorities retained the right to interfere and to impose a fair price.[13] In order to straighten out the existing confusion, it will also be shown how this doctrine was translated into policy, particularly in connection with the guilds.

For the inception of the scholastic doctrine of the just price, one of the fundamental texts is the canon *Placuit*, which is really a capitulary issued in 884 by Karloman, King of France,[14] but incorporated by Raymond of Pennaforte (1180–1278) in the canon law.[15] This canon states that parish priests should admonish their flocks not to charge wayfarers more than the price obtainable in the local market (*quam in mercato vendere possint*). Otherwise, the wayfarers can complain to the priest, who is then required to set a price with "humanity." This text, it seems to me, clearly equates just price with market price

and does not lend itself to a different interpretation.

In the works of Albertus Magnus (1193–1280) and especially in those of Thomas Aquinas (1226–1274), the passages relating to price are so scattered and seemingly so conflicting that they have given rise to varying interpretations. By selecting only those passages favorable to their thesis, certain writers even reached the conclusion that Albertus Magnus and Thomas Aquinas had a labor theory of value and adumbrated Karl Marx (1818–1883).[16] To prove their point these writers used chiefly the comments of the two theologians on Aristotle's *Nicomachean Ethics*, where it is stated that commutative or contractual justice requires strict equivalence between what is received and what is given and that any exchange violating this rule is unfair. This is then construed in a Marxian sense as meaning that price, to be just, should always correspond to cost, which in the Middle Ages was chiefly labor cost.[17] The trouble is that such an explanation contradicts statements made elsewhere by Albertus Magnus and Thomas Aquinas. Moreover, the texts in question are open to another interpretation which would do away with any inconsistency. In their comments on Aristotle both Albertus and Aquinas insist that arts and crafts would be doomed to destruction if the producer did not recover his outlays in the sale of his product.[18] In other words, the market

---

[13] The same point of view is represented by Joseph Höffner (note 12) and by John T. Noonan, Jr., *The Scholastic Analysis of Usury* (Cambridge: Harvard University Press, 1957), p. 86.

[14] Alfredius Boretius and Victor Krause, eds., *Capitularia Regum Francorum* (Monumenta Germaniae Historica, Legum, Sec. II, Hanover, 1892), 375. This capitulary found its way into the canon law through the collections of Burchard of Worms and Yvo of Chartres.

[15] *Corpus juris canonici, Decretales: in X*, III, 17, 1.

[16] The main exponent of this thesis is Selma Hagenauer, *Das "justum pretium" bei Thomas von Aquino* (Stuttgart: W. Kohlhammer, 1931). Cf. Tawney, *Religion*, p. 36.

[17] As a matter of fact, Aquinas comes close to saying that any exchange of two commodities should be based on the ratio between the amounts of labor expended on each. Thomas Aquinas, *Commentaria in X libros ethicorum ad Nicomachum*, lib. V, lect. 7, 8, 9 (Parma edition of *Opera omnia*, XXI, 168, 171, 172).

[18] Albertus Magnus, *Liber V ethicorum*, tract. 2, cap. 7, No. 28, in his *Opera omnia* (Paris, 1891), VII, 353; Aquinas, *Comment. in X libros ethicorum*, lib. V, lect. 7, 8.

price could not fall permanently below cost. If so, there is no contradiction, since the market price would then tend to coincide with cost or to oscillate around this point like the swing of a pendulum. Besides, Thomas Aquinas himself recognizes that the just price cannot be determined with precision, but can vary within a certain range, so that minor deviations do not involve any injustice.[19] This second interpretation, of course, is not in accord with Marxian dialectics; but it agrees with classical and neoclassical economic analysis. It is also consonant with the later development of scholastic thought.

Whatever the meaning of these obscure passages, Albertus Magnus and Thomas Aquinas are more explicit, if less analytical, in other works where they give their own opinions and do not try to elucidate Aristotle's. The first, in his comments on the *Sentences* of Peter Lombard, defines the just price as follows: What goods are worth according to the estimation of the market (*secundum aestimationem fori*) at the time of the sale.[20] Thomas Aquinas nowhere puts the matter so clearly, but he tells the story of a merchant who brings wheat to a country where there is dearth and knows that others are following with more. May this merchant, Aquinas asks, sell his wheat at the prevailing price (*pretium quod invenit*) or should he announce the arrival of fresh supplies and thus cause the price to fall? The answer is that he may sell his wheat at the current price without infringing the rules of justice, although, Aquinas adds almost as an afterthought, he would act more virtuously by notifying the buyers. In my opinion this passage destroys

with a single blow the thesis of those who try to make Aquinas into a Marxist, and proves beyond doubt that he considered the market price as just.[21]

This interpretation, moreover, agrees with that of Cardinal Cajetan (1468–1534), the authoritative commentator on the *Summa*. In connection with question 77 *secunda secundae*, which deals with the sales contract, he concludes that according to Aquinas the just price is "the one, which at a given time, can be gotten from the buyers, assuming common knowledge and in the absence of all fraud and coercion." [22] He then goes on to describe the market mechanism and to show how prices rise or fall in response to changes in demand or supply.

Those who say Thomas Aquinas favored cost of production rather than market valuation as the criterion of justice claim that the later scholastic doctors, yielding to the pressure of rising capitalism, modified his doctrine in this respect.[23] Since Aquinas upheld market valuation instead of cost, however, there was no change, but a continuous tradition involving, it is true, elaboration and refinement as economic development raised new problems and as discussion revealed flaws in previous analysis.

Some of the most valuable contributions were made by Bernardino of Siena (1380–1444), perhaps the ablest economist of the Middle Ages. Although usually a follower of John Duns Scotus, he espouses the

[19] *Summa theologica*, II, ii, qu. 77, art. 1, ad. 1. Cf. Arthur E. Monroe, *Early Economic Thought* (Cambridge: Harvard University Press, 1948), p. 56.
[20] Albertus Magnus, *Commentarii in IV sententiarum Petri Lombardi*, Dist. 16, art. 46, in *Opera omnia*, XXIX (Paris, 1894), 638. Cf. J. B. Kraus, S.J., *Scholastik, Puritanismus, und Kapitalismus* (Leipzig: Duncker & Humblot, 1930), p. 53.

[21] *Summa theologica*, II, ii, qu. 77, art. 3, ad. 4. The story is taken from Cicero, *De officiis*, iii. 12. My conclusion agrees with that of Armando Sapori, "Il giusto prezzo nella dottrina di san Tommaso e nella pratica del suo tempo," *Studi di storia economica (secoli XIII–XIV–XV)* (3d rev. ed.; 2 vols.; Florence: Sansoni, 1955), I, 279.
[22] Comments on *Summa theologica*, II, II, qu. 77, art. 1 (Leonine edition, VI, 149). Cf. Lewis Watt, "The Theory Lying Behind the Historical Conception of the Just Price," in V. A. Demant, ed., *The Just Price* (London: Student Christian Movement Press, 1930), p. 69.
[23] Tawney, *Religion*, p. 40; Tarde, *Juste prix*, pp. 51–52.

Thomist position on price. According to San Bernardino, price is a social phenomenon and is set not by the arbitrary decision of individuals, but *communiter*, that is, by the community.[24] How? There are two possibilities: The price of a commodity can be fixed either by the public authorities for the common good, or by the estimation currently arrived at in the market (*secundum aestimationem fori occurentis*).[25] The first is the legal price; the second is called later the natural price. Citing Henricus Hostiensis (d. 1271), San Bernardino stresses the fact that the market price has to be accepted by the producer and is fair whether he gains or loses, whether it is above or below cost.[26] This point was further elaborated by the Dominican friar, Tommaso Buoninsegni (d. 1609). In his treatise on licit traffics he points out that the just price does not have gradations, because buyers, if they are well informed, as they usually are in a wholesale market, will not pay more than the current price.[27] In other words, for the same commodity there can be only one price in the same market.

By the sixteenth century the majority of the scholastic doctors agreed that the just price was either fixed by law or determined by common estimation (*communis aestimatio*). There has been some discussion about the meaning of this phrase, but it appears to be identical with *aestimatio fori*, or market valuation, since the two expressions were used interchangeably by the scholastics.[28] Moreover, it is not clear how a community acting collectively could arrive at a price except by the chaffering of the market, certainly not by taking a vote, for example.

The dissenters were only a few followers of John Duns Scotus (1265–1308), such as John Mayor (1469–1550), another Scot, and Johannes Consobrinus, or João Sobrinho (d. 1486), a Portuguese who taught for some time in England.[29] Like their leader, they maintained that the just price corresponded to cost including normal profit and compensation for risk.[30] Unlike Langenstein, they did not worry about social status.

The theory of Duns Scotus was denounced most vehemently as fallacious by the School of Salamanca, founded by the great jurist, Francisco de Vitoria (*ca.* 1480–1546). More than ever emphasis was put on the fairness of the current market price. Without exception, Vitoria and his disciples insist that attention be paid only to supply and demand, without regard for labor costs, expenses, or incurred risks; inefficient producers or unfortunate specula-

---

[24] This was the traditional doctrine derived from the Roman law. Accursius (1182–1260), *Glossa ordinaria* to *Digest*, XXXV, 2, 63: "Res tantum valet quantum vendi potest, sed communiter" ("Goods are worth as much as they can be sold for, commonly").

[25] San Bernardino of Siena, *De evangelio aeterno*, sermon 35, art. 2, cap. 2, and sermon 33, art. 2, cap. 7, part 2, §5, in his *Opera omnia*, IV (Florence–Quaracchi: St. Bonaventure Press, 1956), 157–58, 197. Cf. Franz Josef Hünermann, *Die wirtschaftsethischen Predigten des hl. Bernardin von Siena* (doct. diss., Münster; Kempen–Niederrhein: Thomas Druckerei, 1939), pp. 80 ff.

[26] Bernardino, *De evangelio*, sermon 33, art. 2, cap. 7, part 2, §5. Cf. Fanfani, *Origini*, p. 13.

[27] Tommaso Buoninsegni, O.P., *Trattato de traffichi giusti et ordinarii* (Venice, 1588), cap. 11, Nos. 1 and 2.

[28] Raymond de Roover, "Joseph A. Schumpeter and Scholastic Economics," *Kyklos*, IX (1957), 133–34. A different interpretation is given by Abram L. Harris, *Economics and Social Reform* (New York: Harper & Brothers, 1958), pp. 318–22. In support of his views he quotes a definition given by Heinrich Pesch (1854–1926), but it is clear that the latter's value theory stems directly or indirectly from Langenstein, whose doctrine is not representative of scholasticism.

[29] John Duns Scotus, O.F.M., *Quaestiones in librum quartum sententiarum*, dist. 15, qu. 2, No. 23, in his *Opera omnia*, XVIII (Paris, 1894), 318; Moses Bensabat Amzalak, *Frei João Sobrinho e as Doutrinas Económicas da Idade Média* (Lisbon: Gráfica Lisbonense, 1945), pp. 257 ff.

[30] Risk is specifically mentioned, since Scotus states that a merchant who suffers damage through shipwreck or fire can recoup this loss on the sale of other goods.

tors should simply bear the consequences of their incompetence, bad luck, or wrong forecasting.[31]

Although the whole discussion on the just price assumed the existence of competitive conditions, it is strange that the word "competition" never occurs in scholastic treatises until the end of the sixteenth century, when it is used by Luis de Molina (1535–1601). Discussing price formation in an open market, he states that "competition (*concurrentium*) among buyers—brisker at one time than at another—and their greater avidity will cause prices to go up, whereas paucity of purchasers will bring them down."[32] The Spanish school accepted as a matter of course the quantity theory of money and the proposition that prices "generally" will rise or fall in response to expansion or contraction of the monetary circulation.[33]

Whenever the free market failed to function properly, the public authorities, according to the scholastic doctrine, had not only the right but the duty to step in by means of price regulation. When there was a legal price, it superseded the market price and was binding, unless the regulations were manifestly out of date or openly disobeyed, with the authorities making no attempt at enforcement.[34] In other words,

the moralists realized perfectly well that it was useless to fix prices by decree if nothing was done to make them effective.

Discussion of this issue does not start until the fourteenth century, and one of the first advocates of price fixing was the Frenchman Jean Gerson (1362–1428), *doctor christianissimus* and at one time chancellor of the University of Paris. He suggested that price fixing be extended to all commodities, on the ground that no one should presume to be wiser than the lawmaker.[35] This suggestion, however, found few supporters, as the impracticality of the whole scheme became apparent. In fact, medieval price regulation usually embraced only a few basic necessities, such as wheat, bread, meat, wine, and beer. Legal prices were usually ceiling prices. But they could be minima, below which a buyer could not go, if the rate was set in favor of the seller.[36]

One weakness of the scholastic doctors was that they were interested only in laying down principles and tended to overlook practical difficulties, which, they claimed, did not concern the theologians but were the province of the "politicians." An extreme position was taken by Martin Azpilcueta (1493–1587), better known as Navarrus, who opposed all price regulation because it was unnecessary in times of plenty and ineffective or harmful in times of dearth.[37] Several others, among them Molina, looked upon price regulation with the same disfavor.

Since scholastic doctrine favored competition, it is logical that all forms of price discrimination were condemned. Already in the thirteenth century both Thomas Aqui-

---

[31] Marjorie Grice-Hutchinson, *The School of Salamanca: Readings in Spanish Monetary Theory, 1544–1605* (Oxford: Clarendon Press, 1952), pp. 48, 72, 81–82, 86; Demetrio Iparraguirre, *Francisco de Vitoria, una teoria social del valor económico* (Publicaciones de la Universidad de Deusto, 1st series, Vol. VIII; Bilbao: Mensajero del Corazón de Jesús, 1957), pp. 55–56, 74–81; Joseph A. Schumpeter, *History of Economic Analysis* (New York: Oxford University Press, 1954), pp. 98–99; Raymond de Roover, "Scholastic Economics: Survival and Lasting Influence from the Sixteenth Century to Adam Smith," *Quarterly Journal of Economics*, LXIX (1955), 169.

[32] Luis de Molina, *De justitia et jure* (Cuença, 1592), Tract. 2 (*De contractibus*), disp. 348, §4.

[33] Grice-Hutchinson, *School of Salamanca*, pp. 51–52, 95, 113.

[34] Alphonsus Liguori (1696–1787), *Theologia moralis*, Book III, Tract. 5, cap. 3, dub. 8, art. 1, No. 803, in his *Opere*, V (Turin, 1888), 645.

[35] Johannes Gerson *De contractibus*, consid. 19 in his *Opera omnia*, III (Antwerp, 1706), col. 175.

[36] This point is emphasized by Leonardus Lessius, S.J., *De justitia et jure* (Paris, 1606), lib. 2, cap. 21, dub. 2, §13.

[37] Cardinal Juan de Lugo, S.J. (1583–1660), *De justitia et jure, disputationes*, disp. 26, sec. 4, No. 50, in his *Opera omnia*, VII (Paris, 1893), 337.

nas and John Duns Scotus formulated the rule that a seller was not allowed to sell dearer because his wares were greatly wanted by a prospective buyer.[38] An even better statement is found in San Bernardino of Siena who, citing the canon *Placuit* mentioned above, underscores the point that price should be the same to all and that no one is allowed to charge strangers more than local customers or to take advantage of a buyer's ignorance, rusticity, or special need.[39] Instead of *Placuit*, certain writers quote a text from the *Digest*, which says that the seller may not exploit a buyer's affection or desire for a particular article, whence the expression *pretium affectionis*, which in scholastic literature designates a discriminatory price.[40] In any case there was no disagreement about the unethical character of price discrimination.

The scholastics, theologians as well as jurists, were also unanimous in regarding monopoly as a deleterious practice, inimical to the commonweal. Monopoly was defined broadly so as to include any pacts or rings formed to keep up or to depress prices above or below the competitive level. Consequently, this concept included what is today called monopsony, oligopoly, and any other monopolistic practices. In the opinion of the scholastics monopoly was an offense against liberty; it assumed a criminal character because it rested usually on collusion or "conspiracy"—this phrase actually occurs again and again in scholastic treatises.[41] Perhaps the best treatment on the subject is found in the writings of the Belgian Jesuit Leonardus Lessius (1554–1623). He admits that not all monopolies are iniquitous and that a prince, if he has good reasons, may grant exclusive privileges. He must then, however, fix a fair price giving due consideration to all attending circumstances (*spectatio circumstanciis omnibus*), such as cost, risk, and market conditions, presumably by striking a compromise between conflicting criteria, as public utility commissions do today.[42] To my mind there is no doubt that the conspiracy idea of the antitrust laws goes back to scholastic precedents and is rooted in the medieval concept of the just price.[43]

The doctrine of the market price of course applied only to staple products, on which competition, to use David Ricardo's phrase, operated without restraint. The scholastics also discussed the case of luxuries, such as thoroughbred dogs, birds of paradise, rare pictures, rich tapestries, and the like, for which there was no regular market. On this subject the doctors were unable to reach an agreement. Some, as for example Francisco de Vitoria, proclaimed that the seller of such superfluities and frivolities could accept what an informed buyer offered to pay, provided of course that there was no fraud, deceit, or coercion.[44] Others, such as Lessius, contended that the price of such articles should be set by experts (*ex judicio intelligentis mercatoris*).[45] The Blessed Angelo Carletti da

[38] Aquinas, *Summa theologica*, II, ii, qu. 77, art. 1, *corpus;* Duns Scotus, *Quaestiones*, lib. IV, dist. 15, qu. 2, No. 16, in *Opera omnia*, XVIII, 289; Monroe, *Economic Thought*, p. 55.

[39] *De evangelio*, sermon 33, art. 2, cap. 5, in *Opera omnia*, IV, 148–49, and Luciano Banchi, ed., *Le prediche volgari di san Bernardino*, III (Siena, 1888), predica 38, 246. Cf. Fanfani, *Origini*, p. 110.

[40] *Corpus juris civilis, Digest*, XXXV, 2, 63. The text really refers to a slave whose father is a freeman; it states that the slave's owner cannot charge more than the market price if the father wants to buy and adopt his offspring. In the Middle Ages this text was stretched to cover all cases of price discrimination.

[41] Bernardino, *De evangelio*, sermon 33, art. 2, cap. 7, part I, §5, in *Opera omnia*, IV, 153. Cf. Joseph Höffner, *Wirtschaftsethik und Monopole im fünfzehnten und sechzehnten Jahrhundert* (Jena: Gustav Fischer, 1941), pp. 53, 135–56.

[42] *De justitia et jure*, lib. 2, cap. 21, dub. 20, §148.

[43] Schumpeter, *History of Economic Analysis*, pp. 154–55; William L. Letwin, "The English Common Law Concerning Monopolies," *The University of Chicago Law Review*, XXI (1953–54), 355–61; Raymond de Roover, "Monopoly Theory Prior to Adam Smith: A Revision," *Quarterly Journal of Economics*, LXV (1951), 501–2, 507.

[44] Iparraguirre, *Francisco de Vitoria*, pp. 59–65.

[45] Lessius, *De justitia*, lib. 2, cap. 21, dub. 3, Nos. 15, 16.

Chivasso (d. 1495) found it difficult to make a rule but thought that the seller should determine the price honestly after considering such pertinent facts as scarcity, trouble, and risk.[46]

For completeness it should perhaps be added that the Reformation wrought little change and that the Protestant divines, Max Weber notwithstanding, continued to expound the scholastic doctrine on the just price without altering it in the least. I do not see; for example, why the Puritan preacher Richard Baxter (1615–1691) should be denounced as an abbeter of capitalism because he mentions that the just price is the market price in the absence of a rate set by law.[47] The doctrine of the just price was brought to the shores of America by the Puritan ministers. As a sample of their doctrines I shall merely mention the five rules for trading proposed by the Reverend John Cotton (1584–1642).[48] They differ from scholastic doctrine only in one respect: the medieval doctors did not approve of price increases on credit sales, because such a practice involved concealed usury.

A few words need to be said about the practical application of the doctrine of the just price. How was it translated into policy? And was this policy consistent with its theoretical postulates? Perhaps the authorities followed a vacillating course and wavered between the enforcement of competition on the one hand and the protection of monopoly on the other hand. In the Middle Ages the implementation of economic policy rested to a large extent, if not exclusively, with the municipal authorities of cities, towns, and boroughs. This is especially true of the Italian city states and the quasi-independent *Reichsstädte* in Germany. In England and France, however, royal government had not entirely renounced its sovereign rights and often took advantage of economic and social conflicts to assert its authority. Nevertheless, even in these two monarchies the towns were the main policy-making agencies. They followed one policy with respect to foodstuffs that they drew from the countryside and another with regard to the manufactured products that were made within the walls. "Thus," in the words of John M. Clark, "there were laws, of town origin, aiming to enforce competition in the things the townsmen bought, while the guild regulations limited and controlled competition in the things they sold."[49] Although this may be an oversimplification, it contains a great deal of truth. One has to remember, however, that realities involve complications too readily overlooked in making general statements.

With regard to victuals the aim of town policy was very simply to secure abundant supplies as cheaply as possible.[50] For this purpose reliance was placed on the enforcement of competition, and the peasants of the surrounding district were encouraged and, if necessary, compelled to bring their products to the market and to sell them directly to the consumer, thereby eliminating all middlemen, hawkers, or brokers.[51] As Hans van Werveke correctly points out,

[46] Angelo da Chivasso, O.F.M., *Somma angelica* (Venice, 1593), Part II, rubr. *Venditione*, §5.
[47] H. M. Robertson, *Aspects of the Rise of Economic Individualism: A Criticism of Max Weber and His School* (Cambridge, Eng.: The University Press, 1933), p. 17.
[48] N. S. B. Gras and Henrietta M. Larson, *Casebook in American Business History* (New York: Crofts, 1939), p. 59; Tawney, *Religion*, pp. 128–30; E. A. J. Johnson, *American Economic Thought in the Seventeenth Century* (London: P. S. King & Son, 1932), pp. 123–30. The latter is surprised to find that supply-and-demand was understood when the doctrine of "just price" was still the dominant note!

[49] *Social Control of Business*, p. 23.
[50] "Ad hoc ut maior copia victualium in civitate habeatur,": quoted from a Florentine statute by Sapori, *Studi*, I, 294.
[51] Henri Pirenne, "Les anciennes démocraties des Pays-Bas," in *Les villes et les institutions urbaines* (6th ed.; 2 vols.; Paris; Félix Alcan, 1939), I, 196–99; idem, "Le consommateur au moyen âge," *Histoire économique de l'Occident médiéval* (Bruges: Desclée de Brouwer, 1951), pp. 532–34.

this provisioning policy (*politique de ravitaillement*) was practiced throughout western Europe from Sicily to England.[52] Everywhere measures were taken against engrossers (*accapareurs*), forestallers (*recoupers*), and regraters (*regrattiers*) who tried to accumulate stocks, to prevent supplies from reaching the market, or to form corners in order to drive prices up.[53] Medieval records are full of references to engrossers or forestallers who were caught, dragged into court, and fined or punished with exposure on the pillory.[54] This applies not only to England but to the Continent as well. Those who escaped conviction in the secular courts were still punishable *in foro conscientiae*; according to canon law, monopoly profits were *turpe lucrum*, which, like usury, was subject to restitution.[55] In dealing with the Middle Ages it would be a grievous error to ignore the confessional as a means of enforcement.

Unfortunately, crop failures created a recurrent problem, especially in the case of grain, because bread was the staple food and there were no suitable substitutes. Since the demand for cereals was highly inelastic, prices went up to fantastic heights in case of dearth.[56] Under those circum-

stances it would have been folly to rely on the automatic operation of competition. In order to avoid bread riots and mass starvation the authorities were forced to resort to regulation, and it is here that difficulties began. The scholastic authors were full of illusions about the omniscience, honesty, and efficiency of public authorities.

The history of price regulation remains to be written, but we know it to be a tale of woe.[57] In the absence of a well-organized system of allocation and rationing, price controls were bound to break down, and it is not surprising that previous to 1800 their administration was often haphazard, vexatious, inefficient, and arbitrary. A crude form of rationing, common all over Europe, was to freeze the price of bread but to vary the size of the loaf with the price of breadstuffs.[58] As the latter increased, the penny or twopenny loaf became smaller and smaller. Price fixing usually made matters worse instead of better and inevitably led to the emergency of a black market and widespread concealment of available stocks. A more successful device was to store supplies in public granaries and to sell them to the poor below market price in time of dearth.[59] The creation of such granaries,

[52] "Les villes belges: histoire des institutions économiques et sociales," in *La ville*, Vol. II: *Institutions économiques et sociales* (Recueils de la Société Jean Bodin, No. 7; Brussels: Editions de la Librairie Encyclopédique, 1955), p. 564. For Sicily: Antonio Petino, *Aspetti e momenti di politica granaria a Catania ed in Sicilia nel Quattrocento* (Catania: Università di Catania, 1952), p. 31.

[53] In German the terms are *Aufkauf, Vorkauf,* and *Wiederkauf*. Jean Schneider, "Les villes allemandes," *La ville*, II, 432–33. It was not always possible to eliminate middlemen entirely.

[54] L. F. Salzman, *English Industries of the Middle Ages* (Oxford: Clarendon Press, 1923), p. 314.

[55] *Corpus juris canonici, Decretum Gratiani*: c. *Quicumque tempore*, Causa xiv, qu. 4, c. 9. This is article 17 of a capitulary issued by Charlemagne in 806.

[56] This statement is fully supported by statistical data. See, for example, Charles Verlinden, J. Craeybeckx, and E. Scholliers, "Mouvements des prix et des salaires en Belgique au XVIᵉ siècle," *Annales* (*Economies, Sociétés, Civilisations*), X (1955), 173–98.

[57] An excellent monograph provided with a valuable bibliography is the following: Hans Conrad Peyer, *Zur Getreidepolitik oberitalienischer Städte im 13. Jahrhundert* (Vienna: Universum, 1950). Other studies of the same kind are: H. G. von Rundstedt, *Die Regelung des Getreidehandels in den Städten Südwestdeutschlands und der deutschen Schweiz im späteren Mittelalter und im Beginn der Neuzeit* (Stuttgart: W. Kohlhammer, 1930) and L. Klaiber, *Beiträge zur Wirtschaftspolitik oberschwäbischer Reichsstädte im ausgehenden Mittelalter* (Stuttgart: Kolhammer, 1927).

[58] Examples abound. For Belgium, see Verlinden et al., art. cited in n. 56, above, p. 185; for Germany, see Klaiber, *Beiträge*, p. 62; for France, see Gustave Fagniez, *Documents relatifs à l'histoire de l'industrie et du commerce en France* (2 vols.; Paris: Alphonse Picard, 1898–1900), II, 291, No. 164; for England, Ashley, *English Economic History*, I, Part I, 188–89; for Italy, Peyer, *Zur Getreidepolitik*, p. 145.

[59] Example in Basel during the fifteenth century: Hermann Bruder, *Die Lebensmittelpolitik der Stadt Basel im Mittelalter* (Achern im Breisgau, 1909), p. 3.

unfortunately, did not become a regular policy until the eighteenth century, when it was adopted by the Prussian state.[60] Another expedient was to appropriate public funds for purchases abroad and to sell the imported grain at a loss in the local market. The result was usually to relieve the situation, to lower prevailing prices, and to bring stocks out of hiding. In many instances panicky authorities were only goaded into action by the fear of mob violence and then proceeded to seize stocks and to find scapegoats among minor offenders.[61]

The public authorities, for all their inefficiency, probably achieved some measure of success in avoiding worse troubles. I am convinced that the problem was not one that could have been solved by reliance on the free operation of competition. The theologians of the Spanish school were doubtless overoptimistic in assuming that removal of controls was the best solution in times of critical shortage of essential commodities. As the experience of two world wars has shown, the institution of controls is an unavoidable measure when demand greatly exceeds the available supply at reasonable prices.

The scholastic writers, in their weighty treatises, rarely mention the guilds, but when they do, it is not to praise them for their humanitarian livelihood policy but to blame them for their monopolistic practices. Thus, San Antonio (1389–1459) accuses the clothiers, or *lanaiuoli*, of Florence of paying their workers in truck or in debased coins.[62] In England John Wycliffe (*ca.* 1324–1384) curses the free masons and other craftsmen because they "conspire" together to ask more than a rightful wage and to oppress other men.[63] An equally virulent attack is found in the so-called *Reformation of Emperor Sigismond* (1437); the author of this proposal would abolish all guilds because they abuse their control of town governments to exploit the public.[64]

Monopoly was the essence of the guild system.[65] This statement applies chiefly to the craft guilds, which were associations of small independent masters. They often entered into secret compacts to fix prices at the expense of the consumer. There was, however, another kind of guild—much less common—which was mainly found in the textile industry. Instead of being composed of independent masters it was made up of artificers, such as weavers, dyers, fullers, or finishers, who worked for wages and combined to protect themselves against exploitation by their employers and to obtain better pay. They even went so far as to organize strikes. This second type resembled more closely the modern labor union. It is important to distinguish between these two kinds of guilds.[66] No such distinction was made by the scholastics, who were not favorably disposed toward any alliances, whether of masters or of workers. Molina,

[60] This is a reference to the *Magazinpolitik*, or ever-normal granary, initiated by Frederick William I, King in Prussia (1713–40) and continued by his son and successor, Frederick the Great (1740–86): R. de Roover, "Monopoly Theory," p. 520. In France beginnings were made with the same policy but did not produce tangible results: Earl J. Hamilton, "Origin and Growth of the National Debt in France and England," *Studi in onore di Gino Luzzatto* (4 vols.; Milan: A. Giuffré, 1950), II, 249.

[61] Enrico Fiumi, "Sui rapporti economici tra città e contado nell'età comunale," *Archivio storico italiano*, CXIV (1956), 58.

[62] *Summa theologica* (Verona, 1740), Part II, tit. 1 (*De avaritia*), cap. 17, §§7, 8. The truck system existed also in Lucca (1419): Giovanni Sercambi, *Croniche*, ed. Salvatore Bongi, III (Lucca, 1892), 252. It was found even in Flanders: Henri Pirenne, *Histoire de Belgique*, I (5th rev. ed.; Brussels: M. Lamertin, 1929), 282.

[63] John Wycliffe, *The Grete Sentence of Curs Expounded*, in Thomas Arnold, ed., *Select English Works of Wyclif*, III (Oxford, 1871), 333. Cf. Tawney, *Religion and Capitalism*, pp. 27, 293.

[64] J. B. Ross and Mary M. McLaughlin, eds., *The Portable Medieval Reader* (New York: Viking Press, 1949), pp. 314–15.

[65] Tawney (*Religion*, p. 27) fully admits this point. Cf. Emile Coornaert, *Les corporations en France avant 1789* (3d ed.; Paris: Gallimard, 1941), p. 265.

[66] Niccolò Rodolico, *La democrazia fiorentina nel suo tramonto, 1378–1382* (Bologna: Nicola Zanichelli, 1905), pp. 95 ff.

for example, condemns them both indiscriminately as detrimental to the commonweal.[67]

In order to avoid confusion it may be desirable to deal first with the ordinary craft guild of independent artisans, such as bakers, butchers, shoemakers, and so forth. It is often asserted that such guilds set prices supposedly enabling their members to earn a decent living.[68] It cannot be denied that they did so in many cases, but it must be stressed that such action was an abuse, unless the rates established by the guilds had received official sanction.[69]

According to scholastic doctrine the fixing of prices was entrusted to the public authorities, but I have not found that this function was delegated to private interests, such as guilds. In this matter practice corresponded to theory. In England at least the law forbade the guilds to set prices "for their singular profit and to the common hurt and damage of the people"; victualers especially were not permitted to form "confederacies" for this purpose.[70] The same rule prevailed in Germany as long as the territorial princes retained some control over the towns.[71] Thus, in Cologne, according to a decision of 1258, the archbishop retained the right to police the market because the guilds depressed prices when they bought and raised prices when they sold.[72] Even in Italy municipal statutes usually restrained the guilds from making any secret agreements to keep prices up or down.[73] The best example is perhaps Florence; although it was a stronghold of the guild system, the ordinances of justice of 1293 and later statutes contained provisions outlawing all "conspiracies," monopolies, leagues, or pacts for the purpose of manipulating prices. Delinquents incurred a heavy fine of £1,000 *di piccioli*, although I know of no instance in which this penalty was ever imposed.[74]

This leniency contrasts sharply with the drastic measures taken in Florence to thwart any attempt by the workers in the woolen and silk industries to form brotherhoods. In both these industries the guild was controlled by the master manufacturers or industrial entrepreneurs. The statutes of these industrial guilds most severely proscribed any conjurations, machinations, or conventicles among the artificers and

[67] *De justitia et jure,* tract. II, disp. 345, §2. I wish to stress the point that accusations of conspiracy were made against both types of guilds, because there has been a confused controversy on this issue: Ernst Kelter, "Die Wirtschaftsgesinnung des mittelalterlichen Zünftlers," *Schmollers Jahrbuch für Gesetzgebung, Verwaltung und Volkswirtschaft im Deutschen Reiche,* LV[2] (1932), 749–75; Adriaan van Vollenhoven, "Die Wirtschaftsgesinnung des mittelalterlichen Zünftlers: eine Kritik," with rejoinder by Kelter, *ibid.,* LIX (1935), 298–316. Van Vollenhoven errs in assuming that indictments of conspiracy were aimed at only the labor-union type of guild: abundant evidence to the contrary is found in the Italian statutes. Kelter rightly emphasizes that guild policy clashed with municipal policy of abundance and cheapness. Cf. Ugo Froese, *Der Wirtschaftswille im deutschen Hochmittelalter* (Giessen, Konrad Triltsch, 1936), pp. 47 ff.

[68] Clune, *Gild System,* p. 56. On the antinomy between subsistence and profit motive as the ruling principle of guild policy see Friedrich Lütge, "Die Preispolitik in München im hohen Mittelater; ein Beitrag zum Streit über das Problem 'Nahrungsprinzip' oder 'Erwerbsstreben,'" *Jahrbuch für Nationalökonomie und Statistik,* CLIII (1941), 162–202.

[69] George Unwin, *The Gilds and Companies of London* (New York: Charles Scribner's Sons, 1909), p. 92; John Clapham, *A Concise History of Britain from the Earliest Times to 1750* (Cambridge, Eng.: University Press, 1951), p. 132.

[70] Statutes of the Realm: 15 Henry VI, c. 6 (1437); 19 Henry VII, c. 7 (1504); and 22 Henry VIII, c. 4 (1531). Cf. Lujo Brentano, "On the History and Development of Gilds," in Toulmin Smith, ed., *English Gilds* (London: Early English Text Society, 1870), pp. cxxxi, cxl, cxlix, clvii.

[71] Kelter, "Wirtschaftsgesinnung," p. 762.

[72] Ernst Kelter, *Geschichte der obrigkeitlichen Preisregelung,* I: *Die obrigkeitliche Preisregelung in der Zeit der mittelalterlichen Stadtwirtschaft* (Jena: Gustav Fischer, 1935), 34. The title of this book is deceptive; it deals chiefly with Cologne.

[73] Gunnar Mickwitz, *Die Kartelfunktionen der Zünfte und ihre Bedeutung bei der Entstehung des Zunftwesens* (Helsingfors: Centraltryckeriet, 1936), pp. 20 ff. Mickwitz also presents evidence relating to England, France, and Germany.

[74] *Statuti populi et communis Florentiae,* I (Florence, 1778), 302–3, 426–27: ordinamenta justitiae (1293), rubr. 21 and statuta (1415), lib. 3, rubr. 87.

journeymen subject to the guilds' jurisdiction.[75] In 1345 a wool carder, Ciuto Brandini, actually suffered capital punishment, although his only crime was that he had tried to organize a confraternity among his fellow workers.[76] In the indictment he is described as a man of ill fame and foul language and is accused of forming an illegal "congregation," threatening peace and order, and imperiling the life and property of the citizens.[77] Similar conditions existed in other textile centers, not only in Italy, but also beyond the Alps, even in Toulouse, a minor center.[78] In Flanders, around 1300 still the major cloth-producing region in Europe, the patricians and clothiers who ran the town governments passed the most cruel legislation to cow the workers, to ban suspicious assemblies, and to put down strikes.[79] In Ypres the penalty

was blinding and perpetual banishment. In 1280 or 1281 ten strikers were thus disfigured.[80] This inhuman punishment did not prevent an outburst which swept the patricians out of power and caused a long period of unrest. In any case, the evidence is clear. The theory of the just price was applied also to wages and was used or misused to brand workers' associations as intolerable conspiracies, even when they were concealed under the form of religious fraternities.[81]

The general conclusion of this study can be briefly stated. The scholastics were more favorable to freedom or competition than is generally assumed. Their hostility toward monopoly was especially marked. Contrary to a widespread belief they certainly did not rely on the price system to maintain the social hierarchy. As a matter of fact, small masters operating under conditions of competition were not likely to accumulate great wealth. Social status in the Middle Ages depended chiefly on inequality in the distribution of property, mainly land, and the levying of dues (feudal payments or tithes) for the benefit of the ruling classes. There was one exception: in Italy the merchants and bankers outrivaled the feudal nobility.[82]

[75] Anna Maria E. Agnoletti, ed., *Statuto dell'Arte della Lana di Firenze, 1317–1319* (Florence: Felice Le Monnier, 1940), pp. 114–15: statute of 1317, lib. 2, art. 19; Umberto Dorini, ed., *Statuti dell'Arte di Por Santa Maria* (Florence: Leo S. Olschki, 1934), pp. 153–54: statute of 1335, rubr. 134. To forbid labor unions this statute invokes the brotherhood of men (!) and the right to work; all artificers are free to exercise their craft without any impediment (*attribuendo libertatem cuilibet artifici de suo misterio exercendo absque impedimento*). This statute was ratified by the Commune to the extent that it contained nothing against (1) the Catholic faith, (2) the usury doctrine, and (3) the antimonopoly legislation (p. 207). The Arte di Calimala or merchants' guild enacted similar provisions against associations of dyers, menders, and finishers. Giovanni Filippi, *L'arte dei mercanti di Calimala in Firenze ed il suo più antico statuto* (Turin, 1889), p. 160: statute of 1301. lib. 5, art. 4.
[76] Rodolico, *Democrazia fiorentina*, pp. 119–20.
[77] The text of the indictment is published by Niccolò Rodolico, *Il popolo minuto* (Bologna: Zanichelli, 1899), pp. 157–60, No. 14.
[78] Rodolico, *Democrazia*, pp. 96–104; Sister Mary Ambrose Mulholland, "Statutes on Cloth-making, Toulouse, 1227," in J. H. Mundy *et al.*, eds., *Essays in Medieval Life and Thought: presented in Honor of Austin P. Evans* (New York: Columbia University Press, 1955), p. 178 (art. 24).
[79] The jurist Phillippe de Beaumanoir (1246–96)

declares all leagues among artificers to be illegal: *Coutumes de Beauvaisis*, I, ch. xxx, art. 884 (Paris: Picard, 1899), 446. This passage is also published in Fagniez, *Documents*, I, 290.
[80] G. Des Marez, "Les luttes sociales à Bruxelles au Moyen Age," *Revue de l'Université de Bruxelles*, XI (1905–6), 298.
[81] Rodolico, *Democrazia*, p. 116.
[82] After this paper had been read, Fritz Redlich kindly called my attention to a little-known enactment of Emperor Frederic I (1158) according to which sutlers who sold their wares to the soldiery at a price higher than the one prevailing in the neighboring markets exposed themselves to severe punishment, including confiscation of their merchandise, whipping, and branding with a hot iron on both cheeks. This is a rather drastic way of enforcing competition and preventing price discrimination! *MGH*, Legum, Sectio IV, I, 241, No. 173, art. 17.

3 The Trade Crisis of the Early 1620's and English Economic Thought

J. D. GOULD

The aim of mercantilism was to create a politically strong and economically wealthy state. Political power and wealth were thought to go hand-in-hand. Since wealth was identified with the possession of precious metals, mercantilistic thinkers looked to the state to promote a variety of policies which would contribute to the maintenance of a favorable balance of payments, thereby increasing the supply of gold. Thus, the era of mercantilism was one during which economic activity became increasingly oriented to the marketplace instead of the household or the private estate.

While mercantilist thinkers were pragmatists, primarily concerned with their personal fortunes and the power struggle of their nation against its rivals, they did originate some theoretical concepts in economics, the most important of which was "the balance of trade." Considerable analysis was involved in mercantilist examination of the relationship between the trade balance, exchange rate levels, and specie movements. Mercantilist writers understood that a nation's volume of imports and exports is dependent on its domestic price level relative to that prevailing in foreign markets, and that international balances are paid in specie. They were also familiar with the generalization known as the "quantity theory of money."

It is generally argued, however, that mercantilist thinkers were unable to integrate these three principles to arrive at the proposition that it is impossible for any nation to maintain a permanently favorable balance of payments. David Hume subsequently established that price level differentials and, therefore, trade balance disequilibria between nations tend to be corrected through the mechanism of international specie flows.

Although most mercantilists were not analytical thinkers, J. D. Gould maintains that Thomas Mun's failure to state the reverse specie flow mechanism, in the manner of later thinkers of the classical school, is not indicative of limited analytical powers. It is argued in "The Trade Crisis in the Early 1620's and English Economic Thought" that Mun did,

Reprinted from J. D. Gould, "The Trade Crisis of the Early 1620's and English Economic Thought," from *The Journal of Economic History*, Vol. XV, No. 2, 1955, pp. 121–133. Dr. Gould is Professor of Economic History, Victoria University of Wellington, New Zealand.

in fact, perceive the relationship between specie movements, price levels, and balances of payment; but that he did not explicitly formulate the self-regulating principle because it would have been at variance with the then available empirical evidence that stable or falling prices can accompany large gold movements into a country under certain conditions. Specifically, if an increase in M is accompanied by an increase in T, significant upward pressure on P is avoided. An increase in domestic trade would have such an effect. But it is more likely that Mun had in mind an increase in entrepôt trade, for he argued that a loss of specie would occur as a result of "not trading with our money." That is, he recommended that gold be used to finance the stockpiling of foreign goods, especially from the East Indies, for subsequent re-export at advantageous prices.

The export crisis of the early 1620's, the causes of which formed the subject of an earlier paper,[1] was without doubt one of the most widely discussed topics of the day. It figured largely in the Parliamentary debates of 1621 and 1624; it gave rise to much official inquiry and unofficial documentary discussion; and it produced a number of books which, though published as frank *livres de circonstance*, have come down to us as representative of the economic views of the period in general. A careful reconsideration of these works in the light of the immediate circumstances that prompted them would help to explain the peculiarity of some of the arguments put forward, and would be a valuable essay on the origins of Mercantilist concepts. The aim of the present paper is to select two particular topics which illustrate how close the connection was between the discussion of immediate issues and what passes for more abstract Mercantilist "theory."

Many contemporary observers explained the trade crisis in terms of some defect of the mechanism of foreign exchange alleged to have resulted in an artificially low rate. In this respect the crisis does not differ from some of its less well-known predecessors, but on this occasion the contrary view— that the low exchange rate was the result, not the cause, of the unbalanced state of trade—was urged cogently and explicitly by one of the most clear-sighted of early

Mercantilists, Thomas Mun. It is generally realized that a considerable part of his magnum opus, *England's Treasure by Forraign Trade*, was devoted to a point-by-point refutation of the arguments of Malynes and his school. It is not so widely appreciated that it was during the trade depression of the 1620's, and in the course of a controversy as to its causes carried on with Malynes and others before the Privy Council, that Mun was first induced to commit his views to paper. The course of this interesting controversy can be traced in some detail in a number of memoranda in the Public Record Office and British Museum collections, but it must suffice here to draw attention to two passages only.

Mun's general argument was, of course, that the low level of England's exchanges was, not the cause, but the result, of the adverse balance of trade. Further, the export of money, complained of as being due to the machinations of astute foreign bankers, was in its turn caused by a fall of the rate of exchange below the specie export point. In the course of this controversy Mun formulated his argument in the following concise and lucid sentences:

To those particular places of our forraigne Trade, from whence wee receave a greater valew in wares then is exported unto them in our Comodities here is alwaies plenty of money to bee delyvered by Exchange.

Where here is plentie of money to bee delyvered by Exchange for any particular place there our moneys bee undervalued in Exchange.

Where our moneys are undervalued in Ex-

[1] J. D. Gould, "The Trade Depression of the Early 1620's," *Economic History Review*, Second Series, Vol. VII, No. 1 (1954), 81–90.

change to those particular places are our moneys exported.[2]

The paper from which we have just quoted is one of considerable importance in the history of economic thought, for it proves how central this trade depression was to the advances in economic analysis which we associate with Mun. After the passage quoted, the paper goes on to consider the probable effects of a strict adherence to the par rate of exchange between all countries. Here Mun makes some extremely interesting remarks regarding the effect of price changes in international trade, and these will be considered later on. Further, the same paper—and even more notably, another dated three weeks later, continuing the same line of inquiry, and clearly representing, as it were, the next stages in Mun's reflections—contain whole passages later incorporated verbatim in *England's Treasure*. To one who has studied the trade depression of the 1620's in detail, and particularly, the part played by Mun in the controversies it aroused, it is clear that a very substantial part of *England's Treasure* represents simply the fruits of reflection on the events and discussion of those years.[3] This alone ought to assure the

crisis a memorable place in the history of economic thought.

Before leaving this topic, however, one further point deserves mention. There is no doubt that in the worst period of the depression, the London rate on foreign centers, particularly Amsterdam, did fall to a level considerably below par, and probably, indeed, well below the normal specie export point. The explanation is that this period witnessed one of the many attempts to tighten up the enforcement of the laws prohibiting the export of specie. Though the events of the early 1620's caused these efforts to be redoubled, they were brought about in the first instance not by an overall export of specie due to an adverse balance of payments, but by the export of silver occasioned by the very high mint ratio adopted in England in 1611.[4] The result was that while no doubt the prohibition did not prove completely effective, the dangers and expense of transporting bullion became for a time considerably greater. The specie export point therefore fell further below par than usual, and permitted the exchanges, under the influence of the adverse balance of payments, to sink to an abnormally low level. There can be no doubt that it was these circumstances that gave rise to the particularly vehement outcry against the machinations of exchange-dealers which characterized these years. The point of most immediate interest here is that the significance of the attempt to make the laws against the export specie more effective did not pass unnoticed. One of the memoranda in which Mun and his adherents sought to counter Malynes' arguments points out that

since the late example made in the Starr chamber upon the exporters of Coyne, the quantities of monye delivered by exchange, have bene greater than formerly when the

[2] British Museum (= BM), Add. MSS. 34,324, fos. 177–78. Several other documents in this volume are relevant to this section of the article. It is justifiable to infer from the pains which the Council took to obtain other views on Malynes' arguments, that they took these arguments seriously. The report originating this discussion was referred to by Malynes in *The Centre of the Circle of Commerce* (London, 1623), whence it appears that those associated with him in this controversy included Lord Mandeville, Sir Robert Cotton, Sir Ralph Maddison, J. Williams (the King's Goldsmith) and W. Sanderson (a prominent Merchant Adventurer). Malynes, therefore, did not lack influential support for his views, and I am by no means convinced that they were quite so foolish as they appear in the light of classical economic theory.

[3] This has been clearly shown in a recent article by B. E. Supple, "Thomas Mun and the Commercial Crisis, 1623," *Bulletin of the Institute of Historical Research*, Vol. XXVII, No. 75 (May 1954).

[4] J. D. Gould, "The Royal Mint in the Early Seventeenth Century," *Economic History Review*, Second Series, Vol. V, No. 2 (1952), 241–42.

same was used to be more freely exported, & this increase of mony hath made the rate of the exchange, to be lower than it was wont to be.[5]

One wonders whether Mun—if, as seems probable, it was he who wrote this sentence —made the point tongue in cheek; for in so far as the Council still entertained an irrational fear of a low exchange rate, the argument could be taken as strengthening his plea for the free export of bullion.

In addition to evoking these important contributions to the theory of foreign exchange, the trade depression of the early 1620's had a less direct, but in some ways more fundamental, importance for the theory of international trade. This affords a striking illustration of the way in which the elements of Mercantilist thought gestated in the womb of changing economic circumstance. We should note, however, that the validity of the argument of the present section does not rest on the accuracy of the analysis of the causes of the trade depression put forward in my earlier paper. If the explanation of the crisis in terms of comparative international prices be correct, the following argument gains something, perhaps, in interest; its truth or falsehood, however, rests on other grounds. The essential starting point is that the trade depression was *in fact* explained, rightly or wrongly, on the ground that English cloth was too dear. This mere fact compelled economic thinkers to re-examine their ideas as to the significance of price in international trade, and it is just this re-thinking with which we are here concerned.

The easiest method of approaching the argument is to start from the well-known proposition used by Hume and his classical successors to discredit Mercantilist belief in the possibility of maintaining, over a long period, a favorable balance of trade. This proposition has been comprehensively,

if not euphoniously, described as "the self-regulating mechanism of specie distribution." If any country, the argument ran, enjoyed for some time a favorable balance of payments, the resultant inflow of bullion would raise prices there (and depress them in the countries from which the bullion came), thus discouraging exports and encouraging imports. The balance of payments would thus become unfavorable, and the bullion would flow back again until equilibrium was restored at a new level.

We are not primarily concerned with the merits of this theory in general, but it is pertinent to cast some doubts on its validity as applied to the early modern period. It ignored, first, the possibility that an inflow of bullion would have some effect on average velocity of circulation. By no means all of the bullion, for example, which flowed in such vast quantities to the East to buy spices, found its way into active circulation. Had it done so, the consequences might well have been a rise of prices in the spice-producing lands which would have altered considerably the pattern of consumption of our seventeenth-century forebears. More particularly, it was assumed that the volume of transactions of the country receiving the influx of bullion remained unchanged. This is precisely what did not happen in the case of the country whose success in attracting bullion it was the aim of the English Mercantilists to emulate. The Dutch contrived, in the very period in which they were regarded as the whirlpool into which the bullion of all nations was sucked, to maintain a stable or even falling level of prices. Finally, the proposition ignored the elasticities both of supply and of demand of the commodities entering into international trade. We should remember that in the early modern period international trade was restricted to a relatively small number of commodities; that if the demand for these was not always inelastic, the supply very frequently was; and that demand could be, and often was,

[5] BM Add. MSS. 34,324, fo. 155.

severely affected by such extraneous factors as sumptuary laws. The *ceteris paribus* conditions in which Hume's proposition would have been a valid criticism of Mercantilist aims did not exist, and it is not therefore surprising that empirical evidence has not in fact been forthcoming to support the theory. In these circumstances, it is time that writers on the history of economic thought stopped using this proposition as though it were in itself a sufficient proof of the futility of Mercantilist trade policy.[6]

The proposition has, nevertheless, an attractive and logical simplicity, and students of Mercantilism have been at some pains to discover why sixteenth- and seventeenth-century thinkers were not tempted to adopt this position themselves. Some have answered that it was because the quantity theory of money was itself unknown, or not sufficiently well-known, at this period. J. W. Angell, for example, has explained in this way the failure both of Malynes and of Mun to arrive at the proposition.[7] This

view cannot be accepted. It is true that in the early seventeenth century the quantity theory was not formulated in any very precise way, and that there was in general a keener awareness of the significance of changes in the volume of money than of changes in the volume of transactions. As it was on the side of money, however, that the most startling changes in the recent past had taken place, this is scarcely remarkable. Mun showed his familiarity with the concept in a famous passage to be discussed shortly—and incidentally claimed that "all men doe consent" to it.[8] Again, some members of the House of Commons in 1621 tended to ascribe the low price of grain to the shortage of silver, rather than to a run of abundant harvests, though in fact the second was in all probability the more important cause of the two.[9] Another writer ascribed the widespread fall of prices early in that decade to shortage of money.[10] These instances could be multiplied almost indefinitely.

To what, then, can the failure to grasp the self-regulating mechanism be ascribed? Jacob Viner, in his important study of pre-Smithian theories of foreign trade,[11] argues that to arrive at the principle four steps are logically necessary. It must be agreed first that volumes of exports and imports depend upon relative prices in different countries, and secondly that international balances are paid in specie. Thirdly, the quantity theory of money must be accepted. The final step is the integration of

---

[6] That it is still, however, so used, readers of R. de Roover's study of Sir Thomas Gresham will be aware. It is interesting to note that Adam Smith, in his painstaking rebuttal of Mercantilist trade policy, did not himself use this particular argument against it. It may also be noted that a few years ago, a group of leading economists expressed doubts as to "whether, even in the heyday of the international gold standard, induced movements in relative price-levels had any major regulatory influence on the balances of international transactions." *National and International Measures for Full Employment*, United Nations, 1949. All this does not, of course, at all mean that Mercantilist trade policy cannot be justifiably attacked on other grounds.

[7] J. W. Angell, *The Theory of International Prices* (Cambridge: Harvard University Press, 1926), pp. 13–15. The part of Professor Angell's book dealing with this period is, unfortunately, of limited usefulness. He was content to rely entirely on published works, and had apparently read only one of Malynes' books, and neither of Misselden's. The work of Chi-Yuen Wu, *An Outline of International Price Theories* (London, 1939), is much more valuable, and indeed displays a real penetration in its insistence on the importance of those few years in the history of economic thought. Dr. Wu was not, however, concerned to show how the reorientation of economic thought originated in changing eco-

nomic circumstances, and he is content to use the self-regulating principle to disparage the constructions of Malynes and of Mun.

[8] T. Mun, *England's Treasure by Forraign Trade* (London, 1664), pp. 43–44.

[9] For example, Mr. Brooke on 8th March, 1621: "that the Cheapness of Corn now, not so much the Plenty of Corn, as the Scarceness of Money," *Journals of the House of Commons*, I, 544–45. Several others made similar observations.

[10] Public Record Office, London (=PRO), S.P. 15/42/96.

[11] J. Viner, "English Theories of Foreign Trade before Adam Smith," *Journal of Political Economy*, Vol. XXXVIII (1930). See esp. pp. 419 ff.

these three propositions into the realization that any change disturbing the balance of payments would work itself out along these lines: (a) redistribution of bullion; (b) readjustment of prices; (c) readjustment of volumes of imports and exports to new position of equilibrium. There is, of course, no doubt that Viner is correct when he says that the second of these propositions was agreed to by all Mercantilists, being, indeed, an integral part of their own doctrines. Further, we have seen that the quantity theory, though not enunciated in any refined way, was so recognized as to make it impossible to explain on this ground the Mercantilists' failure to grasp the principle. We are, therefore, driven back upon one of two possibilities: either the first of Viner's propositions was not held, or the final integration was not forthcoming. Viner himself accepts the second of these alternatives; he claims that the first of his four steps was "accepted by most Mercantilists, early and late, and explicitly rejected by none." [12]

It may be doubted whether this is wholly correct. Though true, perhaps, in some cases, it seems probable that other thinkers had more positive reasons for refusing to accept the arguments used by Hume and his followers to attack the Mercantilist structure. Malynes, for example, certainly got so far as to realize that a prolonged adverse balance, by depleting the bullion

[12] E. F. Heckscher adopts the same view: *Mercantilism* (trans. London, 1935), II, 249–50, and so apparently does J. A. Schumpeter: *History of Economic Analysis* (New York, Oxford University Press, 1954). The latter work did not appear until after the writing of the present paper. Had it been available earlier, reference to the views of that great scholar would certainly have been made in the text. Despite the difference of view just mentioned, the present writer is greatly encouraged by the similarity of some of Schumpeter's judgments on this period to his own: see, for example, his sympathetic remarks on Malynes (pp. 344–45). Readers should note, however, that the chapter on "The 'Mercantilist' Literature" is apparently one which Schumpeter would have revised had he lived to complete the work (Editor's Appendix, p. 1185).

stocks of a country, would lower prices relatively to those elsewhere. "Had he proceeded," Viner says, "to consider the effect of these price-changes on the balance of trade and on the flow of specie, he would have presented a complete formulation of a full-cycle of the self-regulating mechanism. He proceeded, instead, to denunciation of the exchangers." In other words, Viner attributed Malynes' failure to grasp the principle to his inability to make the final integration, and claimed that it was his obsession with a particular hobbyhorse which caused his argument to go astray.

Surely, the general tenor of that argument suggests the other alternative? Malynes repeatedly stressed that the "overbalance," as he called it (of imports over exports), arose from the fact that prices of imports were high relative to those of exports—rather than that England was not exporting enough by volume. In his most important book he claimed that within the past seventy years, prices abroad had risen faster than those at home, and that it was this which explained the imbalance of English trade. He went to some length to combat the view that "selling our home Commodities good cheap maketh a lively trade" —a view against which he found ammunition to hand in the circumstances of the trade depression then at its worst point— and stated emphatically that "the underselling of our Clothes will not make them more vendible." He repeatedly gives the impression that he thought English exports, far from being too dear, were being sold too *cheaply*. Finally, a long passage in one of his earlier works can only be interpreted as meaning that he thought the loss of bullion and fall of prices consequent on an adverse balance would have, not an equilibrating, but a snowfall effect, since the fall of prices would make the balance not less, but more, adverse. In short, he assumed that the demand for English cloth was, in both directions, and within limits which, it is true, he never attempted to analyze, em-

phatically inelastic.[13] What, then, we have
to ask in order to explain the peculiarities
of Malynes' system of thought is this: was
there any justification for this basic assumption of inelastic demand? There are
in fact important grounds for believing that
it may have been true of at least the late
sixteenth century, the period during which
Malynes was actively engaged in trade, and
the conditions of which are clearly reflected
in his work.

First, and perhaps most important, English prices, as we have noted elsewhere,[14]
tended during the first half-century of the
price revolution to lag behind those of most
countries of Western Europe, and we must
explain to some degree on this ground the
relative scarcity of complaints during that
period as to the price of English cloth, and
also the frequent plea of the trading companies that their organizations served to
keep export prices *up*. Secondly, we must
remember that under the Tudors a very
high proportion of English cloth was exported unfinished, the finishing processes
being carried out by workers in various
localities on the Continent. These finishing
industries thus formed vested interests favoring stable imports of English cloth.
Thirdly, thanks mainly, no doubt, to the
wars that ravaged France and the Low
Countries, English cloth enjoyed during
this period a relative absence of competition.

In the early seventeenth century circumstances were becoming less favorable from

the English point of view under all of these
headings. In the first place, English prices
continued to rise, while on the Continent
the rise became less pronounced and in
some places prices actually fell.[15] Further,
as contemporaries never tired of bemoan-
ing, continental cloth industries developed
apace, and thanks in part to the protective
policy of the Low Countries, English production turned more and more from the
staple unfinished broadcloth to the so-
called "New Draperies." The number of
people dependent for their livelihood on
regular imports of unfinished English cloth
would therefore decline. In any case, the
possibilities of substituting one sort of
cloth for another, and cloth of one country
for that of another, greatly increased. For
all of these reasons, overseas buyers inevitably became more and more sensitive to
price as a determinant of their purchases
of English cloth.

That we have hit on the right view of the
peculiarities of Malynes' system of thought
is confirmed by two facts, first, that he himself was aware, and indeed strongly insisted, that the terms of trade had worsened
for England—a valid and important point
largely overlooked by his contemporaries

---

[13] G. Malynes, *Lex Mercatoria* (3rd ed., London, 1686), p. 65; *Maintenance of Free Trade*
(London, 1622), pp. 22 and 45–46; *A Treatise of
the Canker of England's Commonwealth* (London, 1601), pp. 11–12 and 53–55. Dr. Wu doubts
whether Malynes' assumption of an inelastic demand for exports was wholly consistent, but his
view seems to me grounded on a misinterpretation.
In any case, that assumption was clearly more
fundamental to his system of thought than its
opposite. In one passage, Malynes went some way
to meet critics of his assumption (*Treatise of the
Canker,* pp. 117–18).

[14] J. D. Gould, "The Trade Depression of the
Early 1620's," *loc. cit.*

[15] Theoretically, of course, the general rise of
prices would not have been incompatible with
stable or even falling prices in the cloth industry,
had the expansion of output in the latter been
accompanied by a more than proportionate in-
jection of capital and the adoption of more productive methods. In practice, though we should
not underestimate the social and economic significance of the well-known capitalist figures of the
industry, it would probably be true to say that
the increase of output was achieved in the main
by using more factors of production, and not by
increasing productivity. It is doubtful whether the
large-scale clothiers used in general more productive methods, except that possibly they achieved
some external economies. There was of course at
this period strong opposition, and it had Government sympathy, to improved methods of a labor-
saving character [see, for example, the outcry
against a "newe devise of a loome for many
peeces at once" (PRO S.P. 14/81/56 and 14/121/
155), and see F. J. Fisher, "London's Export
Trade in the Early Seventeenth Century," *Economic History Review,* Second Series, Vol. III
(1950), No. 3].

—and secondly, that his assumption of inelastic demand was made, at any rate consciously, only in the case of England's exports, not in that of her imports. If this interpretation is to hold, however, we must clearly face up to the problem: how was it that at a time, when, as we have seen, it was almost universally insisted that English cloth was too dear, so acute a thinker as Mun could yet fail to arrive at the self-regulating principle?

Let us first note that Mun, though decidedly rejecting the assumption of inelastic demand, had not yet formed any definite views as to the precise relationship between price and quantity sold. In a manuscript "Note" on the exchanges, preserved at the British Museum, he expressed the fear that if imports became (say) 10 per cent cheaper, England might "very likely" spend "at least 20 per cent more in the quantity"; and conversely, if England tried to sell cloth 10 per cent dearer, she might "peradventure" lose (say) 40 per cent of the quantity.[16] The very tentative way in which these suppositions are formulated, and the fact that in incorporating passages of this document, as he later did, in *England's Treasure*, Mun omitted these figures, suggest that he realized the lack of any convincing reasons for making such precise assumptions as to the relationship between price and quantity. But it is clear from this that the facts of contemporary economic life had forced him to abandon the belief that demand for English cloth was insensitive to price changes. Further, it is clear from a passage in *England's Treasure* that he understood in a general way how the relationship between price and quantity could vary in the case of different commodities, and on what factors these variations might depend:

> upon the wares which they cannot want, nor yet be furnished thereof elsewhere, we may . . . gain so much of the manufacture as we can, and also endeavour to sell them dear, so

far forth as the high price cause not a less vent in the quantity. But the superfluity of our commodities which strangers use, and may also have the same from other Nations, or may abate their vent by the use of some such like wares from other places, and with little inconvenience; we must in this case strive to sell as cheap as possible we can, rather than to lose the utterance of such wares.

He recognized in particular that foreigners would make their own cloth if English cloth was too dear, and therefore advocated in this case a policy of low prices, laying down that in general "it is vain to expect a greater revenue of our wares than their condition will afford." [17]

Assuming, however, as he appears to have done, that the demand for England's chief export was now much more sensitive to price changes, how was it that Mun was not tempted to adopt the self-regulating thesis? Has he not, indeed, arrived at it in the following well-known passage in *England's Treasure*:

> shall this [that is, trying to keep a great store of money in the country] cause other Nations to spend more of our commodities than formerly they have done, whereby we might say that our trade is Quickned and Enlarged? no verily, it will produce no such good effect: but rather according to the alteration of times by their true causes wee may expect the contrary; for all men doe consent that plenty of mony in a Kingdom doth make the native commodities dearer, which as it is to the profit of some private men in their revenues, so is it directly against the benefit of the Publique in the quantity of the trade.

Note that this passage does not state explicitly that a rise in prices such as he envisages would bring about an adverse balance, but the sense of the passage as a whole is certainly that it is vain to try to aim at a permanently favorable balance, save under one condition. That condition is indicated when he pointed the moral, adding that he was sure "it is a true lesson for

---

[16] BM Add. MSS, 34,324, fos. 171–72.

[17] Mun, *England's Treasure*, pp. 17 ff.

all the land to observe, lest when wee have gained some store of money by trade, wee lose it again by *not trading with our money*" (italics mine).[18] In other words, his argument is that a substantial inflow of bullion, by raising internal prices, would lead to a decline of exports (and ultimately, though this is not explicitly stated, to an outflow of bullion), *unless* the increased stock of bullion was used as liquid capital to finance a greater volume of trade (in which case, the implication is, the rise of prices need not occur). It seems then that Mun thought as far as the self-regulating principle, but that on the grounds just discussed he consciously rejected it. There seems to the present writer no doubt that for the period in question, at least, this concept is both theoretically sound and empirically supported. Is it surprising, however, that Mun should quite calmly have made what to us appears, perhaps, a bold theoretical leap? The answer is surely no: for how often did seventeenth-century observers refer enviously to the success of the Dutch in attracting the gold and silver of all states to them—at a time when, as contemporaries were again perfectly aware, the Dutch level of prices was either stable or falling, a fact which in its turn was seen to explain in large part the commercial success which English writers, in particular, so wistfully recognized. Had anyone in the early seventeenth century formulated a theory of specie equilibrium similar to that of Hume, he would have found the facts of contemporary Dutch economic development hard to square with it. No such empirical, and therefore no conceptual, difficulty stood in the way of Mun's version.

That the analysis put forward here is substantially correct seems to be corroborated by a change of emphasis as between the schools of Malynes and of Mun as to the chief function of money. No doubt most competent thinkers of the period, if pinned down, would have agreed on the

two main aspects of money. With the older school, however, it was the measure of value rather than the medium of exchange function on which most emphasis was placed. This harmonizes in an obvious way with their preoccupation with the exchanges. Malynes' central contention was that money could not act as a reliable measure of exchange in foreign trade if exchange manipulators drove rates from the true par and thus rendered different currencies incommensurable. The phrase repeatedly employed by this school to characterize the function of money was *communis rerum mensura*.

With the newer school of thought, the exchanges were left to look after themselves, and attention was diverted to the balance of trade, and to the benefit which a positive balance could confer in furnishing an increased supply of liquid capital. Parallel with this change, we find the emphasis transferred from the "measure of value" to the "medium of exchange" aspect of money. Not all those who spoke of the effect of a greater store of money in quickening commercial activity had any precise views as to how this effect came about, but there was certainly a widespread emphasis on the necessity of a smooth and rapid circulation of money. The views of this school might be summed up in Bacon's aphorism: "Money is like muck, not good except it be spread," or as the author of a "proposal" in the State Papers put it, "the gathering togeather of a masse of mony makes a stoppe of trade till it bee dispersed againe." [19] The phrases most often used by such people to characterize money were that it was that "which driveth the wheel of trade about"; "the cause of the subjects employment it is the wheele that sette all on worke"; or as Misselden called it, "the vitall spirit of trade." [20]

<hr>

[18] *Ibid.*, pp. 43–44.

[19] PRO S.P. 16/44/38.

[20] PRO S.P. 16/155/53; BM Hargrave MSS. 321, fo. 38; Misselden, *Free Trade; or, the Meanes to make trade florish* (London, 1622), p. 28.

The attempt to show how these interconnected ideas fared in the later seventeenth and early eighteenth centuries must await separate treatment; but it may be said here that the main interest of writers on economic affairs in these periods was concentrated on other topics. Not until the middle of the eighteenth century was the line of analysis hinted at, rather than developed, by Thomas Mun brought from its obscurity and consciously elaborated by certain French writers in an attempt to explain away the apparent paradox of Mercantilist monetary doctrines, and it was then too late to save the central theoretical edifice from collapse.[21] It is true that most of the elements of the complex of ideas we have been investigating were restated from time to time. Potter is remembered for his emphasis on the circulating medium aspect of money. Pollexfen, Child, and Davenant all stressed the need for low export prices; Petty, Davenant, and North were all clear that there might be too much money in a country. Law argued that an expanding currency would create additional employment, an exportable surplus, and thus a more positive balance. But in general, immediate economic circumstances did not compel so close a degree of attention to the problem of international prices as the depression of the early 1620's made imperative.

It is, therefore, a matter of some interest to wonder what might have ensued had *England's Treasure* been published when it was first written,[22] or had the fragmentary memoranda by the same writer, noticed in this article, been made public. For in the circumstances of those days, it is probable that attention would have been focused on quite a different aspect of Mun's thought from that which has excited most comment in our own day. Mun's famous work was published posthumously in support of the Restoration policy of freeing the export of bullion, and it is the part of the work advocating such freedom, and refuting one by one the bullionist policies which had held sway until the early modern period, that has been most noticed by modern commentators. Whatever may have been, however, the greatest influence of his book on economic *policy*, Mun's most suggestive contribution to the evolution of economic *analysis* lies in the arguments with which we have been concerned in the major part of this article. It is one of the most interesting, and not one of the least important, "might-have-beens" in the history of economic theory to wonder whether, had the whole of Mun's arguments been made public at the time they were first formulated, the subsequent evolution of the theory of international trade and foreign exchange might have taken a quite different course.

[21] Angell, *Theory of International Prices*, pp. 211 ff.

[22] See "The Date of *England's Treasure by Forraign Trade*," *The Journal of Economic History*, 1955, pp. 160–161.

4 Natural Law and the Rise of Economic Individualism in England

ALFRED F. CHALK

The second half of the seventeenth century brought reactions against mercantilist principles and practices which reflected both the changing English institutional environment and the evolution of a new attitude of economic individualism. This attitude mirrored the reinterpretation of the ancient natural law doctrine by sixteenth- and seventeenth-century thinkers. Whereas Aristotle and the schoolmen derived their justification of the existing social and economic status quo from the doctrine of the natural order, the thinkers of the transition period between mercantilism and classicism made this same doctrine the foundation for the thesis that individual freedom to pursue one's own economic interests would simultaneously serve the best interests of the social whole. They regarded the economic system as a self-regulating organism which functioned best when individual economic activity was freed from the central authority of the state and the church. Thus, the medieval attitude that acquisition, particularly in the form of usury, was sinful, was superseded by a hedonistic psychology which viewed man's seeking after material goods as being not only proper but necessary for progress.

This article, "Natural Law and the Rise of Economic Individualism in England" by Alfred F. Chalk, traces the evolution of the natural-law doctrine in sixteenth- and seventeenth-century England and relates it to the evolution of the classical tradition. He shows that, while the thinkers of the transition period had not yet wholly discarded their mercantilist ideas, many drew on the principle of the natural order to support their arguments that man-made laws regulating economic life are not only ineffective but also harmful, whereas economic freedom is beneficial to individuals as well as to society. Their analysis of the behavior of market forces, particularly in connection with international movements of precious metals and the determination of prices and interest rates, was deduced from their conception of a beneficent and automatically functioning natural order. Their isolated arguments were eventually systemized and became an integral part of classical economics.

Reprinted from "Natural Law and the Rise of Economic Individualism in England," by Alfred F. Chalk by permission of the University of Chicago Press. Originally published in the *Journal of Political Economy*, Vol. 59, August 1951, pp. 330–347. Dr. Chalk is Professor of Economics at Texas A & M University.

All students of the history of economic thought are aware of the important role played by the "laws of nature" in the classical pattern of economic ideas. Little attention has been devoted, however, to the origin and early development of the interpretation of natural law that is typified in Smith's *Wealth of Nations*. Those works which deal with various aspects of the rise of economic individualism usually refer to natural law only in the form of *obiter dicta.*[1] Although numerous specialized studies are available which deal with the place of the law of nature in ancient and medieval thought, no thorough analysis has yet been made of the new interpretation of natural law that evolved during the sixteenth and seventeenth centuries. The purpose of the present paper is to sketch briefly the early development of this new interpretation, which was destined to become an integral part of classical economics.[2]

During the later Middle Ages, theologian-philosophers began to synthesize Christian theology and Aristotelian philosophy. The most famous of these syntheses was that of Thomas Aquinas, whose *Summa theologica* is still regarded as authoritative in Catholic circles. In essence, natural law was used by Aquinas and other Scholastics as the basis for a rationalization of static social and economic relationships. In the Thomistic system, economic inequalities were justified because they existed by virtue of the laws of nature and providence. Thus the Stoic tradition of equality was broken, for Aquinas agreed with Aristotle that slavery and social inequality were in accord with natural law. As regards trade and commerce, the medieval belief was that economic activity motivated primarily by a desire for gain or profit violated both natural and divine law. Hence the church attempted to establish moral precepts which would at all times take precedence over the expediency of market forces. In brief, the spirit of Thomism was, in most respects, the antithesis of that which was later to prevail during the liberal revolution.

It was during the latter half of the sixteenth century that the new ("liberal") interpretation of natural law began to evolve in England. About that date, for the first time in the history of natural-law doctrine, writers began to argue that man's freedom to pursue his own economic interests would, through the operation of natural law, promote social welfare. In portions of *A Discourse of the Common Weal of This Realm of England* (1549), there is only an implicit acceptance of this view. Almost a century and a half later, however, the new theory of natural law was to be more explicitly formulated in the various works of William Petty and John Locke. During this interval, therefore, a theory was developing which would provide much of the foundation for the eighteenth-century conception of a "natural" identity of private and social interests. Not only did this new interpretation run counter to the medieval point of view, but it likewise obstructed the efforts of early Puritan leaders to establish religious and moral precepts as guides for economic behavior. The form in which natural-law

[1] Two good examples are Harold Laski's *The Rise of European Liberalism* (London: George Allen & Unwin, 1936) and H. M. Robertson's *Aspects of the Rise of Economic Individualism* (Cambridge: At the University Press, 1933). Although spokesmen for economic individualism used natural law as a basic analytical tool, the authors of such works as the above make few explicit references to the role played by the laws of nature. Of course, no treatment of the growth of economic individualism could fail to recognize implicitly the importance of natural-law doctrine. The present paper may be regarded, therefore, as an effort to give more explicit attention to the place of natural law in the evolution of the philosophy of individualism.

[2] Limitation of space has precluded reference to Continental authors who contributed to the formation of this theory. Despite their importance, it is probably true that the major contributions were made by English writers. For support of this point see n. 85.

doctrine began to evolve during the sixteenth century thus constituted a sharp
break with the past and presaged the victory of a revolutionary new conception of
economic morality.

The period encompassed by the present
paper (approximately 1550–1690) was one
during which the mercantilist point of view
predominated in the economic speculations
of English writers.[3] Throughout this period,
however, mercantilist doctrine contained a
dualism which has special relevance for
a study of the history of natural-law theory. On the one hand, mercantilists favored
the extensive use of statutory law to control many aspects of economic life. This
interventionist phase of mercantilist theory
has received major attention, but it is no
less true, on the other hand, that English
mercantilist literature contained much that
can be properly regarded as an anticipation of laissez faire theory.[4] This dualism
can be best appreciated if one recalls that
many of the mercantilist tracts contained
sharp criticisms of government efforts to
control domestic trade, prices, etc.

As a matter of fact, during the entire
mercantilist period frequent and vigorous
protests were made against the restrictive
legislation which had resulted from the

rise of the national state and the granting
of monopoly privileges to certain companies and individuals. One economic historian has described mercantilism as an
intended "alliance between the state and
growing capitalist interests."[5] This alliance was unsuccessful partly because it
was an effort to extend the "medieval idea
of privilege as the basis of activity."[6] From
its inception, the practice of granting monopoly privileges called forth sharp criticism, and it was out of these early protests against monopoly that a theory of
natural law developed which purported to
prove that the free play of market forces
would have beneficent effects. During the
sixteenth and seventeenth centuries an increasing number of writers spoke of the
futility of trying to legislate concerning
prices, the flow of trade, and similar matters.

This distrust of legislation as a solution of economic problems found expression in economic literature in the middle
of the sixteenth century. Among the economic tracts published during this century,
the *Discourse of the Common Weal* probably expressed more clearly than any other
the conviction that much of the state
regulation of economic life was both futile
and harmful. Although the author of this
work emphasized the need for state action
to assure an abundant supply of the precious metals, he nevertheless doubted the
efficacy of state regulation in many other
fields of economic activity.[7]

---

[3] Any fixed dates which might be given for the
origin and decline of mercantilist ideas would be
arbitrary. It is nonetheless true that mercantilism,
as a body of economic rationalizations, began to
assume importance in England by the middle of
the sixteenth century. For example, Eli Heckscher
(*Mercantilism,* trans. Mendel Shapiro [London:
George Allen & Unwin, 1934], II, 227) refers to
the *Discourse of the Common Weal* (1549) as
"the first work representing, on the whole, the
outlook of a mature mercantilism." Furthermore,
many authorities agree that the popularity of
mercantilist ideas began to decline after the publication of the works of such men as Dudley
North, Charles Davenant, and Nicholas Barbon.

[4] The "anticipation" of liberalism in mercantilist
doctrine has been neglected by some authorities.
Perhaps the best treatment of this aspect of mercantilist thought is contained in Heckscher, *op.
cit.,* II, 269–316. Another good discussion of this
dualism is contained in E. Lipson, *The Economic
History of England* (London: Adam & Charles
Black, 1948), II, lxxiv–cxlix.

[5] Robertson, *op. cit.,* p. 76.

[6] *Ibid.,* p. 77.

[7] *A Discourse of the Common Weal of This
Realm of England,* ed. E. Lamond (Cambridge:
At the University Press, 1929), pp. 48–60. Miss
Lamond established the probability that this
dialogue was written in 1549, although it was first
published in 1581. The authorship of the tract has
been widely disputed since its original publication,
and conclusive evidence of authorship is not yet
available. Most modern authorities have accepted
the opinion of Miss Lamond that John Hales was
the author, but a French writer, Jean-Yves Le
Branchu (*Écrits notables sur la monnaie* [Paris:
Librairie Félix Alcan, 1934], I, lxvi–lxxx), has

One of the most distinctive features of the *Discourse* is the analysis of various problems arising from the enclosure movement. The conversion of arable to pasture land was one of the most debated issues of the sixteenth century, and much space in this dialogue is devoted to a discussion of possible solutions of the problem. In this connection the thesis is developed that market forces are more powerful determinants of prices than are any legislative enactments. Furthermore, the operation of these market forces is apparently regarded as the functioning of inexorable natural laws, which provide the best possible guide for economic policy.

Fundamentally, the author's position is that the profit motive should be the incentive used to solve any "dearthes" that may arise in an economy. We find in this tract one of the earliest detailed arguments supporting the theory that the primary motivation for economic activity must be pecuniary considerations. In this respect, one of the basic presuppositions of classical economic thought is made explicit. The importance attributed to the profit motive is, in turn, implicitly treated as a corollary of the free market, wherein the forces of supply and demand are not restricted in any manner by legislative enactment. In the quotations which follow, a respect for the profit motive can easily be discerned. Furthermore, it will be shown below that the analysis of price adjustments in the *Discourse* anticipated much of the price theory of later economists.

In the second dialogue of the *Discourse*, the Doctor says the solution of the problem of the conversion of arable to pasture land lies in providing a sufficient profit incentive to induce the greater cultivation of land. Thus he argues that, whenever people "find more proffitt by pasture then by tillage, they will still inclose, and turne arrable landes to pasture." [8] This process of conversion will continue, therefore, just so long as pecuniary rewards are greater for the use of land as pasture, and no legislation will be of any avail in remedying the situation. A disbelief in the efficacy of legislation concerning such economic problems is repeated so often that the meaning is not subject to doubt:

> For euerie man will seke wheare most advauntage is, and they see theire is most advantage in grasinge and breedinge than in husbandrie and tillage, by a great deale. And so longe as it is so, the pasture shall [evere] encroche vpon the tillage, for all the lawes that euer can be made to the contrarie.[9]

The same thesis is echoed in the following passage, where the Doctor is speaking of the profit motive and the futility of legislating concerning the enclosures:

> I wote well thei doe not, and therefore it weare hard to make a lawe therein, (so manie as haue proffitt by that matter resistinge it). And yf such a law weare made, yet men studiinge still there most proffit, would defraud the lawe by one meane or other.[10]

The argument concerning the profit motive is not meant to apply only to agricultural matters. It is rather postulated as a universal law of human behavior, which decrees that man will always seek to maximize profits. Profit "nourishes" the best faculties in man, and the profit motive is

attributed authorship to Sir Thomas Smith. The case presented by Le Branchu is so strong that it very seriously weakens the position taken by Miss Lamond. However, no documentary evidence has yet been presented which definitely establishes the authorship of this work. The issue may be resolved when a careful study is made of the Hatfield MS, which was discovered after the death of Miss Lamond.

[8] *Discourse of the Common Weal*, p. 50.

[9] *Ibid.*, p. 53. During the last half of the sixteenth century a new criterion began to be offered as the basis for determining whether land was being used to best advantage. The conviction soon prevailed that the use of land should "be determined by considerations of what was most profitable," and the landowner was "encouraged to give free reins to the promptings of personal gain" (Lipson, *op. cit.*, II, lxviii).

[10] *Discourse of the Common Weal*, p. 50.

therefore beneficent in its effects. The aspect of beneficence is made explicit in the *Discourse*: "Is it not an old saying in [latten], honos alit artes, that is to saie, proffitt or advauncement norishethe euerie facultie; which sayinge is so true, that it is allowed by the common Judgement of all men." [11]

The answer to the enclosure problem thus becomes obvious. A solution can be found only if we "make the proffitt of the plow to be as good, rate for rate, as the proffit of the graisiers and shepmasters." [12] The author's regard for the profit motive is such that he can say that all men should "be prouoked to good deades by rewardes and price." [13] In brief, the whole process of providing incentives for economic activity is to be found in the natural law of self-interest, for "everie man naturally will folow that whearin he seeth most proffit." [14] This is surely a very close approximation to Adam Smith's views concerning the self-interest motive in economic activity.

There is evidence in the *Discourse* that the effort to identify private and social interests had already begun in the middle of the sixteenth century. In the second dialogue the Knight argues that what is "proffitable to one maie be proffitable to another," and he further indicates that this argument was widely used in defense of the enclosure movement:

> I haue hard oftentimes much Reasoninge in this matter; and some, in mainteyninge these Inclosures, would make this Reason. Euerie man is a member of the common weale, and that that is proffitable to one maie be proffitable to another, yf he would exercise the same feat. Therefore that is proffitable to one, and so to a nother, maie be proffitable to all, and so to the common wealth. [15]

The dialogue contains certain precon-

ceptions regarding human nature which were to be developed and refined at a later date by economists and philosophers. For example, self-interest is regarded as the most, if not the only, reliable motivating force in economic behavior. Furthermore, the author apparently believes human nature is determined by certain universal laws which are more powerful than environmental factors which may influence individual behavior. His assertion that men should be "prouoked to good deades by rewards and price" is a clear indication of the extent to which medieval economic ideas were being undermined. In such fashion was the surrender of religious precepts to the rule of economic expediency beginning to take place in English economic thought. [16]

Not only is the desire for profit the natural and universal guide for economic activity, but the mechanism of a free market automatically adjusts prices in such a way as to assure the public of an abundant supply of goods at low prices. The author of the *Discourse* anticipates much of the theory of later orthodox economists, for he emphasizes the automatic adjustment of relative prices, which ostensibly allocates productive resources in the most efficient manner possible. In order to increase the amount of cultivated land in relation to pasture, it would be necessary only to permit the price of corn to rise and fall as the free-market forces dictate, and the farmers would, on the basis of the market price, make the necessary adjustment in the volume of corn produced:

> Knight: How could youe haue them better cherished to vse the plowghe?
> Doctor: To let them haue more proffitt by it then they haue, and libertie to sell it at all times, and to all places, as frely as men maie doe theire otheir thinges. But then no

[11] *Ibid.*, p. 57.
[12] *Ibid.*, p. 53.
[13] *Ibid.*, p. 59.
[14] *Ibid.*, p. 60.
[15] *Ibid.*, p. 50.

[16] For a penetrating discussion of the "amoral" character of mercantilist doctrine see Heckscher, *op. cit.*, II, 286–302. In mercantilist literature the law of nature was simply divested of almost all its religious, and even ethical, overtones.

dowbt the price of corne would rise, specially at the first more then at the lengthe; yet that price would provoke everie man to set plowghe in the ground, to husband waste groundes, yea to turne the landes which he Inclosed from pasture to arable lande; for every man will the gladder folow that whearin they se the more proffit and gaines.[17]

One of the most interesting aspects of the *Discourse* relates to the contrasting views that are presented with respect to the functioning of a free market in domestic and in international trade. Although the author thought "natural" market forces would solve many of the problems of internal trade, he was nevertheless convinced of the necessity for state intervention in the area of international markets. Thus in foreign trade we must "alwaies take hede that we bie no more of strangers then we sell them," since by that process we "sholde empouerishe owr selves and enriche theme."[18] The principle of the free play of market forces is not applicable, therefore, to international trade, for treasure might be lost through an import balance of trade.[19]

As one might surmise, the influence of Aristotle is apparent throughout much of the *Discourse*. The effort to rationalize self-interest on the basis of natural law is developed at greater length than in the works of any previous writer, but much of this economic individualism is adumbrated in Aristotle's *Politics*. One should remember that it was Aristotle who said

"the love of self is a feeling implanted by nature,"[20] and it was also Aristotle who used natural-law theory to defend vigorously the right of private property against the attacks of Plato in the *Republic*. Evidence of Aristotle's influence is contained in the third dialogue of the *Discourse*, where the Doctor says that Aristotle is "the sharpest philosopher of witt that ever was."[21] Much of Aristotle's economic individualism, which had been rejected or ignored by the medieval divines, was revived in the sixteenth and seventeenth centuries by those who spoke for the new commercial class.

The idea that natural market forces should be allowed freedom to function was by no means confined to a small group of reformers. On the contrary, a number of sixteenth- and early-seventeenth-century documents testify to the growing belief in the beneficent effects of prices which are established through the free play of market forces. Some brief quotations from a few of these documents will illustrate the trend that economic thought was beginning to take during this period.

In a document written in 1549, an unknown writer cautioned repeatedly against efforts to control prices by legislative decree.[22] Although the general tenor of the work is of an interventionist character, the author advises against the attempts of the government to set maximum prices for certain basic foodstuffs. In fact, he is of the opinion that the high price of food has been partly a *result* of governmental regulations:

But ther is yet one other thinge which wolde helpe somewhat for the chepnes of

---

[17] *Discourse of the Common Weal*, p. 59.

[18] *Ibid.*, p. 63. Another clear statement of mercantilist foreign-trade doctrine occurs on pp. 66–67, wherein the Knight and the Doctor agree concerning the desirability of prohibiting the importation of any goods which might be produced in the home market.

[19] This is not to imply that mercantilists consistently favored the abandonment of efforts to control all internal prices. For example, most mercantilists thought positive measures should be taken to assure continued low wages. For a thorough documentation of this point see Edgar Furniss, *The Position of the Laborer in a System of Nationalism* (New York: Houghton Mifflin Co., 1920), pp. 117–56.

[20] Aristotle *Politics*, Jowett trans. (London: Oxford University Press, 1916), p. 57.

[21] *Discourse of the Common Weal*, p. 109. For other references to Aristotle, see pp. 73 and 108.

[22] "Policies To Reduce This Realme of Englande unto a Prosperus Wealthe and Estate" (1549), included in *Tudor Economic Documents*, ed. R. H. Tawney and E. Power (London: Longmans, Green & Co., 1924), III, 311–45.

victuall, and that is, yf neyther the lorde
Mayour of London nor no other officer might
haue none auctorrite to sette euery price of
victuall.[23]

The author of the tract becomes even
more explicit when he argues against price
controls on the basis of past experience:

I marvell therfor that this foresaid auctorrite is not taken a waye frome the foresaid
officers, seinge that the longe experience
haue so well declarid that the foresaid settinge of prices of victuall, do nothing at all
bringe downe the highe price thereof . . . but
surely it is not the settinge of lowe prices
that will aney thinge a mende the matter.[24]

The foregoing argument is virtually du-
plicated in an economic document dated
December 4, 1550. When John Mason wrote
a friend about the problem of high prices,
he alleged that high prices could not be
remedied by legislation, since nature's
forces were too strong to be resisted:

I have seen so many experiences of such
ordinances; and ever the end is dearth, and
lack of the thing that we seek to make *good
cheap*. Nature will have her course, etiam si
furea expellatur; and never shall you drive
her to consent that a *penny*-worth of new
shall be sold for a farthing. . . . For who
will keep a cow that may not sell the milk for
so much as the merchant and he can agree
upon?[25]

Here the meaning of the argument is
beyond question, for the essential attribute
of all natural-law theory is contained in
the statement that "nature will have her
course." Furthermore, in such passages as
the foregoing, there is the beginning of an
entirely new interpretation of the function
or purpose of natural law. The medieval
interpretation, as typified in the writings
of Aquinas, was that natural law should
be subsumed under the divine law. For
Aquinas, the exercise of economic controls
was in most instances in strict accord with
the principles of both natural and divine

law. The medieval doctrine of natural law
did not give free play to the self-interest
of a group of "economic men" bargaining
in a free market. In most respects, the new
sixteenth-century doctrine of the merchant
class was the antithesis of the Thomistic
view that the church and/or the state
should regulate prices whenever they
caused undue hardships. The change in
point of view during the sixteenth century
has been described by Tawney in his remarks concerning the moral confusion of
the common man during this period of
English history: "A century before he had
practiced extortion and been told that it
was wrong: for it was contrary to the law
of God. A century later he was to practice
it and be told that it was right: for it was
in accordance with the law of nature."[26]

In other words, it was the "whole conception of a social theory based ultimately
on religion which was being discredited."[27]
Thus the merchant, in Thomas Wilson's
dialogue, is made to express the view that
the activities of merchants must not be
"over thwarted by preachers and others,
that can not skill of their dealings."[28] The
Puritan divines of the sixteenth century
were by no means willing to accept the new
commercial morality of their day, and the
merchant in Wilson's dialogue represents
the growing opposition of the commercial
class to the efforts of religious leaders to
exercise moral authority and control over
business transactions. It is worth noting
that the merchant in Wilson's *Discourse*
expresses sentiments quite similar to those
found in the *Discourse of the Common
Weal*:

For, I pray you, what trade or bargayning
can there be among marchants, or what lending or borrowing among al men, if you take
awaye the assurance and hope of gayne?
What man is so madde to deliver his moneye

[23] *Ibid.,* p. 339.
[24] *Ibid.,* p. 340.
[25] *Tudor Economic Documents,* II, 188.

[26] R. H. Tawney, Introduction to Thomas Wilson, *A Discourse upon Usury* (London: B. Bell &
Sons, Ltd., 1925), p. 121.
[27] *Ibid.,* p. 170.
[28] *Ibid.,* p. 250.

out of his owne possession for naughte? or whoe is he that will not make of his owne the best he can? or who is he that will lende to others and want him self? You see all men now are so wise, that none will lend for moone shine in the water; and therefore, if you forbid gaine, you destroy entercourse of merchandize, you over throwe bargaining.[29]

The foregoing argument is, of course, directed against the laws prohibiting usury, but the same traditional arguments concerning free markets are found in Wilson's work. The merchant in the dialogue epitomizes the new economic morality of the businessman, who insisted that the "hope of gayne make the men industrious and, where no gayne ys to bee had, men will not take paynes." [30] In business transactions there can be no moral rules which preclude the taking of whatever the impersonal forces of the market will permit, for "a man may take as much for hys owne wares as he can gette." [31] Such was the attitude which finally prevailed more than two hundred years after Wilson wrote his book.

Continuing evidence of the importance of this revolt against economic controls can be found in speeches made by Sir Walter Raleigh in 1601. He frequently appeals for political and economic freedom, and he advises against efforts which were being made to prescribe the type of crops which landowners might produce: "For my part, I do not like this constraining of men to use their groundes at our wills. Rather let every man use his ground to that which it is most fit for, and therin use his own discretion." [32] His position is summarized quite succinctly when he says the best policy with respect to agriculture is to "set corn at liberty and leave every man free." [33]

[29] *Ibid.*, p. 249.
[30] *Ibid.*, p. 250.
[31] *Ibid.*, p. 251.
[32] Edward Edwards, *The Life of Sir Walter Raleigh* (London: Macmillan & Co., 1868), I, 272.
[33] *Ibid.*, p. 273.

The emphasis on freedom and natural rights in the economic sphere was quite clearly evident in the report of a committee of the House of Commons in 1604. This report emphasized the necessity of giving men economic freedom and criticized the granting of monopoly rights as a violation of natural rights:

> All free subjects are born inheritable, as to their land, so also to the free exercise of their industry, in those trades whereto they apply themselves and whereby they are to live. Merchandise being the chief and richest of all other, and of greater extent and importance than all the rest, it is against the natural right and liberty of the subjects of England to restrain it into the hands of some few.[34]

When a committee of the House of Commons speaks of economic restraints as being "against the natural right and liberty" of the people, one may be reasonably sure that natural-law doctrine was being accepted by an important segment of English society. The interests of the merchant class were thus being consulted at every turn, and the criticisms of the use of monopoly power by a few trading companies were being based on natural-law theory to an increasing degree.

In a memorandum dated July 5, 1607, certain problems concerning the enclosure movement were discussed in a manner quite similar to that used in the *Discourse of the Common Weal*. The sentiment expressed in this memorandum is strongly in favor of reliance upon free-market forces

[34] *Commons' Journals* (May 21, 1604), I, 218. In this same passage an attack against monopolies is based upon "natural-right" doctrine. Thus the report criticizes a monopoly which restrains a commodity "into the hands of so few, in proportion, to the Prejudice of all others, who, by Law and natural Right, might have interest therein."

It was during this period that the common-law rule against restraint of trade began to crystallize. For a brief discussion of early court decisions which established this rule see Walton Hamilton, "Common Right, Due Process, and Antitrust," *Law and Contemporary Problems*, VII (1940), 26–29.

as the basis for determining the relative amounts of different agricultural commodities which should be produced. The profit motive is held to be the desirable guiding force in productive activity. Furthermore, the identity-of-interests argument is rather clearly stated, for it is asserted that "the good individuall is the good generall." [35] In this document the author argues that the amount of corn produced will continue at a high level because the farmer has been receiving a high price and "his only ende is profite." [36] This is the manner in which the appeal was being made to self-interest in both agricultural and commercial activities.

During the early decades of the seventeenth century the conviction that the flow of trade was subject to inexorable natural laws was becoming a commonplace. Thus the famous mercantilist Edward Misselden remarked: "Trade has in it such a kind of natural liberty in the course and use thereof, as it will not endure to be fors't by any." [37] The memoirs of Thomas Papillon, a seventeenth-century merchant, reveal that he had similar convictions regarding governmental efforts to regulate the flow of trade.[38] He argues, for example, that "trade will not be forced but will have its course; If it meets with a Stop in one place, it will find a Vent another way." [39] The apparently irresistible power of nature's processes was becoming almost a fetish among the authors of economic tracts.

Such quotations clearly indicate the direction which natural-law theory was tak-

ing during the early part of the seventeenth century. Not only was the theory gradually becoming more explicit, but it was also being applied to a greater variety of economic problems. Yet this trend did not result in the formulation of an integrated philosophy of laissez faire during the seventeenth century. As early as the middle of the century, however, one finds the law of nature being used to support the argument that social and private interests are identical. Thus Joseph Lee, a country clergyman, says it is "an undeniable maxime, that every one by the light of nature and reason will do that which makes for his greatest advantage." [40] He then proceeds to develop the identification-of-interests argument:

> The advancement of private persons will be the advantage of the publick: if Merchants do buy an advantagious commodity, hath not the Common-wealth an advantage thereby, as well as themselves? . . . So whatsoever benefit we make to ourselves, tends to the publick good.[41]

Although Lee's statement of the identity-of-interests doctrine was unusually clear for that period, it is nevertheless true that natural-law theory was being used more and more frequently in support of the growing spirit of economic individualism. A steady stream of criticism was directed against efforts to legislate concerning prices, the flow of trade, etc. In almost all these critical remarks, there was an explicit or implicit acceptance of the view that economic activity was subject to universal, immutable laws. Roger Coke voiced an increasingly popular sentiment when he said he would "never believe that any man or Nation ever well attain their ends by forceable means against the Nature and Order of things." [42]

The growth of a spirit of economic indi-

[35] "A Consideration of the Cause in Question before the Lords Touchinge Depopulation" (1607), included in the appendix of W. Cunningham's *The Growth of English Industry and Commerce* (Cambridge: At the University Press, 1903), III, 899.
[36] *Ibid.*
[37] Edward Misselden, *Circle of Commerce* (1623 ed.), p. 112.
[38] A. F. W. Papillon, *Memoirs of Thomas Papillon* (Reading, England: J. J. Beecroft, 1887).
[39] *Ibid.*, p. 142.

[40] Joseph Lee, *A Vindication of a Regulated Enclosure* (London, 1656), p. 9.
[41] *Ibid.*, p. 22.
[42] Roger Coke, *Treatise III*, p. 57, quoted in Heckscher, *op. cit.*, II, 309.

vidualism during this period is clearly reflected in an increasing tendency to glorify the role played by self-interest in economic affairs. Authors of economic tracts repeatedly asserted that any efforts to legislate against the pursuit of self-interest would be both futile and harmful. In pursuing their own interests, men were said to be acting in accord with a universal law of human nature. The unknown author of *Britannia languens* expressed this idea rather bluntly when he said that "no *Statutes,* Nay, or *Preaching,* though never so *learned* or *florid,* can prevail with necessitous men." [43] Samuel Fortrey was developing a similar thesis when he argued that "interest more than reason commonly sways most men's affections." [44]

More specifically, a large number of seventeenth-century writers regarded the desire for profit as the most salutary basis for economic action. This attitude was nowhere more prevalent than in discussions concerning the advisability of preventing the free movement of bullion between nations. From the establishment of the East India Company in 1600, the prohibition against the exporting bullion had been the subject of increasing controversy. In 1660, for example, antagonism toward such restrictions was reflected in a report of the Council of Trade. It is significant that this group objected to the restrictions largely on the basis of the alleged futility of forbidding the exportation of the precious metals when it would be "profitable" to traders. The consensus of the council was that trade could not be "forced" by the passage of laws, for merchants would always find a way of avoiding the regulations when it was profitable to do so. [45] The opin-

ion of the Council of Trade is expressed in the following excerpt from its report:

> The result at last would be no more but what experience hath already taught, that Money and Bullion have always forced their way against the several laws; that the trade of the world will not be forced, but will find or make its own way free to all appearances of profit. [46]

The desire of the traders for profit thus dictates the movement of the precious metals, for "it is impossible by any laws to restrain Money and Bullion against the use that traffic finds for the same." [47] All legislation concerning this problem would, in the words of Thomas Mun, be "not only fruitless but also hurtful." [48] For Mun and many of his contemporaries the forces of the market thus assumed the character of inexorable laws of nature. No legislation could effectively prevent the movement of metals to the places where traders could earn the highest profit. We may refer again to the work of Fortrey for a clear statement of this thesis:

> And our gold being of less value at home then it is abroad it hath been all conveyed away within these few years: and laws to prevent it shall always prove fruitless, when it is advantageous to do it; there being means sufficient to be found to effect it, by such as shall find it profitable. [49]

The excerpts given above indicate the "piecemeal" and inconsistent fashion in

---

[43] *Britannia languens* (1680), reprinted in *Early English Tracts on Commerce,* ed. J. R. McCulloch (London, 1856), p. 376. The authorship of this tract is commonly attributed to William Petyt.

[44] Samuel Fortrey, *England's Interest and Improvement* (1663), reprinted in *Early English Tracts on Commerce,* p. 219.

[45] Many such arguments were obviously made by spokesmen for the large trading companies. What-

ever may have been their motives for such arguments, the important fact is that the rationalizations postulated the existence of more or less impersonal, universal laws over which men could exercise control. These laws were, of course, "laws of nature."

[46] *Advice of His Majesty's Council of Trade* (1660), reprinted in *A Select Collection of Scarce and Valuable Tracts on Money,* ed. J. R. McCulloch (London, 1856), pp. 148–49.

[47] *Ibid.,* p. 149.

[48] Thomas Mun, *England's Treasure by Forraign Trade* (1664) (London: Basil Blackwell, 1928), p. 87. In this same passage Mun says the supply of the precious metals adjusts itself to the balance of trade and this "must come to pass by a Necessity beyond all resistance."

[49] Fortrey, *op. cit.,* p. 240.

which the new interpretation of natural law had begun to insinuate itself into economic literature. Thus some writers had used natural-law doctrine to support their arguments in favor of the enclosure movement. Others had occasionally resorted to this doctrine in their attacks against efforts to control internal prices. Still others had argued that attempts to regulate the flow of gold and silver were futile because they violated the laws of nature. However, such isolated arguments were soon to be integrated into a more or less consistent system of economic theory. This movement toward integration began during the last quarter of the seventeenth century, and its rapid progress is well known to those who have studied the development of economic thought.

One of the earliest, and certainly one of the best, examples of the new trend in economic thought is found in the works of Sir William Petty, who wrote during the period of "transition" from mercantilism to laissez faire.[50] Although Petty subscribed to a number of mercantilist ideas, the general "tone" of his works reflects the extent to which economic individualism was gaining the upper hand in English thought. At the heart of this increasingly popular philosophy of individualism lay a belief in universal and beneficent laws of society.

Petty is probably best known in the history of economic thought for his consistent efforts to find an empirical basis for economic theory. As an avowed empiricist, he was fully aware that his methodology constituted a new approach to economics. Thus he boldly asserted that his economic theory, unlike that of his predecessors, was based exclusively upon observed facts:

The Method I take to do this, is not yet very usual; for instead of using only comparative and superlative Words, and intellec-

tual Arguments, I have taken the course . . . to express myself in terms of *Number, Weight,* or *Measure;* to use only Arguments of Sense, and to consider only such Causes, as have visible Foundations in Nature.[51]

Petty was quite clearly making an effort to avoid the pitfalls of what he regarded as the traditional metaphysical approach to economic theory. Despite his effort to be a thoroughgoing empiricist, however, he frequently resorted to the use of metaphysical absolutes. This was, of course, merely a reflection of his intellectual environment, for the greatest scientists and philosophers of that period used similar analytical tools.[52] If such a renowned physicist as Newton could speculate freely about "absolute" space and time, it is not difficult to understand why social theorists should have assumed the existence of absolute social laws.

The works of Petty offer an excellent illustration of the impact of natural science on social theory during the latter part of the seventeenth century. In this "century of genius," no writer could long remain unaffected by the revolutionary developments in such fields as biology, physics, and mathematics. However, Petty was influenced more than most social scientists of his day because his training and experience gave him an unusually clear appreciation of the accomplishments of natural science. As a doctor of medicine, he acquired an early interest in biology, and his knowledge of mathematics was at least sufficient to enable him to become renowned for his work as a surveyor in Ireland. Perhaps even more important were the associations

---

[50] The term "transition" is that used by Heckscher (*op. cit.,* II, 323).

[51] *Economic Writings of Sir William Petty,* ed. C. H. Hull (Cambridge: At the University Press, 1899), I, 244. Subsequent references to Petty's writings are from this edition of his works.

[52] For an excellent discussion of the metaphysical content of the physical sciences, e.g., Newton's physics, see E. A. Burtt, *The Metaphysical Foundations of Modern Physical Science* (New York: Harcourt, Brace & Co., 1927).

he had with members of the Royal Society, of which he was a charter member.

In an important sense the pioneering work in statistics by John Graunt, Petty, and Gregory King was a reflection of the influence exerted by natural science on the study of social phenomena.[53] Although most of these early studies were confined to the area of statistical demography, they prepared the way for subsequent empirical research in related fields. In any case the interest in quantitative measurement of social data indicates that social scientists were beginning to appeal to facts in much the same fashion that biologists and physicists were basing their theories upon the experimental facts of the laboratory. It was not mere chance that Petty chose to call one of his important works *Political Arithmetick*.

From the point of view of the development of economic theory, the emergence of a scientific philosophy of determinism was possibly the most significant fact of the seventeenth century. The great creative minds in mathematics, biology, physics, etc., gradually came to view the world as an intricate machine in which each part played a role that was rigidly predetermined by inexorable laws.[54] Newton's *Principia*, published in 1687, provided the basis for a mechanistic outlook which would encompass the universe.[55] In such a

climate of opinion, social scientists began to search for a body of laws which would reveal a harmonious social order similar to that which physical scientists had discovered in their researches.[56]

The influences referred to above come into clear focus in Petty's writings, for his favorite thesis is that the natural laws of society are so powerful that they can never be circumvented by "positive" laws. He speaks, for instance, of the "vanity and fruitlessness of making Civil Positive Laws against the Laws of Nature." [57] His general regard for the functioning of natural law is indicated in the following passage:

> We must consider in general, that as wiser Physicians tamper not excessively with their Patients, rather observing and complying with the motions of nature, then contradicting it with vehement Administrations of their own; so in Politicks and Oconomicks the same must be used.[58]

His diagnosis of what had been ailing the economy of England is based upon the assumption that the regulatory, positive laws of the state are usually inimical to the welfare of the people. In England, too many matters "have been regulated by Laws, which Nature, long Custom, and general Consent, ought only to have governed." [59] He complains of efforts to "perswade Water to rise of itself above its natural Spring," and he is likewise critical of those who make "that infinite clutter about resisting . . . Nature, stopping up the windes and seas." [60] In such passages, Petty's terminology frequently reveals the imprint which natural science had made on

---

[53] For a discussion of the importance of the work done by these men see A. Wolf, *A History of Science, Technology, and Philosophy in the Sixteenth and Seventeenth Centuries* (New York: Macmillan Co., 1935), pp. 587–613.

[54] See A. N. Whitehead's discussion of the emergence of "materialistic mechanism" in his *Science and the Modern World* (New York: Macmillan Co., 1935), pp. 66–75.

[55] Many prominent scientists of the late seventeenth century did not adhere to a mechanistic philosophy, although their work was frequently used by others as the basis for this type of philosophy. Thus Newton thought his work strengthened "a spiritual view of reality" (Cecil Dampier, *A History of Science* [New York: Macmillan Co., 1944], p. 187). Even before Newton published his work, however, the mechanistic point of view was well established, e.g., in Hobbes's philosophy.

[56] Mechanistic overtones are found in economic literature at least as far back as the middle of the sixteenth century. In the *Discourse of the Common Weal* (pp. 98–100), for example, there is a long passage in which the author discusses economic activity in terms of an analogy with the mechanism of a clock.

[57] *Economic Writings*, I, 48.

[58] *Ibid.*, p. 60.

[59] *Ibid.*, p. 243.

[60] *Ibid.*, p. 60.

his thinking.[61] It is quite apparent that he thought the laws of society were virtually as inexorable as the Newtonian laws of physics.

One of the specific applications of Petty's natural-law theory appears in his discussion of questions concerning money and interest. He does not accept the early mercantilist views regarding the export of bullion, for he clearly states that any law prohibiting the export of the precious metals is both harmful and futile. Money has a "natural" value, which is determined on the same basis as the value of other commodities. Just as it is wrong to interfere with the natural prices of goods sold in domestic trade, so it is wrong to interfere with the movement of bullion to those countries where its price is highest. When asked whether England's laws limiting the export of bullion were good laws, he replied:

> Perhaps they are against the Laws of Nature, and, also impracticable: For we see that the Countries which abound with Money and all other Commodities, have followed no such Laws: and contrary wise, that the Countries which have forbid these Exportations under the highest penalties, are very destitute both of Money and Merchandize.[62]

Petty's solution of the problem of what

the rate of interest should be is likewise handled in terms of free-market theory. For example, he argues that any effort to prescribe the rate of interest by legislative enactment is doomed to failure, for natural market forces are too strong to be resisted. Hence the "natural" rate of interest can fall only in response to an increase in the supply of money:

> As to Mony, the Interest thereof was within this fifty years, at 10 l. *per Cent* forty years ago at 8 l. and now at 6 l. no thanks to any Laws which have been made to that purpose, forasmuch as those who can give security, may now have it at less: But the natural fall of interest is the effect of the increase of Mony.[63]

The fact that he objected to laws prohibiting usury has no special significance, for other writers had previously voiced opposition to such legislation. Even the Puritans, such as Richard Baxter, had begun to weaken in their strictures against usury. In Petty, however, the idea is clearly developed that statutory laws regulating the rate of interest do violence to the beneficent laws of nature.

To an important extent, John Locke represents the culmination of a trend in natural-law thinking which had begun during the sixteenth century. As previously noted, this new trend involved a significant change in the meaning attributed to natural law. During the medieval period the law of nature had been invoked "as a moral restraint upon self-interest," whereas, by the time of Locke, nature was largely identified with human appetites, and natural law was invoked "as a reason why self-interest should be given free play." [64] It is in connection with the rise of the new philosophy of individualism that Locke occupies a prominent position in the history of economic thought.

Locke's eclecticism is such that he vir-

---

[61] A multitude of terms might be used to illustrate the influence of natural science on economic thought. Of all those adopted by social theorists, perhaps the term "equilibrium" was destined to be most widely adopted in economic literature. The French economist, Pierre Boisguilbert, was among the first to use the concept of equilibrium as a basic analytical tool. For Boisguilbert, as for later economists, the equilibrium price signified both normality and beneficence. The importance which he attributed to equilibrium is indicated in the following statement: "Only equilibrium can save everyone; and nature alone, to repeat, can achieve this" (*Economistes financiers du XVIII siècle,* ed. E. Daire [Paris, 1843], p. 390).

G. N. Clark briefly describes the early influence of natural science on economic and political terminology in his *Science and Welfare in the Age of Newton* (London: Oxford University Press, 1949), pp. 118–19.

[62] *Economic Writings,* II, 445.

[63] *Ibid.,* I, 304.

[64] R. H. Tawney, *Religion and the Rise of Capitalism* (London: John Murray, 1948), p. 180.

tually defies classification with respect to any particular "school" of economic thought. One writer has asserted that Locke's economic "theory" was a "retrogression from Petty to Aristotle and the schoolmen," whereas his "practice" was that of "an adherence to mercantilism at a time when its foundations were being undermined." [65] It was J. M. Keynes who described Locke as "standing with one foot in the mercantilist world and with one foot in the classical world." [66] But, despite the inconsistencies which most writers find in his writings, the fact remains that there is almost universal recognition of the paramount contribution which Locke made in providing the philosophic foundation for economic individualism.

The role played by nature in Locke's philosophy is very clearly revealed in his epistemology, for the impact of nature on man forms the basis of his whole theory of knowledge. If the doctrine of the rationalists concerning the existence of innate ideas was to be abandoned, nature had to play a more active, and the mind a more passive, role than had been the case in previous systems of philosophy. In Locke's system, therefore, "the mind, in respect of its simple ideas, is wholly passive." [67] In other words, "perception is the first operation of our intellectual faculties, and the inlet of all knowledge into our minds." [68] The mind of man can play an active part in the formation of complex ideas, but all knowledge must be derived ultimately from simple ideas. In short, for Locke the "mind of man is entirely a product of his environment." [69]

Just as Locke holds that our knowledge of the physical world does not entail the use of any innate ideas, so he argues that the mind is not endowed with any innate moral knowledge. We are assured of a correct basis for our moral judgments only by means of the functioning of "natural tendencies." These are not to be confused with innate principles, for the "tendencies" are, in Locke's system, conceived to be only a *means* of acquiring moral knowledge, not innate impressions on the mind of moral knowledge itself. [70] When he writes that things "are good or evil only in reference to pleasure or pain," [71] he is anticipating much of the utilitarian theory of morals. Furthermore, since pleasure and pain are simple ideas which are derived only from experience, [72] the mind is passive with respect to both physical and moral knowledge.

Locke uses this sensationalism as the basis for building an individualist philosophy. If our moral concepts are to be derived from sense experience, then the sensations of pleasure and pain are the guides to moral behavior. Whatever gives an individual pleasure is therefore good for him. So it is that men "may choose different things, and yet all choose right." [73] There is, therefore, no universal standard of good and evil to which men may refer in making moral decisions.

What prevents such moral theorizing from becoming "pure" relativism is, of course, the role plyed by nature in Locke's system. Efforts to find a universal standard of value are doomed to failure because

[65] Max Beer, *Early British Economics* (London: G. Allen & Unwin, 1938), p. 234. It is interesting to note that Laski (*op. cit.,* p. 117) argues that the "very illogic of Locke is his strength."

At least one writer has taken exception to the traditional view of Locke's inconsistencies. This unique interpretation is contained in Werner Stark's *The Ideal Foundations of Economic Thought* (New York: Oxford University Press, 1944), pp. 1–26. He unequivocally asserts (p. 24) that Locke "was a master of consistency."

[66] J. M. Keynes, *The General Theory of Employment, Interest, and Money* (New York: Harcourt, Brace & Co.), p. 343.

[67] John Locke, *An Essay concerning Human Understanding* (London: Ward, Lock & Co., n.d.), p. 203.

[68] *Ibid.,* p. 96.

[69] Stark, *op. cit.,* p. 2.

[70] Locke, *op. cit.,* pp. 27–28.

[71] *Ibid.,* p. 160.

[72] *Ibid.*

[73] *Ibid.,* p. 180.

nature has provided for differences among individuals as regards their sensations of pleasure and pain. This does not result in a kind of moral anarchy only because Locke assumes that "natural tendencies" guide the individual in such a manner that he will usually choose the socially and ethically correct course of action. In his theory of morals, therefore, Locke provided what later came to be regarded as a virtually decisive justification for an economic system which would permit wide freedom of choice for the individual.

The importance which Locke attributes to the laws of nature can be seen even more clearly in his theory of property rights. His entire analysis of property rights is based on the assumption that natural law justifies private property. In chapter v of the *Second Treatise of Civil Government,* he discusses the problem of property in both a "state of nature" and in "modern" society. His conclusion is that the same fundamental law of nature justifies private property regardless of the state of social development.

For Locke, "natural reason" tells us that every man has a "property in his own person." [74] Therefore, when a man removes something from the "state Nature hath provided and left it in," he has "mixed" his labor with it, and ". . . thereby makes it his property." [75] In other words, man has "in himself the great foundation of property," and "labour, in the beginning, gave a right of property." [76]

A question immediately arises, however, concerning the amount of property a person has a right to possess. In answering this question, he first discusses the problem in relation to primitive society, and he then provides an answer for modern society. As for the state of nature, his answer is clear and unequivocal, and it is stated in terms

of a "law of Nature": "The same law of Nature that does by this means give us property, does also bound that property too. . . . As much as any one can make use of to any advantage of life before it spoils, so much he may by his labour fix a property in. Whatever is beyond this is more than his share, and belongs to others." [77]

It is important to recall that, for Locke, most of the "things really useful to the life of man" are "generally things of short duration" which will "decay and perish of themselves." [78] He deprecates the importance of the precious metals, diamonds, etc., for they are "things that fancy or agreement hath put the value on." [79] In accumulating such things as trinkets and jewelry, primitive man did not violate the law of nature. He might "heap up as much of these durable things as he pleased," because the law of nature did not limit the mere "largeness of his possession." [80] Natural law only dictated that nothing should be wasted as a result of accumulation.

Locke does not think the introduction of money in "modern" society necessitates any alteration of the basic law of nature concerning property rights, for money (i.e., "gold and silver") is "little useful to the life of man." [81] Modern man, therefore, can "rightfully and without injury, possess more than he himself can make use of by receiving gold and silver." [82] Inequality of wealth is justified on the basis of his assumption that people would always have free access to the economic resources required in the production of "useful" goods.[83] There is no recognition in his writings of a conflict between the law of nature as it applied in primitive and in modern society, for, in either case, inequality of wealth is sanctioned.

[77] *Ibid.,* p. 131.
[78] *Ibid.,* p. 139.
[79] *Ibid.*
[80] *Ibid.*
[81] *Ibid.,* p. 140.
[82] *Ibid.*
[83] *Ibid.,* pp. 138–39.

[74] John Locke, *Two Treatises of Government* (London: J. M. Dent & Sons, 1947), p. 130.
[75] *Ibid.*
[76] *Ibid.,* p. 138.

Locke's sensationalist psychology, combined with his theory of morals, provided much of the intellectual foundation for the utilitarian philosophy of Beccaria, Helvetius, and Bentham. Furthermore, his individualist ethics furnished much of the justification for a social organization which would permit a high degree of freedom for the individual. His theory of property, likewise based on natural-law doctrine, was destined to be a cornerstone in the foundation of economic liberalism.[84]

It is well known that Locke's economic theory did not consistently reflect the basic assumptions of his individualist philosophy. What is important for the present inquiry, however, is that Locke used natural law as a basic analytical tool in his philosophic system. His writings were a source of inspiration for almost all eighteenth-century social theorists, and the systemization of laissez faire theory was, to an important extent, little more than a projection of Locke's individualist philosophy into the field of economic theory.

The rapid movement toward an integrated system of laissez faire which followed the publication of Locke's works is a familiar chapter in the development of economic thought. Illustrations of the pace of this development are found in the writings of such men as North, Davenant, and Mandeville. Indeed, there is much justification for F. B. Kaye's assertion that Mandeville's *Fable of the Bees* is the first *systematic* presentation of the laissez faire philosophy.[85] Be this as it may, the eco-

nomic liberals of eighteenth-century England were obsessed with the idea that the social benefits of permitting each individual to pursue freely his own interests would flow spontaneously from a system of "natural" liberty. I have tried to indicate that the origin of this view dates at least as far back as the middle of the sixteenth century. What had begun as opportunistic and sporadic protests against commercial controls thus emerged, almost two centuries later, in the form of a systematized philosophy of economic individualism which proclaimed the beneficence of the laws of nature.

---

sharper focus in his political theory, e.g., his belief in "natural liberty," "natural rights," etc.

[85] For a discussion of this point see F. B. Kaye's edition of Bernard Mandeville, *The Fable of the Bees* (Oxford: Oxford University Press, 1924), I, xcviii–ciii. In the *Fable,* Mandeville applies the principle of self-interest to virtually all spheres of economic activity. The unifying thread is, of course, natural law, for the beneficent social effects of the pursuit of self-interest flow "naturally" and spontaneously from the operation of a laissez faire system.

For another interesting comment on the decisive influence of Mandeville in the development of economic individualism see F. A. Hayek, *Individualism and Economic Order* (Chicago: University of Chicago Press, 1948), p. 9. Hayek's position is that Mandeville was the first to formulate clearly the central idea of "true" individualism. The type of individualism which culminated in the work of Adam Smith is contrasted with that which derived from Cartesian rationalism and was most clearly reflected in the writings of the Encyclopedists and the Physiocrats. The latter type, according to Hayek, leads toward collectivism. At least two modern studies of physiocracy lend support to this interpretation: Norman Ware, "The Physiocrats: A Study in Economic Rationalization," *American Economic Review,* XXI (1931), 607–19, and Max Beer, *An Inquiry into Physiocracy* (London: George Allen & Unwin, 1939).

[84] The pervasive character of natural-law theory in Locke's system is, of course, brought into even

5 Physiocracy and
Classicism in Britain

RONALD L. MEEK

Although there are significant differences between the Physiocratic system and Smith's *Wealth of Nations,* both express the eighteenth century reaction against stringent government regulation of economic life. The Physiocrats, believing that labor was capable of yielding a net product or surplus only in the primary industries, protested against what they regarded as a misdirection of resources away from agriculture and other primary pursuits into the production of handicrafts and foreign trade. Smith, attacking the English commercial system to expose the fallacies of seeking a favorable balance of trade to augment the nation's gold supply, reasoned that, if foreign commerce contributed to wealth at all, it was because it added to the nation's supply of goods. Labor devoted to agriculture, manufacture, or domestic trade would, Smith believed, be more productive of vendible commodities than that devoted to foreign commerce. But he did not share the Physiocratic idea that only labor employed on the land was productive, even though he implied that land was an inherently superior source of surplus because, in agriculture, "nature labors along with man." He did not, however, view the primary industries as the only source of additions to the capital stock. Manufacturing also gave rise to a surplus. Profit, therefore, emerged in the Smithian system as an independent source of surplus which was separate and distinct from the rent of land.

The Physiocrats had more in common with Pre-Smithian English writers than they had with Smith himself and there was a prevalence of Physiocratic ideas in England, particularly during the early nineteenth century, that is seldom recognized. Ronald L. Meek's article, *Physiocracy and Classicism in Britain,* explores the reasons why the classical attitude of the ninteenth century, of which Physiocracy and Smithianism are both expressions, did not assume the Physiocratic form when it was eventually systemized in England.

Reprinted from Ronald L. Meek, "Physiocracy and Classicism in Britain," from the *Economic Journal,* March 1951, pp. 26–47. Dr. Meek is Professor of Economics, The University of Leicester, England.

"That system," Lauderdale noted in 1805, "which represents the produce of land as the sole source of the revenue, and the wealth of a nation, has long had its disciples in this country." [1] Lauderdale and his contemporaries found little difficulty in tracing many instances where earlier British writers had substantially anticipated certain of the basic doctrines of Quesnay. In the early years of the nineteenth century, indeed, it would have been virtually impossible for any British economist to regard Physiocracy as an eccentric, ephemeral and peculiarly French body of thought. For these were the years of the great debates over the validity of Physiocratic economic principles. Attempts were being made by numbers of publicists to popularise Physiocratic doctrines in various forms; polemics were being written in reply, some of them by men of considerable ability; and there was scarcely an economist writing in Britain at this time who did not feel impelled to give his opinion on the issues at stake.

It was largely in the course of these debates that British political economy was finally purged of the Physiocratic elements which had often characterised it in the past and moulded into something like the form it was eventually to assume in the hands of Ricardo. The present article begins with a discussion of the broad theoretical and historical relationships between the Physiocratic viewpoint and that adopted by Adam Smith and his followers. It then proceeds to its main task—to examine the nature and significance of the British Physiocratic controversies, with special reference to the manner in which they stimulated the development and refinement of Classical theory during the twenty years prior to the publication of Ricardo's *Principles*.

PHYSIOCRACY AND CLASSICISM

To Quesnay, as to Smith, the fundamental economic problem seemed to be that of the nature and causes of the wealth of nations. Of what did wealth consist? How was it produced and increased? And, in particular, what action should be taken to maximise its rate of increase? Both Quesnay and Smith believed that it was impossible to answer such questions as these unless one began by making a clear distinction between the two portions into which the annual produce "naturally divides itself" when it first comes into the hands of those to whom it directly accrues. One portion of the produce (or its value) has to be used to replace or compensate for the items which have been physically used up in the process of production during the period which has just ended. The second portion, the surplus over what Ricardo called "the absolutely necessary expenses of production," [2] represents the net social gain on the period's working. This surplus is "disposable" in the sense that it does not have to be expended in *maintaining intact* the productive powers of the community, but may at the option of the community be either consumed "unproductively" or employed to *increase* its productive powers. [3] In French Physiocracy the second portion of the produce figured, of course, as the famous *"produit net."* In the systems of Adam Smith and his followers it figured variously as the "net real income," "net revenue," "disposable income," or simply "surplus."

Upon the size of the social surplus, it was often assumed, the prosperity of the community largely depended. This assumption was based, at least in part, upon the belief that the surplus was the only possible source from which new capital could be

[1] *An Inquiry into the Nature and Origin of Public Wealth*, p. 112. Cf. Dugald Stewart, "Lectures on Political Economy," in *Collected Works*, Vol. 1, at pp. 298–301.

[2] *Works* (ed. McCulloch), p. 210, footnote.
[3] Cf. J. S. Mill, *Essays on Some Unsettled Questions of Political Economy* (L.S.E. reprint), p. 89.

accumulated. The importance of this idea
is obvious enough in the *Wealth of Nations,*
but it is not so immediately apparent in
the work of the French Physiocrats. Yet
the Physiocrats' analysis of the various
forms of capital was surely one of their
most significant contributions to economic
thought. Quesnay himself was concerned
above all with the application of capitalist
methods to agriculture, but this one-sided
approach was fairly soon corrected when
the agricultural school founded by Quesnay and Mirabeau was amalgamated with
—or absorbed by—the *"école-sœur"* allegedly founded by Gournay. When Du
Pont, Baudeau and Turgot, who were
mainly responsible for removing the feudal
trappings from Quesnay's system, began to
call energetically for the application of
capitalist methods to manufacture as well
as to agriculture, the essential character of
Physiocracy became easier to discern. But
even in the earlier works of the founders of
the agricultural school the emphasis on the
importance of capital is quite unmistaka-
ble. Quesnay's first economic article,
"Fermiers," was a plea for the adoption of
la grande culture by a small number of
rich farmers rather than *la petite culture*
by a host of poor metayers; and in his
second article, *"Grains,"* he made it clear
that he visualised his rich farmer not as a
superior sort of labourer but as *"un entrepreneur qui gouverne."* [4] It was not so much
men who were required in the country,
Quesnay insisted—it was rather wealth.[5]
In the Tableau the great kingdom, *"porté
à son plus haut degré d'agriculture,"* [6] was
obviously intended to represent a France
of the future in which *la grande culture*
which Quesnay had seen in operation in
certain French provinces[7] had been extended throughout the whole realm. And
Quesnay also made it clear that the capital
required to bring the kingdom *"à son plus
haut degré d'agriculture"* must come, gen-

erally speaking, from the *produit net.* "The
more agriculture languishes," he wrote,
"the more necessary it is that a portion of
the disposable revenue should be devoted
to its rehabilitation." [8]

Both Quesnay and Smith, then, and the
schools which they represent, were primarily concerned with the scientific analysis
of *capitalist production.* Both were interested in securing an increase in national
wealth per medium of an extension of
capitalist methods, and both realised that
freedom of trade, internal and external,
was a necessary precondition of this. In
their theoretical analyses they both tended
to concentrate much of their attention on
the question of the origin and disposition
of the social surplus, which they regarded
as the only possible source of new capital.
In this common interest and emphasis,
they are so sharply distinguished, on the
one hand from the Mercantilist writers
who preceded them, and on the other hand
from the Marginalist writers who followed
them, that it seems proper for the historian
of economic thought to stress their community by treating them as working within
a broadly similar framework of aims and
concepts. The most convenient name for
this framework is probably "Classicism."
Physiocracy and the type of theory pro-
pounded by Smith and his followers are
best regarded, I suggest, as two different
species of the genus Classicism.[9]

[4] *Oeuvres* (ed. Oncken), p. 219.
[5] *Ibid.,* p. 333.
[6] *Ibid.,* p. 309.
[7] *Ibid.,* p. 196.
[8] *Ibid.,* p. 317. Cf. the *"troisième observation,"* pp. 318–19. It was in this connection that one of the fundamental contradictions inherent in the Physiocratic tenets was later to reveal itself. Quesnay often argued (*e.g.,* pp. 313–14) that the "interest" which the farmer received on his capital was merely a compensation for wear and tear, etc., and contained no element of *produit net.* On the other hand, he often tended to visualise the farmers, rather than the landlords, as the poten-
tial agents of agricultural reform. How, then, if the farmers' income included no element of *produit net,* could they accumulate the capital necessary to accomplish the reform? One possible explanation was given by Quesnay (pp. 507–8), but it was hardly satisfactory.
[9] This view roughly coincides with the original use of the term "Classical" by Marx. Cf. his *Critique of Political Economy* (Kerr edition), p. 56.

But the differences between these two species of Classical thought were nevertheless profound. The root of the essential difference between them lay in the distinct assumption which each school made concerning the *form* taken by the social surplus. The Physiocrats assumed that the surplus took the form of land-rent and land-rent alone. The earth is the unique source of wealth; agriculture is productive and manufacture sterile; the *produit net* alone constitutes wealth—such propositions as these are simply different ways of saying that land-rent is the only form which the social surplus assumes. To the earlier Physiocrats there was no such category of income as *net* profit at all. The capitalist farmer certainly received "interest" on his capital, but this "interest" was usually regarded as being only just sufficient to compensate for wear and tear and the damage done by acts of God, etc.—that is, it was conceived simply as a refund of certain necessary costs of cultivation. The industrial entrepreneur, again, sometimes received an income which appeared to be in the nature of a net profit, but upon analysis this income was revealed either as a superior sort of wage (in which case it entered into necessary costs) or else as a portion of the *produit net* which the entrepreneur was able to extort from the landowner by selling commodities to him at a price greater than their real value.[10] Any "profit" received which was not resolvable into wages was generally regarded as being dependent upon and paid out of rent, the only true *produit net*. In the work of Quesnay and Mirabeau this view no doubt to some extent reflected the subordinate position of manufacture and the backward condition of agriculture under the *ancien*

régime in the middle of the eighteenth century. But its significance is wider than this. It is a view which is likely to be extensively held in any society which is passing through a particular historical stage—the stage in which profit on capital exists but has not yet emerged as a *normal* category of income.[11] And it is a view which is likely to disintegrate once this stage has been passed.

Whereas the Physiocrats considered rent to be the only income in the nature of a surplus, the Smithian school afforded that status to profit as well as to rent. To Smith himself it seemed clear that that second portion of the annual produce which represented the social surplus over cost consisted of both rent and profits. One part of the produce, he wrote, is "destined for replacing a capital, or for renewing the provisions, materials, and finished work, which had been withdrawn from a capital; the other for constituting a revenue either to the owner of this capital, as the profit of his stock, or to some other person, as the rent of his land."[12] The Physiocratic controversies which are examined later in this article resulted in the eventual confirmation of this viewpoint and in the partial elaboration of a set of techniques capable of giving it theoretical expression. And they also stimulated an important advance beyond this viewpoint.

In British economic thought before Adam Smith, those writers who were interested in questions relating to the analysis of the process of production (as distinct from the process of exchange) occasionally adopted a Physiocratic viewpoint—that is, they tended to regard profits (and interest) as being paid out of and dependent upon the

[10] He could only do this, it was often suggested, if he possessed "exclusive privileges" of some kind or other. Cf. Du Pont's statement quoted in Weulersse, *Le Mouvement Physiocratique,* Vol. 1, p. 298. As Weulersse remarks (p. 295), manufacture is regarded as being burdensome when it ceases to be sterile.

[11] The passing of this stage is likely to be marked by the gradual disappearance of the idea of "profit" as the reward for a special kind of labour, and the emergence of the concept of a normal *rate* of profit, calculated by relating net income not to the amount of labour performed by the owner of the capital but to the amount of capital employed by him. Cf. Smith, *Wealth of Nations* (Everyman edition), Vol. 1, p. 43.

[12] *Wealth of Nations,* Vol. 1, p. 290.

rent of land. Cantillon, for example, believed that "all classes and individuals in a state subsist or are enriched at the expense of the proprietors of land." [13] A seventeenth-century pamphleteer asserted that the landowners "are masters and proprietors of the foundation of all the wealth of this nation, all the profits arising out of the ground which is theirs." [14] Petty, and to some extent Locke, seem to have regarded profits as included in rent, and interest as derived from rent.[15] It is easy enough to detect, in some of the earlier efforts to define the Classical framework and to work within it, a definite Physiocratic bias. Why was it, then, that the eventual *systematisation* of the Classical attitude in Britain did not assume a Physiocratic form? And why was it that the Classical attitude was *first* systematised in France (where the system could hardly help assuming a Physiocratic form), rather than in Britain, whose economy was considerably more advanced than that of France?

[13] *Essai* (R. E. S. reprint), p. 43.
[14] Quoted in Beer, *An Inquiry into Physiocracy*, p. 74.
[15] Cf. Marx, *Theorien* (French edition), Vol. 1, pp. 4 and 21–2. It should perhaps be pointed out here that I do not regard statements to the effect that the earth is "properly the fountaine and mother of all the riches and abundance of the world," etc., or panegyrics in praise of the agricultural surplus, as being necessarily Physiocratic, in the sense in which I am using the word —although they may often be associated with a Physiocratic outlook. There is obviously an important sense in which it is universally true to say that all wealth springs from the earth, and that the agricultural surplus "maintains" all those who do not work on the land. I count as Physiocrats only those who, at a time when profit on capital is a recognised (though not necessarily a regular or normal) category of income, treat it not as an original and independent income but as being in some way dependent upon or "paid out of" land-rent, which alone constitutes the social surplus. This definition, while it leaves us with some difficult border-line cases like Paley and Steuart, at least prevents our having to acknowledge Aristotle and Artaxerxes as pioneers of Physiocracy—which William Spence was quite prepared to do! (See Cobbett's *Weekly Political Register*, December 12, 1807, p. 923.)

Let us deal with the latter question first. The predecessors of Adam Smith, like Smith himself, were mainly interested in the problem of increasing national wealth, but in the conditions of their time it was only natural that their attention should have been chiefly directed to the relative "surplus" yielded in foreign trade rather than to the positive surplus yielded in production. The gains from foreign trade were so manifest and so considerable, and their importance as a source of capital accumulation so obvious, that the commercial classes inevitably regarded the prosperity of the country as being largely dependent upon the size of their own profits. And, as Mr. Dobb has pointed out, conditions were such that they still found it difficult "to imagine any substantial profit being 'naturally' made by investment in production." [16] If, therefore, the revenue from the sale of a commodity exceeded the cost of producing or acquiring it, the excess was regarded as originating, not in the process of production, but in the act of exchange. All industrial and commercial profit, in other words, was "profit upon alienation." For example, Cary explained that when manufactured goods were sold abroad "the necessity and humour of the buyers" sometimes enabled the merchant to sell his commodities at a price greater than the "true value of the materials and labour." [17] It was widely realised, of course, that if such a situation were to persist, it was necessary that the seller should be protected as far as possible against competition—a task which the State was expected to undertake.[18] For these reasons, then, in the last century of the Mercantilist era in Britain the economic analysis of production was almost always subordinated to the analysis of exchange. In France, on the other hand, the gains

[16] *Studies in the Development of Capitalism*, p. 199. Cf. Engels, *Engels on "Capital,"* pp. 110–11.
[17] John Cary, *An Essay Towards Regulating the Trade and Employing the Poor in this Kingdom* (2nd edition, 1719), pp. 11–12.
[18] M. H. Dobb, *op. cit.*, p. 200.

from foreign trade were of little economic importance, and it was possible for the foundations of the Classical analysis, with its emphasis on production, to be laid at a time when the capitalist order was only just beginning to emerge from feudal society.

To answer the other question—why the eventual systematisation of the Classical attitude in Britain did not assume a Physiocratic form—it is necessary to ask why the Mercantilist emphasis on exchange gradually gave way in this country to the Classical emphasis on production. Two interrelated developments in the eighteenth century contributed largely to this radical change of viewpoint. First, British merchants began to experience more serious competition in foreign trade, and attention was increasingly directed towards the reduction of costs in the manufactory rather than towards the strengthening of their monopolistic position in the foreign market[19]—a change of attitude which was, of course, greatly encouraged by the contemporary developments in industrial technique. Second, net profit on capital slowly began to emerge as a distinct and normal category of income, receivable at more or less the same rate per cent on capital employed not only in commerce but also in manufacture and agriculture—and receivable, too, even under conditions approaching perfect competition. Under these conditions, the notion of "profit upon alienation" could hardly hope to survive. Economists gradually began to regard profit as *originating* in the process of production and as merely being *realised* in the act of sale. Under these circumstances, economists naturally began to seek for the origin of the social surplus in the sphere of production rather than in the sphere of exchange. But the very conditions which induced this movement towards Classicism were such as to make it virtually impossible for the

eventual systematisation of the Classical attitude in Britain to assume a Physiocratic form. By the time British economists came to analyse capitalist production, capitalist production itself had developed to such an extent that the basic Physiocratic assumptions seemed quite inconsistent with economic reality.

THE PHYSIOCRATIC CONTROVERSIES

If we look at the *Wealth of Nations* from the vantage point of Ricardo's *Principles* it is not difficult to pick out the concepts which were destined to play the most prominent part in the development of political economy in the early nineteenth century. In the first place, Smith defined clearly the aim of the science. "Political economy," he said, "considered as a branch of the science of a statesman or legislator, proposes . . . to enrich both the people and the sovereign."[20] Secondly, he suggested that the size of the annual produce per head in any country—the best measure of its degree of enrichment—is regulated by two factors—"first, by the skill, dexterity, and judgment with which its labour is generally applied; and, secondly, by the proportion between the number of those who are employed in useful labour, and that of those who are not so employed."[21] Thirdly, he insisted that both of these factors are largely dependent upon the quantity of capital—in the first case because the accumulation of capital is not only a historical precondition of the division of labour but also greatly encourages the extension of the division of labour, and in the second case because the number of useful labourers "is everywhere in proportion to the quantity of capital stock which is employed in setting them to work, and to the particular way in which it is so employed."[22]

---

[19] Cf. E. S. Furniss, *The Position of the Laborer in a System of Nationalism*, pp. 165–7.

[20] *Wealth of Nations*, Vol. 1, p. 375.
[21] *Ibid.*, p. 1.
[22] *Ibid.*, pp. 241–2, and p. 2.

Smith's main theoretical interest lay, therefore, in the sphere of capitalist production, and particularly in the problems relating to the accumulation of capital. The analytical tools which he developed were designed to deal with the questions arising in this sphere. His account of accumulation, for example, is formulated in terms of two basic theoretical concepts— the notion of surplus and the distinction between productive and unproductive labour. The social surplus of produce over cost, assuming the dual form of rent and profits, is regarded as the only possible source of funds for accumulation, and labour is described as "productive" or "unproductive" according to whether it actually helps to create this surplus or merely shares in it.[23]

In Smith's system, as opposed to that of the Physiocrats, labour employed in manufacture is assumed to be productive—in other words, industrial profit is regarded as being an income in the nature of a surplus. Profit now stands on its own, quite independent of rent—a "real primitive increase of national wealth," as a later economist was to describe it,[24] originating in the process of production and regularly yielded even under competitive conditions. Smith intuitively recognised, I think, that if profit was to be regarded in this way a new theory of value had to be evolved. Roughly speaking (and with several notable exceptions) previous writers had conceived of the "value" of a commodity in terms of the

physical items which had been used up in order to produce it. The value of a finished commodity equalled the value of the raw materials embodied in it, plus the value of the subsistence goods consumed during the process of production by the men who worked up the raw materials. This crude theory of value—which we can perhaps call the "physical cost" theory to distinguish it from the Ricardian "labour cost" theory—was, of course, quite inadequate to deal with the theoretical problems arising out of the new way of looking at profit. In the first place, the physical cost theory implied that the "value" of what went into the productive process was exactly the same as the "value" of what came out—that is, it implied that no surplus was yielded *in production*. And in the second place, on the basis of the physical cost theory the existence of profit could be accounted for only by conceiving commodities as being customarily sold *above their value*. But as capitalism developed, and markets became more and more competitive, economists became increasingly impressed by the fact that the actual prices received for a commodity tended to oscillate around a sort of mean or average price, and a new notion of value began to take the place of the old. It began to be felt that value ought to be conceived, not as something which a commodity usually sold *above*, but as something which under competition it tended to sell *at*. The physical cost theory, then, was incapable of giving theoretical expression to the idea of profit as a value-surplus which originated in the activity of production and which was realised when the commodity was sold "at its value" on a market. A new theory of value had to be developed. Smith's own attempt to develop such a theory was no doubt confused and ambiguous, but it did at least have the merit of directing inquiry away from the physical cost theory and towards the labour cost theory eventually adopted by Ricardo.

[23] This, I believe, is the basic idea which Smith had in mind when making his distinction. It is surely implied in the very title of the chapter in which he discusses the question—"Of the Accumulation of Capital, or of Productive and Unproductive Labour." The criterion of distinction usually emphasised by Smith's critics to-day—that relating to the material or immaterial character of the commodity produced—probably owed its origin to the fact that in Smith's time almost all the labourers employed on a capitalist basis were engaged in the production of material goods.
[24] Daniel Boileau, *Introduction to the Study of Political Economy* (1811), p. 164.

And although Smith seems to have decided that the labour cost theory was inapplicable under conditions of developed capitalism, he did apply it fairly consistently in his account of the origin of profit. "The value which the workmen add to the materials," he wrote, "resolves itself . . . into two parts, of which the one pays their wages, the other the profits of their employer upon the whole stock of materials and wages which he advanced." [25]

But these aspects of the *Wealth of Nations* appear especially significant only if, as I have suggested, we look at Smith's work from the viewpoint of Ricardo's *Principles*. It is easy to exaggerate the extent of Smith's emancipation from Physiocratic notions. Taking the *Wealth of Nations* as a whole, Smith looks backwards towards the Physiocrats almost as often as he looks forward towards Ricardo. In a number of passages, for example, he stresses the primacy of the agricultural surplus. "It is the surplus produce of the country only," he writes in his chapter on the progress of opulence, "or what is over and above the maintenance of the cultivators, that constitutes the subsistence of the town, which can therefore increase only with the increase of this surplus produce." [26] Such statements are not in themselves Physiocratic, but they may easily lead to the adoption of a Physiocratic viewpoint. Smith asserted that the great landed pro-

prietor, when he uses his rent-surplus to purchase manufactured goods from tradesmen and artificers, "indirectly pays all (their) wages and profits and thus indirectly contributes to the maintenance of all the workmen and their employers." [27] And in another passage, which Spence was later to find useful, Smith argued that the produce of "lands, mines, and fisheries" replaces with a profit not only the capitals required in these spheres "but all the others in the society." [28] Smith's leanings towards Physiocracy are even more clearly revealed in his well-known comparison between the productive powers of labour in manufacture and in agriculture. In manufacture the labourers occasion only "the reproduction of a value equal to their own consumption, or to the capital which employs them, together with its owners' profits"; but in agriculture, "over and above the capital of the farmer and all its profits, they regularly occasion the reproduction of the rent of the landlord." The generation of this additional surplus in agriculture is ascribed to the fact that it is only in agriculture that "nature labours along with man." [29] In view of these statements, it is not surprising that Smith should have believed that the interest of the landlords is "strictly and inseparably connected with the general interest of the society." [30] Nor is it surprising that his direct critique of Physiocracy at the end of Book IV should have been so unsatisfactory.

In a predominantly agricultural society, it may seem quite natural to regard land-rent as the primary and original category of income and profit as a secondary and derivative category. In a developed capitalist economy, on the other hand, in which capital and capitalist organisation have been extended to embrace every field of

[25] *Wealth of Nations*, Vol. 1, p. 42. It should be noted that the Physiocrats did not need a theory of value at all in order to give expression to the idea of *rent* as a surplus. In early agricultural production, as distinct from manufacture, the commodities comprising the input are likely to be qualitatively similar to those comprising the output, so that the creation of the surplus can be plausibly described in *real* terms without the intervention of a value theory. Cf. Malthus, *Principles* (L.S.E. reprint), pp. 262–4; Ramsay, *An Essay on the Distribution of Wealth* (1836), pp. 137–8 and 146; Marx, *Theorien*, Vol. 1, pp. 44–5; and M. H. Dobb, *Political Economy and Capitalism*, pp. 31–2.
[26] *Ibid.*, Vol. 1, p. 337.

[27] *Ibid.*, p. 367.
[28] *Ibid.*, p. 249.
[29] *Ibid.*, Vol. 1, p. 324.
[30] *Ibid.*, p. 230.

productive activity, including agriculture, it may seem more appropriate to regard profit on capital as the primary and land-rent as the secondary income.[31] From this point of view, Smith's thought was essentially transitional. Although he partially succeeded in emancipating profit from its former state of dependence upon rent, he was content merely to afford it an equal status, and did not seek to assert its superiority over rent. In fact, as we have just seen, rent in his system often retained some of its old pre-eminence. Smith's genius enabled him to discern the broad outlines of the capitalist form of economic organisation rather in advance of its complete realisation, but he could hardly have been expected to anticipate certain fundamental social attitudes which emerged only when the industrial revolution was well under way.

The more abstract sections of the *Wealth of Nations* did not excite much interest until the end of the century. Then, however, a number of factors combined to attract a considerable amount of attention to the question of the origin of capitalist profit and its relation to land-rent. The startling increase in productivity and profit in the manufacturing industries and the threat to Britain's commerce during the Napoleonic wars were obviously influential factors. The promulgation of the Malthusian theory of population may perhaps be regarded as another: Malthus had drawn popular attention to the relationship between subsistence and population, and thence to the relationship of dependence between the agricultural surplus and the nonagricultural population.[32] But the most important influence, overlapping the others and in part dictating the attitudes adopted by the participants in controversies over more ephemeral issues, was un-

doubtedly the sharpening of the political struggle between the recipients of rents and the recipients of profits. This struggle, culminating in the passing of the Reform Bill, may be said to have marked the consummation of the victory of the capitalist order in Britain. The question of the origin of profit and the nature of the interdependence between rent and profit began to be regarded as *politically* significant. If the agricultural surplus was in fact the basic income out of which all the other incomes were ultimately paid, this might be presumptive evidence in favour of special discriminatory measures protecting agriculture and the recipients of rent. If, on the other hand, profit on capital—particularly capital employed in manufacture—actually represented "a real primitive increase of national wealth," there was no longer any necessary presumption in favour of the landed proprietors: if manufacture was truly productive, it was truly independent.

The first important work to be considered is John Gray's pamphlet *The Essential Principles of the Wealth of Nations*, published in 1797. "The principal and most essential cause of the prosperity of a state," Gray argues, "is the ingenuity and labour of its inhabitants exercised upon the fertility of the soil."[33] Agricultural labour is truly productive—*i.e.*, productive of a surplus; but "no augmentation of the revenue of society arises from the labour of a manufacturer," since "the buyer precisely loses not only what the manufacturer gains, but the amount of the wages, and of the price of the raw materials besides."[34] Adam Smith and other notable writers have been misled into believing that manufacturing labour produces a surplus because of the obvious fact that many master-manufacturers do somehow manage to get rich. But profit actually originates, not in the process of production, but in the act of exchange. "When the manufacturer

---

[31] Cf. S. N. Patten, "The Interpretation of Ricardo," *Quarterly Journal of Economics*, April 1893, *passim*.

[32] See, *e.g.*, the second edition of Malthus's *Essay* (1803), pp. 435–6.

[33] *Essential Principles*, p. 4.

[34] *Ibid.*, p. 36.

ceases to be a seller," Gray asserts, "his profits are immediately at a stand, because they are not natural profits, but artificial." [35]

Two special aspects of Gray's argument deserve comment. In the first place, Gray regards manufacture as unproductive from the point of view of the nation as a whole only if the goods are sold at home. If they are exported, then "the profit of the exporter becomes the profit of the nation where he lives"—a thorough-going Mercantilist conclusion.[36] In the second place, Gray uses Physiocracy not to defend but to attack the landed interests. The labourers in manufacture, he says, may be unproductive, but they are at least a necessary and useful class. But the landlords, because they have separated the rent of land from "the constitutional purpose of the defence of the state," have now rendered themselves "one of the most unessential and most burdensome classes in society." [37] Gray was not the only economist to make Physiocratic principles serve radical ends. The idea that the incomes of the landowners were nothing but a monstrous exaction from the produce of the labour of the agricultural workers, and that upon this primary exaction were based the claims of numerous other parasitical elements, became quite common in the radical literature of the period. Charles Hall, Piercy Ravenstone and Thomas Hopkins were among those who founded their main arguments on this thesis.[38]

Daniel Wakefield, an uncle of Edward Gibbon Wakefield, published a reply to Gray in 1799, of which a second edition, virtually a new work, appeared five years later. The main problem which excited Wakefield's interest was "whether labour employed in manufactures does produce, as well as labour employed in agriculture, a surplus value." [39] He personifies agriculture by a "cultivator" and manufacture by a "manufacturer," both of whom, at least in the earlier stages of the argument, are assumed to combine in their own persons the qualities of entrepreneur and labourer. The "cultivator" is apparently assumed to operate with his own "cattle for work, implements, sheds, &c." and to rent land from a proprietor, while the "manufacturer" is assumed "to exercise his industry on a borrowed capital." The cultivator during the process of production "annihilates" certain things in order to obtain his product. He annihilates: (1) "his own intermediate support, between seed time and harvest"; (2) "the wear of his stock advances"; and (3) "the seed sown." The value of his "rude produce" will be sufficient to replace the value of the three items "annihilated" and in addition to provide a "surplus value, or surplus production," divided into "the profits of his stock, and the rent of his land." The manufacturer similarly "annihilates": (1) "his own intermediate support between the beginning and completion of the manufacture"; (2) "the wear of his stock advances"; and (3) "the raw material used." The value of his "finished manufacture" will also be sufficient to replace the value of the three items "annihilated" and in addition to provide a "surplus value" divided into "the profits of his stock, and the interest of his capital." [40] Wakefield believes that this argument proves that "both rent of land and interest of capital . . . are equally caused by the labour and ingenuity of man producing a surplus, or more than his support and expence, whether

[35] *Ibid.*, p. 39.

[36] Cf. Davenant, *An Essay on the East-India-Trade* (1697), p. 31.

[37] *Essential Principles*, p. 51.

[38] Charles Hall, at least, was quite conscious of the affiliation. In a letter written in 1808 to Arthur Young he complains that Spence and Cobbett "took their ideas" from his *Effects of Civilisation* (B.M. Addl. 35,130, f. 128).

[39] *An Inquiry into the Truth of the Two Positions of the French Oeconomists, etc.* (1799), pp. 6–7.

[40] *An Essay upon Political Oeconomy* (1804), pp. 9–11.

employed on land, or capital: in agriculture, or manufacturers." [41]

This was not a new argument. It had been anticipated in a casual remark made by Smith,[42] and Alexander Hamilton had used a variant of it as a weapon against Physiocracy in his *Report on Manufactures* in 1791.[43] And, of course, the analogy between rent and interest is not very happily drawn: if the cultivator operates with his own capital, his net receipts will obviously include a payment for interest,[44] and rent remains as an income of a unique type whose appearance in agriculture alone has still to be explained. But the fact that Wakefield looked at the problem in terms of cost and surplus value led him to put forward a number of subsidiary arguments which are of rather more interest. In the first place, he realised that an adequate answer to the Physiocrats required the intervention of a theory of value, and he endeavoured to supply such a theory himself. The Physiocrats assert, Wakefield argues, that "the increase of the Manufacturer is only nominal: that, though to him it is an increase, to the community it is only a transfer of produce, from the class of Cultivators to that of Manufacturers." But, he asks, "how is it ascertained, that the increase of the Cultivator is not equally nominal?" Surely it is wrong to consider "not any thing to be valuable but food." The labour of the manufacturer, like that of the cultivator, yields a surplus value— that is, it is "worth more in the estimation of the Consumer" than the items annihilated in the process of production. If the

estimation of the consumer is not to be taken as evidence of the value of the product, "what shall be considered as evidence?" [45] Wakefield's attempt to link a subjective theory of value with his main analysis is not particularly successful, but a number of the by-products of his attempt are interesting—notably his concept of "relative cost" (roughly equivalent to our opportunity cost),[46] his statement that the wages of "every kind of educated labour" constitute a "monopoly price," [47] and his recognition of the fact that anything which the labourers and capitalists receive over and above the supply price of labour and capital is in the nature of a rent.[48] In the second place, Wakefield laid considerable emphasis on the role of *labour* in production. "All value," he says, "is the result of an exertion of human wit and industry," supporting this contention with extensive quotations from Garnier, Locke and Priestley. He stresses the fact that even in agriculture and the extractive industries labour plays a prominent and active role—an argument which was to become increasingly familiar during the next decade.[49]

Interest in these problems among economists must have been widespread in the opening years of the nineteenth century. In 1801 William Spence was reading to a literary society a paper in which he maintained "all the main positions" subsequently taken up in his *Britain Independent of Commerce*.[50] In 1803 Malthus's second edi-

[41] *Inquiry*, pp. 14–15.
[42] *Wealth of Nations*, Vol. II, p. 329.
[43] *Papers on Public Credit, Commerce and Finance* (ed. S. McKee), pp. 184–5. Hamilton, like Turgot, emphasised the fact that rent may be regarded as interest on the capital sunk in land. The rent paid on land "advanced" to the farmer by the landlord, therefore, did not differ qualitatively from the interest paid on the capital advanced to the manufacturer.
[44] Wakefield recognised clearly enough that this would be the case if the *manufacturer* worked with his own capital: *Essay*, p. 11.

[45] *Essay*, pp. 12–14.
[46] *Ibid.*, pp. 51–3.
[47] *Ibid.*, p. 67.
[48] *Ibid.*, p. 69. Cf. Buchanan, *Observations on the Subjects Treated in Dr. Smith's Inquiry* (1814), pp. 39–41.
[49] *Ibid.*, p. 56 and pp. 40–6. This argument, that labour is very important in agriculture, was sometimes associated with another—that nature is very important in manufacture. Ricardo used it in his *Principles* (Works, pp. 39–40, footnote); it is also to be found in Hamilton's *Report on Manufactures* (*op. cit.*, p. 183); and in a review of Lauderdale's *Inquiry* in the *Edinburgh Review*, July 1804, p. 359.
[50] Cf. Spence's letter in Cobbett's *Weekly Political Register*, December 5, 1807, pp. 921–2.

tion appeared. Lauderdale's *Inquiry*, with its critique of Physiocracy and its new theory of profit, was published in 1804; and in the same year, apparently, Simon Gray wrote his *Happiness of States*. And Dugald Stewart was including in his influential lectures a long discussion on the distinction between productive and unproductive labour, in which he tended to side with the Physiocrats rather than with Adam Smith. But the publication of Spence's *Britain Independent of Commerce* in 1807, the advocacy of Spence's views by Cobbett in his *Political Register*, and the entrance of Mill, Torrens and Chalmers into the arena, brought the controversy to the notice of a much wider public.

Spence's work, considered in itself, is not particularly interesting. It caused a great popular stir, of course, largely because Spence put forward the comfortable view that the destruction of Britain's overseas trade by Napoleon would make little difference to national welfare. As an exposition of the theory of Physiocracy it is inferior to Gray's pamphlet. Spence tried to explain the origin of industrial profit by arguing, more or less as the French Physiocrats had done, that the cultivator may give more for a manufactured article than its "real value"—its "real value" being conceived (in physical cost terms) as being equivalent to "the raw produce and food consumed in producing it."[51] The master-manufacturer may in this manner receive a surplus over his costs of production, and may even be able to accumulate part of his profits and thus acquire great riches—but even then "the whole of his gains would be at the expense of the land proprietors, and no addition would be made to the national wealth."[52] Cobbett's extensive advocacy of Spence's views (under the provocative title "Perish Commerce") did not contribute a great deal towards a solution of the theo-

retical problem involved, although one of his correspondents was acute enough to realise that its solution depended upon regarding value as being "constituted by labour, or the difficulty of producing any commodity."[53]

Torrens's reply to Spence, *The Economists Refuted*, contains some interesting passages which have sometimes been construed as an anticipation of the doctrine of comparative costs,[54] but in general it is much less effective than James Mill's *Commerce Defended*. Mill's chapter on Consumption is a remarkable piece of work. It is quite consciously imbued with the main ideas associated with the mature Classical outlook—that production is primary and consumption secondary, that the economic progress of society depends upon the accumulation of capital, and that the only possible source of funds for accumulation is the social surplus.[55] The main purpose of the chapter is to attack Spence's contentions that "expenditure, not parsimony, is the province of the class of land proprietors," and that "for the constantly progressive maintenance of the prosperity of the community, it is absolutely requisite that this class should go on progressively increasing its expenditure."[56] Mill saw Spence's argument for what it was—an attack upon capital accumulation, and denied vehemently that it was possible for capital to increase too fast. "Obstacles enow exist to the augmentation of capital," he said, "without the operation of ridiculous speculations."[57] To support his attack on this part of Spence's book, Mill refurbished a well-known dictum of Smith's[58] in order to assure Spence that "the whole annual

[51] Spence, *Tracts on Political Economy* (1822), p. 148.
[52] *Ibid.*, p. 14.

[53] *Register*, January 23, 1808, pp. 130 ff. See also the letter in the issue of February 6, 1808, pp. 218 ff.
[54] See Viner, *Studies in the Theory of International Trade*, pp. 441–4.
[55] *Commerce Defended* (1808), pp. 79, 70–4, and *passim*.
[56] Spence, *Tracts*, pp. 32–3.
[57] *Commerce Defended*, p. 88.
[58] *Wealth of Nations*, Vol. I, p. 302.

produce of the country will be always very completely consumed, whether his landlords choose to spend or to accumulate." [59] Mill then proceeded to develop his famous exposition of what subsequently came to be known as Say's Law. The most interesting thing about this controversy (continued by Spence in his tract *Agriculture the Source of the Wealth of Great Britain*) is, of course, the way in which it foreshadowed the later and greater one between Ricardo and Malthus. Malthus, like Spence (and indeed like Chalmers too), seems to have based his under-consumptionist doctrine on the Physiocratic contention that "the unproductive consumption of the landlords and capitalists" should be "proportioned to the natural surplus of the society";[60] and Ricardo, like Mill, based his reply on an elaboration of Smith's dictum and on Say's Law.

Two more Physiocratic tracts remain to be noticed.[61] One of them, the anonymous pamphlet *Sketches on Political Economy* (1809), has often been commented upon, and little need be said about it here. The author uses Physiocracy (plus a version of the labour theory of value) to attack Lauderdale's theory of the productivity of capital. Capital is merely "accumulated labour," it is urged, and "can only reproduce itself without addition." [62] The most curious thing about the pamphlet is the manner in which the author vacillates between different theories of value. He begins by flirting with something like a subjective theory based on diminishing utility; then he asserts that value "may safely be defined *labour*" and that "in the exchange of commodities, the worth of each in relation to the other, is estimated by the time employed in fabricating it";[63] and finally, he seems to discard the labour theory and adopts Spence's Physiocratic concept of "real value." The pamphlet, like Wakefield's, at least has the merit of recognising that to explain surplus value *some* theory of value is necessary.

The other Physiocratic work, Thomas Chalmers' *Enquiry into the Extent and Stability of National Resources*, was published in 1808. It was inspired by the same set of circumstances which stimulated Spence's pamphlet, but according to Chalmers he did not see the latter until his own work was nearly completed.[64] Chalmers' intention was to prove that "a much larger proportion of the wealth of the country may be transferred to the augmentation of the public revenue, and that . . . a much larger proportion of the population of the country may be transferred to the augmentation of its naval and military establishments." [65] His main analysis is divided into three parts. First, he considers "the case of a country that carries on no foreign trade." He argues that the population of a country consists of: (1) the *Agricultural Population*, upon whom devolves the labour of providing food for the whole community; (2) the *Secondary Population*, who are engaged in providing strict necessities other than food (clothing, housing, etc.) for the whole community; and (3) the balance, the *Disposable Population*. This third group is "disposable" in the sense that it is maintained out of the

---

[59] *Commerce Defended*, p. 71.

[60] From a letter from Malthus to Ricardo of July 16, 1821, quoted by Keynes in *Essays in Biography*, p. 144.

[61] Traces of the Physiocratic outlook may be found in the work of men like Thomas Joplin and J. S. Reynolds, as well as in that of a number of the radical economists and Malthusian underconsumptionists. Haney has claimed Egerton Brydges as a Physiocrat, but the allegedly Physiocratic passages are so vague that the claim seems to be hardly justified. (Brydges is more notable for a clear statement of the relation between price and marginal cost—see his *Population and Riches* (1819), pp. 21-2 and *passim*.) The only other out-and-out Physiocrat I have been able to trace was William Reid, who published a defence of Physiocracy in 1833 (*Inquiry into the Causes of the Present Distress*).

[62] *Sketches*, pp. 19–28.

[63] *Sketches*, pp. 1–3.

[64] *Enquiry*, p. 343.

[65] *Ibid.*, p. 295.

"surplus food of the country," which is, in the first instance, "at the disposal of its proprietor." The proprietor assigns the agricultural surplus to the disposable population, who, in return, "contribute in various ways to his comforts and enjoyments." The master gives the orders and the servants obey. If the country carries on no foreign trade, then, it follows from this view of the economy that the destruction of a particular manufacture is a matter of little concern. The agricultural surplus— the subsistence fund for the disposable population—is still in existence, and since "it will infallibly be expended" by the landed proprietor, the displaced workmen will soon be given "the same maintenance as before, in another capacity." All that will happen is that a section of the disposable population will be put on to producing a different commodity. And if the government taxes the landed proprietor, "and appropriates to itself part of that fund which is expended on the maintenance of the disposable population," the position is similar: the proprietor has to dismiss a section of the disposable population, but the government will soon re-employ them in another capacity. If it employs them as soldiers, the country will lose the commodities they were formerly producing, but will gain in return a different commodity, which at the present time is far more precious—security against invasion. "There is no creative, no inherent virtue in the manufacture: It is the consumer who contributes the revenue." [66]

Secondly, Chalmers considers "the case of a country which carries on foreign trade, but is subsisted by its own agricultural produce." The landed proprietor, it is contended, "may also conceive a liking for an article of foreign manufacture." Owing to the heavy transport costs involved, he will not send his surplus produce abroad to pay for the foreign goods—he will instead "maintain labourers at home, and send

over their work as an equivalent." The idea that those who live by foreign trade form "an independent interest," and that their wealth "is an original and not a derived wealth," is simply an illusion. The practical conclusions arrived at in the first case also apply to the second. [67]

Thirdly, Chalmers considers "the case of a country which has to import agricultural produce." This is obviously a much more difficult case than the second one, and Chalmers' method of dealing with it is ingenious, although hardly satisfactory. He begins by asserting that "the inhabitants of a whole country are seldom accumulated to any great degree beyond the limits of its own agricultural produce." [68] He then suggests, with the aid of a somewhat dubious calculation, that the "redundant population" of Great Britain (that is, the population subsisted by imported food) "does not amount to above one-thirtieth of the natural population of the island." [69] It is true, he admits, that the destruction of Britain's foreign trade would render the redundant population jobless, and reduce the national income. But this is not a cause for despair: their contribution is negligible, and in any event it would probably be quite easy to introduce improvements in agriculture which would increase the surplus of food sufficiently to maintain them. [70]

The passages in which Chalmers discusses the origin of industrial and commercial profit are consistently Physiocratic. It may be asked, he argues, how it is possible to distinguish between "original and derived wealth" when there appears on the surface to be a "mutual dependence" between buyers and sellers. It may be asked whether he has not "all along overlooked a very important element, the profit of our capitalists." But such criticisms ignore the

[66] *Enquiry,* Chapter I, *passim.*

[67] *Ibid.,* Chapter 2, *passim.*
[68] *Ibid.,* p. 145. Cf. Dugald Stewart, *Works,* Vol. I, p. 270.
[69] *Ibid.,* p. 147. Cf. Ricardo, *Works,* p. 383, and Chalmers, *Political Economy* (1832), p. 227.
[70] *Ibid.,* Chapter 3, *passim.*

vital fact that "the proprietors of the necessaries of life compose the original and independent interest." And profit is simply a wage for the "higher species of service" rendered by the capitalist—a wage which, like that of all the others who labour in manufactures, is paid by the "original proprietors of the necessaries of existence." The capitalist may secure a profit which is more than sufficient "to make up to him the maintenance of a labourer," so that he, as well as the landed proprietor, may be able to "command the services of so many of the disposable population." But even so, the wealth of the merchant or manufacturer is necessarily derived, whereas that of the landed proprietor is original.[71]

Between Chalmers' *Enquiry* and Ricardo's *Principles* there lies a deep gulf. Whereas Chalmers thinks of the surplus as a flow of *commodities* of a particular type, Ricardo thinks of it as a flow of *value*, and the physical attributes of the commodities produced in the economy become irrelevant to the problem of the increase of wealth. Then again, while both Chalmers and Ricardo regard the power and prosperity of a country as being largely dependent upon the size of its net revenue,[72] Chalmers regards the surplus as consisting of rent alone, and Ricardo regards it as consisting of both rent and profits. And finally, whereas Chalmers treats profit as being paid out of rent, there is an important sense in which Ricardo treats profit as the primary, and rent as the derivative, income.

Ricardo's *Principles* reflects a new social attitude which had been struggling for adequate theoretical expression for some time. Chalmers himself was haunted by it, and, since his book was written to combat it, often stated it fairly precisely. Manufactures, he said, "are looked up to as an original and independent interest, as possessing in themselves some native and

inherent ability, and as if the very existence of the country depended upon their prosperity and extension."[73] Again, "the interest of the country is supposed to be identical with the interest of its traders and shopkeepers; and as profit is the grand source of their revenue, so profit . . . is supposed to be one of the grand sources of the revenue of the public."[74] As capitalist methods spread throughout the economy, as striking increases in productivity followed one upon the other, and as accumulation came to be made more and more out of profits and less and less out of rents, the idea naturally became current that profits were not just equally as important as rents, but somehow superior to them.

It was more difficult than it might appear to give theoretical expression to this new attitude. For one thing, the claims of agriculture to pre-eminence were hard to dispute. No one could deny that agriculture was historically prior to industry and commerce, and that, at least in the absence of international trade, the size of the agricultural surplus did still effectively limit the extension of industry and commerce. And whereas the production of a surplus in agriculture could easily enough be visualised in physical terms, it was difficult to visualise a similar process taking place in manufacture, where the elements of input and output usually consisted of entirely different commodities. The production of a surplus in manufacture could be visualized only in terms of *value*, which required quite a considerable development in the use of abstraction in economic analysis; and an abstraction from the physical attributes of the commodities produced could become plausible only when the territorial division of labour had become recognised as a normal and natural feature of the world economic scene, and when it had been al-

[71] *Enquiry*, Chapters 2 and 4, *passim*.
[72] *Ibid.*, p. 224; Ricardo, *Works*, pp. 210–12.
[73] *Enquiry*, p. 54. Cf. Hollander, *David Ricardo*, p. 16.
[74] *Ibid.*, p. 169.

lowed that "there is always abundance of food in the world"[75] for which Britain's manufactured exports could be exchanged. For these reasons, it was difficult enough to establish even the independence of profit, let alone its superiority over rent.

Nevertheless, as a result of the Physiocratic controversies, the independence of profit was successfully maintained. It became widely accepted that labour was able to produce a surplus in manufacture as well as in agriculture, and that agriculture was not even *especially* productive. Nature's labour is important in manufacture; man's labour is important in agriculture; rent of land is qualitatively similar to interest on capital; elements akin to rent are found in profit and wages—all these were arguments put forward to prove that there was nothing sacrosanct about rent and nothing unique about agriculture. The next stage was to turn the tables completely on the Physiocrats and to treat profit, rather than rent, as the primary and original income.[76] For this principle to be embodied in a theoretical system, two pieces of apparatus required to be evolved. First, a *theory of*

value was needed—a theory which would be free from any bias towards the old physical cost concept, and which was capable of distinguishing between cost and surplus in manufacture as well as in agriculture. Smith and some of the anti-Physiocrats had pointed in the direction of the labour theory which Ricardo was to adopt; and any ties which still existed between the physical cost and labour cost concepts were decisively broken in Ricardo's first chapterheading. Second, a *theory of rent* was needed—a theory which would suggest that rent was not an original but a derivative income. Ricardo consistently interpreted his new theory of rent in this way. Whereas Malthus always regarded rent as an agricultural surplus beneficently provided by Nature, Ricardo always regarded it as a deduction from profits—a deduction made possible only because Nature had been *less* beneficent in supplying fertile land than she had been in supplying such things as air and water. Rent, by the operation of natural laws, had come to be a part of the social surplus, but it had gained this position only at the expense of profits. Building on the ground which had been cleared during the Physiocratic controversies, Ricardo was at last able to give precise theoretical expression to the mature Classical outlook.

---

[75] Ricardo, *Works*, p. 191, footnote.

[76] Buchanan made an attempt to do this in 1814: see his *Observations,* p. 135. Ricardo was apparently impressed by these passages: see *Works*, p. 243.

6 Adam Smith on the Division of Labour: Two Views or One?

NATHAN ROSENBERG[1]

Among the numerous developments which Adam Smith conceived to emerge spontaneously from the natural order, none is more widely known than the "division of labor." The principle of division of labor is first encountered in Book I of the *Wealth of Nations,* where it is attributed not to any human wisdom or regulation by the state but to man's inherent propensity to "truck and barter." Smith attributes most improvements in man's productive powers—among them increases in skill, dexterity, and judgment—to division of labor, which also "saves time" and encourages mechanization and invention by specialists. These specialists are "philosophers or men of speculation, whose trade it is not to do anything but to observe everybody. . . ." Indeed, division of labor is conceived to be the fundamental basis of economic progress, for it stimulates man's mental ability as it multiplies the quantity of goods produced.

There is, however, an alternative interpretation of Smith's conception of the impact of division of labor. This second interpretation is sociological rather than economic in nature. Its basis is the point-of-view encountered in Book V, in which Smith appears to be critical of division of labor on the ground that it renders people "stupid and ignorant" unless government intervenes and introduces public education.

What are the implications of these two points-of-view about the impact of division of labor on the intellectual and moral quality of the labor force and on the prospects for continued technical progress? Much depends on our conception of the inventive process. There is, on the one hand, the capacity to invent, given an existing technology; and, on the other, a capacity to invent on a level that constitutes a new "breakthrough." Capacity to invent in the latter sense is essential to technical progress but is blunted by increasing division of labor. Is it possible for society to nurture this capacity among some of its members while others experience the stultifying impact of division of labor? In "Adam Smith on the Division of Labour: Two Views or One?", Nathan Rosenberg weighs the prospects for an affirmative answer.

Reprinted from Nathan Rosenberg, "Adam Smith on the Division of Labour: Two Views or One?" from *Economica,* Vol. XXXII, May 1965, pp. 127–140. Dr. Rosenberg is with the Harvard University Program on Technology and Society.

[1] The author is indebted to his colleague, June Flanders, for helpful suggestions.

Adam Smith's treatment of the division of labour has intrigued readers and commentators for many years. On the one hand it provided a masterful analysis of the gains from specialization and exchange upon which, it is no exaggeration to say, the discipline of economics was nurtured. On the other hand, Smith's apparent afterthoughts of Book V, where he refers to the deleterious effects of the division of labour upon the work force, constitute a major source of inspiration for the socialist critique of capitalist institutions, as Marx himself acknowledged. For Smith states here, in part:

> In the progress of the division of labour, the employment of the far greater part of those who live by labour, that is, the great body of the people, comes to be confined to a few very simple operations, frequently to one or two. But the understandings of the greater part of men are necessarily formed by their ordinary employments. The man whose whole life is spent in performing a few simple operations, of which the effects too are, perhaps, always the same, or very nearly the same, has no occasion to exert his understanding, or to exercise his invention in finding out expedients for removing difficulties which never occur. He naturally loses, therefore, the habit of such exertion, and generally becomes as stupid and ignorant as it is possible for a human creature to become. . . . His dexterity at his own particular trade seems . . . to be acquired at the expense of his intellectual, social, and martial virtues. But in every improved and civilised society this is the state into which the labouring poor, that is, the great body of the people, must necessarily fall, unless government takes some pains to prevent it.[2]

The apparent contradiction between the views of Book I and Book V has often been commented upon. Marx observes in *Capital* that Adam Smith ". . . opens his work with an apotheosis on the division of labour. Afterwards, in the last book which

treats of the sources of public revenue, he occasionally repeats the denunciations of the division of labour made by his teacher, A. Ferguson."[3] More recently, in a reappraisal of this subject, Dr. E. G. West presents a confrontation of "Adam Smith's Two Views on the Division of Labour" which he regards as "contradictory," "incompatible," and involving a "striking inconsistency."[4] Since the issues involved are intrinsically important in addition to playing a seminal role both in the development of economic thought and in the critique of capitalist institutions and capitalist development, I propose to re-examine Smith's treatment of division of labour primarily as it relates to one central issue: the determinants of inventive activity. I will show that Smith's treatment of this problem is, in certain respects, considerably more complex and interesting than it has previously been made out to be. Furthermore, I hope to demonstrate that his analysis is free of the inconsistencies and contradictions which have been attributed to it. The issues at stake are of considerable importance, since Smith's long-term prognosis for capitalism is centred upon its capacity for generating technical change and thus substantially raising *per capita* income. This capacity, in turn, is made by Smith to depend overwhelmingly—indeed one may almost say exclusively—upon the division of labour and the consequences flowing from it. As Schumpeter has stated, ". . . nobody, either before or after A. Smith, ever thought of putting such a burden upon division of labor. With A. Smith it is practically the only factor in economic progress."[5]

[2] Adam Smith, *Wealth of Nations*, Modern Library edition, edited by Edwin Cannan, pp. 734–5. All subsequent references are to this edition.

[3] Karl Marx, *Capital*, Foreign Languages Publishing House, Moscow, 1961, p. 123. Marx's curious notion, that Adam Smith was heavily indebted to Adam Ferguson in his analysis of the consequences of division of labour, will be dealt with in a later footnote.

[4] E. G. West, "Adam Smith's Two Views on the Division of Labour," *Economica*, February 1964, pp. 23–32.

[5] Joseph A. Schumpeter, *History of Economic Analysis*, New York, 1954, p. 187.

A difficulty which most commentators seem to encounter with Smith's views on division of labour results from interpreting the discussion in Book I to mean that invention is the sole product of workers' intelligence.[6] Then, having shown by quotation from Book V that Smith believed that workers become increasingly "stupid and ignorant" as a result of division of labour, the inference is drawn that Smith is involved in a contradiction. This view of Smith is inadequate and misleading on several important counts.

We need, first, to enlarge the scope of our discussion by recognizing that Smith looks upon inventive activity as a process which has several dimensions. Increasing division of labour encourages invention in a variety of ways. It does this, first of all, by sharpening the attention of the worker and focusing it more forcefully than before upon a narrow range of processes. By narrowing down the range the worker is enabled to lavish greater care as well as curiosity upon his work. His mind is subjected to fewer distractions. In the absence of the need to make frequent readjustments by moving from one sort of activity to another, the worker proceeds in a spirit of "vigorous application."[7]

> The division of labour no doubt first gave occasion to the invention of machines. If a man's business in life is the performance of two or three things, the bent of his mind will be to find out the cleverest way of doing it; but when the force of his mind is divided it cannot be expected that he should be so successful.[8]

[6] In his opening paragraph, for example, West states: "The reader is first reminded of the discussion in Book I of the economic effects of the division of labour, and of its favourable moral and intellectual effects on the workers" (*West, loc. cit.,* p. 23). And later: "The argument of Book I clearly suggests that the division of labour enhances man's mental stature as it increases the quantity of goods produced" (p. 25).

[7] *Wealth of Nations,* pp. 8–9.

[8] *Lectures on Justice, Police, Revenue and Arms delivered in the University of Glasgow by Adam Smith,* edited by Edwin Cannan, 1896, p. 167 (subsequently referred to as *Lectures*). Cf. also

The worker's perception of mechanical deficiencies and of possibilities for improving the efficiency of an operation is heightened by the unrelieved intensity in the focus of his attention. Smith's apocryphal story of the young boy who, anxious to get off and give vent to his youthful exuberance with his playfellows, invented a device which opened and closed the valves of a steam engine without his assistance, is surely compelling evidence that Smith regarded the invention as a consequence of a narrow focusing of interest and attention rather than of a mature or developed intelligence.

A further important aspect of Smith's view of inventive activity, as his story of the boy and the steam engine makes clear, is motivation. One of the major themes of the *Wealth of Nations,* of course, is its exhaustive examination of the manner in which institutional arrangements structure the decision-making of the individual, sometimes in a manner which harmonizes private interest and social interest, and sometimes in a manner which disrupts them.[9] Smith has a great deal to say, for example, on the impact of different systems of land ownership on the introduction of

_____

Wealth of Nations, pp. 9–10, and an early draft of the *Wealth of Nations,* which appears in W. R. Scott, *Adam Smith as Student and Professor,* Glasgow 1937, p. 336 (subsequently referred to as *Early Draft*). West recognizes the effect of increasing division of labour in performing these functions. My objection to his treatment is in his insistence that the progressive division of labour increases intelligence as well as alertness. "It is, however, in the third proposition, that invention and mechanization are encouraged by the division of labour, where we find Smith's most philosophical and conclusive case for favourable effects upon intelligence and alertness." West, *op. cit.,* p. 25. I find no evidence, either in the quotations cited by West, or in my own reading of Book I of the *Wealth of Nations* or elsewhere in Smith's writings, to support the interpretation that increasing division of labour improves either the worker's intelligence or understanding. Dexterity, certainly; alertness, yes; intelligence, no.

[9] This problem has been examined in some detail in Nathan Rosenberg, "Some Institutional Aspects of the *Wealth of Nations*", *Journal of Political Economy,* December 1960, pp. 557–70.

agricultural improvements. Although his reference here is primarily to capital formation, rather than invention, the importance of motivation in stimulating certain types of economic behaviour shows up clearly, and is applicable to the issue of the determinants of invention and innovation as well.

On the one hand the large landowner is corrupted by his easy and luxuriant style of life:

> To improve land with profit, like all other commercial projects, requires an exact attention to small savings and small gains, of which a man born to a great fortune, even though naturally frugal, is very seldom capable. The situation of such a person naturally disposes him to attend rather to ornament which pleases his fancy than to profit for which he has so little occasion.[10]

On the other hand, the varying forms of tenantry had, historically, discouraged improvement on the part of the cultivator. "It could never . . . be the interest even of this last species of cultivators [metayers] to lay out, in the further improvement of the land, any part of the little stock which they might save from their own share of the produce, because the lord, who laid out nothing, was to get one-half of whatever it produced." [11]

Where a system of farmers developed, as in England, with legal protections and security of tenure, considerable improvements might be undertaken.[12] For the motivation of the farmer is strengthened by the reasonable assurance that he will himself enjoy the fruits of his own initiative, ingenuity and industry. In fact, "after small proprietors . . . rich and great farmers are, in every country, the principal im-

provers." [13] Small proprietors are, however, unsurpassed.

> A small proprietor . . . who knows every part of his little territory, who views it all with the affection which property, especially small property, naturally inspires, and who upon that account takes pleasure not only in cultivating but in adorning it, is generally of all improvers the most industrious, the most intelligent, and the most successful.[14]

Perhaps the most extreme example of the impairment of the incentive to invent is the case of slavery. For here the individual is deprived of all possibility of "bettering his condition" and has scarcely any motive for improving his productivity. "A person who can acquire no property, can have no other interest but to eat as much, and to labour as little as possible." [15] Interestingly enough, Smith seems to have vacillated a good deal on the precise handling of this issue. In the *Early Draft* he tentatively attributes an invention to a slave.

> Some miserable slave, condemned to grind corn between two stones by the meer strength of his arms, pretty much in the same manner as painters bray their colours at present, was probably the first who thought of supporting the upper stone by a spindle and of turning it round by a crank or handle which moved horizontally, according to what seems to have been the original, rude form of hand mills. . . .[16]

---

[13] *Ibid.,* p. 371.

[14] *Ibid.,* p. 392. Elsewhere Smith heaps praise upon successful merchants who have turned country gentlemen. "Merchants are commonly ambitious of becoming country gentlemen, and when they do, they are generally the best of all improvers" (p. 384). For the successful merchant has been subjected to the rigours and discipline of commercial life and has acquired the values and habits essential to the successful introduction of improvements. "The habits . . . of order, oeconomy and attention, to which mercantile business naturally forms a merchant, render him fitter to execute, with profit and success, any project of improvement" (p. 385).

[15] *Ibid.,* p. 365. Cf. *Lectures,* p. 225: "When lands . . . are cultivated by slaves, they cannot be greatly improven, as they have no motive to industry."

[16] *Early Draft,* pp. 336-7.

[10] *Wealth of Nations,* p. 364. In *Lectures* Smith had stated (p. 228): "Great and ancient families have seldom either stock or inclination to improve their estates, except a small piece of pleasure-ground about their house."

[11] *Wealth of Nations,* p. 367.

[12] " . . . The yeomanry of England are rendered as secure, as independent, and as respectable as law can make them." *Ibid.,* p. 394.

In the *Lectures,* however, he at one point repeats the "probable" attribution of the upper spindle to a slave[17] while later in the volume he asserts that ". . . slaves . . . can have no motive to labour but the dread of punishment, and can never invent any machines for facilitating their business."[18] Finally, in the *Wealth of Nations,* although Smith does not much modify his basic scepticism toward slaves, he hedges his statement, in characteristic Smithian fashion, with qualifying phrases: "Slaves . . . are *very seldom* inventive; and all the *most important* improvements, either in machinery, or in the arrangement and distribution of work, which facilitate and abridge labour, have been the discoveries of freemen."[19]

This quotation suggests our next point, which is of considerable importance to Smith's understanding of the relationship between division of labour and invention. Adam Smith clearly recognised the existence of a hierarchy of inventions involving varying degrees of complexity, and requir-

ing differing amounts of technical competence, analytical sophistication and creative and synthesizing intellect. Similarly, he distinguished between the ingenuity required to produce any particular invention on the one hand, and to modify it, improve it, or to apply it to new uses on the other. Interestingly enough, Smith's most detailed treatment is in the *Early Draft*; less appears in the *Lectures* and in the *Wealth of Nations.*[20] With the only slight exception of his treatment of slavery, however, there is no internal evidence that Smith altered his position between the *Early Draft* and the *Wealth of Nations.*

It should be noticed, first of all, that although Smith's attempt to reconstruct the past with respect to the invention of machines takes the form, in his exposition, of conjectural history, he nevertheless shows a clear awareness of the evolutionary process in the development of human artifacts. After surveying some of the basic inventions in agriculture and in grinding mills, he states: "These different improvements were probably not all of them the inventions of one man, but the successive discoveries of time and experience, and of the ingenuity of many different artists." Also: "We have not, nor cannot have, any complete history of the invention of machines, because most of them are at first imperfect, and receive gradual improvements and increase of powers from those who use them."[21]

---

[17] "Some miserable slave who had perhaps been employed for a long time in grinding corn between two stones, probably first found out the method of supporting the upper stone by a spindle." *Lectures,* p. 167.

[18] *Ibid.,* p. 231. Smith was surely a bit unreasonable concerning the motivation of a slave to undertake inventions. When the only consequence is to reduce his master's costs, the slave may be assumed to be uninterested; but when the invention improves the conditions of work in some respect, surely the slave has such a motive. It is obviously in the personal interest of the slave to devise inventions which eliminate the most irksome and backbreaking varieties of work typically performed by slaves—such as the early methods of grinding corn. See *Early Draft,* pp. 336–37.

[19] *Wealth of Nations,* p. 648. Emphasis added. The quotation continues: "Should a slave propose any improvement of this kind, his master would be very apt to consider the proposal as the suggestion of laziness, and of a desire to save his own labour at the master's expense. The poor slave, instead of reward, would probably meet with much abuse, perhaps with some punishment. In the manufactures carried on by slaves, therefore, more labour must generally have been employed to execute the same quantity of work, than in those carried on by freemen."

[20] The most relevant passages are pp. 336–8 of the *Early Draft,* pp. 167–8 of the *Lectures,* and pp. 9–10 of the *Wealth of Nations.*

[21] *Early Draft,* p. 337, and *Lectures,* p. 167. Smith's evolutionist position here is strongly reminiscent of Mandeville: ". . . We often ascribe to the Excellency of Man's Genius, and the Depth of his Penetration, what is in Reality owing to length of Time, and the Experience of many Generations, all of them very little differing from one another in natural Parts and Sagacity." *Fable of the Bees,* ed. F. B. Kaye, 1924, volume II, p. 142. Also ". . . the Works of Art and human Invention are all very lame and defective, and most of them pitifully mean at first: Our knowledge is advanced by slow Degrees, and some Arts and Sciences require the Experience

At the rudest and lowest level, some simple inventions were, as indicated earlier, within the capacity of a common slave to invent. In the past many inventions of not too great complexity were made by common workmen. "A great part of the machines made use of in those manufactures in which labour is most subdivided, were originally the inventions of common workmen, who, being each of them employed in some very simple operation, naturally turned their thoughts towards finding out easier and readier methods of performing it." [22]

Reverting to the operation of the grinding mill, Smith is prepared to concede that the simpler inventions (he cites the feeder and shoe) might have been developed by the miller himself. However, the more complex inventions were probably beyond the limited vision and capacity of the miller. Here Smith suggests that such sophisticated innovations as the cogwheel and the trundle were probably the work of millwrights. For these inventions ". . . bear the most evident marks of the ingenuity of a very intelligent artist." Smith shows here[23] an awareness of the vital role to be played by the capital-goods industries as a source of technological change. Such possibilities, he argues, however, are limited by the size of the market for capital goods which, in turn, determines when (and whether) capital-goods production can be undertaken as a specialized trade. "All the improvements in machinery . . . have by no means been the inventions of those who had occasion to use the machines. Many improvements have been made by the ingenuity of the makers of the machines, when to make them became the business of a peculiar trade. . . ." [24]

Continuing up the scale of complexity and sophistication, invention at the highest levels involves acts of insight, creative synthesis, and the capacity to draw upon diverse fields of knowledge. The most important inventions of all are the works of philosophers, who perceive and exploit new relationships and natural phenomena to human advantage.[25] A philosopher or "meer man of speculation" is

> one of these people whose trade it is, not to do any thing but to observe every thing, and who are upon that account capable of combining together the powers of the most opposite and distant objects. To apply in the most advantageous manner those powers, which are allready known and which have already been applyed to a particular purpose, does not exceed the capacity of an ingenious artist. But to think of the application of new powers, which are altogether unknown, and which have never before been applied to any similar purpose, belongs to those only who have a greater range of thought and more extensive views of things than naturally fall to the share of a meer artist.[26]

The loftiest pinnacles of inventive activity, then, are occupied by philosophers, and the less rarefied heights are inhabited

---

of many Ages, before they can be brought to any tolerable Perfection." *Ibid.*, pp. 186–7. For further discussion of Mandeville's evolutionist views of social development, see Nathan Rosenberg, "Mandeville and Laissez-faire," *Journal of the History of Ideas*, April–June 1963, pp. 183–96.

[22] *Wealth of Nations*, p. 9.

[23] *Early Draft*, p. 337. Smith's preoccupation with technological change in milling operations is shared by Marx, who states that "the whole history of the development of machinery can be traced in the history of the corn mill." *Capital*, p. 348.

[24] *Wealth of Nations*, p. 10.

[25] In his "History of Astronomy" Smith defines philosophy as ". . . the science of the connecting principles of nature . . . as in those sounds, which to the greater part of men seem perfectly agreeable to measure and harmony, the nicer ear of a musician will discover a want, both of the most exact time, and of the most perfect coincidence: so the more practised thought of a philosopher, who has spent his whole life in the study of the connecting principles of nature, will often feel an interval betwixt two objects, which, to more careless observers, seem very strictly conjoined." Adam Smith, "History of Astronomy," in *Essays on Philosophical Subjects*, pp. 19 and 20. It is this ability to perceive gaps and to formulate problems which, for Smith, constitutes the critical step in scientific inquiry and also in the discovery and application of useful knowledge.

[26] *Early Draft*, pp. 337–8.

by artists whose activities involve less novelty and creative insight and who engage also in improving upon the inventions of more illustrious men.

> It was a real philosopher only who could invent the fire engine,[27] and first form the idea of producing so great an effect, by a power in nature which had never before been thought of. Many inferior artists, employed in the fabric of this wonderful machine may after wards discover more happy methods of applying that power than those first made use of by its illustrious inventor. It must have been a philosopher who, in the same manner first invented, those now common and therefore disregarded, machines, wind and water mills. Many inferior artists may have afterwards improved them.[28]

In short, the "capacity to invent" cannot be assessed or measured in absolute terms; the concept is meaningful only in relation to the complexity of the existing technology and the degree of creative imagination required in order for new "breakthroughs" to occur. Presumably, then, even if the alertness and intellectual capacity of the common labourer remained constant, or increased somewhat, it would be inadequate to perform the increasingly complicated intellectual feats required of an inventor in a technically progressive society.

A strategic determinant, within Smith's framework, of the *capacity* to invent is now clear. Major inventions involve the ability to draw upon diverse areas of human knowledge and experience and to combine them in a unique fashion to serve some specific purpose. The ideal intellectual equipment for such synthesis is possessed by ". . . philosophers or men of speculation, whose trade it is not to do any thing, but to observe every thing; and who, upon that account, are often capable of combining together the powers of the most distant and dissimilar objects." [29] This is, of course,

precisely the talent which workmen become progressively *less* capable of exerting as the increasing division of labour continually narrows the range of the worker's activities (and therefore, since ". . . the understandings of the greater part of men are necessarily formed by their ordinary employments," [30] of his comprehension). Although, therefore, division of labour strengthens the force of a worker's attention upon a narrow range of activities and perhaps as a result increases his capacity for instituting small improvements, it is likely to disable him completely for the task of undertaking major inventions which involve drawing upon ranges of knowledge and experience to which he is less and less likely to be exposed. Originally, therefore, when production involved a relatively simple technology, increasing division of labour, by sharpening and concentrating the focus of a worker's attention, made it easier for him to invent and to institute non-fundamental improvements within the existing technology. As technology becomes increasingly complex, however, and as the solutions to problems require the ability to draw upon sources of knowledge and experience from a wide range of areas or disciplines, the worker is likely to be increasingly inadequate because of the exceedingly narrow repertory of materials from which he can draw.

But though Smith visualized the worker as becoming increasingly stupid and ignorant as a result of further division of labour, there is no reason to believe that this was necessarily inconsistent or incompatible with the possibilities for continuing technical progress and invention. This, in fact, brings us to a major point of this article. Smith looked upon the growing division of labour as a process which had not only an historical but necessarily also an important social dimension. Therefore, to concentrate solely on the impact of the division of la-

---

[27] I.e., steam engine.
[28] *Early Draft*, p. 338. Cf. also *Lectures*, pp. 167–8.
[29] *Wealth of Nations*, p. 10.

[30] *Ibid.*, p. 734.

bour upon the working class leads to the adoption of a very partial and misleading view of the economic and social consequence of division of labour. This can be seen most forcefully if we look at the changing structure of the social division of labour as a society moves from a primitive to a civilized condition.

The movement from a primitive to a civilized society is characterized by an enormous proliferation in the number of productive activities performed in society. In a primitive—i.e., unspecialized—economy each worker is, in general, obliged to perform a significant fraction of the total number of activities. As society progresses toward a more civilized state the number of separate activities grows prodigiously but the number performed by each individual worker declines. In an advanced society, then, there are many more activities going on in the economy but the individual worker is confined to a very narrow range. While the structure of the social division of labour becomes more complex, the individual worker's rôle becomes more simple. In the extreme case, and in contemporary jargon, the individual worker becomes the cheapest non-linear servo-mechanism. This was the prospect over which Smith (and later Marx) was so much exercised.[31] There

are, however, important forces working in the opposite direction, for the collective intelligence of society grows *as a result of the very process* which causes the understanding of the "inferior ranks of people" to become increasingly defective.[32] For the increased productivity resulting from specialization and division of labour is evident too in those trades which are concerned with the production of new knowledge.

> In the progress of society, philosophy or speculation becomes, like every other employment, the principal or sole trade and occupation of

[31] "The knowledge, the judgment, and the will, which, though in ever so small a degree, are practised by the independent peasant or handicraftsman, in the same way as the savage makes the whole art of war consist in the exercise of his personal cunning—these faculties are now required only for the workshop as a whole. Intelligence in production expands in one direction, because it vanishes in many others. What is lost by the detail labourers, is concentrated in the capital that employs them. It is a result of the division of labour in manufactures that the labourer is brought face to face with the intellectual potencies of the material process of production, as the property of another, and as a ruling power. This separation begins in simple co-operation, where the capitalist represents to the single workman the oneness and the will of the associated labour. It is developed in manufacture which cuts down the labourer into a detail labourer. It is completed in modern industry, which makes science a productive force distinct from labour and

presses it into the service of capital". Karl Marx, *Capital*, p. 361.

[32] Adam Ferguson had some striking observations on this same process: "It may even be doubted, whether the measure of national capacity increases with the advancement of arts. Many mechanical arts, indeed, require no capacity; they succeed best under a total suppression of sentiment and reason; and ignorance is the mother of industry as well as of superstition. Reflection and fancy are subject to err; but a habit of moving the hand, or the foot, is independent of either. Manufactures, accordingly, prosper most where the mind is least consulted, and where the workshop may, without any great effort of imagination, be considered as an engine, the parts of which are men. . . . But if many parts in the practice of every art, and in the detail of every department, require no abilities, or actually tend to contract and to limit the views of the mind, there are others which lead to general reflections, and to enlargement of thought. Even in manufacture, the genious of the master, perhaps, is cultivated, while that of the inferior workman lies waste. . . . The practitioner of every art and profession may afford matter of general speculation to the man of science; and thinking itself, in this age of separations, may become a peculiar craft." Adam Ferguson, *An Essay on the History of Civil Society*, sixth edition, London, 1793, pp. 305–6. In his discussion of the division of labour in *Capital*, Marx suggests (p. 362) that Adam Smith learned about "the disadvantageous effects of division of labour" from Ferguson, and that he merely "reproduces" Ferguson in Book V of the *Wealth of Nations*. Earlier (p. 354) Marx even refers to "A. Ferguson, the master of Adam Smith." Presumably Marx had in mind the fact that the first edition of Ferguson's *An Essay on the History of Civil Society* was published in 1767, nine years before the *Wealth of Nations*. The discovery of the 1763 *Lectures*, however, sufficiently establishes Smith's priority in this matter. Cf. also Karl Marx, *The Poverty of Philosophy*, Foreign Languages Publishing House, Moscow, no date, pp. 129–30.

a particular class of citizens. Like every other employment too, it is sub-divided into a great number of different branches, each of which affords occupation to a peculiar tribe or class of philosophers; and this subdivision of employment in philosophy, as well as in every other business, improves dexterity, and saves time. Each individual becomes more expert in his own peculiar branch, more work is done upon the whole, and the quantity of science is considerably increased by it.[33]

We can express this in an admittedly over-simplified chronological sequence. In all societies antecedent to the development of an extensive division of labour in manufactures, the level of knowledge and understanding of the majority of the population is "considerable", but the dispersion is small, and there are few individuals with attainments and abilities far above the average.

> In such a society indeed, no man can well acquire that improved and refined understanding, which a few men sometimes possess in a more civilized state. Though in a rude society there is a good deal of variety in the occupations of every individual, there is not a great deal in those of the whole society. Every man does, or is capable of doing, almost every thing which any other man does, or is capable of doing. Every man has a considerable degree of knowledge, ingenuity, and invention; but scarce any man has a great

degree. The degree, however, which is commonly possessed, is generally sufficient for conducting the whole simple business of the society.[34]

In an advanced society with an extensive division of labour, however, the intellectual attainments of the "labouring poor" are hopelessly stultified and corrupted by the monopoly and uniformity of the work process. On the other hand, such a society is made up of an endlessly variegated number of such activities, and although the worker's own personal assignment may be unchallenging and lacking in significant opportunities, the sum total of the occupations in society presents extraordinary opportunities for the detached and contemplative philosophers.[35] Although then the *modal* level of understanding is very low, the *highest* levels of scientific attainment permitted by the extensive specialization in the production of knowledge are quite remarkable. The *collective* intelligence of the civilized society, then, is very great and presents unique and unprecedented opportunities for further technical progress.

> In a civilized state . . . though there is little variety in the occupations of the greater part of individuals, there is an almost infinite variety in those of the whole society. These varied occupations present an almost infinite variety of objects to the contemplation of those few, who, being attached to no particular occupation themselves, have leisure and inclination to examine the occupations of other people. The contemplation of so great a

---

[33] *Wealth of Nations*, p. 10. Smith had expressed this same view as far back as the writing of the *Early Draft* (p. 338): "Philosophy or speculation, in the progress of society, naturally becomes, like every other employment, the sole occupation of a particular class of citizens. Like every other trade it is subdivided into many different branches, and we have mechanical, chemical, astronomical, physical, metaphysical, moral, political, commercial and critical philosophers. In philosophy, as in every other business, this subdivision of employment improves dexterity and saves time. Each individual is more expert at his particular branch. More work is done upon the whole and the quantity of science is considerably increased by it." More succinctly, Smith stated a few pages later (p. 344): "In opulent and commercial societies . . . to think or to reason comes to be, like every other employment, a particular business, which is carried on by a very few people, who furnish the public with all the thought and reason possessed by the vast multitudes that labour."

[34] *Wealth of Nations*, p. 735.
[35] At this point Smith parts company with Mandeville who, characteristically, is reluctant to attribute a beneficent social rôle to the man of pure knowledge; ". . . They are very seldom the same Sort of People, those that invent Arts, and Improvements in them, and those that enquire into the Reason of Things: this latter is most commonly practis'd by such, as are idle and indolent, that are fond of Retirement, hate Business, and take delight in Speculation: whereas none succeed oftener in the first, than active, stirring, and laborious Men, such as will put their Hand to the Plough, try Experiments, and give all their Attention to what they are about". Mandeville, *op. cit.*, vol. II, p. 144.

variety of objects necessarily exercises their minds in endless comparisons and combinations, and renders their understandings, in an extraordinary degree, both acute and comprehensive.[36]

We can now complete our analysis by calling attention to two further points, both of which reinforce the interpretation of Smith presented here. First of all, the more extreme debilitating consequences of the division of labour do not make themselves felt upon those employed in agriculture. This is owing to the fact that the dependence of agriculture upon the changing of the seasons imposes constraints upon the extent to which division of labour can be carried in that sector.[37] Precisely because the division of labour has failed to make the extensive inroads upon agricultural practices that it did upon manufacturing, Smith insists that the understanding of the inhabitants of the countryside is superior to that of their counterparts in manufacturing. Indeed, "after what are called the fine arts, and the liberal professions . . . there is perhaps no trade which requires so great a variety of knowledge and experience." [38] Smith contrasts invidiously the knowledge, judgment and experience required in the common mechanic trades with that required in agriculture. Furthermore, "not only the art of the farmer, the general direction of the operations of husbandry, but many inferior branches of country labour, require much more skill and experience than the greater part of mechanic trades." [39] Smith clearly believes that the agricultural worker avoids the "drowsy stupidity" of his urban cousins because the changing requirements of his work are continually imposing demands upon his judgment and discretion, and therefore keeping alive those mental capacities which the urban worker

eventually loses through sheer desuetude.[40] Even

> the common ploughman, though generally regarded as the pattern of stupidity and ignorance, is seldom defective in this judgment and discretion. He is less accustomed, indeed, to social intercourse than the mechanic who lives in a town. His voice and language are more uncouth and more difficult to be understood by those who are not used to them. His understanding, however, being accustomed to consider a greater variety of objects, is generally much superior to that of the other, whose whole attention from morning till night is commonly occupied in performing one or two very simple operations. How much the lower ranks of people in the country are really superior to those of the town, is well known to every man whom either business or curiosity has led to converse much with both.[41]

Our final point is that Smith sees the upper ranks of society as a group which is thoroughly insulated from the ravages of the division of labour. Whereas the agricultural population is exempted from the worst ravages of division of labour by inherent limits upon the extent to which such division can be carried in agriculture, people "of some rank or fortune" are exempted by virtue of the simple fact that they are not compelled to earn their livelihoods through prolonged drudgery and exertions at relatively menial activities.

[40] Smith may well have been prejudiced against urban life, as West has suggested, but it should now be clear that it is not necessary to resort to such a *deus ex machina* in order to account for Smith's views. West states: ". . . it seems likely that Smith's complaint of moral and intellectual degeneration was directed more against town life as such than against the factory which was only one aspect of it" (West, p. 30). In the light of the interpretation set forward here, it seems much easier to regard Smith's complaints as a logical consequence of the differential incidence of division of labour upon rural and urban populations. Furthermore, of course, Smith objects to towns because, in large measure as a result of geographic concentration, the spirit of monopoly and restraints upon the competitive process develop much more readily in urban than in rural areas. See *Wealth of Nations*, pp. 126–7.

[36] *Wealth of Nations*, pp. 735–6.
[37] *Ibid.*, p. 6; *Lectures*, p. 164; *Early Draft*, pp. 329–30.
[38] *Wealth of Nations*, p. 126.
[39] *Ibid.*, p. 127.

[41] *Ibid.*, p. 127.

The employments . . . in which people of some rank or fortune spend the greater part of their lives, are not, like those of the common people, simple and uniform. They are almost all of them extremely complicated, and such as exercise the head more than the hands. The understandings of those who are engaged in such employments can seldom grow torpid for want of exercise. The employments of people of some rank and fortune, besides, are seldom such as harass them from morning to night. They generally have a good deal of leisure, during which they may perfect themselves in every branch either of useful or ornamental knowledge of which they may have laid the foundation, or for which they may have acquired some taste in the earlier part of life.[42]

It is clear, then, that although the division of labour has potentially disastrous effects upon the moral and intellectual qualities of the labour force, and although Smith was seriously concerned with these effects, he did not fear that such developments would constitute a serious impediment to continued technological change.[43]

Thus Smith shows an acute perception of the social and human as well as the economic consequences of the division of labour in society. Whatever merit or demerit his analysis may have (it is my opinion that it has considerable merit) it is certainly free of serious contradictions. The main thrust of his analysis, as I have argued, is that, as a direct result of increasing division of labour, the creativity of society as a whole grows while that of the labouring poor (". . . that is, the great body of the people") declines. Marx was deeply appreciative of the nice dialectic of Smith's analysis, and certainly learned a good deal from it, although he referred scornfully to Smith's modest proposals for educating the workers as consisting only of the administration of "homoeopathic doses." [44] Be that as it may, there are many who would contend that the broader aspects of the process with which Smith was attempting to come to grips—the causes and the consequences of technical progress—still constitute some of the most serious problems of industrializing societies.

---

[42] *Ibid.*, pp. 736–7.

[43] Smith, perhaps somewhat optimistically, regarded philosophical inquiries as a natural development among leisured classes of societies which had achieved some minimum degree of order, stability and wealth. "Those of liberal fortunes, whose attention is not much occupied either with business or with pleasure, can fill up the void of their imagination, which is thus disengaged from the ordinary affairs of life, no other way than by attending to that train of events which passes around them. While the great objects of nature thus pass in review before them, many things occur in an order to which they have not been accustomed. Their imagination, which accompanies with ease and delight the regular progress of nature, is stopped and embarrassed by those seeming incoherences; they excite their wonder and seem to require some chain of intermediate

events, which, by connecting them with something that has gone before, may thus render the whole course of the universe consistent and of a piece. Wonder, therefore, and not any expectation of advantage from its discoveries, is the first principle which prompts mankind to the study of Philosophy, of that science which pretends to lay open the concealed connexions that unite the various appearances of nature; and they pursue this study for its own sake, as an original pleasure or good in itself, without regarding its tendency to procure them the means of many other pleasures." "History of Astronomy," *op. cit.*, pp. 33–4.

[44] *Capital*, p. 362.

7 Malthus on Money
Wages and Welfare

WILLIAM D. GRAMPP*

The controversy over the Corn Laws which followed the conclusion of the Napoleonic Wars in 1815 was the most far-reaching economic and political issue of the nineteenth century. These laws, which were originally intended to stabilize grain prices, provided for a duty on imports whenever the domestic corn price fell below a specified level. Throughout the war, the demand for corn was such that prices were high without the duty being called into effect. After the war, severe unemployment and falling grain prices led landlords to argue that the duties specified by the Corn Laws should be invoked to restore high corn prices and rents. Businessmen, on the other hand, seeking to preserve low wage rates, which they conceived to be contingent chiefly on low corn prices, called for the abolition of the Corn Laws. The laboring classes, uncertain whether their interests were best served by high or low prices, supported first one side and then the other.

Thomas Malthus and David Ricardo were among the antagonists who engaged in the Corn Law controversy on a theoretical level. The latter, who believed that low grain prices were in the workers' best interests, favored a free corn trade. Malthus, on the other hand, reasoning that the laboring classes would be better off if corn prices were high, supported the Corn Laws. The logic behind his position is explored in "Malthus on Money Wages and Welfare" by William D. Grampp. Utilizing the technique of indifference curves, Grampp demonstrates that rising corn prices are in the workers' best interests, precisely as Malthus had argued, *if* money wages vary with the price of corn and the prices of substitutes do not. However, the welfare effect of rising corn prices will be quite different if money wages are not regulated exclusively by the price of corn, as Malthus had assumed them to be.

Reprinted from William D. Grampp, "Malthus on Money Wages and Welfare," from the *American Economic Review*, Vol. 46, December 1956, pp. 924–936. Dr. Grampp is Professor of Economics at the College of Business Administration, University of Illinois at Chicago Circle.

*The author wishes to thank T. W. Hutchison of the London School of Economics and Eugene Rotwein of the University of Wisconsin for their very careful reading of this paper and for the assistance which they provided on Part II. Both pointed to implications which had not been seen in the idea and showed how they could be represented on indifference curves. The author expresses great indebtedness to them, and adds that neither however is responsible for any misuse to which their comments may have been put.

In the exchange between the classical economists over the Corn Laws, the most interesting contention was that the working class is better off when the price of necessities is high than when it is low. It came from Malthus and led him to support the tariff on grain. The idea is worth examining because it helps to understand a historical period and some current issues as well, and the occasion is appropriate because of the continuing interest in all aspects of Malthus' work.[1]

The reasoning is fairly simple. Suppose, as Malthus does, that the worker is an agricultural laborer who is paid in corn and that he receives the same quantity when the price is high as when it is low. He consumes some of the corn and exchanges the rest for other goods. As the price of corn rises and the prices of other goods (some of them substitutes for corn) do not rise as much, the worker can do two things: (a) He can consume the same quantity of corn as when its price was low and exchange the rest for a larger quantity of other goods. (b) He can reduce his consumption of corn, because it has become relatively expensive, and consume a larger quantity of other goods, because they have become relatively cheap. His welfare again will have increased, because he will have a quantity of corn plus other goods which together yield him as much satisfaction as corn alone yielded when its price was low, and in addition he will have a larger amount of other goods than he had when corn was cheap.

Conversely, as the price of corn falls and brings his money wages down with it (*i.e.*, the money value of a constant quantity of corn), while the prices of other goods do

not fall or fall less, there is a decline in the quantity of other goods which a given quantity of corn will buy. His welfare will decrease if: (a) his consumption of corn is constant and the consumption of other goods declines or (b) if his consumption of corn increases and his consumption of other goods declines still more.

The wage earner then is better off when corn becomes expensive and worse off when its price falls. What makes him so is the assumption (a) that his money wage varies with the price of corn, and the further assumption (b) that the prices of substitutes do not vary with the price of corn. If the assumptions are granted, the conclusion follows; and one cannot look to his logic to find a fallacy in Malthus' theory. The objection, as I shall describe later, is in the realism of the first assumption. However, the theory still is illuminating.

THE WELFARE RESULTS OF WAGE FIXING

His conclusion follows from defining money wages as equal to a constant quantity of a single commodity. It suggests two other ways of defining them. (1) By the Malthus definition, money wages are regulated by the price of corn. (2) They can be regulated by the price of corn and a substitute (or substitutes), which will make them equal to a constant quantity of two (or more) commodities. (3) They can be regulated by an ideal standard of welfare which will keep the worker always in the same welfare position.

If money wages are regulated in the second way, the welfare of the worker increases when the price of corn rises more than the price of substitutes *and* when the price of corn falls more. The result is that which is produced by tying money wages to a price index using base-year weights. In a rising corn market, his money wage is increased by an amount which enables him to buy the same quantity of corn and of the substitute as he bought before. He in fact

¹ *E.g.*, D. V. Glass, ed., *Introduction to Malthus* (London, 1953); Kenneth Smith, *The Malthusian Controversy* (London, 1951); G. F. McCleary, *The Malthusian Population Theory* (London, 1953); Ronald L. Meek, ed., *Marx and Engels on Malthus* (London, 1953), and a brilliant article by Gertrude Himmelfarb on "Malthus" in *Encounter*, Aug. 1955, pp. 53–60.

will not buy the same quantities, but more of the substitute and less corn; and the gain in satisfaction from the former will exceed the loss from the latter. (The gain in welfare is not as great as it is when money wages are regulated by a single commodity.) In a falling market his money wage is decreased, the consumption of corn increases relative to the consumption of the substitute, and again there is a net gain. In a falling market, the result is the opposite of that which follows from regulating money wages by a single commodity, for by that method welfare declines.

The third result follows from adjusting money wages in order to hold welfare constant. It is the result which would be achieved if a perfect index number could be devised, one which measures the cost of a given amount of welfare (produced by varying rather than constant quantities of goods). In a rising market money wages would be increased by an amount enabling the worker to buy an additional quantity of the substitute which would just compensate for the decrease in his consumption of corn. In a falling market, his money wage would be decreased in order that his consumption of the substitute would be reduced sufficiently to compensate for the increased consumption of corn, leaving him in the same welfare position as before.

The three results can be shown on indifference curves. In both diagrams, the ordinate measures the amount of the commodity in which money wages are fixed and which I shall call corn. The abscissa measures the amount of the commodity, X, which is substituted for corn.

The Malthusian Result

In Figure 7-1, let OA be the quantity of corn and OB the quantity of the substitute X which is purchasable by a given money wage. The price-ratio line is AB and is tangent to indifference curve, I_1, at Q which indicates the amount of corn and of X purchased. Now let the price of corn rise and

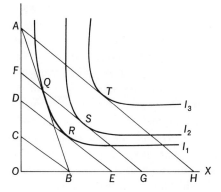

FIGURE 7-1

the price of X be constant. The quantity of corn purchasable by the original money wage falls to OC while the amount of X purchasable is constant at OB. In order that the quantity of corn purchasable be constant at OA (which Malthus supposed), the money wage must be increased. The quantity of X purchasable then increases to OH. A new price-ratio line, AH, is obtained, parallel to CB, and tangent to I_3 at T, showing an increase in welfare.

The result of a decrease in price is shown on Figure 7-2. AB is the price-ratio line

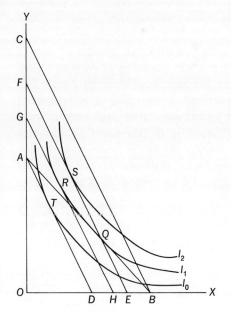

FIGURE 7-2

appropriate to the original money wage and is tangent to I_1 at Q. As the price of corn falls while the price of X is constant, the quantity of corn purchasable by the original money wage rises to OC and the quantity of X purchasable is constant at OB. The money wage is decreased in order to keep the quantity purchasable of corn constant at OA, and the decrease reduces the quantity of X purchasable to OD. The price-ratio line now is AD and is tangent to I_0 at T, showing a decrease in welfare.

The Base-year Weight Result

Consider first the effect of an increase in the price of corn and the money wage (Figure 7-1). At the initial corn price and money wage, the quantities of corn and X are indicated by Q (the point of tangency of AB and I_1). When the price of corn increases, the price of X being constant, the money wage must be increased so that the worker can afford to buy the same quantity of corn and of X as previously. The new price-ratio line then is FG and passes through Q. It is tangent to I_2 at S, and I_2 represents greater welfare than I_1, the indifference curve appropriate to the original money wage and corn price, but less welfare than I_3, the indifference curve relevant to the Malthusian result.

A decrease in the price of corn also produces an increase in welfare. In Figure 7-2, the quantities of corn and of X consumed at the initial corn price and money wage are indicated by Q (the point of tangency of AB and I_1). After the price of corn falls, the money wage is decreased, and the price-ratio line FE is obtained which passes through Q and is tangent to I_2 at S, representing greater welfare than that yielded by the initial money wage and still greater than that produced by the Malthusian result.

The Constant Welfare Result

It is produced by adjusting the money

wage so that a price-ratio line is obtained which is tangent to the initial indifference curve. In Figure 7-1, depicting a rising market, the required price-ratio line is DE and is tangent to I_1 at R. The required money wage measured in corn is OD and in X is OE. In a falling market (Figure 7-2) the required price-ratio line is GH and is tangent to I_1 at R. The required money wage is OG units of corn or OH units of X.

WHAT THE RESULTS SIGNIFY

Malthus' wage theory is more helpful in explaining a policy issue of the nineteenth century than any of the twentieth. However, it has an implication which is relevant to two current practices. The point is best explained by experts in welfare economics. I mention it in order to indicate that the theory is not entirely of historical interest and having done so shall return to a consideration of its place in the nineteenth century. It is common to compute real income by dividing money income by the index of consumer prices. The index uses base-year weights and if it changes in the same proportion as money income, real income is constant. Yet it was shown above that in these circumstances welfare is not constant. If the money of an individual increases as much as the index of prices of the things he buys and if not all prices change in the same proportion, he will substitute, in so far as he can, for the commodities which have risen more those which have risen less in price, and his new money income will buy him more satisfaction than the old. Likewise, when his money income falls as much as the index he will substitute for those commodities which have fallen less those which have fallen more, and again his welfare will increase. The point is relevant to the measurement of real income and consumption and to the position of workers whose money wages are tied to the cost of living. It seems to me that, in inflation or deflation, such workers improve their welfare. Had the allowance system, by which wages were regulated in Malthus' day, been based on something like the consumer price index of the Bureau of Labor Statistics, he could not logically have opposed the repeal of the Corn Laws.

He did so because like many others he believed repeal would injure the laboring classes. There were other reasons for the opposition to free trade, a very important one being the obvious damage it would do to the economic and political interests of the agricultural classes. But the argument which was repeated over and again and which enlisted whatever popular support protection had was the argument that the manufacturers wanted free trade so that they could lower money wages. Once the radical section of the working class was persuaded, it abandoned its support of free trade and often was in open alliance with the Tories. Cobden and the Anti-Corn Law League had less difficulty in breaking down the opposition of the agricultural interest than in persuading the workers that lower bread prices would not injure them. Whether or not the free traders actually wanted to lower money wages (and I do not think they did) is unimportant beside the fact that everyone thought they did.

A reader who today goes through the controversy over the Corn Laws is at first puzzled. He wonders why the free traders didn't make the obvious reply: that real wages would not fall if money wages fell only as much as the price of bread and other commodities. He then begins to wonder if behind the assertion of the protectionists—which today seems odd, to say the least—there might be some kind of reasoning to support it. There indeed was, and Malthus supplied it. It was a deduction from an idea in classical economics and had much support among public figures. It was that in the long run the "corn wages" of labor must be constant. If corn wages were to fall, the population eventually would

decline, the supply of labor and the demand for corn would decrease, raising money wages and lowering corn prices, until the ratio of the two was adequate to support an "optimal" population.

In one or another form the idea appears in Smith, Ricardo, and the writings of many others. Malthus himself expressed it ambiguously. In the *Essay on Population*, he wrote that there is a tendency for corn wages to be constant because the population must adjust itself "to the state of the real funds for the maintenance of labor."[2] In his review of Tooke's *Thoughts and Details on the High and Low Prices of the Last Thirty Years* (1923), he wrote:

Now, though it is well known that a year of scarcity or even two years, may pass over without a rise in the price of labour, yet when the rise of provisions is very considerable in itself, and extends over a considerable period, a rise in the money price of labour must follow, or the population will be quite unable to support itself, and the price of corn must fall again from the destruction of consumers.[3]

When the first two volumes of his *History of Prices* were published in 1833, Tooke denied the contention entirely and said there was no evidence at all that "high prices of agricultural produce tend . . . to extended employment and higher wages to the working population."[4] Tooke seems to have been right in his facts and Malthus wrong. If one compares money wages and wheat prices between 1790 and 1815, one finds they were not correlated at all, and the "index" of corn wages varies between 50 and 124, for most of the period being below

[2] *An Essay on the Principle of Population, etc.*, 6th ed. [1826] (London, 1890), p. 340.
[3] Art. VIII, *Quart. Rev.*, Apr. 1823, XXIX, 233, reprinted in T. R. Malthus, *Five Papers on Political Economy*, ed. Cyril Renwick (Sydney, 1953), pp. 41–67.
[4] Thomas Tooke, *A History of Prices, and of the State of the Circulation, from 1793 to 1837, etc.* (London, 1838), II, 256.

100.[5] Malthus himself was elusive about the amount of time required to bring wages and prices into a constant ratio, but nowhere in his writing on the Corn Laws placed it at more than 25 years.[6]

In the usage of the economists, the word corn usually meant necessities, occasionally meant grain, and sometimes bread. Malthus used it to mean bread. However, even if it were taken to mean all necessities, his assumption of constant corn wages was mistaken. Between 1790 and 1815, the cost of living and money wages did not move together.

That the facts controverted the wage theory in no way lessened its power. Most economists, the public, and its leaders were as wrong in their facts as Malthus was. They believed money wages were regulated by the price of corn, with a conviction usually reserved for articles of faith. One senses the strength of the belief from the way it was asserted and also from the helplessness of the free traders when they tried to disprove it.[7]

[5] I have computed such an "index" from the money wage series of Rufus S. Tucker, "Real Wages of Artisans in London, 1729–1835," *Jour. Am. Stat. Assoc.*, Mar. 1936, XXXI, 78–79; and from the wheat prices reported by W. W. Rostow, "Business Cycles, Harvests, and Politics: 1790–1850," *Jour. Econ. Hist.*, Nov. 1941, I, 2, 220–21.

How firmly it was believed that money wages were determined by the price of corn is explained very well by Mark Blaug in "The Empirical Content of Ricardian Economics," *Jour. Pol. Econ.*, Feb. 1956, LXIV, 42–43. He is mistaken in thinking "this belief was broadly consonant with experience," but the mistake is small indeed beside the excellence of his article.

[6] The error places Malthus in an odd relation to his contemporaries, most of whom were stronger at deduction than in the realism of their premises or the predictions made from them, while Malthus was known from the start "for talking of what actually exists in nature or may be put to practical use," as his friend, Otter, said. In the review of Tooke's work, which was unsigned according to custom, Malthus wrote of "Mr. Malthus . . . [and] . . . his usual and laudable habits of attending to facts and experience" (p. 221).

[7] Here for example is Cobden to a London crowd: "Oh, you have been most grossly bamboozled—most grossly deceived and gulled! most effectually practised on by the monopolists in

A few writers, like Tooke, presented the facts. But not even he, "the schoolmaster of the House of Commons," could disturb the belief. When the Corn Laws were repealed in 1846, it was for other reasons: the potato famine in Ireland, the disaffection of a part of the agricultural classes, the mounting political power of the Anti-Corn Law League, and a historical trend toward free trade. It is true that Peel in carrying the abolition of the laws said that he had come to his position after having been convinced at last that cheap bread would not reduce money wages. The Duke of Wellington had another explanation: "Damned rotten potatoes put Peel in his fright."

There was indeed some small justification in fact for believing that money wages were affected by the price of corn. And along with the authority of received economic opinion it is some mitigation for the error of Malthus. It was the practice of supplementing the wages of agricultural laborers by family allowances determined by the price of corn. It was a part of the system of poor relief which began in the eighteenth century in Speenhamland and continued into the nineteenth century until after the Corn Laws were repealed. The Speenhamland or allowance system did in fact fix the money wages of a large number of workers in a way which made their corn wages constant. It is not unlikely that in predominantly agricultural areas the wages of all workers were affected. Such was Malthus' contention.[8] The system was

London about the factory system! . . . You have been told that the people engaged in this agitation are a mere set of factory owners and mill owners who want, for their own purposes to pull down wages." Henry Ashworth, *Recollections of Richard Cobden, M.P., and the Anti-Corn-Law League* (London, 1876), p. 223.

[8] "To Pierre Prevost, Dec. 23, 1822," in "Six Letters from Malthus to Pierre Prevost," ed. George William Zinke, *Jour. Econ. Hist.*, Nov. 1942, II, 2, 184. It should be stated that Malthus believed the effect of the allowance system was to *lower* money and corn wages and that he was

practiced for so long that it became a part of the public's consciousness (and conscience as well) and was brought to its attention in an arresting way in 1834 when Parliament declared the system must be ended. Actually, the New Poor Law of 1834 failed to end it, and wage supplements continued to be paid.

THE HISTORY OF THE IDEA

The wage theory has a rather jumbled history, because Malthus explained it poorly and his contemporaries never considered it in its entirety. The first statement of it of which I know is in *Observations on the Effects of the Corn Laws, etc.,* a pamphlet he published in 1814. It may have been on his mind before. Francis Horner, one of the founders of the *Edinburgh Review* and its authority on economics, wrote to Lord Seymour Webb in 1807 about Malthus: "There is a new speculation of his, about the importance of the people being fed dear, which I wish you were here to discuss; it has the look of a paradox, and like most of his views, is revolting to the common belief; but I have not yet detected the fallacy, if there is one. I will explain it to you in my next letter." [9] The next letter, if there was one, is not included in Horner's

Memoirs (he did however comment on the idea several years later). In the 1814 pamphlet the theory is described in a few paragraphs, which are unaltered in the second and third editions of the pamphlet published in 1815. The purpose of the *Observations* was to set forth in a disinterested way the ruling considerations on the Corn Laws. One was their effect on the welfare of the working class, and the wage theory was mentioned quite briefly, almost cryptically. A year after the first edition he wrote *The Grounds of an Opinion on the Policy of Restricting the Importation of Corn,* which was intended as an appendix to the *Observations* and was published separately. He said the principal consideration was the welfare of the working class and he supported the laws.[10] But he did not explain the wage doctrine at all well, in fact so obscurely as to make it incomprehensible to anyone who had not read the *Observations.* In 1815 he also published *An Inquiry into the Nature and Progress of Rent, etc.* and there expressed the doctrine more intelligibly than anywhere.[11] Yet when he again took up the defense of the Corn Laws in the last edition of the *Essay on Population* (1826), he ignored the point completely, though it is suggested in the final edition of his *Principles* written shortly before his death in 1834.[12]

---

opposed to it, because he believed "the price of labour . . . [should be] . . . left to find its natural level" (subject of course to his qualification about free trade). *Essay on Population,* p. 339.

John Rooke presented tables showing the number of quarts of wheat purchasable by weekly money wages between 1799 and 1832. For agricultural workers in Cumberland the number was remarkably stable at about 41 quarts for long periods while it was extremely variable for cotton weavers. *Free Trade and Safe Government, etc.* (London, 1835), p. 182.

[9] *Memoirs and Correspondence of Francis Horner, M.P.,* ed. Leonard Horner (Boston, 1853), I, 434.

Malthus must have developed the idea after 1800, because in that year he believed a rise in money wages following on a higher price of corn would not improve the position of the workers. *An Investigation of the Cause of the Present High Price of Provisions, etc.* (London, 1800), p. 17.

[10] "If I were convinced, that to open our ports, would be permanently to improve the condition of the labouring classes of society, I should consider the question as at once determined in favour of such a measure." *The Grounds of an Opinion, etc.* (London, 1815), p. 23.

[11] ". . . the high price of corn . . . so far from being a disadvantage to them [the laboring classes], is a positive and unquestionable advantage . . . if they are able to command the same quantity of necessaries [e.g., corn], and receive a money price for their labour, proportioned to their advanced price, there is no doubt that, with regard to all the objects of convenience and comfort, which do not rise in proportion to corn (and there are many such consumed by the poor) their condition will be most decidedly improved." *An Inquiry, etc.* (London, 1815), pp. 48–49.

[12] *Principles of Political Economy, etc.,* 2nd ed. (London, 1836), pp. 219–20.

It was in reply to the pamphlet on rent that Ricardo wrote *An Essay on the Influence of a Low Price of Corn on the Profits of Stock, etc.* He said that Malthus' rent theory taken with his own theory of profit led him to oppose the Corn Laws. (He did not however ask for their immediate and total repeal—as the Anti-Corn Law League did later—nor did any other economist except Torrens, and then only after having supported them for 23 years). Ricardo seems to have agreed with Malthus about wages. He wrote that money wages "must" fall when the price of corn falls, and in the *Principles* he stated that money wages always buy the same quantity of necessities. Of Malthus' wage doctrine, he wrote in the pamphlet: "Some of his observations on this subject are certainly of great weight." But, he added, whatever workers lost as a result of the eventual repeal of the laws would be more than restored to them by the increased productivity arising from "a better distribution of the national capital." [13] I take this to mean that the price of substitutes for corn would fall more than money wages.

Malthus' two pamphlets were noticed in the *Edinburgh Review* in 1815.[14] The reviewer said that Malthus had misunderstood the classical idea of constant corn wages to mean that the quantity of corn purchasable by the total money wage is constant while in fact the idea means that when the price of corn rises the money wage will rise in smaller proportion and only enough to enable the worker to buy the same amount of corn he previously

bought. The point is not well made. It means that the money wage of the worker will change so that he always can buy the same quantity of all commodities. It was shown above, in the second result to which the Malthus theory leads, that in such circumstances the welfare of the worker is improved in a rising market. It also is improved in a falling market, and hence lower corn prices would not reduce welfare —a point which the reviewer did not make, however. He also stated that whatever is meant by the idea of constant corn wages, the fact is that they are not constant because money wages are not influenced by the price of corn. He was on solid ground here.

In the same month in which the review appeared, Horner wrote to Malthus thanking him for copies of the pamphlets and regretting his support of protection. He noticed the wage doctrine again and now thought he had found a fallacy. He agreed that lower corn prices would mean lower money wages, but stated that the prices of other commodities also would fall, presumably in the same proportion, leaving wages constant in either corn or any other commodity. The result, he properly said, would be to leave the worker in the same position he was in when all prices and money wages were higher.[15] However, what Horner contested was not Malthus' logic but his facts, and the fallacy he detected was not in Malthus' reasoning. Horner altered the premise in order to arrive at a constant welfare wage (which, it was shown above, is the third result to which Malthus' doctrine leads).

In 1816 Torrens wrote *An Essay on the External Corn Trade* in which he tried to confront Malthus directly. He said that an increase in the price of corn would not be

[13] *An Essay on the . . . Profits of Stock, etc.* (London, 1815), p. 40. The pamphlet is in volume IV, pp. 9–41, of the Sraffa edition of Ricardo's works.

[14] Art. XIII, *Edinburgh Rev.,* Feb. 1815, No. 48, 491–505. The review may have been written by David Buchanan, a Scottish journalist and editor of the first complete edition of Smith's works, according to F. W. Fetter, "The Authorship of Economic Articles in the *Edinburgh Review, 1802–47," Jour. Pol. Econ.,* June 1953, LXI, 248, 237.

[15] Horner, *op. cit.,* II, 226. A few days before, Horner had written to J. A. Murray and criticized the wage doctrine more strongly than he had to Malthus himself. He also told Murray that Malthus' support of the Corn Laws "staggers me." *Ibid.,* II, 221.

followed by an increase in money wages of the same percentage but by an amount just sufficient to enable the worker to buy the same quantity of corn he previously bought and the same quantity of other goods. It was the point made by the critic in the *Edinburgh Review*. Torrens again contested the issue in the third edition of his *Essay* (1826). He now accepted Malthus' factual assumption, of a constant quantity of corn purchasable by the total money wage, but denied that money wages would yield more welfare in a rising than in a falling market. He said there was an absolute, fixed, quantity of necessities (corn) which the workers had to have in order to subsist and therefore they were unable to substitute other goods for necessities (corn) when the latter became relatively cheap. Actually in both editions Torrens denied the possibility of substitution, in the first because commodities other than necessities did not become relatively cheap and in the third because substitution was technically impossible. Both Torrens and Malthus believed substitutability was a question of fact, and it is interesting that both referred to the same work in support of their facts, the study of the living conditions of the poor made by Frederick Morton Eden.[16]

Many years later, in 1885, James Bonar wrote a careful and sympathetic book on *Malthus and His Work*, and for long it was the definitive work. Yet on the wage doctrine it is brief and disappointing.[17] Bonar said the doctrine was invalid, and the reasons he gave showed he was no closer to its logic than were the critics of Malthus' time. Bonar simply denied that money wages are equal to a fixed quantity of corn.

It was just this which Sir Edward West did in his pamphlet of 1826. *Price of Corn and Wages of Labour*. It says some pertinent things about the relation of money

wages to prices (and presents a clear statement of the elasticity of demand). However they were pertinent only to the factual assumption of Malthus and not to his logic. West stated that money wages and the price of necessities were not closely correlated over any period of time in which analysis is profitable.

Horner, Ricardo, Torrens, West, and the critic in the *Edinburgh Review* are the only contemporaries of Malthus who (to my knowledge) commented on his wage doctrine explicitly. The remark of Tooke which is quoted above (that money wages and corn prices do not move together) may suggest a familiarity with it or may have been a reply to Malthus' review of Tooke's earlier work. M'Culloch in 1824 wrote on the Corn Laws in the *Edinburgh Review* and declared that corn wages must be constant but denied that artificially high prices were ever justifiable. It was the nearest he came to indicating a familiarity with the doctrine, although in many ways he kept a sharp eye on Malthus whom he regarded as a great rival. He wrote on the Corn Laws again in 1834 and in 1841, both times proposing a moderate, fixed duty to compensate the landlords for their being taxed higher than manufacturers.[18] Senior wrote on the same subject in the *Quarterly Review* in 1821 and expressly took issue with Ricardo, but nowhere commented on Malthus.[19] Nor did William T. Thornton in 1841. He said that repeal would not lower money wages, but even if it did the working class would not suffer because its corn wages would be constant. By corn wages he could have meant what Malthus did, in which event he was wrong, or what Torrens

---

[16] *The State of the Poor: or an History, etc.* London, 1797).

[17] James Bonar, *Malthus and His Work* (London, 1885), p. 226.

[18] Art. III, *Edinburgh Rev.*, Oct. 1824, No. 81, 55–78; Art. I, *Edinburgh Rev.*, Jan. 1834, No. 118, 271–307; *Statements Illustrative of the Policy and Probable Consequences of the Proposed Repeal of the Existing Corn Laws, etc.*, 6th ed. (London, 1841). The *Edinburgh Review* articles are attributed to M'Culloch by Fetter.

[19] Art. IX, *Quart. Rev.*, July 1821, XXV, 466–504.

meant in the first edition of his *Essay* and again he would have been wrong though for a different reason. He seems to have meant the latter, for he stated that when there was a scarcity of corn it was the consumption of the middle and wealthy classes alone which fell.[20]

After Malthus' death, the wage doctrine was almost entirely neglected. The interesting exception was Marx. In 1848 (when one would have thought him taken up with more important matters) he sought a place among the speakers at an international conference of free traders in Brussels. He was refused, and he then read his prepared address to the Democratic Club of Brussels, a workingmen's orgnization.

> And do not believe, gentlemen [he said], that it is a matter of indifference to the workingman whether he receives only four francs on account of corn being cheaper, when he had been receiving five francs before. . . . So long as the price of corn was higher and wages also were higher, a small saving in the consumption of bread sufficed to procure him other enjoyments. But as soon as bread is cheap, and wages are therefore low, he can save almost nothing on bread, for the purchase of other articles.[21]

[20] *The Consequences of the Repeal of the Corn Laws* (London, 1841), pp. 15, 26. That the scarcity of corn should be borne by the middle and wealthy classes and not by the workingman is a blessing, he said, and "it is . . . remarkable that it should not have been pointed out by some Christian writer, as one of the most striking among the merciful dispensations of Providence." One wonders how his friend Mill responded to this.
[21] *Free Trade*, trans. Florence Kelley Wishnewetzky (Boston, 1888), p. 31. But Engels' view was altogether different. He said the repeal of the Corn Laws would increase English exports, the demand for labor, and improve the welfare of the working class—all in the short run. In the long run the population will increase, and real wages will fall: "All this the proletarians understand very well." *The Condition of the Working Class in England in 1844* (London, 1892), p. 280.

The similarity is so close that one cannot but think the idea was suggested to Marx by his reading of Malthus, a reading which is known to have been a close one.[22]

The way Marx expressed the idea is even less impressive than the way Malthus did. In none of his works did Malthus explain it completely, let alone clearly, and it must be pieced together from remarks in all of them. Moreover, he used the word corn to mean grain and also to mean all necessities; he used necessities to mean luxuries as well as necessities, and comforts and conveniences each to mean both necessities and luxuries. His book on methodology is no help except for the unintentionally mocking title, *Definitions in Political Economy, Preceded by an Inquiry into the Rules which Ought to Guide Political Economists in the Definition and Use of their Terms; with Remarks on the Deviation from these Rules in their Writings*. In the first chapter he lays down four rules of definition. His use of the simple word corn breaks all of them.

Another reason for the neglect of the wage theory is its having been developed in the last part of his life, many years after the *Essay on Population* first appeared and when he had lost his taste for controversy. There were new editions of the *Essay* when he was writing on economics, and he may have reserved his failing powers of battle to defend his famous population theory. Bonar says that when Malthus engaged the economists his forces were not in order. Had they been, he might have undertaken to read lessons to Ricardo as he had done to Godwin and to defend his doctrine of wages against Torrens, West, and others.

[22] Marx accused Malthus of "shameless and mechanical plagiarism."

8 A Re-interpretation
of Ricardo on Value

JOHN M. CASSELS

While the theory of distribution is the center of Ricardo's system, no aspect of his thinking has stirred greater controversy than his theory of value. His closest associates thought he accepted a labor theory of value. His explanation of rent as a differential surplus is compatible with such a theory. But there are many passages in his writings which make it clear that Ricardo regarded profits, as well as wages, as among the costs it is always necessary for price to include. For example, he denied Smith's premise that there was once an early and rude state of society in which capital stock had not yet become accumulated, for "Without some weapon, neither the beaver nor the deer could be destroyed, and therefore, the value of these animals would be regulated not solely by the time labor necessary for providing the hunter's capital, the weapon, by the aid of which their destruction was effected." [1] He thus rejected an absolute labor cost theory. However, he reasoned that the exchange values of goods tended to be proportionate to the amounts of labor involved in their production. This is the basis for the long-prevailing view that Ricardo held a labor theory of relative value.

John M. Cassels in "A Re-interpretation of Ricardo on Value" argues that although the preceding interpretation of Ricardo's theory of value is widely accepted, it reflects a misunderstanding of the context within which Ricardo examined the value problem. His concern with the value problem is incidental to the central problem of distribution. That is, his primary focal point is the problem of the relative share going to landlords, wage earners and capitalists. Thus, his chapter on value is not concerned with explaining *how* values are established but rather to explain how ratios of exchange are *altered* over time. Variations in these ratios affect the distributive shares, and it is *this* aspect of the value problem, Cassels argues, which particularly concerned Ricardo.

Reprinted by permission of the publishers from John M. Cassels, "A Re-interpretation of Ricardo on Value," *The Quarterly Journal of Economics*, May 1935, Cambridge, Mass.: Harvard University Press, Copyright 1935, 1963 by the President and Fellows of Harvard College. Dr. Cassels is Professor of Economics, University of Colorado, Boulder.
[1] Ricardo, D. *Principles of Political Economy and Taxation*, P. Sraffa, ed. Cambridge University Press, Cambridge, Mass., 1953, Vol. 1, p. 23.

For over a century now Ricardo's views on value have been very commonly misunderstood. It is the purpose of the present paper to show that, altho his work did undoubtedly contribute in a very important way to the subsequent development of the labor theory of value, it is a complete mistake to regard Ricardo himself as either an adherent or an exponent of that theory. There are, it is true, many passages in his chapter on value which seem at first sight to indicate an acceptance of the labor theory. But on closer examination it will be found that most of them refer not to values but to variations in values, that almost all the others refer to special simplified cases, and that the few remaining statements which do relate to the actual valuation process are merely survivals from the earlier stages of his thinking and are entirely contradicted by what he wrote later in the amended editions of his book and in his letters. It is a curious anomaly that Ricardo, whose rare intellectual honesty and keen discernment are nowhere more admirably displayed than in his critical rejection of this theory, should have come to be regarded as one of its most distinguished exponents.

In what follows it will be shown that his famous chapter on value was never intended as an exposition of any theory of value in the accepted sense of the term but was written for the special purpose of providing him with a particular logical link that was required in his elaborate chain of reasoning about the dynamics of distribution; that, since in his analysis of distribution he was primarily concerned to show how the Corn Laws would benefit the landlord class at the expense of the capitalist class, it was sufficient for his purpose to demonstrate how the value of corn would be *changed* by a *change* in the amount of labor required for its production, without the necessity of his explaining how the actual value of corn was determined at any particular time either in the presence or in the absence of the duties; that the theory of value which Ricardo quite evidently regarded as axiomatic was an expenses of production theory in which profits are included among the necessary costs; and finally, that, altho he undoubtedly began by basing his deductions on a labor theory of value suggested by his reading of The Wealth of Nations, he subsequently discarded this theory as invalid and developed in its place a demonstration, based directly on his own money cost theory, to prove merely that *variations* in the quantities of labor expended in producing different commodities must of necessity produce approximately proportionate *variations* in their relative values.

The difficulties which have been encountered all along in finding a satisfactory interpretation of Ricardo's Principles have been due not only to the intricacy of his reasoning and the obscurity of his writing, but also to the preconceived ideas with which his readers have invariably approached his work. We have naturally expected to find in the chapter on value in a book entitled The Principles of Political Economy an explanation of *how* values are determined. We have looked for a discussion of the forces which determine how much of one good shall be given, at any particular time, in exchange for another; we have looked for a discussion of the principles according to which, at any one time, the ratios of exchange for various commodities are established. This is what we have found in the corresponding chapters of other books and this is what we have insisted on finding in the first chapter of Ricardo.

This, however, was certainly not what Ricardo meant to give us. Altho in his chapters "on natural and market price," "on profits," "on the influence of supply and demand on prices" and elsewhere in his writings he shows that he understood very well the operation of the forces of supply and demand, in his chapter "on value" they receive no more than a passing reference. Again, altho he regarded "cost of production including profits" as the "ultimate" determinant of exchange values for all goods that are freely reproducible by human effort, the only account we are given of *how* costs are related to values was added as an afterthought in chapter XXX, almost at the end of the book. When Ricardo wrote his chapter on value he was concerned not with the ratios of exchange which might exist at any one time but with the changes in those ratios which might take place between two periods of time. He was not interested in the fact that one piece of cloth might be exchanged, at any particular time, for two quarters of corn but he was intensely interested in the possibility that, ten years later, one piece of cloth might be exchanging for only one quarter of corn. Ricardo stated his own position as follows: "The inquiry to which I wish to draw the reader's attention relates to the effects of variations in the relative value of commodities." So engrossing, indeed, was his interest in this question of the *"variations in relative value"* that those very words or their equivalents occur no less than 200 times in this one short chapter, an average of 7 times on every page.

Why was Ricardo so interested in these variations in value? Because they affected the distribution of the national income among the landlords, the capitalists and the laborers. He says in his preface that "to determine the laws which regulate this distribution is the principal problem of Political Economy." What was uppermost in his mind was undoubtedly the effect of the Corn Laws on the relative prosperity of the landlords and the capitalists. His Principles developed out of earlier papers which dealt more explicitly with this particular problem. He realized, as did many others of his class, that the protective duties so beneficial to the rent-receivers were distinctly disadvantageous to those

who drew their income in the form of profits. To prove this by incontrovertible logic was the ultimate object of Ricardo's endeavor. The result, as we shall see, was a remarkable intellectual structure, at the foundation of which was his celebrated principle of diminishing returns, and for which the keystone was found in the close relationship between the changes in the quantity of labor embodied in commodities and the variations that take place in their relative values.

More specifically, what he undertook to show was that the operation of the principle of diminishing returns enforced by restrictions on the importation of corn would inevitably result in a decrease in the *proportion* of the total national income going to the capitalist class. The steps in his reasoning were as follows:

1. As society advances population increases and the number of laborers increases proportionately.
2. If we measure quantity of labor simply by working time it follows that the total quantity of labor employed in producing the national income increases in the same proportion.
3. Since corn is the staple food of the people and its consumption per capita cannot be materially reduced the total corn crop (if importation is prevented) must also be increased in about the same proportion.
4. Because of "the laws of nature which have limited the productive powers of the land" the production of each additional quarter involves a greater expenditure of labor, and the amount of labor embodied in the corn crop as a whole increases in greater proportion than the total quantity of labor available for the production of the national income.
5. Since the quantity of labor embodied in the corn crop has increased relatively to the quantity embodied in all other commodities it follows that, if the variation in exchange values is proportionate to the changes in the quantities of labor embodied, the corn crop now represents a larger share than formerly of the total income of the community measured in terms of general purchasing power.
6. As the margin of production is pushed farther and farther beyond the point of di-

minishing returns the *landlords* receive as rent (according to Ricardo's figures) a larger and larger share of the corn crop and consequently a share of the total income which is increased in even greater proportion.

7. Since the *laborers'* per capita consumption of corn cannot be reduced the total physical quantity necessarily going to that class must increase in proportion as the corn crop itself. Assuming then, as Ricardo does, that the other elements in their subsistence are produced under the same conditions as before (i.e. at the same labor cost) it follows that the wage-earnings' share of the total income measured in terms of general purchasing power is substantially increased.

8. Thus we arrive at the conclusion that, since each of the other classes gets a larger share of the national income, the *capitalists*, as the residual legatees, are left with a smaller proportion than they formerly obtained.[2]

From the foregoing outline it is evident that Ricardo's discussion of value was subsidiary to his discussion of distribution. It is only when this is realized that the peculiarities of the opening chapter can be satisfactorily accounted for. His whole analysis of distribution depends for its validity upon his ability to establish at least an approximate correspondence between the variations in the exchange values of commodities and the changes in the quantities of labor time necessary to produce them (see step 5). It was in order to establish this vital point that he wrote his chapter "on value."

The reason that these fundamental steps

[2] There is one additional step to which we may refer, altho it really carries us beyond the field of distribution as Ricardo had defined it. Having satisfied himself that the proportion of the national income going to the capitalist class must inevitably decline, he goes on to speak as if the rate (%) of return on capital must also fall. He uses the term "fall in profits" ambiguously to refer to either of these changes and his language suggests that the one follows necessarily from the other, whereas in fact the validity of this final step depends not so much on his analysis of distribution as upon his belief that saving is only slightly affected by a reduction in the rate of return on investment. He seems to have been misled here partly because he had based his analysis on an individual farm instead of dealing with the community as a whole.

in Ricardo's demonstration do not stand out more clearly in the text itself is that he stated them there in a curiously cryptic way. Instead of dealing directly with the distribution of the whole national income he based his analysis on the distribution of agricultural produce from a single farm between the farmer, his landlord and his hired laborers. The link between the distribution on an individual farm and distribution in the community as a whole is to be found in his concept of an ideal invariable standard of value. If we succeed in keeping its significance constantly in mind as we study the chapters dealing with distribution (especially the chapter on profits) we discover that the underlying logic of his argument is essentially the same as that outlined above. The difficulty is that this is the most elusive link in the whole chain of his reasoning—so elusive indeed that it is commonly supposed to be missing entirely. Even Professor Cannan has written that Ricardo "always appears to treat *a farm* as a kind of type of the industry of the whole country and to *suppose* that the division of the whole produce can be easily inferred from the distribution on the farm." (The italics are mine.)

The employment of the idea of an invariable standard of value was the most natural thing in the world for an economist of the early nineteenth century. It was one of the central concepts of economic theory in Ricardo's day and no doubt imposed itself upon his thought without any conscious choice on his part. We may be pretty sure, moreover, that it added to the difficulty of his own thinking in much the same way that it has added since to the difficulties of those who have tried to understand him. In spite of the complications introduced by this troublesome concept the logic of his deductions appears to be perfectly sound. The particular standard of value which he set up was a purely hypothetical one and was specially designed to suit the purpose he had in hand. "To facilitate the object of this enquiry," he says, "altho I fully allow that money made of gold is subject to most of the variations of other things *I shall suppose* it to be invariable." [3] (The italics are mine.)

This imaginary ideal money of which he assumed himself to be possessed was designed to measure the variations in the quantity of labor embodied in different commodities. It follows from this assumption that total national income measured in terms of price (ideal) can only vary in proportion to the changes in the total amount of labor expended in producing it. That being so it is clear that, since the amount of corn produced is always proportionate to the total labor of the community, a rise in its price (ideal) per quarter must mean that the crop as a whole has come to represent a larger proportion than formerly of the total national income measured in terms of this ideal money. It follows further from the nature of this arbitrary standard, and from the relations established between the variations in quantities of labor expended and the variations in value, that the corn crop represents a larger proportion of the national income in terms of general purchasing power. From this point on his analysis follows closely the outline given above. [4]

[3] It is true, as Professor Hollander has pointed out, that Ricardo was later drawn into the current controversy about the best practical measure of value, but as far as this book is concerned the idea of an invariable standard served merely as a form in which to express his thought and contributed nothing itself to the logic of his argument. It was essential to the presentation of his case in the form he chose but was quite unessential to its fundamental logic. His whole chain of reasoning was independent of this concept and he realized quite clearly that the existence or nonexistence of such a standard in actual fact did not matter to him in the least. "Of such a measure," he says, "it is impossible to be possessed, because there is no commodity which is not itself exposed to the same variations as the things the value of which is to be ascertained."
[4] The ideal standard is no more essential to the logic of the chapter on value than it is to the discussion of distribution. The prominent position it is given in section I of the *Principles* is un-

In the light of the foregoing discussion of Ricardo's methods and objectives his perplexing chapter on value become intelligible. Striking verbal inconsistencies remain because of his failure to rewrite the text completely as his thinking of the subject progressed, but the real significance of these contradictory statements and the underlying meaning of the chapter as a whole become perfectly clear. It will help us in reëxamining this chapter if we recognize three different stages in the development of his thought: first, the stage in which he based his conclusions about the variations in values on Adam Smith's theory that actual values correspond to the quantities of labor embodied in the products; second, the transitional stage in which, altho he had renounced the labor theory as such because it was inconsistent with his own money cost theory, he was still inclined to argue that the exchange values of goods would be *proportionate* to the amounts of labor bestowed on their production; and finally, the stage in which he gave up even this claim that values would be proportionate and derived directly from the money cost theory itself the relations he required to establish between the *variations* in values and the *variations* in the quantities of labor expended in producing the goods.

Of the first stage only a few traces remain, at the very beginning of the chapter on value. There can be little doubt that the idea of a fundamental relation between labor and value was suggested to him by an early reading of The Wealth of Nations. Being a hard-headed business man rather than a philosopher he did not share Adam Smith's interest in the ethical significance of a labor theory value, but when he came to work out the principles of his own economic system he was naturally attracted to an idea which fitted into it so nicely.

warranted and our understanding of Ricardo's reasoning is greatly facilitated if we skip from the end of the tenth paragraph in section I to the beginning of section II.

Thus we find him quoting with approval near the beginning of the chapter Smith's statement that "labor was the first price . . . the original purchase money paid for all things." A little later he himself says that the labor expended in producing commodities "is really the foundation of the exchangeable value of all things, excepting those which cannot be increased by human industry." There follows immediately after this a statement which is highly significant because it indicates the real nature of his interest in the labor theory of value. He writes *"if* the quantities of labor realized in commodities regulate their exchangeable value, every *increase* in the quantity of labor must *augment* the value of that commodity on which it is exercised, as every *diminution* must *lower* it." (The italics are mine.)

Several passages representative of the second stage in the development of Ricardo's thought are to be found in the third edition of the Principles. From a comparison of this edition with the earlier ones it is clear that his views had undergone considerable modification between the time that these passages were originally written and the time that the final edition was published. Ricardo's objective during the transitional stage in which these passages were written was, it will be remembered, to show that on the basis of a money cost theory values would be *proportionate* to the quantities of labor expended on the commodities. His first step was to eliminate rent from among the costs. This he did by pointing out that it is the marginal cost of a commodity that affects its price—the cost on no-rent land. That being so the costs of production which affect value are reduced to two, wages and profits. His adherence to a cost of production theory in this form is explicitly avowed in a footnote as follows: "Mr. Malthus appears to think that it is part of my doctrine that the cost and value of a thing should be the same; it is, if he means by cost, 'cost of

production' including profits." He explains in this connection that in measuring the quantity of labor embodied in commodities we must include not cnly the labor expended "on their immediate production" but also that which was bestowed "on all those implements and machines" which contributed to their manufacture. Having thus eliminated rent and reduced capital to past labor the temptation to treat profits merely as a percentage of wages and to suppose that total costs would, therefore, always be proportionate to the wage-bills paid must have been almost irresistible. Ricardo did for a time succumb to this temptation and wrote in a well-known passage: "I have not said, because one commodity has so much labor bestowed upon it as will cost £1,000, and another so much as will cost £2,000, that therefore one would be of the value of £1,000, and the other of the value of £2,000; but I have said that their value will be to each other as two to one." He did not identify costs with wages. He made no attempt to eliminate profits as he had eliminated rent. He was content with his claim that the inclusion of profits would not disturb the proportional relationship between wages and costs.

A further step was necessary in order to reach the conclusion required for the main purpose of his investigation. He had to slip from the use of the term "wages" to the use of the term "quantity of labor" (measured by time). This was an entirely illogical step but Ricardo took it. We find in more than one place the statement that the relative values of commodities are "regulated" or "governed" by the "relative quantities of labor bestowed on their production."

It is to Ricardo's credit that he himself perceived later the error into which he had fallen. In a letter to McCulloch in the summer of 1820 he wrote, "I sometimes think that if I were to write the chapter on value again which is in my book, I should acknowledge that the relative value of commodities was regulated by two causes instead of one, namely, by the relative quantity of labor necessary to produce the commodities in question, and by the rate of profit for the time that the capital remained dormant, and until the commodities were brought to market."

About the same time in a letter to Malthus he admitted the weakness of this step in his proof but defended the validity of his final conclusions about the effects of the increasing cost of corn on the distribution of the national income among the different classes of society. He recognized that his proposition about quantity of labor regulating value was "not rigidly true." "But," he says, "the doctrine is less liable to objections when employed not to measure the whole absolute value of the commodities compared, but the *variations* which from time to time take place in relative value." (The italics are mine.)

This statement in his letter to Malthus was characteristic of the third phase in the development of his thought on the subject of values and value relations. The essential elements of the direct proof which he used to relate *variations* in values to *variations* in labor inputs measured by time, while present in the first and second editions of the work, were given the greatest prominence in the final edition. The superiority of this proof over that which we have just been examining lies in the fact that whereas no logical link was found between wage-bills and quantities of labor (time), such a link was discovered between *variations* in the wage-bills and the *variations* in quantities of labor (time). In section II of the chapter on value Ricardo explains why in dealing with the variations in the relative values of commodities between two different periods he is justified in ignoring differences in the qualities of labor altho these differences in quality admittedly affect the relative values themselves. "The estimation," he says, "in which

different qualities of labor are held comes soon to be adjusted in the market with sufficient precision for all practical purposes and . . . The scale, when once formed, is liable to little variation. If a day's labor of a working jeweller be more valuable than a day's labor of a common laborer, it has long ago been adjusted and placed in its proper position in the scale of value. In comparing, therefore, the value of the same commodity at different periods of time, the consideration of the comparative skill and intensity of labor required for that particular commodity needs scarcely to be attended to, as it operates equally in both periods."

Wage-bills depend, of course, on two factors, the length of time worked and the rate of pay per unit of time. The first of these is, according to Ricardian terminology, the *"quantity"* of labor. It is evident then that if the rates of pay remain the same (or change proportionately through some common cause) the changes in the wage-bills will correspond exactly with changes in the quantity of labor expended. This was the link in his reasoning that Ricardo required and the subsequent steps in his deductions are logically supported by it, altho the connection between this step and the later ones is obscured by the particular method of exposition he adopted. What he did from this point on in his discussion was to treat labor as if it were all of the same quality. In all the numerical illustrations which are introduced the rates of remuneration for labor are uniform regardless of the nature of the work which is being done. While this procedure is logically valid it is obviously liable to be misleading. There can be no doubt that the treacherous step in Ricardo's transitional deductions referred to above resulted, in part at least, from his adoption of this dangerous procedure and that many of his readers have been misled in exactly the same way into the belief that he had demonstrated a correspondence between actual values and the quantities of labor expended.

Before leaving this particular subject we may well consider for a moment why Ricardo should have attached to the term "quantity of labor" the meaning that he did. By defining it as a quantity measurable purely by time he made it impossible to relate it to value and difficult to relate it even to variations in value. Why should he not have made it a quantity measurable by wages? The answer is simple. From an earlier part of our study we discovered how important it was for him to bring into as direct relationship as possible the total food supply and the total quantity of labor. The fact that the amount of subsistence required and the amount of work done are both dependent on time provided him with the necessary link between them and determined immediately the meaning that should be attached to the term "quantity of labor."

In the development of his argument Ricardo proceeds from the consideration of a hypothetical case in which no capital at all is employed in production to the consideration of an exceptional case in which it happens that labor and waiting (to use the term now familiar) are combined in the same proportions in all industries and finally to the consideration of more realistic cases in which labor and waiting are combined in different proportions in different industries. The first case is dismissed almost without discussion; the second is dealt with in the latter part of section III; and the realistic cases are dealt with in sections IV and V.

Unfortunately for his readers Ricardo, a pioneer in this field of investigtion, did not have at his disposal the precise concepts and the carefully considered terminology which are available to economists today. He was obliged to struggle along with such cumbersome concepts as "the proportions of fixed and circulating capital," "the degree of durability of fixed capi-

tal," "the time which must elapse before it (the product) can be brought to market," "the rapidity with which it (the capital) is returned to its employer," and so on. We naturally have some difficulty in grasping the significance of this unfamiliar language but a careful study of his explanations and his illustrations enables us to see that the idea he had in mind was what Jevons would have referred to as "the amount of investment of capital." This "amount of investment of capital" or this "amount of waiting" is a quantity of two dimensions, value and time, obtained by multiplying together the amount of money invested and the length of time that elapses before it is returned to the investor.

Stated in modern terms, then, Ricardo's conclusions were: (1) that where the proportions of labor and waiting (both measured by money) are the same in the different industries concerned, the variations in the values of the products will be exactly proportionate to the changes in the quantity of labor (time) expended on them; (2) that even where labor and waiting enter in unequal proportions the correspondence, altho not exact, will be sufficiently close to afford a basis for the deductions he wished to make about the dynamics of distribution. Referring to the effects on values of a change in the rate of profits he wrote, "The reader should remark that this cause of the variation of commodities is comparatively slight in its effects." This factor he believed to be limited in the range of its effect to 6 or 7 per cent. "Not so," he says, in contrast, "with the other great cause of variation in the value of commodities, namely the increase or diminution in the quantity of labor necessary to produce them. If to produce the corn eighty instead of one hundred men should be required, the value of the corn would fall 20 per cent . . . An alteration in the permanent rate of profits, to any great amount, is the effect of causes which do not operate but in the course of years, whereas alterations in the quantity of labor necessary to produce commodities are of daily occurrence." Therefore, he declares, "*I shall consider all the great variations which take place in the relative value of commodities to be produced by the greater or less quantity of labor which may be required from time to time to produce them.*"

This arbitrary disregard of the minor variations may appear at first sight to be a rather high-handed method of dealing with a troublesome discrepancy. But it involves no relaxation in the logic of his analysis. Since he was concerned with the variations in the value of corn, a commodity "chiefly produced by labor," the recognition of the effects of changes in the rate of profits would have strengthened rather than weakened his case. The falling rate of profits found (according to Ricardo) in an advancing society would affect the value of corn in exactly the same way as the increase in the quantity of labor necessary for its production and would contribute in like manner to the redistribution of the national income with which we are here concerned. In making the above assumption Ricardo's object was not to gain any dialectic advantage but merely to simplify the presentation of his argument.

A more important assumption than this, however, is made in these sections without any explicit mention whatever. In all the reasoning involved in his direct proof he has taken for granted that the proportions in which labor and waiting are combined in the different industries remain constant between the two periods under consideration. It was not necessary for him to assume, as is sometimes supposed, that the proportions are the same in all industries but it was necessary to assume that they were constant. This means, in the language of Bohm-Bawerk, that "the period of production" for each commodity must remain unaltered, i.e. that the "roundaboutness" of the process in each industry

must remain the same. It allows for no fundamental changes in the methods of production. Altho this assumption is only made implicitly we have no reason to doubt Ricardo's willingness to accept the conditions implied. The case is closely parallel to that in which he assumed that the qualities of labor would remain the same in different industries. Both of these assumptions seem more reasonable when we realize that, in spite of his references to the gradual advance of society, he really had in mind the effects which would be brought about in a relatively short time by the imposition of a high tariff on corn. In speaking of the qualities of labor he says, "the variation is very inconsiderable from year to year, and therefore can have little effect, for short periods, on the relative value of commodities." The same might well have been said of the arts of production.

The reinterpretation here suggested of Ricardo's chapter on value is not only logically consistent with all he wrote but is also psychologically consistent with what we know of his own character and background. He was a retired business man, actively engaged in politics, and keenly interested in the practical economic problems of his day, who had a remarkably penetrating and logical mind but was absolutely untrained in the arts of academic men and was persuaded to write his book only by the insistent pressure of his friends. He undertook this task only a few years before his death and he continued to reconsider his views to the very end. He was not interested in expounding any theory of value for its own sake—least of all a labor theory. He took over the idea of a labor theory from Adam Smith but he can never have believed himself that labor "created" value directly by its embodiment in commodities. He was not even interested in the "real costs" of production. His deductions are all based on money costs and the farthest that he ever went in the direction of a labor theory was to say (carelessly) that costs would be proportionate to labor expended. Even in this relation he had no direct interest; he used it merely as a means of reaching his conclusions about variations in value; and recognizing in the end the error in this step of his reasoning he eliminated it from the main chain of his deductions. The real significance of Ricardo's chapter on value lies not in the fact that occasional passages seem to support a labor theory but rather in the evidence it gives us that he had examined this theory critically and was finally led to reject it entirely.

9 The Wages Fund Controversy: A Diagrammatic Exposition

WILLIAM BREIT

The wages-fund doctrine is among the most fundamental tenets of classical economics. From Smith until the ultimate rejection of the doctrine by John Stuart Mill, wage rates were explained according to the principle that their level depends on the number of workers seeking employment relative to the size of the wages fund available. The wages fund was conceived of as a stock of wage goods, principally food products, which becomes available at successive harvests and is advanced to workers during the production process. Since these wage goods were viewed as part of the economy's real capital, which was continuously being used up to furnish the worker's subsistence and then replenished from the sale of his output, the wages-fund doctrine served, though not without criticism, both as a theory of wages and a theory of capital.

The main source of controversy and confusion about the doctrine concerned the relationship between it and the general law of demand and supply. Some writers, among them Frances Longe and W. T. Thornton, conceived of the demand for labor as a specific magnitude representing the quantity of circulating capital offered in relation to a given supply of labor. According to this interpretation the general rate of wages is uniquely determined; that is, only one equilibrium rate is possible. Mill's application of the demand and supply apparatus to the labor market, on the other hand, is compatible with various equilibria. He conceived of the quantity of labor demanded and supplied in a schedule sense, so that the equilibrium wage is one at which the quantity demanded just equals the quantity supplied.

Mill's critics tried to undermine the wages-fund doctrine by demonstrating the inadequacy of the demand and supply principle as an explanation for the phenomenon of price.[1] However, as William Breit has shown, the wages-fund doctrine is perfectly compatible with demand and supply analysis in the Millian sense.

Reprinted from William Breit, "The Wages Fund Controversy Revisited" from *The Canadian Journal of Economics*, Vol. 33, No. 4, November 1967, pp. 523–528. William Breit is Associate Professor of Economics at the University of Virginia, Charlottesville.

[1] "Thornton on Labor and Its Claims," *Fortnightly Review*, No. XXIX and XXX, May and June 1869, pp. 505–518–700. Thornton's argument is generally regarded as having persuaded Mill to recant the wages-fund doctrine.

Diagrammatic formulation of the classical system can assist in solving a problem that was never settled in the wages fund theory debate, namely, what relation exists between the wages fund theory and supply and demand theory? It will be demonstrated that, contrary to Longe and Thornton, the analysis can be stated in terms of supply and demand, although through a rather circuitous route.

A functional representation of the theoretical system of the classical economics would be as follows:

(1) $R = R(W)$
(2) $I = I(R)$
(3) $Ld = Ld(I)$
(4) $L_s = L_s(W)$
(5) $L_d = L_s$

where

R = rate of profit
W = wage rate
I = investment (net additions to capital stock)
L_d = demand for labour
L_s = supply of labour

Equation (1) is the Ricardian residual theory of profits, which says that there is an inverse relation between wages and profits. To Ricardo the rate of profit is the ratio of surplus produce to invested capital. An increase in wages meant a decline in profits since profit was conceived of as a residual. According to Ricardo, wages represent the product of so much labour: when high, they are equivalent to the output of much labour; when low, the equivalent of little labour. With a given output and capital stock, an increase in the wage rate reduces the rate of profit, since surplus produce available to the capitalist must be less.

Equation (2) expresses the theory of capital accumulation, wherein profits determine the amount of net investment. Virtually all classicists took it for granted that capitalists make investments because they expect to earn profits; what they expect in the future is a function of present profits. By investment is meant net investment; that is, net additions to the stock of capital. Thus $I = I(R)$ where R is the return on fixed factors of production, or profit. By definition, net investment is represented by the increase in capital stock. Part of the net addition to capital stock hires workers, and is called "circulating capital." The other part, called "technological" or "fixed capital" consists of machines, buildings, and inventories of non-wage goods. The classical economists generally assumed that both wage capital (circulating) and technological capital (fixed) increase together.

Equation (3) is the wages fund theory. It says that wages are a part of capital stock used in support of labour during the current period of production; part of this period's output will be used to hire workers in the next productive period. Workers producing goods today are replenishing those goods consumed in the current period. The new wage goods will then be used to tide workers over the next period of production. Hence, they determine the quantity of labour demanded in the next period.

Equation (4) represents the Mathusian theory of population, and says that the labour force is a function of real wages. As real wages rise, population and therefore the supply of labour increases. A discussion of the shape of this function will be reserved for later.

Equation (5) is the equilibrium condition.

The model is represented graphically in Figure 9-1. All directions in Figure 9-1 should be taken as positive. Quadrant A shows the wage-profit relation assumed by classical theory. Since for each wage rate there is a corresponding profit rate, the curve shows all possible combinations of wage rates and profit rates consistent with a particular state of the arts and a given output. From this curve is found the rate of profit consistent with any given rate of

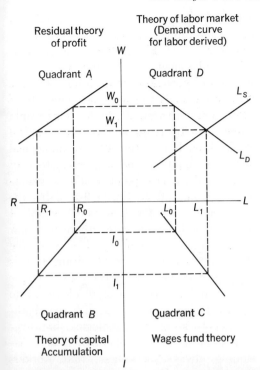

Residual theory
of profit

Theory of labor market
(Demand curve
for labor derived)

Quadrant A

Quadrant D

Quadrant B

Quadrant C

Theory of capital
Accumulation

Wages fund theory

FIGURE 9-1

in Figure 9-1. The purpose of the four quadrants is to show how the aggregate demand function for labour may be distilled from the postulates of the classical model. The point is to relate the demand for labour to the wage rate. Starting with Quadrant A, assume the wage rate is W_0. The corresponding rate of profit is R_0. It can be seen from Quadrant B that a profit rate of R_0 results in an amount of investment equal to I_0. Part of this net addition to capital stock will be in the form of wage goods, and, as seen from Quadrant C, will hire the quantity of workers, L_0. The coordinates of L_0 and W_0 yield a point on the demand curve for labour, in Quadrant D, showing that the demand for labour is a function of the wage rate.

Another point on the demand curve can be generated by repeating the process starting with arbitrary wage rate, W_1. Following the same procedure as before, another point on our demand curve is derived. Connecting the points, there is a demand curve for labour consistent with our given wage-profit function, profit-investment function, capital stock-labour demand function. It is seen that the demand curve for labour slopes downward and to the right, consistent with the usual conception of a demand curve.

It is now a simple matter to add a labour supply curve (L_s) showing the functional relationship of labour and the average wage rate. In Quadrant D of Figure 9-1, the curve for labour supply slopes upward and to the right, meaning that higher rate is associated with a larger labour force. Since this is a long-run analysis it might be assumed that the supply function should be represented by a horizontal line at a subsistence wage rate. But the truth is that it is difficult to find such an interpretation in classical economics itself. The classicals were well aware that higher wages could lead to a different standard of living and new fertility rates arising from changes in values and mores. So the classical long-run

wages. The rate of profit in Quadrant A is projected to Quadrant B, which shows the amount of investment stimulated by present profit. As has been pointed out, investment means net additions to capital stock. This variable is a function of present profit, and it is necessary to specify as to shape of the curve only that it is a straight line showing that greater profits will stimulate greater investment. The slope of the line showing net investment is positive.

Since investment adds to capital stock, its increase means a rise in the stock of all kinds of capital, circulating as well as fixed. But the demand for labour is a function of the growth of circulating capital and can be read off the horizontal axis common to both Quadrants C and D. If we assume that the proportion of circulating capital is relatively large, an increase in capital would support a larger quantity of labour.

The aggregate demand curve for labour may now be derived. The process is shown

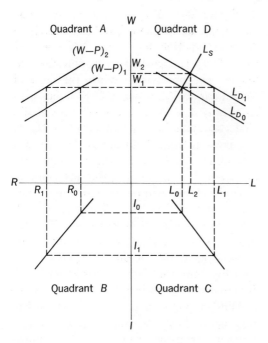

FIGURE 9-2

involves an upward and outward shift of the wage-profit function, as shown in Quadrant A of Figure 9-2. The previous full employment equilibrium wage rate, W_1, would now leave more profits (profits being a residual) to capitalists. The rate of profit increases from R_0 to R_1. This would induce employers to add to their capital stock through investment in technological and wage capital. With a greater stock of wage goods, a new point would be generated in Quadrant D, Figure 9-2. Using the new wage-profit function in Quadrant A for all possible wage rates, there is a new demand curve for labour, which is to the right of the old one. In Quadrant D this has led to an increase in the rate of wages to W_2, and the volume of employment to L_2, a conclusion consistent with the classical hypothesis that technological improvements accrue to the benefit of labour, assuming always, of course, that workers limit their numbers. From the model, therefore, it can be concluded that an increase

supply curve of labour need not be perfectly elastic at subsistence. Of course, if drawn perfectly elastic then the dismal science would be dismal indeed, and any policy recommendations which merely acted upon the rate of profit would be futile. This would mean that the belief of the wages fund adherent that higher profits stimulate capital accumulation and greater wages could only be a very short-run expectation. But, since the classical school had strong views on economic policy regarding the accumulation of capital as a means of salvation of the labouring classes, it is clear that they implicitly assumed an elasticity in the labour supply curve of less than infinity.

A better understanding of the model and of the diagrams will come from analysing the effects on the equilibrium values of the several variables of some changes in parameters. For example, consider the effects of an increase in the productivity of labour. An increase in the productivity of labour

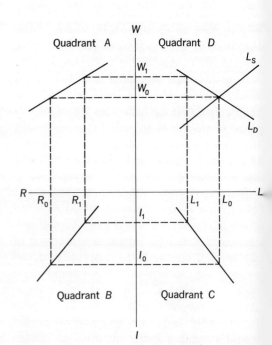

FIGURE 9-3

in productivity raises profits, increases capital accumulation, the wage rate, and employment.

Now consider the effect of imperfect competition in the labour market. As already indicated, many economists and public officials were in agreement that labour unions could not in the long run help the working class. The reasoning behind this proposition can be clarified by the model.

Consider the situation as shown in Figure 9-3. In Quadrant D, there is an equilibrium real wage rate of W_0 consistent with full employment at L_0. But suppose that the wage rate is artificially fixed by a trade union at W_1, above the current equilibrium rate. In the long run, what will be the new level of R, I, and L? It can be seen that the rate of profit would fall, investment would be reduced to I_1, and hence less capital produced. The quantity of labour demanded would then fall to L_1, while the quantity of labour supplied would increase. Unemployment would result. Moreover, this conclusion would be magnified if the artificial increase in wages resulted in a "Ricardo effect," that is, a substitution of capital for labour. Such an effect would involve a shift to the left of the wages fund function in Quadrant C. The effect of this substitution would be to shift the aggregate demand curve for labour to the left. Thus we may sum up by saying that labour unions would reduce the quantity of labour demanded at the higher artificial wage, and perhaps shift the labour demand curve to the left, thereby aggravating the problem of unemployment.

This model demonstrates that there is a consistent version of the classical theory of employment, based on the residual theory of profits, the theory of capital accumulation, and the wages fund theory.

What is more, the diagrammatic formulation of the theory helps solve a problem never settled in the wages fund debates; namely, what relation, if any, exists between the wages fund theory and supply and demand theory? We now see that, contrary to Longe and Thornton, the analysis can be put in terms of supply and demand schedules, although through a rather indirect route. Further, the insistence on the part of some interpreters (including Mill of the "recantation") that the wages fund theory involves a unitary elastic demand curve is seen to be in error. Moreover, one of the most important special insights of the wages fund theory, the dependence of future wages on present profits, is made clear by use of the model presented here. Finally, in answering the criticisms made during Mill's lifetime, we have implied that the properly stated form of the theory, and its policy implications, remain valid today.

The obvious danger of rehearsing the history of a theoretical controversy is that of getting so engrossed in the subtleties of the arguments that the essence of the theory itself is forgotten. This simplified model should help bring out the real meaning of the wages fund theory within the total schema of the classical system.

10 Mill and the Wages Fund

A. C. PIGOU

The requirements for raising the average level of wages for labor as a whole has long been an intriguing question. Most contemporary theorists would agree with the classicists' conclusion that, with a given population and a given level of technology, the average rate of wages can be raised only if the size of the capital stock increases. They would, however, explain the increase in the wage level as resulting from an increase in the marginal productivity of labor when it is combined with more capital, rather than as a result of an increase in that portion of the capital stock represented by the wages fund.

The classicists typically exhorted capitalists to practice parsimony in order to increase the wages fund and enhance the employment of productive labor. But, they also generally accepted the principle that the tendency for population to increase with increases in the availability of physical subsistence limits the prospect for substantially increasing the wages of labor as a whole, unless workers can be educated to the importance of controlling the sizes of the labor market. This too is a conclusion with which modern thinkers would generally agree, though they would relate low wages, not to large numbers per se, but to the effect of large numbers on labors' productivity.

While the conclusions to which the wages fund theory led the classicists were not without validity, the doctrine itself lost adherents after J. S. Mill recanted it in 1869 in his well-known dispute with Henry Thornton. Mill later retained the doctrine in the final edition of his *Principles of Political Economy* which suggests that his position *vis a vis* Thornton stemmed largely from his sympathy for the union movement. He also analyzed the effect on the wages fund of several phenomena, among them industrial fluctuation and governmental borrowing. In "Mill and the Wages Fund," written on the one hundredth anniversary of the publication of Mill's *Principles of Political Economy*, A. C. Pigou reexamined some of these applications and reviewed and enlarged on the theoretical basis for rejecting the wages fund.

Reprinted from A. C. Pigou, "Mill and the Wages Fund" from *The Economic Journal*, Vol. 57, 1949, pp. 171–180. Reprinted by permission of the publisher. The late Professor Pigou was affiliated with King's College, Cambridge.

Mill's *Principles of Political Economy* were first published in 1848, a hundred years ago as I write this. Now is, therefore, a (sentimentally) appropriate time for a comment. Summary and laudation are both dull. Discussion is a more worthy tribute; and for discussion we want some theme that has caused puzzlement and roused controversy. What better could there be than the celebrated doctrine of the wages fund?

Before attacking that theme, however, I should like to call attention to an aspect of Mill's view, not on the wages fund, but on capital in general, which has an important bearing on the present situation in Europe. He argues that, when a country has been devastated, for example, by war, the damage is much less than might be thought at first sight, because the structures destroyed would in any event have been worn out and have required replacement in a short time. It is a wasting, not a permanent, asset that has been devastated. "What the enemy has destroyed would have been destroyed in a little time by the inhabitants themselves; the wealth which they so rapidly replace would have needed to be reproduced, and would have been reproduced in any case and probably in as short a time."[1] There is, of course, a very important element of truth in this. Nevertheless, Mill's argument, as he puts it, while it corrects excess pessimism, is itself weighted with excess optimism. For suppose that we start with 1,000 machines, a hundred of which would normally wear out in each of the ten succeeding years. Mill's statement suggests that, were the 1,000 machines destroyed, the whole of the devastation could without any extra effort be made good in ten years. This is not so. For it is very much harder to make a hundred machines in a year when there are no machines, or only a few machines, to help make them than when there are nine hundred available for that. Mill's argument neglects this very important fact. Destruc-

tion of three fourths of a country's capital equipment is more than twice as bad as destruction of three eighths of that equipment.

That, however, is a digression. Let us pass to the main theme. Everybody agrees that in any year there is a certain wages flow—a sum of wage goods that are actually handed out to wage-earners in payment for their work during that year. This does not, however, imply that a stock of wage goods of that amount was stored up beforehand, which, without addition or subtraction, must be paid out to labour in that year. Indeed, it says nothing at all about the relation between the wages flow and the previously stored stock of wage goods. A study of that relation may perhaps even now contribute a little towards clarifying our ideas.

Mill defines as "circulating capital" that part of capital, "which, after being once used, exists no longer as capital; is no longer capable of rendering service to production, or at least not the same service nor to the same sort of production."[2] It thus includes materials, and consumable goods held in store ready to be handed over to labour as wages for work. This latter element—we may call it wage-goods capital—is thus a part of circulating capital. Together with "funds which, without forming a part of capital, are paid in exchange for labour, such as the wages of soldiers, domestic servants and other unproductive labour"[3]—these, following Mill's own example, I shall disregard—it constitutes the wages fund. This fund is not always the

---

[1] *Principles of Political Economy,* Ashley's edition, p. 75.

[2] *Principles,* p. 91.

[3] *Principles,* p. 344. Elsewhere (*Essays on some Unsettled Questions of Political Economy,* p. 91) Mill seems to deny that what I have called wage-goods capital is productive of anything. "Wages do not contribute along with labour to the production of commodities, no more than the price of tools contributes along with the tools themselves." But surely the food, etc., that is used to sustain labour when at work corresponds to the tools themselves and *is* productive. The money price (value) of this stock, like the money price of the tools, must not, of course, be counted as a further productive element.

same. It is likely to grow larger as wealth expands. But at any given moment it is a *predetermined amount*. It is the fund *destined* to maintain labour in production.[4] It is "a sum of wealth unconditionally devoted to the payment of labour."[5] In the passage of the *Dissertations* describing, after he had abandoned it, what his conception of the fund was, Mill says that the whole of it available in any period must actually be paid out in that period; that is to say, the wages flow in any period must be exactly equal to the wages fund. More than the wages fund "the wage earning classes cannot possibly divide among them; that amount and no less they cannot but obtain. So that, the sum to be divided being fixed, the wage of each depends solely on the divisor, the number of participants."[6] Elsewhere, however, he concedes that it is not necessary for the whole of the wages fund available in any period to be used in that period. In bad times a part of it may be "locked up in crowded warehouses."[7] On this version the size of the fund proper to any year does not rigidly determine the amount of the wages flow. *But on either version it does set a ceiling to it*. Beyond the amount of the fund it is impossible for any agency, government, trade union or anything else to force up the wages of labour as a whole. They may, of course, force up the wages of a particular group of wage-earners, but that can only be at the expense of other groups.

Before inquiring into the validity of this doctrine it is convenient to describe some of the chief applications which Mill makes on it. In the *Principles* he adopts the second of the two versions distinguished above. Working out that version, he supposes that in a depression there is a continuing excess of wages fund over wages flow. In this way the stock of wage goods gets continually larger, till, as it were, the dam

bursts. The penned-up water is then released in a wages flow larger, not merely than it was during the period of depression, but larger than its average amount. Thus Mill writes: "When a few years have elapsed without a crisis and no new and tempting channel for investment has been opened in the meantime, there is always found to have occured in these few years so large an increase in capital seeking investment as to have lowered considerably the rate of interest."[8] This, however, is a very dubious thesis. For we have no assurance that during the period of depression the unused part of the wages fund *will* be piled up in a growing store. If, as a result of being offered less aggregate pay, the number of wage-earners at work is reduced, or those employed work fewer hours per day, or less strenuously, the reduction in their pay will be partly offset by a reduction in their output, and the excess of wages fund over wages flow will be *pro tanto* diminished. Moreover, such excess as there is may be consumed by non-wage-earners or handed to wage-earners, not in wages, but through charity, the poor-law or unemployment benefit; in which case it will be consumed by them just as effectively as if it had been handed to them as wages. Thus it is not necessary *a priori* that a piling up of wage goods shall have taken place. Nor does the fact that the rate of interest in periods of depression is low prove *a posteriori* that there has been such a piling up. For we know that in these periods the demand for investment is abnormally low; and this would by itself make interest rates low without supply having to be abnormally high. Whether there is a piling up of wage capital in bad times cannot, therefore, be determined by general reasoning; appeal must be made to records of fact. These unfortunately are very scanty. That immediately after the breaking of a boom stocks pile up is, indeed, evident. For the outgoing stream of

4 *Ibid.*
5 *Dissertations*, vol. 4, p. 43.
6 *Ibid.*
7 *Principles*, p. 344.

8 *Principles*, p. 641–2.

wage goods passing to work-people is reduced, while, since the first cut in employment is likely to be made in the earliest stages of production, and not in respect of partially finished goods that are nearly complete, the inflowing stream into store is not at once affected. But this does not tell us what happens over the main body of a representative period of depression. On the whole, the evidence is unfavourable to Mill's thesis. As a depression proceeds, "the accumulated stocks of goods carried over from the preceding period of prosperity are gradually disposed of. Even when consumption is small, manufacturers and merchants can reduce their stocks of raw material and finished wares by filling orders chiefly from what is on hand, and confining purchases to the small quantities needed to keep full assortments." [9] Thus, in spite of the fact that the consumption of wage-earners is lower than it was before, stocks of consumable commodities go on falling until after the revival has begun. More generally, booms are characterised by the "production of goods in excess of the current rate of consumption, with consequent accumulation of stocks," and depressions by "curtailment of production below current consumption with consequent depletion of stocks." [10] If this view is correct, the later part of the period of depression is responsible, not only for no accumulation of stocks of consumable goods, but for an actual reduction in the stocks left over from the preceding period of boom. [11]

Apart from this problem of industrial fluctuations Mill makes use of the wages-fund doctrine in connection with three principal matters. In one of its applications it led him to his highly paradoxical "fourth fundamental proposition concerning capital"; that "a demand for commodities is not a demand for labour." "What supports and employs productive labour is the capital expended in setting it to work, and not the demand of purchasers for the produce of the labour when completed." [12] This entails that, if I spend £100 on the direct hire of labour, I benefit labour in a way that I do not if I spend the same sum on a commodity—even though no part of the price of the commodity goes to the management. This is clearly wrong. No doubt, if in buying for consumption a labour-made commodity, I make my payment when the commodity is finished and if in buying labour direct I make it when the labour does its work, the second plan is more advantageous to labour because on the first it has to borrow at interest while the commodity is being made. But, if I pay for the commodity in advance, or if, hiring labour direct, I delay payment for the appropriate length of time, the two plans affect labour in exactly the same way. In practice the payments to labour are usually dated differently and this *does* affect the advantage labour gets. But with the same dating it is immaterial which plan is adopted.[13] Contrary to Mill's view, a demand for commodities *is* a demand for labour.

---

[9] Cf. Mitchell, *Business Cycles*, pp. 565–6; cf. also *Business Cycles and Unemployment*, p. 8.

[10] Persons, Hardy and others. *The Problem of Business Forecasting*, p. 305.

[11] A certain confusion on this matter arises, I think, from the fact that the term "capital" is sometimes used to cover people's money claims, *e.g.*, on the banks. Thus Mill himself speaks in one place of the capital to finance recovery being drawn in part "from the deposits in banks" (*Principles*, p. 643). It may well be that in times of depression business men and others pile up "savings deposits" which are afterwards drawn on, or, in other words, that in these times the income velocity of money is low and in times of activity high. Insofar as there are stores of wage goods available to be drawn on, drawing on deposits and banks may well be a chief means by which, in periods of activity, they are called into play. But this in no way implies—and, unless real circulating capital and holdings of money claims are confused cannot be supposed to imply—that in periods of depression, characterised by large savings deposits, the stocks of wage goods available to be drawn on are larger than they are in times of activity, characterised by small savings deposits.

[12] *Principles*, p. 79.

[13] Cf. Marshall, *Principles*, fifth edition, p. 828.

A second application of the wages-fund doctrine has to do with the consequences of government borrowing when the borrowing is of such a sort that it does not lead to any change in the quantity of employment. If what the Government takes is derived from a foreign loan, or, being raised at home, comes from what would have been lent abroad or from what would not have come into existence—"would not have been saved at all,"—or from what, if saved, would have been wasted in unproductive enterprises, then, Mill agrees, the aggregate wages of work-people will not be affected.[14] Otherwise, he holds, what the Government takes must be abstracted from funds either engaged in production or destined to be employed in it; so that its diversion from that purpose is equivalent to taking it from the wages of the labouring classes.[15] Moreover, according to him, if the rate of interest rises, this indicates that the escape channels are not being used and so that labour is in fact being mulcted. This is a hard saying. The most obvious answer is that the "capital," which, by the Government's borrowing, private persons are prevented from spending on labour, will, in general, be devoted to that purpose by the Government itself; so that *prima facie* labour suffers no damage. But a deeper analysis is wanted. When Government raises money, whether by borrowing or by taxing, and uses it for a public purpose, a war or anything else, then, provided that the volume of employment is unaffected, it thereby diverts productive power from other uses to serve that purpose. Let us— as is proper when the Government requires extra resources for waging a war—ignore any benefit that the community may get from its use of these resources. Then there will be less total output of consumption goods and investment goods together available for the community as a whole. By sufficient cuts, however, in investment and

in the consumption of non-wage-earners commonsense affirms—though the strict wages-fund doctrine denies—that the consumption of wage-earners might be maintained. It *might* even—and that apart from foreign borrowing—be increased. That, indeed, is very unlikely. The chances are that wage-earners as a whole will find the prices of the things they buy raised more than in proportion to their money wages. But there is no *necessity* for that to happen.

The last application of the wages-fund doctrine on which I shall comment is concerned with the consequences for labour of the employing classes' deciding in some one year to switch over so much labour from making consumption goods to maintain stocks to making capital goods. This decision does not, of course, entail any addition to net saving on their part. Mill assumes further that it does not affect the total number of work-people in employment. He postulates that employers, having control of a certain wage fund, say nine hundred quarters of wheat, available to pay over to their work-people—a fixed number—in the next year, decide to require from them in return a machine, instead of, as hitherto, a thousand quarters of wheat, of which normally, say a hundred quarters would have accrued to and been consumed by themselves in payment for the service of management, and nine hundred put back into the wages fund to keep it at its original level. It follows that, while this decision does not affect the work-people's wages this year, next year there are nine hundred quarters less wages fund. Therefore wage-earners must in that year be injured. This conclusion is mitigated by the fact that, on account of the new machine, there is a slight addition to the yield of wheat, part of which is likely to be turned into the wages fund. Thus that fund for the second year is not less by nine hundred quarters than in the first, but by a little less than that. This, however, is a trivial point. In

[14] *Principles*, p. 874.
[15] *Ibid.*, p. 873.

the main, the extent of the injury to work-people depends on what proportion of men previously engaged in making wheat are switched over to making machines. Since investment is normally only a small part of total output and, consequently, the switch only a very small part of it, the damage per head to wage-earners brought about in this way in any year is likely to be very small. Still that there will be some damage to them—if we like, we may say some forced saving imposed on them—is clear. This could only be avoided through the non-wage-earning classes cutting their consumption in a measure large enough to provide wage goods at the old rate for all work-people engaged in making the new machine. That, even though we allow—what again on the strict wages-fund doctrine we ought not to do—that it would be effective, entails net saving on their part, which, for the purposes of this argument, we are assuming that they do not undertake. So much for the second year. In the third and subsequent years, provided that the same number of work-people are at work, they produce a little more than they did originally, on account of having the machine to work with. Thus they—and along with them non-wage-earners also—are enabled to consume a little more in compensation for their having been obliged in the second year to consume less so as to enable the machine to be made. All this follows logically *provided that the wages-fund doctrine is correct.*

After these illustrations of the way in which Mill applied his doctrine let us pass to the doctrine itself. It avers, as we have seen, that the wages flow in any year has to be equal to the pre-determined wages fund, subject only to the limitation that, on one version of it, a part of the fund, instead of appearing in the flow, may be "locked up in crowded warehouses." Leaving this limitation aside, we encounter at once the objection that non-wage-earners, employers or others, when the wages fund is given,

may, if they choose, make the wages flow larger or smaller by varying the amounts of their own consumption; by, for example, in any year cutting down their consumption and handing over what they would have consumed in extra real wages to work-people.

This objection is plainly fatal. How was it that Mill prior to his recantation failed to see the force of it? In one passage, indeed, in the *Principles* he did do that. In arguing against the view that, if the richer classes cut their spending and make investments instead, there may be no market for the output due to these investments, he wrote: "When these classes turn their income into capital, they do not thereby annihilate their power of consumption; they do but transfer it from themselves to the labourers to whom they give employment." [16] What is this but to allow that their action adds to the wages flow, which is, therefore, not pre-determined? In general, however, Mill does not apparently allow that this sort of thing may happen. What can have made him blind to it? Possibly he may have been misled by the sharp distinction which he drew between the wages of labour and the wages of managers—and, it would logically follow, the earnings of shareholders. Work-people's wages are paid, he held, in advance of labour's yield, out of what has been previously accumulated; the earnings of managers "are not paid in advance out of capital like the wages of all other labour, but merge in the profit and are not realised until the production is completed." [17] Now, certainly particular capitalists might have in effect to borrow goods from shops in order to pay their labourers, and would not need to in order to pay their managers. But, granted—Mill, as we shall see in a moment, tacitly assumes this—that output only emerges once a year, all consumption

[16] *Principles*, p. 68.
[17] *Essays on some Unsettled Questions in Political Economy*, p. 108.

by managers no less than by labourers has to come out of stock previously accumulated. Unless managers own such stocks, *they* have to borrow from shops or, what comes to the same thing, to borrow money with which to buy them, just as the capitalists have to do for their labourers. The different dating of the several payments is, therefore, in the present connection without significance; though, indeed, in the event of a catastrophe labourers, being paid synchronously with their work, can be sure that they *will* be paid for it in a way that managers and shareholders cannot be.

Eventually, of course, Mill did see the force of our objection; and, in consequence, renounced his wages-fund doctrine altogether. In his reply to Thornton in 1869 he wrote "Is there such a thing as a wages fund in the sense here employed? Exists there any fixed amount which, and neither more nor less than which, is destined to be employed in wages?" [18] And he answers, No. He concedes that non-wage-earners can make the amount of wages paid greater or less by varying the amount of their own consumption. Therefore there is no predetermined wages fund.

There is, however, in the way of the wages-fund doctrine a difficulty more deep-seated than this; one that would still be there even though the doctrine were so modified as to take account of what has just been said. This has to do with a factual premise which underlies Mill's analysis. In working out that analysis he was influenced by the accidents that, when he wrote, the predominant part of wage goods consisted of food, and that the predominant part of this food became available, not continuously, but in annual jets at English harvest time. In these conditions immediately after harvest the wages fund consists of the harvest yield minus such part of it as non-wage-earners elect to keep for themselves. As the year proceeds, it dwindles, being gradually converted into

[18] *Dissertations*, vol. 4, p. 44.

an equivalent value of agricultural goods in process. In the middle of the year it is half what it was at the beginning; at the end it is nothing; and then with the new harvest, Phœnix-like, it reconstitutes itself. As things now are, this conception is highly unrealistic. No doubt, some sorts of wage goods do emerge ready for use, all of them at the same time, in large jets once a year. But for a great many the inflow is more or less continuous. It is more proper today to assume that all of them, rather than none of them, become available in a nearly constant stream. At all events, it is worth while enquiring what will follow if we make that assumption. Let us suppose then that there are so many work-people altogether and that, for the average man, the interval between his work and its emergence in output is so many days. It is plain that before operations under this system can start there must be in existence a stock of wage goods sufficient to sustain all these work-people until the flow of the output due to them has begun and some of them until it has reached the (constant) level that is proper to it. Until that has happened the initial stock of wage goods is in course of being transformed into a stock of "goods in process"; and, when it has happened, the stock, *qua* stock of wage goods, has disappeared. Henceforward what is needed for wages is provided by the continuous inflow of newly-made wage goods. Thus, while a capital of goods in process is always essential, there is no need for any stock of wage goods at all—for any wages fund, pre-determined or otherwise! [19]

[19] In consequence of this, it may be remarked in passing, the conclusion reached at the bottom of p. 176 about the effects of a decision by employers to switch labour from making wage goods for stock to making a machine, without themselves undertaking any savings, is not applicable to actual conditions. With continuous production, instead of production in annual jets, wage-earners need not suffer damage in any year. All that need happen is that, from the second year onwards, the stock of capital is larger than it used to be by one machine and smaller by an equivalent value of wage goods held in store.

Of course, the picture sketched above is an idealised one. Wage goods, when finished on the farms or in the factories, do not pass immediately into the hands of consumers. Besides the machine of process there is a machine of distribution—a pipe-line—; and there are always finished goods, wage goods and others, standing in that. Moreover, besides the pipe-line stocks there are pretty sure in normal times to be some further emergency stocks held against unforeseen disasters and unforeseen opportunities. All these constitute, along with the content of the machine of process, the community's working capital. The sum of the stocks of wage goods held in these several ways has, of course, in any given period some average arithmetical relation to the annual or monthly wages flow. But it is in no sense a determinant of—it would be truer to say that it is determined by—that flow. The wages fund as Mill conceived it, is thus sunk without trace.

But the wages flow remains. In any time interval the principal element in it is the inflow of wage goods from the machine of process, through the machine of distribution, into consumption. It may be added to or subtracted from according as the non-wage-earners purchase and consume a smaller or a larger quantity of wage goods. It can be inflated, too, by borrowing from abroad; and by borrowing from pipe-line stocks and emergency stocks. Converse processes are available for deflating the wages flow. If, throughout, employment is held fixed, this is all. Variations in the wages flow are simply reflected in equi-proportionate variations in the real rate of wages. An increase in the wages flow may, however, well be partly taken out in an increase, and a decrease in a decrease, of employment. In this case two things happen. First a new element making for variations in the wages flow is introduced. For during periods of expansion wage goods are set free from the payment of unemployment benefit in respect of men ceasing to be unemployed; and conversely in depressions. This enables the wages flow to vary more widely than it would do otherwise. Secondly, as the case may be, national income will be expanded or contracted. This allows expansions and contractions in investment to take place without being accompanied by equivalent contractions or expansions in consumption. But to carry this analysis further would be to trespass beyond my title—Mill and the Wages Fund.

11   Marx's "Increasing Misery" Doctrine

THOMAS SOWELL

Marx's *Communist Manifesto* begins with the observation that "the history of all hitherto existing society is the history of class struggles"—struggles whose origin he perceived to be economic. The classical economists, Ricardo in particular, were also concerned with the economic source of class conflict but, unlike Marx, viewed the basic antagonism in society to be between the landholding and industrial classes. They traced the origin of conflict to the inexorable tendency of industrial profits to fall as land rents and money wages rise. These trends were the consequences of the pressure of increasing population and diminishing returns on food costs at the margin of cultivation. Marx, however, regarded the classical emphasis on land and rent to be inappropriate in a bourgeois society. He reasoned that in such a society the relationship between the owners of capital and the proletariat determined the mode of production and therefore the character and future of the entire society. The objective of his analysis was, then, to focus on capital-labor relationships.

The essence of the capital-labor relationship, according to Marx, was the exchange of "labor power." Since the bourgeoisie owned the means of production in a capitalist system, labor power was the only commodity which the proletariat had for sale. The exchange process in a capitalist system was, therefore, essentially different from the historically simpler system of commodity production, in which workers owned their own means of production and exchanged the commodities they produced for money which commanded other commodities. Marx represented this process symbolically as $C - M - C$. Under capitalism, however, the exchange process was initiated by capitalists, who purchased both labor power and means of production in which labor power was congealed in order to convert the commodities they produced once again into money. This process was represented symbolically by Marx as $M - C - M'$. The difference between M and M' was identified as surplus value.

Surplus value, whose creation was the objective of the production process, was, then, inherent in a system in which workers, propertyless except for their labor power, had

Reprinted from Thomas Sowell, "Marx's 'Increasing Misery' Doctrine" from *The American Economic Review*, December 1960, pp. 111–120. Thomas Sowell is Professor of Economics at Cornell University.

no choice except to sell that labor power to employers at the going competitive market wage rate. Because this rate tended to reflect the labor cost of producing subsistence—that is, the socially required minimum as opposed to the minimum required for survival, it afforded surplus value. The capitalist, who bought labor power and paid its competitively-determined exchange value, received its "use value" for a working day, whose length usually exceeded the number of labor hours socially necessary to produce the equivalent of its own subsistence. The output derived from necessary labor accrued to the worker in the form of wages, but the product of surplus labor was realized as surplus value by the bourgeoisie. The longer the working day, the greater the productivity of labor; and the lower the real wages of labor, the greater the rate at which surplus value was created, hence, at which labor was exploited. Exploitation and "the misery of the proletariat" increased with the advancement of capitalism because the same factors which increased the worker's output reduced the value of the labor required to produce his subsistence, thus depressing the exchange value of his labor power.

Does the "increasing misery" doctrine imply that the absolute level of labor will deteriorate with the advance of capitalism or, rather, that its position relative to other classes will decline? The following article by Thomas Sowell, "Marx's 'Increasing Misery' Doctrine," reviews the economic basis for each interpretation and argues that only increasing misery in an absolute sense is compatible with the *noneconomic* aspect of Marx's thinking, which emphasizes the crucial role of work in human self-realization.

Economists often assume as almost self-evident that Karl Marx's prediction of ever-increasing misery for the workers under capitalism refers to a decline in the amount of goods and services they will receive. Some writers have implied that only the intellectually dishonest could deny this view. It is readily inferred that the interpretation of Marx to mean a decline in labor's relative share is only an afterthought of latter-day Marxists seeking to salvage something from the ruins of the prediction [18, p. 383]* [1, p. 213] [23, pp. 155–57] [3, p. 324] [22, pp. 34–35] [16, p. 61]. While labor's relative share has not declined, this at least has the dignity of a plausible prediction which went unfulfilled, while a theory of absolute misery would be thoroughly discredited by history. That some consideration of this sort has in fact provided the subjective motivation for some statements on this point by latter-day Marxists is probable, but to say that this is the only possible basis for the "relative misery" interpretation is something very different. It will be argued here that relative misery was precisely what Marx's prediction referred to, in so far as it was

concerned with the purely economic aspect of the workers' condition. It will be further argued that Marx was not solely concerned with this aspect.

A standard argument against the relative-misery interpretation is that while "some passages in Marx . . . bear interpretation in this sense, this clearly violates the meaning of most" [22, p. 35]. In order to avoid this charge, the argument that follows will not cite passages from Marx which "bear interpretation" as relative misery, but only such passages as bear interpretation in no other way. This argument, however, will not be simply a passage-quoting one, but will attempt to show how the substantive meaning of Marx's increasing misery prediction turns in part on the Marxian conception of the "value of wages"—which depends in turn on the whole value framework of Marxian economics, derived from Ricardian economics, whose peculiar conceptual framework caused similar misunderstandings of Ricardo long before Marx wrote *Capital*.

It will be shown that Marx was fully aware of Ricardo's peculiar conception of the value of wages, and explicitly endorsed it. In addition to exploring (1) the meaning of the value of wages in Ricardian-Marxian

* Editor's note: Numbers in brackets refer to references at end of reading.

terms, and especially the meaning of a rise or a fall of wages in such terms, it will be necessary to consider (2) the meaning of Marxian "subsistence" and its relevance here, as well as (3) some of the arguments used to support the absolute misery interpretation, and (4) the noneconomic dimension of Marxian "misery."

THE VALUE OF WAGES

Conventional economic theory has long made a distinction between the amount of money which the worker receives as wages, and the amount of goods and services which this money will buy. Adam Smith spoke of "real wages" and "nominal wages" in this sense.[1] David Ricardo, from whom much of Marx's economic apparatus is derived, also used the terms "real wages" and "nominal wages," but because of the nature of his system, they meant something very different. What Adam Smith and other economists called "real wages" was included under "nominal wages" by Ricardo [24, p. 50]. Real wages, in Ricardo's terminology, meant the value of wages, that is, the amount of *labor* contained in the commodities which the worker received. Ricardian real wages measured the degree to which the workers shared in total output, not the absolute amount of goods and services which they received.[2] If, due to increased productivity, the workers should receive a greater quantity of goods representing a smaller share of output, then—in Ricardian terms—wages would have *fallen*.

[1] He was not always consistent as to the basis for the dichotomy.

[2] [24, pp. 49-50]. The point is more succinctly expressed by J. S. Mill: "In his [Ricardo's] language wages were only said to rise, when they rose not in mere quantity but in *value*. . . . Mr. Ricardo, therefore, would not have said that wages had risen, because a labourer could obtain two pecks of flour instead of one, for a day's labour. . . . A rise of wages, with Mr. Ricardo, meant an increase in the cost of production of wages . . . an increase in the proportion of the fruits of labour which the labourer receives for his own share . . ." [17, pp. 96-97].

Ricardo declared that "it will not the less be a real fall, because they might furnish him with a greater quantity of cheap commodities than his former wages" [24, p. 50]. Marx follows this same line of reasoning:

> . . . it is possible with an increasing productiveness of labour, for the price of labour-power to keep on falling, and yet this fall to be accompanied by a constant growth in the mass of the labourer's means of subsistence [5, p. 573].

More important than such parallel statements is the fact that Marx saw the peculiarity of the Ricardian conception of wages and deliberately made it his own, not simply as an accidental by-product of using Ricardo's so-called "labor theory of value," but because he, Marx, felt that there was a valid social philosophy implicit in this conception:

> The value of wages has to be reckoned not on the basis of the quantity of necessaries which the worker receives, but on the basis of the quantity of labour which these necessaries cost—actually the proportion of the working day which he appropriates for himself . . . It is possible that, reckoned in use value (quantity of commodities or money), his wages may rise as productivity increases, and yet reckoned in value they may fall . . . It is one of Ricardo's greatest merits that he made an examination of relative wages and established them as a definite category. Previously wages had always been looked upon as a simple element, and consequently the worker had been regarded as an animal. In Ricardo, however, he is considered in his social relationship. The position of the classes in relation to each other depends to a greater extent on the proportion which the wage forms than on the absolute amount of the wage. [10, p. 320]

Marx seemed particularly concerned to emphasize the relative-share approach because of the economic prerequisites of increased wages under capitalism:

> A noticeable increase in wages presupposes a rapid growth of productive capital. The rapid growth of productive capital brings

about an equally rapid growth of wealth, luxury, social needs, social enjoyments. Thus, although the enjoyments of the worker have risen, the social satisfaction that they give has fallen in comparison with the state of development of society in general. Our needs and enjoyments spring from society; we measure them, therefore, by society and not by the objects which serve for their satisfaction. Because they are of a social nature, they are of a relative nature. [12, Sec. IV, p. 37]

But while it is clear that Marx regarded a relative decline in wages as a real fall in wages, this does not dispose of the possibility that he may have, in addition, felt that real wages in the conventional sense would also fall over time under capitalism. And in fact, the evidence seems to indicate that at an early period in his writings, probably up through the time of the *Communist Manifesto* in 1848, he did in fact believe that absolute impoverishment would be the lot of the working class under capitalism. The *Manifesto* flatly declared: "The modern labourer . . . instead of rising with the progress of industry, sinks deeper and deeper below the conditions of existence of his own class" [13, p. 36]. Marx's unfinished manuscripts of this period also seem to suggest a belief in either stable or declining real wages (again, in the conventional sense) [4, pp. 274–79] [15, p. 351]. All of this, however, was written before Marx's long years of study in the British Museum, and also at a time ("the hungry 'forties") when in fact the standard of living of workers seemed to be either unchanging or deteriorating.

Between this period in the 1840's and the publication of the first volume of *Capital* in 1867, German socialists and communists put forth the so-called "iron law of wages," which declared that wages could not rise under capitalism. Some latter-day critics have attempted to associate Marx with this "iron law" [21, pp. 531–32] [3, p. 311], but in fact Marx heaped scorn and ridicule on it in his *Critique of the Gotha Programme* in 1875. Significantly, he char-

acterized it as a view that was now outmoded and constituted an "outrageous retrogression" in the light of recent, more "scientific" understanding of wages [7, Sec. II, p. 15]. Engels was less indirect in referring to the publication of the first volume of *Capital* which, he declared, now showed that the laws of wages "are in no sense iron but on the contrary very elastic," in contrast to the "antiquated economic view" represented by Lassalle's "iron law" [14, p. 335]. These vague and oblique references to "antiquated" ideas and "retrogression" only hinted at what Engels was later to state openly, that Lassalle's iron law was derived from his and Marx's writings of the 1840's and represented views now discarded.[3]

From the point of view of the developed Marxian theories, Lassalle's iron law represented not merely a false statement but, more importantly, a false issue. It was the exploitation of the worker that was the central issue to Marx, who declared that this exploitation must grow worse, *regardless* of whether wages go up or down:

> . . . the wage worker has permission to work for his own life, i.e., to *live*, only in so far as he works for a certain time gratis for the capitalist . . . consequently, the system of wage labour is a system of slavery, and indeed of a slavery which becomes more severe in proportion as the social productive forces of labour develop, whether the worker receives better or worse payment. . . .
> It is as if, among slaves who have at last got behind the secret of slavery and broken out in rebellion, a slave still in thrall to obsolete notions were to inscribe on the programme

[3] Marx declared in *The Poverty of Philosophy* (1847): "The natural price of labour is no other than the wage minimum." Engels, in the German edition of 1885, attached to this statement of Marx's the following footnote: "The thesis that the 'natural,' *i.e.*, normal, price of labour power coincides with the equivalent in value of the means of subsistence absolutely indispensable for the life and reproduction of the worker was first put forward by me [in 1844]. . . . As seen here, Marx *at that time* accepted the thesis. Lassalle took it over from both of us" [8, p. 45n] (emphasis added).

of the rebellion: Slavery must be abolished because the upkeep of slaves in the system of slavery cannot exceed a certain low maximum! [7, Sec. II, p. 15]

The idea that increasing misery accompanies the growth of capitalism "whether the worker receives better or worse payment" occurs also in *Capital*, where Marx declares that "in proportion as capital accumulates, the lot of the labourer, be his payment high or low, must grow worse" [5, pp. 708–9]. In fact, this statement occurs in the very same paragraph as that statement so often quoted to support the interpretation of the "absolute misery" school:

> Accumulation of wealth at one pole is, therefore, at the same time accumulation of misery, agony of toil, slavery, ignorance, brutality, mental degradation at the opposite pole . . . [5, p. 709]

This and similar statements do not support either interpretation, since it is precisely the meaning of such statements which is at issue.

SUBSISTENCE

An increasing misery which can occur in spite of increasing wages (in the ordinary sense) does not, however, preclude decreasing wages. Neither does the definition of rises and falls in relative terms, of itself, preclude absolute misery, since relative misery carried beyond a certain point would also be absolute misery. In order to see what limits, if any, Marx assigned to this relative misery, some consideration of Marxian "subsistence" is required.

Marx's subsistence has sometimes been regarded as being minimum physical subsistence, or something very close to it—or, at least, something *fixed* at a definite level. Some writers have extended this idea to mean that Marx assumes a subsistence level toward which wages might tend to fall over time [20, pp. 908–11, esp. 910n.]. But this particular theory is entirely absent from

Marx. There is not a secular tendency for wages to fall *to* subsistence; rather, workers tend to be *at* subsistence, but the content of this subsistence changes, consisting as it does of both "natural wants" and "so-called necessary wants" which are "the product of historical development" [5, p. 190]. However one might object to Marx's (and other economists') use of subsistence in this sense, the substance of his meaning is plain. The value of a worker's labor-power is that "value" or embodied labor "required for the conservation and reproduction of his labour-power, regardless of whether the conditions of this conservation and reproduction are scanty or bountiful, favorable or unfavorable" [6, p. 956]. It is sometimes claimed that a wage level fixed at subsistence (in the ordinary sense) is a necessary condition for Marx's theory of surplus value [23, p. 94], but in fact it is only necessary to show a difference between the output of labor and the output required to sustain the laborer.[4]

Marx's picture of the worker at subsistence, therefore, does not preclude increases in real wages in the conventional sense. Once a new higher standard of living becomes established, it too becomes subsistence, and represents the new value of labor-power, i.e., the real-wage level. Marx does not have a determinate theory of wages; how labor shares in the increasing productivity is a matter of bargaining power: it "depends on the relative weight, which the pressure of capital on the one side, and the resistance of the labourer on the other, throws into the scale" [5, pp. 572–73]. The

---

[4] Marx made this point in his criticism of the Physiocrats who assumed a fixed subsistence or value of labor-power: "If they made the further mistake of conceiving the wage as an unchangeable amount, in their view entirely determined by nature—and not by the stage of historical development, a magnitude itself subject to fluctuations—this in no way affects the abstract correctness of their conclusions, since the difference between the value and the profitable use of labor power does not in any way depend on whether the value is assumed to be great or small" [10, p. 45].

Ricardian-Marxian conception is here manifested in the word "resistance." The worker is resisting a *fall* in wages, although Marx declares that the "lowest limit" of this fall is a wage which will purchase the former sum of commodities [5, p. 572]. If wages fall to any point above "the lowest possible point consistent with its new value," then despite this fall, "this lower price would represent an increased mass of necessaries" [5, p. 573]. Marx credits Ricardo with the original formulation of this law. Far from being a law of increasing misery in the conventional sense, it represents a law of a customary floor under wages, which would *prevent* such an occurrence.

A crucial but unstated assumption in Marx's increasing misery doctrine is that the workers themselves will judge wage movements from this relative point of view; otherwise Marxian "misery" when accompanied by material prosperity need never provoke revolution. Another assumption in both Marxian and Ricardian illustrations is a falling price level with increased productivity, so that it is meaningful for them to speak of a fall in wages in money terms, as well as in value terms, and to speak of a "cheapening" of commodities.

ARGUMENTS FOR THE "ABSOLUTE MISERY" INTERPRETATION

It is sometimes asserted that Marx's theory was that increasing productivity with the same capital-labor ratio would raise wages, but that capital-intensive (labor-saving) growth tended to decrease wages by causing technological unemployment, with the "reserve army of the unemployed" dragging down wages. This is true as long as it is kept in mind that wage movements are in value terms, and may be said to fall in money terms only on the Ricardian-Marxian assumption of increasing purchasing power of money with growing productivity. Moreover, capital-intensive growth introduced an element of *absolute* misery for those particular workers displaced by new technology. Marx brings this point in against those who argue a necessary connection between the growth of capital and the material well-being of the worker [12, Sec. V, p. 43]. He is further concerned to explode the contention that this is only a "temporary" inconvenience, by asserting that "since machinery is continually seizing upon new fields of production, its temporary effect is really permanent" [5, p. 471]. Capital-intensive growth, for Marx, not only deprives the worker of his rightful share in increasing productivity by lowering his ability to "resist" the capitalist's encroachments, it causes an absolute decline in living standards for those displaced by machinery.

Marx's theory of the growth of what he calls "official pauperism" is sometimes cited as an argument for the "absolute misery" interpretation. However, as Marx defines his terms, "official pauperism" covers those no longer in the labor force, that is, "that part of the working-class which has forfeited its condition of existence (the sale of labour-power) and vegetates upon public alms" [5, p. 717]. The view that this group will tend to increase with the growth of capitalism is not the same thing as a theory of increasing absolute misery for the working class as a whole, and in fact is only a small part of Marx's picture.

Marx often speaks of a "tendency" of capitalists, or capitalism, to reduce wages in terms which suggest absolute impoverishment. The other side of Marx's coin, however, is the countertendency of the workers to increase wages as much as possible. He speaks of

> . . . the continuous struggle between capital and labour, the capitalist constantly tending to reduce wages to their physical minimum, and to extend the working day to its physical maximum, while the working man constantly presses in the opposite direction.

The matter resolves itself into a question of the respective powers of the combatants. [11, Sec. XIV, p. 67] [cf. 5, pp. 657–58]

Although Marx seems to have a purely "bargaining power" theory of wages, the possible range of wages is limited by the customary standard of living as a floor, and by a ceiling representing wages high enough to threaten the existence of capitalism itself: "the oscillation of wages is penned within limits satisfactory to capitalist exploitation" [5, p. 843].

It has been claimed that Marx's increasing misery theory is logically inconsistent with his theory of a falling rate of profit [19, p. 36]. Obviously if one dichotomizes output into wage income and property income, both cannot fall simultaneously (unless output declines). But here again Marx's theory must be understood in Marx's terms. He divides output *three* ways: into wage income ("variable capital"), property income ("surplus value") and replacement of depreciated machinery and raw materials, etc. ("constant capital"). There is nothing to prevent the proportions of the first two from being less in later periods than in earlier periods, with a secular rise in the proportion of the third. In the Marxian theory it is the *rate* of profit which tends to decline, while the mass increases,[5] and the share of labor that falls rather than ordinary real wages.

THE NONECONOMIC DIMENSION OF "MISERY"

The noneconomic aspect of increasing misery rests on Marx's philosophical approach and his underlying conception of man. The Marxian mode of analysis follows the Hegelian dialectical approach in so far as it tends to analyze things not simply as they are, but as they are potentially. This applies not only to social and

[5] "The same laws, then produce for the social capital an increase in the absolute mass of profit and a falling rate of profit" [6, p. 256].

economic systems, but also to man in general and the worker in particular. Thus the extent to which the worker is given scope for unfolding his inner potentialities is a vital part—if not *the* vital part—of his well-being.

Work, to Marx, is precisely the instrumentality of this realization of his potentiality by the individual, as well as by mankind. Work is not a mere disutility to be endured for the sake of satisfying material human wants—in which case material production would then be the measure of (absolute or relative) well-being. On the contrary, work is itself "life's prime want" [7, Sec. I, 3, p. 10], because it contributes to the development of the individual. This is dialectical development: "A caterpillar *grows* into a bigger caterpillar; it *develops* into a butterfly" [2, p. 80]. Not so the worker under capitalism: "If the silk worm were to spin in order to continue its existence as a caterpillar, it would be a complete wage-worker" [12, Sec. I, p. 22]. Yet work can be an end in itself, and its performance a satisfaction: "Milton produced *Paradise Lost* for the same reason that a silk worm produces silk. It was an activity of his nature" [10, p. 186]. Marx was annoyed at economists like Adam Smith who treated the expenditure of labor time "as the mere sacrifice of rest, freedom and happiness, not as [at] the same time the normal activity of living beings [5, p. 54n.]. World history, for Marx, represents the drama of "the creation of man by human labour . . ." [9, p. 246].

Under capitalism, Marx argues, work no longer fulfills its vital role in the lives of the people. The division of labor under capitalism "attacks the individual at the very roots of his life" [5, p. 399]. It converts the worker into "a crippled monstrosity" by developing his manual dexterity in a narrow detail "at the expense of a world of productive capabilities and instincts; just as in the States of La Plata they butcher a whole beast for the sake of his hide or his tallow" [5, p. 396]. What is more relevant to the present question, Marx declares that this must grow worse over time under capitalism. The same methods which increase productivity are methods which "mutilate the labourer into a fragment of a man" and "estrange from him the intellectual potentialities of the labour-process in the same proportion as science is incorporated in it as an independent power [5, p. 708]. This is a vital part of the picture which leads Marx directly to the conclusion that "in proportion as capital accumulates, the lot of the labourer, be his payment high or low, must grow worse" [5, pp. 708–9].

Although this aspect of well-being (or lack of well-being) is often overlooked by his interpreters, it was supremely important to Marx himself. He described it as "a question of life and death" that the worker under capitalism, "crippled by life-long repetition of one and the same trivial operation, and thus reduced, to the mere fragment of a man" be replaced by "the fully developed individual . . . to whom the different social functions he performs are but so many modes of giving free scope to his own natural and acquired powers" [5, p. 534].

CONCLUDING REMARKS

Because Marx saw a tendency for industry to become more capital-intensive, he postulated a secular decline in the proportion of outlays on wages (variable capital) to outlays on plant and equipment (constant capital) and property incomes (surplus value)—a "fall" in wages. This fall might conceivably go so far as to deprive the workers of any increase in their standard of living, but whether it would go that far depended upon the relative bargaining power of capital and labor, the latter "resisting" the fall in wages through trade unions, etc. If the fall could be arrested at any point above the previously existing subsistence level, then the "lower" wages would represent an increased quantity of goods, although the value of these goods would be less—that is, the workers would be spending less of their working day producing their own livelihood and more of it producing surplus value for the capitalists.

A more important question to Marx than the movement of wages, even in relative terms, was the question of the self-realization of men through their practical physical and mental exertions. Man, as the sum total of his potentialities, is only successively revealed through the exercise of his faculties. Under capitalism, Marx argues, the worker "does not fulfill himself in his work, but denies himself" and "has a feeling of misery . . ." [9, p. 169]. This misery becomes progressively worse with the growth of capitalism as the worker is increasingly estranged "from the intellectual potentialities of the labour-process. . . ." For Marx this is a fundamental deprivation which cannot be remedied by higher wages.[6]

References

1. M. M. Bober, *Karl Marx's Interpretation of History*. Cambridge, Mass. 1948.
2. M. Cornfortii, *Materialism and the Dialectical Method*. New York 1953.
3. A. Gray, *The Socialist Tradition*. London 1947.
4. H. Marcuse, *Reason and Revolution*. New York 1954.
5. K. Marx, *Capital*, Vol. I. Chicago 1906.
6. ———, *Capital*, Vol. III. Chicago 1909.
7. ———, *Critique of the Gotha Programme*. New York 1938.
8. ———, *The Poverty of Philosophy*. Moscow 1935.
9. ———, *Selected Writings in Sociology and Social Philosophy*, ed. T. B. Bottomore and M. Rubel. London 1956.

[6] Marx asserts that this is the situation for the class, but does not deny that gifted individuals may escape he class situation. His attitude towards social mobility in this context is distinctly negative, since he sees it as strengthening and perpetuating the system as a whole: "The more a ruling class is able to assimilate the most prominent men of a ruled class, the more solid and dangerous is its rule" [6, p. 706].

10. ———, *Theories of Surplus Value*. New York 1952.

11. ———, *Value, Price and Profit*. Moscow 1947.

12. ———, *Wage, Labour and Capital*. Moscow 1947.

13. ——— and F. Engels, "The Communist Manifesto," *A Handbook of Marxism*, ed. E. Burns, New York 1935, pp. 21–59.

14. ———, *Selected Correspondence*. New York 1942.

15. F. Mehring, *Karl Marx*. New York 1935.

16. G. Meier and R. Baldwin, *Economic Development*. New York 1957.

17. J. S. Mill, *Essays on Some Unsettled Questions of Political Economy*. London 1877.

18. L. von Mises, *Socialism*. London 1936.

19. J. ROBINSON, *An Essay on Marxian Economics*. London 1947.

20. P. A. Samuelson, "Wages and Interest: Marxian Economic Models," *Am. Econ. Rev.*, Dec. 1957, *47*, 884–912.

21. ———, *Ecnomics—An Introductory Analysis*. New York 1955.

22. J. A. Schumpeter, *Capitalism, Socialism and Democracy*. New York 1950.

23. J. Strachey, *Contemporary Capitalism*. London 1956.

24. *The Works and Correspondence of David Ricardo*, ed. P. Straffa. Vol. I: *On the Principles of Political Economy and Taxation*. Cambridge 1951.

12 The Classical Theory of Economic Growth

ADOLPH LOWE

Contemporary economic model-builders typically conceive of the growth phenomenon in terms of changes in the stock of capital or employment of labor in response to changing profit expectations. Thus, their models proceed by abstracting the influence of non-economic factors, such as innovations and population and labor force changes on the growth process. But noneconomic factors cannot indefinitely be laid aside, for they are among the factors affecting economic growth; furthermore, economic growth is only one aspect of the whole process of development. The problem of economic growth serves, perhaps more forcefully than any other, to make us conscious of the limitations inherent in economic science, which derive from its being essentially concerned with examining phenomena and relationships which lend themselves to being expressed in terms of pecuniary gains and losses.

Contemporary theorists, therefore, have much to learn from studying the growth theories of classical thinkers. The classicists fully appreciated the need to deal with relationships between purely economic magnitudes and the meta-economic variables comprising nature and society. This is the contention of Adolph Lowe in "The Classical Theory of Economic Growth." He shows that classical thinkers, unlike most of their contemporary counterparts, constructed theories of economic change which specifically incorporated the natural, social, and technical environment to explain consumer and investor demands, factor supplies, production techniques, the distribution of income and wealth and their changes through time. Though the substance of their theories of economic development admittedly may have little to contribute to current thinking, their methodology anticipated the current emphasis on interdisciplinary research.

Reprinted from Adolph Lowe, "The Classical Theory of Economic Growth," from *Social Research*, Summer 1954, pp. 127–158. Dr. Lowe is Professor Emeritus of Economics, Graduate Faculty, New School for Social Research, New York.

One of the most satisfying prospects that the newly awakened interest in economic growth has opened up is the advance in the direction of an integrated social analysis as contrasted with the rigorously circumscribed economic analysis of neoclassical theory. Even in dealing with a relatively short-term problem like business cycles, one can doubt the wisdom of treating behavior patterns and the institutional environment as fixed once and for all. Certainly when we turn our attention to growth processes, such as the rise of the industrial system or the secular development of capitalism, systematic mutations in the meta-economic conditions have to be taken into account as much as changes in the economic field proper.

This is all plain and commonly accepted. Yet when one tries to proceed beyond fine, methodological postulates to the actual work of integration, truly formidable difficulties arise. Not only is the number of meta-economic variables legion—and they comprise the whole realm of nature and society. But even if the individual sciences —from geology, physics, and chemistry, through technology and biology to psychology, sociology, political science, law, and the humanistic sciences of man—could establish a systematic catalogue of these variables as they appear in the context of the respective indigenous field of each science, there would still remain the task of "translating" their "meaning" into the conceptual framework of economics.

What this amounts to can best be illustrated by an example. For many centuries the idea of "monopoly" was known as a sociopolitical concept, pointing toward a certain manner in which power is exercised, with some notion of exploitation thrown in. But neither power nor exploitation is a manageable concept in the framework of traditional market analysis. Only when monopoly was understood as a change in the nature of the price-quantity relationship—compared with the nature of this relationship under fully competitive conditions—did it become a tool in economic analysis. Failure to perform such a translation, whenever concepts indigenous to one dimension of science are to be introduced into another dimension, is mainly responsible for the fact that experiments with "integration" have only rarely carried us beyond description into the realm of genuine causal analysis.

One might expect to find some enlightenment about the problem raised here in the recent writings on economic dynamics. Indeed, a lively discussion is under way, clarifying the nature of processes, the types of change, and the role of time, in their influence on human behavior.[1] But the time-honored distinction between dependent and independent variables—that is, between an economic process and the underlying meta-economic forces which drive it on and change it—is generally maintained. We find an exception to this general approach, however, in what Professor Frisch and his followers have called "dynamic process analysis." There certain relations are stressed which may exist between variables at different points of time, and which —because of the prevailing "lags"—can create self-enforcing processes, even if the variables themselves do not change. Such movements, which may be damped, cyclical, or explosive, are designated as "endogenous," in contrast with the other type of changes, which arise from "exogenous" stimuli represented by independent variables.

It is only fair to say that this modern notion of "endogeneity" is but a dim reflection of a much more ambitious method of analysis that dominated an earlier epoch.

[1] See, for example, Paul A. Samuelson, *Foundations of Economic Analysis* (Cambridge, Mass. 1947) chap. 11; R. F. Harrod, *Towards a Dynamic Economics* (London 1948) Lecture I; J. Tinbergen and J. J. Polak, *The Dynamics of Business Cycles* (Chicago 1950) chap. 9; J. R. Hicks, *A Contribution to the Theory of the Trade Cycle* (Oxford 1950) p. 10, as well as his earlier *Value and Capital* (Oxford 1939) chap. 9; William J. Baumol, *Economic Dynamics* (New York 1951) chap 1.

of theoretical economics. As a matter of fact, upon this issue of endogeneity versus exogenity, rather than upon conflicting theories of value, hinges the main difference between genuine classical theory and post-Millian economic reasoning, including all versions of neo-classical analysis. The problem and its relevance for the theory of dynamics was probably realized most clearly by the late Joseph Schumpeter, who stated it, a quarter of a century ago, as follows.

After describing economic theory in terms of Marshall's "tool chest," Schumpeter asserted that it arose from something quite different, namely, from a "theory . . . which claimed to contain the essence of all fundamental knowledge about the economy, and also the solution of its main empirical problems. The practical success as well as the grand defeat of the doctrine of the classical economists . . . are bound up with the fact that they aimed at just this goal, and that to reach it they established, in youthful recklessness, fundamental assertions and postulates without any real basis. . . . The characteristic example . . . is the quite uncritical manner in which Ricardo used an alleged connection between wage level and subsistence level as a substitute for a theory of wages. . . . Modern theory differs from classical theory not simply in not asserting any longer the existence of that particular relationship, for the reason that it cannot be verified. More important is the fact that modern theory does not establish any such propositions at all. Rather it offers a formal framework, into which any conceivable relationship, e.g., the opposite one, can be inserted *casuistically as a special datum.* . . . However no particular relationship as such is indispensable for the validity of the framework itself" (italics mine).[2]

Leaving alone the value judgment expressed in Schumpeter's remarks, we must

admit that they do indeed point to a fundamental difference between the classical and the modern approach. What is at stake is no less than the entire possible range of deductive reasoning.

Let us be quite explicit about the disputed region. It concerns the whole natural, social, and technical environment of the economic system, that is, the conditions that determine the quality and quantity of demand on the part of consumers and investors, the supply of productive factors, the prevailing technique of production, social distribution, the bargaining behavior of consumers and producers, and last but not least, the changes in all these elements through time. Modern theory, by treating these conditions once and for all as data, can never give us more than a catalogue of all *possible* movements of the economic system, derived from, and arranged according to, hypothetical sets of data combinations. It does not and cannot claim to tell us which particular set, and consequently which specific movement deduced from it, corresponds to reality. To make deduction applicable to reality, we must in each case first assess, by methods of induction, the order of data ruling in the particular situation. Only then are we in a position to select from our catalogue of hypothetical deductions the one that comes closest to the actual constellation.

This sounds quite trivial to the contemporary economist brought up in the modern tradition. All he may wonder is how one could proceed in any other way. Yet another method was in fact applied for a full century, during which deductive reasoning was not confined to conclusions drawn from sets of data postulated anew whenever analysis took another step. Rather, the explanation of the order and changes of these data itself formed part of the theoretical work of economists.

Of course, every process of deduction must ultimately start from some set of "synthetic" propositions, which classical economics too could arrive at only by

[2] Joseph A. Schumpeter, *Die Wirtschaftstheorie der Gegenwart* (Vienna 1927) vol. 1, pp. 6–7. The rather free translation from the German is mine.

means of induction. But whereas the modern economist is compelled to begin every deductive operation, if it is to have realistic bearing, with another empirical investigation of the relevant data, the classical economist did so only once—namely, when he described the primeval state of affairs from which the economic process was supposed to have started. Different notions as to the nature of this original reality produced contrasting images of economic evolution in the different classical systems. But for each classical system separately the empirical stage was, at least in principle, set once and for all with these initial assumptions. From there on the economic process could be deduced by an unbroken chain of reasoning. In this sense Ricardo's assertion that the stationary state is the ultimate goal of economic development, or Marx's "general law of capitalist accumulation," proclaims explicitly what is implicitly contained in all classical systems.

Obviously this classical procedure results in an "endogenous" dynamics of a much more comprehensive nature than that offered by modern process analysis. Underlying these classical constructions is a belief in the cognitive power of deduction, and a notion of society and history, that seem to contradict all ideas concerning the relationship between science and reality that prevail today. Yet in studying economic growth, at least as it develops under capitalism, the conceptional range of classical theory seems more appropriate than the delimitations of modern theory.

The central problem of capitalism has often been defined as the question of how order rather than chaos ensues from the undirected action of innumerable individuals. We can give this question a time shape by asking what interaction of forces has determined the particular course that capitalist development has taken over the decades. If this development had been "planned," as may well be the case with the future development of the Western economic system, the problem of an "endog-

enous" dynamics would hardly arise. The basic "data" and their major changes would have been set by conscious decision, and would rightly have to be treated as independent variables of the economic process that has been set in motion by them. But over the last two hundred years we have been confronted with a self-propelling secular process, in the course of which not only did the data change "spontaneously," but in addition these changes displayed striking regularities.

As we look at this secular process in retrospect today, our analysis of it may receive little help from the *substance* of the classical theory of economic development. This does not in itself reflect upon the dynamic *method* which the leading classical economists applied.[3] To realize this, more is required, of course, than a cursory statement of the classical procedure. The latter will have to be elaborated in all its ramifications by the study of some of its most significant protagonists. I begin with the earliest, and in many ways the most lucid example: the theory of economic development as contained in Adam Smith's *Wealth of Nations*. I shall then consider certain modifications that Ricardo and the early "anti-harmonist" writers introduced into the original model, and shall complete the survey with a detailed examination of Marx. In a concluding section, centered on J. S. Mill, I shall deal briefly with the reasons for the subsequent abandonment of the classical method of growth analysis.

SMITH

I pointed above to the truism that however far the range of deduction may be ex-

[3] I first took this position in my *Economics and Sociology* (London 1935) chaps. 4 and 5. Since then valuable support has been given to this view by B. S. Keirstead in his *Theory of Economic Change* (Toronto 1948), especially in Parts I and II of that work.

tended, it must start from some original set of propositions. In all classical theories of development these propositions are "historical"; that is, they refer to an "original" order of society from which the economic process is supposed to spring. Smith never defined these original data systematically, but the context of his work leaves no doubt as to what he considered them to be. Division of labor and exchange, allegedly the "consequence of a certain propensity in human nature," [4] represent the basic pattern of economic behavior. They operate within the institutional framework of a competitive class society: private property in the means of production, including land, which are unequally distributed after the "early and rude state of society" [5] has passed, and full mobility of the factors of production, safeguarded by the watchmen of the public interest. As our investigation progresses we shall meet some additional assumptions, which round off the set of historical constants.

Now in order to set the economic process in motion and give it the direction which Smith attributes to actual economic development, these constants have to generate the factors of production in the appropriate quantity and quality: an adequate supply of labor, of natural resources, and of capital, and a steady increase in productivity. In contrast with the constants themselves from which they spring, these factors cannot be regarded as given once and for all by nature and history. They are continuously being drained off and replenished according to certain laws of motion.

At this point we encounter the main peculiarity of classical analysis. Again neither the problem at stake nor its solution has been explicitly formulated by Smith. Both

[4] Adam Smith, *Wealth of Nations,* ed. by Edwin Cannan (London 1930) Book I, chap. 2. Subsequent references to Smith are to this edition.

[5] *Op. cit.,* Book I, chap. 6. This chapter contains the rather naive but methodologically essential hypotheses suggesting how this original state—the basic set of data—was transformed into the civilized state defined by the above conditions.

have to be inferred from scattered passages, which are found mainly in Chapters 1, 2, 3, 8, and 9, of the first book of *Wealth of Nations,* and in Chapters 3 to 5 of the second book.

First of all, there is a law governing the *supply of labor* (Book I, chap. 8). It is based on two complementary hypotheses. On the one hand, forces are at work that tend to reduce, over the secular period, the level of real wages to the subsistence level. The causal nexus is identical with what was later called the "iron law of wages": variations in the level of real wages evoke counteracting changes in the size of the working population. On the other hand, real wages can and do rise, as long as the natural and technical conditions of a country permit a steady increase in its wealth. Not that the systematic link between the level of real wages and the size of the population is destroyed for good in a progressive society. But demand for labor, as expressed in "the funds which are destined for the payment of wages," can overtake supply. And with the increase of real wages population grows, since "the demand for men, like that for any other commodity, necessarily regulates the production of men."

Thus labor supply is ultimately dominated by the cooperation of two balancing forces: the propensity to procreate, which is seen as a composite of a biological urge and a rational calculation of the "value of children," and the available wage fund. The former is another constant of the socio-economic process, but one which by itself would cause the system to "run down" to a constant level of labor supply and thus of real output. This tendency is counteracted by the latter force, which is a variable. What forces rule its changes?

The answer is given by Smith's law of *accumulation.* The funds which govern the variations in labor supply are the result of saving, which itself arises from another alleged human propensity or constant of the social mechanism: "the desire of bettering our condition" (Book II, chap. 3). Of course, it is not by the act of saving itself, but by the use they make of their savings, that people fulfill this desire. Accumulation, comprising both saving and investing, "is the most likely way of augmenting their fortune," provided a "neat or clear profit" or a rate of interest "in proportion to the clear profit" can be earned (Book I, chap. 9).

The level of profit and interest, however, is as precarious a magnitude as the level of wages. "In a country which had acquired that full complement of riches which the nature of its soil and climate, and situation with respect to other countries allowed it to acquire, which could, therefore, advance no further, and which was not going backwards, both the wages of labour and the profits of stock would, probably, be very low" (Book I, chap. 9). The reason is seen in the competition among capitalists once a country is "fully stocked in proportion to all the business it had to transact." As is the case with wages, "it is not the actual greatness of national wealth, but its continuous increase" (Book I, chap. 8) that favors profits. Since the notion of capital-deepening lies outside the field of Smith's vision—and for better reasons than the later classical economists can adduce for themselves—only a continuous widening of the capital structure can sustain profits and thus accumulation, and can keep real wages above the subsistence level. Such widening or economic growth, however, can be stimulated only by a rise in productivity, because the other growth factor, population increase, is regarded, as we saw, as a response rather than a stimulus to accumulation. Thus the psychological constant again makes the system "run down" to a constant level, unless its tendency is counteracted by changes in the variable factor, this time productivity. In this factor we now encounter the strategic variable of the whole system.

If one places side by side the many remarks on productivity and economic progress which are contained in *Wealth of Nations*, one can collect the whole list of factors that Schumpeter classifies as "innovations": extension and improvement of machinery, increased division of labor, new branches of trade, and territorial expansion. But the emphasis with which these various factors are treated differs markedly. It is technical progress in the narrower sense that is in the center.

Among the conditions for such improvement of productive power is, first of all, a country's equipment in terms of natural resources and its geographic position. The threat of the exhaustion of natural wealth is regarded as far distant. As to the interim period, Smith is little concerned about decreasing returns, so that for the foreseeable future he can again treat the whole complex of natural conditions as a constant of the dynamic model. The decisive variable is a particular form of technology, namely, "division of labor."

It has always been recognized that for Smith division of labor is the true dynamic force. Yet in our context we do well to distinguish between the general phenomenon which, as we have already seen, he traces back to a psychological constant, and the varying forms in which this phenomenon materializes throughout history. The latter comprise for Smith all types of technical progress, in particular the introduction of improved machinery. At the same time, his notion of technical progress is defined by the characteristics of the economies of specialization, as he describes them in his first three chapters. Above all, mechanization, like specialization, is supposed to "facilitate and abridge labour," but not to displace the worker who performs it. Quite to the contrary, in the introduction to Book II Smith even asserts that division of labor in this inclusive sense is conditional upon a prior increase in labor supply. The passage is important enough to be quoted in full: "As the division of labour advances, therefore, in order to give constant employment to an equal number of workmen, an equal stock of provisions, and a greater stock of materials and tools than would have been necessary in a ruder state of things, must be accumulated beforehand. But the number of workmen in every branch of business generally increases with the division of labour in that branch, or *rather it is the increase of their number which enables them to class and subdivide themselves in this manner*" (italics mine).

In other words, the machine is regarded as a complement of labor rather than a substitute for it, a definitely pre-industrial notion of technology. To find such ideas in *Wealth of Nations* is hardly surprising, if we remember the date of publication of the book. They fit well with Smith's distrust of large-scale organization of industry and of long apprenticeship, both of which he evaluates by pre-industrial standards (Book I, chap. 10).

This identification of technical progress generally with specialization has far-reaching consequences for Smith's model of economic development. The improvements that determine the rate of economic progress, and thus the rate of profit, do not arise from spontaneous shifts in the production function, catering to the pre-existing level of demand. Their introduction depends rather on the opening of new sources of demand, a proposition that is expressly stated in the title of the famous Chapter 3 of the first book: "That the Division of Labour is limited by the Extent of the Market." Far from being an independent variable, technical progress as understood by Smith develops "in proportion to the riches and populousness" of the country in question, and in proportion to its trade with other countries. It is the rate of increase in aggregate demand that governs the rate of technical progress.

Furthermore, Smith leaves no doubt about where the source of such continuous increase in demand is to be found. It is true that hardly any one before him has

put equal emphasis on the advantages of international division of labor, and he sees in foreign commerce the stimulus to most modern improvements in manufacture and even in agriculture. And yet he calls this causal nexus an "unnatural and retrograde order." "According to the natural course of things, therefore, the greater part of the capital of every growing society is first directed to agriculture, afterwards to manufactures, and last of all to foreign commerce" (Book III, chap. 1). Thus pride of place belongs to the domestic market, that is, to a continuous increase of population, equipped with sufficient buying power. With this our argument has turned a full circle.

Here it may be helpful to restate the sequence of this circular, or rather "spiral," process, and the strategic points in it where the constants exert their recurring influence. We have to remember that we find ourselves confronted with a process *in development*. Therefore in order to describe the sequence of events we have to break the chain of interdependent links artificially at some point. The most opportune place to do so is the point where the increase of aggregate employment, owing to the preceding "turn of the spiral," has raised aggregate demand, thus providing new investment opportunities for further division of labor. These opportunities are bound to raise profit expectations and thus demand for money capital, which will keep the level of the rate of interest above the minimum, and, together with the propensity for "betterment," will stimulate a positive rate of savings. These savings offered for investment represent demand for additional labor and keep real wages above the subsistence level. Under the influence of the propensity to procreate, labor supply responds to the wage stimulus, so that the investment opportunities can actually be realized through increase in employment. At the same time the additional payrolls expand the market beyond the expectations held at the beginning of the spiral turn that is under observation. This creates new investment opportunities, and the next turn begins.

The main center of interest in this causal chain is the factors of production, on the growth of which the development of the economic process depends. There we must distinguish between the supply of natural resources on one hand, and on the other hand the supply of labor and savings and the changes in the technique of production. The former is treated as a natural constant, at least up to the point when the system has utilized to the full its given stock of resources. The supply of the other factors, and especially all changes in such supply, is a function of the dynamic process itself, together with the operation of certain constants. Labor supply is fully determined by the interaction of a bio-psychological constant with the market price of labor, as savings are determined by a psychological constant and the market price of savings. Technological change, finally, is induced by the expansion of what Smith calls "national wealth" (comparable with what is today called "national income"), the continual increase of which is the inevitable result of the spiral process.

What is decisive is the fact that this process of development is not distorted by any independent variables. Therefore it is not only open to exact prediction but, in the absence of any possible disturbances from without, it moves in dynamic equilibrium. True, the absence of outside shocks is only a necessary condition for such equilibrium, and is not in itself sufficient to insure it; to clinch the argument in favor of a self-propelling harmonious dynamics, proof had to be given that the spiral chain would never be broken from within. Here lies the systematic significance of the specific form of technology that dominates Smith's dynamic model. Only a technology that is labor-attracting insures the steady expansion of the market, and thus the un-broken continuity of the "upward spiral."

The so-called "optimism" of Smith's vision of economic development hinges on his treatment of technical progress. Otherwise, as we saw, all the "pessimistic" arguments are present which in the hands of his successors turned the expanding secular process into the dismal stationary state. The bio-psychological constants, as conceived by Smith, would cause the mechanism to run down, were it not for the counteracting force of technology. But only by linking technical progress strictly with the growth of the system can the mechanism be made to "run up" steadily, until the full utilization of the natural environment prevents further expansion of aggregate and per capita income.[6]

One element, and only one, in the customary set of data retains in Smith's dynamics the role of an independent variable: consumer tastes. The *bi-polar shifts* of the productive factors according to the variations in these tastes exhaust what employment fluctuations the system can undergo, and they are of a sectorial and short-run nature only. The rigid manner in which *aggregate changes* in factor supply are linked with one another in a regular sequence precludes any aggregate fluctuations over the long run, and this for two reasons. Not only are such changes in factor supply always a response to a preceding change in demand, and therefore in the nature of a self-correcting adjustment, but they are

---

[6] Looking at this axiom of Smith's model from the vantage point of a fully developed industrial system, it is easy to raise the objection that it is unrealistic. But the axiom is an indispensable condition for the twin postulates of "autonomy" and "harmony" on which both the theory and the policy recommendations of Smith's economics rest. To have missed this central point is the main defect in Keirstead's otherwise valuable exposition of Smith's dynamics (see *Theory of Economic Change*, cited above, note 3, pp. 69–77). In linking moving equilibrium with a peculiar type of technology, Smith has shown an insight into the operation of the market mechanism that is sadly lacking in the work of most of his classical and all of his neo-classical successors.

also of necessity slow, thus permitting steady absorption. The rhythm of change is ultimately limited by the rearing period of children. Though these periods overlap in a continuous process of growth, making the influx of additional labor into the market a continuous process, they keep the rate of growth slow and steady.

This consideration gives to the hypothesis of "other things remaining equal," which underlies all classical analysis of short-term processes, a more than methodological significance. In a spiral process of development, as conceived by Smith, all factors other than bi-polar changes in taste do in fact remain equal over the short run. Far from assuming the function of controlled experiments, as it does in modern economics, in the context of original classical economics the *ceteris paribus* rule is a pronouncement on reality—at least on the aspired-to reality of perfect competition.

In summary, we can say that Smith's theory of economic development is composed of two kinds of building blocks: a set of natural, psychological, and institutional constants, and a circular mechanism that links the changes in the supply data with the course of the economic process in reciprocal causation. This reciprocity of cause and effect over time—though at any given moment cause and effect are clearly separable—raises economic analysis to the level of more comprehensive social analysis, at least so far as the supply conditions of the factors of production reflect the social process. The other social forces, as embodied in the constants, are not drawn into the circular mechanism of causation. We shall see that in this respect at least one later classical system, that of Marx, goes much further in establishing "laws of interdependence." But though for Smith the constants only affect the process of development, without themselves being affected by it, their nature as constants prevents them from prejudicing either the

stability or the calculability of the economic process. They belong to the "natural order," in the twofold meaning which this term has in the social philosophy of the Enlightenment. Therefore their mode of operation can be known, and the resulting model of economic dynamics is the image of a fully predictable process of "natural" development. Social economics was indeed raised by Smith to the formal level of a true science.

RICARDO AND THE EARLY "ANTI-HARMONISTS"

It is not my intention to present a systematic survey of all the variants that the classical theory of economic development exhibits, or to trace the influence that different writers exerted on one another in formulating their ideas. Our concern with the problem is methodological rather than historical, and for such a purpose a random selection of a few further hypotheses is quite sufficient. The reason for this is that Smith's model has remained the formal pattern for the "liberal" strand of classical economics, though the later models differ substantially from it and also from one another. The differences arise either from a change in the constants assumed, or from the weakening of the circular mechanism through the introduction of certain independent variables.

The outstanding example in both respects is Ricardo. By substituting the law of diminishing returns on land for Smith's assumption of constant returns, the trend of economic development is radically changed. Ricardo's "pessimism," as expressed in the first two editions of the *Principles*, is exclusively due to this modification of Smith's model. The idea of an *ultimate* running-down of the system is integral to the Smith model also, as we saw above. All that Ricardo did was to move forward into the present the point of time when the stinginess of nature asserts itself.

Not only does this place the level of real wages under a constant threat, which can be removed only temporarily by technical progress; but in addition Ricardo presents a new theory of profits, according to which the same tendency threatens their persistence also. It is no longer competition among capitalists, but the rise of money wages—inevitable under the pressure of decreasing returns—that cuts into profits. More and more this strangles accumulation, and thus the whole process of expansion.

Nevertheless, the strictness of the spiral process was in no way affected by this change. A "downward" spiral was added to the initial "upward" spiral, and this has important consequences for functional distribution; but the process as such remains fully determinate and calculable.

A much more serious modification was introduced in the third edition of the *Principles*, with the new chapter, "On Machinery." By taking note of the labor-displacing effects of industrial technology, Ricardo removes the cornerstone of the Smithian structure.[7] As in Smith, profits still depend on technical advance, and even more so when decreasing returns continuously tend to push up money wages. But though the prospects of innovation profits stimulate saving, their investment, which is still taken for granted, no longer assures growing aggregate employment. The displacement effect threatens to diminish the "gross produce"—that is, the size of the market—and steady growth is no longer assured. Ricardo did not himself draw the far-reaching conclusions regarding the secular process that this new notion of the technical factor suggests. The new insight expressed in the critical Chapter 31—in itself a rare case of self-destructive intellectual honesty—is hardly compatible with the notion of a system which, though "run-

ning down" in terms of real output, is free from any aggregate fluctuations.

It has become customary in recent years to attribute the first genuine insight into the causes of such fluctuations to Malthus. This emphasis is less than fair to some of his forerunners, and more than fair to Malthus' capacity to understand what indeed he saw. On both scores Lord Lauderdale and Sismondi deserve to be reinstated in the position that they held in the history of economic doctrines before Keynes traced to Malthus the introduction into "respectable circles" of the principle of effective demand.[8]

However this may be, the formal procedure of all these writers is the same. They break the link that—in Smith as well as in Ricardo, and prior to him in Say—had fastened savings firmly to investment. By stressing the "propensity" element in the creation of savings over and against the circular effect of profit expectations, savings themselves become an independent variable, to which investment may, or may not, adjust itself spontaneously.

With this the stability of economic development is undermined, though not necessarily its upward trend. If Malthus has a claim to originality in this respect, it lies in his demonstration that aggregate fluctuations are compatible with an upward trend of real output and employment. His law of population is much less strict than the hypothesis that underlies Smith's iron law of wages. "Moral restraint" is capable of breaking the circular chain at the most critical point—where the supply of labor is related to the level of real wages—trans-

---

[7] The fallacies contained in Ricardo's proof of the displacement effect do not alter the systematic consequences of his conclusion.

[8] For a balanced treatment of the relative merits of Malthus and Lord Lauderdale, see A. H. Hansen, *Business Cycles and National Income* (New York 1951) chap. 14. But in concentrating on the notion of "voluntary" underconsumption or "oversaving," Hansen disregards the importance of Sismondi in stressing the complementary role, and for the past history of capitalism the more important role, of "forced" underconsumption due to pressure on the wage level.

forming the latter into an independent variable. This second break in the circular chain may then undo part of the social evils brought about by the first, though it further reduces the determinateness and thus the predictability of the process of development.

MARX

We can say that in order to approximate their models to the complexities of the real world, the early nineteenth-century writers felt compelled to relax the strictness of the original circular mechanism. Marx's methodological position is unique because, although writing half a century later, he went in the other direction far beyond Smith. He transformed almost all the original constants into dependent variables. For this reason his model is the outstanding case of "endogenous dynamics," whatever reservations may have to be made about the substance of some of his most essential propositions.

To gain insight into the mechanism of Marx's model, we can best begin by considering those elements for which equivalents can be found in Smith's model. The process of development that Marx tries to formulate in the "general law of capitalist accumulation" [9] is kept moving, as in Smith, by the interaction of a law of population, a law of accumulation, and a law of technical change. But the social forces that replenish the stock of productive factors through these laws are quite different from those postulated by Smith.

To start with the law of population or labor supply, for Marx it is "relative surplus population" as created by technological displacement, rather than the "absolute surplus population" due to natural increase, that determines the state of the

[9] *Capital* (Kerr Edition, Chicago 1906, 1909) vol. 1, chap. 25. Subsequent references to Marx are to this edition.

labor market and the level of real wages (vol. 1, chap. 25). Since the introduction of labor-displacing technical changes can be geared to the demand for labor, labor supply can be kept at such a level that it is always available at minimum cost, that is, at wages near the subsistence level.[10]

Now the force that makes the capitalist-entrepreneur use the weapon of innovation in this manner operates through the "special" law of accumulation, the latter term to be understood in the classical sense of saving-plus-investment. But for Marx—in contradistinction to the earlier classical writers—accumulation is not stimulated by an innate propensity, but by the social pressure of a competitive society. Smith's psychological constant is transformed into a dependent variable of the institutional environment, which compels the capitalist "to keep continuously extending his capital, in order to preserve it" (vol. 1, chap. 24).

But Marx is in full agreement with both Smith and Ricardo that accumulation alone is not sufficient for the capitalist to survive. This is so, at least, if accumulation takes the form of "accumulation with constant organic composition of capital"—Marx's term for a "pure widening" of the capital structure. As will be shown below, in this case profits are threatened from two sides: through price decreases due to the competition of fellow-capitalists (Smith's argument), and through wage increases, since in this case the demand for labor rises without a simultaneous increase in supply

[10] It is a controversial point whether Marx regarded the industrial reserve army as a necessary condition for the pressure on the level of real wages, or merely as a force supplementary to the operation of the law of surplus value. The decision depends on what state of competition, pure or monopsonistic, one attributes to the labor market. Only if one assumes pure competition—hardly Marx's assumption—is the existence of a reserve army a necessary condition. We shall treat it as such, in order not to become involved in Marx's theory of value.

(Ricardo's argument). Only accumulation with "rising organic composition of capital"—capital-attracting technical progress, in modern terminology—can sustain the level of profit and with it the process of accumulation and development. And as we shall see presently, even this type of accumulation ultimately defeats its own ends.

Thus in Marx, as in all classical systems, it is technical progress that provides the ultimate dynamic force. But there the resemblance ceases. Before Marx technical progress was regarded as the vehicle of social progress and of market stability. It was supposed to create additional employment and thus to extend the market; to overcome, at least temporarily, the stinginess of nature; to stimulate investment and thus to banish the specter of oversaving. But to Marx modern technology is a Janus-faced phenomenon. While sustaining accumulation and thus growth, it maintains and even increases mass misery, breaks the stability of the economic process by blocking the extension of the market, and ultimately even jeopardizes profits.

We saw that it was a specific type of technical progress—specialization—that produced the harmonistic effects of the Smithian model. Another peculiar type creates the ambivalent tendencies in Marx's model. Its characteristics are two: it is labor-displacing and capital-intensifying.

I have already referred to the first characteristic in discussing Marx's law of population. In elaborating the earlier suggestions of Barton and Ricardo, Marx demonstrated that, as a rule, the reabsorption of technological unemployment is, under industrial conditions, not a question of short-run adjustment but of secular growth, conditional on prior formation of real capital. The significance of this proposition for the operation of Marx's model is twofold. On the one hand, by periodically flooding the labor market the industrial reserve army prevents the masses from participating in the benefits that increasing

productivity potentially offers. On the other hand, it prevents aggregate consumption from rising in proportion to aggregate output, thus threatening the system with (forced) underconsumption.

The second characteristic of technical progress, as Marx sees it, is progressive capital intensification, that is, an increase in the value of capital relative to the wages paid out over a stated period.[11] On this assumption he builds a supplementary theory of profits, in which the paradoxical effects of technical progress find their climax. This "law of the falling tendency of the rate of profits" is probably the most controversial of Marx's propositions,[12] although it follows logically from any consistent theory of labor value. If aggregate profits are the difference between the value of output and aggregate payrolls, then the rate of profit (that is, the ratio of aggregate profits to the value of total capital stock) is bound to fall whenever capital intensification raises the value of fixed capital at a higher rate than payrolls—at least so long as it is possible for labor's share in aggregate income to be maintained.[13]

[11] In some of Marx's statements, stocks and flows are badly confused. But there is no doubt that the above formulation renders the meaning of what he wanted to express.

[12] See, for example, the critique of this law contained in P. M. Sweezy, *The Theory of Capitalist Development* (New York 1942) chap. 6, a book that is certainly sympathetic to the general trend of Marx's ideas.

[13] It is quite another question, which has been much discussed in recent years (Sweezy, Joan Robinson), whether real wages, and thus labor's share in aggregate income, must not rise under these assumptions. This conclusion would then obviate Marx's whole deduction of the "catastrophic trend" of capitalist development. Now it is quite true that *per capita* real wages must rise with increasing productivity, unless money wages fall at the same time, which would in turn restore the level of profits. But this need not be true for *aggregate* real wages, unless aggregate employment is maintained. This condition, however, runs counter to Marx's intentions, since he derives an economic crisis from the fall of the profit rate. Whatever may happen to the real wages of the employed, therefore, growing misery of the working class as a whole is quite compatible with such a fall.

We must ask, of course, why capitalists introduce innovations if the result is a fall rather than a rise of the profit rate. To this Marx has three answers. First, there are a number of counteracting factors that reduce the "law" to a "tendency." The most important of these factors are the reduction of the value of the fixed capital stock (in spite of its physical increase) as a consequence of rising productivity, and the secondary effect of labor displacement on wages, namely, a fall in real wages. But these counteracting forces operate obviously ex post facto. Therefore Marx's other two reasons are more convincing from the standpoint of a capitalist who is confronted with the investment decision. On the one hand, Marx is fully aware (vol. 3, chaps. 13 and 15) of the temporary "pioneer profits" that form the center of Schumpeter's profit theory; although competition is bound to wipe these out over the long run, until it does so they raise the rate of profit. On the other hand, a fall in the rate of profit is fully compatible with a rise in its volume. This, of course, can be a stimulus only for the borrower, not for the lender, whose remuneration is calculated in terms of the rate. Whenever the rate falls, therefore, especially disturbing effects arise from the behavior of the capitalist (in the narrower sense), who succumbs to a sort of liquidity preference (vol. 3, chap. 15).

I have dwelt at some length on this supplementation of the classical theory of profit, since its simple meaning is shrouded in a fog of verbiage spread over it by Marx himself and subsequently by his critics. But again, we are not interested here in the substantive truth of the proposition, but in its significance for the logic of Marx's model.[14] What is new in Marx's law of technical change, compared with the corresponding propositions of his predecessors, is the combination of progressive with regressive tendencies that it describes. Only through its operation can profits, accumulation, and employment, and thus economic development, be stimulated—the same phenomena that are also checked by its operation. The result is an endogenous cycle of expansion and contraction, which takes the place of the steady running "up" or "down" of the classical mechanism. In this manner Marx's general law of accumulation makes regular fluctuations an inherent property of economic growth.

This modification invests the model with a degree of realism never before attained by any theory of development. But it makes the exposition of the underlying process rather complicated. And this all the more so, since Marx visualizes at least two different types of business cycles. As in many of his propositions, he left his cycle theory as a torso. But Sweezy (*op. cit.*, chap. 10) is probably right in asserting that Marx was fully aware of the two types, which nowadays pass as "overinvestment" and "underconsumption" cycles, the action of the falling rate of profit being associated with the latter. And far from playing one off against the other, as has become the modern fashion, he treats them as equivalent forms of the economic process.

We shall not pursue here a detailed examination of the manner in which Marx derives the sequence of cyclical phases for each of the two types. The main methodological significance of his cyclical model of growth lies in the fact that, once the cycle has started, it operates as the law of circular motion, according to which the factors of production are drained off and replenished in calculable fashion.

All that is needed to set the cycle going is an institutional environment, very like the one that figures in Smith's model, and the availability of innovational projects of the type described. The former developed out of the breakdown of mediaeval so-

---

[14] The substantive conclusion as to the instability of the level of profits can also be derived from the underconsumption effects that labor-displacing innovations exert.

ciety, which also provided the original investment funds for what Marx calls the process of "primitive accumulation" (vol. 1, chaps. 26–32). The latter is a consequence of the industrial revolution. The social pressure of the institutional order assures the appropriate motive force, whereas a continuous stream of inventions is the material for the profit motive to actualize itself through the fundamental economic behavior: accumulation. No additional channels are required to feed outside forces—biological or psychological—into the economic mechanism. The factors that sustain it, especially labor and capital, are recreated by the mechanism itself.

Again we have to break into a continuous process at an arbitrarily chosen point, in order to describe the circular mechanism. We select the point where availability of new projects, together with a large supply of idle labor and capital, induce what is today called "autonomous investment," thus starting a new revival. What form the ensuing upswing takes, and in what manner it ends, depends on the relative weight, in total investment, of "pure widening" projects and technical improvements respectively. If the former dominate, the labor pool inherited from the preceding depression will be gradually exhausted and wages will rise. This creates the "overinvestment" dilemma, resulting in general cut-throat competition.[15] Conversely, a sufficient supply of genuine improvements will, during the upswing, continuously refill the labor pool, thus preventing wage rises. But by this very fact it will drive the system in the end into the underconsump-

tion dilemma.[16] It is characteristic of the end phase of either type of upswing that profits decline. This brings accumulation to a temporary stop, leading to general contradiction and the recreation of the large factor pools, which are the condition for a new revival.

When examined from the aspect of determinateness and predictability, Marx's model gains upon Smith's by freeing the circular mechanism from all exogenous biological and psychological constants. As a cycle, the economic process recreates all conditions necessary for its continuation. Up to this point, however, it is difficult to see that the resulting secular process can be anything else but a sequence of cycles, distinguished at best by different types of upswings and crises, but without any specific trend of development. This gap is filled by Marx's most original contribution: the linking up of even the institutional environment with the cyclical process.

The decisive link is the "capital-intensifying" nature of technical progress, as understood by Marx. First of all, from cycle to cycle it raises the degree of "concentration"—that is, the average amount of capital per firm, and possibly the average size of the labor force per firm also. Second, and even more important for the dynamic process, it promotes "centralization" of production, namely, an increase in the share of large concerns in capital stock, aggregate output, and employment. This transformation is brought about by the periodic downswings, and derives from the

---

[15] The relevant passages (vol. 1, chap. 25, and vol. 3, chap. 15), in which a fall in profits, the stoppage of further accumulation, and thus the outbreak of the crisis, are derived from the wage rise, are open to criticism. We know today that overinvestment can arise only to the extent that factor specificity prevents a short-period adjustment of disproportionalities in the structure of production, a line of reasoning that is alien to Marx's thinking.

[16] The scattered passages in Marx referring to underconsumption are so vague that this problem has become a fertile field for both text interpretation and controversy; see Sweezy (cited above, note 12) chap. 10. Some neo-Marxists, notably Otto Bauer and Sweezy, have tried to construct from the available building blocks a consistent theory of "forced underconsumption." These constructions are defective, because they try to prove with purely "mechanical" arguments what can be demonstrated only with due regard to "changes in expectations."

greater crisis resistance of the larger and thus the more efficient firms. These retain, even during the depression, a certain volume of profits, whereas the general fall of the rate eliminates the smaller and less efficient firms.

This economic effect of the depression, however, is the cause of much more fundamental social effects. The process of competitive elimination gradually transforms a widely stratified society, originally composed of many independent producers, into two starkly antagonistic groups: a few "capital magnates," and the large mass of the proletarianized people. But again this process is Janus-faced. Misery and exploitation mount, as does underconsumption, making the periodic crises worse and worse. Yet at the same time centralization furthers the rationalization and planning of the productive process and the international unification of markets. It cannot help training the laboring masses in the "cooperative form" of production, and organizing them in self-defense. "Centralization of the means of production and socialization of labor at last reach a point where they become incompatible with their capitalist integument. This integument is burst asunder" (vol. 1, chap. 32). From this point on, the autonomous mechanism of the capitalist process gives way to planned direction.[17]

Thus the trend of socio-economic development follows from the interaction of two apparently contradictory tendencies. Both are inherent in labor-displacing, capital-intensifying technical change, when applied in a society that has gone through the process of "primitive accumulation." A constructive tendency—progressive accumulation, concentration, centralization, proletarian training and self-organization —plays against a destructive tendency— displacement, increasing misery, growing underconsumption, and worsening crises. The final catastrophe requires, of course, a "voluntaristic" stimulus—the "wrathful indignation" of the proletariat. But even this is traced back to the pressure of the social environment and treated as an inevitable response to it, as is the case with capitalists' profit incentive and its behavioral expression—accumulation. Later Marxists, notably Hilferding, Luxemburg, Sternberg, and Sweezy, have extended and refined the argument by applying it to the explanation of monopolistic tendencies and the related behavior patterns, as well as to the rise of a non-revolutionary working class and a new middle class in the leading capitalistic countries. But the determinateness of the socio-economic circular mechanism is unimpaired, as long as the effects follow from the operation of the basic variable "technology" in a historically given, but endogenously changing environment.[18]

For this reason clarity about the logical position of these ultimate "causes" is crucial for full understanding of the model. The case is simple as far as the environmental factors are concerned. They are the passive element in the process of development. Originally a set of data given by nature and history, they change slowly under the influence of the cyclical process, which they in turn affect through the channel of behavior. Once the economic process has started, the environment enters into a fully endogenous relationship with it.

The active factor, technology, is a more complex phenomenon. We must distinguish between the scientific-technological process of invention, and innovation as the economic application of invention. The latter is endogenously related to the move-

[17] This is true even though under socialism the sphere of material production remains a "realm of necessity," as Marx maintains (vol. 3, chap. 48) against some of his more utopian disciples.

[18] Luxemburg and Sternberg have added to the institutional factors of the environment the geographical-historical element of a "non-capitalist space," which is gradually being filled up. Marx's own stand in this respect is not clear.

ments of the cycle, and can be regarded as "bunched" in reverse proportion to the rate of profit. Invention, on the other hand, seems to be less closely bound up with the socio-economic process. Certainly modern technology generally is a child of the age and cultural climate in which modern capitalism arose. One might even assert that the constant flow of ever-new inventions is stimulated by the crumbs from the tables of the earners of profit, which fall to the inventor. But this motive can hardly be taken as his sole stimulus, and in any event it operates as a "carrot" rather than as a "stick." Finally and above all, the particular form that the invention has to take in order to direct the dynamic process in the historically ordained direction cannot be attributed to endogenous forces only. That Marx's capitalist should prefer labor-saving to labor-attracting devices agrees with the circular mechanism of the system as well as with the postulated trend of evolution. This is not true of the other characteristic of these devices: their "capital-intensifying" nature. This feature is indeed indispensable as a causal link in the chain of events, which lead through concentration and centralization to the self-organization of socialism in the "womb of the old society." But it cannot be derived with equal cogency from the basic behavior pattern of the capitalist. His ultimate aim would be served much better by capital-saving devices, which tend—at least in Marx's interpretation—to raise the profit rate. Exactly as in Smith, a very specific technology is an indispensable condition for the evolutionary process taking its postulated course. But again as in Smith, this variable has been introduced into the system from without rather than having been derived from the operation of the circular mechanism.[19]

[19] See also Lewis S. Feuer, "Indeterminacy and Economic Development," in *Philosophy of Science,* vol. 15, no. 3 (October 1948) pp. 225–41.

It is an interesting task to criticize the Marxian model by confronting each one of its "links" with the actual process of capitalist development. But though the course of history has refuted the prediction of the ultimate catastrophe—at least in the terms conceived by Marx—it has not by this refuted the method by whose help Marx attempted to establish a scientific theory of the development of the industrial market economy. We may well deny every single one of his substantive propositions, and yet regard the methodological lesson of his work as a challenge that no responsible social scientist can afford to evade.

I can vindicate this position by citing a witness who, in view of his earlier pronouncements quoted above, should be accepted as impartial: ". . . there is one truly great achievement to be set against Marx's theoretical misdemeanours . . . the idea of a theory, not merely of an indefinite number of disjointed individual patterns or of the logic of economic quantities in general, but of the *actual* sequence of these patterns or of the economic process as it goes on under its own steam, in *historic* time, producing at every instant that state which will of itself determine the next one. Thus, the author of so many misconceptions was also the first to visualize what even at the present time is still the economic theory of the future for which we are slowly and laboriously accumulating stone and mortar, statistical facts and functional equations" (italics mine).[20]

THE CLASSICAL THEORY OF GROWTH ABANDONED

It is an open question whether "theoretical misdemeanors" alone are responsible for the fact that to this day "respectable circles" have not taken note of Marx's methodological daring, and that men like

[20] Joseph A. Schumpeter, *Capitalism, Socialism and Democracy* (New York 1942) p. 43.

Silvio Gesell and Major Douglas could crowd him out of the most important treatise written in this generation. The latter fact seems all the more paradoxical since, judged in methodological terms, Keynes' *General Theory* is much nearer, if not to Marx himself, at least to his prototype Smith than anything written in academic economics since the days of Mill—a point to which I shall return presently.

But it is true that when *Capital* appeared, the main stream of classical economics had already abandoned not only the original approach to the problem of secular development but even any concern with it at all. The reasons for this were never explicitly stated, and must be inferred from the context of the later classical writings.

An illuminating phase of transition is represented by Book IV of Mill's *Principles*. Chapters 4 to 6 of this Book, dealing with the tendency of profits to fall to a minimum, and with the stationary state, are written much in the old vein, combining the Ricardian "runing down" tendency of the system with the Malthusian alleviations referred to. But these chapters are preceded by the extremely interesting Chapter 3, in which five hypothetical cases of the behavior of the factors of production are analyzed in a thoroughly modern fashion. Changes in factor supply (constant or increasing population combined with constant or increasing capital and constant or increasing productivity) are discussed in a "catalogue of permutations" that would do honor to any modern textbook.

Apparently Mill regarded all these cases as empirically possible, with little to choose between them on a priori grounds. This agnostic position follows quite logically from the destruction that had been dealt (by Malthus and by Mill himself) to the "laws of data changes," especially the iron law of wages and its descendant, the wage-fund theory; to the naive theory of accu-

mulation (by Lauderdale, Sismondi, and Wakefield); and to the optimistic interpretation of technical progress (abandoned by Ricardo, and restored by Mill himself only with many qualifications). The existence of business cycles had by Mill's time been fully realized, but no one had succeeded in integrating an explanation of them with the general theory of price and distribution. Even the purely physical tendencies of real output seemed more complex than they had appeared to the optimist Smith or to the pessimist Ricardo. For Mill the outcome depended on a "conflict between two tendencies" (Book IV, chap. 2), namely, technical progress and diminishing returns on land, an outcome that he regarded as unpredictable.

In short, the former "constants"—natural, psychological, and technological—had revealed themselves as so many variables. And since Marx's idea of relating them in circular fashion to the institutional environment contradicted what was still left of the original notion of a "natural order," they could only be regarded as independent variables. This is the manner in which neoclassical economics has treated them ever since, no longer attempting to account for the regular form that the capitalist process has taken during the secular period of two hundred years.

I agree with Keirstead (*op. cit.*, chap. 4) that Schumpeter's "Theory of Economic Development" is no exception to this rule. What Schumpeter has done is to put forth an explanation of the business cycle on the basis of a theory of innovations. But not only are innovations treated as an independent variable; their effect on the labor market is completely disregarded. Since Schumpeter insists that, in principle at least, every new cycle starts from equilibrium, the economic process as such has no causal function. Of his later works, *Business Cycles* stresses the role of historical causes at the expense of any circular mechanism. By building his model of the secular process on the dubious foundation of Kondratieff's hypothesis, Schumpeter at best *describes* a movement without being able to *explain* it.

His last book, *Capitalism, Socialism and Democracy,* contains a number of highly interesting suggestions about the interaction between the economic process and the social order in late capitalism. But Baumol is certainly right in pointing to the "somewhat loose and conversational manner which makes it almost impossible to discern the details of the analytical framework." [21] Thus the man who alone among recent academic economists recognized the meaning, and in the end the lasting importance also, of the Smith-Marx scientific procedure, himself did very little to revive it. The leadership fell to a man who was strangely unaware of the tradition that he followed.

What places Keynes, in spite of his railing against "classical" economics, squarely within the classical frame of reference is, on the one hand, his return to macro-economics (in the Quesnay-Marx tradition rather than in the Smith-Ricardo tradition) and, on the other hand, his replacing some of the independent variables of neo-classicism by constants, in the manner of Smith.[22] I refer, of course, to Keynes' revival of specific "propensities," "preferences," and "expectations," with whose help the *actual* course of the economic process is analyzed and predicted, at least for the short run. Certainly the functions that describe the Keynesian system can, in principle, assume any values. To that extent the theory is indeed general and its apparatus purely formal. But when it comes to analyzing the actual process of

capitalism and its inherent autonomous tendencies, Keynes no longer has recourse to the procedure by which neo-classicism tried to "apply" its apparatus, namely, by empirically determining the "data" from case to case. General propositions are put forth about how people at large divide an increment of income between consumption and saving, how movements of the rate of interest affect the demand for cash, and how long-term expectations affect investment. In scattered remarks, which refer to the secular process, a truly Marxian position is taken.[23] And the conclusions drawn regarding an industrial market left to its autonomous devices are hardly more reassuring.

All this, and also the recent attempts to build a more specific and more exact theory of economic growth on Keynesian foundations (Harrod, Hicks), requires detailed discussion beyond the range of this paper. But enough has been said to suggest to the reader that closer study of the classical apparatus, far from having merely historical significance, leads straight into the center of research in contemporary theoretical economics.

With this we have returned to our starting point: how to construct a verifiable theory of economic growth that adequately combines social with economic analysis. The lesson to be drawn from the foregoing investigation cannot be a call for the return to the "closed" circular mechanism of classical economics. Rather, the problem

---

[21] Baumol, *Economic Dynamics* (cited above, note 1) p. 20, note 2.

[22] To realize Keynes' position one must distinguish, of course, first, between classical and neo-classical economics, and second, between the substantive propositions of classical macro-economics and the method by which they were developed.

[23] It is true that the systematic elaboration of what is now called "maturity" theory is the work of some of Keynes' disciples. But all the elements of this theory are present in the three pages of the *General Theory* that deal more extensively with economic development (chap. 21, sec. VII). Keynes calls this a question "for historical generalization rather than for pure theory." This is precisely the analytical level on which the classical theory of development moves. The apparent difference in generality is exclusively due to the early classical belief in "natural" parameters, whereas Keynes and his followers are satisfied, like Marx, with generalizing about certain historical periods.

consists in establishing the criteria by which those areas where the economic process does indeed interact with its environment can be distinguished from fields where the "underlying forces" operate as independent variables. In some instances, as in the theory of expectations, elements belonging to both areas may well be active. At this stage we do not possess such criteria, nor does our ability to handle circular mechanisms transcend the rather crude determinism of dynamic process analysis in its modern version.[24] But the

growing concern with "endogeneity" is certainly in accord with sound methodological principles. After all, the limits of endogenous explanation coincide with the limits of our understanding of the social process.

---

[24] See, for example, Paul A. Samuelson's contribution in Howard S. Ellis, ed., *A Survey of Contemporary Economics* (Philadelphia 1948) pp. 352–81. It remains to be seen whether social scientists will profit from the theory of "servomechanisms" or "feedback systems," which play an increasingly important role in modern physical research. See Richard M. Goodwin's contribution to Alvin H. Hansen, *Business Cycles and National Income* (cited above, note 8) pp. 417–68. That the notion of a "circular mechanism" is much older than these constructs of modern physics, and is indigenous to social research, should not be doubtful after the foregoing observations.

13   The Retarded
Acceptance of the
Marginal Utility Theory

EMIL KAUDER

While classical economists recognized that a commodity must have value in use in order to have value in exchange, their failure to understand the relationship between use value and exchange value caused them to overlook the role of utility and demand in the determination of value. Nor did they understand the significance of the marginal increment in determining value. Continental thinkers, on the other hand, appreciated the role of the want-satisfying power of goods and the importance of the marginal increment in establishing exchange value considerably earlier than their English counterparts. Thus, Italian and French thinkers formulated subjective or utility-oriented theories of value, while William Petty, John Locke, and Adam Smith expounded cost of production theories which emphasized the role of labor in the value-creating process.

It is interesting to speculate why Continental thinkers had an earlier appreciation than English writers of the role of utility in the determination of value. The article which follows, "The Retarded Acceptance of the Marginal Utility Theory" by Emil Kauder, suggests that there was a relationship between the religious and philosophical convictions of a thinker and the pattern of his economic thought. Thus, the Aristotelian-Thomistic philosophy of the Italian and French schools was reflected in the Continental thinkers' subjective explanation of the valuation process, whereas in England, Protestant emphasis on the virtue of work led to a labor-oriented theory of value. These patterns were perpetuated even after the relationship between economic and religious thought became tenuous. It was not until the 1870s that English economic analysis was revolutionized by William Jevon's formulation of a theory of exchange value based on the principle of diminishing marginal utility. Similar theories were presented, almost simultaneously, in Switzerland and Austria by Leon Walras and Carl Menger.

Reprinted by permission of the publishers from Emil Kauder, "The Retarded Acceptance of Marginal Utility Theory," *The Quarterly Journal of Economics,* Vol. LXVII, November 1953, pp. 564–575, Cambridge, Mass.: Harvard University Press. Copyright 1953 by the President and Fellows of Harvard College. Dr. Kauder is Professor of Economics at the College of Business Administration, University of Southern Florida, Tampa.

Before 1870 the history of the theory of value shows rather strange features, not easily paralelled in the history of any other science. In the same field two diverse schools were working completely secluded from each other. One group discovered and developed the theory of value-in-use, the other continued to cling tenaciously to the theory of objective value, especially labor value. Our science might have developed much faster if the British classicists had given up their fruitless search for an objective value and had paid attention to the other school, which was exploring utility theory.

Much earlier than is generally assumed the theorists of subjective value had discovered the principles of marginal utility.[1] At the time of Adam Smith, Italian and French economists already considered it self-evident that the interplay of utility and scarcity explains the value of consumer goods, money, and the level of wages; Turgot had sketched a price theory very similar to Wicksell's analysis of much later date, and Bernoulli presented a mathematical analysis of marginal utility.[2]

These French, Italian, and Swiss writers had solved all problems of marginal utility except one; no one saw the connection between marginal utility and the individual value of equal units. The correct relation was discovered in 1834 by William F. Lloyd. Fourteen years later John Stuart Mill, in his Principles (unaware of Lloyd's achievement) expounded a somewhat weak mixture of objective and subjective elements in his theory of value. Mill, like the British Mercantilists, Petty and Locke, the classicists, Adam Smith, Ricardo before him and Karl Marx after him, either by-passed the utility approach or paid scant attention to it.

Why did they do this? Ignorance of literature alone cannot have been the reason for the nonacceptance. Neither the Mercantilists nor the Classicists may have read the Italian economists, yet Locke knew Pufendorf and Adam Smith was acquainted with Grotius and Pufendorf.[3] Adam Smith discussed economy with Turgot, and may have gotten at least some inkling about the directions in which Galiani and Turgot had moved in trying to solve the value problem.[4]

In the seventeenth and eighteenth centuries it was not ignorance which accounted for the dividing line between the two opposing points of view, but rather the antagonism between the Aristotelian-Thomistic and the Protestant social schools of thought. It was no coincidence that the members of the Italo-French subjective value school were Catholics and that the

[1] The history of marginal utility theory from Aristotle to Gossen has a substantial literature. We mention only two significant works: Augusto Graziani, *Storia critica della teoria del valore in Italia* (Milano, 1889); Otto Weinberger, *Die Grenznutzenschule* (Halberstadt, 1926). See also Emil Kauder, "Genesis of the Marginal Utility Theory," *Economic Journal*, September 1953.

The best documentation for the Italian writers from the end of the sixteenth century until about 1800 can be found in the voluminous collection: *Scrittori Classici Italiani Di Economia Politica* (Milano, 1804).

[2] Ferdinando Galiani, *Della Moneta* (the first anonymous edition was not available to me), ed. Fausto Nicolini (Bari, 1915), Book I, chap. II, p. 25; Book V, chap. I, p. 289. Graziani, *op. cit.*, p. 99. *Oeuvres de Turgot*, ed. Daire (Paris, 1844), Vol. I, "Valeurs et Monnaies," p. 72. Daniel Bernoulli, *Versuch einer neuen Theorie der Wertbestimmung von Glücksfällen*, ed. A. Pringsheim under the title: *Die Grundlagen der modernen Wertlehre*. Brentano und Leser, *Sammlung alterer und neuerer staatswissenschaftlicher Schriften des In- und Auslandes* (Leipsic, 1896). (Original edition and title, "Specimen Theoriae Novaede Mensur a sortis," 1738, not used.)

[3] Raymond de Roover, "Monopoly Theory prior to Adam Smith: A Revision," *The Quarterly Journal of Economics*, Vol. LXV (1951), p. 521.

[4] Dugald Stewart, "Account of the Life and Writings of Adam Smith," *The Works of Adam Smith*, Vol. V (London, 1811), p. 467. I. Jastrow. "Ein neuer Adam Smith Fund und der Aufbau des nationalökonomischen Lehrgebäudes," *Zeitschrift für Nationalökonomie*, Vol. VIII (Vienna, 1937). This paper contains, in the notes, a very good survey of the literature.

defenders of the cost theory of value were Protestants, as indicated in the following table:

TABLE   13-1

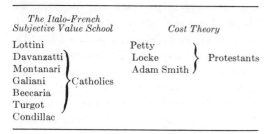

The Italo-French Subjective Value School	Cost Theory
Lottini	Petty
Davanzatti	Locke
Montanari	Adam Smith } Protestants
Galiani } Catholics	
Beccaria	
Turgot	
Condillac	

It seems likely that different religious backgrounds help to explain the fact that the French and Italian economists worked at cross-purposes with the British economists. Of course, the religion of their forefathers should explain only partly the thinking and writing of the mature authors. These latter can by no means be classified simply as either Catholics or Protestants without qualification, for they may hold religious convictions which are at variance with the faith of their youth. Thus the young Galiani, when he wrote his *Treatise on Money,* was influenced by Vico,[5] by Catholic theology,[6] and by the deism of the eighteenth century.[7] Condillac was one of the main interpreters of sensualistic philosophy. In the British camp Locke and Adam Smith combined deism with sensualism. But all these variegated views of sensualism, deism, etc., were grafted onto either a Catholic-Thomistic or a Protestant-Puritan pattern of thought. The point is that early education leaves its permanent impression on our minds, regardless of how we may change our convictions at a later date. These indelible fundamentals created specific social outlooks which separated the two camps.

According to Max Weber, Calvin and his disciples placed work in the center of their social thoelogy.[8] This earth is the place where man has to strive, by incessant labor, for the greater glory of God.[9] All work in this society is invested with divine approval. Any social philosopher or economist exposed to Calvinism will be tempted to give labor an exalted position in his social or economic treatise, and no better way of extolling labor can be found than by combining work with value theory, traditionally the very basis of an economic system. Thus value becomes labor value, which is not merely a scientific device for measuring exchange rates but also the spiritual tie combining Divine Will with economic everyday life.

Generally authors are not fully aware of the connection between their ideas and their early education. Locke and Adam Smith did not see clearly the relation between their theory of labor value and Calvin's glorification of work, although traces thereof can be found in their writings. Locke wrote: "God . . . commanded man also to labor. . . ." Man must follow this command, continues Locke, to improve the world which God has given men for their own benefit.[10] Labor, divinely ordained, be-

---

[5] See Fausto Nicolini, "Giambattista Vico e Ferdinando Galiani. Ricerca storica," *Giornale Storico Della Letteratura Italiana,* Vol. LXXI (10 semestre 1918), p. 142.

[6] See especially his polemic against the Protestant theory of usury and his defense of Catholic censorship. Galiani, "Della Moneta," *Early Economic Thought,* ed. Arthur Eli Monroe (Cambridge, 1945), p. 300. A short time before he wrote an essay on the immaculate conception. See S. G. Tallentyre (pseud. for Evelyn Beatrice Hall), *The Friends of Voltaire* (New York, 1907), p. 64. Apparently the young Galiani was not the skeptical freethinker of his later days.

[7] Galiani defends the theory of social harmony, one of the most important principles of deism. "Della Moneta," A. E. Monroe, *op. cit.,* p. 288.

[8] Max Weber, "Die protestantische Ethik und der Geist des Kapitalismus," *Gesammelte Aufsätze zur Religions-soziologie,* Vol. I (Tübingen, 1920), p. 17. See also Talcott Parsons, *The Structure of Social Action* (Glencoe, Illinois, 1949), p. 500.

[9] J. B. Kraus, S.J., *Scholastik, Puritanismus und Kapitalismus* (Munich, 1930), p. 243.

[10] John Locke, "The Second Treatise on Civil Government," Nos. 31, 33, in *John Locke on Politics and Education* (New York, 1947), p. 90. About Locke's Puritan family see Alexander

comes the measure of market exchange. This conclusion had been drawn already by Locke and much more clearly by Adam Smith who, in spite of being a deist, showed during his entire lifetime, a deep sympathy for Presbyterianism.[11]

The author of the *Wealth of Nations* believed that the hidden hand of Providence must be guiding economic action in order to insure just prices. Fair prices are reached if the amount of labor in the exchanged goods is the same. Like many other defenders of the labor theory, Adam Smith combined the Calvinistic glorification of labor with the Aristotelian-Scholastic the-

Campbell Fraser, *Locke* (Philadelphia, 1890), p. 5. Even as a student at Oxford Locke had doubtless revolted against "Presbyterian dogmatism" and "Congregational fanaticism," but this revolution did not erase the social convictions of Calvinistic teaching.

[11] Adam Smith was born in the town of Kirkcaldy, whose inhabitants had fought for the Covenant in the battle of Tippermuir. See Francis Hirst, *Adam Smith* (London, 1904), p. 1. In the Burgh School of Kirkcaldy he came into contact with young Scottish Presbyterians, e.g., John Drysdale who held twice "the helm of the Scotch Church as Moderator of its general Assembly. . . ." (*Ibid.*, p. 3.) His mother wanted him to become an Episcopalian clergyman; with the help of the Snell Exhibition he was sent to Oxford. However, he refused to become a clergyman (*Ibid.*, p. 8). His Episcopalian baptism did not prevent him from signing the Westminster Confession before the Presbytery of Glasgow when he became professor at Glasgow in 1750 (*Ibid.*, p. 23). His deep sympathy for the Presbytery is plainly expressed in *The Wealth of Nations*: "There is scarce, perhaps, to be found anywhere in Europe, a more learned, decent, independent, and respectable set of men than the greater part of the Presbyterian clergy of Holland, Geneva, Switzerland and Scotland." *The Wealth of Nations* (Oxford, 1928), Vol. II, p. 453. Already in his time his favorable attitude toward Presbyterianism was noted and unfavorably criticized by one of his friends, Hugh Blair: "You are, I think, by much too favorable to Presbytery" (Letter of Hugh Blair to Adam Smith. Edinburgh, 3 April 1776, quoted in W. R. Scott, "A Manuscript Criticism of the Wealth of Nations," *Economic History*, Vol. III, p. 52). These remarks are not meant to prove that Adam Smith was a pious man in the sense of denominationalism, but to show how far he was exposed to the Scottish brand of Puritanism.

ory of the fair price. No doubt Locke and Smith, both of whom studied in the British stronghold of Aristotelianism, in Oxford, knew the Greek philosopher.[12] Thus they were able to combine Puritan social philosophy with the traditional Aristotelian theory of value. This combination was possible because Aristotle and the schoolmen had presented a value concept with two sides: the subjective utility aspect, which was explored by the Italo-French school, and the objective aspect, i.e., intrinsic value and just price, which fitted into the Puritan social pattern.

The Puritan theologians claimed that business is not only a morally acceptable, but also a divinely commanded, activity, on condition that economic value is identical with the just price and that just price is equal to the amount of labor in the commodities. This harmony between just price, valuation, and the full share of divinely commanded labor will be realized by free competition. The Aristotelian and Thomistic idea of fair price was not dead in the British camp, but by weaving just price together with a higher estimate of this world and the glorification of labor, a new social philosophy was originated. The Puritan philosophy was at variance with the social philosophy which was still dominant in Italy and France.

Until the middle of the eighteenth century the future authors of the Italo-French school were trained by professors of philosophy who often were also members of religious orders (Carmelites, Dominicans, and Jesuits). These teachers presented a combination of Aristotelianism and Thomism which generally was not touched by

[12] About English universities and their teachings in the seventeenth century see Fraser, *op. cit.*, pp. 10–11; in the eighteeth century: Leslie Stephen, *The English Utilitarians* (London, 1900), reprint of the London School, p. 43. Adam Smith must have acquired a very thorough knowledge of Aristotle. The existent fragment of his inaugural dissertation, "de Origine idearum," is proof of it. See Hirst, *op. cit.*, p. 23.

any modern "hereticism." [13] The young students were not exposed at all to any glorification of labor. Work, according to the schoolmen and their followers, is not a divine vocation but is necessary in order to maintain one's place in the given natural order of society. There was no compulsion to integrate labor costs into the social order, or into the philosophy of economic value.[14]

Instead of work, moderate pleasure-seeking and happiness form the center of economic actions, according to Aristotelian and Thomistic philosophy. A certain bal-

anced hedonism is an integrated part of the Aristotelian theory of the good life.[15] If pleasure in a moderate form is the purpose of economics, then following the Aristotelian concept of the final cause, all principles of economics including valuation must be derived from it.[16] In this pattern of Aristotelian and Thomistic thinking, valuation has the function of showing how much pleasure can be derived from economic goods.

In Italy and France, Aristotelian "Good Life" and finalism formed the background for the development of one theory of value, whereas in Great Britain, moral recognition of economics and the glorification of labor led to quite a different theory of value. This, in my opinion, is the final reason why John Locke and Adam Smith were not interested in the work of their Italian and French contemporaries and vice versa. I am very well aware of the fact that this explanation is a conjecture, but it is a conjecture which does account for the opposing attitudes of the two camps.[17]

My theory has, however, an important limitation. The belated acceptance of marginal utility in the nineteenth century cannot be explained by the Aristotelian-Calvinistic dichotomy. Other conditions prevailed. Economists in general no longer thought in accordance with their religious backgrounds. Only a dwindling minority were influenced by religious convictions. To this small group belonged Alfred Marshall,

[13] Apparently Aristotelianism had a dominant position in the universities of France and Italy until the middle of the eighteenth century. Any attempt before that time to throw off the shackles of Aristotelian philosophy aroused the ire of religious orthodoxy and led to the persecution of the innovator. Aristotle was the only philosopher who could be taught according to the study plans of the Jesuits. ("Commentariolus" to the "ratio studiorum" of 1586.) See Paul Barth, *Geschichte der Erziehung* (5th and 6th ed.; Leipsic, 1925), p. 333. The Jesuits had an essential influence on Spanish and Italian education. Although French Jesuits and the College Royal de France were not on the best of terms, they joined forces against Descartes, Jansenism, and Quietism, and propagated the exclusive teaching of Aristotelianism during the whole seventeenth century. See Barth, *op. cit.*, pp. 349, 515, 735; Ernst von Sallwürk, "Bildung und Bildungswesen in Frankreich während des 17. und 18. Jahrhunderts," *Geschichte der Erziehung vom Anfang an bis auf unsere Zeit*, ed. K. A. Schmid and Georg Schmid (Stuttgart, 1896, Vol. IV, Part I, pp. 416; 431; 435; 437. A similar situation existed also in Italy during the seventeenth and the first quarter of the eighteenh century. During the lifetime of Giambattista Vico, the great Neapolitan philosopher, the inquisition tried to suppress Cartesians, Epicureans, and atheists (between 1683 and 1744). Max Harold Fisch and Thomas Goddard Bergin, *The Autobiography of Giambattista Vico* (Ithaca, N.Y., 1944), p. 34. N. Cortese, "L'Età Spagnuola," *Storia della Universita di Napoli* (Naples, 1924), pp. 428, 430. The attempts to break away from Aristotle were apparently successful only in the second part of the eighteenth century. In Pavia under Austrian domination, Minister Kaunitz emphasized in a reform program of 1772 that philosophy should be taught according to Bacon, Locke, Condillac, and Bonnet. Baldo Perroni, "La riforma dell' Universita di Pavia ne settecento," *Contributo alla Storia dell' Universita di Pavia* (Pavia, 1925), p. 147.

[14] Kraus, *op. cit.*, p. 72.

[15] Léon Robin claims that the place for pleasure is not clearly designated in Aristotle's ethics. "Three main ideas are presented: (1) pleasure is never a good (Speusippus); (2) some pleasures are good, but the majority are bad (all those which are neither true nor pure (Philebus); (3) even if all pleasures were good it still would be impossible that pleasure is the supreme good . . ." Léon Robin, *Aristotle* (Paris, 1944), p. 215. (My translation.) It seems that most of our writers are interested in Aristotle's positive evaluation of pleasure seeking.

[16] W. D. Ross, *Aristotle* (London, 1930), p. 190.

[17] I presented this explanation for the first time in a paper read before the midwestern section of the American Economic Association (Milwaukee, April 1951).

to whom Talcott Parsons has drawn my attention.[18] The Evangelicalism of his dominating father left a strong imprint on the thinking of Alfred Marshall.[19] Evangelicalism was a Calvinistic revival movement which gained a foothold in many Protestant churches of America and Great Britain during the nineteenth century. The Evangelicals demanded the consecration of Christians to valuable and zealous action and the condemnation of luxury.[20]

Marshall, as a mature personality, became an agnostic yet he retained a deep feeling for religious values,[21] and his welfare policy was patterned after the moral postulates of Evangelicalism. "Work in its best sense, the healthy energetic exercise of faculties is the aim of life, is life itself," comfort is "a mere increase of artificial wants." [22] Transferring this Calvinistic appreciation of activity for its own sake and depreciation of comfort into economic theory produces a dilemma which has been ably analyzed by Professor Parsons. On the one hand, Marshall was one of the independent discoverers of marginal utility. On the other hand, his glorification of labor attracted him to the cost problem. The result was the unbalanced character of his price and value theory. He failed to make fullest use of the marginal utility

theory,[23] and he defended valiantly Ricardo's objective value theory.

Marshall stressed costs and supply rather than demand in his famous explanation of price-equilibrium. Calvinism in its evangelical form was still strong enough to unbalance the system but no longer powerful enough to eliminate the marginal utility approach entirely. Even the son of an evangelical father no longer suppressed scientific interest for the sake of religious postulates. Marshall's dilemma was rarely found.

Educational background was no longer a sufficient explanation of the trend in the nineteenth century. The tie between specific religious or philosophical convictions and a particular pattern of economic thinking became weaker and weaker. For example, most of the outstanding analysts of subjective value theory in the nineteenth century do not fit into the Aristotelian-Thomistic pattern. Lloyd and Longfield were Protestants, Gossen was an outstanding Anti-Catholic, Beccaria, Verri, and later Ferrara, who grew up in an intellectual climate which was still influenced by Catholic ideas, showed outspoken sympathies for the British cost theory.

The reasons for the delayed acceptance of marginal utility in the nineteenth century can be found only in the history of economic science itself. This statement contradicts customary explanations. Sociologists, philosophers, and economists claimed that either sensualism (Northrop and Gunnar Myrdal),[24] or the return to Kantianism

---

[18] In recent correspondence.

[19] His father was "cast in the mould of the strictest Evangelicals." John M. Keynes, "Alfred Marshall, 1842–1924," *Memorials of Alfred Marshall*, ed. A. C. Pigou (London, 1925), p. 1.

[20] About Evangelicalism: A *Dictionary of English Church History*, ed. S. L. Ollard and Gordon Crosse (London, 1921), pp. 211, 215; *Encyclopedia of Religion and Ethics*, ed. James Hastings (New York, 1920), Vol. V, p. 602.

[21] *Memorials, op. cit.*, p. 7.

[22] Quoted from *Memorials* and from Marshall's *Principles* in Talcott Parsons, *The Structure of Social Action* (Glencoe, Ill., 1949), p. 141, n. 1, and p. 140. Marshall's remark on his beloved chess game is typical of his Puritan abstinence from luxury. "We are not at liberty to play chess games, or exercise ourselves upon subtleties that lead nowhere. It is well for the young to enjoy the mere pleasure of action, physical or intellectual. But the time presses; the responsibility on us is heavy." *Memorials, op. cit.*, p. 2.

[23] It is worthy of note that Marshall presents the whole marginal utility theory on two and one half pages in his Principles, a book dedicated mainly to the explanation of price theory. Alfred Marshall, *Principles of Economics* (8th ed.; London 1930), pp. 92–94.

[24] C. Northrop, *The Meeting of East and West* (New York, 1946), p. 131. Gunnar Myrdal, *Das Politische Element in der national-ökonomischen Doktrinbildung* (Berlin, 1932), p. 125. See Canina, "Valore e rarita nel pensiero di G. Montanari," *Istituto Lombardo di Scienze e Lettere* (Milano, 1943–44), LXXVII, p. 166, note 1.

(Stark),[25] or the changed interests of the leading social classes (Nikolai Bukharin and Fritz Behrens)[26] helped marginalism to establish its dominant position in economics. It seems to me that all three explanations are insufficient.

Most plausible is the first interpretation connecting hedonism with marginal utility. Marginal utility, according to Northrop and Myrdal, is a specific application of the hedonistic pain and pleasure calculus. It was when hedonism was adopted as a philosophical background by the majority of economists, Myrdal and Northrop claim, that the marginal value system got its central position in economic thinking.[27] This statement is an oversimplification. From the Middle Ages until the end of the eighteenth century the contact between hedonism and marginal utility was rather infrequent and accidental. Not even the young abbé Galiani can be considered a hedonist,[28] and only one of his followers, Condillac, bases the value-in-use concept on the pain and pleasure principle.[29] But in the nineteenth century the situation was somewhat different. Gossen and Jevons were strict disciples of this philosophy. Yet

Lloyd,[30] Menger, and Walras[31] were not sensualists. So the acceptance of marginal utility cannot be explained by the conversion of the majority of economists to sensualism.

Still less important than sensualism was the influence of the Kant-revival in spite of Stark's interesting thesis. He claims that, at least in Germany, both the acceptance of marginal utility and the contemporary renaissance of Kantianism are phenomena of the same kind, i.e., reaction to positivism and the reawakening of introspection and theory.[32] Yet Vienna, the center of the new theoretical studies in the German language zone, was not touched by the new enthusiasm for Kant—instead of Kant, Aristotelianism and especially neo-positivism were taught.[33]

---

[25] W. Stark, *The History of Economics* (New York, 1944), p. 3.

[26] Nikolai Bukharin, *The Economic Theory of the Leisure Class* (New York, 1927), pp. 8, 17. Fritz Behrens, "Hermann Heinrich Gossen oder die Geburt der wissenschaftlichen Apologetik des Kapitalismus," *Leipziger Schriften zur Gesellschaftswissenschaft*, 1. Heft (Leipsic, 1949). Fritz Behrens, using the same approach as Bukharin, does not quote Bukharin at all.

[27] "The marginal utility theory adopts the hedonistic and psychological concept of valuation at a time in which the psychological experts all over the world are trying to eliminate hedonistic formulas and to establish more realistic methods." Gunnar Myrdal, *Das politische Element . . . ,* op. cit., p. 127 (my translation).

[28] See p. 566, note 6.

[29] On sensualism, materialism, and enlightenment the following works were used: Friedrich Albert Lange, *Geschichte des Materialismus* (3d ed.; Iserlohn, 1876). Baron Cay von Brockdorff, *Die englische Aufklärungsphilosophie* (Munich, 1924).

[30] No documentary proof can be given that Bentham had influenced his younger countryman, Lloyd. No doubt, Bentham and the Oxford professor of economics had much in common; Bentham knew the law of diminishing utility and so did Lloyd; Lloyd read the *Westminster Review,* the mouthpiece of the Benthamites. He did not, however, quote Bentham at all. Lloyd is a rather meticulous scholar; in his lectures he quotes each available source, even Daniel Defoe's *Robinson Crusoe* and some anonymous writers.

In a letter of October 22, 1951, Professor Roy Harrod, Oxford, who is very familiar with the local history, emphasizes that Lloyd cannot have been a Benthamite. "Lloyd was a clergyman and brother of a famous divine, and the circles in which he lived would hold Bentham in pretty good contempt. . . ." (letter addressed to author).

[31] A fragmentary chapter intended for the second edition of his *Principles* makes it quite clear that Menger was not a sensualist. He distinguishes between physiological, egotistical, and altruistical wants. Carl Menger, *Grundsätze der Volkswirtschaftslehre* (2d ed., Vienna, 1923), pp. 4 ff., note.

About Walras' philosophy see Leon Walras, *Éléments d'Économie Pure* (Paris, 1926), p. 16. Walras was apparently strongly influenced by Descartes and Comte.

[32] Stark, *op. cit.*, p. 3.

[33] Roy Wood Sellars, "Positivism in Contemporary Philosophic Thought," *American Sociological Review,* Vol. IV (1939), p. 34.

Kant was not the leading Austrian philosopher, as Heinrich Ritter von Srbik has shown in his subtle analysis of the Austrian intellectual climate

Neither was the marginal utility theory the expression of bourgeois economic interest, as the Marxians claimed. The theory had been accepted not only by convinced defenders of existing society but also by socialists, including agricultural socialists (Gossen and Walras), and even by anarchists. Only a theory without a class bias could be used by such diversified political and economic groups.

Not hedonism, nor neo-Kantianism, nor the peculiarities of class-consciousness, but only the development of economic thinking during the first seventy years of the nineteenth century can explain the belated acceptance of the marginal utility theory. First the classical theory of value and later the historical school delayed the acceptance of the subjective theory of value.

At the beginning of the classical era Adam Smith, David Ricardo, and their disciples had gained a political and scientific ascendancy.[34] Defenders of the value-in-use theory lost their influence and were forgotten. Even before 1800, the Italian and French writers had already been drawn into the orbit of British classical thinking. An attempted synthesis of utility theory and cost theory was the main object of later Italian writers.[35]

A number of authors bound neither by school nor leadership were original and independent enough to avoid the well-worn track of classical thinking. Lauderdale saw as early as 1819 the inconsistencies of the classical value concept: "After this philosopher's stone [i.e., labor value as a form of objective measure] many have been in search; and not a few, distinguished for their knowledge and their talents, have imagined that in *labour* they had discovered what constituted a real measure of value."[36] Lauderdale's sarcastic remarks were of no avail.

Ricardo, at least, knew that he had not found the invariable yardstick, and that the "embodied" labor was nothing but a workable substitute for a perfect measure.[37] Yet he, his immediate followers, J. R. McCulloch and James Mill, and even his personal friend and scientific opponent, Malthus, remained so absorbed in this search, that no other approach found room in their pattern of thinking. I venture to say that Ricardo and his contemporaries believed that economics could only reach the dignity of a science if it could be based on objective measures like the Newtonian

---

since 1800. Since that time, he writes, Austrian thinking, based on Catholic tradition, was opposed to the idealism of Kant and his followers. Leibniz' monadology, an ontological and not a transcendental logic, form the framework of Bernhard Bolzano's logic, and of the writings of Bolzano's followers, Exner and Robert Zimmermann. Traces of this attitude survive even after 1890. Heinrich Ritter von Srbik, *Geist und Geschichte. Vom Deutschen Humanismus bis zur Gegenwart.* Vol. II (Munich, 1951), p. 85. See Robert Mühlher, "Ontologie und Monadologie in der österreichischen Literatur des 19. Jahrhunderts," *Die Österreichische Nationalbibliothek, Festschrift* (Vienna, 1948), pp. 488 ff.

The connection between Menger, Böhm-Bawerk, and the Austrian intellectual climate has not been completely investigated. Some relations have been discovered by Manuel Gottlieb, *The Ideological Influence in Schumpeter's Theory of Capitalism* (paper, not published, submitted for discussion at the midwestern section of the American Economics Association, Cedar Rapids, 1953), p. 31, note 109.

[34] About the rising Ricardian influence see Schumpeter, "Review of the Troops," this *Journal*, Vol. LXV (1951), p. 162.

[35] Augusto Graziani, "Le idee economiche degli scrittori Emiliani e Romagnoli sino al 1848," *Memorie della Regia Accademia di Scienze, Lettere ed Arti in Modena* (Modena, 1893), Serie II, Vol. X, p. 478.

[36] James Maitland, the eighth Earl of Lauderdale, *An Inquiry into the Nature and Origin of Public Wealth. . . .* (2d ed.; Edinburgh, 1819), p. 21 (italics in original); cf. also p. viii.

[37] Ricardo's letter to John Ramsay McCulloch (Aug. 21, 1823), *The Works and Correspondence of David Ricardo*, ed. Piero Sraffa, Vol. IX (Cambridge, 1952), p. 358. Ricardo's letter to Hutches Trower (Aug. 31, 1823). *Ibid.*, p. 377. David Ricardo, "Absolute Value and Exchangeable Value. A Rough Draft," *ibid.*, Vol. IV (Cambridge, 1951), pp. 361 ff.

physics.[38] When, eleven years after the death of Ricardo, the writings of Lloyd and Longfield were published, neither the students of Ricardo nor other leading economists were able to see the new possibilities. The Ricardian pattern of thinking prevented it.

Twenty-two years later Gossen published his work. This time other circumstances prevented recognition and acceptance. Gossen was a retired Prussian official without prestige and not a member of the universities. Academic outsiders can nowhere count on a great audience of scholars. Moreover, Gossen had the bad luck to write and publish in the era of the emerging historical school, when would-be readers could not be attracted by purely theoretical discussion.[39] This double handicap must have kept the circle of attentive readers rather small. Up to the present time only one writer who mentioned Gossen's work before 1870 has been found: the Hungarian professor Julius Kautz.[40]

The successful triumvirate, Menger, Jevons, and Walras, worked eighteen years later under much better social and intellectual conditions than Gossen. Their words carried weight because they were professors at well-established universities and not men without jobs and out of luck, like Gossen. Their Austrian, French, and British readers lived outside the very center of the historical school in Germany, and were therefore not biased against theoretical studies. Menger's Austria, although tied to the "Reich" by common language and cultural tradition, was only slightly influenced by the historical school.[41] In these three countries, especially in France and in England, the predilection for theoretical studies, so well-established by Adam Smith, John Stuart Mill, Jean Baptiste Say, and others, was still existent. The theoretical tradition was kept alive but not the objective value theory of Adam Smith and David Ricardo. Already the last leaders of the classical school, Nassau Senior and John Stuart Mill, had given up the rigid labor theory and had adopted an empirical cost theory. The attempt to find an invariable unit of measurement was abandoned. The question, "what are the principles of economic valuation?" was put anew before the forum of economists. A new answer was presented in 1870. The long period of delay had ended.

[38] In this connection it is noteworthy that Ricardo from his early youth, was very much interested in natural science, "mathematics, chemistry, geology, and mineralogy." Jacob Hollander, "David Ricardo. A Centenary Estimate." *Johns Hopkins University Studies in Historical and Political Science.* Series XXVIII, No. 4 (Baltimore, 1910), p. 35. The search for an objective measure may be a carry-over from Ricardo's scientific studies. Moreover the scholarly conviction of that time was that any investigation of scientific character must follow the pattern of the natural sciences.

[39] Concerning the fate of Gossen's book, see F. A. Hayek, *Hermann Heinrich Gossen. Eine Darstellung seines Lebens und seiner Lehre* (Berlin, 1928), p. 5.

[40] Kautz read Gossen's work rather thoroughly but he was apparently not aware of its importance. Julius (Gyula) Kautz, *Theorie und Ge-*

schichte der Nationalökonomik. I. Die National-ökonomik als Wissenschaft (Vienna, 1858), p. 9, note 1; II. *Die geschichtliche Entwicklung der Nationalökonomik und ihrer Literatur* (Vienna, 1860), p. 704. Cf. Hayek, *op. cit.*

[41] See Menger's analysis of the intellectual situation in his preface to the second edition of his *Principles.* Menger, *op. cit.*, p. vii.

14 Leon Walras and
His Economic System

MILTON FRIEDMAN

Instead of seeking to establish the equilibrium rate of exchange between two commodities, which was the procedure generally used by Marshall, Walras' general equilibrium analysis undertakes the simultaneous determination of four sets of unknowns. These are: (1) the quantities of n productive services offered for sale, (2) the quantities of m finished goods demanded, (3) the prices of n productive services, and (4) the prices of m finished goods. The price of one of the m commodities is used as a *numeraire* or common denominator in terms of which all other prices are expressed, so there are $2m + 2n - 1$ unknowns for which a value must be established. This analysis requires an equal number of independent equations which Walras constructs from four sets of data. These are: (1) the quantities of m finished goods available for consumption per unit of time, (2) the supplies of n factors of production available for employment, (3) the *rareté*, or marginal utility functions of individuals for goods and factor services self-employed by owners, and (4) the technical coefficients of production. It follows from the principle of simultaneous equations that sufficient data are available to establish values mutually and simultaneously for the unknowns being sought. Analogously, general equilibrium in all markets, commodity as well as factor, requires simultaneous individual equilibriums. This demonstration is a singular achievement for which credit belongs exclusively to Walras.

Milton Friedman's review of the William Jaffe translation of Walras' *Elements of Pure Economics*, which follows, puts this contribution into perspective by describing it as a "framework for organizing our ideas" about the interdependence of consumer and factor markets. While it is without substantive content itself, this framework has facilitated the conceptualization of substantive knowledge about price determination—much of which has been established with the aid of the Marshallian tools of particular price determination.

Reprinted from Milton Friedman, "Leon Walras and His Economic System," *The American Economic Review*, December 1955, pp. 900–909. Dr. Friedman is Professor of Economics at the University of Chicago.

"Thus the system of the economic universe reveals itself, at last, in all its grandeur and complexity: a system at once vast and simple, which, for sheer beauty, resembles the astronomic universe." Leon Walras.[1]

The appearance of William Jaffé's loving translation of Leon Walras' *Elements of Pure Economics* offers an excuse for re-examining that great work some eighty odd years after its original publication. Though in so far as this is a review, it is a review of Walras and not of Jaffé, I cannot refrain from prefacing it with a word of thanks to Jaffé for his translation, which is a model of its kind: careful, accurate, and marked throughout by an unobtrusive attention to detail. His notes on the collation of editions are an important aid to research; his translator's notes illuminate many points of the text as well as directing the reader's attention to much recent writing that is relevant to its interpretation.

Though I regard as somewhat extravagant Schumpeter's judgment that, "so far as pure theory is concerned, Walras is . . . the greatest of all economists," [2] there can be no doubt that the *Elements* is a great work which marked an important step forward in the development of economics as a science, and which still plays an important role in economic thinking. It is well worth having a translation even at this late date in order to make it more readily accessible both to the profession at large and particularly to students learning to become economists: it belongs on their "five foot shelf." The comments that follow deal with the book in this context, as a piece of living literature, rather than with its role in the history of economic thought.

On the broadest level of generality, there are two main themes in the *Elements*: the

analysis of *rareté*, or marginal utility; and the theory of general equilibrium. Walras regarded the two as fitting together in one harmonious whole, which is certainly tenable; he also viewed the marginal utility analysis as indispensable for the study of general equilibrium, which seems much more dubious. The marginal utility analysis impresses the modern reader as "dated," as important primarily in understanding the development of economic ideas rather than in directly extending his horizons as a scientist. For this reason I shall discuss the marginal utility analysis first, in order to clear the ground for the theory of general equilibrium.

RARETÉ

Walras essentially completes his analysis of the "Theory of Exchange of Two Commodities for Each Other," the title of Part 2 of the *Elements*, before he introduces utility analysis at all. Prior to that point, he has derived demand curves and offer curves, discussed their typical shapes, and considered the meaning of their points of intersection, distinguishing stable from unstable equilibria. These topics are described as revealing the "nature of exchange"; and utility curves are then introduced in order to examine "the cause" of exchange. Similarly, at each successive stage in the analysis—the extension of the theory of exchange of two commodities to several commodities, and the expansion of the system to include successively production, capital formation and credit,[3] and circulation and

[1] *Elements of Pure Economics,* translated by William Jaffé, published for The American Economic Association and the Royal Economic Society. (Homewood, Ill.: Richard Irwin, 1954. Pp. 374.) All subsequent page references not otherwise identified are to this volume.

[2] J. Schumpeter, *History of Economic Analysis* (New York, 1954), p. 827.

[3] As Jaffé remarks, the analysis of utility considerations in connection with the theory of capital formation and credit is in parts "obscure to the point of almost complete incomprehensibility." Jaffé gives an extensive reconstruction in an attempt to render the argument intelligible in his translator's note [2] to Lesson 27 (pp. 536–39). I find it difficult to accept this reconstruction in one important respect, namely, Jaffé's interpretation of the argument as applying to a stationary state and his resulting assignment of an essential role to expenditures on the replacement of capital

money—utility considerations strike the reader as something introduced rather artificially, as being on a different level from the rest of the analysis and capable of being extracted from it bodily without in any way altering its essence—a step that Cassel took in his reformulation of the Walrasian system.

Yet this is clearly not the way it seemed to Walras or to his contemporaries, Jevons and Menger. Today, Walras' primary contribution would surely be regarded as general equilibrium theory, of which at best only pale reflections can be found in Jevons or Menger; yet the three linked themselves together and were linked together by others as the pioneers of "marginal utility." Walras writes as an italicized theorem, "The exchange of two commodities for each other in a perfectly competitive market is an operation by which all holders of either one, or of both, of the two commodities can obtain the greatest possible satisfaction of their wants consistent with the condition that the two commodities are bought and sold at one and the same rate of exchange throughout the market," and goes on to say, "The main object of the theory of social wealth is to generalize this proposition. . . . We may say . . . that this proposition embraces the whole of pure and applied economics" (p. 143).

It is hard now for us to understand why this marginal utility analysis should have been regarded as so vital and revolutionary. We can repeat the formulae of the histories of economic thought that it gave a meaningful solution to the diamond-water paradox and so permitted demand to be assigned its proper role and the shackles of the cost of production or, even worse, labor theory of value to be overthrown. But I do not believe that such formulae carry real conviction or understanding. Partly, this is for the usual reason that an error, once pointed out, seems obvious to those who never held it, though it may have taken a real stroke of genius to discover the error and though simply pointing it out did not make it obvious to those who had the error imbedded in the fabric of their thought. But I suspect the main reason is quite different, namely, the change in our general philosophical and methodological outlook that has been wrought, though by no means directly, by the developments in physical science, in particular, by the replacement of the physics of Newton by the physics of Einstein. Surely this is why a chapter title like that of Lesson 10, "*Rareté*, the Cause of Value in Exchange," strikes us as an anachronism.

The almost purely metaphysical role of *rareté* in Walras is brought out very well by his discussion of measurement:

> The above analysis is incomplete; and it seems impossible, at first glance, to pursue it further, because intensive utility, consid-

---

goods. I am inclined to go to the opposite extreme. It seems to me that Walras here, as elsewhere, thought initially in terms of capital goods that were permanent, required no maintenance or replacement, and gave rise to a permanent flow of services. The question he seems to me to be asking in the section at issue is: given a certain amount of productive power to be used in producing an additional set of permanent capital goods of this kind, what bundle of capital goods will produce the additional stream of consumer goods having the greatest utility. His proof is correct, provided one consistently treats the capital goods as permanent and interprets his differential coefficients or ratios between them as rates of substitution—which seems to me also required in Lesson 26 and to explain what puzzles Jaffé in his translator's note [1] to that lesson (p. 533). The equations labeled [ε] at the bottom of p. 297 are not simultaneously valid; they are alternatives, showing that if (A) is substituted for (T), and all other quantities are unchanged, the quantity of (A) acquired must equal in value the quantity of (T) given up; and so on for every possible pair. That this is intended seems to me even clearer from the wording of earlier editions.

The tendency for Walras to work his argument out initially in terms of permanent capital goods requiring no replacement seems to me to explain also how the difficulty arose which Jaffé deals with in his translator's note [3] to Lesson 27 pp. 539–41). Having arrived at a result for this case, Walras generalized it without full proof to the case of nonpermanent capital goods, in the process making what Jaffé terms—correctly, I believe—a "slip."

ered absolutely, is so elusive, since it has no direct or measurable relation to space or time, as do extensive utility [the quantity that will be taken at a price zero] and the quantity of a commodity possessed. Still, this difficulty is not insurmountable. We need only assume that such a direct and measurable relationship does exist, and we shall find ourselves in a position to give an exact, mathematical account of the respective influences on prices of extensive utility, intensive utility and the initial stock possessed. I shall, therefore, assume the existence of a standard measure of intensity of wants or intensive utility . . . (p. 117).

In a modern writer, one would expect this to be followed by a statement that such an assumption, combined presumably with others, has observable implications of a kind that will enable utility, though "it has no direct or measurable relation to space or time," to be assigned numerical values that are inferred from what are regarded as its manifestations. Walras, of course, does not take this line. He says nothing more on the subject and simply proceeds to take for granted that there is something called *rareté* which has numerical values that can be plotted, averaged, and so on, and can be identified with "satisfaction" in a sense that is relevent for welfare purposes.

In a way, Walras' ready acceptance of the nonmeasurability by physical operations of his *rareté* is somewhat ironical. For, like the other pioneers of marginal utility, he made a subsidiary assumption about utility functions that, if accepted, gives a relatively straightforward method of assigning numbers to utility. Walras throughout assumes that the total utility of a collection of commodities can be written as the sum of functions, each containing as a variable the quantity of only one commodity. Indeed, one gets the impression that it may well have been this feature of his utility function that was to him the main justification for regarding *rareté* as *the* cause of value in exchange; for *rareté*

was "absolute," depending only on the quantity of the one commodity itself, whereas value in exchanging was "relative," the ratio of two such absolutes; and along the same lines, the utility curve for a particular commodity was more fundamental, because a function of only one variable, than the demand function which had to be regarded as depending on several. However, if a consumer's preferences can be validly represented by a sum of one-variable functions, a convenient measuring rod for utility is at hand; one need only take the utility added by some specified unit of one commodity, say the utility added by the tenth slice of bread, as the basic unit, and the utility of all other commodities can be expressed in terms of it— essentially the procedure that both Fisher and Frisch experimented with at a later date.

The reason why this method of measuring utility has not been adopted is, of course, because a utility function consisting of a sum of one-variable functions has implications for consumer behavior that are contradicted by observation, the most striking, perhaps, being the implication that the higher the income of a consumer the more he will consume of every commodity separately, *i.e.*, that there are no inferior goods. Needless to say, Walras does not explore such implications, though he does record the corresponding implication that a demand curve for one commodity is always negatively sloped for given amounts possessed of other commodities (which is equivalent to given money income and other prices). However, he asserts this (on p. 91) prior to introducing his marginal utility analysis, giving little justification for it, apparently because he regarded it as obvious.

One must conclude, I think, that this part of Walras' book has interest almost solely for the student of economic thought. In so far as utility theory plays a role in modern economic analysis, it does so in a more sophisticated, albeit empirically emptier, form than in Walras, though it should perhaps be recorded that there is much current literature that has not advanced beyond Walras in its understanding of the meaning and role of the measurability of utility.

THE THEORY OF GENERAL EQUILIBRIUM

Cournot writes in Chapter 11 of his *Researches,*

> So far we have studied how, for each commodity by itself, the law of demand in connection with the conditions of production of that commodity, determines the price of it and regulates the incomes of its producers. We considered as given and invariable the prices of other commodities and the incomes of other producers; but in reality the economic system is a whole of which all the parts are connected and react on each other. An increase in the income of the producers of commodity A will affect the demand for commodities B, C, etc., and the incomes of their producers, and, by its reaction, will involve a change in the demand for commodity A. It seems, therefore, as if, for a complete and rigorous solution of the problems relative to some parts of the economic system, it were indispensable to take the entire system into consideration. But this would surpass the powers of mathematical analysis and of our practical methods of calculation, even if the values of all the constants could be assigned to them numerically.[4]

It is Walras' great and living achievement to have constructed a mathematical system displaying in considerable detail precisely the interrelationships emphasized by Cournot. Did he thereby show Cournot to be wrong in supposing that the task sur-

passed the powers of mathematical analysis? I believe not. For there is a fundamental, if subtle, difference between the task Cournot outlined and the task Walras accomplished; an understanding of this difference is essential to an assessment of both the positive contribution of Walras and the limitations to that contribution; and failure to recognize the difference seems to me a primary source of methodological confusion in economics. It is clear from Cournot's references to "practical methods of calculation" and to the assignment of numerical values to constants that the "rigorous solution" he had in mind was not a solution "in principle," but a numerical solution to a specific problem. His goal was an analysis that would, given the relevant statistical material, yield specific answers to specific empirical questions, such as the effects of a specified tax on a specified product; answers that could be confronted by observation and confirmed or contradicted. And surely there can be little doubt that a "complete and rigorous solution" of this kind does "surpass the powers of mathematical analysis and of our practical methods of calculation" even today despite the enormous advances in methods of calculation. Cournot was quite right that *for his problem* a "complete and rigorous" solution was out of the question, that the thing to do was, "while maintaining a certain kind of approximation, . . . to carry on . . . a useful analysis."[5]

Walras solved a different, though no less important, problem. He emptied Cournot's problem of its empirical content and produced a "complete and rigorous" solution "in principle," making no pretense that it could be used directly in numerical calculations. His problem is the problem of form, not of content: of displaying an idealized picture of the economic system, not of constructing an engine for analyzing concrete

[4] Augustin Cournot, *Researches into the Mathematical Principles of the Theory of Wealth* 1838), transl. by Nathaniel T. Bacon (New York, 1897), p. 127.

[5] *Ibid.*, pp. 127–28.

problems.[6] His achievement cannot but impress the reader with its beauty, its grandeur, its architectonic structure; it would verge on the ludicrous to describe it as a demonstration how to calculate the numerical solution to a numerically specified set

[6] Walras comments that "when we pass from the realm of pure theory to that of applied theory or to actual practice, . . . the variations in the unknown quantities will be effects of either the first or the second order, that is to say, effects which need or need not be taken into consideration, according as they arise from variations in the special or the general data" (pp. 307-8; see also similar comment on p. 431). In a translator's note, Jaffé cites this sentence as evidence that I "drew too sharp a contrast between Marshall and Walras" in my article "The Marshallian Demand Curve," *Jour. Pol. Econ.* Dec., 1949, LVII, 463–95; reprinted in my *Essays in Positive Economics* (Chicago, 1953), pp. 47–99. He goes on to say, "There one gets the impression that Walras's sole preoccupation was the achievement of 'abstractness, generality and mathematical elegance' (p. 490), while Marshall sought 'an engine for the discovery of concrete truth.' A more valid and important distinction between Walras and Marshall resides in the fact that the former always took great care not to confuse pure theory with applied theory, while the latter gloried in fusing the two" (p. 542).

In his final sentence, Jaffé speaks like a true Walrasian in methodology. One first constructs a pure theory, somehow on purely formal considerations without introducing any empirical content; one then turns to the "real" world, fills in the empty boxes, assigns numerical values to constants, and neglects "second-order" effects at this stage. As I have argued extensively elsewhere [particularly in "The Methodology of Positive Economics" and "Lange on Price Flexibility and Employment: A Methodological Criticism," both in my *Essays,* pp. 3–43, 277–300, the latter reprinted from this *Review,* Sept., 1946, XXXVI, pp. 613–31], this seems to me a basically false view. Without denying the importance of what Jaffé and Walras call "pure theory" (see my comments below), I deny that it is the whole of "pure theory." More important in the present context, two largely parenthetical comments in the *Elements* to the effect that second-order effects will have to be or can be neglected in application seem a rather thin basis on which to claim that Walras was concerned with the construction of "an engine for the discovery of concrete truth." As I argue in the text, I remain of my original opinion; indeed, I am confirmed therein by the careful rereading of Walras to which I was led by the request to write this article, by Jaffé's critical comment, and by similar comments in reviews of my *Essays.*

of equations. The difference is brought out clearly by the further developments along Walras' line that have been—and rightly—regarded as improvements in his system. These have all consisted in making the system still more general and elegant, in eliminating empirically specializing assumptions. The clearest example is, of course, in the theory of production: Walras assumed constant coefficients of production, recognizing that this was an "approximation" and in later editions suggesting the route to generalize the analysis. Pareto generalized Walrus' solution to cover variable as well as constant coefficients of production. The recent reintroduction of the assumption of constant coefficients of production in connection with input-output analysis has not been a further development of Walras' pure theory. It has rather been an attempt—so far largely unsuccessful—to use Walrasian constructs in solving Cournot's problem.

Emphasis on pure form has an important role to play in economics in two rather different respects. One, the easier to specify, is the role of mathematics or pure logic in general, namely, to help us to avoid contradictory statements—to avoid mistakes in arithmetic, as it were. This role is immediately recognized and granted, and for that reason tends to be passed over rapidly; yet it deserves to be emphasized how many, how important, and sometimes how difficult to detect, are the fallacies in economics of this kind; fallacies that consist in the assertion that contradictory statements are simultaneously valid, that we can have our cake and eat it too. The ability to think clearly and exactly is a scarce resource for which, unfortunately there seems no adequate substitute. Walras discussion of bimetallism (Lessons 31 and 32) and of Ricardo's and Mill's theories of rent and wages (Lessons 39 and 40) are excellent examples, largely peripheral to his own general equilibrium theory, of how useful emphasis on pure form can be. By translating vague statements into symbolic form and using very elementary mathematics indeed, Walras is able to clear away much irrelevant material, show that some widely accepted statements are mutually contradictory, and specify the conditions under which others are valid.

The other respect in which emphasis on pure form has an important role to play is in providing a language, a classificatory scheme to use in organizing materials—labels, as it were, for the compartments of our analytical filing box. This is Walras' great contribution. His general equilibrium system gives a bird's-eye view of the economic system as a whole, which has not only an extraordinary aesthetic appeal as a beautifully articulated abstraction but also a utilitarian appeal as providing relevant, meaningful, and mutually exhaustive categories. This bird's-eye view rests fundamentally on two dichotomies: between services and sources of services or between income and capital; and between the markets for consumer services or goods and for productive services or goods. A third dichotomy might almost be added: between entrepreneurs and consumer units, though this seems somewhat less fundamental. Each consumer unit and entrepreneur is conceived as operating in both markets: in terms of markets for services, a consumer unit sells productive services of the capital sources he owns in the resource market and buys consumer services in the consumption market; an entrepreneur buys productive services in the resource market and sells consumer services in the consumption market either directly or indirectly. The distinction between markets thus leads naturally and directly to the distinction between demand and supply.

This classificatory scheme is developed in considerable detail, with extraordinary skill and ingenuity, great attention being devoted to showing, or attempting to show, that it is internally consistent and exhaustive (*i.e.*, that the system of equations has

a solution that tends to be attained and maintained by the operation of market forces). I have described this analysis as involving emphasis on pure form, which I think in a meaningful way it does. Yet I do not mean thereby to imply either that it lacks importance for economics as a substantive science, or that empirical considerations play no role in its construction and use. Quite to the contrary. Walras' picture is not pure mathematics but economics precisely because it was constructed to provide a framework for organizing substantive material of an economic character; the classifications it employs reflect a judgment about the empirically important characteristics of the economic structure; the usefulness of the picture, though not its logical coherence, depends on the extent to which this judgment is confirmed by experience. One cannot read Walras, it seems to me, without recognizing that he was an economist first and a mathematician and logician second; he accomplished what he did not because he was a mathematical genius but despite inferior mathematical equipment—reading the *Elements* gives no reason to doubt the fairness of the examiners who failed him twice in the mathematics examination for entry to the Ecole Polytechnique.[7] In some ways, indeed, "despite" might perhaps be replaced by "because." Walras' necessity to work things out rather cumbrously, from the simplest cases to the more complicated, must have forced him to give much more attention to the economic significance and meaning of his categories than he would have if he had been able to proceed on a still higher level of abstraction. I hasten to add that I do not mean to be urging that bad mathematics is better than good but only that each task requires its own tools. A hand spade may well be better than a

[7] I am indebted for this tidbit to Richard S. Howey, *The Rise of the Marginal Utility School, 1870–1889*, unpublished Ph.D. dissertation at the University of Chicago, 1955.

modern steam shovel for some kinds of work; pure mathematicians are notoriously bad at simple arithmetic.

Though emphasis on form can and does play a vital role in economic analysis, it can also be mischievous if it is not illuminated by empirical judgment and understanding. An excellent example is Walras' utility analysis of savings. This analysis was first introduced into the fourth edition, which appeared in 1900, about a quarter of a century after the first edition. In this edition, Walras yielded to the temptation, which has claimed so many lesser men, of treating "savings" like a consumer good and simply carrying over mechanically the formal analysis applicable to consumer goods. So he defines a commodity (E) consisting of a perpetual net income stream, a unit of (E) being one unit of *numeraire* per unit of time indefinitely, writes down for each individual a marginal utility function for (E), and regards him as possessing a certain quantity of (E) and maximizing his utility subject to a budget constraint which includes expenditures on (E) along with expenditures on other commodities. He regards this process as yielding a demand function for (E) like other demand functions (pp. 274 and 275).

In symbols, this looks like a simple extension of Walras' general analysis and one is led to ask why it was that he did not discover this obvious yet important extension for a quarter of a century. But the moment one digs beneath the symbols and asks why, as economists, we regard it as important to distinguish savings from current consumption, it becomes clear that Walras' procedure is fallacious and involves precisely the kind of confusion between stocks and flows that Walras elsewhere so carefully avoids and indeed underlines. I can perhaps illustrate this best by Walras' utility function for (E) which, in deriving the demand curve, he writes as

$$\Phi_e(q_e + d_e), \qquad (14.1)$$

where q_e is the initial quantity of (E) possessed, d_e, the quantity purchased or sold during the time unit in question. Now q_e and d_e are of different dimensions and cannot be added: q_e is the number of units of (E) that the individual possesses, *i.e.*, the number of units of *numeraire* per unit of time that the individual can receive indefinitely if he so chooses—for simplicity, let us say the number of dollars per year that is yielded by his existing stock of wealth; d_e is the number of dollars per year that he is going to add to this flow as income on the savings he accumulates during the time period in question (see p. 117), say a year, so that savings during that period are $p_e d_e$, where p_e is the price of a dollar a year indefinitely. In other words, q_e is of the dimension of dollars per year; d_e, of the dimension of dollars per year per year. Let the time period in question be half a year instead of a year; the same numerical value of d_e means that he saves twice as large a fraction of his income. q_e and d_e simply cannot be added: an individual will not be indifferent, as Walras' equation implies that he is, between a situation in which he starts with an income of $10,000 a year and adds $100 a year income to it by saving $2,000 during the year in question, which means that the rate of interest is 5 per cent, and a situation in which he starts with an income of $9,700 a year and adds $400 a year to it by saving $8,000 during the year in question. Savings cannot be assimilated directly to current consumption, precisely because their whole function is to provide a stream of consumer services.

In the earlier editions of the *Elements*, Walras made no attempt to derive the demand for savings from utility analysis. He simply wrote down as an empirical datum an individual savings function, and noted, quite correctly, that in order to derive it from utility considerations it would be necessary "to consider utility under a new aspect, distinguishing present utility from future utility." [8] This was no oversight and the change in the fourth edition no belated discovery of a neglected truth. Surely, the explanation must be that when Walras made the change in the fourth edition, he no longer had his system and its meaning and its role in his bones the way he did when he developed it; he was taken in by considerations of pure form; the substance which the form was to represent was no longer part of him. It would be hard to find a better example of the nonsense to which even a great economist can be led by the divorce of form from substance.

CONCLUSION

Walras has done more than perhaps any other economist to give us a framework for organizing our ideas, a way of looking at the economic system and describing it that facilitates the avoidance of mistakes in logic. It is no derogation of this contribution to emphasize that it is not by itself enough for a fruitful and meaningful economic theory; division of labor is appropriate in economic theory too. Economics not only requires a framework for organizing our ideas, it requires also ideas to be organized. We need the right kind of language; we also need something to say. Substantive hypotheses about economic phenomena of the kind that were the goal of

Cournot are an essential ingredient of a fruitful and meaningful economic theory. Walras has little to contribute in this direction; for this we must turn to other economists, notably, of course, to Alfred Marshall.

The large and substantial immediate rewards from Walras' concentration on form; the prestige and intellectual appeal of mathematics; the difficulty of making experiments in economics and the consequent laboriousness and seeming unproductiveness of substantive work devoted to filling in our analytical filing boxes—all these have combined to favor the Walrasian emphasis on form, to make it seem not only an essential part of a full-blown economic theory, but that economic theory itself. This conception—or misconception—of economic theory has helped to produce an economics that is far better equipped in respect of form than of substance. In consequence, the major work that needs now to be done is Marshallian rather than Walrasian in character—itself a tribute to Walras' impact.

I am tempted, in concluding this rather discursive commentary, to paraphrase Mill's comment that "A person is not likely to be a good economist who is nothing else." [9] A person is not likely to be a good economist who does not have a firm command of Walrasian economics; equally, he is not likely to be a good economist if he knows nothing else.

---

[8] Jaffé's Collation of Editions, note [*h*] to Lesson 23, p. 587; my translation from Jaffé's quotation in French.

[9] From *On Comte,* p. 82, as quoted by Alfred Marshall, *Principles of Economics,* 8th ed. (London, 1920), p. 771.

15 Marshall and
the Trade Cycle[1]

J. N. WOLFE

It is generally agreed that Alfred Marshall was more interested in the "normal" equilibrium tendencies of the economy than in its tendency to generate crises and cycles. The main analytical problem of his best-known work, *The Principles of Economics* (1890), is that of price determination and the allocation of resources among alternative uses. It is, however, a misconception of the range of Marshall's theoretical interests to interpret the limited inquiry into the problem of fluctuation found in *The Principles* as indicative of a lack of concern about fluctuation. Marshall not only recognized the possibility of short-run fluctuations in industry and trade; he offered an explanatory hypothesis for these phenomena, a fact which is seldom recognized because only the microeconomic aspects of Marshall's works are widely studied.

How then do the macroeconomic aspects of Marshall's work compare with Keynesian and contemporary inquiries into the problem of fluctuation? The main difference between them appears to be in the role which they conceive short-run changes in the general price level to play in initiating and propagating disturbances. While price changes are the center of Marshall's analysis, Keynes and most contemporary writers view them as having little significance.

In "Marshall and the Trade Cycle," J. N. Wolfe offers several reasons for this shift in emphasis, and asks whether writers on the problem of fluctuation have perhaps gone too far in deemphasizing the role of price changes in explaining changes in the level of economic activity.

Reprinted from J. N. Wolfe, "Marshall and the Trade Cycle," *Oxford Economic Papers*, Vol. 8, February 1956, pp. 90–101. Reprinted by permission of The Clarendon Press, Oxford. J.N. Wolfe is Professor of Economics at the University of Edinburgh.

[1] I have been working on this subject for about five years and am therefore under obligation to a great number of people. I am afraid, however, that this paper will please none of them, and I present it with diffidence as an interim report. My greatest debts are to Professor J. R. Hicks, Dr. F. Cyril James, and Professor Sir Dennis Robertson.
Where I speak of Lord Keynes's work, I refer to his *General Theory of Employment, Interest and Money* (Macmillan, 1936).

Most of those who have discussed the relation of Keynes's *General Theory* with that of his predecessors have concentrated on contrasting the Keynesian theory, considered as a static system, with various 'Classical' static systems. This approach is, no doubt, very useful, but as an assessment of the development of economic thought it seems open to objection. It may be argued that what really interested Keynes was not so much his static model of the economy as a theory of the business *cycle*. And if that is the case, the appropriate comparison is not with a 'Classical' stationary state, but rather with 'Classical' accounts of the trade cycle.[2] This rather obvious difficulty has sometimes been surmounted by suggesting that the existence of a business cycle was not acknowledged by 'classical' writers, or that it was in any case clearly incompatible with their theoretical structures. The simplest way to test such a proposition is, clearly, to examine the work of earlier theorists, and the most obvious case to take is to compare the writings of Marshall on this point with those of Keynes himself. It may therefore seem surprising that one can only find scattered fragments of such a comparison

in the literature of the last twenty years,[3] but there are two very good reasons why that should be so. Firstly, Marshall's observations on the trade cycle are scattered throughout his work, and hidden in the minutes of evidence of several Royal Commissions. Secondly, and more important, those economists who were principally concerned to evaluate the *General Theory* on its first appearance were themselves so familiar with Marshall's work that they saw no reason for any explicit formalization of it, or comparison of it with Keynes's theory. Their attitude was, without doubt, justified at the time. But by now a new generation of economists has grown up, a generation which cannot be assumed to have the same familiarity with Marshall. For that reason alone it appears to me useful to set down the essentials of his views on the cycle, and to compare and contrast them with the views of certain later writers. Such a course seems to be particularly useful because some of the conclusions of this analysis seem to contradict certain widely held beliefs.

We may perhaps summarize certain main points of our analysis:

1. The trade cycle is given explicit and extensive treatment by Marshall.
2. Short-run movements of the general price-level are in Marshall the principal mechanism for the propagation of cyclical disturbances.
3. Keynes and later writers have almost completely ignored the role of price movements in trade-cycle propagation. Some reasons are suggested for the acceptance of this change in attitude, but it is criticized on several grounds.
4. Marshall uses a loanable-funds theory of interest in explaining short-term fluctuations in general prices.
5. The use of the quantity theory of money is reserved by Marshall for a discussion of

---

[2] The *General Theory* was regarded by its author as 'a natural evolution' from the *Treatise on Money* (*General Theory*, p. vi). It is seldom suggested that the latter was anything but an attempt at the development of a theory of the trade cycle, and it seems unreasonable to believe that the *General Theory* differed very much in this respect. Perhaps the chief reason why a different view has commonly been taken is the widespread belief that Keynes intended to provide an analysis appropriate to a period of 'secular stagnation'. But the evidence for this is certainly very limited—one reference in the *General Theory* (pp. 307–8), and a few sentences in two magazine articles written some time later (*Eugenics Review*, Apr. 1937, and *New Republic*, July 1940). I am inclined to the view that even in these places Keynes went no farther than the suggestion that the business cycle might continue to fluctuate about a fairly low average level. I conclude, therefore, that to treat the *General Theory* as no more than a static model is to confuse method with result.

[3] On the interpretation of Marshall's trade-cycle theory, compare and contrast Milton Friedman, *Essays in Positive Economics* (University of Chicago Press, Chicago, 1953), pp. 65–68.

those long-run movements in prices which are not associated with the business cycle.

6. Keynes, in contrast to Marshall, treats the business cycle as though it took place without any expansion of credit.

A central feature of Marshall's account of the course of the trade cycle is his emphasis on movements in the general price-level. When the general price-level is assumed to be stable, as in the *Principles* and the early parts of the *Economics of Industry,* the trade cycle is in abeyance.[4]

Marshall is anxious to distinguish between gradual price movements and those which are more violent. The former have no significant effect upon employment and general prosperity, although they may improve the standard of living of the working man. Violent price changes are far more injurious.[5]

The effects of price movements fall into two chief classes. First of all, some prices are bound to move less quickly than others:

> It however very seldom happens in fact that the expenses which a manufacturer has to pay out fall as much in proportion as the price which he gets for his goods. For when prices are rising, the rise in the price of the finished commodity is generally more rapid than that in the price of the raw material, always more rapid than that in the price of labour; and when prices are falling, the fall in the price of the finished commodity is generally more rapid than that in the price of the raw material, always more rapid than that in the price of labour. And, therefore, when prices are falling the manufacturers' receipts are sometimes scarcely sufficient even to repay him for his outlay on raw materials, wages and other forms of Circulating Capital; they seldom give him in addition enough to pay interest on the Fixed Capital and Earnings of Management for himself.[6]

The second influence of a fall of prices is that it causes business men to expect a further fall, and so to refrain from production.

> Even if the prices of labour and raw materials fall as rapidly as those of finished goods, the manufacturer will lose by continuing production if the fall has not come to an end. He may pay for raw materials and labour at a time when prices generally have fallen by one-sixth; but if, by the time he comes to sell, prices have fallen by another sixth, his receipts may be less than is sufficient to cover his outlay.[7]

Of course, the same thing holds *a fortiori* if production requires the use of borrowed capital. Marshall's famous suggestion for a commodity standard of value was put forward to mitigate this evil.[8] We shall consider this problem in more detail later on.[9]

Marshall was, of course, aware of other factors at work in the trade cycle. The most obvious of these is the effect of growing unemployment in one trade in reducing sales in another and so causing unemployment to spread.[10] But price movements seem almost to stand as prior conditions to such a development.

It has been widely argued that Marshall's account of the determination of the general level of prices is contained in his Quantity Theory of Money. I should like to suggest that, although this may be true for the gradual movements of prices which do *not* affect employment, it is not true for those violent fluctuations of prices which form the key to the trade cycle. In the short run he seems to regard credit expansion or con-

---

[4] Alfred Marshall, *Principles of Economics,* 8th edn. (Macmillan, 1947), pp. 593 and 62 note. See also Alfred Marshall and Mary Paley Marshall, *Economics of Industry* (2nd edn., Macmillan, 1886), pp. 68–69 and 150. A. C. Pigou (Ed.), *Memorials of Alfred Marshall* (Macmillan, 1925), p. 192.

[5] Alfred Marshall, *Official Papers* (Macmillan, 1926), pp. 9 and 20.

[6] *Economics of Industry,* p. 156.

[7] Ibid.

[8] Alfred Marshall, 'Remedies for Fluctuation of General Prices,' *Contemporary Review,* 1887.

[9] In view of the adverse effects postulated for price reductions, it is not altogether easy to defend Marshall's assertion in at least one place that a reduction of wages in the depression might improve employment. It is probable from the context, however, that he has in mind reductions in specific industries in which prices have become relatively high; cf. *Principles,* p. 710.

[10] Ibid., pp. 711–12.

traction as the usual cause of a rise or fall in prices.[11] He even goes so far at one point as to call his description of the trade cycle 'The Ordinary Course of a Fluctuation of Commercial Credit'.[12] This alone would not necessarily argue against the view that the quantity theory was being applied; but the way in which a change in credit affects prices is clearly seen to be through its effect on the interest rate. Such subtlety is far beyond the range of the quantity theory.[13]

The mechanism involved is most easily understood if we consider the way in which an influx of gold by increasing the supply of credit increases prices:

> Equilibrium is found at that rate of interest . . . which equates supply and demand. But next, this equilibrium being established, we set ourselves to enquire what will be the result of a new disturbance, viz. the influx of a good deal of bullion into the City. This does not increase the amount of capital in the strictest sense of the word; it does not increase the amount of building materials, machinery, etc. But it does increase the amount

of command over capital, which is in the hands of those whose business it is to lend to speculative enterprise. Having this extra supply, the lenders lower still more the rate which they charge for loans, and they keep on lowering it until a point is reached at which the demand will carry off the larger supply. When this has been done there is more capital in the hands of speculative investors, who come on the market for goods as buyers, and so raise prices.[14]

The theory here sketched may be said to rely upon the movement of the rate of interest to give an impulse to the trade cycle, and upon the resultant price changes to propagate the movement once it has started. In fact, of course, the impulse will usually be given by some real cause, a war or a good harvest,[15] for example, or by the mere growth or passing away of suspicion among lenders,[16] without any particular change in the rate of interest.[17] This is the basis of the resolution of one of the principal 'paradoxes' of Marshall's monetary theory: whereas a simple theory seems to indicate that interest-rates ought to move up in depression, and down in booms, they operate in the reverse fashion. Marshall's solution of the paradox consists in making the demand for (and supply of) funds move in the appropriate directions under the influence of changing confidence.[18]

It must be noted that the interest mechanism operates not only to give an impulse to the system, but also to give the price fluctuations which propagate that impulse much of their characteristic effect. This can best be appreciated by considering Marshall's use of the 'real rate of in-

---

[11] See *Official Papers*, pp. 21 and 23, and also Alfred Marshall, *Money, Credit and Commerce* (Macmillan, 1924), p. 19 (hereafter *M.C.C.*). But contrast *Official Papers*, p. 285, in which, for once, the expansion of the currency supply is given equal place with credit expansion.

[12] *M.C.C.*, p. 249.

[13] Cf. Knut Wicksell, *Interest and Prices* (London, 1936), p. 76. This account of the matter is, I think, formally compatible with Marshall's assumption that the money balances which individuals were prepared to hold were at any time uniquely determined by the level of money income. Keynes's more subtle account, which makes these balances a function of the rate of interest as well, appears to be mainly useful as an exploration of the varying response of the rate of interest with respect to changes in the quantity of money. Part at least of this difference in outlook of the two writers may be due to the different ways in which they were picturing the money being put into circulation. Marshall is probably thinking of the expansion of bank loans to business, while Keynes has in mind the purchase of government securities by the banking system. The Marshallian assumptions might, however, lay his system open to the charge that a fall in prices might be self-limiting because of the increase in the real value of stocks of wealth. But it is, I think, unlikely that Marshall would have thought this of practical importance in the trade cycle.

[14] *Official Papers*, p. 51.

[15] *M.C.C.*, p. 249.

[16] Or because of an external drain of currency. See *M.C.C.* p. 251. But it may be surprising to readers of Professor Hawtrey that Marshall nowhere, so far as I can discover, attaches any significance to the *internal* drain of gold as a cause of the turning-points. Apparently, therefore, the size of the gold supply does not set a limit to prices *in the short run*. Cf. *Official Papers*, pp. 38–39.

[17] Ibid., pp. 50–51.

[18] Ibid., pp. 273–4.

terest' as an element in his trade-cycle theory.

> When we come to discuss the causes of alternating periods of inflation and depression of commercial activity, we shall find that they are intimately connected with those variations in the real rate of interest which are caused by changes in the purchasing power of money. For when prices are likely to rise, people rush to borrow money and buy goods and thus help prices to rise; business is inflated and is managed recklessly and wastefully; those working on borrowed capital pay back less real capital than they borrowed, and enrich themselves at the expense of the community. When afterwards credit is shaken and prices begin to fall, everyone wants to get rid of commodities, and get hold of money which is rapidly rising in value; this makes credit fall all the faster, and the further fall makes credit shrink even more; and thus for a long time prices fall because prices have fallen.[19]

Superficially, this doctrine seems a straightforward extension of the argument about the depressing effect of price declines to cover entrepreneurs operating with borrowed money. But its force depends upon the implicit assumption that the money rate of interest remains relatively fixed while prices rise or fall. And how can the money rate remain even relatively stable if both borrowers and lenders expect prices to move in the same direction? [20]

Such a situation must arise because the greater willingness of lenders to lend in periods of rising prices (and consequent prosperity) helps to keep the effective money rate of interest from rising sufficiently to keep the real rate stable, and vice versa.[21]

It is interesting to notice that there is implicit in this real rate of interest doctrine a rejection of what some have called the 'classical' interest mechanism.[22] The existence of that mechanism depends upon the

assumption that savings will always appear on the market for securities as soon as they are decided upon, and that no other sources of demand for new securities exist. The fact that lenders may alter their willingness to lend and that credit may be increased or reduced shows that such assumptions do not hold in the Marshallian world. Marshall's doctrine of the rate of interest resembles very closely, in fact, the modern loanable funds theory.

It appears useful at this point to examine the cyclical turning-points more carefully.

> An improvement in credit may have its rise in the opening out of foreign markets after a war, in a good harvest, or in some other definite change; but more often it arises from the mere passing away of old causes of distrust, which had their origin in some previous misfortune or mismanagement. Whatever its origin, when once begun it tends to grow.[23]

In *Money, Credit and Commerce* the cause of the downturn is set out in detail. Here the first step is seen to be the growing desire of lenders to decrease their loans as the boom progresses since they 'are among the first to read the signs of the times'.[24] The fear of lenders may be due to the increasingly unfavourable state of the exchange. 'An adverse movement of the exchange is often both a symptom and a cause of a slackening of the flow of credit.' [25] But whatever the cause of the growing reluctance of lenders to lend,

> the lenders of capital already wish to contract their loans; and the demand for more loans raises the rate of interest very high; distrust increases, those who have lent become eager to secure themselves; and refuse to renew their loans on easy or on any terms. Some speculators have to sell goods in order to pay their debts; and by so doing they check the rise of prices. This check makes all

---

[19] *Principles,* pp. 594–5.
[20] Cf. R. F. Harrod, *Economic Essays* (Macmillan, London, 1952), pp. 227–8.
[21] *M.C.C.,* pp. 249, 250 et seq.
[22] *Principles,* p. 711.

[23] *M.C.C.,* p. 249.
[24] *M.C.C.,* p. 250.
[25] Ibid., p. 251.

other speculators anxious, and they rush in to sell.[26]

The effect of this increase in the discount rate has a considerable role to play in bringing about a downturn, for it is apt to induce at least some bulls to sell out, rather than to carry their stock-exchange holdings over at the higher rate. This might be of little significance by itself, but the fact that bulls are expected to behave that way causes the bears to increase their pressure, and the bulls to become more pessimistic yet. If the market is in a nervous state, the fall in security prices may be appreciable, and may even become cumulative. This has, of course, a tendency to make credit much tighter, and thus to exacerbate a commercial crisis.[27]

So prices begin to fall, and creditors to demand payment at once. This causes some to fail, and 'failure and panic breed panic and failure. The commercial storm leaves its path strewn with ruin.'[28] But— and this is important—

> The immediate *occasion* of a commercial crisis has often been a few business failures, that would have been unimportant if the solid framework of business had not been overlaid by much rather loose credit: but the real *cause* of the crises was not to be found in those small failures. It lay in the slender hold which much credit at the time had on solid foundations.[29]

Finally, a word about the cause of the long continuation of certain periods of depression:

> The chief cause of the evil is a want of confidence. The greater part of it could be removed almost in an instant if confidence could return, touch all industries with her

[26] Ibid., p. 250.
[27] Ibid., p. 258. Marshall does not expand on the effect of changes in stock-exchange prices. Keynes, on the other hand, makes such changes important in two ways: first of all, they change the effective rate of interest at which existing firms can obtain more funds, and, secondly, they change the price at which new enterprises can be sold to the public. See *General Theory*, p. 151.
[28] *M.C.C.*, p. 250.
[29] Ibid., p. 251.

magic wand, and make them continue their production, and their demand for the wares of others.[30]

There is no natural periodicity in Marshall's cycle (in contrast with that of Keynes),[31] but it is clear that each phase is usually, if not always, a natural result of the phase which preceded it.

We are now in a position to contrast the views on the trade cycle of Marshall and Keynes. One thing is clear from the start: whatever differences may exist, they are certainly not over the *possibility* of a trade cycle.

The most obvious difference between these theories is the place which movements of the price-level occupy in them. Keynes's functions are expressed in terms of wage units, i.e. his theory is more or less independent of the price-level.[32] Mar-

[30] *Principles*, p. 710.
[31] *General Theory*, pp. 314 and 317.
[32] Deflating consumption, investment, and income by the wage unit comes to much the same thing as expressing them in real terms, that is, independently of the price-level, under certain quite simple assumptions. Assuming with Keynes that prices move in the same direction and in the same proportion as wages, this holds good whether the wage unit is expressed as a sum of money or as a basket of goods. Of course, in the later parts of his book Keynes drops this assumption and argues that, in so far as each worker is not paid on the basis of efficiency earnings, the employment of less efficient workers will, with constant money wage rates, drive prices up. (We may alternatively say, either that the wage basket is reduced and the level of the variables, expressed in real wage units, is consequently increased, or that the level of the variables expressed in money wage units becomes less than their level expressed in dollars of constant purchasing power.) Such price rises do not, however, have any marked effect on the course of the cycle as sketched by Keynes. They seem to be caused by preceding changes in output, and it is not suggested that they have any considerable role to play in determining subsequent changes, except as outlined in the paragraph below.

The important functions expressed in wage units are the marginal efficiency of capital, the propensity to consume, the supply of money, and the liquidity preference function. The supply curve of labour is, of course, given in money terms, at least before full employment is reached. Keynes makes the propagation of the cycle largely dependent upon shifts in the marginal efficiency of

shall, as we have seen, laid great emphasis upon commodity-price changes as the means by which the cycle was propagated. The great importance attached by Marshall to price fluctuations is certainly characteristic, but it would be a mistake to believe that this attitude was not widely shared. Wicksell made the 'cumulative process' or movement of prices the centre of his work, and justifies this by remarking that when prices fall business is paralysed, and growing unemployment and falling wages result.[33] Keynes was fully aware of the effects on employment of a fall in prices when in 1923 he wrote *A Tract on Monetary Reform*.[34] Professor Robertson, writing in 1926 on *Banking Policy and the Price Level*, saw fit to subtitle his work 'An Essay in the Theory of the Trade Cycle'.[35] And the theme of Professor Hicks's *Value and Capital* is, of course, very similar.[36] It may, in fact, be argued that the concentration upon price movements as basic to the propagation of the trade cycle is sufficiently important to set these writers off as a separate school of neo-classical business-cycle theory.

A consideration of the factors which may have made such an *approach* unfashionable does much to show why it is reasonable to regard Keynes's major revolution as the development of a theory to explain how the level of economic activity might change *without* any appreciable change in the commodity price-level. These factors are quite varied, but may be summarized under four headings:

Theoretical

Price changes were for a long time the only ones which could be definitely established as features of the trade cycle. The figures for output and employment were, until well into the present century, both sketchy and unreliable. It seems to be a characteristic of theoretical reasoning that it is usually directed to the provision of explanations for phenomena that are known beyond any doubt. So when output and employment variations became subject to easy measurement it was only natural for theory to take a new direction.

Factual

It seems probable that with the growth of trade unions and the solidification of trade associations the movement of prices at less than full employment levels of output has become less pronounced. At any rate the fluctuations of employment and output must have seemed (in the period of the thirties at any rate) to have become *relatively* more pronounced, and to warrant a shift in the emphasis of theory. To this consideration must be added the fact that later experience seemed to indicate that, in the early stages of an upswing at least, output tends to grow before prices rise very considerably. So that for this stage of the cycle at least, a price-orientated theory is clearly undesirable.

Other Developments in Theory

As long as value theory was organized on the basis of industries and an industry price under more or less perfect competition, it was only natural that changes in output should be regarded as dependent on previous price changes. As soon, however, as the development of theories of imperfect

capital schedule due rather to the sudden changes of mood on the stock exchange and changes in the real factors influencing investment than to expected price changes. There is, however, one major exception to this rule. On p. 317 of the *General Theory* Keynes indicates that the rising cost of production of capital goods may provide firm ground for the sudden reversal of the stock exchange's views on the future which tends to characterize the downturn.

[33] Wicksell, op. cit., p. 2.

[34] Reprinted in J. M. Keynes, *Essays in Persuasion* (Rupert Hart-Davis, London, 1951), p. 101.

[35] D. H. Robertson, *Banking Policy and the Price Level* (P. S. King & Son, London, 3rd impression, revised, 1932).

[36] J. R. Hicks, *Value and Capital* (Oxford, 1939).

and monopolistic competition focused attention on the elasticity and position of each firm's particular demand curve, this assumption was no longer logically satisfactory. It has almost certainly been the case that the ease with which the theory of imperfect competition can be integrated with Keynes's approach has helped increase the popularity of the latter. It seems, however, from the lack of explicit reference to this problem, almost equally certain that this aspect of Keynes's system was an entirely accidental (or perhaps unconscious) development.

Organization of the Theoretical Structure

So far the factors we have advanced are fairly substantial in nature. It may be, however, that even more influence must be attributed to Keynes's desire to change the organization and approach of business-cycle theory. Marshall was content to divide his theory into two parts, one dealing with an economy having a stable price-level, the other with one without it. By assuming the relative stability of the rate of interest expressed in money terms (the variability of the real rate of interest) he causes the latter system to produce unemployment and reduce output. Keynes, on the other hand, can be conceived of as approaching the whole problem from the side of the theory of money. By showing the radical flaw in the mechanism for establishing the rate of interest which makes it insensitive to current business influences, he establishes the possibility of variations in effective demand. From that point it is not far to the division of the theory into two parts, one assuming full employment, the other under-employed resources. The principal difference between these two alternative forms of organization is the policy prescriptions that leap to mind in examining them: in the one case the stabilization of prices, perhaps by an accounting formula, in the other measures designed to increase the volume of effective demand directly.[37]

There is some reason to believe that the reaction against price orientation has gone too far. After all, commodity prices do usually move during the cycle, and an ideal theory ought to give due weight to this fact. It is interesting to notice that Marshall's system, as we have expounded it, bears a striking resemblance to that of Professor Hicks in *Value and Capital*. The former relies, however, upon an elasticity of expectations which is greater than unity, while the latter concentrates attention on the case of unit elasticity. Because he does so, Professor Hicks is prevented from making the anticipation of future price changes a cause of unemployment. He is instead forced to place all his emphasis upon the effects of sticky wages in causing a substitution away from labour and towards other factors. But Professor Hicks has not explained how such substitution could reach significant proportions in the short run.

Marshall's implied assumption that the elasticity of expectations is greater than unity throws some very revealing light on modern developments in trade-cycle theory. Because of this assumption, Marshall had no difficulty in explaining how an upward or downward movement, when once it had started, could go on and gather force. In fact, on this assumption, the real problem is how to explain the fact that such movements eventually slacken and even reverse themselves.

Now one of the reasons which has been advanced for using modern multiplier-accelerator theories of the trade cycle is that they provide a convenient account of this cumulative process.[38] It can be seen,

[37] Cf. the remarkable scheme proposed by Mr. Harrod, who seems here to have gone back to a Marshallian approach. R. F. Harrod, *Towards a Dynamic Economics* (Macmillan, London, 1949), pp. 161–9.

[38] J. R. Hicks, *A Contribution to the Theory of the Trade Cycle* (Oxford, 1949).

however, that no matter how much it may add to our knowledge, the acceleration principle is not *necessary* to the *existence* of a cumulative process. It only becomes so if there are no price changes, or if the elasticity of expectations is less than unity. We need not, then, *rely* on the action of the accelerator except as an auxiliary force moving us up (or, on some accounts, down) in the cycle. This consideration appears to be important when we remember the objections of those practical people who regard the value of the accelerator as in any case too low to produce the desired effect.[39]

The field of employment of the accelerator could, then, easily be restricted to the explanation of the turning-points of the cycle, and more particularly the upper turning-point. The foregoing discussion appears, moreover, to open up a whole new set of possible explanations for a downturn, especially if we regard price expectations as themselves dependent to some extent on the level of investment and the rate of growth of economic activity. For example, a boom might be killed because price expectations ceased for some reason (say, a decrease in the rate of growth of income) to be elastic, and because the accelerator mechanism was not then able by itself to support the upswing.

This reduced emphasis on the accelerator is made more acceptable because of another change in trade-cycle theory. At one time the accelerator was thought essential because it could explain the greater relative amplitude of the fluctuations in investment goods industries. Nowadays, the peculiar shape and relative stability of the consumption function is often regarded as sufficient explanation of this phenomenon.[40]

From another point of view the accounts of Marshall and of Keynes stand together in contrast with much recent theory of the trade cycle. Both of these writers emphasize the volatility of expectations and the importance of confidence on the course of the trade cycle. More recently, it has become fashionable to minimize the importance of such elements, and to rely instead on certain 'real' forces which the cycle is itself said to generate. It is not easy to explain this change in opinion, but it may be that it is partly the result of a growing belief in the regular periodicity of the trade cycle. Perhaps of equal importance is the greater opportunity such non-psychological factors seem to offer to econometric testing. This may possibly be regarded (*pace* Professor Samuelson) as an interesting (if wrong-headed) result of the growing demand for having theories cast in an 'empirically meaningful' form!

An important point in which Marshall's theory appears to differ from that of Keynes's is in the role which credit plays in their account of the cycle. For Marshall the expansion and contraction of credit is a central feature of the cycle. It is itself almost a necessary condition for the price movements which are the immediate causes of cyclical fluctuations of employment. But in the *General Theory* the creation of credit plays a much smaller role in causing the cycle. It is the change, or the expected

---

[39] J. Tinbergen, 'Statistical Evidence on the Acceleration Principle,' *Economica* (N.S.), 1938, pp. 164–76.

[40] It is interesting to notice that Marshall does not blame the principle of acceleration for the fact that fluctuations are apt to be greatest in capital goods industries. It is the fact that credit is used for expansion, and that credit restriction (or a mere cessation of the growth of credit) will

reduce this expansion, which appears to be crucial. This is only one aspect of a tendency to place a good deal of weight on the effect of changes in the supply of capital.

'For while credit is expanding, the extra purchasing power which credit gains goes chiefly to trades and trading companies, who, whether they want it to begin or extend their business, are sure to spend a great part of it on machinery, buildings, ships, railway material, and other forms of Fixed Capital. On the other hand, where credit is contracting, many find their means of purchasing altogether cut off, while those whose means are not straitened do not care to invest in Fixed Capital until they think prices have nearly reached their turning point.' (*Economics of Industry*, p. 163.)

change, in profitability which causes changes in the amount of investment. The money market does not, apparently, offer any resistance to such a change in investment. The rate of interest may indeed be affected, but only as the result of a change in the amount of money required for transaction purposes, a change which can, by hypothesis, come about only *after* the change in activity brought about by the change in investment has had time to manifest itself. Keynes's later introduction of 'finance'—the money required to bridge the gap between the planning and execution of investment decisions—goes some way to restore the importance of credit expansion in the theory of the trade cycle. Yet he does not stress the fact that since the saving engendered by investment may be done by people different from those who perform the investment, the intercession of the banking system may be necessary to sustain even relatively stable interest rates. This is because money may be held as a form of savings, as well as for transaction purposes, and therefore the demand for it may increase much more than in proportion to income as savings rise. It is almost as though Keynes were attempting to show that a trade cycle is *possible* without any creation of new money. If that were his intention, there is no doubt that he has succeeded (given certain assumptions about the speculative demand for cash balances). But it may be asked whether our knowledge of the *usual* course of the cycle has been much increased.

That Keynes himself believed in the importance of the separation of trade-cycle theory from a theory of monetary expansion is, I believe, borne out by his later reflections on his own work. He seems to imply in one place that the great novelty of his theory lies in the assertion that the equality of saving and investment frees economic expansion from the limitations sometimes thought to be characteristic of an appeal to the money market.[41]

These limitations were thought to be due to the inability of credit creation to call forth real savings to support the investment decisions which it facilitated. In slightly differing forms this appears to be the basis of both the so-called 'Treasury View'— that a public works programme would only result in the diversion of investment from one sector to another—and of the view that the crisis was due to the ephemeral nature of credit-induced 'forced saving.' But these objections are not Marshallian. In opposing them Keynes made no break with traditional Cambridge theory.

There are, of course, many more points of difference between Marshall and Keynes. One could mention the role of the stock exchange, the assumptions about the effects of wage cuts, and so on. I suspect, however, that an expedition into such well-mapped territory is unlikely to add very much to our present knowledge.

[41] J. M. Keynes, 'Alternative Theories of the Rate of Interest,' *Economic Journal*, vol. xlvii (1937), pp. 248–50.

16 Institutionalism and American Economic Theory: A Case of Interpenetration[1]

FRITZ KARL MANN

The analytical tools, concepts, and laws with which phenomena, economic or otherwise, are explained, comprise the "science" of a discipline. To study the history of a science is primarily to investigate the additions and refinements which successive generations have made to its substantive content. But this study is, of necessity, also concerned with the methodology or philosophy which underlies theoretical speculation and becomes embodied in its substantive content. The influence of philosophy on content is subtle; so subtle, in fact, that controversy about methodology seems usually to arise within a broader context, which also involves controversy about the substantive content of a discipline. The American Institutionalist movement is an example of this kind of dual intellectual controversy.

Although the American Institutionalist movement to reconstruct economic science is a development of the present century, contemporary students are generally less well-acquainted with its basic tenets than they are with those of the historically much older classical and neoclassical schools against which the revolt was directed. One is scarcely aware of the intellectual orientation within which the economic heterodoxy of Veblen, Commons, Mitchell, and their younger disciples developed in the micro- and macro-economic principles on which the present generation is typically nurtured. It is likely that few students fully appreciate the possibility, contemplated by Fritz Karl Mann, that Institutionalism has survived via interpenetration, that is, by having been absorbed into the fabric of current economic inquiry. This student deficiency may perhaps be partially alleviated by reviewing briefly the origin and scope of the reconstruction which Veblen and his fellow critics of economic orthodoxy conceived to be necessary.

The intellectual orientation of this group of thinkers seems the most appropriate starting point because it penetrates the root of their quarrel with the classical and neoclassical school. Nineteenth and early twentieth century academic economic thought

Reprinted from Fritz Karl Mann, "Institutionalism and American Economic Theory: A Case of Interpenetration," *Kylos*, Vol. 13, 1960, pp. 307–322. Dr. Mann is Professor of Economics at the American University of Washington, D.C.

[1] The author is indebted to Professor Goetz A. Briefs of Georgetown University, Washington, D.C., for useful suggestions.

in the United States, as in England, was premised on the eighteenth-century conception of a natural order whose functioning was thought to manifest itself in relatively few unchanging universal propositions or laws. The Institutionalists rejected this Newtonian *Weltanschauung* and adopted, in its stead, an antimechanistic view of the world order predicated on the thinking of Herbert Spencer and Charles Darwin. Because their biologically-oriented conception envisaged the world order as a process or continuum, rather than as a stable mechanism, it nurtured inquiry into phenomena of change instead of focusing on equilibrium economics.

The hedonistic psychology of orthodox thinkers, which conceived of individual behavior as being rational and maximizing, was equally inconsistent with the Institutionalist's view of the economic order as an organism in which an ongoing evolutionary process took place. The Institutionalists favored a sociopsychological view of the individual which made him part of the collective whole. Concern with the whole was likewise reflected in the substitution of a total or overall approach to the functioning of the economy, as opposed to the atomistic approach so much in evidence in neoclassical price theory. Thus, the Institutionalists recommended that the traditional boundaries of economics be disregarded and that other disciplines, particularly psychology and sociology, be drawn upon for information and insights which traditional economics is incapable of providing.

The finished product of this revolution was to be a cultural, pragmatic science, as opposed to the formal pure theory derived from deductive analysis. Since this product never fully emerged, contemporary commentators on the present state of Institutional economics are, perhaps, quite right in thinking of the movement as moribund. And yet, there is much of Institutionalism that has survived as a result of the process of interpenetration. The following article by Professor Mann, "Institutionalism and American Economic Theory: A Case of Interpenetration," identifies some of the areas in which this process appears to have taken place.

At the threshold of the 20th century, American Institutionalism made its successful debut as an independent school of thought. Although neither its exaggerations nor its contradictions were overlooked, the system was received with a rising wave of sympathy. It appealed to professional economists who had grown impatient with the sophisticated and abstract message of Neo-Classicism and were looking for a short-cut to a "realistic" science. It appealed especially to that group of economists who by congeniality or education leaned towards German Historism. Many of them were convinced that Karl Marx was the stormy petrel of Institutionalism, that Historism was another move, although too timid, in the same direction, and that American Institutionalists could refer to Max Weber and Werner Sombart as their active supporters.[2] The future predominance of the system in the USA seemed assured for intellectual as well as practical reasons. The approach of the Institutionalists was in line with American trends in philosophy and political ideology. The new principles could be applied to pressing economic and social needs and, as some of their proponents anticipated, would eventually be integrated into an organon of public policy. Institutionalism also gratified national pride as the only school of economic thought with an uncontested American birth certificate.

Since its formative years, however, the prestige of Institutionalism has considerably declined. If present American economists should be asked by a Gallup poll to state their relation to schools of thought, most of them would decline to be distinguished as Institutionalists. They would prefer to be linked with economic theorists, mathematical economists, econometricians, empiricists, economic planners, or with that large, amorphous, and unreliable group,

[2] See Abram L. Harris, "Types of Institutionalism," *Journal of Political Economy*, Vol. XL (1932), pp. 721–749.

euphemistically termed eclectics. Many writers like to say that Institutionalism has run its course.[3] As Eric Roll discreetly put it, Institutionalism is "almost completely dead." [4] Even the cause of its agony has been ascertained. According to Frank H. Knight, Institutionalism was "largely drowned by discussion of the depression, or perhaps boom and depression, and especially by the literature of the Keynesian revolution." [5]

We may wonder, however, whether the time for obituaries has yet arrived. A more sceptical attitude could seem pertinent for the following reasons:

(1) At no time was Institutionalism an integrated whole like Physiocracy, Classicism, Marginalism, or Marxism. From its start it was fragmentary, contradictory, and torn by dissensions.
(2) Only rarely in history have theoretical systems and ideologies preserved their initial purity over several generations. Regularly their substance has been mixed with other ingredients—sometimes so effectively as to prevent identification. Did such a process of adjustment and amalgamation play a significant role in the experience of Institutionalism?
(3) We need hardly mention that neo-classical theory has shifted positions; perhaps it shifted more radically during the past few decades than Classicism did in the course of an entire century. Were those shifts caused by the sparks kindled in the camp of the Institutionalists? Or, to go beyond this point, did institutionalist ideas infiltrate the territory of Neo-Classicism?

If all our questions were answered in the affirmative, we would face a typical case of interpenetration.

Evidently those possibilities range too far over the entire field of economics to be fully explored in a brief essay. No attempt can be made to present any full documentation, but some tentative conclusions may be reached.

To prevent customary misunderstandings, I begin with a few comments on the diversification of institutional thought.

PATTERNS OF INSTITUTIONALISM

Its first architects, Thorsten B. Veblen and John Rogers Commons, provided Institutionalism with a roof broad enough to shelter several scientific structures. In addition, the ambiguity of its name spread confusion. It has played some part in stirring up family quarrels. Like some other economic terms, the word "institution" has been used with extreme inconsistency. Generally, the Institutionalists were agreed on one point only: to consider institutions not merely as a background, but as *"dramatis personae"* in the economic play of forces.[6] However, the task of identifying those actors was left to the vision of the individual author.

Here a first conflict arose between the co-founders. When Veblen chose to call his system "Institutionalism," he conceived of institutions as accustomed ways of doing and thinking, "habits of action and thought widely current in a social group." Commons rejected this notion as summarily as all other conventional concepts. When he proudly submitted the first comprehensive treatise bearing the name "Institutional Economics," [7] he insisted that institutions did not signify exogenous conditions of economic activities "analogous to a building, a sort of framework of laws and regulations, within which individuals act like in-

[3] See for example, John M. Ferguson, *Landmarks of Economic Thought,* 2nd ed., New York 1950, p. 260; John Fred Bell, *A History of Economic Thought,* New York 1953, p. 566.

[4] Eric Roll, *A History of Economic Thought,* 3rd ed., New York 1956, p. 453.

[5] Frank H. Knight, "Institutionalism and Empiricism in Economics," *American Economic Review,* Vol. XLII, No. 2 (May 1952), p. 45 (Papers and Proceedings).

[6] William Jaffé in the debate on "Economic Theory and Institutionalism" at the meeting of the American Economic Association in 1930 (*American Economic Review,* Vol. XXI, No. 1, Supplement, March 1931, Papers and Proceedings, p. 138).

[7] John R. Commons, *Institutional Economics: Its Place in Political Economy,* New York 1934.

mates." Nor should they be defined as in Veblen's work, as "the 'behavior' of the inmates themselves."[8] Commons wavered, however, in taking a final stand. Sometimes he identified institutions with the activities of organizations, sometimes defined them as all types of transactions brought together in a larger unit of economic investigation. Those units of investigation were described also as "Going Concerns." In any case, "Going Concerns" were identical with "institutions." Commons conceded, of course, that organizations or units of economic investigation differed in structure and functions. They embraced the family, the corporation, the trade union, the trade association, and the State itself. On the contrary, all of those institutions were engaged in "collective action"—and "collective action," in its turn, was to Commons the central theme of economic theory. In other words, collective action was related to the "Going Concern" rather than to the social group. As Commons drastically put it, the passive concept was the "group," the active concept the "Going Concern." With this limitation, institutional economics could be described as a "science of activity"[9] or "a theory of the human will" or "a system of volitional economics."

Veblen's and Commons' systems differed equally in method and scope of scientific inquiry. In his challenge to Neo-Classicism, Veblen insisted that economics should be transformed into a genuine evolutionary science. He postulated that economic activities represented an unfolding process of life, and he analyzed institutions in the light of Darwinism. We thus call his system *Darwinian Economics.*

Since Veblen wished to transform economics into a natural and evolutionary science, he dismissed idealistic philosophy, abstract premises, and static analysis. Concentrating on habits of thought and action,

he derived his findings partly from behavioristic psychology and partly from cultural history and anthropology.

Although Commons' version bore an identical name and was equally considered as a challenge to orthodox thought, it differed from Veblen's system in philosophy, substance, and purpose. Commons discarded again the natural science approach and, more particularly, the Darwinian concept of evolution. He leaned heavily on pragmatic philosophy, though he labored in vain to free himself from the eggshell of metaphysics. To him, scientific inquiry was no end in itself. Contrary to Veblen's "Olympian detachment,"[10] he considered economic studies as a means for securing economic progress and social welfare. Therefore his system—which I characterize as *Pragmatic Economics*—reached its climax in presenting a guide to "collective action."[11] And collective action was to result in "collective control." These terms, however, were used with remarkable sophistication. They did not suggest any need for "overall dirigism." Although—as Commons declared—collective action served to control individual action, it was "literally the means to liberty."[12] If all social groups would pursue their egoistic interests (which, in Commons' view, was legitimate) permanent economic struggle, if not chaos, was inevitable. He suggested, therefore, that opposing interests should be reconciled by collective action. Such a policy would provide for economic liberty, economic growth, and social progress.

Finally, in contrast to Veblen, Commons did not think of Institutionalism as the heir presumptive of the orthodox school. Limited in scope as it was, it could not replace a science that had covered all aspects

---

[8] *Ibid.,* p. 69.
[9] John R. Commons, *The Economics of Collective Action,* New York 1950, p. 34.

[10] John Maurice Clark, *Economic Institutions and Human Culture,* New York 1957, p. 57.
[11] Therefore Common's last treatise which he had left untitled was by its editor: *The Economics of Collective Action* (New York 1950).
[12] *Ibid.,* p. 35.

of economic life. Institutionalism cultivated a major province of economics, but left the remainder to a more conventional scheme that deserved the traditional name "Political Economy."

The two institutional patterns, Darwinian and Pragmatic Economics, had been barely completed when a loosely knit group of economists, claiming to represent "the younger generation"[13] overhauled their foundations. Guiding spirit of the group was Wesley G. Mitchell (1874–1948); among his associates were Walton H. Hamilton, Frederic C. Mills, Rexford Guy Tugwell, Morris A. Copeland, Gardiner C. Means, Clarence E. Ayres, and Arthur F. Burns. These revisionists proceeded by elimination as well as by supplementation. The Darwinian concept of evolution, the role of irrational motivation, the idea of collective action, and other paraphernalia of the earlier versions were either de-emphasized or eliminated. Only a few members of the group stressed the impact of legal systems and practices as much as Commons did. Nor did they blend economic theory with economic sociology as fully as Veblen had suggested. Equally significant was their mellowing of the former anti-theoretical position. Finally, "the younger generation" supported enthusiastically some political and social objectives of their time. They joined forces with modern "welfare economists" and actively participated in public life.

So the tree of American Institutionalism burst into a third blossoming, more exuberantly than its earlier blooms. For the lack of a better name, I suggest referring to it as *Neo-Institutionalism.*[14]

SHIFTS IN NEO-CLASSICAL POSITIONS

The rapprochement of the rival schools was mutual. I turn first to those areas in which neo-classical theorists, partly under the spell of the Keynesian revolution, have made major concessions.

In the past few decades, for example, macro-economics has emerged as a pre-eminent, if not vital, subject of the theoretical inquiry. In so far, neo-classical theorists now concur with the views held by their former adversaries. This does not imply that the aggregative approach was of equal significance for all patterns of Institutionalism. Neither Veblen nor Commons were its leading exponents. Veblen, of course, showed some interest. In his later years, he suggested current surveys of available physical resources as a tool of total planning. Yet those surveys, termed "organizational tables," were conceived in too primitive a fashion to be useful as a point of departure.[15] More consistently, Mitchell and his group relied on the aggregative approach. If, as they believed, economics was a genuine social science it was primarily concerned with mass phenomena. These in turn, could be best disclosed by a study of aggregates.[16]

Equally significant was another shift in the camp of the theorists; a shift from the search for economic laws to the short-run analysis. This shift, too, was intensified, if not initiated, by the Keynesian revolution. We shall deal with it more explicitly in the following section.

The two rival schools have been pulling together in a third controversial field. From their early beginnings, Institutionalists conceived of economic change or of cumulative

---

[13] Rexford Guy Tugwell, for instance, called his representative symposium: *The Trend of Economics* (New York 1924), "a manifesto of the younger generation." (Introduction, p. IX.)

[14] For a supplement of this section, see my article "Wirtschaftstheorie und Institutionalismus in den Vereinigten Staaten," in *Die Einheit der Sozialwissenschaften, Franz Eulenburg zum Gedächtnis,* ed. by Wilhelm Bernsdorf and Gottfried Eisermann, Stuttgart 1955, pp. 201–213.

[15] Th. B. Veblen, "Memorandum on a practicable Soviet of Technicians," reprinted in his collection of essays: *The Engineers and the Price System,* New York 1921, pp. 138–169.

[16] Wesley C. Mitchell, "Quantitative Analysis in Economic Theory," Presidential Address to the American Economic Association (1924), reprinted in *The Backward Art of Spending Money,* New York 1937, pp. 22–36.

change as the foremost theme of their science. Also here, neo-classical positions have been shifted. Questions of economic expansion, economic development, or economic growth loom too paramount in our time to deserve a second place. Probably no technical term has been used by professional economists of this generation as enthusiastically (and ambiguously) as the term "economic growth." At the same time, the conventional distinction between Statics and Dynamics has become somewhat blurred. As we gather from a recent study of economic semantics, both learned terms show a "truly kaleidoscopic variety of meanings." [17] Apparently, Paul A. Samuelson was right in his caustic remark some time ago that those two technical terms have been used as synonyms for good and bad, realistic and unrealistic, simple and complex: "We damn another man's theory by terming it static, and advertise our own by calling it dynamic." [18]

Also the Neo-Institutionalists must be credited with having expedited a final compromise on this issue. They debunked the Darwinian concept of evolution. They regarded it as a liability rather than an asset of their new economics and stressed both its empirical and its philosophical deficiencies. The Darwinian concept of evolution—they thought—contradicted experience in the realms of economic and social life. While institutions changed rapidly, biological evolution was infinitely slow. Furthermore, economic Darwinism meant a relapse into metaphysics or, as Mitchell put it, "a sort of theology." [19] Nevertheless the school has continued to speak of economic evolution

as a synonym of economic development, without any biological connotation. [20]

Pragmatism and Relativism

Other affinities of the two rival schools rest, to a large extent, on some common philosophical convictions. Both Neo-Classicists and Neo-Institutionalists have been anointed with a large dose of pragmatic oil. They are looking for theories that can "work." Most of them would accept William James' well known dictum: that the two phrases—that an idea or belief was useful because it was true and that an idea or belief was true because it was useful—meant exactly the same thing: that here was an idea that had been fulfilled and could be verified. [21]

Therefore most economists were inclined to forego any search for "natural" laws. Theories that can work do not need to be absolutely true. They are valid in the future only if all relevant economic and social data will remain the same. Broadly speaking, pragmatism is based upon a "relativity concept of truth." Consequently economic research reaches its climax in subjecting theories to an "applicability test." After having passed such a test, theories are regarded as fit to be transmuted into economic and social practice. [22]

In this way, the pragmatic creed provided the economist with a simple device for selection. Thus, for instance, Morris A. Copeland declared, economic theories should enable one to say *a priori* what he expected to find under certain specific

[17] Fritz Machlup, "Statics and Dynamics: Kaleidoscopic Words," *Southern Economic Journal*, Vol. XXVI, No. 2 (October 1959), pp. 91–110.

[18] Paul A. Samuelson, Foundations of Economic Analysis, Cambridge (Mass.) 1947, p. 311.

[19] Wesley C. Mitchell, "The Prospects of Economics," in *The Trend of Economics*, New York 1924, p. 26, and his letter of August 9, 1928 to John Maurice Clark, in *Wesley Clair Mitchell: The Economic Scientist*, New York 1952, pp. 93–99.

[20] More recently Albert O. Hirschman suggested segregating the two terms of development and growth by applying the first to underdeveloped and the second to economically advanced countries. (*The Strategy of Economic Development*, New Haven 1958, p. 29.)

[21] William James, *Pragmatism: A New Name for Some Old Ways of Thinking*, London 1907, p. 204.

[22] See, for instance, Joseph J. Spengler's remarks at the debate of the American Economic Association in 1930, *loc. cit.*, p. 137.

conditions, of course, "within the limits of accuracy of the generalization." Inversely, the economist is committed to strike off the roster of valid notions any theory that is contradicted by experience.[23] Since, however, the social and economic environment is in permanent flux, theories that were right in the past must be expected to be wrong at a later time; and vice versa.

At this point, various writers made significant reservations. They still stuck to their right to more lasting generalizations since, as they contended, relevant economic or social data should be taken *sub specie naturae humanae.* Wesley C. Mitchell, for one, was convinced that human nature has remained substantially the same over the millenniums.[24] This position, however, was challenged by those who—like Clarence E. Ayres—insisted that there was no such thing as the original nature of men. "Except for the organic functions which man shares with other animals, man is a creature of society. The content of human behavior is a cultural content.[25]

Even if we disregard those and similar platitudes, neo-institutionalistic views on this subject still do not strike us as original. Long ago, relativism and scepticism gained a foothold in economics. They inspired the recurrent attacks on the validity of economic laws, which reached a climax in the era of historism. Hildebrand spoke of "abstract cosmopolitism,"[26] Knies more contemptuously of "absolutism of theory."[27]

Following both writers, any institution or policy that in a previous setup hampered the well-being of the human race could become a boon to society in the case of a change of material or nonmaterial conditions. Economic theory should claim only "relative truth." Therefore the search for immutable natural laws should be abandoned. As later the English historical economist William James Ashley proclaimed, political economy was not "a body of absolute true doctrines," but "a number of more or less valuable theories and generalizations." [28]

As in similar cases, however, the absence of novelty in the institutionalistic approach did not interfere with its wide appeal. Apparently, economic relativism is endorsed by the great majority of American economists. Its impact has been enhanced by its affiliation with pragmatic philosophy. Still we should notice that a similar trend prevails in some countries abroad. We refer to two closely related contributions; first, to Spiethoff's concept of the sequence of "economic styles," each of which requires its own valid system of economics; second, to Neumark's propositions recently advanced in this journal that, in order to be "general," economic theories should explain "normal phenomena" in a "predominant economy"; and that they must be revised *pari passu* with its structural changes and, of course, must be overhauled if a new "predominant economy" should emerge.[29]

EXPLANATORY HYPOTHESES

The concessions of the Neo-Classicists vis-à-vis Pragmatism and Relativism have

[23] Morris A. Copeland, *Facts and Theory in Economics: The Testament of an Institutionalist,* ed. by Chandler Morse, Ithaca, New York, 1958, p. 38.

[24] Wesley C. Mitchell, "Quantitative Analysis in Economic Theory," *loc. cit.,* p. 30.

[25] Clarence E. Ayres, *The Industrial Economy: Its Technological Basis and Institutional Destiny,* Boston 1952, p. 28.

[26] Bruno Hildebrand, *Die Nationalökonomie der Gegenwart und Zukunft,* 1848; republished with other of his articles under the title: *Die Nationalökonomie der Gegenwart und Zukunft und andere gesammelte Schriften,* Jena 1922, pp. 22–23.

[27] Karl Knies, *Die politische Ökonomie vom Standpunkt der geschichtlichen Methode,* Braun-

schweig 1853, p. 19. See also Wilhelm Roscher, *Grundriss zu Vorlesungen über die Staatswirtschaft nach geschichtlicher Methode,* Göttingen 1843, pp. IV–V.

[28] William James Ashley, *An Introduction to Economic History and Theory,* 11th impression, London 1923, pp. X–XI (Preface).

[29] Fritz Neumark, "Gedanken zur Allgemeinheit der Wirtschaftstheorie," *Kyklos,* Vol. XII, 1959, Fasc. 3, pp. 472–491.

been matched by concessions of the Neo-Institutionalists with regard to the use of generalizations. Although emotional pronouncements against abstract reasoning are still widely acclaimed, economic theory was permitted to establish, so to speak, several bridgeheads within institutionalistic territory. To elaborate on those developments, we must start with some commonplace observations.

No empiricist, of course, can explore a mountain of facts and figures without knowing in advance what he is looking for.[30] To identify his subject, to evaluate its significance, and to make economic behavior plausible, he relies on a conceptual framework. In so far, successful empirical research depends on economic theory; or, more specifically, on notions not derived from experience. Following Mitchell's terminology, the economist should embark on "analytic description."[31] Also Mitchell's successor Arthur F. Burns, though using institutionalistic verbiage, stressed the complementarity of empirical work and conceptual reasoning: "Like the formal theorist, the realistic investigator must have the ability to formulate economic concepts and to think through economic relations precisely."[32]

More debatable, however, was another concession of the Neo-Institutionalists: their reliance on economic theory in its capacity of a heuristic principle or an "as-if proposition." Occasionally, this concession has been belittled on the ground that the use of "explanatory hypotheses" (Mitchell) was a harmless variant of the customary trial and error approach of the empiricist. It committed the investigator

to address questions to his statistical data, with the willingness to reformulate them in the light of accumulative evidence. If an analytical tool failed to work, it was either modified or replaced. Therefore economic research was a continuous "process of constructing an analytical framework, seeking out observations, processing them, reshaping the framework, seeking out new observations, and so on."[33]

In any case, this approach was appraised with considerable optimism. It involved, as Mitchell suggested, "a great deal more passing back and forth between hypothesis and observation, each modifying and enriching the other"[34] than there was acceptable to neo-classical economics.

Of course, reasoning in this twilight zone of abstraction and observation does not guarantee scientific results. Not only may explanatory hypotheses be false, but their validity may be indeterminate or impossible to determine.[35] Often enough, the "world of realities" differs too much from the premises of the analytical model to be used as a test of their truth.

Notwithstanding those limitations, explanatory hypotheses led to remarkable findings. One of them was the acceleration principle of John Maurice Clark, stated in 1917 prior to Keynes' multiplier. This original contribution was a model of neo-institutionalistic reasoning.

Clark proceeded in two distinct steps. First, he derived a hypothetical law of demand for intermediate products under imaginary conditions, namely an industry reduced to a mere machine. Second, he tested this hypothetical law by comparing it with railway traffic and purchases of cars of American railroads over a period of 15 years (1901–1916). It was questionable,

[30] See John R. Hicks and Albert G. Hart, *The Social Framework of the American Economy*, New York 1945, p. 9.

[31] See, for instance, the preface of his book on *Business Cycles*, Berkeley 1913.

[32] Arthur F. Burns in his "Report on the National Bureau's Work (1948)," in *The Frontiers of Economic Knowledge, Essays by Arthur F. Burns,* Princeton 1954, p. 50 (National Bureau of Economic Research, No. 57, General Series).

[33] *Ibid.*, p. 50.

[34] See the letter of Mitchell to John Maurice Clark of August 9, 1928, reproduced by Lucy Sprague Mitchell, "A Personal Sketch," in *Wesley Clair Mitchell, op. cit.*, p. 98.

[35] Compare Paul A. Samuelson, Foundations, *op. cit.*, p. 4.

however, whether his railroad statistics, covering such a limited period of time, could be used as a test for a general trend. Clark's empirical test was also shaky on some other grounds: the behavior of American railroads was no standard for the behavior of American industry and still less indicative for the behavior of industry in general. Actually Clark conceded those defects of his performance and acknowledged, moreover, its hidden bias. In the frame of his argument—Clark admitted—railroads furnished the most favorable case, for instance, because they could not "make to stock" in slack periods like the manufacturer and were under obligation to carry whatever traffic offered at the time it was offered. In spite of those scruples, however, Clark believed he had found an "exact formulation to the relationship, in quantity and in time, between demand for products and demand for the means of production." [36]

One of the explanatory hypotheses widely used by neo-institutional writers was the equation of exchange, stated partly in elementary, partly in more sophisticated terms. Nobody could deny—according to Mitchell—that the quantity of money affected the price level. Despite some objections, he endorsed the use of the formula on a tentative or experimental basis. [37] Still more hopefully, Copeland embarked on its verification. [38] However, in his case too, the empirical data could be criticized. They referred to a limited period of time, to a single country, and to an extraordinary economic configuration. The experience of the United States during the hectic period from 1919 through 1927 could be regarded as unique. Possibly the verification rested on factors unaccounted for in the formula.

Characteristically, Neo-Institutionalists have been reluctant to acknowledge the service of their theoretical tools. Mitchell himself was no exception. Schumpeter's remark that Mitchell's great book on *Business Cycles* (1913), as far as the bare bones of the argument were concerned, was an exercise in the dynamic theory of equilibrium caused Mitchell a speechless surprise. [39] Actually Mitchell's picture of business cycles showed its theoretical undercoat also in other places. Therefore a more theoretical mind like Friedman, thought it worthwhile to restate Mitchell's business cycle theory in mathematical terms. [40]

COMMON TARGETS

As a symptom of interpenetration I may mention also some cases in which both rival schools aimed at identical targets, though each used its own ammunition. Among those targets were oligopoly and monopolistic competition. To the Neo-Institutionalists, Chamberlin's theory signified an admission that institutional aspects of the market were unduly neglected by the orthodox school. Copeland praised Chamberlin's work for having opened new vistas for "the pure, abstract, or deductive economics" and for probing the logical implications of alternative assumptions. [41] Equally indicative are some overlappings of Chamberlin's theory and Means' concept of "ad-

[36] John Maurice Clark, "Business Acceleration and the Law of Demand: A Technical Factor in Economic Cycles," *Journal of Political Economy*, Vol. xxv, March 1917, pp. 217–235.

[37] Wesley C. Mitchell, *Business Cycles: The Problem and Its Setting*, New York 1927, p. 138; *Idem*, "The Real Issues in the Quantity Theory of Money," *Journal of Political Economy*, xii (1904), pp. 403–408.

[38] Morris A. Copeland, "The Equation of Exchange: An Empirical Analysis (1928)," in *Facts and Theory in Economics, op. cit.*, pp. 95–107.

[39] Joseph A. Schumpeter, "Wesley Clair Mitchell," in *Ten Great Economists*, New York 1951, p. 248.

[40] Milton Friedman, "The Economic Theorist," in *Wesley Clair Mitchell: The Economic Scientist, op. cit.*, pp. 275–282.

[41] Morris A. Copeland, "The Theory of Monopolistic Competition" (1934) and his own supplement entitled: "Competing Products and Monopolistic Competition" (1940), both reprinted in *Facts and Theory in Economics, op. cit.*, pp. 247–287.

ministered prices." Means, of course, would deny any duplication. Following his argument, "administered prices" tend towards price inflexibility while a rigorous application of Chamberlin's doctrine leads to the expectation of flexible prices.[42]

QUANTIFICATION AND CORRELATION

Finally, I refer to an area in which members of the opposite schools pulled so closely together as to form almost a united front. Most post-classical theorists take it for granted that the explanation of the magnitudes of economic quantities and their correlation are their main task. They thus share the preoccupation of Neo-Institutionalists with quantification and correlation.

We should indicate, however, that those tools were not always regarded as the magic wand of institutionalistic research. Neither Veblen nor Commons derived major conclusions from statistical laws or from functional relations. Instead they relied on psychology, anthropology, cultural history, and law.

Contrary to their forerunners, Neo-Institutionalists lean heavily on time series, possibly supplemented by experimentation. Observations of specific conditions, as careful as they may be, cannot be generalized. Furthermore, empirical findings may suffer from a subjective bent of the individual investigator, from his preconceptions and prejudices. Finally, quantification is consistent with the neo-institutionalistic concept of economics. Since it deals with mass phenomena[43] and since mass phenomena, in their turn, can be counted and expressed in figures, economic data must be properly verified by statistics.[44]

This approach, of course, does not leave any room for the classical generalizations. It abandons as well the search for sole causes. "Time series"—even combined with "analytic description"—are concerned with probable and approximate relations or with stochastic regularities. Therefore economic analysis is essentially a study of correlations or, to use Frederic C. Mills' phrase, a measurement of the degree of association found in experience between related phenomena. Broadly speaking, causation is replaced by association and correlation.[45]

From the same empirical point of view, Neo-Institutionalists pursued another perspective: the discovery of "concrete theories." Obviously, this term fails to meet logical requirements. Since abstraction is the heartbeat of all forms of theorizing, "concrete theory" means a *contradictio in adjecto*. Yet this possibility fascinated quantitative workers looking for a modicum of generalizations. In this context, Mitchell commended the "concrete laws of demand" for representative crops as derived by Henry L. Moore from statistics.[46] These laws were epitomized in equations that expressed the quantitative relation between the demands for and the prices of representative crops. With their help the elasticity of demand for each crop could be measured and therefore its price could be predicted.[47] Mitchell expected that an application of such an econometric approach

---

[42] See Gardiner C. Means in *American Economic Review*, Vol. XLIX, No. 2 (May 1959), p. 451 (Papers and Proceedings). Compare also John M. Blair, "Administered Prices: A Phenomenon in Search of a Theory," *ibid.*, pp. 431–450.

[43] See above p. 312.

[44] Wesley C. Mitchell, "Quantitative Analysis," *loc. cit.*, pp. 22–36.

[45] Frederic C. Mills, "On Measurement in Economics," in *The Trend of Economics, op. cit.*, pp. 43, 46.

[46] Wesley C. Mitchell, "Quantitative Analysis," *loc. cit.*, pp. 22–36.

[47] Henry Ludwell Moore, *Economic Cycles. Their Law and Cause*, New York 1914, pp. 62–92 (Chapter IV: The Law of Demand). See also his earlier book: *Laws of Wages, An Essay in Statistical Economics* (New York 1911) that, in line with Pareto's suggestion to explore empirical laws, derived the shape of the demand curve for labor from empirical data on coal mining in France. Compare further Moore's book: *Synthetic Economics*, New York 1929.

to numerous commodities would eventually yield a superior theory of demand.[48]

In this area, interpenetration of the two rival schools reaches its climax. Many theorists have subscribed to the need for quantification and concretism. They anticipate that by filling the "empty boxes of abstract theories" with actual statistical data, the objectivity, realism, and applicability of their science will be maximized.[49]

INCONGRUITIES AND LACUNAE

It remains to be seen whether the concessions made by Neo-Institutionalists and theorists signify lasting improvements. As in other cases, compromises may spell contradictions without settling basic issues. Nor may interpenetration lead to an integrated whole. My concluding remarks are too brief to provide for a general appraisal. I shall touch, however, on some obvious defects of the present mixture—and reserve the right to elaborate on them for another occasion.

First, a broad hiatus persists in the methodological field. Notwithstanding their empiricistic convictions, Neo-Institutionalists base their inquiries on a broad conceptual apparatus, not derived from experience. Abstract theorems, furthermore, are permitted to reenter the scene through the back door, primarily in the guise of explanatory hypotheses. Neo-Institutionalists, furthermore, approve of some half-way generalizations such as "concrete theories" of demand, whose validity, of course, does not extend beyond the limits of observation.[50] It is difficult, however, to accept the premise that the extensive classical generalizations are fallacious, but that a little generalization is valid.

Second, other incongruities arise from the fundamental concessions to pragmatism. If economists are committed to prepare practical solutions, they must concentrate on such notions as will "work" in the short, intermediate, or long run. More specifically, economic theory must supply propositions that will yield sufficiently accurate predictions under current conditions.[51] Lack of accuracy is condoned as a minor evil.

This pragmatic bent, however, calls for a coordination of economic considerations with social and ethical standards. We refer to the views of a staunch advocate of economic pragmatism: Charles H. Cooley declared that a social science that was not, in its central principles, an ethical science, was unfaithful to its deepest responsibility.[52] The indifference of economists towards social and ethical norms can hardly be excused on the ground that those norms were data, for example, by assuming a general consensus on social and ethical objectives. It is still more questionable to rely on a *l'art pour l'art* approach following the suggestion that it is "a legitimate exercise of economic analysis to examine the consequences of various value judgments, whether or not they are shared by the economist." [53] Certainly, conclusions based on the contradictory definitions of economic and total welfare do not breed confidence in a neutral approach.

A *third* observation applies to an incongruity more conspicuous in current economic research than in principles stated by leading economists. I agree with Schumpeter's formulation that economics is a science and that this science has one important quantitative aspect.[54] But his

[48] Wesley C. Mitchell, "Quantitative Analysis," *loc. cit.,* p. 24.

[49] See Wassily Leontief, "Econometrics," in *A Survey of Contemporary Economics,* ed. by Howard S. Ellis, Philadelphia 1948, p. 390.

[50] See Henry L. Moore, *Laws of Wages, op. cit.,* p. 22.

[51] Milton Friedman, *Essays in Positive Economics,* Chicago 1953, p. 15.

[52] Charles Horton Cooley, "Political Economy and Social Process" (1918), in *Sociological Theory and Social Research,* New York 1930, pp. 257–258.

[53] Paul A. Samuelson, *Foundations, op. cit.,* p. 220.

[54] Joseph A. Schumpeter, "The Common Sense of Econometrics" (1933), in his *Essays,* Cambridge (Mass.) 1951, p. 100.

paper on "Common Sense of Econometrics" implied that distinctions of quality should not be neglected on behalf of distinctions in numbers.

We should notice as well that the present mixture does not indicate major progress in the integration of economics with the other social sciences. Many studies, indeed, are concerned with specific interrelations of the economic process and its social and political framework. While at least some of these inquiries should be highly commended, they are generally a far cry from a system of economic behavior or a system of "economic sociology" as envisaged by Veblen and Max Weber. Neither pretentious book titles nor recurrent exposures of the evils of "compartmentalization" are sufficient to bridge the existing gap. As a matter of fact, most economists, Institutionalists as well as theorists, still prefer the cultivation of a limited area, not too different from the traditional field of "Political Economy."

We may finally mention that the growing affinity of the two rival schools, though still far from a consolidation, should intensify some existing trends. Specialization will probably grow at an unprecedented scale. Although, in contra-distinction to some products of postclassical theory, pragmatism may avoid academic "hair splitting," it is setting a premium on the splitting of subjects of inquiry.

Such an outlook dims our hopes for a new and provocative synthesis. As it seems to me, the era of system building in the United States, represented by such illustrious names as John Bates Clark and Joseph A. Schumpeter, and by the architects of Institutionalism, draws to its close. Mitchell's prediction of an uninspiring future of economics may be vindicated:

"Knowledge will grow by accretion as it grows in the natural sciences, rather than by the excogitation of new systems . . . It will be harder for any one to cover the whole field, perhaps quite impossible. From time to time someone will try to give a comprehensive survey of the results of quantitative research, but such books will not have the prestige won by the treatises by Adam Smith, Ricardo, Mill, and Marshall." [55]

[55] Wesley C. Mitchell, "Quantitative Analysis," *loc. cit.*, pp. 28–29.

17   Perfect Competition,
Historically Contemplated

GEORGE J. STIGLER

The explanation, given in Book V of Alfred Marshall's *Principles of Economics*, of the nature of demand and supply and their interaction to establish prices was accepted as definitive until the early decades of this century. The pricing situation on which Marshall's greatest attention was focused relates to the individual industry that is so small, relative to the rest of the economy, that industry demand and supply curves, which are completely independent of one another, can be drawn up. An industry demand curve implies that the outputs of various firms are homogeneous from the point of view of their buyers so that there is no reason for anyone to prefer the output of a particular firm. Its interaction with the industry supply curve results in a single market price at which the individual firm has an infinitely elastic demand. Thus, Marshall saw no need for separate examination of the price behavior of any firm, unless it is a monopolist, because it is essentially the same as that of every other firm in the industry.

While Marshall himself never used the term "perfect competition" or "pure competition," the pricing situations with which he was most concerned have become associated with them. The reformulation of value theory accomplished by Joan Robinson's *Economics of Imperfect Competition* and Edward Chamberlin's *Theory of Monopolistic Competition*, published almost simultaneously in England and the United States in 1933, was undertaken as an indictment of the perfectly competitive models associated with neoclassicism.

What exactly are the minimum requirements of "perfect competition"? Marshall, perhaps wisely, refrained from setting forth the specific assumptions on which his analytical model of the industry is constructed. And it is precisely because change is ever present that George Stigler, who elsewhere has made a case for the continued usefulness of the perfectly competitive model, maintains that a definitive statement of the minimum requirements of perfect competition is impossible. The article, "Perfect Competition Historically Contemplated," reveals the concept of competition as among the most venerable in economics; its history is an excellent reflector not only of the changes which have taken place since Smith's time in market phenomena but also in the discipline which seeks to explain them.

Reprinted from George J. Stigler, "Perfect Competition, Historically Contemplated," *The Journal of Political Economy*, Vol. LXV, No. 1, February 1957, pp. 1–16. Dr. Stigler is Professor of Economics at the School of Business, University of Chicago.

No concept in economics—or elsewhere—is ever defined fully, in the sense that its meaning under every conceivable circumstance is clear. Even a word with a wholly arbitrary meaning in economics, like "elasticity," raises questions which the person who defined it (in this case, Marshall) never faced: for example, how does the concept apply to finite changes or to discontinuous or stochastic or multiple-valued functions? And of course a word like "competition," which is shared with the whole population, is even less likely to be loaded with restrictions or elaborations to forestall unfelt ambiguities.

Still, it is a remarkable fact that the concept of competition did not begin to receive explicit and systematic attention in the main stream of economics until 1871. This concept—as pervasive and fundamental as any in the whole structure of classical and neoclassical economic theory—was long treated with the kindly casualness with which one treats of the intuitively obvious. Only slowly did the elaborate and complex concept of perfect competition evolve, and it was not until after the first World War that it was finally received into general theoretical literature. The evolution of the concept and the steps by which it became confused with a perfect market, uniqueness of equilibrium, and stationary conditions are the subject of this essay.

THE CLASSICAL ECONOMISTS

"Competition" entered economics from common discourse, and for long it connoted only the independent rivalry of two or more persons. When Adam Smith wished to explain why a reduced supply led to a higher price, he referred to the "competition [which] will immediately begin" among buyers; when the supply is excessive, the price will sink more, the greater "the competition of the sellers, or according as it happens to be more or less important to them to get immediately rid of the commodity."[1] It will be noticed that "competition" is here (and usually) used in the sense of rivalry in a race—a race to get limited supplies or a race to be rid of excess supplies. Competition is a process of responding to a new force and a method of reaching a new equilibrium.

Smith observed that economic rivals were more likely to strive for gain by under- or overbidding one another, the more numerous they were:

> The trades which employ but a small number of hands, run most easily into such combinations.
> If this capital [sufficient to trade in a town] is divided between two different grocers, their competition will tend to make both of them sell cheaper, than if it were in the hands of one only; and if it were divided among twenty, their competition would be just so much the greater, and the chance of their combining together, in order to raise the price, just so much the less.[2]

This is all that Smith has to say of the number of rivals.

Of course something more is implicit, and partially explicit, in Smith's treatment of competition, but this "something more" is not easy to state precisely, for it was not precise in Smith's mind. But the concept of competition seemed to embrace also several other elements:

> 1. The economic units must possess tolerable knowledge of the conditions of employment of their resources in various industries. "This equality [of remuneration] can take place only in those employments which are well known, and have been long established in the neighbourhood."[3] But the necessary information was usually available: "Secrets

[1] *The Wealth of Nations* (Modern Library ed.), pp. 56–57.
[2] *Ibid.*, pp. 126 and 342.
[3] *Ibid.*, p. 114.

. . . , it must be acknowledged, can seldom be long kept; and the extraordinary profit can last very little longer than they are kept."[4]

2. Competition achieved its results only in the long run: "This equality in the whole of the advantages and disadvantages of the different employments of labour and stock, can take place only in the ordinary, or what may be called the natural state of those employments."[5]

3. There must be freedom of trade; the economic unit must be free to enter or leave any trade. The exclusive privileges or corporations which exclude men from trades, and the restrictions imposed on mobility by the settlement provisions of the poor law, are examples of such interferences with "free competition."

In sum, then, Smith had five conditions of competition:

1. The rivals must act independently, not collusively.
2. The number of rivals, potential as well as present, must be sufficient to eliminate extraordinary gains.
3. The economic units must possess tolerable knowledge of the market opportunities.
4. There must be freedom (from social restraints) to act on this knowledge.
5. Sufficient time must elapse for resources to flow in the directions and quantities desired by their owners.

The modern economist has a strong tendency to read more into such statements than they meant to Smith and his contemporaries. The fact that he (and many successors) was willing to call the ownership of land a monopoly—although the market in agricultural land met all these conditions—simply because the total supply of land was believed to be fixed is sufficient testimony to the fact that he was not punctilious in his language.[6]

[4] *Ibid.*, p. 60.
[5] *Ibid.*, p. 115.
[6] *Ibid.*, p. 145. Perhaps this is not the ideal illustration of the laxness of the period in the use of the competitive concept, for several readers of this paper have sympathized with this usage. But, to repeat, competition is consistent with a zero elasticity of supply: the fact of windfall gains from unexpected increases in demand is characteristic of all commodities with less than infinitely elastic supplies.

Smith did not state how he was led to these elements of a concept of competition. We may reasonably infer that the conditions of numerous rivals and of independence of action of these rivals were matters of direct observation. Every informed person knew, at least in a general way, what competition was, and the essence of this knowledge was the striving of rivals to gain advantages relative to one another.

The other elements of competition, on the contrary, appear to be the necessary conditions for the validity of a proposition which was to be associated with competition: the equalization of returns in various directions open to an entrepreneur or investor or laborer. If one postulates equality of returns as the equilibrium state under competition, then adequacy of numbers and independence of rivals are not enough for equilibrium. The entrepreneur (or other agents) must know what returns are obtainable in various fields, he must be allowed to enter the fields promising high rates of return, and he must be given time to make his presence felt in these fields. These conditions were thus prerequisites of an analytical theorem, although their reasonableness was no doubt enhanced by the fact that they corresponded more or less closely to observable conditions.

This sketch of a concept of competition was not amplified or challenged in any significant respect for the next three-quarters of a century by any important member of the English school. A close study of the literature, such as I have not made, would no doubt reveal many isolated passages on the formal properties or realism of the concept, especially when the theory was applied to concrete problems. For example, Senior was more interested in methodology than most of his contemporaries, and he commented:

But though, under free competition, cost of production is the regulator of price, it influence is subject to much occasional interruption. Its operation can be supposed to b perfect only if we suppose that there are no disturbing causes, that capital and labour can be at once transferred, and without loss, from one employment to another, and that every producer has full information of the profit to be derived from every mode of production. But it is obvious that these suppositions have no resemblance to the truth. A large portion of the capital essential to production consists of buildings, machinery, and other implements, the results of much time and labour, and of little service for any except their existing purposes. . . . Few capitalists can estimate, except upon an average of some years, the amounts of their own profits, and still fewer can estimate those of their neighbours.[7]

Senior made no use of the concept of perfect competition hinted at in this passage, and he was wholly promiscuous in his use of the concept of monopoly.

Cairnes, the last important English economist to write in the classical tradition, did break away from the Smithian concept of competition. He defined a state of free competition as one in which commodities exchanged in proportion to the sacrifices (of labor and capital) in their production.[8] This condition was amply fulfilled, he believed, so far as capital was concerned, for there was a large stock of disposable capital which quickly flowed into unusually remunerative fields.[9] The condition was only partly fulfilled in the case of labor, however, for there existed a hierarchy of occupational classes ("non-competing industrial groups") which the laborer found it most difficult to ascend.[10] Even the extra rewards of skill beyond those which paid for the sacrifices in obtaining training were a monopoly return.[11] This approach was not analytically rigorous—Cairnes did not tell how to equate the sacrifices of capital-

ists and laborers—nor was it empirically fruitful.

Cairnes labeled as "industrial competition" the force which effects the proportioning of prices to psychological costs which takes place to the extent that the products are made in one non-competing group, and he called on the reciprocal demand theory of international trade to explain exchanges of products between non-competing groups. Hence we might call industrial competition the competition within non-competing groups, and commercial competition that between non-competing groups. But Sidgwick and Edgeworth attribute the opposite concepts to Cairnes: commercial competition is competition within an industry, and industrial competition requires the ability of resources to flow between industries.[12] Their nomenclature seems more appropriate; I have not been able to find Cairnes's discussion of commercial competition and doubt that it exists.[13]

THE CRITICS OF PRIVATE ENTERPRISE

The main claims for a private-enterprise system rest upon the workings of competition, and it would not have been unnatural for critics of this system to focus much attention on the competitive concept. They might have argued that Smith's assumptions were not strong enough to insure optimum results or that, even if perfect competition were formulated as the basis of the theory, certain deviations from optimum results (such as those associated with external economies) could occur. The critics did not make this type of criticism, however, possibly simply because they were

---

[7] N. W. Senior, *Political Economy* (New York, 1939), p. 102.

[8] *Some Leading Principles of Political Economy Newly Expounded* (London, 1874), p. 79.

[9] *Ibid.*, p. 68.

[10] *Ibid.*, p. 72.

[11] *Ibid.*, p. 85. Thus Cairnes tacitly labeled all differences in native ability as "monopolistic."

[12] Henry Sidgwick, *Principles of Political Economy* (London, 1883), p. 182; F. Y. Edgeworth, *Papers Relating to Political Economy* (London, 1925), II, 280, 311.

[13] Karl Marx once distinguished interindustry from intraindustry competition in *Theorien über den Mehrwert* (Stuttgart, 1905), II, Part 2, 14 n.

not first-class analysts; and for this type of development we must return to the main line of theorists, consisting mostly of politically conservative economists.

Or, at another pole, the critics might simply have denied that competition was the basic form of market organization. In the nineteenth century, however, this was only a minor and sporadic charge.[14] The Marxists did not press this point: both the labor theory of value and the doctrine of equalization of profit rates require competition.[15] The early Fabian essayists were also prepared to make their charges rest upon the deficiencies in the workings of competition rather than its absence.[16] The charge that competition was non-existent or vanishing did not become commonplace until the end of the nineteenth century.

The critics, to the extent that they took account of competition at all, emphasized the evil tendencies which they believed flowed from its workings. It would be interesting to examine their criticisms systematically with a view to their treatment of competition; it is my impression that their most common, and most influential,

charge was that competition led to a highly objectionable, and perhaps continuously deteriorating, distribution of income by size.[17] In their explanations of the workings of a competitive economy the most striking deficiency of the classical economists was their failure to work out the theory of the effects of competition on the distribution of income.

THE MATHEMATICAL SCHOOL

The first steps in the analytical refinement of the concept of competition were made by the mathematical economists. This stage in the history of the concept is of special interest because it reveals both the types of advances that were achieved by this approach and the manner in which alien elements were introduced into the concept.

When an algebraically inclined economist seeks to maximize the profits of a producer, he is led to write the equation

$$\text{Profits} = \text{Revenue} - \text{Cost}$$

and then to maximize this expression; that is, to set the derivative of profits with respect to output equal to zero. He then faces the question: How does revenue (say, pq) vary with output (q)? The natural answer is to *define* competition as that situation in which p does not vary with q—in which the demand curve facing the firm is horizontal. This is precisely what Cournot did:

> The effects of competition have reached their limit, when each of the partial productions D_k [the output of producer k] in inappreciable, not only with reference to the total production $D = F(p)$, but also with reference to the derivative $F'(p)$, so that the partial production D_k could be subtracted from

---

[14] For example, Leslie repeatedly denied that resource owners possessed sufficient knowledge to effect an equalization of the rates of return (see T. E. Cliffe Leslie, *Essays in Political and Moral Philosophy* [London, 1888], pp. 47, 48, 81, 158–59, 184–85).

[15] See especially Volume III of *Das Kapital* and also F. Engels, *The Condition of the Working-Classes in England*, reprinted in Karl Marx and Friedrich Engels, *On Britain* (London, 1954), pp. 109 ff. The Marxian theory of the increasing concentration of capital was a minor and inconsistent dissent from the main position (see *Capital* [Modern Library ed.], pp. 684 ff.).

[16] See *Fabian Essays* (Jubilee ed.; London, 1948), especially those by Shaw and Webb. But the attention devoted to monopoly was increasing, and the essay by Clarke argued that "combination is absorbing commerce" (*ibid.*, p. 84). A few years later the Webbs used a competitive model in their celebrated discussion of "higgling in the market" and then went on to describe the formation of monopolistic structures as defences erected against the competitive pressures the Webbs did not quite understand (see *Industrial Democracy* [London, 1920], Part III, chap. ii).

[17] A second main criticism became increasingly more prominent in the second half of the nineteenth century: that a private-enterprise system allowed or compelled large fluctuations in employment. For some critics (e.g., Engels), competition was an important cause of these fluctuations.

D without any appreciable variation resulting in the price of the commodity.[18]

This definition of competition was especially appropriate in Cournot's system because, according to his theory of oligopoly, the excess of price over marginal cost approached zero as the number of like producers became large.[19] Cournot believed that this condition of competition was fulfilled "for a multitude of products, and, among them, for the most important products." [20]

Cournot's definition was enormously more precise and elegant than Smith's so far as the treatment of numbers was concerned. A market departed from unlimited competition to the extent that price exceeded the marginal cost of the firm, and the difference approached zero as the number of rivals approached infinity. But the refinement was one-sided: Cournot paid no attention to conditions of entry and so his definition of competition held also for industries with numerous firms even though no more firms could enter.

The role of knowledge was made somewhat more prominent in Jevons' exposition. His concept of competition was a part of

his concept of a market, and a perfect market was characterized by two conditions:

[1.] A market, then, is theoretically perfect only when all traders have perfect knowledge of the conditions of supply and demand, and the consequent ratio of exchange; . . .

[2.] . . . there must be perfectly free competition, so that anyone will exchange with any one else upon the slightest advantage appearing. There must be no conspiracies for absorbing and holding supplies to produce unnatural ratios of exchange.[21]

One might interpret this ambiguous second condition in several ways, for the pursuit of advantages is not inconsistent with conspiracies. At a minimum, Jevons assumes complete independence of action by every trader for a corollary of the perfect market in that "in the same market, at any moment, there cannot be two prices for the same kind of article." [22] This rule of a single price (it is called the "law of indifference" in the second edition) excludes price discrimination and probably requires that the market have numerous buyers and sellers, but the condition is not made explicit. The presence of large numbers is clearly implied, however, when we are told that "a single trader . . . must buy and sell at the current prices, which he cannot in an appreciable degree affect." [23]

[18] *Mathematical Principles of the Theory of Wealth* (New York, 1929), p. 90. It is sufficient to assume that D_k is small relative to D if one assumes that the demand function is continuous, for then "the variations of the demand will be sensibly proportional to the variations in price so long as these last are small fractions of the original price" (*ibid.*, p. 50).

[19] Let the revenue of the firm be $q_i p$, and let all firms have the same marginal costs, MC. Then the equation for maximum profits for one firm would be

$$p + q_i \frac{dp}{dq} = MC.$$

The sum of n such equations would be

$$np + q \frac{dp}{dq} = nMC,$$

or $nq_i = q$. This least equation may be written,

$$p = MC - \frac{p}{nE},$$

where E is the elasticity of market demand (*ibid.*, p. 84).

[20] *Ibid.*, p. 90.

[21] *Theory of Political Economy* (1st ed.; London, 1871), pp. 87 and 86.

[22] *Ibid.*, p. 92. This is restated as the proposition that the last increments of an act of exchange (i.e., the last exchange in a competitive market) must be proportional to the total quantities exchanged, or that dy exchanges for dx in the same proportion that y exchanges for x, or

$$\frac{dy}{dx} = \frac{y}{x}.$$

It would have been better for Jevons simply to assert that, if x_i exchanges for y_i, then for all i

$$\frac{x_i}{y_i} = \frac{P_y}{P_x}.$$

[23] *Ibid.*, p. 111. In the Preface to the second edition, where on most subjects Jevons was farseeing, the conceptual treatment of competition deteriorated: "Property is only another name for monopoly . . . Thus monopoly is limited by competition . . ." (*Theory* [4th ed.], pp. xlvi–xlvii).

The merging of the concepts of competition and the market was unfortunate, for each deserved a full and separate treatment. A market is an institution for the consummation of transactions. It performs this function efficiently when every buyer who will pay more than the minimum realized price for any class of commodities succeeds in buying the commodity, and every seller who will sell for less than the maximum realized price succeeds in selling the commodity. A market performs these tasks more efficiently if the commodities are well specified and if buyers and sellers are fully informed of their properties and prices. Possibly also a perfect market allows buyers and sellers to act on differing expectations of future prices. A market may be perfect and monopolistic or imperfect and competitive. Jevons' mixture of the two has been widely imitated by successors, of course, so that even today a market is commonly treated as a concept subsidiary to competition.

Edgeworth was the first to attempt a systematic and rigorous definition of perfect competition. His exposition deserves the closest scrutiny in spite of the fact that few economists of his time or ours have attempted to disentangle and uncover the theorems and conjectures of the *Mathematical Psychics*, probably the most elusively written book of importance in the history of economics. For his allegations and demonstrations seem to be the parents of widespread beliefs on the nature of perfect competition.

The conditions of perfect competition are stated as follows:

> The *field of competition* with reference to a contract, or contracts, under consideration consists of all individuals who are willing and able to recontract about the articles under consideration. . . .
> There is free communication throughout a normal competitive field. You might suppose the constituent individuals collected at a point, or connected by telephones—an ideal supposition [1881], but sufficiently approxi-

mate to existence or tendency for the purposes of abstract science.
> A *perfect* field of competition professes in addition certain properties peculiarly favourable to mathematical calculation; . . . The conditions of a *perfect* field are four; the first pair referrible to the heading *multiplicity* or continuity, the second *dividedness* or fluidity.
> I. An individual is free to *recontract* with any out of an indefinite number, . . .
> II. Any individual is free to *contract* (at the same time) with an indefinite number; . . . This condition combined with the first appears to involve the indefinite divisibility of each *article* of contract (if any X deal with an indefinite number of Y's he must give each an indefinitely small portion of x); which might be erected into a separate condition.
> III. Any individual is free to *recontract* with another independently of, *without* the consent being required of, any third party, . . .
> IV. Any individual is free to *contract* with another independently of a third party; . . .
> The failure of the first [condition] involves the failure of the second, but not *vice versa*; and the third and fourth are similarly related.[24]

The natural question to put to such a list of conditions of competition is: Are the conditions necessary and sufficient to achieve what intuitively or pragmatically seems to be a useful concept of competition? Edgeworth replies, in effect, that the conditions are both necessary and sufficient. More specifically, competition requires (1) indefinitely large numbers of participants on both sides of the market; (2) complete absence of limitations upon individual self seeking behavior; and (3) complete divisibility of the commodities traded.[25]

The rationale of the requirement of indefinite numbers is as follows. With bilateral monopoly, the transaction will be indeterminate—equilibrium can be anywhere on the contract curve.[26] If we add

[24] *Mathematical Psychics* (London, 1881), pp. 17–19.
[25] Edgeworth's emphasis upon recontract, the institution which allows tentative contracts to be broken without penalty, is motivated by a desire to assure that equilibrium will be achieved and will not be affected by the route by which it is achieved. It will not be examined here.
[26] *Ibid.*, pp. 20 ff.

second buyer and seller, it is shown that the range of permissible equilibriums (the length of the tenable contract curve) will shrink.[27] By intuitive induction, with infinitely many traders it will shrink to a single point; a single price must rule in the market.[28]

Before we discuss this argument, we may take account also of the condition that individual traders are free to act independently. Edgeworth shows that combinations reduce the effective number of traders and that "combiners *stand to gain.*"[29] In effect, then, he must assume that the individual trader not only is free to act independently but will in fact do so.

The proof of the need for indefinite numbers has serious weaknesses. The range of indeterminacy shrinks only because one seller or buyer tries to cut out the other by offering better terms.[30] Edgeworth fails to show that such price competition (which is palpably self-defeating) will occur or that, if it does occur, why the process should stop before the parties reach a unique (competitive) equilibrium. Like all his descendants, he treated the small-numbers case unsatisfactorily.

It is intuitively plausible that with infinite numbers all monopoly power (and indeterminacy) will vanish, and Edgeworth essentially postulates rather than proves this. But a simple demonstration, in case of sellers of equal size, would amount only to showing that

Marginal revenue = Price

$$+ \frac{\text{Price}}{\text{Number of sellers} \times \text{Market elasticity}}$$

and that this last term goes to zero as the number of sellers increases indefinitely.[31] This was implicitly Cournot's argument.

But why do we require divisibility of the traded commodity?

> Suppose a market, consisting of an equal number of masters and servants, offering respectively wages and service; subject to the condition that no man can serve two masters, no master employ more than one man; or suppose equilibrium already established between such parties to be disturbed by any sudden influx of wealth into the hands of the masters. Then there is no determinate, and very generally unique, arrangement towards which the system tends under the operation of, may we say, a law of Nature, and which would be predictable if we knew beforehand the real requirements of each, or of the average, dealer; . . .[32]

Consider the simple example: a thousand masters will each employ a man at any wage below 100; a thousand laborers will each work for any wage above 50. There will be a single wage rate: knowledge and numbers are sufficient to lead a worker to seek a master paying more than the going rate or a master to seek out a worker receiving less than the market rate. But any rate between 50 and 100 is a possible equilibrium.[33]

It is not the lack of uniqueness that is troublesome, however, for a market can be perfectly competitive even though there be a dozen possible stable equilibrium posi-

---

[27] *Ibid.,* pp. 35 ff.
[28] *Ibid.,* pp. 37–39.
[29] *Ibid.,* p. 43.
[30] " . . . It will in general be possible for *one* of the *Y*s (without the consent of other) to recontract with the two *X*s, so that for all those three parties the recontract is more advantageous than the previously existing contract" (*ibid.,* p. 35).

[31] Let one seller dispose of q_i, the other sellers each disposing of q. Then the seller's marginal revenue is

$$\frac{d(pq_i)}{dq_i} = p + q_i \frac{dp}{dQ} \frac{dQ}{dq_i},$$

where Q is total sales, and $dQ/dq_i = 1$. Letting $Q = nq_i = nq$, and writing E for

$$\frac{dQ}{dp} \frac{p}{Q},$$

we obtain the expression in the text.
[32] *Mathematical Psychics,* p. 46.
[33] Of course, let there be one extra worker, and the wage will be 50; one extra master, and it will be 100.

tions.[34] Rather, the difficulty arises because the demand (or supply) functions do not possess continuous derivatives: the withdrawal of even one unit will lead to a large change in price, so that the individual trader—even though he has numerous independent rivals—can exert a perceptible influence upon price.

The element of market control arising out of the non-continuity is easily eliminated, of course. If the article which is traded is divisible, then equalities replace inequalities in the conditions of equilibrium: the individual trader can no longer influence the market price. A master may employ a variable amount of labor, and he will therefore bid for additional units so long as the wage rate is below his marginal demand price. A worker may have several employers, and he will therefore supply additional labor so long as any employer will pay more than his marginal supply price. "If the labour of the assistants can be sold by the hour, or other sort of differential dose, the phenomenon of determinate equilibrium will reappear." [35] Divisibility was introduced to achieve determinateness, which it fails to do, but it is required to eliminate monopoly power.

Divisibility had a possible second role in the assumptions, which, however, was never made explicit. If there are infinitely many possessors of a commodity, presumably each must have only an infinitesimal quantity of it if the existing total stock is to be finite. But no economist placed em-

phasis upon the strict mathematical implications of concepts like infinity, and this word was used to convey only the notion of an indefinitely large number of traders.

The remainder of the mathematical economists of the period did not extend, or for that matter even reach, the level of precision of Edgeworth. Walras gave no adequate definition of competition.[36] Pareto noticed the possible effects of social controls over purchases and sales.[37] Henry Moore, in what may have been the first article on the formal definition of competition,[38] listed five "implicit hypotheses" of competition:

I. Each economic factor seeks a maximum net income.
II. There is but one price for commodities of the same quality in the same market.
III. The influence of the product of any one producer upon the price per unit of the total product is negligible.
IV. The output of any one producer is negligible as compared with the total output.
V. Each producer orders the amount of his product without regard to the effect of his act upon the conduct of his competitors.[39]

This list of conditions is noteworthy chiefly because it marked an unsuccessful attempt to revert to the narrower competitive concept of Jevons.

MARSHALL

Marshall as usual refused to float on the tide of theory, and his treatment of competition was much closer to Adam Smith's than to that of his contemporaries. Indeed,

[34] Since chance should operate in the choice of the equilibrium actually attained, it is not proper to say, as Edgeworth does (in a wider context), that the dice will be "loaded with villainy" (*ibid.*, p. 50).
[35] *Collected Papers Relating to Political Economy* (London, 1925), I, 36. One might also seek to eliminate the indeterminateness by appeal to the varying demand-and-supply prices of individual traders; this is the path chosen by Hicks in "Edgeworth, Marshall, and the Indeterminateness of Wages," *Economic Journal*, XL (1930), 45–31. This, however, is a complicated solution; one must make special hypotheses about the distribution of these demand-and-supply prices.

[36] *Elements of Pure Economics*, trans. Jaffé (Homewood, Ill., 1954), pp. 83 and 185. It is indicative that the word "competition" is not indexed.
[37] *Cours d'économie politique* (Lausanne, 1896, 1897), §§46, 87, 705, 814; cf. also *Manuel d'économie politique* (2d ed.; Paris, 1927), pp. 163, 210, 230.
[38] "Paradoxes of Competition," *Quarterly Journal of Economics*, XX (1905–6), 209–30. Most of the article is concerned with duopoly.
[39] *Ibid.*, pp. 213–14. The fifth statement is held to be a corollary of III and IV; but see p. 13 below.

Marshall's exposition was almost as informal and unsystematic as Smith's in this area. His main statement was:

> We are investigating the equilibrium of normal demand and normal supply in their most general form: we are neglecting those features which are special to particular parts of economic science, and are confining our attention to those broad relations which are common to nearly the whole of it. Thus we assume that the forces of demand and supply have free play in a perfect market; there is no combination among dealers on either side, but each acts for himself: and there is free competition; that is, buyers compete freely with buyers, and sellers compete freely with sellers. But though everyone acts for himself, his knowledge of what others are doing is supposed to be sufficient to prevent him from taking a lower price or paying a higher price than others are doing; . . .[40]

If this quotation suggests that Marshall was invoking a strict concept of competition, we must remember that he discussed the "fear of spoiling the market" and the firms with negatively sloping demand curves in the main chapters on competition[41] and that the only time perfect competition was mentioned was when it was expressly spurned.[42]

Soon he yielded a bit to the trend toward refinement of the concept. Beginning with the third (1895) edition, he explicitly introduced the horizontal demand curve for the individual firm as the normal case and gave it the same mathematical formulation as did Cournot.[43] But these were patchwork revisions, and they were not carried over into the many passages where looser concepts of competition had been employed.

Marshall's most significant contribution was indirect: he gave the most powerful analysis up to his time of the relationship

of competition to optimum economic organization (Book V. chap. xiii, on the doctrine of maximum satisfaction). There he found the competitive results to have not only the well-known qualification that the distribution of resources must be taken as a datum, and the precious exception that only one of several multiple stable equilibriums could be the maximum,[44] but also a new and possibly extremely important exception, arising out of external economies and diseconomies. The doctrine of external economies in effect asserts that in important areas the choices of an individual are governed by only part of the consequences, and inevitably the doctrine opens up a wide range of competitive equilibriums which depart from conventional criteria of optimum arrangement. It was left for Pigou to elaborate, and exaggerate, the importance of this source of disharmonies in *Wealth and Welfare*.

THE COMPLETE FORMULATION CLARK AND KNIGHT

Only two new elements needed to be added to the Edgeworth conditions for competition in order to reach the modern concept of perfect competition. They pertained to the nobility of resources and the model of the stationary economy, and both were presented, not first,[45] but most influentially, by John Bates Clark.

Clark, in his well-known development of the concept of a static economy, ascribed all dynamic disturbances to five forces:

1. Population is increasing.
2. Capital is increasing.
3. Methods of production are improving.

[40] *Principles of Economics* (1st ed.; London, 1890), p. 402. A comparison with the corresponding passage in the eighth edition (*op. cit.*, p. 341) will reveal the curious changes which were later made in the description of competition.

[41] *Principles* (8th ed.; London, 1929), pp. 374 and 458.

[42] *Ibid.*, p. 540.

[43] *Ibid.*, pp. 517 and 849–50.

[44] Both of these qualifications were of course recognized by predecessors such as Walras and Edgeworth.

[45] In the mathematical exposition of theory it was natural to postulate stable supply and demand functions, and therefore stable technologies and tastes, so one could trace a gradually expanding concept of the stationary economy in Walras, Auspitz and Lieben, and Irving Fisher.

4. The forms of industrial establishments are changing: . . .

5. The wants of consumers are multiplying.[46]

The main purpose of his treatise was to analyze the stationary economy in which these forces were suppressed, and for this analysis the assumption of competition was basic:

> There is an ideal arrangement of the elements of society, to which the force of competition, acting on individual men, would make the society conform. The producing mechanism actually shapes itself about this model, and at no time does it vary greatly from it.
>
> We must use assumptions boldly and advisedly, making labor and capital absolutely mobile, and letting competition work in ideal perfection.[47]

Although the concepts of a stationary economy and of competition are completely independent of each other, Clark somehow believed that competition was an element of static analysis:

> The statement made in the foregoing chapter that a static state excludes true entrepreneurs' profits does not deny that a legal monopoly might secure to an entrepreneur a profit that would be permanent as the law that should create it—and that, too, in a social condition which, at first glance, might appear to be static. The agents, labor and capital, would be prevented from moving into the favored industry, though economic forces, if they had been left unhindered, would have caused them to move in. This condition, however, is not a true static state, as it has been defined. . . . Industrial groups are in a truly static state when the industrial agents, labor and capital, show a perfect mobility, but no motion. A legal monopoly destroys at a certain point this mobility. . . .[48]

I shall return to this identification of competition with stationary equilibrium at a later point.

The introduction of perfect mobility of resources as an assumption of competition

was new, and Clark offers no real explanation for the assumption. One could simply eliminate his five dynamic influences, and then equilibrium would be reached after a time even with "friction" (or less than instantaneous mobility). Clark was aware of this possible approach but merely said that "it is best to assume" that there is no friction.[49] The only gain in his subsequent work, of course, is the avoidance of an occasional "in the long run."

Mobility of resources had always been an implicit assumption of competition, and in fact the conditions of adequate knowledge of earning opportunities and absence of contrived barriers to movement were believed to be adequate to insure mobility. But there exist also technological limitations to the rate at which resources can move from one place or industry to another, and these limitations were in fact the basis of Marshall's concept of the short-run normal period. Once this fact was generally recognized, it became inevitable that mobility of resources be given an explicit time dimension, although of course it was highly accidental that instantaneous mobility was postulated.

The concept of perfect competition received its complete formulation in Frank Knight's *Risk, Uncertainty and Profit* (1921). It was the meticulous discussion in this work that did most to drive home to economists generally the austere nature of the rigorously defined concept[50] and so prepared the way for the widespread reaction against it in the 1930's.

Knight sought to establish the precise nature of an economy with complete knowl-

---

[46] *The Distribution of Wealth* (New York, 1899), p. 56.

[47] *Ibid.*, pp. 68 and 71.

[48] *Ibid.*, p. 76; cf. also p. 78.

[49] *Ibid.*, p. 81.

[50] Although Pigou was not concerned with the formal definition of competition, he must also be accounted an influential figure in the popularization of the concept of perfect competition. In his *Wealth and Welfare* (1912), he devoted individual chapters to the effects of immobility (with incorrect knowledge as one component) and indivisibility upon the ability of a resource to receive an equal rate of return in all uses (*ibid.*, Part II, chaps. iv and v).

edge as a preliminary step in the analysis of the impact of uncertainty. Clark's procedure of eliminating historical changes was shown to be neither necessary nor sufficient: a stationary economy was not necessary to achieve complete competitive equilibrium if men had complete foresight; and it was not sufficient to achieve this equilibrium, because there might still be non-historical fluctuations, owing, for example, to drought or flood, which were imperfectly anticipated.[51] Complete, errorless adjustments required full knowledge of all relevant circumstances, which realistically can be possessed only when these circumstances do not change; that is, when the economy is stationary.

The assumptions necessary to competition are presented as part of a list that describes the pure enterprise economy, and I quote those that are especially germane to competition:

> 2. We assume that the members of the society act with complete "rationality." By this we do not mean that they are to be "as angels, knowing good from evil"; we assume ordinary human motives . . . ; but they are supposed to "know what they want" and to seek it "intelligently." . . . They are supposed to know absolutely the consequence of their acts when they are performed, and to perform them in the light of the consequences. . . .
> 4. We must also assume complete absence of physical obstacles to the making, execution, and changing of plans at will; that is, there must be "perfect mobility" in all economic adjustments, no cost involved in movements or changes. To realize this ideal all the elements entering into economic calculations —effort, commodities, etc.—must be continuously variable, divisible without limit. . . . The exchange of commodities must be virtually instantaneous and costless.
> 5. It follows as a corollary from number 4 that there is perfect competition. There must be perfect, continuous, costless intercommunication between all individual members of the society. Every potential buyer of a good constantly knows and chooses among the offers

of all potential sellers, and conversely. Every commodity, it will be recalled, is divisible into an indefinite number of units which must be separately owned and compete effectually with each other.
> 6. Every member of the society is to act as an individual only, in entire independence of all other persons. . . . And in exchanges between individuals, no interests of persons not parties to the exchange are to be concerned, either for good or for ill. Individual independence in action excludes all forms of collusion, all degrees of monopoly or tendency to monopoly. . . .
> 9. All given factors and conditions are for the purposes of this and the following chapter and until notice to the contrary is expressly given, to remain absolutely unchanged. They must be free from periodic or progressive modification as well as irregular fluctuation. The connection between this specification and number 2 (perfect knowledge) is clear. Under static conditions every person would soon find out, if he did not already know, everything in his situation and surroundings which affected his conduct. . . .
> The above assumptions, especially the first eight, are idealizations or purifications or tendencies which hold good more or less in reality. They are the conditions necessary to perfect competition. The ninth, as we shall see, is on a somewhat different footing. Only its corollary of perfect knowledge (specification number 2) which may be present even when change takes place is necessary for perfect competition.[52]

This list of requirements of perfect competition is by no means a statement of the *minimum* requirements, and in fact no one is able to state the minimum requirements.

Consider first complete knowledge. If each seller in a market knows any n buyers, and each seller knows a different (but overlapping) set of buyers, then there will be perfect competition if the set of n buyers is large enough to exclude joint action. Or let there be indefinitely many brokers in any market, and let each broker know many buyers and sellers, and also let each buyer or seller know many brokers—again we have perfect competition. Since entrepreneurs in a stationary economy are essen-

[51] *Risk, Uncertainty and Profit* (New York, 1921), pp. 35–38.

[52] *Ibid.*, pp. 76–79; cf. also p. 148.

tially brokers between resource owners and consumers, it is sufficient for competition if they meet this condition. That is, resource owners and consumers could dwell in complete ignorance of all save the bids of many entrepreneurs. Hence knowledge possessed by any one trader need not be complete; it is sufficient if the knowledge possessed by the ensemble of individuals in the market is in a sense comprehensive.

And now, mobility. Rigid immobility of every trader is compatible with perfect competition if we wish to have this concept denote only equilibrium which is not affected by the actions of individual traders: large numbers (in any market) and comprehensive knowledge are sufficient to eliminate monopoly power. If we wish perfect competition to denote also that a resource will obtain equal returns in all possible uses, mobility becomes essential, but not for all resources. If one resource were immobile and all others mobile, clearly the returns of all resources in all uses could be equalized. Even if all resources were immobile, under certain conditions free transport of consumers' goods would lead to equalization of returns.[53] Even in the general case in which mobility of resources is required, not all the units of a resource need be mobile. If some units of each resource are mobile, the economic system will display complete mobility for all displacements up to a limit that depends upon the proportion of mobile units and the nature of the displacement.

The condition that there be no costs of movement of resources is not necessary in order to reach maximum output for an economy; under competition only those movements of resources will take place for which the additional return equals or exceeds the cost of movement. But costless

movement is necessary if equality is to obtain in the return to a resource in all uses: if the movement between A and B costs $1.00 (per unit of time), the return to a resource at A can vary within $1.00 of either direction of its return at B. Equilibrium could be reached anywhere within these limits (but would be uniquely determined), and this equilibrium would depend upon the historical distribution of resources and consumers.

Next, divisibility. It is not enough to have a large number of informed traders in a market: price must change continuously with quantity if an individual trader is to have only an imperceptible influence upon the market rate, and this will generally require divisibility of the commodity traded. Infinite divisibility, however, is not necessary to eliminate significant control over price by the individual trader, and divisibility of time in the use of a resource is a substitute for divisibility in its quantity. Divisibility, however, is not sufficient to insure uniqueness of equilibriums; even in the simpler problems one must also require that the relevant economic functions display strict monotonicity, but this has nothing to do with competition.

And homogeneity. The formal condition that there be many producers of *a* commodity assumes homogeneity of this commodity (Knight's assumption 5). Certain forms of heterogeneity are of course unimportant because they are superficial: potatoes need not be of the same size if they are sold by the pound; laborers do not have to be equally efficient if the differences in their productivity are measurable. As these examples may suggest, heterogeneity can be a substitute for divisibility.

The final assumption, concerning collusion, is especially troublesome. If one merely postulates the absence of collusion, then why not postulate also that even two rivals can behave in such a way as to reach competitive equilibrium? Instead, one usually requires that the number of traders

[53] See P. A. Samuelson, "International Factor-Price Equalization Once Again," *Economie Journal*, LIX (1949), 181–97; and S. F. James and I. F. Pierce, "The Factor Price Equalization Myth," *Review of Economic Studies*, XIX (1951–52), 111–22.

be large enough so that collusion will not appear. To determine this number, one must have a theory of the conditions under which collusion occurs. Economists have generally emphasized two barriers to collusion. The first is imperfect knowledge, especially of the consequences of rivalry and of the policy which would maximize profits for the group, and of course neither of these difficulties would arise in the stationary economy with perfect knowledge. The second barrier is the difficulty of determining the division of profits among colluders, and we simply do not know whether this difficulty would increase with the number of traders under the conditions we are examining. Hence it seems essential to assume the absence of collusion as a supplement to the presence of large numbers: one of the assumptions of perfect competition is the existence of a Sherman Act.

It is therefore no occasion for complaint that Knight did not state the minimum requirements for perfect competition; this statement was impossible in 1921, and it is impossible today. The minimum assumptions for a theoretical model can be stated with precision only when the complete theory of that model is known. The complete theory of competition cannot be known because it is an open-ended theory; it is always possible that a new range of problems will be posed in this framework, and then, no matter how well developed the theory was with respect to the earlier range of problems, it may require extensive elaboration in respects which previously it glossed over or ignored.

The analytical appeal of a definition of competition does not depend upon its economy of assumptions, although gratuitously wide assumptions are objectionable.[54] We

[54] They are objectionable chiefly because they mislead some user or abusers of the concept as to its domain of applicability. That dreadful list of assumptions of perfect competition which textbooks in labor economics so often employ to dismiss the marginal productivity theory is a case in point.

wish the definition to specify with tolerable clarity—with such clarity as the state of the science affords—a model which can be used by practitioners in a great variety of theoretical researches, so that the foundations of the science need not be debated in every extension or application of theory. We wish the definition to capture the essential general content of important markets, so the predictions drawn from the theory will have wide empirical reliability. And we wish a concept with normative properties that will allow us to judge the efficiency of policies. That the concept of perfect competition has served these varied needs as well as it has is providential.

CONCLUDING REFLECTIONS

If we were free to redefine competition at this late date, a persuasive case could be made that it should be restricted to meaning the absence of monopoly power in a market. This is an important concept that deserves a name, and "competition" would be the appropriate name. But it would be idle to propose such a restricted signification for a word which has so long been used in a wide sense, and at best we may hope to denote the narrower concept by a suggestive phrase. I propose that we call this narrower concept *market competition*.

Perfect market competition will prevail when there are indefinitely many traders (no one of which controls an appreciable share of demand or supply) acting independently in a perfect market. A perfect market is one in which the traders have full knowledge of all offer and bid prices. I have already remarked that it was unfortunate that a perfect market was made a subsidiary characteristic of competition, for a perfect market may also exist under monopoly. Indeed, in realistic cases a perfect market may be more likely to exist under monopoly, since complete knowledge is easier to achieve under monopoly.

Market competition can exist even

though resources or traders cannot enter or leave the market in question. Hence market competition can rule in an industry which is not in long-run competitive equilibrium and is compatible with the existence of large profits or losses.

It is interesting to note that Chamberlin's definition of "pure" competition is identical with my definition of market competition: "competition unalloyed with monopoly elements." [55] But Chamberlin implied that pure competition could rule in an imperfect market; the only conditions he postulated were large numbers of traders and a standardized commodity. The conditions are incomplete: if one million buyers dealt with one million sellers of a homogeneous product, each pair dealing in ignorance of all others, we should simply have one million instances of bilateral monopoly. Hence pure competition cannot be contrasted with perfect competition, for the former also requires "perfect" knowledge (subject to qualifications I have previously discussed), and for this reason I prefer the term "market competition."

The broad concept of perfect competition is defined by the condition that the rate of return (value of the marginal product) of each resource be equal in all uses. If we wish to distinguish this concept from market competition, we may call it (after the terminology attributed to Cairnes) *industrial competition*. Industrial competition requires (1) that there be market competition within each industry; (2) that owners of resources be informed of the returns obtainable in each industry; and (3) that they be free to enter or leave any industry. In addition, the resources must be infinitely divisible if there is to be strict equality in the rate of return on a resource in all uses.

An industrial competitive equilibrium will obtain continuously if resources are instantaneously mobile or in the long run if they move at a finite time rate. Since the

[55] *The Theory of Monopolistic Competition* (1st ed. Cambridge, Mass., 1933), p. 6.

concept of long-run competitive equilibrium is deeply imbedded in modern economic theory, it seems most desirable that we interpret industrial competition as a long-run concept. It may be noticed that a time period did not have to figure explicitly in the pre-Marshallian theory because that theory did not separate and devote special attention to a short-run normal period in which only a portion of the resources were mobile: the basic classical theory was a long-run theory.

The concept of industrial competition has a natural affinity to the static economy even though our definition does not pay any explicit attention to this problem. Rates of return on resources will be equalized only if their owners have complete knowledge of future returns (in the case of durable resources), and it seems improper to assume complete knowledge of the future in a changing economy. Not only is it misleading to endow the population with this gift of prophecy but also it would often be inconsistent to have people foresee a future event and still have that event remain in the future.

One method by which we might seek to adapt the definition to a historically evolving economy is to replace the equalization of rates of return by *expected* rates of return. But it is not an irresistably attractive method. There are troublesome questions of what entrepreneurs seek to maximize under these conditions and of whether risk or uncertainty premiums also enter into their calculations. A more important difficulty is that this formulation implies that the historically evolving industry is in equilibrium in long-run normal periods, and there is no strong reason to believe that such long-run normal periods can be defined for the historically evolving industry. If all economic progress took the form of a secularly smooth development, we could continue to use the Marshallian long-run normal period, and indeed much progress does take this form. But often, and sooner or later always, the historical changes come in vast surges, followed by quiescent periods or worse, and it is harder to assume that the fits and starts can be foreseen with tolerable confidence or that they will come frequently enough to average out within economically relevant time periods.

It seems preferable, therefore, to adapt the concept of competition to changing conditions by another method: to insist only upon the absence of barriers to entry and exit from an industry in the long-run normal period; that is, in the period long enough to allow substantial changes in the quantities of even the most durable and specialized resources. Then we may still expect that some sort of expected return will tend to be equalized under conditions of reasonably steady change, although much work remains to be done before we can specify exactly what this return will be.[56]

The way in which the competitive concept loses precision when historically changing conditions are taken into account is apparent. It is also easily explained: the competitive concept can be no better than the economic theory with which it is used, and until we have a much better theory of economic development we shall not have a much better theory of competition under conditions of non-repetitive change.

The normative role of the competitive concept arises from the fact that the equality of rate of return on each resource in all uses which defines competition is also the condition for maximum output from given resources. The outputs are measured in market prices, and the maximum is rela-

tive to the distribution of ownership of resources. This well-known restriction of the competitive optimum to production, it may be remarked, should be qualified by the fact that the effects of competition on distribution have not been studied. A competitive system affects the distribution of the ownership of resources, and—given a stable distribution of human abilities—a competitive system would probably lead eventually to a stable income distribution whose characteristics are unknown. The theory of this distribution might have substantial normative value.

The vitality of the competitive concept in its normative role has been remarkable. One might have expected that, as economic analysis became more precise and as the range of problems to which it was applied widened, a growing list of disparities between the competitive allocation of resources and the maximum-output allocation would develop. Yet to date there have been only two major criticisms of the norm.[57] The first is that the competitive individual ignores external economies and diseconomies, which—rightly or wrongly—most economists are still content to treat as an exception to be dealt with in individual cases. The second, and more recent, criticism is that the competitive system will not provide the right amount (and possibly not the right types) of economic progress, and this is still an undocumented charge. The time may well come when the competitive concept suitable to positive analysis is not suitable to normative analysis, but it is still in the future.

Finally, we should notice the most common and the most important criticism of the concept of perfect competition—that it is unrealistic. This criticism has been widespread since the concept was completely

[56] It is worth noticing that even under static conditions the definition of the return is modified to suit the facts and that mobility of resources is the basic competitive requirement. Thus we say that laborers move so that the net advantages, not the current money return, of various occupations are equalized. The suggestion in the text is essentially that we find the appropriate definition of net advantages for the historically evolving economy.

[57] In a wider framework there have of course been criticisms of the competitive norm with respect to (i) the ability of individuals to judge their own interests and (ii) the ability of a competitive system to achieve a continuously high level of employment of resources.

formulated and underlies the warm reception which the profession gave to the doctrines of imperfect and monopolistic competition in the 1930's. One could reply to this criticism that all concepts sufficiently general and sufficiently precise to be useful in scientific analysis must be abstract: that, if a science is to deal with a large class of phenomena, clearly it cannot work with concepts that are faithfully descriptive of even one phenomenon, for then they will be grotesquely undescriptive of others. This conventional line of defense for all abstract concepts is completely valid, but there is another defense, or rather another form of this defense, that may be more persuasive.

This second defense is that the concept of perfect competition has defeated its newer rivals in the decisive area: the day-to-day work of the economic theorist. Since the 1930's, when the rival doctrines of imperfect and monopolistic competition were in their heyday, economists have increasingly reverted to the use of the concept of perfect competition as their standard model for analysis. Today the concept of perfect competition is being used more widely by the profession in its theoretical work than at any time in the past. The vitality of the concept is strongly spoken for by this triumph.

Of course, this is not counsel of complacency. I have cited areas in which much work must be done before important aspects of the definition of competition can be clarified. My fundamental thesis, in fact, is that hardly any important improvement in general economic theory can fail to affect the concept of competition. But it has proved to be a tough and resilient concept, and it will stay with us in recognizable form for a long time to come.

18 Monopolistic Competition After Thirty Years: The Impact on General Theory

ROBERT L. BISHOP

Joan Robinson's *Economics of Imperfect Competition* (1933) and Edward Chamberlin's *Theory of Monopolistic Competition* (1933) comprise the foundation on which most contemporary contributions to microeconomic analysis have been built. Both writers are equally recognized as pioneers in the theory of pricing situations that are intermediate between pure competition and monopoly. One such situation is oligopoly which results from the absence of large numbers of competitors. A second, usually referred to as monopolistic competition, occurs when buyers are not indifferent with respect to the seller from whom they buy a particular commodity.

The implications of buyer preferences for the outputs of specific firms are several. One is that it is difficult to classify a particular group of objects as constituting a "commodity" and a particular group producing a "commodity" as an "industry." Thus, the microcosm on which contemporary analysis typically focuses is the firm rather than the industry. A second implication of product differentiation is that a firm's cost curves and demand curves are interdependent because expenditures for advertising, for example, are incurred specifically to create consumer preferences for particular commodities. Individual firms are, therefore, confronted not with infinitely elastic demand curves for their products, as is the case when competition is perfect or pure, but with curves that are downward-sloping. It follows that even if there is freedom for new firms to enter the market, so that pure profit tends to be eliminated in the long run, selling price will equal average cost but not marginal cost.

While there is general agreement about the preceding substantive content of the theories of nonperfect competition, there are those few who question whether the Chamberlinian and Robinsonian contributions have revolutionized the microeconomic area. Some of the reasons for their dissent from the majority view are examined and evaluated by Robert Bishop in the following article.

Reprinted from Robert L. Bishop, "Monopolistic Competition After Thirty Years: The Impact on General Theory," from *The American Economic Review Proceedings,* May 1964, pp. 33–43. Professor Bishop is Dean, School of Humanities and Social Sciences at the Massachusetts Institute of Technology, Cambridge.

The character and importance of the impact that the theories of monopolistic and imperfect competition have had on general theory obviously depend on whose general theory it is. As I judge the consensus of economists, Chamberlin's *Theory of Monopolistic Competition* and Mrs. Robinson's *Economics of Imperfect Competition* are acknowledged to have touched off, in 1933, a theoretical revolution whose relative importance in the microeconomic area was comparable to that of Keynesian analysis in macroeconomics. But there are also some significant minorities in the profession who would minimize or reject completely the positive value of the Chamberlinian and Robinsonian doctrines; so, for anyone like myself that happens to hold these theories in high esteem, it is important to test that judgment against the counterarguments of the opposition. Accordingly, I shall divide my remarks between, first, a brief characterization of the merits and positive significance of Chamberlin's and Robinson's contributions and, second, a consideration of the nature and worth of some of the dissenting views.

Let me begin on a personal note. I was privileged to begin my own study of economics, as a freshman at Harvard, just before the Chamberlin-Robinson revolution —in the very year that their pioneering works were published. I confess that I was a better student of the received doctrines that were set before me than I was an observer of reality; and, among other things I absorbed quickly the notion that "supply and demand" were the key to an understanding of how any market operates, including the occasional monopolistic one that was subject to a control and restriction of supply. Then, sometime during that first year, I heard someone talking about a distinction between buyers' markets and sellers' markets, according as buyers found it easy to buy or sellers to sell. My own instant reaction was to classify the speaker as an economic illiterate;

for it seemed perfectly apparent that, in any "competitive" market, the equilibrium price had to be at the level where demand and supply were equal, so that every buyer could readily buy, and every seller could no less readily sell, whatever respective quantities they pleased. When I subsequently learned that the speaker was indeed talking about relevant economic phenomena, not only did I make a belated mental apology to him for my similarly unspoken slur on his intelligence, but I also felt that I had acquired a justifiable grievance against the analytical tradition that had trapped me into placing my faith in the universality of the law of supply and demand. By this time, of course, I had become a student of monopolistic competition, having found readily convincing the judgment that the demands relevant for most sellers' price decisions were significantly less than perfectly elastic. This was a conclusion that seemed to me then, and still seems to me now, essentially inescapable as soon as the equilibrium of the individual firm was subjected to a more explicit and cogent analysis than, say, in Marshall's fuzzy device of a "representative firm."

Now I do not mean to suggest for a minute that my betters among pre-1933 economists were all equally and uniformly guilty of the same overliteralness in their understanding and analytical use of the law of supply and demand than I was as a freshman. I do believe, however, that they were frequently victims of the state of affairs in which their only explicit theory of competition involved what is now called pure or perfect competition. Furthermore, having only that theory, they were also subject to the persistent analytical bias of a wishful thinking that the world did indeed conform well enough, for the most part, to the conditions necessary for a relevant application of the only theory at their command. Nor has this bias altogether disappeared; it is still very much alive, for example, in such citadels as the University of Chicago. As always, it takes a theory to lick a theory. Accordingly, whether we call the phenomenon "monopolistic competition" as in this Cambridge or "imperfect competition" as in the other one, the intensive theoretical treatments of Chamberlin and Mrs. Robinson were essential in order to force upon the attention of the economics profession due regard for the fact that most product markets differ significantly from the traditional models of either simple monopoly or pure competition.

I can afford to sketch only briefly, and with a few selected examples, some of the ways in which these doctrines have made a difference in economic theory and in the views that most of us entertain as to the economic world around us. Example: as late as 1932, even as excellent an economist as J. R. Hicks was able to write a *Theory of Wages* in which he was still telling us that wages are typically equal to the value of labor's marginal product. In the commentary that he has recently published on that early work, he has himself acknowledged to some extent the seriousness of the defects attributable to his having so consistently and uncritically assumed perfect competition in both product and factor markets.[1]

A few examples concerning Marshall's economic theory are especially appropriate; for he was probably without peer in the delicate art of not letting his inadequate theory get too much in the way of his sensible view of reality. As to retail trade, for example, he was usually careful to mention that the competitive theory he was talking about did not apply.[2] Now, of course, we have a theoretical framework into which an analysis of many different kinds of retail trade can be fitted. Or con-

sider the famous category of the decreasing-cost industry, whose existence Marshall had to explain by means of a very confusing set of comments about the internal and external economies reaped by the representative firm when demand for the industry's product went up, despite the fact (which he uneasily recognized) that unexhausted internal economies of scale are incompatible with purely competitive equilibrium. With product differentiation or oligopoly (or both), the possibility that increased demand may lead to lower prices becomes eminently comprehensible and plausible, without recourse to any mystique about an especially dubious type of external economy. Finally, consider the anomalousness of Marshall's view that price typically equals marginal cost except when demand is too low for the firm to cover its full costs, whereupon misgivings about "spoiling the market" are dragged in to explain why the firm does not suffer the even greater loss that would be implied if it were to continue to equate price to marginal cost (at least down to minimum average variable cost). This conception is revealed in all its naked implausibility by Frisch's graphical interpretation of Marshall's verbal exposition.[3]

As soon as we recognize that there are comparatively few markets in which "demand and supply" operate in the essentially symmetrical way that is the essence of that famous law, many things become analytically clear for the first time. Thus, in product markets where buyers are passive and prices are unilaterally administered by sellers, the normal condition of price in excess of marginal cost explains why it is the sellers rather than the buyers who are eager for more transactions. Not only does this open the door to such phenomena as advertising and other forms of non-price competition, but it also helps explain why we are a race of eager sellers and coy

[1] J. R. Hicks, *The Theory of Wages* (2nd ed., 1963), p. 310.
[2] A. Marshall, *Principles of Economics* (8th ed., 1920), p. 328.
[3] R. Frisch, "Alfred Marshall's Theory of Value," *Q.J.E.*, 1950, pp. 495–524.

buyers, with purchasing agents getting the Christmas presents from the salesmen rather than the other way around, and with "salesmanship" a familiar concept while "purchasemanship" does not even appear in the dictionary. We find here also, I am convinced, part of the explanation— even though not the whole—of the persistent producer-orientation of so many of the world's mercantilist policies, both ancient and modern, international and domestic.

Not the least of the contributions of these doctrines, in my opinion, is the improved sense that they make out of the major propositions that have emerged from Keynesian macroeconomic analysis. Keynes himself, of course, was still sufficiently Marshallian when he wrote the *General Theory* so that he based his theory on an assumption of universal pure competition, but with the anomalous extra feature of a perfectly elastic labor supply up to the full employment quantity, as based on a peculiarly strong and implausible "money illusion" on the part of the labor suppliers. This was Keynes' way of explaining how an underemployment equilibrium was possible without a persistent price deflation. In contrast to that rationalization, how much more natural and plausible it is to explain the necessary price and wage rigidities or "stickiness" with reference to the fact that the world is not predominantly purely competitive.

Similarly, it is only with reference to these doctrines that we can make analytical sense out of the more modern dilemma that really full employment is very hard to achieve without at least a creeping inflation. The difficulty is not at all that some prices and wage rates rise for the good competitive reason that otherwise there would be an excess of demand over supply, but rather that other prices not only fail to fall but are even capable of being increased when the opposite condition prevails. This asymmetry, whereby many

prices and wage rates go up much more readily than they go down (save only in the deepest depression), is again traceable to the basic facts that (1) our price-determining machinery is preponderantly seller-dominated, and (2) the normal condition of such markets is that supply exceeds demand—in the relevant sense that sellers (whether of goods or labor) are willing and eager to sell more than they can actually sell at their current prices. To investigate the conflicting claims of demand-pull and cost-push theories of inflation without due regard for these considerations, as some scholars still do, is to omit a most important ingredient of the analysis.[4]

Widely accepted though the theories of monopolistic or imperfect competition have been, there are still some determined pockets of resistance. I turn, accordingly, to an examination of some of the views entertained in those quarters. The various misgivings can be disentangled to some extent, I think, under such headings as (1) ideological, (2) methodological, and (3) factual.

Even though ideological precommitment is a poor influence in shaping anyone's evaluation of a new theory, such ideological contamination has played a not inconsiderable role in just such areas as the present one. As always, ideology cuts at least two ways. Thus, in the atmosphere of the depressed 1930's, so conducive to the deepest disillusionment with the current performance of capitalist free enterprise, it was not surprising that many young Turks —and some old ones as well—were strongly predisposed to find in the theories of monopolistic or imperfect competition, not only a legitimate analytical framework, but also a device for dramatizing in an exaggerated way at least some of the sins of capitalism. Mrs. Robinson herself, I am told, has testified that the central motiva-

---

[4] For example, R. T. Selden, "Cost-Push versus Demand-Pull Inflation, 1955–57," *J.P.E.*, Feb., 1959, pp. 1–20.

tion for her own book was to demonstrate the pervasiveness of the exploitation of labor; and her bias is further apparent in her failure to give a corresponding attention to monopoly power in labor markets. It is sometimes inadequately appreciated that, no matter how much labor a great corporation may hire, it exerts no monopsony power at all unless it is unable to get as much labor as desired at the current wage rate; conversely, if there is an excess of job seekers at that wage, the predominating influence in the situation is monopolistic, not monopsonistic.

On the other side, the central ideological resistance to a due acknowledgement of the widespread relevance of monopolistic competition comes from those theorists who have a strong emotional stake in an absolute and uncompromising defense of the optimality of unregulated markets. This is illustrated, for example, in the writings of Mises and Hayek. To Mises, imperfect or monopolistic competition is "mythology" (*Human Action*, 1949, p. 378). His argument is a curious one, however, for he concedes the existence of all of the basic phenomena with which the theory of monopolistic competition is concerned, including product differentiation and oligopoly (e.g., pp. 354–61). Indeed, he even concedes that "almost all consumers' goods are included in the class of monopolized goods" (p. 357). But, even more curiously, he also argues that it does not follow by any means that monopolists necessarily, or even presumptively, charge monopoly prices (e.g., p. 356). Now it should not be thought that Mises is talking about the *curiosum* of a "monopolist" who faces a perfectly elastic demand; for he is ludicrously confused about this. Thus, a bit farther on (pp. 381–82), in speaking of the various ways in which the individual consumer may react to monopoly prices, he says of one of the possibilities: "The consumer restricts his purchase of the monopolized commodity to such an extent that he spends less for it than he would have spent under the competitive price; he buys with the money thus saved goods which he would not have bought otherwise. (If all people were to react in this way, the seller would harm his interests by substituting a higher price for the competitive price; no monopoly price could emerge. . . .)" The cream of this little jest, of course, is that a monopolist with positive marginal cost maximizes his profit only where marginal revenue is also positive, or where demand exhibits the relative elasticity that Mises' case implies.

But if Mises' own discussion founders in this type of futility, he also invokes the aid of a much more careful and competent analyst when he cites (p. 278, n.) as "a refutation of the fashionable doctrines of imperfect and of monopolistic competition" two essays by Hayek in his *Individualism and Economic Order* (1948; pp. 92–118). Actually, however, Hayek's unhappiness with the concept of an "imperfect" market really rests primarily on his misgivings as to the unreal character of a "perfect" one and on what he describes as "the so-called theory of 'perfect competition'" (p. 92). Thus, his quarrel would seem to me to be less with Chamberlin and Mrs. Robinson than with such theorists as Friedman and Stigler, who defend the application of the perfectly competitive model in many situations where others of us regard it as very dubiously applicable.

Specifically, Hayek argues "that what the theory of perfect competition discusses has little claim to be called 'competition' at all and that its conclusions are of little use as guides to policy" (p. 92). This reflects a methodological complaint that "the modern theory of competition deals almost exclusively with a state of what is called 'competitive equilibrium' in which it is assumed that the data for the different individuals are fully adjusted to each other, while the problem which requires explanation is the nature of the process by which the data are thus adjusted" (p. 94). In reply, it seems to me that no competent theorist regards static-equilibrium theory as the last word of economic analysis. Moreover, part of our interest in static equilibria concerns their stability conditions, from which the more general comparative-statics theorems are generated; and, beyond that, everyone stands ready to move on to explicitly dynamic analysis whenever necessary. But to argue, as Hayek seems to, that dynamic analysis can be wholly divorced from concepts of equilibrium seems to me anything but fruitful. In other words, even the dynamics of a market remain quite incomprehensible except as we can analyze them as movements toward or away from some equilibrium position, even when the data are changing so rapidly that at least the longer-run types of equilibria are never actually attained. In short, Hayek's discussion is less a "refutation" of what others call imperfections of competition—like Mises, he also willingly acknowledges the phenomena and balks only at what they are called—than it is an obcurantist effort to undermine all of the standard techniques of economic analysis.

On the other hand, Hayek is too sensible a man to hold consistently to his rejection of equilibrium analysis. Thus, his methodology does not prevent him from comparing "an 'imperfect' market . . . with a relatively 'perfect' market as that of, say, grain" (p. 102), despite his previous argument that competition has to be not only dynamic but personal (pp. 96–97). On the latter point, he cites as "remarkable" Stigler's eminently perceptive statement that "economic relationships are never perfectly competitive if they involve any personal relationships between economic units" (in the sense, of course, that when demand equals supply in a perfectly competitive market, it makes no difference to any buyer or seller as to the identity of the other party or parties with whom he deals, and

also in the sense that no buyer or seller is thereby frustrating any other person in his desire to make a similar purchase or sale at the competitive equilibrium price). My final comment is that, if Hayek finds such impersonal equilibria unrealistic, he is more than welcome to join the ranks of the converts to the theory of monopolistic competition. Nor, if he were to accept this invitation, should he fear that he would thereby be forced to give up what he cites as the "practical lesson of all this, . . . that he should worry much less about whether competition in a given case is perfect and worry much more whether there is competition at all" (p. 105). Surely, many of his presumed opponents agree wholeheartedly with that sentiment, and also with his further remark that "much more serious than the fact that prices may not correspond to marginal cost is the fact that, with an intrenched monopoly, costs are likely to be higher than necessary." To this I would only add that so may they be when oligopolists invite excess capacity with high-price policies and deliberately create excess capacity to discourage further entry, or when monopolistic competitors of any kind inflate their costs with certain types of sales-effort expenditures as an alternative to cutting prices. But even if Hayek rejects this invitation, the rest of us must at least be pardoned if we conclude that his discussion constitutes a pale and unconvincing "refutation" of the doctrines in question.

A quite different motive for either ignoring or minimizing market imperfections is rooted in the theorist's methodological bias in favor of the assumption of pure competition, because of its analytically tractable features. Sometimes this assumption is made in a properly apologetic way, as by Hicks in *Value and Capital*. Still, this does not keep him from consoling himself with the comforting thought: "I do not myself believe that the more important results of this work are much damaged by this omission [of imperfectly competitive influences]" (p. 7). And later, when he acknowledges that certain considerations do indeed have "to be met by sacrificing the assumption of perfect competition," he adds unhappily, "yet it has to be recognized that a general abandonment of the assumption of perfect competition, a universal adoption of the assumption of monopoly, must have very destructive consequences for economic theory" (p. 83). In other words, he feels that it is better to have a neat, inapplicable theory than to face up to the difficulties of formulating some relevant ones.

Where Hicks is at least frankly apologetic and defensive, however, others such as Friedman assume an aggressive initiative, even to the extent of finding positive merit in the failures of the purely competitive model to conform better than it does to the facts of a great variety of situations. If I understand him aright, Friedman imposes on himself the heroic act of self-denial of choosing to work with only two abstract models (*Essays in Positive Economics*, pp. 35ff.). These involve: (1) a "competitive" firm, where "the demand curve for its output is infinitely elastic with respect to its own price for some price and all outputs, given the prices charged by all other firms"; and (2) a "monopolistic" firm, where "the demand curve for its output is not infinitely elastic at some price for all outputs." In a footnote, however, he breaks the latter category down into two types: (1) "the monopolistic firm proper, if the demand curve is nowhere infinitely elastic (except possibly at zero output)," and (2) "the oligopolistic firm, if the demand curve for its output is infinitely elastic at some price for some but not all outputs."

As to this weird oligopoly concept, it may first be noticed that oligopolistic suppliers of merely close (but not perfect) substitute products are not oligopolists at all to Friedman, but just monopolists. Thus, there is apparently no competition worth analyzing at all between Ford and General Motors. Second, there is not even a clear distinction between competition and oligopoly in Friedman's scheme; for, whether the suppliers of perfect substitutes are two or two thousand, the demand confronting any one of them (with other prices constant, as Friedman specifies) is perfectly elastic only up to the total quantity demanded in the market as a whole at the common price. On the other hand, Friedman never puts his oligopolistic model to any analytical use anyway; so it does not really constitute a third model as an addition to the two basic ones.

Having only two such models at his disposal, then, he naturally needs a good deal of leeway in the discretion that he allows himself as to their use. Thus, as he makes perfectly clear in an example relating to the cigarette industry (pp. 37–38), either model is relevantly applicable depending on the problem at hand. First, however, no guidance whatever is offered as to the principles that might determine which of the two models is relevant, in advance of applying one or the other. Second, there is obviously a lot of room here for self-deception as to whether either model really applies at all satisfactorily. Thus Friedman says: "Suppose the problem is to determine the effect on retail prices of cigarettes of an increase, expected to be permanent, in the federal cigarette tax. I venture to predict that broadly correct results will be obtained by treating cigarette firms as if they were producing an identical product and were in perfect competition." There are some problems, however, as to how this conjecture might be tested. Thus, depending perhaps on the period allowed for the industry's adjustment, the gross price paid by consumers will presumably rise; but any such reaction can be tautologically rationalized after the fact with reference to either competitive or monopolistic theory, whether the price rises by an amount greater than, equal to, or less than the tax. Clearly, if competitive theory is to be relevantly applicable, Friedman must first find not only *a* supply curve for the cigarette industry, but the whole collection of successively relevant short-run and long-run supply curves; and he must then find that the cigarette industry does indeed behave "as if" it were constantly equating demand and supply. Now, actually, there is a test that can at least disprove what Friedman ventures to predict. In an industry that really is purely competitive, with the basic demand and cost data constant, a tax may cause the price to rise little, if at all, in a very short run; then it causes the price to rise more in each successively longer short run; and finally it rises most in the long run. But monopolists and oligopolists, in their wisdom as dynamic profit maximizers, often respond to a tax with an immediate, once-and-for-all price increase —quite unlike pure competitors. My own ventured prediction is that cigarette manufacturers do indeed respond in this oligopolistic manner, perhaps even rescinding part of the price increase in the longer run if a reduction of factor prices is induced by the curtailment of factor demand.

The same sort of determination to divide both reality and its economic analysis into the two neat boxes of competition and simple monopoly is also illustrated in Stigler's work. Thus, in one of his *Five Lectures on Economic Problems* (1950), he concludes that the theory of monopolistic competition is a "failure" (p. 22) because it embraces too many diverse conditions for any single, neat theory to cope with in a fruitful way. Then, in the last lecture, he gallantly undertakes to classify as best he can the industries of the United States into the two categories of "competition" and "monopoly" (with a monopolistic subcategory of "compulsory cartels"). "A competitive situation," he says (p. 48), "is characterized by price or product competition of the individual firm, leading to approximate

equality of price and marginal cost in the long run." This is a constructive start, but it has two weaknesses: (1) the standard of "approximate equality" is not clear (should it be no more than a 2 percent disparity, for example, or would 10 percent be acceptable too?), and (2) what is the meaning and the justification of limiting the prescription to the long run? As to the first point, it is also important to appreciate that, with production divided into various vertical stages, the magnitude of price minus marginal cost is more relevantly compared with value added than with price. As to the reference to the long run, if this means only that price may temporarily exceed marginal cost by an appreciable percentage, for example in the early stages of major innovative change, then well and good; but if it means, as I fear it does, that price may acceptably be only slightly higher than long-run marginal cost at the same time that it is persistently or predominantly higher than short-run marginal cost by a much larger percentage, then I must respectfully protest. The point involved is an important one and the subject of quite widespread confusion, so I should like to spell out its implications.

First, in an industry that is really purely competitive, there is no need to indulge in any apologetics about short-run equilibrium. In any purely competitive equilibrium, whether short-run or long-run, price is always equal to the respectively relevant marginal cost. Furthermore, in long-run equilibrium, price is equal to both long-run and short-run marginal cost (provided only that they are both determinate). This follows, of course, from the tangency or envelope relationship between long-run and short-run total cost. Then, according as output in the short run is either above or below the long-run equilibrium level, short-run marginal cost is also either above or below long-run marginal cost, respectively. Thus it does not follow that short-run marginal cost is either necessarily or presumptively below long-run marginal cost, despite a widespread belief to the contrary even among theorists who should know better. Accordingly, in any evaluation as to how "nearly" purely competitive a given industry may be, the relevant test is how nearly price corresponds to short-run marginal cost on the average through time. Therefore, an industry or firm which keeps price not too far above some version of long-run marginal cost on the average, but which consistently exhibits an appreciably higher excess of price over short-run marginal cost, should not get very good marks as to the closeness of its approximation to pure competition. Under these conditions, in other words, there is an unfailing indication that capacity is persistently in excess of what it should be for either purely competitive or efficient equilibrium. On the other hand, as already suggested above in connection with Hayek's observation about cost inflation, this is by no means an unusual case under conditions that are other than purely competitive.

Stigler's estimate as to the number of industries that adequately approximate pure competition or, as he puts it, "in which monopoly power is inappreciable" (p. 47), is further biased by his willingness to certify an industry as "competitive" if either of two conditions are met. The first concerns an industry's structure and the second concerns its performance (p. 47): "(1) It must possess a large number of independent firms, none dominant in size, and additional firms can enter the industry. (2) It may possess few firms, or a few firms of relatively large size, but the departures from a competitive situation are not large." I have already indicated my misgivings as to the excessive leniency of the second condition, since it rests on the "approximate equality of price and marginal cost in the long run." Furthermore, the first condition

is also too lenient, in that it allows an industry to qualify as "competitive" even if the gap between price and marginal cost is substantial. This may well be the case (1) because product differentiation alone is capable of raising price appreciably above marginal cost, even when the rival firms are numerous and entry is easy, and (2) because local oligopolistic relationships may also exist, even when firms are numerous throughout a broadly and loosely defined "industry."

Let me conclude with the almost obligatory reference to what remains for future research. Despite the methodological differences just indicated, it still seems to me that the basic conflicts between Cambridge and Chicago in this area are primarily factual, at least to the extent that we seem to agree that the relationships of price and marginal cost are of central importance. What we ideally need, accordingly, is a kind of profile of price, marginal-cost, and value-added relationships throughout the economy. Even if the whole job would be a staggering one, it would still be worth while to have it done if only on a piecemeal sampling basis. Only then would we really be in a position to evaluate definitively, for example, Stigler's conclusion that the U.S. economy is about 70 percent "competitive" or Harberger's ingenious but extraordinarily naïve estimate that resource misallocation in American manufacturing entails a cost of only about $2.00 per capita.[5] My own hostage to fortune is that the relevant data would reveal the disparities between price and marginal cost throughout the U.S. economy to be far greater than they are thought to be in Chicago.

[5] A. C. Harberger, "Monopoly and Resource Allocation," *A.E.R.*, May, 1954, pp. 77-87, esp. p. 84.

19 Monopolistic Competition
and Welfare Economics*

WILLIAM J. BAUMOL

It is generally agreed that welfare questions in their broadest sense involve value judgments which lie outside the province of the economist qua economist. It has become customary, therefore, to conceive of *economic* welfare as being maximized when an economic system functions at maximum efficiency to satisfy given ends with available resources. This conception is intended to make it analytically possible to separate questions about the efficiency of resource use from questions about the justice or desirability of using resources for one alternative rather than another.

Achievement of the economic optimum requires that certain conditions known as marginal or first-order conditions be satisfied. Optimum in the consuming sector requires that the marginal rate of substitution between each pair of goods be equal to the ratio of their prices for each consumer. It is then not possible for any consumer to move to a higher indifference curve except at the expense of someone else. Optimum in the producing sector requires that all firms producing the same two goods, and paying the same prices for their factor inputs, equate both their marginal rates of transformation between the goods and the marginal rate of substitution between factors to the ratio of their marginal costs. Otherwise a reorganization of production could increase the output of either or both products without any change in total factor input or the output of other commodities.

It is apparent that simultaneous satisfaction of the marginal conditions in both the consuming sector and the producing sector requires that the prices to which consumers equate the ratios of the marginal rates of substitution be the same as those to which producers equate their marginal rates of transformation and substitution in the process of maximizing profits. This can take place only if commodity prices are everywhere equal to marginal cost, and factor prices are everywhere equal to the value of their marginal products. It follows that the marginal or first-order conditions cannot be satisfied under nonperfect competition because the negative slope of a firm's average and marginal revenue curves

Reprinted from William J. Baumol, "Monopolistic Competition and Welfare Economics," in *The American Economic Review* of May 1964, pp. 44–52. Dr. Baumol is Professor of Economics at Princeton University.

* The author would like to express his thanks to the National Science Foundation whose grant greatly facilitated the completion of this paper.

will then result in a price which is consistently above marginal cost and an output which is smaller than optimum, even in an equilibrium situation.

What are the welfare implications of market situations in which the marginal conditions are violated? The article "Monopolistic Competition and Welfare Economics" by William Baumol suggests that the matter is not nearly as simple and straightforward as it might first appear. Specifically, the implications of business behavior aimed at sales maximization are different from those aimed at profit maximization. Further, the welfare significance of the excess-capacity theorem is difficult to assess because of the variety of interpretations to which it is subject.

Definitive reappraisals of a major theoretical contribution are like a soprano's final farewell appearance. They come frequently and sometimes with monotonous regularity. It would not be easy to estimate the number of conclusive evaluations of Professor Chamberlin's contribution [4] but their rate of appearance seems recently to have been stepped up. This paper will no doubt quietly take its place in this massive and spontaneous tribute to the impact of the *Theory of Monopolistic Competition.*

It must be emphasized here that even the writings of those who would minimize the contribution of monopolistic competition, by their very number and vociferousness combine to constitute an encomiast, as it were, praising by strong (and frequent) damns.

To deal with the subject which has been assigned to me—the contribution of monopolistic competition to welfare economics— I feel I must probe into ancient history. For in recent years it has become unfashionable for the welfare economist to speak about anything so substantive. Rather, he has grown exceedingly introspective and has been spending much of his time determining the circumstances under which he has any right to speak at all. No longer does he ask whether monopolistic competition is good for the country, but tries, instead, to construct criteria of increasing subtlety which, if the circumstances were right, and the appropriate data and value judgments were available, would permit him to break his stubborn silence on more applicable matters. Fortunately, monopolistic competition theory antedates this

period and so we can be somewhat sanguine as we proceed to look at the literature.

MONOPOLISTIC COMPETITION AND THE ALLOCATION OF RESOURCES

One of the main substantive areas of contribution of welfare theory is its analysis of the allocation of resources under different market structures and its comparison with the social optimum—the so-called "ideal output." However, most results which have emerged have dealt with the case of universal pure competition or with the presence of a single monopolist in a world otherwise unsullied by the presence of monopolistic elements.[1]

One need not seek far for the reason monopolistic competition has failed to make a stronger showing here. Resource allocation among industries and among products is, after all, intrinsically a matter for general equilibrium (or general disequilibrium) analysis. One cannot say in absolute terms that the output of a single product, taken in isolation, is ideal. Only if its producers have kept out of the hands of the makers of other commodities neither too large nor too small a collection of inputs can we say that their output levels are consistent with maximal social well-being. In other words, to pass judgment on the allocation of resources one must be able to account for the interrelationships among the outputs of the various industries. But it is here that monopolistic competition is notoriously weak. Despite Professor Trif-

[1] Two noteworthy exceptions are Chap. **27** in Mrs. Robinson's classic volume [9] and R. A. Berry's unpublished dissertation [3].

fin's noble attempt, it must be recognized that general equilibrium theory remains, by and large, a theory of pure competition.

PRODUCT DIFFERENTIATION AND RESOURCE ALLOCATION

The case of product differentiation has proved particularly resistant to general equilibrium analysis. Where we can propose no satisfactory criterion by which one can recognize either an industry or a product, it is perhaps too much to expect that we can say much by way of rigorous analysis about the allocation of resources among industries and products. The theory of product differentiation has been and remains a theory of the firm.

OLIGOPOLY AND RESOURCE ALLOCATION

Rather more hopeful is the case of the oligopolistic industry whose product is homogeneous. And, indeed, the literature does contain models which offer some (rather limited) welfare implications. For example, the Cournot theory tells us that oligopolists who behave in accord with its model will produce an output smaller than that which would be yielded by a comparable competitive industry. From this we may infer that in suitably specified circumstances oligopoly will lead to a misallocation of resources and an inadequate output of the oligopolized product.

But when we recognize the number of conditions which are required by this argument we are left deriving small comfort from it. Not only must our industry be composed exclusively of unreconstructable Cournot oligopolists who never learn by experience that their output decisions affect those of their rivals, but all other industries must be uncontaminated either by elements of monopoly or by external economies and diseconomies. In Mrs. Robinson's "world of monopolies" all bets are off. For with a given level of employment of resources (the fundamental assumption of allocation theory) it is impossible for all industries simultaneously to use too small a proportion of society's resources. If all industries demands for resources are weaker than would be those of their competitive equivalents, the allocation of resources may nevertheless conceivably remain unaffected,[2] and in any event it is not easy to predict or evaluate such changes in allocation as will occur.

Moreover, in such a world our efforts at prescription are further hampered by the exacting requirements of the Lipsey-Lancaster theory of the second best. For they have argued that in circumstances in which some necessary conditions for an optimum are violated, there is little to be said for enforcement of the remaining necessary conditions. It is not difficult to construct a persuasive resource allocation illustration for this view. In a two-industry world, as we have seen, if both industries are monopolized, there is no reason to assume that a serious misallocation of resources will result. But enforcement of marginal cost pricing on one of these industries is a sure way to produce a maldistribution of resources.[3] It is at least arguable that the relatively competitive circumstances of American agriculture in pre-New Deal days aggravated significantly the misallocation of the nation's inputs.

SALES MAXIMIZATION AND RESOURCE ALLOCATION

One somewhat personal postscript may perhaps be permissible before leaving our discussion of allocation. In recent months a number of prominent economists and I have received an unpublished paper in which my sales maximization hypothesis ([2], Chaps. 6–8) is denounced as an at-

[2] For a more detailed argument see Berry [3], Chap. II.
[3] Cf. Berry, *loc. cit.*

tack on the profit system. I must admit that this rather took me by surprise because I had been more fearful that my hypothesis would be considered by some to be a piece of capitalist apologetics. For it seems clear enough from the preceding discussion, and indeed it is a commonplace, that profit maximizing behavior in the presence of monopoly elements can frequently yield results which are not optimal from the point of view of society as a whole.

By contrast, if oligopolists seek to maximize their sales (total revenue), the consequences may be somewhat more commendable. This is suggested by a crude view of the matter, utilizing the theorem that sales (total revenue) maximization will yield outputs larger than those which maximize profits. For, if the trouble with profit maximizing monopolistic and oligopolistic outputs is that they are too small, then (if only they do not overcompensate) the larger sales maximizing output levels have some presumption in their favor.

A somewhat more subtle argument (which should not be taken very seriously but is perhaps a bit more amusing) takes as its view that sales maximizing oligopolists seek to return to their stockholders no more (or less) than "normal" profits; i.e., the rate of interest on capital plus some compensation for risk. If this were so and if all firms were to succeed in this goal, then a mixed world of competitors and oligopolists might yet produce the ideal output, provided, of course, that it were untouched by externalities.

THE EXCESS CAPACITY THEOREM: INTERPRETATION

The analysis of product differentiation, while it has had little to say about the allocation of resources among industries, has yielded one celebrated theorem with much noted welfare implications. This is Professor Chamberlin's excess capacity theorem which rests on the argument that

high profits will lead to the manufacture of new substitute products and that a sufficient rate of entry can force the total elimination of profits. Since this requires tangency between the company's average cost and revenue curves and since the demand (average revenue) curve will have a negative slope under monopolistic competition, the equilibrium point must lie on a negatively inclined portion of the average cost curve; i.e., the company must be able to reduce its unit costs by increasing its production.

Mr. Kaldor [7] has long ago discussed, in some detail, the plausibility of the assumptions which lie behind this argument, and in a similar spirit Professor Machlup ([8], pp. 311–44) has proposed several alternative interpretations of the theorem:

1. Tautological interpretation: The profits of the firm under monopolistic competition must be imputed to one or more of its inputs, and if this rent is included in cost, the company's net profit must necessarily be zero. The tangency result and the excess capacity theorem therefore follow inescapably. It is worth noting that Mrs. Robinson's version of the theorem is of this variety, which, as Machlup has shown, is not entirely without welfare implications, despite its tautological character.

2. A second variant of the theorem asserts that it is valid only where firms are sufficiently similar, small, and numerous. This interpretation restricts the range of relevance of the theorem very severely, not only because such circumstances are far from universal, but also because then the typical company's demand curve may plausibly be expected to be quite flat and excess capacity correspondingly insignificant.

3. A final interpretation of the theorem treats it as an approximation which indicates a tendency expected to be observed in most circumstances characterized by product differentiation. This is by far the most attractive variant of the theorem but

it then becomes a matter for empirical verification.

Returning now to the tautological version of the theorem, we note that Professor Machlup has divided the rents imputed to the profit yielding inputs into those which are socially "allowable" and those which must be rejected because they represent no real significance for the social product. For example, if the firm enjoys a monopolistic advantage because it employs a really scarce input (such as a uniquely advantageous site), then this input service constitutes a very real advantage to the firm and to the community, and the rent is accordingly considered an allowable element in the relevant social unit cost curve. On the other hand, where the firm's product is differentiated by an ability to create an illusory quality advantage, e.g., by salesmanship, then no social rent can be imputed to the input in question and the social unit cost curve may fail to be tangent to the average revenue curve, so that equilibrium need not involve declining average social costs (there need be no excess capacity). Professor Machlup concludes rather despondently that we are then damned in the one case and damned in the other. In the one circumstance, where the rents are "real," excess capacity must also be very real; while in the other eventuality, where we may escape true excess capacity, we are likely to become tributaries to the artful producer of artificial monopolistic elements.

THE EXCESS CAPACITY THEOREM: VALIDITY OF ITS WELFARE IMPLICATIONS

Recently, the very validity of the welfare implications usually drawn from the excess capacity theorem has come under attack, even in circumstances satisfying the assumptions of the theorem. It is appropriate to review and evaluate the objections which have been raised. Harold Demsetz [5] has argued that the theorem is undermined by the multiplicity of variables which enter the profit function under monopolistic competition. Professor Chamberlin's argument shows merely that a small increase in output from its equilibrium level must reduce average cost only if all other things remain constant. But, says Demsetz, other things cannot be expected to remain equal. Self-interest will usually induce managements to reconsider their advertising outlays whenever they add to their outputs. The net effect of a combined change in advertising and production levels cannot be predicted from the Chamberlinian analysis.

Suppose this much is granted. Demsetz on his side readily agrees that the *ceteris paribus* consequence of an output change from an equilibrium point will reduce unit costs. The question to be settled then, is, which assertion has the action—which of them is pertinent for welfare analysis?

Here, it seems to me, the logic of the matter rules against Demsetz. If any partial derivative of the average cost function is negative at the equilibrium point, we cannot be at an optimum. Lower unit operating costs are necessarily possible and the productive arrangements must necessarily be wasteful in the sense which will presently be specified. True, if the firm is left to adjust by itself to a decree which requires it to increase output, the result may be even worse than it was initially. If it increases its advertising along with its production, its unit costs may well rise. But this does not mean that the initial equilibrium, however much less costly it may have been, was sufficiently large to yield minimum costs. On the contrary, granting its premises, the Chamberlin argument shows conclusively that his equilibrium point is characterized by unused opportunities for cost reduction.

A second attack on the validity of the excess capacity theorem was mounted by G. C. Archibald ([1], pp. 18–19). Archibald also rests his case on the multivariate character of decision making under product differentiation. But he argues that the average cost curve which Chamberlin shows to be downward sloping at the equilibrium point is an aggregation of production and advertising outlays. However, this negative slope is perfectly compatible with rising unit output costs, provided only that advertising costs are falling with sufficient rapidity to offset any rise in per-unit production outlays. "Hence," he concludes, "when advertising is introduced, tangency is consistent with production at less than or more than minimum cost of production." One can hardly quarrel with the logic of Mr. Archibald's argument, and it must be emphasized that he carries it no further and makes no attempt to draw any welfare implication from his brief discussion.

One may, then, agree with him and yet simultaneously warn the reader against jumping to conclusions about the consequence of his analysis. For, so long as the combined curve of output and advertising costs slopes downward, it surely follows that an increase in the firm's production level can reduce the real resources tied up in a unit of its product, whether these resources are expended in the factory or by way of Madison Avenue. Chamberlin's negative slope remains a strike against the efficiency of unregulated product differentiation.

Very recently, Professor Friedman has also loosed one of his formidable thunderbolts upon the theorem. He argues ([6], p. 67):

In a world of specialized resources, and certainly in one of monopolies whatever their source, [average cost equals average revenue] is either a convention of accounting (total costs equal total receipts) or, if defined to be an equilibrium condition, is imposed on the firm by the capital market via the revaluation of specialized resources. This is what renders the tangency condition irrelevant to productive adjustments and makes the alleged implications about "excess capacity and unexploited economies of scale"—with or

without advertising—highly misleading if not downright wrong.

Professor Friedman, of course, has a valid point when he later expresses his dislike of the use of the term "capacity" for the minimum point on the average cost curve. But the fact remains that the excess capacity hypothesis (note I now do not call it a theorem) if not interpreted in accord with the Kaldor-Machlup tautological version, can still indicate that all is not quite for the best in a best of all possible economies. If small firms with heterogeneous products do, in fact, tend to drive one another's profits down to zero with no monopoly rents included (and as one who grew up among small retailers I can only consider this an understatement), then very likely each firm will be left so small a segment of the market that it must proceed at an uneconomically small scale of operation. Crude observation suggests that this phenomenon occurs all too often and that the tangency analysis can offer a meaningful hypothesis to explain it. The essence of the matter is an empirical hypothesis about the nature of entry under monopolistic competition, which, if valid, will prevent any substantial monopoly rents and hence any material revaluation of resources by the capital market. Of course, observation may show that the required entry behavior very rarely or perhaps, even, never occurs. But then the model will be shown to be false, but it still will neither be empty nor devoid of welfare implications.

STANDARD CAVEAT RE THE WELFARE IMPLICATIONS

There is little need to review in detail the standard reservations regarding the welfare implications of the excess capacity theorem. We have often been warned of its pitfalls and the caution which is required in its interpretation. The two main points in this matter may quickly be summarized:

1. The excess capacity theorem is not a

statement about the desirability of the allocation of resources among industries. It does not say that there will be too little produced by an industry (however defined) whose products are differentiated. Rather, the theorem tells us that the organization of the "industry" into firms is apt to be wasteful. It suggests that the same total output if produced by a smaller number of more sizable firms, can be provided at a lower real cost per unit, and hence a smaller total use of society's scarce resources.

2. The second relevant reservation refers to the social costs of standardization. If there is a reduction in the number of firms producing differentiated outputs, the variety of products available to the consumer must fall. Whether the resulting saving in resources is then to be considered a net gain is a matter of judgment which will doubtless vary from case to case. In other words, the excess capacity theorem represents a real social cost only if the increased choice which it offers consumers does not provide adequate psychic compensation for the added costs which it imposes.

MEASURES FOR THE ELIMINATION OF EXCESS CAPACITY

Where excess capacity is considered undesirable, one may well ask what can be done about it. Aside from direct nationalization and abolition of excess capacity by fiat, an obvious means for going about it is a licensing system whereby the number of firms is restricted to any level deemed desirable by the authorities. Clearly such an enforced reduction in the number of companies can impart an upward shift to the demand curve of each surviving firm, and by skillful choice of the number of licenses issued the marginal revenue curve can be forced near the minimum point on the original average cost curve where the corresponding marginal cost curve is always to be found. Hence the profit maximizing output will coincide with the competitive output level for the firm and excess capacity will have been eliminated.

One new result in this area also merits some note. Mr. L. G. Sandberg [10] has recently shown in a neat argument that price ceilings can be used to induce monopolistic competitors to produce "competitive" (least average cost) outputs. It is merely necessary to set the price ceiling at the level of minimum average cost. At any other output, firms must, then, lose money. Suppose the demand before the typical firm is insufficient to permit it to sell the least average cost output. Some companies will then be forced to leave the field and the demand curves of the remaining firms will shift to the right. This process will continue until each remaining firm can just sell the least cost output and there the equilibrium point will be found.

CONCLUDING COMMENTS

This seems to be about all we can say about the specific welfare implications of the theory of monopolistic competition. It may well seem to the reader that more might have been expected especially in the first flush of enthusiasm for the newborn and more general model of the firm. But it must be remembered that the paucity of welfare results may be as much a commentary on the state of welfare theory as on the theory of that monopolistically competitive firm.

More important, it should be recognized that some of the most significant consequences of Chamberlin's contribution are less tangible and come by way of its negative implications. One prominent member of our profession has described Chamberlin's book as the most influential single work ever produced by an American economist. The continuing impact of the book consists primarily in the habits of mind and point of view which it has engendered.

Few economists today would accept, hastily and uncritically, welfare conclusions derived exclusively from a purely competitive construct. Moreover, we have learned to recognize a wide variety of types of monopolistic element and have at least formed intuitive judgments about their social consequences. No doubt, many of these judgments were implicit long ago in the thoughts and writings of some of the wisest members of our profession. But this detracts nothing from Professor Chamberlin's contribution. For it is the nature of a revolution in a body of analysis, that it renders tangible and readily available ideas which *dogmengeschichte* later shows to have been floating about well before the revolutionaries came into power.

References

1. G. C. Archibald, "Chamberlin versus Chicago," *Rev. of Econ. Studies*, Oct., 1961.
2. W. J. Baumol, *Business Behvior, Value and Growth* (Macmillan, 1959).
3. R. A. Berry, "Welfare Implications of Monopoly" (Ph.D. dissertation, Princeton, 1963, unpublished).
4. E. H. Chamberlin, *The Theory of Monopolistic Competition* (5th ed., Harvard Univ. Press, 1947).
5. Harold Demsetz, "The Nature of Equilibrium in Monopolistic Competition," *J.P.E.*, Feb., 1959.
6. Milton Friedman, "More on Archibald versus Chicago," *Rev. of Econ. Studies*, Feb., 1963.
7. Nicholas Kaldor, "Market Imperfection and Excess Capacity," *Economica*, N.S. Vol. II, 1935.
8. Fritz Machlup, *The Economics of Sellers' Competition* (Johns Hopkins, 1952).
9. Joan Robinson, *The Economics of Imperfect Competition* (Macmillan, London, 1933).
10. L. G. Sandberg, "A Note on the Effect of Price Controls on *The Theory of Monopolistic Competition*," *American Economist*, 1963.

20 Classic and Current Notions of "Measurable Utility"

DANIEL ELLSBERG

The "marginal revolution" of the 1870s established the principle of diminishing marginal utility as the basis for explaining the exchange ratios which tended to be established between commodities in competitive markets. While the subjective nature of the marginal utility concept was recognized, most discussions implied that utility could be measured in cardinal terms. Even though the technique of the indifference curve, which required only the assumption that utilities could be ranked ordinally instead of measured cardinally, was developed in the 1880s, the assumption of cardinally measurable utility persisted and became typical of neoclassical economics.

The indifference curve technique did not come into general use until Professors J. R Hicks and R. G. D. Allen demonstrated, in their *Reconsideration of the Theory of Value* (1934), that it is possible to explain the downward slope of the demand curve without reference to the assumption of diminishing marginal utility and the notion of cardinally measurable utility.* Their formulation led to a lengthy controversy in which critics of the indifference curve approach argued that a consumer could not know to which of several combinations he is indifferent unless he could estimate the magnitude of utility each combination represented.** Some suggested this could be accomplished by establishing the marginal rate of substitution between one good and the dollar value of the best combination of other goods, for this is equivalent to expressing the utility of that good in money

The "measurability" controversy had not yet been brought to a definitive end when some ten years later, the issue was raised anew. Professors von Neumann and Morgenstern in their *The Theory of Games* (1944), demonstrated that if an individual's preference among sure (nonrisky) outcomes were expressed in terms of arbitrarily assigned numbers it would be possible to give numerical expression to the "utility" of other outcomes whose

Reprinted from Daniel Ellsberg, "Classic and Current Notions of 'Measurable Utility,'" *The Economic Journal*, September 1954, pp. 528–556. Dr. Ellsberg is a member of the Economic Department of the Rand Corporation in Santa Monica.

* *Economica*, 1934, pp. 14, 52–76, 196–219.
** O. Lange, "Note on the Determinateness of the Utility Function," *Review of Economi Studies*, 1934, pp. 2, 75–77; Phelps-Brown E. H. "Note on Determinateness of Utility Func tion," *Review of Economic Studies*, 1934, pp. 2, 66–69.

occurrence was uncertain. Provided that preferences among sure outcomes were consistent, they could serve as limits within which it would be possible to find utility index numbers expressing preferences for noncertain outcomes. These could then be used as a basis for predicting choice.

Although the von Neumann-Morgenstern demonstration of measurable utility represented a new theoretical achievement, it unfortunately introduced further confusion into a long-standing controversy. The article "Classic and Current Notions of 'Measurable Utility'" by Daniel Ellsberg, which follows, suggests that the confusion derived at least in part from the fact that the cardinal utility which the von Neumann-Morgenstern index measured was operationally different from that of the Marginalists. The latter conceived of the measurement of utility as taking place in the subject's mind and as relating to alternatives that do not involve risk. The von Neumann-Morgenstern index, by contrast, was intended for predicting choice among alternatives involving risk. It is cardinal and, therefore, "measurable" in the sense that calculating mathematical expectations on the basis of these numbers is a numerical operation which is empirically meaningful because it is related to observable behavior.

It is ten years since von Neumann and Morgenstern, in their famous aside to the economic profession, announced they had succeeded in synthesising "measurable utility." That feat split their audience along old party lines. It appeared that a mathematician had performed some elegant sleight-of-hand and produced, instead of a rabbit, a dead horse.

The most common reaction was dismay. To "literary" economists who had freshly amputated their intuitive feelings of cardinal utility at the bidding of some *other* mathematicians, it seemed wanton of von Neumann and Morgenstern so soon to sprinkle salt in their wounds with the statement: [1] "It can be shown that under the conditions on which the indifference curve analysis is based very little extra effort is needed to reach a numerical utility." To others, who had said all along that surgery was unnecessary, the verdict was no surprise but still welcome, coming as it did from an unexpected (non-Cambridge) source. But before long both these groups had joined in expressing doubts that von Neumann and Morgenstern had succeeded in doing what (these readers believed) they had set out to do. The spokesman for the "cardinalists," interpreting their cause as his own, was forced to conclude that they

"seem to me to have done as much harm as good to the cause to which they have lent their distinguished aid." [2]

However, it is now clear that the impression that von Neumann and Morgenstern were leading a reactionary movement was erroneous. Their cause, if it can be so dignified, is a new one, not that to which Professor Robertson alluded. The operations that define their concepts are essentially new, and their results are neither intended nor suited to fill the main functions of the older, more familiar brands of "cardinal utility." It is unfortunate that old terms have been retained, for their associations arouse both hopes and antagonisms that have no real roots in the new context.

In the latest writings the theory has been formulated unambiguously, so that the subject presents little difficulty to one approaching it now for the first time. This article is directed, instead, at readers who came early to the controversy, and who followed the theory in its various stages closely enough to become thoroughly confused.

By concentrating their discussion on the general concept of "measurability," von Neumann and Morgenstern unfortunately obscured the unique features of their par-

[1] Von Neumann and Morgenstern, *The Theory of Games* (Princeton, 1944), p. 17.

[2] Professor D. H. Robertson, *Utility and all That* (London, 1952), p. 28.

ticular construction. Later expositions have tended to follow them in this,[3] or to stress the empirical content of the von Neumann-Morgenstern results.[4] Very little attention has been given to the major source of mis-understandings: ambiguity concerning the differences in derivation and application between the new notion of "measurable utility" and the concept of the same name implied in the writings, say, of Marshall and Jevons. This article will attempt to distinguish clearly between the two concepts, chiefly by examining the different operations by which they are defined and tested.[5]

This procedure may provide some valuable exercise in the use of the operational approach, which in economic literature has been honored chiefly in footnotes. This approach regards the basic definition of a technical concept in scientific usage as: "What is measured by" a particular set of operations. Two different sets of operations are presumed to measure two different "things," although under certain conditions (discussed later) it is justifiable to treat the two concepts as identical. A scientific proposition is operationally meaningful if definite conceivable results of given operations are defined which would *refute* the statement; if it does not *restrict* the class of results which are to be expected, it cannot be useful for scientific purposes. The meaningfulness of concepts and propositions is a necessary, though not a sufficient, condition for their scientific usefulness.[6] This point of view will prove useful in the concluding section in clarifying the *difference* in meaning of two concepts bearing the same name.

The next section will describe the similarities between the old and new approaches to a "cardinal utility" and will present, in advance, some of the conclusions to be drawn as to their points of contrast. The next two parts examine the operational bases of the two theories, and the final section will analyse in detail the peculiarities of the von Neumann-Morgenstern construction.

Suppose that a man who prefers A to B, B to C and A to C must choose between having B for certain or having a "lottery ticket" offering A with probability p or C with probability $1 - p$.[7] Without asking him outright, is it possible to predict his choice? If so, what sort of data are necessary?

Economists of the school of Jevons, Menger, Walras and Marshall, on the one hand, and on the other those following von Neumann and Morgenstern would answer "Yes" to the first question. But their pre-

[3] This is the only shortcoming of the otherwise excellent article by Alchian, "The Measuring of Utility Measurement," *American Economic Review*, March 1953, p. 26. The present paper may serve as a complement to Alchian's.

[4] Friedman and Savage, "The Utility Analysis of Choices Involving Risk," *Journal of Political Economy*, August 1948, p. 279. Mosteller and Nogee, "An Experimental Measurement of Utility," *Journal of Political Economy*, October 1951, p. 371. I have also benefited from reading as yet unpublished papers by Professors Bishop, Marschak and Allais.

[5] This paper was originally written as the first chapter in a thesis, entitled "Theories of Rational Choice Under Uncertainty: The Contributions of von Neumann and Morgenstern," submitted for undergraduate honors at Harvard University, April 1952. The thesis was written under the valuable guidance of Professor John Chipman. I am also greatly indebted to Professors Paul Samuelson, Robert Bishop, Oskar Morgenstern and Frederick Mosteller for the opportunity to discuss problems and to read unpublished writings on the subject, and to Mr. Nicholas Kaldor for his comments.

[6] These concepts and the general point of view were first formulated explicitly by Percy W Bridgman, in *The Logic of Modern Physics* (New York, 1927), who declared them to be implicit in the thinking of modern physicists. The terms, and the emphasis on restrictiveness and refutability of propositions, have become familiar to economists largely through Samuelson's *Foundation of Economic Analysis* (Cambridge, 1948), but the other main propositions are less well known.

[7] A "lottery ticket" of this sort, offering a set of alternative outcomes with stated probabilities summing to unity, will hereafter be known as a *prospect*. If one outcome is offered with unit probability, i.e., with no uncertainty, it will be known as a *sure outcome*.

dictions would be based on quite different types of data.

For von Neumann and Morgenstern, it would be necessary to observe the man's behavior in other risk-situations, involving different outcomes or the same outcomes with different probabilities. The older economists, of whom we will take Marshall as typical, would ask no knowledge of his other risk-behavior. They assumed it possible, by observation or interrogation, to discover a man's intensities of liking for sure outcomes; on the basis of this knowledge alone, they were ready either to predict or to prescribe his choice between prospects.

This divergence is concealed by the fact that both schools would summarise the results of their investigations in the same symbolic shorthand, arriving at expressions that are formally identical. Under both procedures the results of experiment would be expressed by assigning a triplet of numbers, U_a, U_b and U_c, to the three outcomes, with the property: $U_a > U_b > U_c$. This triplet is a utility index for the three outcomes, since their order of magnitude reflects the order of preference. Next, both Marshall and von Neumann-Morgenstern would form the expression:

$$1 \cdot U_b \gtreqless p \cdot U_a + (1 - p)U_c \quad (20.1)$$

where p and $1 - p$ are the respective probabilities of A and C. Each side of this relationship is a sum of the utility numbers corresponding to the outcomes of a given prospect multiplied by their respective probability numbers. Since the probabilities sum to unity, the result is a weighted arithmetic mean of the utilities, variously known as the mathematical expectation of utility, the expected utility, the moral expectation, moral expectancy, actuarial value of utility and the first moment of the utility-probability distribution.[8]

---

[8] Of these, "mathematical expectation of utility" and its shorter form, "moral expectation," will be

In each case the prediction (or advice) would have the man choose the prospect with the highest mathematical expectation of utility. Or, if the two sides of the relationship (20.1) were equal, he should be indifferent between the two prospects. A man whose behavior conformed to this rule could be said to be "maximising the mathematical expectation of utility."

With this much similarity between the two approaches, it is natural that they should commonly be confused. Yet the most misleading point of similarity remains: the fact that in both cases "utility" is said to be "measurable." The necessity of this assumption is seen more clearly if the left-hand side of expression (20.1) is rewritten $p \cdot U_b + (1 - p)U_b$ and terms collected to form the relationship:

$$p(U_a - U_b) - (1 - p)(U_b - U_c) \gtreqless 0 \quad (20.2)$$

This is merely relationship (20.1) in a different form. The rule would now have the man accept the prospective offering A or C if the left-hand side of (20.2) were positive, reject it if the left-hand side were negative, or be indifferent between it and the sure outcome B if the left-hand side were equal to zero. The important point here is that relationship (20.2) shows clearly that the rules rely on comparing *differences* in utility.

If only preferences were known, the triplet of utility numbers could be replaced by another with the same ordinal relationships. In general, such a monotonic transformation would not preserve equality, or given inequalities, among differences between utility numbers. The rule of maximising expected utility would lead to prediction or advice which would depend on the particular index used, and if preferences were the only guide, the choice of

---

used below. Both must be carefully distinguished from the "mathematical expectation of *money*," which is a weighted sum of the money outcomes, rather than of their utility numbers.

index would be arbitrary. The rule would be meaningless, therefore useless.

In order for the rule to give definite results, it would be necessary to find some "natural"[9] operation that would give meaning to differences in utility numbers, hence to the numerical operations implied by the rule. The new index, summarising the results of the additional operation as well as preferences, would belong to a more restricted set of indices than the set of all ordinal utility indices. Any two indices in which corresponding differences as well as absolute utilities satisfied the same inequalities would be related by a linear, and not merely any monotonic, transformation.[10] It is, then, necessary to find some aspect of behavior that can be described only by a set of numbers determined up to a linear transformation: a set, moreover, which is one of those expressing preferences. So much is necessary in order for the rule of maximising expected utility to be meaningful. Its usefulness, if any, must depend on the particular aspect of behavior which serves this purpose, if one can be found.

To say that both Marshallian and the von Neumann-Morgenstern theories require a "measurable utility" is precisely to say that they require a utility index determined up to a linear transformation. At

this point the similarity ends. In general, the order of magnitude of the differences between corresponding numbers would be different for the two indices; therefore, predictions based on the rule of maximising moral expectation would differ for the two approaches. Moreover, it might be possible to find a measurable index by one method and not the other. Even if both should "exist," they would be in general monotonic, and not linear, transformations of each other.

Such theorists as Jevons, Menger, Walras and Marshall conceived of the crucial natural operation in the measurement of utility as taking place within the mind of a subject; it was a process of weighing introspectively the amounts of "satisfaction" associated with different outcomes.

Such an operation appeared more of an objective basis for theory to them than it would to modern economists. In their view in the realm of reasonable men one man's introspection was as good as another's, and the theorist's own internal calculations were likely to correspond roughly to those of his subject; to this extent the results of the subject's operation were "observable." However, if challenged to produce less subjective evidence, it would undoubtedly have occurred to Jevons that the most natural way to obtain the results of the man's introspective measurements would be to ask for them.

The first rough outline of the subject's pattern of "satisfaction" would emerge from an "indifference-map" experiment, in which he is asked to rank the events, A, B and C in order of preference. If he can compare the events and if his preferences are transitive ("consistent"), e.g., if he prefers A to B, B to C and A to C, the results of this experiment are summarised by any triplet of numbers satisfying: $U_a > U_b > U_c$. This triplet is a "non-measurable" utility index, determined up to monotonic transformation.

[9] Von Neumann and Morgenstern use this term to signify an operation other than numerical or logical manipulation of a mathematical model. A mathematical model is useful if the results of a "natural" operation can be correlated with numbers in such a way that numerical operations can symbolise and substitute for the "natural" operation.

[10] For an excellent exposition of the concepts of linear and monotonic transformations, the reader is referred to the article by Alchian, *op. cit.* Briefly, two indices are related by a linear transformation if for every point x on one index, the corresponding point y on the other index satisfies a relationship of the form: $y = ax + b$, where a and b are constants. The two indices differ only with respect to scale and origin.

If the difference between two numbers in one index is greater than, less than or equal to the difference between two other numbers, the corresponding differences in the other index will have the same ordinal relationship.

In what we will call a "Jevonsian" [11] experiment the man would next be asked to rank his preferences of A to B and his preference of B to C. If he finds that he can state, for example, that his preference of A to B exceeds his preference of B to C, we could summarise this information by any triplet of numbers satisfying the two inequalities: (a) $U_a > U_b > U_c$, and (b) $U_a - U_b > U_b - U_c$.

Finally, if A and B were sums of money, we could ask the man to vary the sum of money represented by B until he could tell us that he found his preference of A to B' equal to his preference of B' to C. If he finds such a B', then the results of this last operation would be expressed by any triplet of numbers satisfying the relationships: (a) $U_a > U_b > U_c$, and (b) $U_a - U_b = U_b - U_c$. Any two triplets obeying these relationships must be related by a linear transformation; they represent utility indices differing only by scale and origin.

The Jevonsian index for the individual, if one can be found, is thus "measurable"; which in this case means nothing more or less than that the subject was able to give consistent answers to these particular questions. It might be objected that in fact subjects will be unable to answer the questions, or will answer them inconsistently. This is an empirical matter. If the events were the possession of (a) one million dollars, (b) two dollars, and (c) one dollar, it seems likely that most people would answer the question (and, moreover, would state specifically that their preference of A to B exceeded their preference of B to C).[12] For such people, the notion of a cardinal utility index would not be "meaningless"; if it had no other meaning, it might at least imply that their answers to this sort of question could be predicted. Inconsistency is to be expected, particularly with respect to utility differences that are almost equal. But inconsistency also appears (in lesser degree) in the "indifference-map" experiment; in each case the most important information gained concerns choices which the subject finds easy to make.[13]

The more damaging attack has been on the usefulness of the method, though here again the case is not conclusive. If the only "consistency" discovered were consistency of answers with other answers, the results would be trivial. But Marshall and his predecessors regarded such answers as revealing the subject's internal measurements of satisfaction.[14] Since they believed the man based his decisions to act on the results of this introspective operation, they hoped to use the results of a Jevonsian experiment to predict his decisions.

As the ordinalists have demonstrated, decisions in the marketplace under conditions of certainty can be predicted on the basis of the "indifference-map" experiment alone. But this is not true of behavior under uncertainty or risk. With a Jevonsian utility index, on the other hand, it is possible to frame meaningful hypotheses placing definite restrictions on observable behavior in risk-situations.

The particular rule which Marshall and Jevons proposed (rather more for normative purposes than descriptive) was that the "rational" man would maximise the mathematical expectation of utility. In terms of the expression (20.1) cited earlier:

$$U_b \gtreqqless p \cdot U_a + (1 - p) U_c \quad (20.1)$$

---

[11] This name is suggested by J. C. Weldon, who points out that it implies no more than that Jevons assumed that preferences could be directly compared. "A Note on Measures of Utility," *Canadian Journal of Economics and Political Science*, May 1950, p. 230.

[12] At least, they would probably do so if asked point-blank and not given time for doubts as to whether the question "meant" anything (induced, perhaps, by the writings of Samuelson). This

could be made part of the conditions of the experiment.

[13] The above discussion follows Weldon, *op. cit.*

[14] Such information might by itself be of interest in welfare economics; it might, though it need not, influence the evaluations on which a social-welfare function must be based.

the rational man should (would) choose the prospect if the right-hand side were greater, the sure outcome B if the left-hand side were greater. If U_b, the utility that can be had for certain if the prospect is rejected, is regarded as the opportunity cost of the prospect, then the expression (20.2):

$$p(U_a - U_b) - (1 - p)(U_b - U_c) \gtreqless 0 \quad (20.2)$$

represents the mathematical expectation of *gain* (measured in utility) associated with the prospect. The first term is the amount of utility that the man stands to win by accepting the gamble (in excess of the utility cost of the gamble) multiplied by the probability of winning, and the second term is the amount of utility he stands to lose multiplied by the probability of losing. The man should take any gambles whose expectation of gain is positive, reject all whose expectation of gain is negative, be indifferent to those whose expectation of gain is zero.

One point about this procedure must be emphasised, for it is in sharp contrast to that of von Neumann and Morgenstern. The utility index, and its measurability, on which the Marshallian predictions were based was not derived from any risk-behavior, and did not depend on any sort of consistency in that behavior. The rule of maximising expected utility on the basis of a Jevonsian index led to prediction, or prescription, of a man's choices among prospects without any previous observation of his behavior in the face of risk.

Actually, in the main field of consumer behavior characterised by risk—gambling —Marshall was not sanguine about the usefulness of the rule as a descriptive hypothesis. He took it as a universal empirical law that answers in the Jevonsian experiment would reveal diminishing marginal utility. In other words, if A, B and C are three sums of money such that $A > B > C$, and if $A - B = B - C$, then he assumed that corresponding utility numbers

would satisfy the inequality: $U_a - U_b < U_b - U_c$. A "fair" gamble is defined as one in which the mathematical expectation of *money* gain is zero, expressed by:

$$p(A - B) - (1 - p)(B - C) = 0 \quad (20.3)$$

where p is the probability of winning A, $1 - p$ the probability of winning C and B is the cost of the gamble (in the above case, p must equal $\frac{1}{2}$). But, granted decreasing marginal utility, the corresponding expectation of *utility* gain is negative, so the rational man would never accept a fair gamble, or, *a fortiori*, an unfair gamble.

As Marshall was well aware, people did accept fair and even unfair gambles; but this behavior disputed their rationality, not (the curvature of) their utility index. The latter was established once and for all by tests that did not involve risk. Because of the existence of "pleasure of gambling"[15] (which Marshall measured by the acceptance of unfair bets), Marshall would have rejected the observation of risk-behavior as an alternative operation for measuring people's intensities of liking for outcomes.

The particular Marshallian rule governing risk-behavior is not implied by his concept of utility or by the methods of measuring it. An early form of the rule is stated by Jevons:[16]

[15] Unfair gambling could be "rationalised" if introspective tests revealed that the happiness derived from gambling outweighed the "expected loss of satisfaction" implied by the odds. However, Marshall wished to retain the normative connotation of "rationality" at the expense of predictive value. In his view, the pleasures of gambling "are likely to engender a restless, feverish character, unsuited for steady work. . . ." (*Principles of Economics* (London, 1925), Mathematical Appendix, Note IX, p. 843.) Granted that marginal utility was decreasing, and that pleasures of gambling could be ignored because "impure," then unfair gambling was unequivocally irrational, an "economic blunder."

[16] W. Stanley Jevons, *The Theory of Political Economy* (London, 1911), p. 36.

"If the probability is only one in ten that I shall have a certain day of pleasure, I ought to anticipate the pleasure with one-tenth of the force which would belong to it if certain. In selecting a course of action which depends on uncertain events, as, in fact, does everything in life, I should multiply the quantity of feeling attaching to every future event by the fraction denoting its probability."

The reliance of this approach on measurability (of "quantity of feeling") is obvious; but it is equally obvious that the measurability of "pleasure," and even the general principle that likings for prospects should be based on likings for outcomes and their probabilities, does not imply this particular rule of decision-making. On the basis of a given Jevonsian index, Marshall or Jevons could just have easily proposed that the rational man base his preference on the mode, the median, the range, variance or other properties of the distribution of utilities. These rules would have been just as meaningful, and possibly more useful (especially if they took into account measures of "risk" as well as "central tendency"). In fact, it was the feeling that the emphasis on mathematical expectation was arbitrary and unrealistic which led to the decline of the concept even before doubts arose that a measurable utility could be discovered to make it meaningful.

What von Neumann and Morgenstern asserted, in their famous digression,[17] was the possibility that the notion of maximising the mathematical expectation of utility might (a) be made meaningful, and (b) describe a wider range of risk-behavior than in its old usage, *if "utility" were measured (defined) in a special way*. Since they were concerned only with risk-behavior, the operation they proposed was the observation of choices in risk-situations. If a person's preferences among *prospects*—described merely in ordinal terms—should satisfy certain, apparently weak, axiomatic restrictions, then von Neumann has proved that it would be possible to find a set of numbers which could express these preferences in a particularly convenient way.

This set of numbers would be *a* utility index, because it would be one among all the sets of numbers (related by monotonic transformations) expressing the person's preferences (*not* "intensities of preference" or "quantities of feeling") among sure outcomes. The novelty would be that this same set of numbers, applying explicitly only to sure outcomes, could also summarise the person's preferences among prospects. In a complete description of the individual's entire preference-structure, it would be unnecessary to list prospects separately or to record explicitly his preferences among prospects; these preferences would be known, through observation, but they could be expressed implicitly by the numbers attached to sure outcomes.

Clearly, the class of indices which could express with such economy preferences both among sure outcomes and among prospects must be smaller than the class of all ordinal utility indices (in most of which it would be necessary to list prospects individually). In fact, it turns out that all indices with this property, if any exist, will be related by linear transformations. Yet the index is not "measurable" in the sense that it is correlated with any significant economic quantity such as quantity of feeling or satisfaction, or intensity, such as intensity of liking or preference. It is derived from *choices*, and describes only *preferences*. It would be "cardinal" ("measurable") only to the extent that the numerical operation of forming mathematical expectations on the basis of these numbers would be related to observable behavior, so as to be empirically meaningful.

[17] The theory which follows occupies only a few pages in the introduction to their book, and plays no role in the theory of games. The latter theory requires a commodity which is not only measurable but intercomparable and freely transferable, so pay-offs are expressed in money, not in von Neumann-Morgenstern "utility."

Von Neumann and Morgenstern might simply have proposed the empirical hypothesis that an index of the desired sort could be found for certain individuals. However, this proposition, which we will call the Hypothesis on Moral Expectations, has little inherent plausibility. The major feat of von Neumann and Morgenstern is to show that the Hypothesis on Moral Expectations is *logically equivalent* to the hypothesis that the behavior of given individuals satifies certain axiomatic restrictions. Since these axioms appear, at first glance, highly "reasonable," the second hypothesis seems far more intuitively appealing than the equivalent Hypothesis on Moral Expectations. It is thus more likely to be accepted on the basis of casual observation and introspection, although the two hypotheses would both be contradicted by exactly the same observations.

Most expositions follow von Neumann and Morgenstern in focusing all attention on the second hypothesis, *i.e.*, on the empirical relevance of the axioms. Once this is accepted, the Hypothesis on Moral Expectations "goes along free" in the form of the Theorem on Moral Expectations, which states conditionally that *if* an individual's behavior conforms to the axioms, a von Neumann-Morgenstern index can be computed for him (this proposition rests on logic rather than observation, and it has been established by several different proofs). Empirical test of the proposition is thus displaced to the axioms which imply it. The logical relationship of the axioms to the Hypothesis is usually left obscure, for the demonstration is too difficult for most readers.[18] Therefore the reader must generally take it on faith that behavior violating a particular axiom conflicts with the possibility of finding a von Neumann-Morgenstern index. Instead, we will follow the straighter, though less persuasive, route of describing how the Hypothesis on Moral Expectations would be tested directly.

We can state the Hypothesis in the following form. For a given individual (it is asserted that) a set of numbers *exists* (*i.e.*, can be found) with the two properties: (1) it is one of the sets expressing the individual's actual preferences among sure outcomes (*i.e.*, it is one of his ordinal utility indices); (2) numbers are assigned to sure outcomes in such a way that, if "moral expectations" of *prospects* were computed on the basis of these numbers, one prospect would have a higher moral expectation than another if, and only if, the person actually preferred the former to the latter, and two prospects would have the same moral expectation if and only if the person were indifferent between them.

If, from the set of all utility indices (related by monotonic transformations) one index can be found such that "moral expectations" computed on the basis of this particular set of "utilities" arrange prospects according to an individual's actual preferences among them, then any other index related to the first by a linear (not merely by any monotonic) transformation will also have this property. Thus, if one such index exists, an infinite set will exist: though still a tiny subset of all indices expressing ordinal preferences among outcomes. The Theorem on Moral Expectations states that such a set does exist, if and when the axioms apply. The Hypothesis states that the index actually does exist for given persons.

[18] Von Neumann and Morgenstern did not present a proof deriving the Theorem from the axioms until the second edition of *The Theory of Games* (1947); they describe it, with terrific understatement, as "rather lengthy and may be somewhat tiring for the mathematically untrained reader" (p. 617). A different, slightly easier proof, is given by Marschak in "Rational Behaviour, Uncertain Prospects, and Measurable Utility," *Econometrica*, April 1950. A genuinely simple proof has finally been presented by Samuelson in "Utility, Preference, and Probability," abstract of paper given before the conference on *Le Fondements et Applications de la Theorie du Risque en Econometrie*, 1952.

Having found such an index, we could submit it to a monotonic increasing transformation—*e.g.*, we could take the square or the log of each number—and the resulting set of numbers would be a perfectly valid utility index of outcomes. But it would not serve any more as a utility index of prospects as well; it would no longer be true that moral expectancies would correspond to the individual's actual preferences among prospects.

Our approach will consist of trying to find an index (hypothetically) with the two properties specified, noting in the process the type of behavior which would make this impossible. The "operational content" of the theory should be most obvious from this point of view, since it is intimately related to the body of behavior "ruled out" by the Hypothesis. The greater the amount and importance of this behavior, the more powerful does the Hypothesis appear, though the less immediately plausible.

The basic operation in deriving a von Neumann-Morgenstern utility index is the observation of an individual's behavior in the very simplest situation involving risk: a choice between a sure outcome and a prospect involving two possible outcomes with given probabilities. The essential restriction the Hypothesis puts on behavior is that, by observing a person's choices in situations of this simple type, it must be possible to predict his choices among sets of prospects each offering a multitude of prizes with complex odds (some of the prizes possibly being other prospects). In the discussion below, the notation $(A, p; B)$ signifies a prospect offering outcome A with probability p or B with probability $1 - p$.

To fix the origin and unit of the utility index we seek, we assign arbitrary numbers to two outcomes (order of magnitude in order of preference); this guarantees that the index, if we can find one, will be unique. For example, let us assign to the money-sums $1,000 and $0 the utility numbers 10 and 0: *i.e.*, $U_{1000} = 10$, $U_0 = 0$. Now we

consider a third sum, say, $500, which the individual ranks between the first two; the problem is to find a utility number U_{500} that satisfies the Hypothesis on Moral Expectations, consistent with his preferences and with the two numbers already assigned arbitrarily. The crucial datum in the procedure is the probability $\dot{p}$ at which the person is indifferent between having $500 with certainty or a prospect ($1,000, $\dot{p}$; $0).[19] Suppose that this $\dot{p}$ is $\frac{8}{10}$; *i.e.*, he tells us, or we observe, that he is indifferent between $500 and ($1,000, $\frac{8}{10}$; $0). The Hypothesis on Moral Expectations then implies that it is possible to find a number U_{500} with the two properties:

$0 < U_{500} < 10$ (since he prefers
$1,000 to $500 and $500 to $0)   (20.4[1])

$$1 \cdot U_{500} = \tfrac{8}{10} \cdot 10 + \tfrac{2}{10} \cdot 0 \quad (20.4[2])$$

Obviously, such a number *can* be found: $U_{500} = 8$. So the Hypothesis has passed the first test.

Even in this first application, the Hypothesis was not tautologous. It was conceivable that the individual would prefer the certainty of $500 to any prospect ($1,000, p; $0) for *any* p whatever; perhaps from extreme conservative principles or moral scruples against gambling. The Hypothesis would then imply that it was possible to find a number U_{500} satisfying both the following two relationships:

$$0 < U_{500} < 10 \quad (20.5[1])$$

and

$U_{500} > p \cdot 10 + (1 - p) \cdot 0,$
$\qquad\qquad$ for *all* p, $0 < p < 1$.   (20.5[2])

But no such number exists; for any given U_{500} satisfying 20.5[1], there would exist a p, such that 20.5[2] would not hold.

[19] The axioms require that he be indifferent at one and only one p. Tests have already shown that this perfect consistency is never encountered, but "indifference" might be defined stochastically (*e.g.*, if an individual rejected a prospect with given odds as often as he accepted it, he might be said to be "indifferent" to it).

Therefore the Hypothesis would be contradicted.

Similarly, the Hypothesis would be contradicted if the individual should prefer any prospect ($1,000, p; $0) to the certainty of $500; say, from an obsession with gambling.

It might seem that such behavior might well occur, thus rejecting the Hypothesis on the basis of one observation. But proponents of the Hypothesis could point out that it is unusual to have such "absolute" likes or dislikes: to feel so strongly either for or against gambling as to ignore entirely the relative stakes and odds.[20] They might suggest that such behavior, though it may exist, is statistically unimportant, so that it is reasonable to hypothesise that there will be *some* $\dot{p}$ at which the subject will be indifferent. A man with a marked taste for security might pick $\dot{p} = 9,999/10,000$; a born gambler might indicate $\dot{p} = 1/1,000$. In either case it would be possible to find a number U_{500} consistent with these preferences.

Thus, the Hypothesis puts very weak limitations in this initial application to the man's preferences among risky alternatives. The drastic test is to investigate whether or not his *other* choices will be "consistent" with this first choice. Let us return to our original result, $U_{500} = 8$. On the basis of our single observation (fixing $\dot{p}$ at $\frac{8}{10}$) we must be able to predict the individual's choice among any set of prospects involving the three outcomes, $1,000, $500 or $0, with any probabilities. Given any set of prospects, we simply compute the moral expectations of each on the basis of the utility numbers (two of which, in this case, were fixed arbitrarily and the third derived from a single observed choice), and pick the prospect with the highest moral expectancy. No rationale for this procedure has been given here. It is

not suggested that the individual makes his choice by a similar calculation. We are merely examining the implications of the hypothesis that it is possible to describe his behavior "as though" he did.

Thus, we compute the moral expectation of the prospect ($1,000, $\frac{1}{2}$; $0) as: $\frac{1}{2} \cdot 10 + \frac{1}{2} \cdot 0 = 5$. If, when confronted with the choice between this prospect and the certainty of $500 ($U_{500} = 8$), our subject does not definitely prefer the latter, then it is not true that moral expectations computed on the basis of our utility numbers arrange prospects according to the individual's actual preference; our triplet does not have properties of a von Neumann-Morgenstern index. More than that, if this triplet is not one of those whose existence is implied by the Moral Expectations Hypothesis, *then no such triplet can be found*, and the hypothesis is thereby invalidated. For, once two numbers had been arbitrarily chosen, the third one was uniquely determined by our initial observation;[21] any other value for U_{500} would be inconsistent (in terms of our hypothesis) with that particular choice.

If, on the contrary, no serious[22] inconsistency appears, we can proceed to find utility numbers for other sums of money. If we observed that the subject was indifferent between $200 and ($500, $\frac{1}{4}$; $0), we would define $U_{500} = 2$. Our set of utility numbers corresponding to $0, $200, $500 and $1,000 is now 0, 2, 8, 10. If these are the unique set implied by the Hypothesis, then the individual should be indifferent between a 50–50 chance of $0 or $1,000, and a 50–50 chance of $200 or $500, since: $\frac{1}{2} \cdot 0 + \frac{1}{2} \cdot 10 = \frac{1}{2} \cdot 2 + \frac{1}{2} \cdot 8$. If, in fact, he prefers one to another, then the existence

---

[20] As John Chipman has put it, this is the "every man has his price" axiom.

[21] Since indices satisfying the Hypothesis are determined "up to two arbitrary constants," the specification of two values determines the index uniquely.

[22] In a real experiment we would have to decide in statistical terms what to regard as a "reasonable" approximation to consistency with the Theorem.

theorem is contradicted; the axioms on which it may be based do not apply to this individual.

More complicated tests can be devised. One of the "prizes" in a prospect might be another prospect, say, a "lottery ticket" offering a $\frac{4}{5}$ chance of $1,000 and a $\frac{1}{5}$ chance of $0; if the other prize is $200, the two prizes being offered at equal odds, this would appear in our notation: ($200, $\frac{1}{2}$; ($1,000, $\frac{4}{5}$; $0)). This "complex" prospect might be compared to the "simple" prospect: ($500, $\frac{5}{8}$; $0). The person "should" be indifferent between them, since:

$$\tfrac{1}{2} \cdot 2 + \tfrac{1}{2}(\tfrac{4}{5} \cdot 10 + \tfrac{1}{5} \cdot 0) = \tfrac{5}{8} \cdot 8 + \tfrac{3}{8} \cdot 0$$

A new test would be to confront the subject with a choice between the above complex prospect and the simple prospect with three prizes: ($1,000, $\frac{2}{5}$; $200, $\frac{1}{2}$; $0, $\frac{1}{10}$). Suppose that U_{200} is yet to be computed, and that the individual is found to prefer the complex "lottery ticket" to the above simple one. Then the Hypothesis would imply that a number U_{200} can be found satisfying both:

$$0 < U_{200} < 10, \qquad (20.6[1])$$

and

$$\tfrac{2}{5}\cdot 10 + \tfrac{1}{10}\cdot 0 + \tfrac{1}{2}\cdot U_{200} < \tfrac{1}{2}(\tfrac{4}{5}\cdot 10 + \tfrac{1}{5}\cdot 0) + \tfrac{1}{2}\cdot U_{200} \qquad (20.6[2])$$

Since 20.6[2] implies $U_{200} < U_{200}$, it is clearly impossible to find a number with the desired properties.

Von Neumann and Morgenstern's controversial Axiom 3: $C : b$[23] rules out this type of behavior by assuming that a person will be indifferent between two prospects which are derivable from each other according to the rules of probabilities. By application of these rules, any complex prospect offering other prospects as prizes may be reduced to a simple prospect, and the axiom requires the individual to be indifferent between this derived prospect and the original one. This implies that the in-

dividual is indifferent to the number of steps taken to determine the outcome. On the contrary, a sensible person might easily prefer a lottery which held several intermediate drawings to determine who was still "in" for the final drawing; in other words, he might be willing to pay for the possibility of winning intermediate drawings and "staying in," even though the chances of winning the pot were not improved thereby. A longer time-period of suspense would usually also be involved, but it need not be. The crucial factor is "pleasure of winning," which may be aroused by intermediate wins even if one subsequently fails to receive the prize. Many, perhaps most, slot-machine players know the odds are very unfavorable, and are not really motivated by hopes of winning the jackpot. They feel that they have had their money's worth if it takes them a long while to lose a modest sum, meanwhile enjoying a number of intermediate wins—which go back into the machine to pay for the pleasure of the next win. Von Neumann and Morgenstern single out Axiom 3: $C : b$, which excludes this type of behavior, as the "really critical" axiom[24] —"that one which gets closest to excluding a 'utility of gambling.'"[25]

The final major test of the Hypothesis would be to give the subject a choice between two such prospects as ($500, p; $1,000) and ($200, p; $1,000), where p is the same in each and where $500 is preferred to $200. For any p he must prefer the first to the second. If, for example, he was indifferent between them at some $p = P$, the Hypothesis would imply that there was a U_{500} such that:

$$2 < U_{500} < 10, \qquad (20.7[1])$$

and

$$P \cdot U_{500} + (1 - P)10 = P \cdot 2 + (1 - P)10. \qquad (20.7[2])$$

[23] Von Neumann and Morgenstern, *op. cit.*, p. 26.

[24] *Ibid.*, p. 632.
[25] *Ibid.*, p. 28.

Together these imply that $U_{500} > 2$ and $U_{500} = 2$, which can be true of no number (we are assuming in this example that U_{500} has not already been determined by some other experiment).

It is the "Strong Independence Axiom" ruling out this sort of preference which Samuelson has emphasised, presenting it as the "crucial" axiom.[26] It seems rather hard to justify this emphasis, since the axiom seems indubitably the most plausible of the lot. After all, all of the axioms are necessary to the final result, and this particular one is almost impregnable (even people who did not follow it in practice would probably admit, on reflection, that they should) whereas others (such as 3: $C : b$) are contradicted by much everyday experience. One might almost suspect Samuelson, who counts himself a "fellow traveller"[27] of the von Neumann-Morgenstern theory, of using the axiom (his invention) as a man-trap, luring critics past the really vulnerable points to waste their strength on the "Independence Assumption."[28]

In all this it has been emphasised that the Hypothesis on Moral Expectations sets a double condition for an acceptable index, the first part being that it must be one of the individual's ordinal utility index. Some critics seem to have overlooked this; for example, I. M. D. Little:[29]

"Suppose that . . . we had given C, A, B, the utility numbers $10\frac{4}{5}$, 10, 9, because the consumer was 'indifferent' between (A certain) and (C with probability $\frac{5}{9}$ or B with probability $\frac{4}{9}$. It follows that . . . if the consumer is given the choice between B and A, A must be taken. In fact B might well be taken."

If, as the last sentence suggests, the consumer preferred B to A (and C to both), we would start the experiment with this information. If we should then observe that he was indifferent between A and $(C, \frac{5}{9}; B)$, then we would not be able to assign any utility number at all to A, for it would be impossible to find one satisfying the two conditions: $U_a < U_b < U_b$ and $U_c = \frac{4}{9} \cdot B + \frac{5}{9} \cdot C$. This behavior contradicts the Hypothesis, but the conflict would show up in the impossibility of finding a von Neumann-Morgenstern index, not in the index, once having been "certified," turning out to be inconsistent with ordinal preferences. This is a small point, but criticism which may be quite pertinent loses force if framed in a way that suggests the critic has not understood the conditions of the experiment.

Another type of criticism that goes wide of the mark uses examples involving only "utils," with no mention of the sums they represent or the particular observations on which they were based Baumol, for example, cites two lottery tickets with prizes expressed in utils (*i.e.*, utility units, rather than money).[30] He computes their moral expectations, but asks, "Yet who is to say" that it is "pathological" for the subject to prefer the one with the lower expectation. To this a defender can retort: (*a*) Baumol gives no indication that the utility numbers were correctly derived; (*b*) it would not, of course, be "pathological" in any case; but (*c*) if it happened that the utility numbers were actually derived, for example, from the person's previous choice between

[26] Samuelson, "Utility, Preference, and Probability," *op. cit.* Also, "Probability, Utility, and the Independence Axiom," *Econometrica*, October 1952, p. 672.

[27] Samuelson, "Probability, Utility, and the Independence Axiom," *op. cit.*, p. 677.

[28] Dr. Alan S. Manne's article, "The Strong Independence Assumption—Gasoline Blends and Probability Mixtures," *Econometrica*, October 1952, p. 665, gives an interesting example of a physical situation in which superposition does not apply, which may be more relevant to linear programming than to the present subject. Although it raises a doubt, I do not think his criticism is really damaging in this context. The argument in the same issue by H. Wold, "Ordinal Preferences or Cardinal Utility?" is definitely invalid.

[29] I. M. D. Little, *A Critique of Welfare Economics* (Oxford, 1950), p. 30.

[30] William Baumol, "The Neumann-Morgenstern Utility Index—An Ordinalist View," *Journal of Political Economy*, February 1951, p. 65.

the very two prospects cited, then it would be "inconsistency" of a sort usually defined as non-rational for him to switch his choice on this occasion. The crux of the matter is that it is impossible to decide on intuitive grounds whether it is "plausible" to choose the prospect with the higher moral expectation if only utils are cited and if the person's past choices are not known, since an appraisal of "plausibility" must be based on the money sums involved and on the person's pattern of behavior in risk-situations.

We have described above the main types of behavior that conflict with the Hypothesis on Moral Expectations. It is possible to give long lists of factors in risk-situations which would lead to these types of behavior.[31] Among those which have not been mentioned earlier are: feelings of skill, or, in general, the feeling that the "real" odds are more favorable than the stated odds (*e.g.*, belief in personal luck, or in "winning streaks"); inability to compute compound probabilities, and thus to derive simple prospects from complex ones; influence of the other elements in the risk-situation besides the money prizes and the probabilities—*e.g.*, the atmosphere of the gaming-room. The Theorem could possibly be framed so as to allow for these considerations, but in any practical application they would undoubtedly have some effect.

Whether or not these factors would lead to *serious* inconsistency is open to question; it seems very likely that they would in the field of gambling, but Samuelson suggests that they may be less important in business and statistical problems.[32]

. The only laboratory test of the Hypothesis has been performed by Professor Frederick Mosteller, who derived utility

curves for a group of subjects on the basis of their choice among simple gambles, and used these data to predict their choices among other and more complicated gambles.[33] The experiment side-stepped pitfalls which could not be avoided· in practical application by abstracting from the major sources of inconsistent behavior: (*a*) all probabilities were known; (*b*) all calculations were performed for the subjects and their misconceptions eliminated;[34] (*c*) only small sums were used; (*d*) no social influences or any "other factors" were present; (*e*) behavior was observed only in one special risk-context (and that an artificial one). The fact that Mosteller found only mild consistency despite these "ideal" conditions might be interpreted as distinctly unfavorable to the hypothesis (though, considered in themselves, the results were inconclusive).

In deriving a "Jevonsian" utility index, we would begin as in the preceding section by assigning two arbitrary values; since, like the von Neumann-Morgenstern index, it is determined up to a linear transformation (if it can be found at all). As before, we might assign the utility numbers 10 and 0 to the outcomes $1,000 and $0. To find U_{500}, instead of confronting the individual with a choice between prospects, we would

[31] Maurice Allais, in "Notes théoriques sur l'Incertitude de l'Avenir et la Risque" (as yet unpublished), and Professor Robert Bishop, in a paper that has not been published as yet, outline these considerations in detail.

[32] Samuelson, "Probability, Utility, and the Independence Axiom," *op. cit.*, p. 677.

[33] Frederick Mosteller and Philip Nogee, "An Experimental Measurement of Utility," *Journal of Political Economy*, October 1951, p. 399.

[34] In the first two sessions subjects were not instructed on computing odds, and calculations were not performed for them. Behavior in these sessions was quite different from behavior in the rest of the experiment. Although these interesting results were not discussed in the article cited, Mosteller informed me that a definite finding of the experiment was that all the subjects behaved very differently before and after they had received lectures on dealing with probabilities. Moreover, their behavior showed a trend factor throughout the experiments as they grew increasingly familiar with the various gambles.

Even if the final conclusions had been much more favorable than they were, these observations would have dictated great caution in extrapolating them to situations outside the laboratory.

ask him to rank his preference of $1,000 to $500 and his preference of $500 to $0. Suppose he should tell us that the two preferences were equal; we would then assign the utility number $U_{500} = 5$. But on the basis of the von Neumann-Morgenstern experiment (let us assume that the same individual was the subject) we assigned the number $U_{500} = 8$. Is there not a conflict here?

To anyone who has skimmed the literature in this field it will not be obvious that the two sets of results are independent, hence do not conflict, for certain passages, particularly in *The Theory of Games*, gives quite the opposite impression. A close examination of the texts can, in fact, settle the question definitely. Instead of referring immediately to the literature, however, it is rewarding to examine a more general type of analysis, which might have made the issues intelligible to economists from the beginning.

Bridgman states the central proposition of the operational approach thus:[35]

"We must demand that the set of operations equivalent to any concept be a unique set, for otherwise there are possibilities of ambiguity in practical applications which we cannot admit. . . .

"If we have more than one set of operations we have more than one concept, and strictly there should be a separate name to correspond to each different set of operations."

The word "should" above should be interpreted as meaning that it is *useful*, in terms of certain specific purposes, to adopt the proposed point of view (this applies as well to the word "should" in this sentence). Because of incautious phrasing in his early

writing, it has often been thought that Bridgman regarded his own definitions and classifications as logical imperatives. Actually (as he has since made explicit), it is not necessary to insist on his approach dogmatically or exclusively; without making any unique claims, it is easy to show the value of his point of view (which admittedly is not the most natural) in helping to avoid certain types of confusion.

Of course, in everyday usage we very commonly use the same term to cover different operations, on the grounds that they measure the "same thing." If we take the strict operational point of view that a "thing" is "what is measured by a particular operation," we need not ban the practice of treating two different operations as measuring the "same thing," but we must insist that it be justified by a direct argument. In an important passage, Bridgman indicates the nature of an adequate justification:[36]

"If we deal with phenomena outside the domain in which we originally defined our concepts, we may find physical hindrances to performing the operations of the original definition, so that the original operations have to be replaced by others. These new operations are, of course, to be chosen so that they give, within experimental error, the same numerical results in the domain in which the two sets of operations may be both applied; but we must recognize in principle that in changing the operations we have really changed the concept. . . . The practical justification for retaining the same name is that within our present experimental limits a numerical difference between the results of the two sorts of operations has not been detected."

It would hardly be possible to find a passage more pertinent to a comparison of the economic theories discussed here. It may be helpful to give some economic il-

---

[35] Percy W. Bridgman, *The Logic of Modern Physics* (New York, 1927). The first sentence is on p. 6, the second on p. 10 (my italics).
Although such notions as the meaningfulness and restrictiveness of hypotheses have been made familiar to many economists by followers of Bridgman, the above proposition and the following ones, which are the very heart of the operational approach, are not widely known among economists.

[36] Percy W. Bridgman, *The Logic of Modern Physics* (New York, 1927); the first two sentences are on p. 23; the third, on p. 16 (in the latter sentence, Bridgman refers to the measurement of length by ordinary and by Einstein's operations).

lustrations; several examples of pairs of operations which differ but are usually treated as equivalent exist within the boundaries of our discussion.

(1) In the indifference map experiment the operations (*a*) of interrogating the individual as to his preferences, or (*b*) observing his actual choices (Samuelson's "revealed preference"), are usually regarded as alternative.

(2) In the "Jevonsian" experiment two operations are usually thought to be involved: (*a*) inquiring of the subject how he ranks his preferences; (*b*) the subject's own subjective process of "weighing" satisfactions. The first is said to measure differences in satisfaction on the assumption that it approximates the results of the second. The basis of this assumption is that in the area where they can both be applied—the area of our own introspection—they give identical results (to the extent that we *can* balance satisfactions and that we tell the truth).

(3) In the von Neumann-Morgenstern experiment we used the operation (*a*) of asking the subject to name a $\dot{p}$ at which he would be indifferent; but we also suggested the possibility (*b*) of observing his choices when confronted with various pairs of prospects many times. Mosteller used the latter operation in his empirical tests.

In each case, the alternative operations are regarded as roughly identical. Actually, most economists who have had practical experience in applied theory are well aware that the results of interrogation and of observing actual behavior are almost never identical. Moreover, minor differences in the operations (such as the wording of questions) do "make a difference."[37] When a pair of operations is accepted as measuring the "same thing" it is because the divergence between the results is not regarded as significant. But as the range of

application of each operation is widened over time, divergences appear in the area of overlap, and as precision increases, small differences become significant. Too often, theorists are unprepared for these phenomena and are thrown into confusion at the emergence of ambiguity and paradox.[38] One who accepts the propositions of the operational approach, on the other hand, not only expects these problems to arise but also knows where to watch for them. This (and nothing more pretentious) is the chief virtue which is claimed for the approach.

The relevance of the above discussion to the present problem can now be stated. Probably many readers of *The Theory of Games* and some later articles have received the impression that the third pair of operations above was being proposed as "measuring the same thing" as the second pair. In other words, many have interpreted the von Neumann-Morgenstern experiment as a more precise or practical, though indirect, approach to the results of the Jevonsian experiment: *i.e.*, basically, to the results of the subjective calculation of satisfactions. But if the operational point of view were more common as a habit of thought, readers would have placed the burden of proof on the (supposed) exponents of such an equivalence, challenging them to exhibit evidence. In fact, as they would have discovered, there are no such exponents. And the evidence does not exist, for in general the two operations do not produce even approximately the same results.

Let us recall the results of our hypothetical von Neumann-Morgenstern experiment: $U_0 = 0$, $U_{200} = 2$, $U_{500} = 8$, $U_{1,000} = 10$. If the von Neumann-Morgenstern index for this individual were plotted as a function of money incomes, interpolating a smooth

---

[37] The operational approach may be useful in reminding us that differently worded questionnaires measure, in general, "different things."

[38] Such confusion was prevalent in physics prior to the revolutionary theories of Einstein and Planck. The operational approach was proposed as a means of avoiding such a state of mind in the future.

curve, the graph would be concave upward between $0 and $500; in this range it would show "increasing marginal utility." This shape would reflect merely the fact that in this range of money outcomes the individual accepted "unfair" bets and that his choices among prospects showed consistency of a certain type.

In contrast to this, Marshall and Jevons predicted almost unconditionally one general feature of a "utility" curve derived from an experiment of the Jevonsian type; it would be concave downward throughout its whole length, exhibiting non-increasing marginal utility at all points. Among those economists who believe that a Jevonsian experiment can have consistent results at all, few have ever disputed this opinion.

If Marshall's prediction does hold, then the numbers inferred from the two experiments will certainly conflict for any person who is observed to accept a gamble at odds which are not distinctly favorable, let alone odds that are actually unfair. If such a person has a von Neumann-Morgenstern index it will have a range of increasing marginal utility, which is assumed to be contradictory to the Jevonsian index. Marshall himself pointed out that there were such people, even among those otherwise "rational."

Thus we can state: the von Neumann-Morgenstern and Jevons-Marshall operations do *not* measure the "same thing." The former do not simply tend to measure the Marshallian "utilities" with greater precision, *i.e.*, to a higher number of significant figures. In general, the ranking of first differences in "utility" as a function of money will be different, depending on which "utility" is being measured; if the functions are continuous, the second derivatives will not in general have the same sign.

To those who accepted the apparent inference that the gambling operation allowed an "estimate" of the results of a Jevonsian experiment, a moment's thought should have suggested the question: Why is an estimate necessary? If risk-behavior

reveals something about differences in satisfaction, presumably it is because those differences in satisfaction are the decisive factor in decision-making. But in that case we might as well ask about satisfactions directly.[39]

This discussion has not established yet that von Neumann and Morgenstern do not themselves regard their operation, mistakenly, as measuring differences in satisfaction. The evidence for this is their repeated rejection of the notion that an individual reaches decisions in risk-situations by calculating differences in utilities, their brand or any other (such as Jevonsian utilities). But much confusion probably stems from the fact that they are prone to write in large, clear type about comparing differences in preferences and to discard such notions in fine print at the bottom of the page. Thus, they formulate their "continuity" axiom (which rules out the "absolute" rejection of lottery tickets or the "absolute" love of gambling discussed earlier) as follows:[40]

> "No matter how much the utility of v exceeds . . . the utility of u, and no matter how little the utility of w exceeds . . . the utility of u, if v is admixed to u with a sufficiently small numerical probability, the dif-

[39] It is perhaps conceivable, though unlikely, that his feelings of satisfaction might be difficult for an individual directly, being only semi-conscious, though influencing his behavior. But if it were true that his risk-behavior was a reliable and convenient guide to his feelings of differences in satisfaction, this would ensure that the Jevonsian experiment *could* always be performed. For even if the subject were an economist, say, who detested introspection, he could note tacitly his reactions to hypothetical lottery tickets (or even, if conscientious, plot his behavior at bingo games and horse races) before replying to questions about differences in satisfaction.

On the other hand, to say that the Jevonsian experiment cannot lead to consistent results is to say that any consistency revealed by the von Neumann-Morgenstern experiment is not closely related to satisfaction.

[40] Von Neumann and Morgenstern, *op. cit.*, p. 630. Since the content of this passage is not under discussion, the reader is advised to pass his eyes over it rather swiftly.

ference that this admixture makes from *u* will be less than the difference of *w* from *u*."

This leaves a strong impression, to put it mildly, that the notions of quantity of utility and differences in quantities are an integral part of the argument . . . unless the reader follows a footnote on to the next page:[41]

"The reader will also note that we are talking of entities like 'the excess of *v* over *u*,' or 'the excess of *u* over *v*' or (to combine the two former) the 'discrepancy of *u* and *v*' (*u*, *v*, being utilities) merely to facilitate the verbal discussion—they are not part of our rigorous, axiomatic system."

One other passage in the "literary" discussion is probably the greatest single source of misunderstanding; it concerns a situation in which an individual is offered a choice between a sure outcome, *A*, and a 50–50 chance of *B* or *C*, where *C* is preferred to *A* and *A* to *B*:[42]

"any assertion about his preference of *A* against the combination contains fundamentally new information. Specifically: If he now prefers *A* to the 50–50 combination of *B* and *C*, this provides a plausible base for the numerical estimate that his preference of *A* over *B* is in excess of his preference of *C* over *A*."

This passage seems clearly to imply that the von Neumann-Morgenstern operation aims at the same "entities" (*i.e.*, utility differences) as the Jevonsian experiment, being merely more indirect. But again, the crucial withdrawal is in the footnote:[43]

"Observe that we have only postulated an individual intuition which permits decision as to which of the two 'events' is preferable. But we have not directly postulated any intuitive estimate of the relative sizes of two preferences—*i.e.*, in the subsequent terminology, of two differences of utilities."

The equivocal word here is "estimate." This implies that the procedure tries to approximate the results of an introspective operation. Actually, in the von Neumann-Morgenstern experiment described above utility differences were not "estimated" but computed exactly. They were related precisely to certain risk-choices; no other evidence, intuitive or otherwise, was allowed to influence the results.

The authors themselves point out the ambiguity:

"Are we not postulating here—or taking it for granted—that one preference may exceed another, *i.e.*, that such statements convey a meaning? Such a view would be a complete misunderstanding of our procedure." [44]

Their procedure is actually to use the risk-choices to *define* the utility differences —to make this notion meaningful in a new way—not to "estimate them." Very likely it was the above passage which led Professor D. H. Robertson to imagine that von Neumann and Morgenstern had proposed a method for estimating relative differences in desirability. It is easy to spot this inference in his critical account of their theory:[45]

"Thus in the case of a man who does not know how to choose—i.e., who chooses by the toss of a mental coin—between the certainty of *B* and an even chance of *A* or *C*, these authors offer 1 as a measure of the ratio of *AB* to *BC*. . . . But it is clear that this would only be *true* for a particular type of man, namely, one who is content to be governed entirely by mathematical expectations. . . ." (My italics.)

[41] *Ibid.*, p. **631** n. This is not the only time in their book that the authors introduce notions in a "literary" discussion of their theorems that they simultaneously disown, informing the reader that it all comes out in the axioms. Of course, the very inclusion of a verbal discussion is a concession to non-mathematicians; but one can do only so much in the name of "heuristic devices." It is not a recommendation of the empirical relevance of axioms to say that they can be made plausible in literary translation only by identifying them with notions (such as subjective utility differences) which are actually irrelevant.

[42] *Op. cit.*, p. 18.
[43] *Ibid.*, p. 18 n.

[44] *Ibid.*, p. 20.
[45] D. H. Robertson, *Utility and All That* (London, 1952), p. 28.

In the case of the behavior described, von Neumann and Morgenstern would *define* the ratio of utility differences as 1; and in a matter of definition there can be no question of truth and falsity. Those standards could be applied only to a *hypothesis* that the scale defined by von Neumann and Morgenstern bore some empirical relation to some other data, not involving risk: for example, the hypothesis that it approximated the results of a Jevonsian measurement. It is clear from the context of Robertson's remarks that he believed, like most readers, such a hypothesis was implied. It has been the argument of this paper that this belief is mistaken.

In the same passage Robertson adopts essentially the Marshallian position:[46] ". . . we can make no sense of his actions in the face of uncertainty without supposing that he can form some estimate of the relative difference in desirability between pairs of situations." Whatever the plausibility of this argument, it has no relevance to the von Neumann-Morgenstern theory. Where Marshall postulated a type of "consistency" between men's risk-choices and their feelings of relative differences in desirability of the outcomes, von Neumann and Morgenstern hypothesise simply a consistency between risk-choices and other risk-choices. By coincidence, it happens that the particular form of "consistency" prescribed by Marshall (he might well have chosen some other rule than the maximisation of "expected utility") would imply von Neumann-Morgenstern "consistency"; though not vice versa. A man who had a Jevonsian index *and* who obeyed Marshall's dictum would have a von Neumann-Morgenstern index; but the existence of the latter index implies neither of the first two conditions (and the existence of the former index implies neither of the last two conditions). Thus the von Neumann-Morgenstern axioms cover all those who

are "rational" in the Marshallian sense; in addition, they may apply to others who would be "irrational" in Marshall's terms, *e.g.*, bettors who accepted unfair bets:[47] and still others for whom no Jevonsian index can be defined.

Von Neumann and Morgenstern describe their procedure thus: "We have practically defined numerical utility as being that thing for which a calculus of mathematical expectations legitimate."[48] The word "practically" is unnecessary; from an operational point of view, they *have* so defined it. Does such a "thing" exist? Friedman and Savage have emphasised the use of the axioms, which put definite restrictions on behavior, as a basis for testable and fairly powerful predictions concerning risk-choices.[49] *Should* it exist? Marschak has proposed that the axioms be regarded as defining "rational" behavior in risk-situations; according to this view, which no other writer has supported, the axioms are of interest for normative purposes, even if no one actually does conform to them.[50]

Von Neumann and Morgenstern cited only the descriptive aspect of the theory. They were not particularly interested in predicting or prescribing people's preferences among prospects, but merely in describing them in terms of mathematical expectation: a necessity in their own theory of games, a convenience in any context. This original view of the subject, by far the least pretentious, is probably the most appropriate. The emphasis by Friedman

---

[46] *Ibid.*, p. 28.

[47] The theory, since it allows for this sort of behavior, cannot be said to rule out all forms of "pleasure in gambling." But proponents have rather overplayed this point. Although acceptance of unfair bets does not contradict the theory, there is ample behavior which does, including some other forms of "pleasure in gambling."

[48] *Op. cit.*, p. 28.

[49] Friedman and Savage, *op. cit.*

[50] Marschak, *op. cit.*, p. 139; also, "Why 'Should' Statisticians and Businessmen Maximise 'Moral Expectation'?" *Proceedings of the Second Berkeley Symposium on Mathematical Statistics and Probability* (Los Angeles, 1951), p. 493.

and Savage on the meaningfulness of the hypothesis obscures the fact that many other hypotheses are just as meaningful, perhaps more useful, and even more convenient for predictive purposes (though not for description). For example, hypotheses in terms of parameters of the *money* distribution, such as mathematical expectation and variance, might produce fully as good predictions as those based on a derived von Neumann-Morgenstern index, and they would certainly be easier to test. As for the normative aspect, there seems very little reason to advise a man who is extremely reckless (or excessively conservative) in some of his risk-choices that he should be consistently reckless (or conservative) in his remaining risk-choices. Nor does it seem that a person who behaves approximately in accordance with a von Neumann-Morgenstern index would be in any sense better off if he behaved *more* in accordance with it. If these conclusions are accepted (and von Neumann and Morgenstern would probably accept them), then one must answer the question, "What does it matter whether such a 'thing' exists?" very conservatively.

At any rate, it should be clear that Baumol's impression that "Neumann and Morgenstern consider the utility index obtained by them as the *only* true one" [51] is quite mistaken. So far as behavior under certainty is concerned, only the ordinal features of the index are relevant. The only numerical operation permitted is that of forming mathematical expectations, which is related to risk-behavior; it makes no sense, for example, to *add* von Neumann-Morgenstern utilities. The cardinal features of the index—the relative differences between utility numbers—are used only to predict or describe risk-behavior, and, moreover, are derived solely from risk-behavior. Therefore the results of a von

Neumann-Morgenstern experiment cannot be "checked" against the results of any experiment not involving risk-choices. This applies to simple introspection, to the Jevonsian experiment, and also to other attempts to base a cardinal utility on consumer behavior.[52] These latter have been rather thoroughly discredited by Samuelson and others because of their use of special unrealistic assumptions. But the existence or non-existence of a von Neumann-Morgenstern index and the existence of "measurable" indices based on these other operations are entirely independent matters. Each method might, out of the whole set of ordinal utility indices, select a different subset of indices reflecting some type of data in addition to preferences; if the indices inside each subset were related by linear transformations, each method would result in a "measurable" utility index. These indices might have entirely different shapes, but so long as they did not entirely overlap in application, there would be no need to single out any one of them as being the "true" utility index. Certainly von Neumann and Morgenstern make no such claims for their construction; they cite only its convenience in formalising risk-behavior. There is no reason to believe that a "measurable utility" derived by some other method could do this;[53] on the other hand, the von Neumann-Morgenstern index could not do the main jobs for which other constructions are intended. It would be of no aid whatsoever in formalising consumer behavior under certainty (the goal of the

---

[51] Baumol, "The Neumann-Morgenstern Utility Index—An Ordinalist View," *Journal of Political Economy*, February 1951, p. 61.

[52] See Robert Bishop, "Consumer's Surplus and Cardinal Utility," *Quarterly Journal of Economics*, May 1943. For criticism of these approaches see Samuelson, *Foundations of Economic Analysis*, pp. 174–9.

[53] Thus, Alchian is mistaken in asserting that "measurability 'up to a linear transform' both *implies* and is implied by the possibility of predicting choices among uncertain prospects, the universal situation" ("The Meaning of Utility Measurement," p. 49 (my italics)). Actually, it is easy to conceive a "measurable" utility index which is neither derived from nor used to predict risk-behavior.

Fisher-Frisch constructions: see Bishop, *op. cit.*), nor would it seem to be of any relevance in welfare evaluations (whereas a Jevonsian index might be).[54] If it is true, as Professor Robertson has complained,

that von Neumann and Morgenstern have actually done harm to "the cause" of creating acceptance for a measurable utility with these last two objectives,[55] this is but a measure of the general misinterpretation of their results: a confusion for which they cannot evade all responsibility.

[54] After I had reached these conclusions, I had the great benefit of conversation with Professor Oskar Morgenstern, who was kind enough to read and discuss with me an earlier version of this paper. Professor Morgenstern confirmed what were then speculations on the implications of the theory; he particularly confirmed that he and von

Neumann had envisioned only limited application, to risk-behavior alone.

[55] Robertson, *op. cit.*, p. 28.

21   Mr. Keynes
and Mr. Marx

SIDNEY S. ALEXANDER

John Maynard Keynes once wrote to George Bernard Shaw that he was at work on a book that would revolutionize the generally accepted conception of the nature of the economic problem. The work to which he was referring was *The General Theory of Employment, Interest and Money*. This work was premised on his criticism of the accepted doctrine that an economy with flexible wages and prices tends automatically to generate full employment. The eventual impact of his theory of "insufficient aggregate demand" as the fundamental impediment to full employment, and the policy recommendations which have been anchored to it, have amply borne out the prediction he made to Shaw. One would need to go back to Karl Marx, whose *Capital* was published a half a century earlier than the *General Theory*, to find a thinker who undertook as substantial a reconstruction of the science of political economy and who had as zealous a group of followers to carry his message to the world.

The article "Mr. Keynes and Mr. Marx" by Sidney S. Alexander, which follows, reminds us that "the law of capitalist motion" which Marx discovered, is surprisingly anticipatory of the later Keynesian conception in which the declining marginal efficiency of capital causes a lack of effective demand. There are, however, important differences between the Marxian and Keynesian systems. For Keynes, the sources of breakdown are derived from basic human propensities rather than from the class structure of the system itself. Marx saw increasingly severe breakdowns as a prelude to the destruction of capitalism; Keynes felt that the destruction of capitalism was neither inevitable nor desirable.

Reprinted from Sidney S. Alexander, "Mr. Keynes and Mr. Marx," *Review of Economic Studies*, February 1940, pp. 123–135. Dr. Alexander is a member of the Economics Department of the Rand Corporation in Santa Monica.

"I am not come to destroy but to fulfill"—
(Matthew, v, 17)

Mr. Keynes has expected that "Those, who are strongly wedded to . . . 'the classical theory,' will fluctuate . . . between a belief that I am quite wrong and a belief that I am saying nothing new." [1] I should expect that one who is wedded to the (perhaps) most prominent non-classical theory, the Marxist, would not fluctuate at all, but hold firmly to the belief that much of what Mr. Keynes is saying is quite true, and quite new for an academic economist.[2] The Keynesian system is not only thoroughly consistent with the Marxian but also supplements it at certain critical points.

Both these men have been singularly blessed in being misunderstood by their critics. And this is no mere accident, nor is it entirely a result of their novelty of approach. Their presentation is involved and, at points, confusing. I cannot hope to have entirely escaped the pitfalls whereinto so many have stumbled, but on the broader phases of the theories there is sufficient clarity of outline to permit confident comparison, and on the detailed points we may depend on verbatim quotations, having due regard for context. The peculiar and private terminology of each of these thinkers raises all the treasons of translation from one system to the other.

Keynes makes but three references to Marx in *The General Theory*: once to refer to his "invention" of the name "classical economists" (p. 3), once to compare him unfavourably to Gesell (p. 355), and once to point out that the "puzzle of Effective Demand" "could only live on furtively, below the surface, in the underworlds of Karl Marx, Silvio Gesell, or Major Douglas." [3] We can safely say that whatever may be the relation of the theories of Marx to those

of Keynes, these theories of Marx had little direct influence on Keynes' formulation of his own doctrines. This is quite in keeping with the tradition of independence and originality in Cambridge economic thought, achieved through a combination of native brilliance and insulation from outside influences.

The General Theory is an analysis of the determination of the total output (total employment) of the community. *Capital* [4] is a study of the nature and development of the economic system. As such its viewpoint is far broader than that of *The General Theory* so that those Marxian theories which we shall discuss must be abstracted from the general background of the Marxian system. This general background can hardly be presented in a few sentences, but some of the main relevant principles may be stated so that the special theories relating to the determination of the total output and related subsidiary topics may be oriented within the Marxian framework.

The (present) capitalist mode of production is a particular stage in economic development characterised chiefly by wage-labour and the corresponding ownership of the means of production by non-labourers. The development of capitalism involves the increase of the numbers of wage labourers and the proportion they bear to the total population; the increase of the amount of capital and an increase in its proportion owned by non-labourers, and furthermore an increase in the size of the industrial unit as well as a concentration of ownership and control in fewer hands.

The total annual gross product of the community is distributed in three portions: one goes to replace the means of production consumed in production, another goes to the maintenance of the workers, and the last (surplus value) goes to the owners of the means of production in the form of profits of enterprise, interest, and rent. This last portion (the surplus value) is only partly

[1] Keynes, J. M.: *The General Theory of Employment, Interest and Money*, New York, 1936; preface, p. v.

[2] Marx may be, in many senses of the word classical, but not in Mr. Keynes' sense.

[3] *General Theory*, p. 32.

[4] Marx, Karl: *Capital*. References are to Kerr Edition, Chicago, 1906, 1909.

taken in the form of consumption goods. The capitalist, in his function as capitalist, seeks to increase his capital.[5] He, therefore, characteristically tends to "reconvert" a portion of his surplus value into new and additional capital so that he may in the future reconvert even more surplus value into capital. But with a growing amount of capital, or rather with a growing proportion of capital goods to the maintenance of the workers (a growing proportion of "constant" to "variable" capital), the rate of profit falls. This in time tends to diminish the rate of accumulation of capital goods, but the relationships of production (the system of income distribution in relation to the production of goods) are not such as to permit the slack to be taken up by the increase of consumption[6] so that there is a gap between the amount of goods and services that are produced and the amount that might be produced if the existing "forces of production" (production potentialities) were not held in check. This is called the contradiction between the forces of production and the relationships of production. Periodical adjustments temporarily narrow the gap while additional accumulation again widens it. As concentration and accumulation proceed, the "contradiction" becomes more pressing. Meanwhile the organisation of industry (capital) is no longer individualised but socialised so that the administrative functions of industry are more and more separated from the capitalist who becomes more and more a pure receiver of surplus value and an accumulator. Thus the stage is set for socialism: since the existing relationships governing the distribution of income act as a fetter on

production, and the organisation of production is separated from the capitalist's function, production already being socialised, it is time, says Marx, for the relations of production to be socialised. This implies the socialisation of the ownership of capital.

According to Keynes, the total output and employment of the community is determined by the propensity to consume and the amount of investment. The amount of investment depends on what I may call the attractiveness of investment which Keynes expresses as the relationship between the schedule of the marginal efficiency of capital[7] and the rate of interest. Under-full-employment equilibrium is normal because with the increase of the amount of capital the attractiveness of investment is diminished, chiefly because the schedule of the marginal efficiency falls. But the "habits of the community" are such that with an increase of income there is an increase of the non-consumed income, which would be earmarked for investment if there were suitable investment opportunities. These opportunities failing, a lower level of income will obtain, corresponding to an under-full-employment equilibrium.

Marx, too, believed that a condition of under-full-employment is normal under capitalism.[8] This he expressed as the conflict between the forces of production and the relations of production. The capitalists, as capitalists, earmark their income chiefly for accumulation. But with the accumulation of capital the rate of profit falls and makes less attractive the accumulation of productive capital so that investment falls off. This "contradiction" works itself out temporarily in adjustment periods (crises) when the capitalists fail to realise profits, and the rate of profit is raised through the depreciation of capital and the fall of real wages. It meanwhile creates and partially

[5] The maximisation of his profit is a corollary of this, since profit is regarded as the flow of income which may be converted into more capital.

[6] "Finally if it is said that the capitalists would only have to exchange and consume those commodities among themselves, then the nature of the capitalist mode of production is forgotten, it is forgotten that the question is merely one of expanding the value of capital, not of consuming it." *Capital*, Vol. III, p. 302.

[7] Its definition is given on page 235, footnote 16.

[8] Not, however, under-full-employment *equilibrium*. Through the inclusion of "laws of motion" of capitalism Marx regards the economic system as dialectically developing, and not tending toward a static equilibrium.

reabsorbs the industrial reserve army (unemployed). There is not an automatic balance of the exchanges between the consumption goods industries and the production goods industries, since there are "one-sided" purchases and sales rather than exchanges. The capitalists may attempt (in vain, as a class) to hold some of their surplus-value (profits) in the form of money, rather than in the purchase of "actual capital" or of "money capital."[9]

Not only are Keynes and Marx in agreement on the normalcy of an under-full-employment situation. There is also a strong correspondence in their visualisations of the forces bringing this about. Keynes' fundamental institutional form of behaviour, expressed in the propensity to consume, or in its obverse the propensity to save, corresponds to Marx's concept of the capitalist as characteristically an accumulator of capital. Both systems depend on the fall of the attractiveness of investment as the depressant of the total output. The agreement of Keynes' general theory of the determination of total .employment with the corresponding elements of Marx on the same level of generality insures the consistency of Keynes' theory with the entire Marxian system. Any further discussion must concern itself with detailed analysis of the components of the respective theories, since their conclusions and the last stages of their arguments are similar. These components can easily be grouped according to Mr. Keynes' three fundamental relationships: the propensity to consume, the marginal efficiency of capital, and liquidity preference. These roughly correspond to the Marxian concepts of capitalist accumulation, the rate of profit, and factors affecting the interest rate, respectively.

THE PROPENSITY TO CONSUME

The "propensity to consume" plays a leading role in the Keynesian system. It is defined as "the functional relationship . . .

between a given level of income in terms of wage units, and . . . the expenditure on consumption out of that level of income."[10] The importance of this concept with regard to the determination of under-full-employment equilibrium depends on the "fundamental psychological law"[11] that only part of an increase in income is spent on consumption. This condition leads to the proposition that larger total incomes require larger total investments, since any given investment will determine that income to which there corresponds a difference between income and consumption, as determined by the propensity to consume, equal to the given amount of investment.

Marx considers investment and net saving as attributes of the capitalists, the workers tending to consume their income.[12] Furthermore, accumulation is the *characteristic* attribute of the capitalist; "so far as he is personified capital, it is not values in use and the enjoyment of them, but exchange-value and its augmentation that spur him into action."[13] "Accumulate, accumulate. That is Moses and the prophets!"[14]

Any increase in the income of the capitalists tends to be, for the most part, accumulated. Thus Marx localises what is for us the most significant feature of the propensity to consume in the capitalist class, and regards it as the fundamental organic behaviour of that class. Keynes clearly

[9] *Capital,* Vol. II, p. 401, et seq.

[10] *General Theory,* p. 90.
[11] Ibid, p. 96.
[12] Indeed, in my opinion, the most fruitful line of interpretation of the Marxian theory that wages are equal to the cost of producing the labour, is not that this is a subsistence theory of wages. It is rather that wages may be regarded as entirely consumed so that surplus value may then be considered the extra product of society above that portion of the product devoted to the maintenance of the producers, whatever their standard of living may be. Surplus value, in this light, may be regarded more consistently as that portion of the total product which is available for the increase of the means of production. These categories are given *value* dimensions in a capitalist society. Cf. Vol. III, p. 102.
[13] *Capital,* Vol. I, p. 649.
[14] Ibid, p. 652.

recognises the distributional aspects of the propensity to consume, but states the problem as a general psychological law rather than as the behaviour of a particular class in a particular stage of economic development. Statistical studies of the spending habits of income recipients with regard to increases of income have little significance in relationship to the Marxian statement of the case, while they may confuse the issue in the Keynesian case. The important feature is the reaction of the community as a whole including institutional elements, such as corporate practices and changes in the proportions of the total income received by different classes. Nor would the problem arise in a socialist state wherein the determination of accumulation and the distribution of surplus value[15] are administered by the state. But the Marxian approach implies that this mode of behaviour is inherent in a system oriented toward profit, while Keynes suggests that an equalisation of income, e.g. through taxation of incomes, would help to smooth out the difficulty. Marx would perhaps maintain that such an equalisation within the capitalist framework would be substantially a reduction in the rate of profit and would therefore intensify the contradiction.

MARGINAL EFFICIENCY OF CAPITAL

The diminishing attractiveness of investment as capital increases is discussed by Marx in terms of the declining rate of profit, by Keynes in terms of the fall of the schedule of the marginal efficiency of capital compared with a less transigent interest rate. The marginal efficiency of capital[16] is composed of two elements, the expected marginal physical productivity and expected future price relationships. But its secular decline is apparently[17] laid at the door of declining marginal physical productivity of capital through the progressive exhaustion of the opportunities for the utilisation of capital goods.

In defining the schedule of the marginal efficiency of capital, and in characterising its slope, Keynes says: "If there is an increased investment in any given type of capital during any period of time, the marginal efficiency of that type of capital will diminish as the investment in it is increased, partly because the prospective yield will fall as the supply of that type of capital is increased, and partly because, as a rule, pressure on the facilities for producing that type of capital will cause its supply price to increase; the second of these factors being usually the more important in producing equilibrium in the short run, but the longer the period in view the more does the first factor take its place. Thus for each type of capital we can build up a schedule showing by how much investment in it will have to increase within the period in order that its marginal efficiency should fall to any given figure. We can then aggregate these schedules for all the different types of capital, so as to provide a schedule relating the rate of aggregate investment to the corresponding marginal efficiency of capital in general which that rate of investment will establish. We shall call this . . . the schedule of the marginal efficiency of capital." [18]

This involves a questionable transition

---

[15] This would be "surplus product" not "surplus value" in the socialist state. It is only within the capitalist mode of production, according to Marx, that this surplus product has a value dimension, just as only there has labour a value dimension; ". . . the social character of labour appears as the money-existence of commodities." *Capital*, Vol. III, p. 607.

[16] Actually not marginal at all. It is defined as the relation (ratio ?) of the prospective yield of an additional unit of capital to its supply price (*General Theory*, p. 135). If this were to be a marginal concept, account would have to be taken of the change in the yields of other units of capital.

[17] I say "apparently," for the alleged historical decline of the schedule of the marginal efficiency of capital is not explained in the *General Theory*.

[18] *General Theory*, p. 134.

from a single industry to the aggregate of all industries, so that changes in effective demand are neglected.[19] As Keynes himself says in another connection,[20] "It is invalid, therefore, to transfer the argument to industry as a whole unless we also transfer our assumption that the aggregate effective demand is fixed. Yet this assumption reduces the argument to an ignoratio elenchi." This is not pointed out solely for the sake of picking flaws. For there is involved throughout the Keynesian analysis the idea that aside from the semi-independent (and usually short period) variations in expectations, the decline and low level of the marginal efficiency of capital proceeds from technological relationships. There is little attention paid at this point to the possibility that the schedule of the marginal efficiency of capital is itself depressed by the income distribution as determined by the institutional relationships (chiefly property rights).[21] Marx, of course, emphasises these institutional relationships:

"The conditions of direct exploitation and those of the realisation of surplus-value are not identical. They are separated logically as well as by time and space. The first are only limited by the productive power of society, the last by the proportional relations of the various lines of production and by the consuming power of society. This last-named power is not determined either by the absolute productive power nor by the absolute consuming power, but by the consuming power based on antagonistic conditions of distribution, which reduces the consumption of the great mass of the population to a variable minimum within more or less narrow limits. The consuming power is furthermore restricted by the tendency to accumulate, the greed for an expansion of capital and a production of surplus-value on an enlarged scale."[22] Also: "Those economists who, like Ricardo, regard the capitalist mode of production as absolute, feel, nevertheless, that this mode of production creates its own limits, and, therefore, they attribute this limit, not to production, but to nature."[23]

This, we are warned,[24] should not be construed as an "underconsumption" theory of crisis or of under-full-employment equilibrium. Such an interpretation would, at least, be inconsistent with what Marx says elsewhere, since an increase in the share of the workers would lower the rate of profit. An under-consumption theory maintains that at full employment there is not enough purchasing power in the hands of consumers to buy up all the consumers' goods produced, and therefore the remedy is to increase the income and thereby the purchasing power of the consumers. Marx, in the above quotation does agree that the workers, from whom alone any additional consumption may be expected, would not be given enough purchasing power at full employment to maintain full employment. But he would also hold that to give them more purchasing power would not help, since this would mean an increase in wage-costs, and therefore a decrease in the rate of profit.[25]

Perhaps this is best interpreted in Keynesian terms as a dependence of the schedule of the marginal efficiency of capital on the schedule of the propensity to consume. That these two are not independ-

---

[19] I do not think there is an excuse for this in the claim that the individual expectations do not involve consideration of changes in aggregate effective demand. These changes are the main component of expectations.

[20] *General Theory*, p. 259.

[21] Keynes most certainly does recognise, as is indicated above, that a redistribution of income affects the propensity to consume, but he does not clearly relate this directly to the marginal efficiency of capital as well. Cf. infra, page 237, note 27.

[22] *Capital*, Vol. III, p. 286.

[23] Ibid., p. 283.

[24] Dobb: *Political Economy and Capitalism*, London, 1937; p. 113 et seq.

[25] Dobb, op. cit., p. 90, f. quotes an unequivocal disavowal by Marx of an underconsumption theory, *Capital*, Vol. II, pp. 475–6.

ent functions will be recognised in the fact that a greater propensity to consume (i.e. an upward shift of the schedule) would lead us to expect a greater marginal efficiency of capital.

Or perhaps, as Dobb suggests,[26] what is meant is that the amount of new investment (or perhaps the amount of capital goods) is "geared" to the increase of (or amount of) the production of consumption goods. In this case accumulation can be converted into capital goods without greatly diminishing the rate of profit only in the face of an expanding market for consumers goods. That is, there are technologically fixed limits to the ratio of the increase of the production of producers goods to the increase of consumers goods. If then the ratio of the increase of income devoted to consumption to that devoted to accumulation fall outside these limits, there will be a maladjustment perhaps leading to a crisis. This would lead to the situation that in order to maintain the rate of profit with capital accumulating, consumption must be increased, but if the rate of profit is maintained income will be distributed so as to discourage the increase of consumption.

This again expresses the dependence of the schedule of the marginal efficiency of capital upon the propensity to consume as well as on the purely technological factors.[27]

Of course there is usually the alternative of "deepening" the capital structure as well as "widening" it as considered above. By deepening the capital structure we mean the use of additional capital to produce an equal output at a lower cost. This must

mean that less labour is required for the production of a given product. According to Marx this tends to displace labour and increase the surplus reserve army (unemployed), and so helps to bring real wages down (at least real wages measured in socially necessary labour time).[28] This tends to check the fall of the rate of profit and may even temporarily raise the rate until the "widening" of capital in reabsorbing the workers again causes the wages to be bid up and the workers get a larger share of the product and the rate of profit again falls.[29]

Keynes differs on this point: "It will be found, I think, that the change in real wages associated with a change in money wages, so far from being usually in the same direction, is almost always in the opposite direction. . . . This is because in the short period, falling money wages and rising real wages are each, for independent reasons, likely to accompany decreasing employment; labour being readier to accept wage-cuts when employment is falling off, yet real wages inevitably rising in the same circumstances on account of the increasing marginal return to a given capital equipment when output is diminished." [30]

Keynes accepts the "classical postulate" that the real wage is equal to the marginal productivity of labour, and therefore the amount of capital and the amount of employment being given, the real rate of wages is determined by technological relationships. Keynes tends to regard this re-

---

[26] Ibid, p. 111.

[27] This Mr. Keynes recognises in discussing the propensity to consume: "Every weakening in the propensity to consume regarded as a permanent habit must weaken the demand for capital as well as the demand for consumption." But Mr. Keynes does not consider the indeterminacy this introduces with regard to the schedule of the marginal efficiency of capital.

[28] I.e. the value of labour-power, in Marxian terms, is reduced; therefore s/v, the rate of surplus value increases.

[29] This is fundamental in Marx's analysis of crisis. That which takes its place in the Keynesian system is the erratic movement of expectations. That is, in the Marxian system the rate of profit (related to the marginal efficiency of capital) is periodically reduced by the rise of real wages as the unemployed are absorbed, helping to bring a downturn. In the Keynesian system the marginal efficiency of capital is subjected to a periodical "collapse," due to revised expectations which lead an almost independent life.

[30] *General Theory*, p. 10.

lationship as working in a one-sided fashion. That is, the money wage level being determined by collective bargaining, output will be determined by the propensity to consume (expressed in terms of wage units), the marginal efficiency of capital and the liquidity-preference schedule, and the quantity of money measured in wage units. The output so determined will correspond to a given level of employment, which, in connection with the amount of capital, determines the marginal productivity of labour and therefore the real wages.[31] Any hopes of an increase of output from a cut in money wages must depend, says Keynes,[32] either on a decreased rate of interest due to the greater quantity of money in terms of wage units or on an upward shift of the schedule of the marginal efficiency of capital based on the expectation that money wages will rise in the future. The possibility is not considered that this cut in money wages may raise the marginal efficiency of capital through the fact that the adjustment may come, not entirely in the form of a fall of prices (which would tend to raise real wages), but partly in an expansion of capital to take advantage of the new relation of prices to wages. This would make the cut in money wages partly a cut in real wages, because employment would then be increased due to the increase of investment.

In other words: wages are cut, entrepreneurs think that this improves their profit position, expands employment, and find that this raises the marginal productivity of capital (due to the increased ratio of labour to capital, to the reduced cost of capital, and to the reduced cost of a dose of capital plus operating labour); and therefore the marginal efficiency of capital

goes up. Investment increases (at least in terms of wage units), and therefore the additional employment can be maintained. Employment will increase more than proportionally to capital so the real wage will be lower than it was before the cut in money wages. Of course, as the wages tend to rise again this widening of capital may yield again to the deepening process. The expectations of the entrepreneurs were justified. If this example be correct, the Marxian theory of the successive widening and deepening of capital with appropriate fluctuations in the rate of profit and in real wages is not inconsistent with the Keynesian model, but merely with the manner in which Keynes manipulates his model. It leads, however, to a questioning of Keynes' conclusion that a reduction of money wages has its chief expansionist influence on the rate of interest. This is of great practical significance when the rate of interest is near its lower limit, when little is to be hoped from the deepening of capital.

Of course, Marx recognises the technological aspects of the fall of the rate of profit also. His argument on this score has often been termed circular, and I shall not defend it against that charge, since I do not believe that the law can be established on purely deductive grounds. Marx connects the fall of the rate of profit with the increase of the proportion of capital to labour[33]: "The rate of profit sinks, not because the labourer is less exploited, but because less labour is employed in proportion to the employed capital in general." [34]

What I call "the attractiveness of investment" is related in Marxian thought to the rate of profit. In Keynes, it is involved in the relation of the schedule of the marginal efficiency of capital to the interest rate. That amount of investment which reduces the marginal efficiency of capital to a level of equality with the rate of interest will be the amount of investment voluntarily

[31] Of course, Keynes' concept of real wages is in some sort of composite commodity which might be identified with an index number. In order to make it clearly comparable with Marx's concept we should have to express this in necessary labour time.

[32] *General Theory*, p. 265.

[33] Vol. III, p. 288.

[34] I.e. with the increase of c/v.

made. It is important in the Keynesian system that the rate of interest is not considered as the variable whose determination equalises the amount of saving with the purchase of new capital goods. The schedule of the propensity to consume must be assumed independent of the rate of interest. Otherwise we would not get under-full-employment equilibrium, for then any (positive) amount of investment might be associated with any income however large since the rate of interest could be determined sufficiently low to insure the appropriate relationship between income and consumption. We pass now to consider how Keynes and Marx explain the determination of the rate of interest.

LIQUIDITY PREFERENCE

Little attention has been paid so far to the rate of interest in spite of the central role it plays in the Keynesian model. Indeed in most of the cases above a given rate of interest was assumed, implicitly. This is largely because Marx paid little attention to the rate of interest in the determination of the total output and employment. But this does not mean that Marx neglected those factors which Keynes handles in his theory of the rate of interest. This theory relates the amount of money in the economic system to the desire to hold money for contemplated future transactions or as an alternative form of holding wealth. This desire to hold money varies with the rate of interest which "is the 'price' which equilibrates the desire to hold wealth in the form of cash with the available quantity of cash." [35] Keynes speaks of a "schedule of liquidity preference" relating the quantity of money which people will wish to hold to the rate of interest. He recognises the fact that this schedule is not independent of the other elements in his system, so that a change in the quantity of

[35] *General Theory*, p. 167.

money may itself lead to a change in the schedule of liquidity preference.[36]

The essential idea is that interest is not the reward for saving but is the reward for not hoarding.[37] Keynes distinguishes between the transaction and speculative motives for holding money.[38] The transactions motive relates to the function of money as a medium of exchange, it governs the amount of money which is held "to bridge the interval between receipt . . . and disbursement." [39] The amount of money held in pursuance of this motive "mainly depends on the level of income." [40] The speculative motive governs the holding of money in preference to other forms of wealth as a bridge from the present to the future. The amount of money so held "mainly depends on the relation between the current rate of interest and the state of expectations." [41] This distinction becomes important with regard to the fact that for an individual all saving need not be spent in the purchase of goods. The concerted net attempt of many individuals to convert wealth or income into money to hold results both in a failure to reproduce income and a rise in the rate of interest which further discourages the purchase of new investment-assets.

Marx has a somewhat similar treatment of these matters, but I do not believe this comparison should be extended very far. He distinguishes between money in circulation and in hoards. Money in circulation is roughly proportional to the volume of transactions. The hoard is a transitional stage in the accumulation of capital. As money is accumulated in hoards it is withdrawn from circulation. There is no difficulty, of course, when withdrawals into hoards equal return

[36] This is comparable to defining a demand curve in such a way that a change in price of the commodity would shift the curve.
[37] *General Theory*, p. 182.
[38] I here lump the precautionary and transactions motives, as Keynes does, p. 199.
[39] Ibid, p. 195.
[40] Ibid, p. 199.
[41] Ibid.

to circulation plus the net increment to the total quantity of money. This is the usual case except in those periods when investment in actual capital is unattractive, at which times accumulated funds are put into the forms of money capital leading to a cyclically recurring plethora of money capital.[42] As for the rate of interest, "The division of profit into interest and profit proper is regulated by demand and supply, that is, by competition,"[43] but since unlike the case of commodities, there is no cost of production for price to fluctuate about, "no such thing as a 'natural' rate of interest exists."[44] But "The rate of interest holds a similar relation to the rate of profit as the market price of a commodity does to its value."[45] The competition which Marx considers here is in the supply of and demand for loan capital. This is not to be confused with the demand for actual (physical or industrial) capital.[46] "In times of stringency the demand after loan capital is a demand for means of payment and nothing else; it is by no means a demand for money as a means of purchase.[47] . . . The demand for means of payment is a mere demand for convertibility into money to the extent that the merchants and producers can offer good security; it is a demand for money capital insofar as . . . an advance of means of payment gives them not merely the form of money, but also the equivalent they lack for making payment in any form."[48] What is it that is missing in such periods of stringency, capital or money in its function as a means of payment? And this is a well-known controversy. . . . It is not a question of a contrast between a demand

for money as a means of payment and a demand for capital. The contrast is rather between capital in its money-form and its commodity-form; and the form which is here demanded, and which can alone perform any function here, is its money-form."[49] In other words, entrepreneurs may borrow in order to acquire actual capital, or they may borrow in order to convert their capital into a money-form.

There is no inconsistency, then, between the Keynesian concept of the rate of interest and the Marxian. Certainly in Marx's theory interest is the payment, not for saving, but for lending.[50] But the emphasis is different, for Marx regards the alternatives which the rate of interest equilibrates as lending and borrowing money.[51] The possibility of absorption in hoards is, according to Marx, only a transitional stage in the acquisition of actual or money capital or a stage in the business cycle. Keynes, on the other hand, envisages the choice as between holding money or holding other assets, with liquidity preference continually operating. Whether the liquidity preference theory of interest advanced by Keynes, and a loanable-funds-supply-and-demand theory such

[42] *Capital*, Vol. III, pp. 595-96. Money capital refers to money used for the purchase of interest-bearing paper (loanable money capital) or the interest-bearing paper itself.
[43] Ibid, p. 419.
[44] Ibid, p. 419.
[45] Ibid, p. 429.
[46] *Capital*, Vol. III, p. 602.
[47] The word purchase is mistranslated as payment in the Kerr Edition.
[48] *Capital*, Vol. III, p. 605.

[49] Ibid., p. 544.
[50] Ibid, p. 495. The "limit" of the rate of interest "is determined by the supply and demand of *money capital as distinguished from the other forms of capital*." (Italicised by Marx.)
[51] *Capital*, Vol. III, p. 595. "As for the other portion of profit, which is not intended to be consumed as revenue, it is converted into money capital only when it is not immediately able to find a place for investment in the expansion of the productive sphere in which it has been made. This may be due to two causes. Either the sphere of production may be saturated with capital. Or it may be because accumulation must first have reached a certain volume, before it can serve as capital, according to the proportions of the investment of new capital required in this sphere. Hence it is converted for a while into loanable money-capital and serves in the expansion of production in other spheres. . . . But if this new accumulation meets with difficulties in its employment, through a lack of spheres for investment, due to the overcrowding of the lines of production and an oversupply of loan capital, then such a plethora of loanable money capital proves merely that capitalist production has its limits."

as that held by Marx are merely alternative formulations, or whether they are fundamentally different is still a controversial question. In general those who hold the loanable-funds-supply-and-demand theory regard it as equivalent to the liquidity preference theory, while those who hold the liquidity preference theory claim that the two theories are inconsistent with each other. Furthermore, Keynes thinks the rate of interest of great importance in the system, while Marx regards it as something rather peripheral, determining chiefly the division of total profit into interest and profits of enterprise, a purely quantitative distinction which is institutionalized into a qualitative one. Marx and Keynes adopt a common attitude (as against the Austrians) in regarding interest as a monetary and not a technological phenomenon. "If there were no money at all, there would certainly be no general rate of interest." [52]

This completes our consideration of Mr. Keynes' three fundamental relationships and their Marxian equivalents. We shall now consider briefly certain side issues of interest.

SAY'S LAW

Mrs. Robinson, writing from a Keynesian viewpoint, maintains that the Marxist theory has adopted an "unexceptionable" proposition in the theory of the tendency of the rate of profit to fall (although "the argument by which this proposition is derived from the labour theory of value is completely circular.")[53] But the Marxian theory is attached to Say's Law, and "the pivot of the whole argument is that investment cannot increase unless consumption declines." [54] If it were not for these errors

the Marxists would see that "when capitalism is rightly understood, the rate of interest will be set at zero, and the major evils of capitalism will disappear." [55]

I do not think that Marx would support Say's law or the proposition that investment cannot increase unless consumption declines. Indeed Marx categorically denies Say's law: He criticises attempts to explain the processes of production and exchange in barter terms, and later says: "The disposal of the various elements of annual reproduction, that is to say, their circulation which must comprise the reproduction of the capital to the point of replacing its various elements, such as constant, variable, fixed, circulating, money, and commodity capital, is not conditioned on the mere purchase of commodities followed by a corresponding sale, or a mere sale followed by a corresponding purchase, so that there would actually be a bare exchange of commodity for commodity, as the political economists assume, especially the free trade school from the time of the physiocrats and Adam Smith." [56]

"But to the extent that only one-sided exchanges are made, a number of mere purchases on one hand, a number of mere sales on the other—and we have seen that the normal disposal of the annual product on the basis of capitalist production requires such one-sided metomorphoses—the balance can be maintained only on the assumption that the value of the one-sided purchases and one-sided sales is the same. The fact that the production of commodities is the general form of capitalist production implies the role which money is playing not only as a medium of circulation, but also as money capital, and creates conditions peculiar for the normal transactions of exchange under this mode of production. . . . These conditions become so many causes of abnormal movements, implying the possibility of crisis, since a bal-

---

[52] *Capital*, Vol. III, p. 495.
[53] Robinson, Joan: *Essays in the Theory of Employment*, New York, 1937; p. 251. It is only fair to say that Mrs. Robinson in discussing Marxist economics refers rather to the works of Mr. John Strachey, than to those of Mr. Karl Marx.
[54] Ibid, p. 252.

[55] *Essays in The Theory of Employment*, p. 255.
[56] *Capital*, Vol. II, p. 577.

ance is an accident under the crude conditions of this production." [57]

A ZERO RATE OF INTEREST

The argument that "investment cannot increase unless consumption declines" is not to be found in Marx's work so far as I know. But the idea of the possible euthanasia of *capitalism* (not only of the rentier) expressed in the suggestion of a zero rate of interest does mark the clash of social viewpoints of Keynes and Marx. This difference of viewpoint may also be read into the above-noted differences between Keynes and Marx with respect to the dependence of the marginal efficiency of capital on the rate of real wages and on the propensity to consume. Dobb maintains[58] that neither the state nor the banking system could be depended upon to bring about a distribution of income contrary to the interest of the capitalist class as a whole. Thus this difference of opinion is reduced to a problem of the practical feasibility of a zero rate of interest in a capitalist system.[59] I think it

is more than this. It is a disagreement on the fundamental working of the economic system, the Marxian view being that a system motivated by profit will not function well, as profit goes toward zero. This remains a question of theory, however great its practical importance. The line between a theoretical and a practical question is limited only by the limits of the theoretical framework.

CONCLUSION

From the general Marxian framework, criticism of Mr. Keynes' system would fall under two headings: (1) Mr. Keynes fails to recognise a law of capitalist development, i.e. his system regards human institutions as data, changing independently, and hence he fails to recognise that the limitations on production are imposed by the capitalist mode of production *itself*. (2) Mr. Keynes' fundamental relationships, as represented in his schedules are not independent of each other nor even of the values of the variables they relate. Analytically this means, for example, that even with the slope of the liquidity preference schedule given as negative, we cannot then say that an increase in the quantity of money will lower the rate of interest. We must first find the effects on the other variables in the system. Pragmatically, it means that these schedules may be altered by the alteration of property and income relationships, although, say the Marxists, to do so would be to transform the capitalist system.

---

[57] *Capital*, Vol. II, p. 578.
[58] Op. cit., p. 110. He also refers to Harrod's view that the banking system may be unable to "influence appropriately" the long term rate of interest.
[59] Of course there is another solution which solves the riddle in a most direct way. The solution is to convert that portion of the total surplus value which is not consumed by the capitalists nor used for replacement, into articles which the state finds desirable and which are capable neither of glutting the market, nor of increasing the amount of capital. Armaments may be considered the archetype of this form of commodity. The state may acquire these commodities either by a direct requisition in the form of taxation or by purchase through funds obtained by inducing the capitalists to convert their unconsumed surplus-value into money-capital (interest-bearing certificates of indebtedness of the state). This inducement may be facilitated by obstructions to or prohibitions of conversion of the surplus value into other forms of capital. This seems to have

been the policy of the Nazi state. The essential background of the solution is a transformation from a dynamic into a static state, or a state dynamic only with regard to the accumulation of money-capital. It is a divorce of the profit motive from the accumulation of capital goods. It is in a very real sense, therefore, that the totalitarian state may be said to "preserve capitalism."

22 The Profit Concept
and Theory: A Restatement
J. FRED WESTON

The first definitive step in the evolution of profit theory was taken when J. B. Say distinguished between profit received by the entrepreneur and interest received by the capitalist. This was an advance over Adam Smith and those who followed him in viewing profit simply as the aggregate income, including interest, which accrued as a noncontractual residual to the social class associated with the ownership of business enterprise. Their attempt at explanation probably reflected the fact that entrepreneurs were usually also capitalists, which blurred the distinction between the profit form of income and interest. A functional view of the activities of owner-capitalists was required to associate profit specifically with entrepreneurship and interest specifically with the function of supplying capital, including the stock of wage goods out of which advances were made to wage workers.

The conception of profit as a residual which remains only temporarily in the absence of monopoly, after contractual costs like wages and rent have been met, was rooted in the association of entrepreneurial activity with the institution of private property. Later, the evolution of the institutional milieu from the predominantly individual-proprietorship type of enterprise to the corporation, with its characteristic separation of ownership and control, facilitated analytical disassociation of the profit form of income from the simple function of ownership. The view that profit is a monopoly return continued to have adherents, but it was challenged by alternative views. One was that profit originates in the entrepreneurial activity of innovation. The other was that profit is a nonfunctional residual which results because uncertainty causes a difference between *ex-ante* and *ex-post* returns. These theories of profit are reviewed and compared in "The Profit Concept and Theory: A Restatement" by J. Fred Weston, who is persuaded that the merits of the uncertainty theory of profit exceed those of its rivals.

Reprinted from J. Fred Weston, "The Profit Concept and Theory: A Restatement," *Journal of Political Economy*, Vol. 62, April 1954, pp. 152–170. Dr. Weston is Chairman of the Department of Business Economics at the University of California at Los Angeles.

Profit theory has long been regarded as a vexed, confused, and unsatisfactory subject.[1] The recent writings in this area continue to present divergent ideas.[2] It appears useful, therefore, to review the areas of dispute, to indicate the reasons for the continuing disagreements, and to attempt a restatement which may secure more general acceptance.[3]

INTRODUCTION

The development of profit theory offers a fascinating study in the history of economic ideas. Since Knight covers the period up to the publication of his own landmark,[4] it is necessary to sketch here only the nature of the subsequent materials, with one notable exception. Although *Risk, Uncertainty, and Profit* includes references to the stationary state of Schumpeter's *The Theory of Economic Development*, it does not discuss his profit theory.[5]

Although only six books on "profit" have been published since 1921,[6] many others included substantial sections on this topic.[7] Especially good are Triffin's discussion of uncertainty, innovation, restrictions on entry, and recontracting and his emphasis on the individual rather than the firm.[8] Statistical studies of accounting net income purport to test some aspects of "profit" theory.[9] Textbook discussions have been influential, but this segment of the liter-

---

[1] For convenience in summarizing and referring to the different views held by the writers in this area, code letters will designate the leading rival theories of profit. This results in extreme oversimplification but serves to indicate the nature of the positions held.

[2] Chronologically: J. F. Weston, "Profit as the Payment for the Function of Uncertainty-bearing," *Journal of Business,* XXII (April, 1949), 106–18; "Enterprise and Profit," *ibid.,* July, 1949, pp. 141–59; "A Generalized Uncertainty Theory of Profit," *American Economic Review,* XL (March, 1950), 40–60 (U); Armen A. Alchian, "Uncertainty, Evolution, and Economic Theory," *Journal of Political Economy,* LVIII (June, 1950), 211–21 (U, A); Jean Marchal, "The Construction of a New Theory of Profit," *American Economic Review,* XLI (September, 1951), 549–65 (MC, A); Stephen Enke, "On Maximizing Profits," *American Economic Review,* XLI (September, 1951), 566–78 (U, A); R. G. Hawtrey, "The Nature of Profit," *Economic Journal,* LXI (September, 1951), 489–504 (A); G. L. S. Shackle, "The Nature and Role of Profit," *Metroeconomica,* III (December, 1951), 101–7 (U); Richard M. Davis, "The Current State of Profit Theory," *American Economic Review,* XLII (June, 1952), 245–64 (U, Q); Boris Ischboldin, "Die Theorie der Quasirente und des Profits," *Schmollers Jahrbuch,* LXXII (1952), 35–51 (U); R. F. Harrod, "Theory of Profit," *Economic Essays* (London: Macmillan & Co., Ltd., 1952), pp. 188–207 (E, U, R); Peter L. Bernstein, "Profit Theory—Where Do We Go from Here?" *Quarterly Journal of Economics,* LXVII (August, 1953), 407–22 (A).

[3] I have greatly benefited from extended discussions with Armen A. Alchian, Martin Bonfenbrenner (by correspondence), Karl Brunner, Harry Markowitz, Frank E. Norton, and R. Clay Sprowls. I am grateful for research assistance to the Bureau of Business and Economic Research, University of California, Los Angeles.

[4] Frank H. Knight, *Risk, Uncertainty, and Profit* (Boston: Houghton Mifflin Co., 1921), pp. 22–50 (U).

[5] Joseph A. Schumpeter, *The Theory of Economic Development,* trans. R. Opie (Cambridge: Harvard University Press, 1934) (E).

[6] William Trufant Foster and Waddill Catchings, *Profits* (1925) (R, E); George O'Brien, *Notes on the Theory of Profit* (1929) (R); Clarence J. Foreman, *Efficiency and Scarcity Profits* (1930) (R, E, MC); H. P. Fairchild, *Profits or Prosperity* (1932) (W); James P. Beddy, *Profits* (1940) (MC); Hastings Lyon, *Risk, Profit, and Loss* (1943) (R).

[7] M. Dobb, *Capitalist Enterprise and Social Progress* (1925) (U, E); J. M. Keynes, *A Treatise on Money* (1930) (U); A. C. Pigou, *Economics of Welfare* (London: Macmillan & Co., Ltd., 1932) (R).

[8] Robert Triffin, *Monopolistic Competition and General Equilibrium Theory* (Cambridge: Harvard University Press, 1941), pp. 158–87 (U, E).

[9] S. H. Nerlove, *A Decade of Corporate Incomes* (Chicago: University of Chicago Press, 1932); R. C. Epstein, *Industrial Profits in the United States* (New York: National Bureau of Economic Research, 1934); R. T. Bowman, *A Statistical Study of Profits* (Philadelphia: University of Pennsylvania Press, 1934); W. L. Crum, *Corporate Size and Earning Power* (Cambridge: Harvard University Press, 1939); M. Taitel, *Profits, Productive Activities, and New Investment* ("T.N.E.C. Monograph," No. 12 [Washington, 1941]).

ature is too diverse for brief treatment.[10]

Surprisingly few journal articles on profit appeared during the thirty-year period, 1921–50.[11] Three contributions have been outstanding: Hicks for his discussion of the nature and role of uncertainty; Gordon for delineating dominant patterns of ideas about profit and for a persuasive formulation of his own; Machlup for a remarkably clear exposition of the relationships between accounting and economic concepts and for his discussion of the many facets of restrictions on entry.

Important issues are raised by both the older and the more recent literature on profit: (1) the use of the profit concept in economic analysis; (2) the nature of risk and uncertainty; (3) the origin or source of profit; (4) empirical testing of profit concepts and theories; (5) innovation, en-

[10] I have not attained complete coverage of the foreign-language literature since 1920. Nor have I attempted to track down all unpublished doctoral dissertations on profit.

[11] L. Kotany, "A Theory of Profit and Interest," *Quarterly Journal of Economics*, 1921–22 (A); R. A. Lehfeldt, "Analysis of Profit," *Journal of Political Economy*, 1925 (R); G. E. Barnett, "The Entrepreneur and the Supply of Capital," *Economic Essays in Honor of John Bates Clark* (1927) (E); C. A. Tuttle, "A Functional Theory of Economic Profit," *Economic Essays in Honor of John Bates Clark* (1927) (E); J. R. Hicks, "The Theory of Uncertainty and Profit," *Economica*, 1931 (U); W. S. Hopkins, "Profit in American Economic Theory," *Review of Economic Studies,* Vol. I (October, 1933) (U, MN, MC); A. C. Littleton, "Contrasting Theories of Profit," *Accounting Review,* 1936 (E, A); R. A. Gordon, "Enterprise, Profits, and the Modern Corporation," *Explorations in Economics* (1936) (U, E, MN, MC); M. A. Hasan, "Enterprise and Profit," *Indian Journal of Economics,* 1937 (E); R. S. Tucker, "Is There a Tendency for Profits To Equalize?" *American Economic Review,* 1937 (A); N. S. Buchanan, "Toward a Theory of Fluctuations in Business Profits," *American Economic Review,* 1941. (A); L. R. Chenault, "Buchanan's Theory of Fluctuations in Business Profits," *American Economic Review,* 1942 (A); M. Kalecki, "A Theory of Profits," *Economic Journal,* 1942 (A); F. Machlup, "Competition, Pliopoly, and Profits," *Economica,* 1942 (R, MN, MC); J. H. Stauss, "The Entrepreneur: The Firm," *Journal of Political Economy,* 1944 (E).

trepreneurship, and profit; (6) profit and monopoly power; (7) profit, imputation, and quasi-rent; (8) profit and the income of social classes; (9) profit maximization; (10) profit and macroeconomics. These topics are discussed in the order listed.

IS A PROFIT CONCEPT USEFUL FOR ECONOMIC ANALYSIS?

Do we need a concept "profit"? A succinct statement of the distribution process provides an answer. Fundamentally, there are two types of payments for productive services—wages and rent. Since personal services cannot be capitalized and sold as a reservoir of services, payments for a stream of current services may be called "wages." The payment for the use of a capital asset is rent. Alternatively, a person may borrow loanable funds to buy a capital good and pay interest on his borrowings. Rent and interest may therefore be regarded as alternative methods of arranging for the possession and use of capital goods. Under perfect competition and complete knowledge, each factor is paid the value of its marginal product. In accordance with Euler's theorem, total product will be exhausted in wage, rent, and interest payments.[12]

Planned total product and planned total costs, however, are likely to differ from those actually realized. If expectations are not realized, residuals will arise. These residuals represent an income-flow element contained in payments to owners of productive services. The residuals are not income flows parallel or correlative with the traditional categories—wages, rent, and interest—but components of these incomes.

[12] Technically, total product is exhausted under two sets of conditions. Under constant returns to scale, this is true at any output. Exhaustion of product in distribution also obtains whenever the production function is tangent to any homogeneous function of the first degree, as is the case at long-run equilibrium.

Thus any income has two elements, a functional segment and a nonfunctional segment, profit. Thus the profit concept is useful for identifying a distinctive income element. This concept of profit is explained further after a discussion of the key factor, uncertainty.

THE NATURE OF RISK AND UNCERTAINTY

Degrees of Information

Marschak has set forth a framework which is useful for making clear the nature of uncertainty.[13] He distinguishes four degrees of information (for convenience of reference, his numbering and symbols are followed):

3.1. The firm does not know (p).[14]
3.2. The firm does not know (p), but it knows data permitting it to estimate (p).
3.3. The firm knows (p).
3.4. The firm knows (p), and every element of (p) is either 0 or 1.

The relationships can be most clearly seen by a tabular summary of his explanatory comments.

Incomplete information, 3.1, nonstochastic case (ignorance)
Incomplete information, 3.2, stochastic case
Complete information, 3.3, stochastic case
Complete information, 3.4, nonstochastic case (certainty)

The stochastic cases are amenable to rational solution through statistical decisions. The extreme cases are relatively unimportant for practical problems. Although Marschak acknowledges "obvious mixed cases" of other degrees of information, one of these mixed cases is of such importance that it deserves recognition as a distinct

category. It is intermediate between his first and second situations and will be referred to here as "situation 3.11."

Under situation 3.11, the firm does not know p; it has some knowledge, but the information is such that p cannot be estimated on the basis of statistical relationships (because, for example, the observations are not drawn from a single or homogeneous universe; the observations are not from a stable universe; there are too few observations; etc.). Situations represented by 3.11 are of the greatest practical importance, since the great majority of important business and economic decisions fall into this category. A danger of Marschak's classification is its implication that business and economic decisions can ordinarily be handled as stochastic problems. One of the goals of statistical analysis and econometrics, of course, is to develop record-keeping and techniques which will transform 3.11 problems into 3.2 problems.[15] But the area of decision-making in which this has not yet been attained remains vast and doubtless will always remain so.

The use of distinct categories (as both Knight and Marschak have observed) is an idealization, since reality is a continuum of cases running from certainty to increasing degrees of uncertainty. Nevertheless, the concepts of uncertainty and risk are amenable to definition.

Definition and Nature of Uncertainty

The necessary condition for uncertainty is either incomplete information or a "short-run" stochastic situation. Differences in degree of uncertainty may be distinguished for stochastic cases by measures of the dispersion of the probability distribution. In the important 3.11 cases of incomplete probability distributions, it may not be meaningful to attempt to compare the degree of uncertainty associated with al-

---

[13] Jacob Marschak, "Role of Liquidity under Complete and Incomplete Information," *American Economic Review*, Suppl. XXXIX (May, 1949), pp. 183–84. Professor Marschak also helped me by commenting on an earlier draft of this section.

[14] (p) is the probability distribution of alternative outcomes.

[15] The recent development of linear programming is an example of such effort.

ternative courses of action. These circumstances pose difficult questions for formalizing the decision-making process, which Shackle seeks to surmount by the concept of the degree of potential surprise.[16] But if the decision-maker cannot assign probability values to alternative outcomes, it is difficult to understand how he can arrive at degrees of potential surprise. Shackle's analysis appears to represent a method of formulating subjective probability judgments.

The causes of uncertainty are (1) innovations, (2) exogenous changes, and (3) interactions between the two. Examples of exogenous changes are wars, alterations in the legislative-legal environment, differences in ability between businessmen (also reflected in innovations), spontaneous changes in tastes (including changes in spending habits of people, changes in preferences between income and leisure, etc.). The interaction of these forces produces changes in the total national product; these changes have unequal impact upon industries and firms, variations in income elasticities of demand being an important variable.

Definition of Risk

Two meanings of risk are in current usage. Many follow Knight, who identified risk with the insurable cases. Others use the word to indicate possible disappointment; in this use, risk is not a category parallel with those of certainty and uncertainty. Since insurable (more generally, transformable) situations no longer involve risk after the risk has been insured (transformed), what Knight calls "risk" may more informatively be referred to as "transformable uncertainty."[17] The word

"risk" may then be reserved to refer to the possibility of an unfavorable outcome of an action taken under uncertainty. It is not necessarily the expected (actuarial) loss, since p may not be known. Risk may be measured in money or utility; or it may be expressed in terms of degrees of surprise, regret, disappointment, unattained pleasures, etc.

THE UNCERTAINTY THEORY OF PROFIT

Under uncertainty, total product may not equal total costs (explicit and implicit) because plans are not fulfilled. How this occurs is briefly indicated. Two classes of owners of productive services are distinguished. First, those with rates of compensation fixed in advance of the determination of the results of operations are called "hired factors" and receive contractual returns. Second, those with rates of compensation dependent upon the results of operations are referred to as "unhired factors," who receive noncontractual or residual returns.[18]

Whatever the basis upon which contractual relationships have been entered, actual results will not have been accurately foreseen, because of uncertainty. Hence, whatever the basis upon which contractual commitments have been made, events actually do not work out that way. This is the significance of economic profit. It is not possible to plan in advance exactly what total product or total costs will be.[19]

Identification of Profit

It is uncertainty which gives rise to profit, yet makes difficult a clear exposition

---

[16] G. L. S. Shackle, *Expectation in Economics* (Cambridge: At the University Press, 1949); also "On the Meaning and Measure of Uncertainty," I, *Metroeconomica,* IV (December, 1952), 99–103.

[17] For elaboration of this position see my "A Generalized Uncertainty Theory of Profit," pp. 43–44.

[18] J. R. Hicks, *The Theory of Wages* (New York: Peter Smith, 1932), pp. 234–35. It will be noted that the above formulation avoids the use of that "mystery man" of economic history whose presence is always felt, who seems to be an important figure in the economic process, and yet whose identity is difficult to establish—the entrepreneur.

[19] Alchian, *op. cit.,* pp. 211–13.

of its nature. Profit is the difference between *ex ante* and *ex post* returns.[20] If all compensation were actually a function of the results of operations, no profit would arise (except in the sense that if some other commitment of time or resources had been made, one's return would have been different, even though dependent upon the results of operations). But, in practice, compensation arrangements involve fixed commitments. Hence, after all protective strategies are taken into account, commitments are made on the basis of some subjective probability distributions. The difference between the expected outcomes defined by the basis upon which contracts are entered into and the results actually realized is a measure of profit.[21] This is what is meant when I state that profit is the difference between *ex ante* and *ex post* returns. It is not implied that the *ex ante* returns represent single-valued expectations or can be expressed as certainty equivalents.[22]

Another aspect of the uncertainty concept of profit is emphasized by means of an example using the concept "utility-equivalent income." [23] Let us postulate that a decision-maker is considering an action whose outcome is uncertain. We could offer him a series of certain incomes to determine the minimum certain income he would take for his uncertain alternative. We would thus determine the point at which he would be indifferent between an income with certainty and the uncertain situation. This income we will call the "utility-equivalent income." Profit may be defined as the difference between the income actually attained and the utility-equivalent income.

However, there is lack of parallelism between the certainty equivalent and the uncertain incomes. If the decision-maker chooses the certain income, that ends the matter. But if he remains in the uncertainty situation, many other kinds of behavior are called for—flexibility, diversification, safety margins, etc. Thus the utility-equivalent-income idea is a useful analytical device, but it has severe limitations for indicating behavior strategy.

The uncertainty concept of profit may be further clarified by considering its emergence under different circumstances. With the aid of the classification presented under the discussion of the nature of uncertainty, the existence of profit under alternative situations may be diagramed (Table 22-1).

The only point requiring explanation, in connection with Table 22-1, is the distinction between profit in the short run and profit in the long run, in cases **3.2** and **3.3**. As long as the problem is a statistical one, statistical errors may occur in the short run (the time dimension is not necessarily identical with the definition of the short-run production period). These errors will be associated with profit (unless perfect canceling occurs).

Profit as Reward for Uncertainty-Bearing

The uncertainty concept of profit is often misunderstood and frequently misrepresented. This is the case when profit is said to be the payment *for bearing* risk or uncertainty. That such a view still has many adherents results from its effective presentation by Pigou.[24] If each of a million people, having a vase worth £100 as a vase, but with equal probability of between 0 and £250 broken, break their vases, national wealth would be increased by £25

[20] "A Generalized Uncertainty Theory of Profit," p. 51.

[21] But, of course, zero profits may occur with wide divergences which happen to cancel out.

[22] Another method of formulating the profit idea is to describe it as the difference between incomes which would have been received if no payments were contractual and incomes when some payments are contractual and others not.

[23] This formulation was suggested to me by Harry Markowitz of Rand Corporation.

[24] Pigou, *op. cit.,* pp. 771–72.

TABLE 22-1

PROFIT UNDER ALTERNATIVE SITUATIONS

Degree of Information	Category	Stochastic Situation?	Uncertainty?	Profit?
Incomplete	3.1	No	Yes	Yes
Incomplete	3.11	No	Yes	Yes
Incomplete	3.2	Yes	Short run—yes; long run—no	Short run—yes; long run—no
Complete	3.3	Yes	Short run—yes; long run—no	Short run—yes; long run—no
Complete	3.4	No	No	No

million.[25] From this example Pigou develops the idea of units of uncertainty-bearing and uncertainty as a fourth factor of production.

The commitment of funds or effort to economic activities is, indeed, analogous to "breaking the vase" in Pigou's example. But it is not bearing uncertainty as such which is the source of the gain. One can envisage many commitments under uncertainty which will involve loss. The source of the gain in Pigou's example is the fact that operations, on the average, yield outputs which exceed inputs. It is the productivity of economic activity which is the source of additional value. The bearing of risk or uncertainty as such is not productive.

Another reason why it is sometimes said that profit is the payment for bearing uncertainty or risk is the observation that higher-risk investments appear to provide higher yields than lower-risk investments. Thus Caa bonds appear to bear higher yields than Aaa bonds. Nominal yields of lower-grade bonds may be higher than nominal yields of higher-grade bonds, but whether they will be higher net of defaults

[25] Calculation of the actuarial value of breaking the vases demonstrates this:

Probability (p)	Gain or Loss (X)	Probability Times Gain or Loss
0.5	0 less 100 = (100)	(50)
0.5	250 less 100 = 150	75
		$E(X) = 25$

is less certain. If a net differential obtained, it would not represent the payment for bearing risk but would represent different relative demand and supply conditions upon which many forces, in addition to the degree of uncertainty, operate.

SOME OBJECTIONS TO THIS UNCERTAINTY CONCEPT OF PROFIT

The Traditional Functions of Profit

One objection to this uncertainty concept of profit is its failure to perform the functions traditionally assigned to profit: (1) to constitute a distinctive distributive share and (2) to guide economic decisions.

Economic profit is not a distinctive share correlative with wages, interest, and rent. It is a component of each of these types of payments. Profit is the difference between the bases upon which the decision-makers choose between alternative courses of action to enter into contractual commitments and the actual outcomes which are experienced. If decision-makers are overoptimistic, their incomes are smaller, and contractual incomes are larger, than they would have been if the decision-makers had possessed more knowledge. If decision-makers are overpessimistic (but not so much so that the total level of economic activity is reduced), the converse will obtain. It follows that profit is an element found in payments to the owners of all types of productive services. Profit should not, therefore, be regarded as a distinct distributive share.

A statement frequently expressed is that profit guides economic decisions, that it is the mechanism for allocating economic resources. It is strange how thinking is compartmentalized at times. A basic teaching of economics is that the price system allocates resources. A utility theory (theory of demand for products) plus a marginal-productivity theory (theory of demand for resources and a statement of the supply conditions of factors) are sufficient to explain simultaneously resource allocation and income distribution. Wage theory, interest theory, and rent theory (to the extent that we have them) in essence are applications of price theory, attempting to take account of differences in market forces in different institutional settings. Such theories are ingredients of the theory of a price system. Price theory involves maximization of incomes.[26] Since price theory and income maximization provide the basis for decisions resulting in resource allocation, it is not necessary to have a profit theory which does this uniquely. In fact, the attempt to do so runs into inconsistencies.

If the uncertainty concept of profit does not perform the traditional functions of profit theory, what function does it perform for economic analysis? First, it states explicitly a fact of economics—the divergence of plans and realizations. Second, it provides a basis for revising plans as in a sequential process. Decisions are based on (1) *ex post* data, (2) expectations with regard to the uncertain future, and (3) utility preferences of the decision-makers. A decision is made. Time elapses. If plans are not fulfilled (profit is the measure of the extent of nonfulfilment), plans will be revised.

Zero profit does not imply that plans may not be revised. The occurrence of zero profit

is an additional amount of information. The subjective probability judgments of decision-makers will be influenced by the increased knowledge. Thus plans for the future will be influenced by (1) the amount of profit, and (2) the additional information upon which a course of action may be formulated.

The uncertainty concept of profit is not unique in this attribute. Many economic decisions involve uncertainty. When the opportunity of revising plans occurs, the decision will be influenced by experience subsequent to the previous decision. Indeed, most of life's activities involve sequential decision processes.

Hence the direct importance of the uncertainty concept of profit for economic theory is modest. What needs underscoring is the de-emphasis of the uncertainty theory on the role of profit, as such, in the economy. Ours is not a profit (and loss) system, as much as it is a (relative) price system. The role of profits (windfalls) is significant at times, but the price mechanism performs the functions ascribed to "profit" by various writers. Profit theory is important, not because of the significance of amounts of profit, but because of the need for a concept consistent with generally accepted economic principles.

What is loosely called "profit theory" is a concept or definition. The uncertainty definition or concept of profit follows from the definitions and theorems of economic doctrine. Theory flows from propositions derived from the profit concept.

Empirical Tests of the Uncertainty Theory

Still, it is averred, the uncertainty theory of profit cannot be tested empirically.[27] Empirical testing of the uncertainty theory

---

[26] Qualification of income maximization under uncertainty and the distinction between profit maximization and income maximization are developed in the section "Is Profit Maximization Meaningful?"

[27] Many citations, of course, can be marshaled to denounce any theory which cannot be so tested. "What is not measurable is not meaningful." A polite but firm reservation ought to be expressed. Some important ideas cannot be quantified and vice versa.

is a task of considerable dimensions, but the nature of the procedure can be briefly sketched. The previous discussion has made clear that payments for productive services of all kinds include profit elements. Hence data on wage, rent, and interest returns would be relevant. For illustrative purposes, we may utilize the studies of business net income data to test the theory.[28]

Stability in earnings would be inconsistent with the uncertainty theory. Great variability of earnings patterns would be consistent with the hypothesis and also would be consistent with some of the alternative profit theories. Epstein's data indicate some stability in the differences between levels of returns of firms in different industries.[29] But these are large firms in which, to a considerable extent, statistical averaging of results may take place. Bowman and Crum, using broader samples, observed great erratic tendencies.[30] In all these empirical studies the dispersion of earnings rates of firms is considerable. The observed diversity of experience and wide changes from year to year are predicted by the uncertainty theory of profit. Further investigations along these lines are indicated.

Another approach to empirical testing of the uncertainty theory utilizes internal accounting records of firms. To the extent that they are genuinely employed, budgets or *pro forma* statements represent expressions of the plans of firms.[31] Variable budgets express these plans not as single-valued certainty equivalents but as expected ranges of the variables. The uncertainty theory predicts that while budgets may provide rough guides to action, budgeted amounts will usually not be realized. The differences between the "plans" expressed in budgets and what actually happens provide a basis for some quantification of profit.

The Significance of the Uncertainty Theory of Profit for Behavior Strategies

The uncertainty concept of profit is significant, whether or not the magnitudes may be directly measured. Like other constructs of economic theory, the uncertainty profit concept is useful if meaningful statements (propositions) can be derived from it. The uncertainty profit idea meets this test better than possible alternatives, because it provides a model of economic behavior which suggests important types of activities that would not exist in the absence of uncertainty.

1. Because of uncertainty, which gives rise to profit, reasonable and prudent men hold different views of the future. The differences in expectations give rise to different forms of contractual relationships. It is differences of opinions (also differences in abilities and tastes) which make markets. This is the motivational significance of the uncertainty concept. Uncertainty leads some to take great chances, to innovate, to attempt to monopolize, etc. It leads some to avoid risky occupations and enterprises, to seek the quiet life.

2. Because of uncertainty, strategies and arrangements which provide some protection against the alternative contingencies are developed and utilized. Some of these devices are flexible machines and plants, diversification in many forms—multiproducts, multiplants, multisales outlets; reduced ratios of fixed to total costs; etc.

3. Since, because of uncertainty, it is not possible to reduce business decisions to virtual

[28] The usual empirical studies of "profit" are actually studies of accounting net income. The main component of this conglomerate of economic returns is an interest return on invested capital. In addition, unimputed wage or rent returns are likely to be included. The "profit" category in national income statistics is aggregated corporate net incomes. Thus empirical studies of "profit" have not centered on the real issues of profit theory.

[29] Epstein, *op. cit.*, pp. 79–86.

[30] Bowman, *op. cit.*, pp. 173–76; Crum, *op. cit.*, pp. 231–34.

[31] They may also represent strategic weapons in intra-firm struggles for allocation of resources. Such problems are highlighted by the discussion of budgeting under a different social setting in J. S. Berliner, "The Informal Organization of the Soviet Firm," *Quarterly Journal of Economics,* LXVI (August, 1952), 347–53.

routine, the operations of a firm require continuous exercise of judgment. Judgment is decision-making on the basis of incomplete information. It is not possible to associate the exercise of judgment with a limited number of key personnel in a firm. Akin to the difference between the abilities of a baseball player in a major league versus one in a minor league, the difference in the extent of judgment exercised by functionaries at different levels in any authority hierarchy is a matter of degree, not of kind.

If these descriptions of the usefulness of the uncertainty concept of profit appear abstract, a practical application may be cited.[32] The uncertainty concept of profit is a basis for a wartime (or period of heightened preparedness) excess profits tax. An excess profits or excess income tax should remove those elements of income in excess of incomes likely to have been earned if the unusual exogenous factors (war, threat of war) had not occurred. For a wartime excess profits tax, this implies the use of historical earnings standards rather than an invested capital standard.[33] While practical problems of implementation abound, a defensible conceptual basis for a wartime excess profits tax is provided.

Other aspects of the uncertainty concept will be developed through a consideration

[32] In this connection cf. Bernstein, *op. cit.,* pp. 407–22. I am sympathetic with Mr. Bernstein's emphasis on the practical aspects of profit theory. But his suggestion to have different profit theories for different circumstances violates any usable theory of knowledge. While behavior implied by a theory may find different forms of expression under differing circumstances, the theory need not be altered to fit different situations. Indeed, profit theory does not explain all kinds of facts and situations. Other theories may be applicable, *but not different profit theories.* The materials he discusses are important, but he needs other elements of economic theory to provide an understanding of some items he discusses. His paper reflects the tendency to attempt to label every explanation of dramatic business activity with the rubric "profit theory."

[33] Those who hold that a wartime excess profits tax should be levied on "high" profits as well as "war" profits will disagree on policy grounds. The applicability of the uncertainty profit concept holds, nevertheless.

of alternative theories of profit. One which has long commanded an important following is the innovation theory of Schumpeter.

INNOVATION, ENTREPRENEURSHIP, AND PROFIT

Schumpeter's System

To explain the innovation theory of profit, it is necessary to summarize (briefly) Schumpeter's entire framework. Innovation is the act of changing production functions. This includes producing new products, improving processes, improving production methods. Schumpeter treats changes in tastes as changed production functions. (Influences from the demand side are thus thrown over into the supply side.) Without innovations, an economy would settle down into a stationary state —the circular flow (unless exogenous forces intervened).

The central figure in Schumpeter's scheme is the entrepreneur. The entrepreneur is defined as one who innovates. (Once Schumpeter has defined innovation, the rest of his system follows.) Profit arises from innovation; it is achieved through entrepreneurial activity; the entrepreneur is its recipient.

Schumpeter does not stop here, however. Because others imitate the innovator, his profits are finally wiped out. Hence the only way an innovator can continuously make profit is to innovate continuously. The tremendous social significance of Schumpeter's innovator is thus seen. He is an instrument of progress. Profit is the reward which induces him to innovate repeatedly, and by this device society is led to continuous progress.

Other central ideas in Schumpeter's theory are summarized in the following succinct statement:

A word about the relation of profit to monopoly revenue. Since the entrepreneur has no competitors when the new products first appear, the determination of their price proceeds wholly, or within certain limits, according to the principles of monopoly price. Thus there is a monopoly element in profit in a capitalist economy. Let us now assume that the new combination consists in establishing a permanent monopoly, perhaps in forming a trust which need fear absolutely no competing outsiders. Then profit is obviously to be considered simply as permanent monopoly revenue and monopoly revenue simply as profit. And yet two quite different economic phenomena exist. The carrying out of the monopolistic organization is an entrepreneurial act and its "product" is expressed in profit. Once it is running smoothly the concern in this case goes on earning a surplus, which henceforth, however, must be imputed to those natural or social forces upon which the monopoly position rests—it has become a monopoly revenue. Profit from founding a business and permanent return are distinguished in practice; the former is the value of the monopoly, the latter is just the return from the monopoly condition.[34]

Here Schumpeter emphasizes the distinction between the act of innovating which results in profit and the continuing differential return which is capitalized or imputed to its sources. Any continuing differential in payments for services is not profit but a differential revenue return.

Comparison between the Profit Theories of Schumpeter and Knight

The theories of Schumpeter and Knight are similar in many respects. Uncertainty and innovation are related. Innovation may be defined more generally than in Schumpeter's presentation (but consistent with it) as changing production *or* utility functions. An ultimate source of uncertainty is therefore innovation. But uncertainty and innovation are not identities, because innovation sets in force a series of influences with concomitant adjustments that, in addition, interact with exogenous factors—wars, new laws, etc.

The innovator positively engages uncertainty. To forsake the tried and familiar in creating change is clearly a situation in

[34] *Op. cit.*, p. 152.

which the decision-maker has incomplete information. But decision-makers not attempting innovations also face uncertainty. Hence both Knight and Schumpeter devote considerable discussion to entrepreneurial activities. For Knight, the entrepreneur makes decisions dealing with uncertainty and then bears responsibility for those decisions. Schumpeter's entrepreneur innovates, an act involving uncertainty as well as a major source of uncertainty. Knight emphasizes that entrepreneurship is fundamentally judgment of men—innovation and other activities can be delegated. Schumpeter's later writing makes a similar emphasis: "Innovation itself is being reduced to routine. Technological progress is increasingly becoming the business of teams of trained specialists who turn out what is required and make it work in predictable ways."[35]

This subsequent agreement suggests that Schumpeter's earlier position on the function of profit requires revision. The economic incentive to creation is seen to be income, whose nature is similar to payments for other types of productive services. This has been clearly stated by Harrod: "In value theory it has proved expedient to relate profit specifically to uncertainty-bearing, ability to direct a business being easily assimilable in theory to the category of highly skilled labour."[36] Machlup expressed the same view equally effectively: "The high 'profit' made by the entrepreneur who performs these services himself is really nothing but an implicit wage or an implicit rent."[37]

Thus, whether the payment is for creative services, whether compensation is on a contractual or residual basis, the return remains functional in nature. It is an income category appropriately labeled wages,

[35] Joseph A. Schumpeter, *Capitalism, Socialism, and Democracy* (2d ed.; New York: Harper & Bros., 1947), p. 132.
[36] *Op. cit.*, p. 192.
[37] *Op. cit.*, p. 15.

rent, or interest; and it is likely to contain a nonfunctional component, profit.

ENTERPRISE AND PROFIT

The discussion of Schumpeter's contribution leads to a treatment of other aspects of the relationship between entrepreneurship and profit. In specifying the unique function of the entrepreneur, writers have described him variously as (*a*) one who organizes and co-ordinates the other factors of production (peak co-ordinator); (*b*) one who exercises the joint and inseparable functions of responsibility (ultimate risk-bearing) and control (ultimate decision-making); (*c*) one who innovates (changing production or utility functions); and (*d*) one who is charged with the responsibility of dealing with uncertainty.[38]

The Nature of Entrepreneurial Returns

Somehow it is felt that, since the acts of organizing, co-ordinating, directing, and changing the scope of enterprise are of special significance, some special terminology should be applied to the returns for these activities. But, regardless of the definition adopted, entrepreneurial activities are functional in nature. The returns to the entrepreneur in connection with his functional activities qua entrepreneur are not, therefore, profit. As the quotations above from Harrod and Machlup emphasize, the returns to entrepreneurs seem best looked upon as wage or rent returns.

This does not deny that executive leadership and creative activity in business are important or that adequate inducements for the performance of these functions

[38] If there is little agreement on the nature of the entrepreneurial function or functions, there is even less on identification of the entrepreneur, i.e., the person performing the functions in different circumstances. Fortunately, it is not necessary to consider these problems here.

should be provided through requisite incentives. If the value of such services could be forecast, compensation could be fixed accordingly. But since such forecasts cannot be made accurately, bonuses, profit-sharing, stock options, pensions, including arrangements to minimize taxes, are widely used in executive compensation arrangements. Executive incomes depend at least in part upon the results of operations; their incomes are partially residual in nature. This is another clear illustration of the proposition that wage returns may include a fluctuating component. The use of incentive payment schemes for piece-workers is still another. We may conclude, therefore, that functional returns to high ability in any form cannot be said to be profit but rather a type of rent or wage return.

The Firm as Entrepreneur

In this connection, Davis has proposed to "define the entrepreneur as the business enterprise itself and profit as the enterprise's net income." [39] While the firm is a useful unit of account and center for organizing economic activity, it is an institution whose function is best understood as a convenience of association for the purpose of achieving particular goals of individuals. As a consequence, the difficulties in adopting the suggested fiction are many.

It is logically fallacious, because the whole is made equal to one of its parts. What scope remains for the operation of the other types of productive services in the firm? The essential qualities of entrepreneurship are blurred. The nature of its origin and development are obscured. The conditions for the successful expression of the entrepreneurial functions cannot be discerned in such an orientation. The error of identifying the goals of the firm with the goals of all participating agents is ag-

[39] Davis, *op. cit.*, pp. 251–52; see also Stauss, *op. cit.*, pp. 112–27.

gravated.[40] While it may appear to be "remarkably convenient" for handling certain problems, it has not been shown that the adoption of this fiction is more useful than adherence to the realities of the situation. All the advantages for its adoption are also attained by regarding entrepreneurship as a function widely diffused among participants in the operation of a firm.

Profit as the Income of a Social Class

It has also been proposed that profit can be identified as the income of a particular social class. Professor Davis states: "For many authors the purpose of distribution theory is to explain the sharing out of the total income among social groups."[41] He observes that this is a basis for the fundamental objection to the orientation of the uncertainty theory of profit.

If ownership of types of productive services coincided even roughly with the composition of social groups, it might be possible to apply distribution theory to the explanation of social incomes, as did the classical economists. But such a coincidence now obtains to an even smaller degree than formerly (for example, the time of the classical economists). To assume it now is not only inaccurate but also leads to a distortion of the basic nature and purpose of distribution theory—the pricing of productive services in their allocation among alternative uses.

Davis suggests that at one end of the spectrum of classification the terms "entre-

preneur" and "businessman" may be treated as roughly equivalent.[42] But this is to define an ambiguous concept with an imprecise expression. What is a businessman? Are all executives businessmen? Do we include only top-level management? Do we include supervisory personnel? Are inactive bondholders businessmen? Are equally inactive common stockholders businessmen?

At the other end, Davis suggests that the firm be identified as the entrepreneur and profit be defined as the firm's net income. Aside from difficulties previously described, such a procedure fails to achieve Davis' objective of associating the receipt of profit with a particular social class. Thus whichever definition is followed, Davis' attempt to identify profit with the income of a social class fails.

With even greater emphasis, Marchal develops the doctrine that profit is the special type of income of a particular social class.[43] The methods by which entrepreneurs ("enterprise" and "entrepreneurship" are not defined) are said to seek to augment their gains are seen, upon reflection, to be those utilized by workers and capital owners alike. But the distinctive behavior of the entrepreneur, Marchal says, is to identify himself with the enterprise.[44] However, this is only asserted, not demonstrated. Even if true, identification of the entrepreneur with the enterprise is without economic significance, for the opportunity cost of the entrepreneur's services must be taken into account.

Furthermore, it should be observed that, although other types of factor owners are not identified with the enterprise, they enter the market and contract in fundamentally the same manner as enterprisers. Owners of other factor services may act on the market structure; they may attempt to

[40] This criticism has been expressed most effectively by Triffin: "In fact, however, the firm is a mere abstraction: profit maximization is the concern, not of the legal entities called firms, but of human beings. Pure theory starts on the assumption that each man tries to maximize his income" (Triffin, *op. cit.*, p. 186; see also M. W. Reder, "A Reconsideration of the Marginal Productivity Theory," *Journal of Political Economy*, LV [October, 1947], 450–58).

[41] Davis, *op. cit.*, p. 248.

[42] *Ibid.*, p. 250.

[43] *Op. cit.*, pp. 549–65.

[44] *Ibid.*, p. 550.

change it; and they may attempt to engage in all types of predatory practices attributed to entrepreneurs by Marchal. Even more important, since elements of predatory behavior exist everywhere in varying proportions, the behavior is of unique relevance not to profit theory but to income distribution generally.

From this analysis of some recent theories of how profit may be related to the incomes of specific social classes, it appears clear that such attempts confuse, rather than clarify, the nature of profit and its significance.

Profit as Property Returns

Another critic has suggested a related approach. There are two types of returns —property returns and nonproperty returns or returns for labor services. Payments for labor services are called "wages." Returns to property involve fixed commitments. These returns are called "profits." This was essentially the practice of the classical economists. Profits formerly included all elements of returns for the contributions of the owners, whether land, capital, or personal services. One development in economic thought has been the peeling-off of the various segments of returns, leaving a pure economic profit element.

Gross residual returns (total receipts less contractual payments for labor services) are akin to accounting net income or profit.[45] However, accounting net income is not an adequate representation of economic profit, because the residual-income receivers contribute productive services. It would not be logical to label as profit the entire amount of the returns of residual-income receivers, when contractual payments for similar functional services performed by hired factors are labeled variously wages or interest. Not only would this be illogical from a classification stand-

point, but it would also be unsound for practical reasons. It would not be possible for owners of a particular type of productive service to know whether the productive service could earn more on a contractual or on a residual basis, when the residual incomes of firms included payments for a combination of different types of productive services. Correct allocation and distribution decisions depend upon knowledge of the value imputed to services sold to the firm on a residual basis.

MONOPOLY AND PROFIT

Most opposing theories of profit existed prior to Knight's first exposition of the uncertainty theory. One of these was the view of profit as a monopoly return—a position which has repeatedly been expressed. Marchal's recent paper, "The Construction of a New Theory of Profit," is another presentation of it.[46]

Marchal's emphasis on improving a firm's situation by changing the economic structure is a useful one. His discussion implies, however, that most of the actual activity along this line has been in the direction of predatory activities by managements. This may be an unwarranted exaggeration for noncontinental economies. But, regardless of the degree of its empirical applicability, Marchal's contribution is not profit theory but rather a description and theory of predatory behavior.

The continued rejection of the uncertainty theory by those who view profit as a monopoly return is both understandable and surprising. It is understandable because the activity of increasing one's income by achieving a monopoly position and by engaging in restrictive activities and monopoly pricing is "obviously widespread." Here is another apparent ground for dissatisfaction with the uncertainty theory of profit—it does not seem to explain enough of the dramatic events of

---

[45] Accountants themselves now avoid calling business net income "profit."

[46] Pp. 489–504.

economic life which press upon our attention.

But the persistence of predatory theories of profit is surprising, since Schumpeter very early pointed out the basis for their invalidity.[47] The attainment of a monopoly situation is an act either of creation (innovation) or of chance (a windfall). But after the monopoly has been established, the prospective monopoly revenues or rents are imputed to the source of the monopoly advantage and/or capitalized. A clear illustration of this can be observed in the fact that when the common stocks of firms possessing such advantages are publicly traded, they sell on a low-yield basis (because of relative stability of prospective earnings and dividends). Although monopoly pricing and monopoly revenues may remain, the yields to current purchasers of the common stock are competitive.

The implications of the uncertainty theory of profit may be further discerned by consideration of three remaining topics: (1) How can the profit element be identified in conventional diagrams of partial equilibrium analysis? (This question may also be expressed in another fashion: What are the nature and role of the imputation process and the implications for choices between alternative kinds of contractual relationships?) (2) Are profits really maximized? (3) What is the significance of profit theory for macroeconomics?

PROFIT AS AN UNIMPUTABLE QUASI-RENT

The first question is most conveniently discussed in connection with the conventional diagram of a situation in which short-run "profits" are obtained (Fig. 22-1). The area $CDEF$, is said to portray economic "profit." It is said to be the unimputed (and unimputable) surplus of the firm. The tale is told best in the following

[47] *Op. cit.,* p. 152; see also Harrod, *op. cit.,* pp. 198–206.

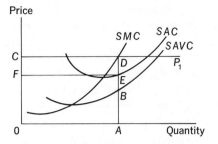

FIGURE 22-1 SHORT-PERIOD EQUILIBRIUM

manner.[48] The future cannot be known with certainty. All resources are not freely and immediately transferable from one use to another. As a consequence of the twin influences of uncertainty and resource immobility, situations of the type portrayed in Figure 22-1 develop.[49] Factor prices are set by the entire framework of competitive conditions. A wholly unanticipated favorable change in demand conditions facing the industry takes place. This new situation facing the individual firm may be considered to be that portrayed by Figure 22-1. The firm has a surplus, DE, over costs, AE, which is called "profit." This "profit" calls forth a resource flow, which tends to eliminate such a surplus in the long run. This is quite a reasonable, appealing, and convincing story; but it leaves a good many elements unsettled.

Does the diagram represent a planned or an *ex post* situation? Drawn in the Marshallian tradition, it is timeless with reference to clock time or represents an unstated arbitrary choice of one of many relevant clock-time periods. The situation is *ex ante*, in that the decision-makers have freedom of action with respect to the quantities of the variable factors which will be employed. With respect to the fixed factors, an unalterable monetary commitment has been made, so it is an *ex post* situation.

[48] Cf. Davis, *op. cit.,* pp. 247–48.
[49] Both uncertainty and immobility are necessary conditions. Without uncertainty, the immobile resources would have been correctly located. Without immobilities, adjustments to change would involve no delays.

Thus the conventional short-run situation is a mixture of *ex ante* and *ex post* elements.

The short period is conventionally defined as one in which it is useful to regard a particular set of costs as nonvariable. The division between the short run and the long run is based on the degree of fixity of costs. Although the Marshallian tradition does not distinguish between short and long run on the basis of demand considerations, it is not likely that demand conditions will remain fixed during the planning period implied by the selection of a particular set of costs for defining a short period.

Thus a contradiction is implied in the diagram. Given that the situation is the result of a wholly anticipated shift in economic conditions, is it realistic or meaningful to make the assumption that no further changes will take place for the duration of the planning period? If the industry is subject to windfall changes of this type, it is not meaningful to draw this type of diagram without showing the sales curve as a range of values.[50]

This leads to the question of imputation of a portion of quasi-rents. Quasi-rents of the firm are generally defined as "simply the excess of receipts over total variable costs."[51] Davis appears to have another definition.[52] He refers to *BD* (Stigler's quasi-rent per unit of output)[53] as the net income of the firm per unit of output. He divides this into two segments. The segment *ED* is said to be unimputed and termed "profit." The segment *BE* is im-

puted to the assets which the firm owns, and this is termed "quasi-rent."

But the segment *ED*, which is often referred to as "profit," is a portion of the quasi-rents per unit of output. To the extent that it is meaningful to use the diagram, what is maximized is quasi-rent, not profit. This is not simply a matter of taste in choice of terminology. The components of total product are wage, rent, or interest returns. It is misleading to label a portion of the total revenues as profit, as distinct from wages, rent, and interest. A profit element may be, and probably is, contained in all three of these other returns. The differential is a temporary supernormal (or subnormal) return for some of the factors. Its allocation is determined by the nature of the contractual arrangements that have been agreed upon.

With regard to imputation, the role of uncertainty must be recognized and its institutional consequences considered. Given that situations of the type portrayed by Figure 22-1 develop because of uncertainty, it would be unrealistic not to acknowledge that owners of productive services are likely to take uncertainty into account in their decisions. Since the future cannot be wholly known, some resource payments cannot be fixed by contract before the results of operations are known. Some income receivers must therefore take a residual-income position.

Whether resource owners take a residual position or a contractual position depends in part upon differences in training, experience, opportunities, asset position, attitudes toward risk, noneconomic considerations, and, in part, differences in anticipations. The practical fact is, however, that the residual-income receivers are the recipients of the amounts remaining after the fixed-income receivers have been fully paid. Given the institutional consequences of uncertainty, the distribution of the element *EB* (as well as *ED*) is not a matter of imputation but a matter of contractual re-

---

[50] Another interpretation is that insiders (firms already in the industry) have knowledge of these favorable conditions but that outsiders do not have this knowledge. However, this would be a permanent differential—a rent rather than a quasi-rent. If it is urged that the favorable conditions are only temporary, then it is not likely that their exact duration can be known, nor can the sales curve be known for the duration of "the" planning period.

[51] George J. Stigler, *The Theory of Price* (rev. ed.; New York: Macmillan Co., 1952), p. 193.

[52] Davis, *op. cit.,* p. 247.

[53] Refer to Fig. 22-1 again.

lationships. Theoretically, any type of arrangement could be envisaged. Wages of workers, salaries of executives, payments to "bond" holders, etc., could all be put on a contingent as well as a fixed basis. Given the presence of uncertainty, however, all returns could not be fixed (but all could be contingent).

The characteristics of contracts differ. The two most important elements of the difference are: (1) whether the return is fixed or residual [54] and (2) if fixed, the terminability of employment or the opportunity of either party for recontracting.

But the noncontractual payments do not represent a different kind of economic return. A profit element, as here defined, may be contained in the returns of either form. The fixed return contains positive or negative profit if the return would have been lower or higher if all returns had been based on *ex post* data (strictly speaking, *mutatis mutandis* considerations make this statement somewhat inaccurate, but it conveys the basic idea). The noncontractual returns contain a positive or negative element of profit for exactly the same reason.

IS PROFIT MAXIMIZATION MEANINGFUL?

From time to time it has been suggested that a wider concept, e.g., preference-function maximization, be substituted for the traditional idea, profit maximization.[55] Al-

ternative motives are cited: leisure or the quiet life, power and prestige, reluctance to experiment (aversion to uncertainty-bearing), and ideas of the "just price." [56] This approach emphasizes the role of noneconomic influences, whose relative importance has not yet been established by factual evidence.

On other grounds, Alchian and Enke discard profit maximization both as a *goal* and as a *criterion* for choosing between different actions.[57] Since unfavorable surprises may threaten the very survival of the firm, the use of expectation "begs the question of uncertainty by disregarding the variance." [58] The maximization of expected profits is therefore not a rational goal under uncertainty.

They set forth in detail the difficulties of profit maximization as a criterion for choosing between alternative actions. Behavior under incomplete knowledge involves the following: (1) the variability of the environment, (2) the multiplicity of factors that call for attention in choice, (3) the uncertainty attaching to all these factors and outcomes, (4) the nonavailability of a trial-and-error process converging to an optimum position, and (5) therefore the absence of an identifiable criterion for decision-making.[59]

The Alchian-Enke framework establishes that, under a complete uncertainty model, the economist can diagnose, predict, or explain resource allocation in the economy as a whole.[60] This is a somewhat surprising conclusion, and its demonstration is a valuable contribution. However, when the implications of such a model for individual decision-making are considered, we confront some difficulties. Under complete uncer-

[54] However, the form of the contractual relationship is not a sufficient basis for distinguishing whether returns will fluctuate or be relatively stable. Uncertainty is associated with both contractual and noncontractual returns. Numerous examples could be cited to demonstrate this. Bondholders receive contractual returns, but very low-grade bonds fluctuate more, pricewise and incomewise, than high-grade common stocks do. Workers receive contractual returns, but what is the relevant time horizon? They receive contractual returns so long as they are employed, but employment may be interrupted.
[55] Cf. Andreas G. Papandreou, "Some Basic Problems in the Theory of the Firm," *Survey of Contemporary Economics,* Vol. II (Homewood, Ill.: Richard D. Irwin, Inc., 1952), p. 207.

[56] *Ibid.,* pp. 207–8.
[57] Alchian, *op. cit.,* pp. 211–12; Enke, *op. cit.,* pp. 569–70.
[58] Alchian, *op. cit.,* p. 213.
[59] *Ibid.,* p. 218.
[60] I am particularly indebted to Karl Brunner for suggestions leading to the materials in this and the following paragraph.

tainty, the optimum behavior strategy for the individual is a procedure which produces random actions. If some knowledge is admitted, but incomplete information remains, what is appropriate decision-making procedure? Alchian suggests imitation, adaptation, and innovation. The present writer would emphasize, in addition, the necessity for businessmen to exercise judgment.

But if profit maximization is denied, what is offered in its place? Some statements of positive position are offered. A maximizing solution is possible only under complete information. When information is complete, the probability distribution is known, so that it is rational to maximize the expected (long-run) value. Under complete information the individual maximizes his long-run income; the firm maximizes its long-run net receipts (the long-run income of the residual-income receivers).[61]

Under incomplete information, it is necessary to adopt some form of minimax[62] strategy. Even under the stochastic case in which the decision-maker knows data permitting him to estimate the probability distributions of alternative outcomes, he will make statistical errors (Type I or Type II).[63] Thus statistical decisions are all minimax procedures. Where only two hypotheses are admitted (h_0 and h_1), we have a special case where h_1 represents the total-ity of unfavorable outcomes.[64] If knowledge is incomplete, the individual minimaxes his long-run income position; the firm minimaxes its long-run net receipts position.

While a situation of uncertainty implies that income maximization is not an appropriate goal or criterion, it does not imply that rational behavior will not be effective. Imitation, adaptation, and innovation are examples of rational strategies in the face of uncertainty. Subjective probability opinions may be formulated; but flexibility, diversification, and safety margins will be employed as well. These are all elements of a minimax strategy. They likewise involve the exercise of judgment and are influenced by the utility preference systems of the decision-makers. Sometimes greater uncertainty will be borne for the possibility of attaining higher income or net receipts, that is, the maximum potential loss possibility some are willing to chance may be greater or less than that of others.[65]

PROFIT AND MACROECONOMICS

Davis' analysis of writings in this area is comprehensive, his criticisms searching, and his major conclusions well established.[66] He shows to be of doubtful validity Kalecki's generalization that gross margins reflect the degree of monopoly, which thus is said to determine the distribution of national income.[67] He points out that

[61] This formulation emphasizes that maximization of net receipts is the maximization of a conglomerate of economic returns, properly included under the broad title of "quasi-rents." Maximization of net receipts is indeed an important motivation. But I object to the undue emphasis on maximization of profits, as though decision-makers of firms were motivated by a particular kind of drive which was unique to them. Income maximization and rational behavior describe equally well the behavior of owners of all types of productive services.

[62] The term is used in the general sense of minimizing maximum regret or maximizing the minimum gain.

[63] A. M. Mood, Introduction to the Theory of Statistics (New York: McGraw-Hill Book Co., 1950), pp. 245–52.

[64] Ibid., p. 246.

[65] To a great degree business decisions are portfolio selection problems. Business behavior represents a combination of activities. If the correlation between outcomes of activities is not unity (positive), diversification exists, and uncertainty is reduced. Much of the analysis of portfolio selection will therefore apply (cf. Harry Markowitz, "Portfolio Selection," Journal of Finance, VII [March, 1952], 77–91).

[66] Davis, op. cit., pp. 252–62.

[67] M. Kalecki, Essays in the Theory of Economic Fluctuations (New York: Farrar & Rinehart, 1939), chap. i, "The Distribution of the National Income."

Boulding's macroeconomic profit theory rests upon an assumption that wage-earners have different consumption, investment, and liquidity preference functions than others.[68] Limited empirical studies raise considerable doubt that such fundamental differences exist. Davis suggests that more significant for macroeconomic theory than a division between total wages and property incomes (miscalled "profits" by many) is the distribution of income between people with large and small incomes, large and small holdings of total assets, and high and low ratios of liquid to other assets. His suggested emphasis on a division between households and firms may have some usefulness but, as he acknowledges, has little relation to the traditional profit theory he espouses.

The uncertainty theory of profit, however, can be shown to have significance for macroeconomics. Since some portions of income are unanticipated or relatively more uncertain than others, spending plans for such income are likely to be more flexible. They probably are influenced by the degrees of fluctuation of these incomes in previous periods as a guide to likely variations in the future. Thus the existence of profit implies an income-spending lag. The larger the absolute aggregate values of profits (and losses), the greater the uncertainty, and the greater are likely to be the portions of incomes which are subject to spending lags.[69]

The relationship of uncertainty (the source of profit) to production lags is mixed. On the one hand, uncertainty causes the disappointment of expectations, mak-

ing the consequence of production lags more serious than otherwise. On the other hand, uncertainty causes decision-makers to introduce a wider amount of flexibility into operations; adjustments are made more quickly to altered market circumstances. Hence production lags are likely to be shorter.

Another aspect of macroeconomics in which the uncertainty theory of profit finds expression is in the divergence of the *ex post* from the *ex ante*. Whenever any of the planned magnitudes differ from the realized magnitudes, the influence of uncertainty is reflected, and profits emerge.

CONCLUSIONS

The uncertainty theory of profit is not likely to secure general acceptance. The writings on profit theory since *Risk, Uncertainty, and Profit* (1921) afford abundant evidence of this. The entrepreneurial theories of profit secure adherents because they deal with dramatic and important economic behavior. The predatory theories offer opportunity for the expression of noble sentiments and moral indignation. Finally, it seems that there ought to be some special recompense for bearing risk and uncertainty.

While the uncertainty theory of profit presents challenges for investigating the many ramifications of the effects of uncertainty, it does not promise that these can be adequately catalogued. Nevertheless, it provides a framework for a better understanding of many types of economic practices and institutions, and it avoids the inconsistencies and dilemmas to which rival theories lead. It can be integrated into, and leads to, correct use of economic doctrine generally.

[68] K. E. Boulding, *A Reconstruction of Economics* (New York: John Wiley & Sons, 1950), chap. xiv, "A Macroeconomic Theory of Distribution."
[69] It should not be implied that this is the only cause of the "Robertson" lag.

23 Alternative Theories of Distribution

NICHOLAS KALDOR

The subject matter of distribution theory in its most comprehensive interpretation explains not only how total income is shared but also how the proportions of these shares behave over time, and what the relationship of this behavior is to the behavior of the macroeconomy. The three basic models which have been developed for dealing with these questions are the classical, the neoclassical, and the Kaldorian. The latter is a macrotheory of relative shares developed from Keynes' theory of employment. The exposition of the classical and neoclassical models given by Kaldor in "Alternative Theories of Distribution," as a prelude to the presentation of his own model, is designed to facilitate exploration of the relative share problem.

A simple way of looking at the relative share problem is in terms of the behavior of the ratios which follow:

$$\frac{W}{P} = \frac{L}{K} \cdot \frac{w}{r}$$

where W is the wages bill, P is total profit, L and K are the quantities of labor and capital respectively, and w and r represent the average wage and the average return to capital. Clearly, the behavior of $\frac{W}{P}$ depends on the behavior of the four variables in the equation

and, hence, on all of the many factors which influence them. This suggests that the relative share problem is, in principle at least, a general equilibrium problem, though the classical, neoclassical, and Kaldorian models do not proceed in this way. They may, nevertheless, be useful, that is, capable of predictions that square with the facts which a relative share theory must explain. These facts appear to be: (1) a secular constancy of the wage and profit shares, (2) a secular constancy of the capital/output ratio, (3) a secular increase in the capital/labor ratio, and (4) a pattern of cyclical variation in which the wage share increases during a downswing and decreases during an upswing.

Kaldor's model focuses on key aggregate magnitudes to "predict" the pattern of relative

Reprinted from Nicholas Kaldor, "Alternative Theories of Distribution," *Review of Economic Studies*, Vol. 7, 1955–1957, pp. 83–100. Professor Kaldor is at King's College, Cambridge, England.

shares and the capital/output ratio over time. It is based on the assumptions that the ratio of investment to output is a variable which is independent of the profit and wage share, that there is full employment, that the propensity to save out of profits is greater than the propensity to save out of wages, and that both propensities are given. The impact of a change in the investment/output ratio on income shares is found to be dependent on the "coefficient of sensitivity of income distribution." The smaller the difference in the marginal propensities to save out of wages and profits, the larger the value of the coefficient and, therefore, the larger the change in income distribution which will be generated by a small change in the investment/output relationship.

The critical assumption of this model is whether the investment/output ratio is, in fact, independent of the shares going into profit and real wages. Kaldor recognizes that there are reasons why the investment/output ratio, which reflects the rate of growth of the full employment ceiling, might be sensitive to changes in the rate of profit instead of being independent of it. However, he reasons that the actual profit rate tends toward a norm as a result of induced changes in the rate of capital accumulation. Thus, the model "predicts" a secular constancy in the capital/output ratio and in the wage and profit share. This coincides with what appears to be the observable facts which a viable theory of distribution must explain, whereas neither the classical nor neoclassical theories yield conclusions that have proven compatible with experience.

According to the Preface of Ricardo's *Principles*, the discovery of the laws which regulate distributive shares is the "principal problem in Political Economy." The purpose of this paper is to present a bird's eye view of the various theoretical attempts, since Ricardo, at solving this "principal problem." Though all attempts at classification in such a vast field are necessarily to some extent arbitrary, and subjective to the writer, in terms of broad classification, one should, I think, distinguish between four main strands of thought, some of which contain important sub-groups. The first of these is the Ricardian, or Classical Theory, the second the Marxian, the third the Neo-Classical or Marginalist Theory and the fourth the Keynesian. The inclusion of a separate "Keynesian" theory in this context may cause surprise. An attempt will be made to show however that the specifically Keynesian apparatus of thought could be applied to the problem of distribution, rather than to the problem of the general level of production; that there is evidence that in its early stages, Keynes' own thinking tended to develop in this direction—only to be diverted from it with the discovery (made some time between the publication of the *Treatise on Money* and the *General The-*

ory) that inflationary and deflationary tendencies could best be analysed in terms of the resulting changes in output and employment, rather than in their effects on prices.

The compression of a whole army of distinguished writers, and schools of thought, between Ricardo and Keynes (Marx aside) under the term of Neo-Classical or Marginalist Theory is harder to justify. For apart from the marginalists proper, the group would have to include such "non-marginalists" or quasi-marginalists (from the point of view of distribution theory) as the Walrasians and the neo-Walrasians,[1] as well as the imperfect competitionists, who though marginalist, do not necessarily hold with the principle of Marginal Prod-

[1] By the term "neo-Walrasians" I mean the American "linear programming" and "Activity analysis" schools, as well as the general equilibrium model of von Neumann (*Review of Economic Studies*, 1945–46, Vol. XIII (1)) whose technique shows certain affinities with Walras even though their basic assumptions (in particular that of the "circularity" of the production process) are quite different. From the point of view of distribution theory however, the approach only yields a solution (in the shape of an equilibrium interest rate) on the assumption of constant real wages (due to an infinitely elastic supply curve of labour); it shows therefore more affinity with the classical models than with the neo-classical theories.

uctivity. But as I shall hope to show, there are important aspects which all these theories have in common,[2] and which justifies bringing them under one broad umbrella.

Ricardo prefaced his statement by a reference to the historical fact that "in different stages of society the proportions of the whole produce of the earth which will be allotted to each of these (three) classes under the names of rent, profit and wages will be essentially *different*."[3] Today, a writer on the problem of distribution, would almost be inclined to say the opposite—that "in different stages of (capitalist) society the proportions of the national income allotted to wages, profits, etc., are *essentially similar*." The famous "historical constancy" of the share of wages in the national income—and the similarity of these shares in different capitalist economies, such as the U.S. and the U.K.—was of course an unsuspected feature of capitalism in Ricardo's day. But to the extent that recent empirical research tends to contradict Ricardo's assumption about the variability of relative shares, it makes the question of what determines these shares, more, rather than less, intriguing. In fact no hypothesis as regards the forces determining distributive shares could be intellectually satisfying unless it succeeds in accounting for the relative stability of these shares in the advanced capitalist economies over the last 100 years or so, despite the phenomenal changes in the techniques of production, in the accumulation of capital relative to labour and in real income per head.

Ricardo's concern in the problem of distribution was not due, or not only due, to the interest in the question of distributive shares *per se*, but to the belief that the theory of distribution holds the key to an understanding of the whole mechanism of the economic system—of the forces governing the rate of progress, of the ultimate incidence of taxation, of the effects of protection, and so on. It was through "the laws which regulate distributive shares" that he was hoping to build what in present-day parlance we would call "a simple macro-economic model."[4] In this respect, if no other, the Ricardian and the "Keynesian" theories are analogous.[5] With the neo-Classical or Marginalist theories, on the other hand, the problem of distribution is merely one aspect of the general pricing process; it has no particular theoretical significance apart from the importance of the question *per se*. Nor do these theories yield a "macro-economic model" of the kind that exhibits the reaction-mechanism of the system through the choice of a strictly limited number of dependent and independent variables.

THE RICARDIAN THEORY

Ricardo's theory was based on two separate principles which we may term the "marginal principle" and the "surplus principle" respectively. The "marginal principle" serves to explain the share of rent, and the "surplus principle" the division of the residue between wages and profits. To explain the Ricardian model, we must first divide the economy into two broad branches, agriculture and industry

[4] "Political Economy" he told Malthus "you think is an enquiry into the nature and causes of wealth—I think it should rather be called an enquiry into the laws which determine the division of the produce of industry amongst the classes who concur in its formation. No law can be laid down respecting quantity, but a tolerably correct one can be laid down respecting proportions. Every day I am more satisfied that the former enquiry is vain and delusive, and the latter only the true objects of the science." (Letter dated 9 Oct., 1820, Works (Sraffa edition) vol. VIII, pp. 278–9.)

[5] And so of course is the Marxian: but then the Marxian theory is really only a simplified version of Ricardo, clothed in a different garb.

[2] With the possible exception of the "neo-Walrasian" group referred to above.

[3] Preface (my italics).

and then show how, on Ricardo's assumptions, the forces operating in agriculture serve to determine distribution in industry.

The agricultural side of the picture can be exhibited in terms of a simple diagram (Fig. 23-1), where Oy measures quantities of

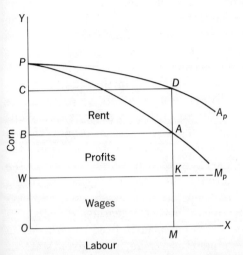

FIGURE 23-1

"corn" (standing for all agricultural produce) and Ox the amount of labour employed in agriculture. At a given state of knowledge and in a given natural environment the curve $p—Ap$ represents the product per unit of labour and the curve $p—Mp$ the marginal product of labour. The existence of these two *separate* curves, is a consequence of a declining tendency in the average product curve—i.e., of the assumption of diminishing returns. Corn-output is thus uniquely determined when the quantity of labour is given:[6] for any given working force, OM, total output is represented by the rectangle $OCDM$. Rent is the difference between the product of labour

on "marginal" land and the product on average land, or (allowing for the intensive, as well as the extensive, margin) the difference between average and marginal labour productivity which depends on the elasticity of the $p—Ap$ curve, i.e., the extent to which diminishing returns operate.

The marginal product of labour (or, in classical parlance, the "produce-minus-rent") is not however equal to the wage, but to the sum of wages and profits. The rate of wages is determined quite independently of marginal productivity by the supply price of labour which Ricardo assumed to be constant in terms of corn. In modern parlance, the Ricardian hypothesis implies an infinitely elastic supply curve of labour at the given supply price, OW.[7] The demand for labour is not determined however by the $p—Mp$ curve, but by the accumulation of capital which determines how many labourers can find employment at the wage rate OW. Hence the equilibrium position is not indicated by the point of intersection between the $p—Mp$ curve and the supply curve of labour, but by the aggregate demand for labour in

---

[6] This abstracts from variations in output per head due to the use of more or less fixed capital relative to labour—otherwise the curves could not be uniquely drawn, relative to a given state of technical knowledge. As between fixed capital and labour therefore the model assumes "fixed coefficients"; as between labour and land, variable coefficients.

[7] The basis of this assumption is the Malthusian theory of population, according to which numbers will increase (indefinitely) when wages are above, and decrease (indefinitely) when they are below, the "subsistence level." In Ricardo's hands this doctrine had lost its sharp focus on a biologically determined quantum of subsistence to which the supply price of labour must be tied; he emphasized that habits of restraint engendered in a civilized environment can permanently secure for labour higher standards of living than the bare minimum for survival. Yet he retained the important operative principle that in any given social and cultural environment there is a *"natural rate of wages"* at which alone population could remain stationary and from which wages can only deviate temporarily. The hypothesis of an infinitely elastic supply curve of labour thus did not necessarily imply that this supply price must be equal to the bare minimum of subsistence. Yet this assumption was inconsistent with another (implied) feature of his model discussed below, that wages are not only *fixed* in terms of "corn" but are entirely (or almost entirely) *spent* on corn.

terms of corn—the "wages fund." [8] As capital accumulates, the labour force will grow, so that any addition to the total wage fund, through capital accumulation—the *agricultural* wages fund is indicated by the area *OWKM*—will tend to be a horizontal addition (pushing the vertical line *KM* to the right) and not a vertical one (pushing the horizontal line *WK* upwards).[9]

For any given *M*, profits are thus a residue, arising from the difference between the marginal product of labour and the rate of wages. The resulting ratio, $\dfrac{\text{Profits}}{\text{Wages}}$, determines the rate of profit per cent on the capital employed; it is moreover *equal* to that ratio, on the assumption that the

[8] Total wages depend on—and are "paid out of" —capital simply because production takes time, and the labourers (unlike the landlords) not being in the position to afford to wait, have their wages "advanced" to them by the capitalists. This is true of fixed as well as circulating capital, but since with the former, the turnover period is relatively long, only a small part of annual wages is paid out of fixed capital; the amount of circulating capital was therefore treated as the proper "wages fund." Despite his analysis of the effect of changes in wages on the amount of fixed capital used relative to labour, i.e., on the proportions of fixed and circulating capital employed in production (Professor Hayk's celebrated "Ricardo effect") for the purpose of his distribution theory this ratio should be taken as given, irrespective of the rate of profit.

[9] The feature which the modern mind may find most difficult to swallow is not that capital accumulation should lead to a rise in population but that the reaction should be taken as something so swift as to ignore the intervening stage, where the increase in the wages fund should raise the rate of wages rather than the numbers employed. The adjustment of population to changes in the demand for labour would normally be treated as a slow long-run effect whereas changes in the demand for labour (caused by capital accumulation) may be swift or sudden. Ricardo however conceived the economy as one which proceeds at a more or less steady rate of growth in time, with the accumulation of capital going on at a (more or less constant) rate; while he conceded that *changes* in the rate of capital accumulation will temporarily raise or lower wages, he assumed that the rate of population growth itself is adapted to a certain rate of capital accumulation which had been going on for some time.

capital is turned over once a year, so that the capital employed is equal to the annual wages-bill. (This latter proposition however is merely a simplification, and not an essential part of the story.)

In a state of equilibrium, the money rate of profit *per cent* earned on capital must be the same in industry and in agriculture, otherwise capital would move from one form of employment to the other. But it is the peculiarity of agriculture that the money rate of profit in that industry cannot diverge from the rate of profit measured in terms of that industry's own product, i.e., the corn-rate of profit. This is because in agriculture both the input (the wage outlay) and the output consist of the same commodity, "corn." In manufacturing industry on the other hand, input and output consist of heterogeneous commodities —the cost per man is fixed in corn, while the product per man, in a given state of technical knowledge, is fixed in terms of manufactured goods. Hence the only way equality in the rate of profit in money terms can be attained as between the two branches is through the prices of industrial goods becoming dearer or cheaper in terms of agricultural products. The money rate of profit in manufacturing industry therefore depends on the corn-rate of profit in agriculture,[10] the latter on the other hand, is entirely a matter of the margin of cultivation, which in turn is a reflection (in a closed economy and in a given state of technical knowledge) of the extent of capital accumulation. Thus "diminishing fertility of the soil," as James Mill put it, "is the great and ultimately only necessary cause of a fall in profit."

To make the whole structure logically consistent it is necessary to suppose, not

[10] The analytical basis for this conclusion, given above, was never, as Sraffa remarks, stated by Ricardo in any of his extant letters and papers though there is evidence from Malthus's remarks that he must have formulated it either in a lost paper on the Profits of Capital or in conversation (cf. *Works*, Vol. I., Introduction, p. xxxi.).

only that wages are fixed in terms of "corn" but that they are entirely spent on "corn," for otherwise any change in the relation between industrial and agricultural prices will alter real wages (in terms of commodities in general) so that the size of the "surplus," and the rate of profit on capital generally, is no longer derivable from the "corn rate of profit"—the relationship between the product of labour and the cost of labour working on marginal land. Assuming that ("corn") agricultural products are wage-goods and manufactured products are non-wage goods (i.e., ignoring that *some* agricultural products are consumed by capitalists, and *some* non-agricultural products by wage-earners), the whole corn-output (the area $OCDM$ in the diagram) can be taken as the annual wages fund, of which $OWKM$ is employed in agriculture and $WCDK$ in the rest of the economy. Any increase in $OWKM$ (caused, e.g., by protection to agriculture) must necessarily lower the rate of profit (which is the source of all accumulation) and thus slow down the rate of growth.[11] Similarly all taxes, other than those levied on land, must ultimately fall on, and be paid out of, profits, and thus slow down the rate of accumulation. Taxation and agricultural protection thus tend to accelerate the tendency (which is in any case inevitable—unless *continued* technical progress manages to shift the $p—Ap$ and $p—Mp$ curves to the right sufficiently to suspend altogether the operation of the Law of Diminishing Returns) to that ultimate state of gloom, the Stationary State, where accumulation ceases simply because "profits are so low as not to afford (the capitalists more than) an adequate compensation for their trouble and the risk which they must necessarily encounter in employing their capital productively." [12]

THE MARXIAN THEORY

The Marxian theory is essentially an adaptation of Ricardo's "surplus theory." The main analytical differences are:—(1) that Marx paid no attention to (and did not believe in) the Law of Diminishing Returns, and hence made no analytical distinction between rent and profits; (2) that Marx regarded the supply price of labour (the "cost of reproduction" of labour) as being fixed, not in terms of "corn," but of commodities in general. Hence he regarded the share of profits (including rent) in output as determined simply by the surplus of the product per unit of labour over the supply price (or cost) of labour—or the surplus of production to the consumption necessary for production.[13]

There are important differences also as between Marx and Ricardo in two other respects. The first of these concerns the reasons for wages being tied to the subsistence level. In Marx's theory this is ensured through the fact that at any one time the supply of labour—the number of workers seeking wage-employment—tends to exceed the demand for labour. The existence of an unemployed fringe—the "reserve army" of labour—prevents wages from rising above the minimum that must be paid to enable the labourers to perform the work. Marx assumed that as capitalist enterprise progresses at the expenses of pre-capitalistic enterprise more labourers are released through the disappearance of the non-capitalist or handi-craft units than are

---

[11] The evil of agricultural protection is thus not only that real income is reduced through the transfer of labour to less productive employments, but that owing to the reduction in the rate of profit, industrial prices fall in terms of agricultural prices; income is thus transferred from the classes which use their wealth productively to classes which use it unproductively.

[12] Ricardo, *Principles,* p. 122 (Sraffa Edition).
[13] Ricardo himself abandoned in the *Principles* the idea that wages *consist* of corn (to the exclusion of manufactures) but whether he also abandoned the idea that the agricultural surplus is critical to the whole distribution process through the fixity of wages in terms of *corn only* is not clear. (Cf. Sraffa, *op. cit.,* pp. xxxii–xxxiii.)

absorbed in the capitalist sector, owing to the difference in productivity per head between the two sectors. As long as the growth of capitalist enterprise is at the cost of a shrinkage of pre-capitalist enterprise the increase in the supply of wage labour will thus tend to run ahead of the increase in the demand for wage labour.

Sooner or later, however, the demand for labour resulting from accumulation by capitalist enterprise will run ahead of the increase in supply; at that stage labour becomes scarce, wages rise, profits are wiped out and capitalism is faced with a "crisis." (The crisis in itself slows down the rate of accumulation and reduces the demand for labour at any given state of accumulation by increasing the "organic composition of capital," so that the "reserve army" will sooner or later be recreated.)

The second important difference relates to the motives behind capital accumulation. For Ricardo this was simply to be explained by the lure of a high rate of profit. Capitalists accumulate voluntarily so long as the rate of profit exceeds the minimum "necessary compensation" for the risks and trouble encountered in the productive employment of capital. For Marx however, accumulation by capitalist enterprise is not a matter of choice but a necessity, due to competition among the capitalists themselves. This in turn was explained by the existence of economies of large scale production (together with the implicit assumption that the amount of capital employed by any particular capitalist is governed by his own accumulation). Given the fact that the larger the scale of operations the more efficient the business, each capitalist is forced to increase the size of his business through the re-investment of his profits if he is not to fall behind in the competitive struggle.

It is only at a later stage, when the increasing concentration of production in the hands of the more successful enterprises re-moved the competitive necessity for accumulation—the stage of "monopoly capitalism"—that in the Marxian scheme there is room for economic crises, not on account of an excessive increase in the demand for labour following on accumulation but on account of an insufficiency of effective demand—the failure of markets resulting from the inability of the capitalists either to spend or to invest the full amount of profits (which Marx called the problem of "realising surplus value").

Marx has also taken over from Ricardo, and the classical economists generally, the idea of a falling rate of profit with the progressive accumulation of capital. But whereas with the classicists this was firmly grounded on the Law of Diminishing Returns, Marx, having discarded that law, had no firm base for it. His own explanation is based on the assumed increase in the ratio of fixed to circulating capital (in Marxian terminology, "constant" to "variable" capital) with the progress of capitalism; but as several authors have pointed out,[14] the law of the falling rate of profit cannot really be derived from the law of the "increasing organic composition" of capital. Since Marx assumes that the supply price of labour remains unchanged in terms of commodities when the organic composition of capital, and hence output per head, rises, there is no more reason to assume that an increase in "organic composition" will yield a lower rate of profit than a higher rate. For even if output per man were assumed to increase more slowly than ("constant" plus "variable") capital per man, the "surplus value" per man (the excess of output per man over the costs of reproduction of labour) will necessarily increase faster than output per man, and may thus secure a rising rate of profit even if there is diminishing productivity to successive additions to fixed capital per unit of labour.

While some of Marx's predictions—such

[14] Cf., in particular, Joan Robinson, *An Essay in Marxian Economics*, pp. 75–82.

as the increasing concentration of production in the hands of large enterprises—proved accurate, his most important thesis, the steady worsening of the living conditions of the working classes—"the immiseration of the proletariat" [15]—has been contradicted by experience, in both the "competitive" and "monopoly" stages of capitalism. On the Marxian model the share of wages in output must necessarily fall with every increase in output per head. The theory can only allow for a rise of wages in terms of commodities as a result of the collective organisation of the working classes which forces the capitalists to reduce the degree of exploitation and to surrender to the workers some of the "surplus value." [16] This hypothesis however will only yield a constant share of wages on the extremely far-fetched assumption that the rate of increase in the bargaining strength of labour, due to the growth of collective organisation, precisely keeps pace with the rate of increase in output per head.

THE NEO-CLASSICAL THEORIES

Marginal Productivity

While Marx's theory thus derives from Ricardo's surplus principle, neo-classical value and distribution theory derives from another part of the Ricardian model: the "marginal principle" introduced for the ex-

[15] It is not clear, in terms of Marx's own theoretical model, why such a progressive immiseration should take place—since the costs of reproduction of labour appear to set an *absolute* limit to the extent to which labour can be exploited. Some parts of *Das Kapital* could however be construed as suggesting that wages can be driven below the (long run) reproduction cost of labour, at the cost of a (long run) shrinkage in the labour force: and with the increasing organic composition of capital, and the rise of monopolies, the demand for labour may show an equally declining tendency.

[16] Marx himself would have conceived a reduction in the "degree of exploitation" in terms of a reduction in the length of the working day rather than a rise in real wages per day. In fact both have occurred side by side.

planation of rent (which explains why both Marx and Marshall are able to claim Ricardo as their precursor). The difference between Ricardo and the neo-classics is (1) that whereas Ricardo employed the "principle of substitution" (or rather, the principle of "limited substitutability"—which is the basic assumption underlying all "marginal" analysis) only as regards the use of labour relative to land, in neo-classical theory this doctrine was formalized and generalized, and assumed to hold true of any factor, in relation to any other; [17] (2) whereas Ricardo employed the principle for showing that a "fixed" factor will earn a surplus, determined by the gap between the average and marginal product of the variable factor, neo-classical theory concentrated on the reverse aspect—i.e., that any factor variable in supply will obtain a remuneration which, under competitive conditions, must correspond to its marginal product. Thus if the total supply of *all* factors (and not only land) is being taken as given, independently of price, and all are assumed to be limited substitutes to one another, the share-out of the whole produce can be regarded as being determined by the marginal rates of substitution

[17] As well as of any particular commodity in the sphere of consumption. The utility theory of value is really Ricardian rent-theory applied to consumption demand. In fact, as Walras has shown, limited substitutability in consumption might in itself be sufficient to determine distributive shares, provided that the proportions in which the different factors are used are different in different industries. His solution of the problem of distribution, based on "fixed coefficients" of production (intended only as a first approximation) is subject however to various snags since the solution of his equations may yield negative prices for the factors as well as positive ones and it cannot be determined beforehand whether this will be the case or not. If the solution of the equations yields negative prices the factors in question have to be excluded as "free goods"; and the operation (if necessary) successive repeated until only factors with positive prices are left. Also, it is necessary to suppose that the number of different "factors" is no greater than the number of different "products" otherwise the solution is indeterminate.

between them. Thus in terms of our diagram, if we assumed that along Ox we measure the quantity of any particular factor of production, x, the quantities of all the others being taken as fixed, $p-Mp$ will exhibit the marginal productivity function of the variable factor. If the actual employment of that factor is taken to be M, AM will represent its demand price per unit, and the rectangle $OBAM$ its share in the total produce. Since this principle could be applied to any factor, it must be true of all (including, as Walras and Wicksell have shown, the factors owned by the entrepreneur himself) hence the rectangle $BCDA$ must be sufficient, and only just sufficient, for remunerating all other factors but x on the basis of their respective marginal productivities. This, as Wicksteed has shown[18] requires the assumption that the production function will be homogeneous of the first degree for all variables taken together— an assumption which he himself regarded as little more than a tautology, if "factors of production" are appropriately defined.[19] From the point of view of the theory, however, the *appropriate* definition of factors involves the elimination of intermediate products and their conversion into "ultimate" or "original" factors, since only on this definition can one assume the properties of divisibility and variability of co-

efficients. When factors are thus defined, the assumption of constant returns to scale is by no means a tautology; it is a restrictive assumption, which may be regarded, however, as being co-extensive with other restrictive assumptions implied by the theory—i.e., the universal rule of perfect competition, and the absence of external economies and diseconomies.

The basic difficulty with the whole approach does not lie, however, in this so-called "adding-up problem" but in the very meaning of "capital" as a factor of production.[20] Whilst land can be measured in acres-per-year and labour in man-hours, capital (as distinct from "capital goods") cannot be measured in terms of physical units.[21] To evaluate the marginal product of labour it is necessary to isolate two situations containing identical "capital" but two different quantities of labour, or identical amounts of labour and two differing quantities of "capital," in precise numerical relationship.[22]

Marshall, without going into the matter in any detail, had shown in several passages that he was dimly aware of this; and in carefully re-defining marginal productivity so as to mean "marginal *net* productivity" (*net* after deduction of all associated expenses on other "factors") he shied away

---

[18] *The Co-ordination of the Laws of Distribution* (1894).

[19] *Ibid.*, p. 53. "We must regard every kind and quality of labour that can be distinguished from other kinds and qualities as a separate factor; and in the same way, every kind of land will be taken as a separate factor. Still more important is it to insist that instead of speaking of so many £ worth of capital we shall speak of so many ploughs, so many tons of manure, and so many horses or footpounds of power. Each of these may be scheduled in its own unit." Under these conditions it is true to say that "doubling all factors will double the product," but since these "factors" are indivisible in varying degrees, it does not mean that the production function is a linear and homogeneous one in relation to incremental variations of output. Also a change in output may be associated with the introduction of *new* factors of production.

[20] For a general equilibrium system, capital goods cannot be regarded as factors of production *per se* (in the manner suggested by Wicksteed) otherwise the same things are simultaneously treated as the parameters and the unknowns of the system.

[21] Measurement in terms of value (as so many £'s of "capital") already assumes a certain rate of interest, on the basis of which services accruing in differing periods in the future, or costs incurred at differing dates in the past, are brought to a measure of equivalence.

[22] The product of the "marginal shepherd" is the difference, in terms of numbers of sheep, between 10 shepherds using 10 crooks and 11 shepherds using 11 slightly inferior crooks, the term "slightly inferior" being taken to mean that the 11 crooks in the one case represent precisely the same amount of "capital" as the 10 crooks in the other case. (Cf. also, Robertson, "Wage Grumbles," in *Economic Fragments*, 1931.)

from the task of putting forward a general theory of distribution altogether.[23]

In fact, in so far as we can speak of a "Marshallian" theory of distribution at all, it is in the sense of a "short period" theory, which regards profits as the "quasi-rents" earned on the use of capital goods of various kinds, the supply of which can be treated as given for the time being, as a heritage of the past. The doctrine of the "quasi-rent" assimilates capital as a factor of production to Ricardian land: the separate *kinds* of capital goods being treated as so many different kinds of "land." Here the problem of the measurement of capital as a factor of production does not arise: since, strictly speaking, no kind of change or reorganization in the stock of intermediate products is permitted in connection with a change in the level or composition of production. It was this aspect of Marshall which, consciously or sub-consciously, provided the "model" for most of the post-Marshallian Cambridge theorizing. Prices are equal to, or determined by, marginal prime costs; profits are determined by the difference between marginal and average prime costs; prime costs, for the system as a whole, are labour costs (since raw-material costs, for a closed economy at any rate, disappear if all branches of industry are taken together); ultimately therefore the division of output between profits and wages is a matter depending on the existence of diminishing returns to labour, as more labour is used in conjunction with a *given* capital equipment; and is determined by the elasticity

of labour's average productivity curve which fixes the share of quasi-rents.

Marshall himself would have disagreed with the use of the quasi-rent doctrine as a distribution theory, holding that distributive shares in the short period are determined by long-period forces.[24] Clearly even if one were to hold strictly to the assumption that "profit margins" are the outcome of short-period profit-maximisation, this "short-period" approach does not really get us anywhere: for the extent to which diminishing returns operate for labour in conjunction with the capital equipment available to-day is itself a function of the price-relationships which have ruled in the past because these have determined the quantities of each of the kinds of equipment available. The theory does not therefore really amount to more than saying that the prices of to-day are derived from the prices of yesterday—a proposition which is the more true and the more trivial the shorter the "day" is conceived to be, in terms of chronological time.

For the true neo-classical attempt to solve the general problem of distribution we must go to Wicksell who thought that by integrating the Austrian approach to capital with Walrasian equilibrium theory he could provide a general solution, treating capital as a two-dimensional quantity, the product of time and labour. The "time" in this case is the investment period or waiting period separating the application of "original" factors from the emergence of the final product, and the marginal productivity of capital the added product resulting from an extension of "time." This attempt, again, came to grief (as Wicksell himself came near to acknowledging late in life[25]) (i) owing to the impossibility of measuring

[23] "The doctrine that the earnings of a worker tend to be equal to the net product of his work, has by itself no real meaning; since in order to estimate the net product, we have to take for granted all the expenses of production of the commodity on which he works, other than his own wages." Similarly, the doctrine that the marginal efficiency of capital will tend to equal the rate of interest "cannot be made into a theory of interest, any more than a theory of wages, without reasoning in a circle." (Cf. *Principles,* 8th edition, Book VI, ch. I, paras. 7–8.)

[24] Cf., in particular, *Principles,* 8th edition, Book V, ch. V, and 6, and Book VI, ch. VIII, para. 4.
[25] Cf. the concluding passage of his posthumous contribution to the Wieser Festschrift. *Die Wirtschaftstheorie der Gegenwart* (1928) Vol. III, pp. 208–9; also his Analysis of Akerman's Problem, reprinted in *Lectures,* Vol. I, p. 270.

that period in terms of an "average" of some kind;[26] (ii) owing to the impossibility of combining the investment periods of different "original" factors in a single measure.[27]

In fact the whole approach which regards the share of wages and of profits in output as being determined by the marginal rate of substitution between Capital and Labour—with its corollary, that the constancy of relative shares is evidence of a unity-Elasticity of Substitution between Capital and Labour[28]—is hardly acceptable to present-day economists. Its inadequacy becomes evident as soon as it is realized that the "marginal rate of substitution" between Capital and Labour—as distinct from the marginal rate of substitution between labour and land—can only be determined once the rate of profit and the rate of wages are already known. The same technical alternatives might yield very different "marginal rates of substitution" according as the ratio of profits to wages is one thing or another. The theory asserts in effect, that the rate of interest in the capital market, (and the associated wage rate in the labour market) is determined by the condition that at any lower interest rate (and higher wage rate) capital would be invested in such "labour-saving" forms as would provide insufficient employment to the available labour; whilst at any higher rate, capital would be invested in forms that offered more places of employment than could be filled with the available labour.

Quite apart from all conceptual difficulties, the theory focuses attention on a rela-

tively unimportant feature of a growing economy. For accumulation does not take the form of "deepening" the structure of capital (at a given state of knowledge) but rather in keeping pace with technical progress and the growth in the labour force. It is difficult to swallow a theory which says, in effect that wages and profits are what they are for otherwise there would be too much deepening or too little deepening (the capital/output ratios would be either too large or too small) to be consistent with simultaneous equilibrium in the savings-investment market and in the labour market.

The "Degree of Monopoly" Theories of Distribution

Monopoly profit was always regarded as a distinct form of revenue in neo-classical theory, though not one of any great quantitative importance since the mass of commodities was thought of as being produced under competitive conditions. But the modern theories of imperfect competition emphasised that monopoly profit is not an isolated feature. Profits in general contain an *element* of monopoly revenue—an element that is best defined as the excess of the actual profit margin in output over what the profit margin would have been under perfectly competitive conditions. Under Marshallian "short-period" assumptions the perfectly-competitive profit margin is given by the excess of marginal cost over average prime costs. The additional monopoly element is indicated by the excess of price over marginal cost. The former, as we have seen, is a derivative of the elasticity of labour's productivity curve where capital equipment of all kinds is treated as given. The latter is a derivative of the elasticity of demand facing the individual firm. The novel feature of imperfect competition theories is to have shown that the increase of profit margins due to this element of monopoly need not imply a corresponding excess in the rates of profit on capital over

---

[26] Since owing to compound interest, the weights to be used in the calculation of the average will themselves be dependent on the rate of interest.

[27] For a more extended treatment cf. my articles on capital theory in *Econometrica*, April 1937 and May 1938; also Joan Robinson, The Production Function in the Theory of Capital, *Review of Economic Studies*, Vol. XXI (1953–54) p. 81, and *Comment* by D. G. Champernowne, *ibid.*, page 112.

[28] Cf. Hicks, *The Theory of Wages* (1932) ch. VI, passim.

the competitive rate; through the generation of excess capacity (i.e., the tendency of demand curves to become "tangential" to the cost curves) the latter may approach a "competitive" or "normal" rate (as a result of the consequential rise in the capital/output ratio) even if the former is above the competitive level.

Kalecki[29] built on this a simplified theory of distribution, where the share of profits in output is shown to be determined by the elasticity of demand alone. This was based on the hypothesis that in the short period, labour and capital equipment are largely "limitational" and not "substitutional" factors, with the result that the short-period prime cost-curve is a reverse —L shaped one (prime costs being constant up to full capacity output). In that case marginal costs are equal to average prime costs; the ratio of price to prime costs (and hence, in a closed economy, the ratio of gross profits to wages) is thus entirely accounted for by the elasticity of the firm's demand curve.

On closer inspection, however, the elasticity of the demand curve facing the individual firm turned out to be no less of a broken reed than its counterpart, the elasticity of substitution between factors. There is no evidence that firms in imperfect markets set their prices by reference to the elasticity of their sales-function, or that short-period pricing is the outcome of any deliberate attempt to maximize profits by reference to an independent revenue and a cost function. Indeed the very notion of a demand curve for the products of a single firm is illegitimate if the prices charged by different firms cannot be assumed to be independent of each other.[30]

In the later versions of his theory Kalecki abandoned the link between the "degree of monopoly" and the elasticity of demand, and was content with a purely tautological approach according to which the ratio of price to prime costs is *defined* simply as the "degree of monopoly." Propositions based on implicit definitions of this kind make of course no assertion about reality and possess no explanatory value. Unless the "degree of monopoly" can be defined in terms of market relationships of some kind (as, for example, in terms of the "cross-elasticities" of demand for the products of the different firms)[31] and an attempt is made to demonstrate how these market relationships determine the relation between prices and costs, the theory does not provide a hypothesis which could be affirmed or refuted.

There is no need, of course, to follow Kalecki in the attempt to lend spurious precision to the doctrine through implicit theorizing—a vice which afflicts all theories which we grouped together as "neo-classical" in varying degrees. Fundamentally, the proposition that the distribution of income between wages and profits depends on market structures, on the strength or weakness of the forces of competition, is not a tautological one; it asserts *something* about reality (which may in principle be proved false) even if that "something" cannot be given a logically precise formulation. Just as the positive content of the marginal productivity theory can be summed up by the statement that the rate of profit on capital (and the margin of profit in output) is governed by the need to prevent the capital/output ratio from being either too

---

[29] The original version appeared in *Econometrica*, April 1938. Subsequent versions appeared in *Essays in the Theory of Economic Fluctuations* (1938) ch. I, *Studies in Economic Dynamics* (1943) ch. 1, and *Theory of Dynamic Economics* (1954) Part 1.
[30] The theory of the "kinked" demand curve is in fact no more than a recognition of the fact that the demand curve of the firm (in the sense required for the purpose of deriving price from

the postulate of profit maximisation) is non-existent. Since the position of the "kink" *depends* on the price, it cannot *determine* the price; it thus leaves the profit margin completely undetermined.
[31] The "cross-elasticities" of demand indicate the degree of interdependence of the markets of different firms and are thus inversely related to monopoly power in the usual sense of the word.

large or too small, the positive content of the "degree of monopoly" theory can be summed up in the sentence that "profit margins are what they are because the forces of competition prevent them from being higher than they are and are not powerful enough to make them lower than they are." Unfortunately neither of these statements gets us very far.

Dissatisfaction with the tautological character and the formalism of the "marginal revenue-equals-marginal cost" type of price theory led to the formulation of the "full cost" theories of pricing,[32] according to which producers in imperfect markets set their prices independently of the character of demand, and solely on the basis of their long run costs of production (including the "normal" rate of profit on their own capital). If these theories asserted no more than that prices in manufacturing industry are *not* determined by the criterion of short-run profit-maximization, and that profit margins can be fairly insensitive to short-period variations in demand,[33] (the

impact effect of changes in demand being on the rate of production, rather than on prices) they would provide a healthy antidote to a great deal of facile theorising. When, however, they go beyond this and assert that prices are determined quite independently of demand, they in effect destroy existing price theory without putting anything else in its place. Quite apart from the fact that a "full cost" theory is quite unable to explain why some firms should be more successful in earning profits than others, the level of the "normal profit" on which the full cost calculations are supposed to be based is left quite undetermined. The very fact that these full cost theories should have received such widespread and serious consideration as an alternative explanation of the pricing process is an indication of the sad state of vagueness and confusion into which the neo-classical value theory had fallen.

THE KEYNESIAN THEORY

Keynes, as far as I know, was never interested in the problem of distribution as such. One may nevertheless christen a particular theory of distribution as "Keynesian" if it can be shown to be an application of the specifically Keynesian apparatus of thought and if evidence can be adduced that at some stage in the development of his ideas, Keynes came near to formulating such a theory.[34] The principle

---

[32] Cf. Hall and Hitch, *Oxford Economic Papers,* 1939; P. M. S. Andrews, *Manufacturing Business* (1949).

[33] This, I believe, was the intention of the original Hall-Hitch article. Cf. Marshall, *Principles,* Book VI, ch. VIII, paragraph 4: "We see then that there is no general tendency of profits on the turnover to equality; but there may be, and as a matter of fact there is, in each trade and in every branch of each trade, a more or less definite rate of profits on the turnover which is regarded as a "fair" or normal rate. Of course these rates are always changing in consequence of changes in the methods of trade; which are generally begun by individuals who desire to do a larger trade at a lower rate of profit on the turnover than has been customary, but at a larger rate of profit per annum on their capital. If however there happens to be no great change of this kind going on, the traditions of the trade that a certain rate of profit on the turnover should be charged for a particular class of work are of great practical service to those in the trade. Such traditions are the outcome of much experience tending to show that, if that rate is charged, a proper allowance will be made for all the costs (supplementary as well as prime) incurred for that particular purpose, and in addition the normal rate of profits per annum in that case of business will be afforded. If they charge a price

which gives much less than this rate of profit on the turnover they can hardly prosper; and if they charge much more they are in danger of losing their custom, since others can afford to undersell them. This is the "fair" rate of profit on the turnover, which an honest man is expected to charge for making goods to order, when no price has been agreed on beforehand; and it is the rate which a court of law will allow in case a dispute should arise between buyer and seller." Cf. also Kahn, *Economic Journal,* 1952, p. 119.

[34] I am referring to the well-known passage on profits being likened to a "widow's cruse" in the *Treatise on Money,* Vol. I, p. 139. "If entrepreneurs choose to spend a portion of their profits on consumption (and there is, of course, nothing to

of the Multiplier (which in some way was anticipated in the *Treatise* but without a clear view of its implications) could be alternatively applied to a determination of the relation between prices and wages, if the level of output and employment is taken as given, or the determination of the level of employment, if distribution (i.e., the relation between prices and wages) is taken as given. The reason why the multiplier-analysis has not been developed as a distribution theory is precisely because it was invented for the purpose of an employment theory—to explain why an economic system can remain in equilibrium in a state of under-employment (or of a general under-utilization of resources), where the classical properties of scarcity-economics are inapplicable. And its use for the one appears to exclude its use for the

prevent them from doing this) the effect is to *increase* the profit on the sale of liquid consumption goods by an amount exactly equal to the amount of profits which have been thus expended . . . Thus however much of their profits entrepreneurs spend on consumption, the increment of wealth belonging to entrepreneurs remain the same as before. Thus profits, as a source of capital increment for entrepreneurs, are a widow's cruse which remains undepleted however much of them may be devoted to riotous living. When on the other hand, entrepreneurs are making losses, and seek to recoup these losses by curtailing their normal expenditure on consumption, i.e., by saving more, the cruse becomes a Danaid jar which can never be filled up; for the effect of this reduced expenditure is to inflict on the producers of consumption-goods a loss of an equal amount. Thus the diminution of their wealth, as a class is as great, in spite of their savings, as it was before." This passage, I think, contains the true seed of the ideas developed in the *General Theory*—as well as showing the length of the road that had to be traversed before arriving at the conceptual framework presented in the latter work. The fact that "profits", "savings" etc. were all defined here in a special sense that was later discarded, and that the argument specifically refers to expenditure on consumption goods, rather than entrepreneurial expenditure in general, should not blind us to the fact that here Keynes regards entrepreneurial incomes as being the resultant of their expenditure decisions, rather than the other way round—which is perhaps the most important difference between "Keynesian" and "pre-Keynesian" habits of thought.

other.[35] If we assume that the balance of savings and investment is brought about through variations in the relationship of prices and costs, we are not only bereft of a principle for explaining variations in output and employment, but the whole idea of separate "aggregate" demand and supply functions—the principle of "effective demand"—falls to the ground; we are back to Say's Law, where output as a whole is limited by available resources, and a fall in effective demand for one kind of commodity (in real terms) generates compensating increases in effective demand (again in real terms) for others. Yet these two uses of the Multiplier principle are not as incompatible as would appear at first sight: the Keynesian technique, as I hope to show, can be used for both purposes, provided the one is conceived as a short-run theory and the other as a long-run theory—or rather, the one is used in the framework of a static model, and the other in the framework of a dynamic growth model.[36]

We shall assume, to begin with, a state of full employment (we shall show later the

[35] Although this application of Keynesian theory has been implicit in several discussions of the problem of inflation. (Cf. *e.g.* A. J. Brown, *The Great Inflation*, Macmillan, 1955.)

[36] I first thought of using the Multiplier technique for purposes of a distribution theory when I attempted the ultimate incidence of profits taxation under full employment conditions in a paper prepared for the Royal Commission on Taxation in 1951. The further development of these ideas, and particularly their relationship to a dynamic theory of growth, owes a great deal to discussions with Mrs. Robinson, whose forthcoming book, *The Accumulation of Capital*, contains a systematic exploration of this field. I should also like to mention here that I owe a great deal of stimulus to a paper by Kalecki, "A Theory of Profits" (*Economic Journal*, June–Sept. 1942) whose approach is in some ways reminiscent of the "widows' cruse" of Keynes' *Treatise* even though Kalecki uses the technique, not for an explanation of the share of profits in output, but for showing why the *level* of output and its fluctuations is peculiarly dependent on entrepreneurial behaviour. (In doing so, he uses the restrictive assumption that savings are entirely supplied out of profits.) I have also been helped by Mr. Harry Johnson and Mr. Robin Marris, both in the working out of the formulae and in general discussion.

conditions under which a state of full employment will *result* from our model) so that total output or income (Y) is given. Income may be divided into two broad categories, Wages and Profits (W and P), where the wage-category comprises not only manual labour but salaries as well, and Profits the income of property owners generally, and not only of entrepreneurs; the important difference between them being in the marginal propensities to consume (or save), wage-earners' marginal savings being small in relation to those of capitalists.[37]

Writing S_w and S_p for aggregate savings out of Wages and Profits, we have the following income identities:

$$Y \equiv W + P$$
$$I \equiv S$$
$$S \equiv S_w + S_p.$$

Taking investment as given, and assuming simple proportional saving functions $S_w = s_w W$ and $S_p = s_p P$, we obtain:

$$I = s_p P + s_w W = s_p P + s_w (Y - P)$$
$$= (s_p - s_w)P + s_w Y$$

Whence $\dfrac{I}{Y} = (s_p - s_w)\dfrac{P}{Y} + s_w$ (23.1)

and $\dfrac{P}{Y} = \dfrac{1}{s_p - s_w}\dfrac{I}{Y} - \dfrac{s_w}{s_p - s_w}$ (23.2)

Thus, given the wage-earners' and the capitalists' propensities to save, the share of profits in income depends simply on the ratio of investment to output.

The interpretative value of the model (as distinct from the formal validity of the equations, or identities) depends on the "Keynesian" hypothesis that investment, or rather, the ratio of investment to output, can be treated as an independent variable, invariant with respect to changes in the two savings propensities s_p and s_w. (We

[37] This may be assumed independently of any skewness in the distribution of property, simply as a consequence of the fact that the bulk of profits accrues in the form of company profits and a high proportion of companies' marginal profits is put to reserve.

shall see later that this assumption can only be true within certain limits, and outside those limits the theory ceases to hold.) This, together with the assumption of "full employment," also implies that the level of prices in relation to the level of money wages is determined by demand: a rise in investment, and thus in total demand, will raise prices and profit margins, and thus reduce real consumption, whilst a fall in investment, and thus in total demand, causes a fall in prices (relatively to the wage level) and thereby generates a compensating rise in real consumption. Assuming flexible prices (or rather flexible profit margins) the system is thus stable at full employment.

The model operates only if the two savings propensities differ and the marginal propensity to save from profits exceeds that from wages, i.e., if:

and $\begin{aligned} s_p &\neq s_w \\ s_p &> s_w \end{aligned}$

The latter is the stability condition. For if $s_p < s_w$, a fall in prices would cause a fall in demand and thus generate a further fall in prices, and equally, a rise in prices would be cumulative. The degree of stability of the system depends on the *difference* of the marginal propensities, i.e., on $\dfrac{1}{s_p - s_w}$ which may be defined as the "coefficient of sensitivity of income distribution," since it indicates the change in the share of profits in income which follows upon a change in the share of investment in output.

If the difference between the marginal propensities is small, the coefficient will be large, and small changes in $\dfrac{I}{Y}$ (the investment/output relationship) will cause relatively large changes in income distribution $\dfrac{P}{Y}$; and *vice versa*.

In the limiting case where $s_w = 0$, the amount of profits is equal to the sum of investment and capitalist consumption, i.e.:

$$P = \frac{1}{s_p} I.$$

This is the assumption implicit in Keynes' parable about the widow's cruse—where a rise in entrepreneurial consumption raises their total profit by an *identical* amount— and of Mr. Kalecki's theory of profits which can be paraphrased by saying that "capitalists earn what they spend, and workers spend what they earn."

This model (i.e., the "special case" where $s_w = 0$) in a sense is the precise opposite of the Ricardian (or Marxian) one —here wages (not profits) are a residue, profits being governed by the propensity to invest and the capitalists' propensity to consume, which represent a kind of "prior charge" on the national output. Whereas in the Ricardian model the ultimate incidence of all taxes (other than taxes on rent) falls on profits, here the incidence of all taxes, taxes on income and profits as well as on commodities, falls on wages.[38]

Assuming however that $\frac{I}{Y}$ and s_p remain constant over time, the share of wages will also remain constant—i.e., real wages will increase automatically, year by year, with the increase in output per man.

If s_w is positive the picture is more complicated. Total profits will be reduced by the amount of workers' savings, S_w; on the other hand, the sensitivity of profits to

changes in the level of investment will be greater, total profits rising (or falling) by a greater amount than the change in investment, owing to the consequential reduction (or increase) in workers' savings.[39]

The critical assumption is that the investment/output ratio is an independent variable. Following Harrod, we can describe the determinants of the investment/output ratio in terms of the rate of growth of output capacity (G) and the capital/output ratio, v:

$$\frac{I}{Y} = Gv \qquad (23.3)$$

In a state of continuous full employment G must be equal to the rate of growth of the "full employment ceiling," i.e., the sum of the rate of technical progress and the growth in working population (Harrod's "natural rate of growth"). For Harrod's second equation:

$$\frac{I}{Y} = s$$

we can now substitute equation (23.1) above:

$$\frac{I}{Y} = (s_p - s_w) \frac{P}{Y} + s_w.$$

Hence the "warranted" and the "natural" rates of growth are not independent of one another; if profit margins are flexible, the

---

[38] The ultimate incidence of taxes can only fall on profits (on this model) in so far as they increase s_p, the propensity to save out of *net* income after tax. Income and profits taxes, through the "double taxation" of savings, have of course the opposite effect: they reduce s_p, and thereby make the share of *net* profits in income larger than it would be in the absence of taxation. On the other hand, discriminatory taxes on dividend distribution, or dividend limitation, by keeping down both dividends and capital gains, have the effect of raising s_p. (All this applies, of course, on the assumption that the Government *spends* the proceeds of the tax—i.e., that it aims at a balanced budget. Taxes which go to augment the budget surplus will lower the share of profits in much the same way as an increase in workers' savings.)

[39] Thus if $s_p = 50\%$, $s_w = 10\%$, $\frac{I}{Y} = 20\%$, $\frac{P}{Y}$ will be 15%; but a rise in $\frac{I}{Y}$ to 21% would raise $\frac{P}{Y}$ to 17.5%. If on the other hand $s_w = 0$, with $s_p = 50\%$, $\frac{P}{Y}$ would become 40%, but an increase in $\frac{I}{Y}$ to 21% would only increase $\frac{P}{Y}$ to 42%. The above formulae assume that average and marginal propensities are identical. Introducing constant terms in the consumption functions alters the relationship between $\frac{P}{Y}$ and $\frac{I}{Y}$, and would reduce the *elasticity* of $\frac{P}{Y}$ with respect to changes in $\frac{I}{Y}$.

former will adjust itself to the latter through a consequential change in $\frac{P}{Y}$.

This does not mean that there will be an *inherent* tendency to a smooth rate of growth in a capitalist economy, only that the causes of cyclical movements lie elsewhere—not in the lack of an adjustment mechanism between s and Gv. As I have attempted to demonstrate elsewhere[40] the causes of cyclical movements should be sought in a disharmony between the entrepreneurs' *desired* growth rate (as influenced by the degree of optimism and the volatility of expectations) which governs the rate of increase of output capacity (let us call it G') and the natural growth rate (dependent on technical progress and the growth of the working population) which governs the rate of growth in output. It is the excess of G' over G—not the excess of s over Gv—which causes periodic breakdowns in the investment process through the growth in output capacity outrunning the growth in production.[41]

Problems of the trade cycle however lie outside the scope of this paper; and having described a model which shows the distribution of income to be determined by the Keynesian investment-savings mechanism, we must now examine its limitations. The model, as I emphasized earlier, shows the share of profits $\frac{P}{Y}$, the rate of profit on in-

[40] *Economic Journal*, March 1954, pp. 53–71.

[41] $\frac{I}{Y}$ will therefore tend to equal $G'v$, not Gv. It may be assumed that taking very long periods G' is largely governed by G but over shorter periods the two are quite distinct, moreover G itself is not independent of G', since technical progress and population growth are both stimulated by the degree of pressure on the "full employment ceiling," which depends on G'. The elasticity of response of G to G' is not infinite however: hence the greater G', the greater will be G (the *actual* trend-rate of growth of the economy over successive cycles) but the greater also the ratio $\frac{G'}{G}$ which measures the strength of cyclical forces.

vestment $\frac{P}{vY}$, and the real wage rate $\frac{W'}{L}$, as functions of $\frac{I}{Y}$ which in turn is determined independently of $\frac{P}{Y}$ or $\frac{W}{L}$.[42] There are four different reasons why this may not be true, or be true only within a certain range.

(1) The first is that the real wage cannot fall below a certain subsistence minimum. Hence $\frac{P}{Y}$ can only attain its indicated value, if the resulting real wage exceeds this minimum rate, w'. Hence the model is subject to the restriction $\frac{W}{L} \geqslant w'$, which we may write in the form:

$$\frac{P}{Y} \leqslant \frac{Y - w'L}{Y} \qquad (23.4)$$

(2) The second is that the indicated share of profits cannot be below the level which yields the minimum rate of profit necessary to induce capitalists to invest their capital, and which we may call the "risk premium rate," r. Hence the restriction:

$$\frac{P}{vY} \geqslant r \qquad (23.5)$$

(3) The third is that apart from a minimum rate of profit on capital there may be a certain minimum rate of profit on turnover—due to imperfections of competition, collusive agreements between traders, etc., and which we may call m, the "degree of monopoly" rate. Hence the restriction:

$$\frac{P}{Y} \geqslant m \qquad (23.6)$$

It is clear that equations (23.5) and (23.6) describe *alternative* restrictions, of which the higher will apply.

(4) The fourth is that the capital/output ratio, v, should not in itself be influenced by the rate of profit, for if it is, the invest-

[42] Where $L =$ labour force.

ment/output ratio Gv will itself be dependent on the rate of profit. A certain degree of dependence follows inevitably from the consideration, mentioned earlier, that the value of particular capital goods in terms of final consumption goods will vary with the rate of profit,[43] so that, even with a *given technique* v will not be independent of $\frac{P}{Y}$. (We shall ignore this point.) There is the further complication that the relation $\frac{P}{Y}$ may affect v through making more or less "labour-saving" techniques profitable. In other words, at any given wage-price relationship, the producers will adopt the technique which maximizes the rate of profit on capital, $\frac{P}{vY}$; this will affect (at a given G) $\frac{I}{Y}$, and hence $\frac{P}{Y}$. Hence any rise in $\frac{P}{Y}$ will reduce v, and thus $\frac{I}{Y}$, and conversely, any rise in $\frac{I}{Y}$ will raise $\frac{P}{Y}$. If the sensitiveness of v to $\frac{P}{Y}$ is great, $\frac{P}{Y}$ can no longer be regarded as being determined by the equations of the model; the *technical* relation between v and $\frac{P}{Y}$ will then govern $\frac{P}{Y}$ whereas the savings equation (equation 23.2 above) will determine $\frac{I}{Y}$ and thus (given G) the value of v.[44] To exclude this

we have to assume that v is invariant to $\frac{P}{Y}$,[45] i.e.:

$$v = \bar{v} \tag{23.7}$$

If equation (23.4) is unsatisfied, we are back at the Ricardian (or Marxian) model. $\frac{I}{Y}$ will suffer a shrinkage, and will no longer correspond to Gv, but to, say, αv where $\alpha < G$. Hence the system will not produce full employment; output will be limited by the available capital, and not by labour; at the same time the classical, and not the Keynesian, reaction-mechanism will be in operation: the size of the "surplus" available for investment determining investment, not investment savings. It is possible however that owing to technical inventions, etc., and starting from a position of excess labour and underemployment (i.e., an elastic total supply of labour) the size of the surplus will grow; hence $\frac{I}{Y}$ and α will grow; and hence α might rise above G (the rate of growth of the "full employment ceiling," given the technical progress and the growth of population) so that in time the excess labour becomes absorbed and full employment is reached. When this happens (which we may call the stage of *developed* capitalism) wages will rise above the subsistence level, and the properties of the system will then follow our model.

If equations (23.5) and (23.6) are unsatisfied, the full employment assumption breaks down, and so will the process of growth; the economy will relapse into a state of

---

[43] Cf. p. 90 above. In fact the whole of the Keynesian and post-Keynesian analysis dodges the problem of the measurement of capital.

[44] This is where the "marginal productivity" principle would come in but it should be emphasized that under the conditions of our model where savings are treated, not as a constant, but as a function of income distribution, $\frac{P}{Y}$, the sensitiveness of v to changes in $\frac{P}{Y}$ would have to be very large to overshadow the influence of G and of s_p and of s_w on $\frac{P}{Y}$. Assuming that it is large,

it is further necessary to suppose that the value of $\frac{P}{Y}$ as dictated by this technical relationship falls within the maximum and minimum values indicated by equations (23.4)–(23.6).

[45] This assumption does not necessarily mean that there are "fixed coefficients" as between capital equipment and labour—only that technical innovations (which are also assumed to be "neutral" in their effects) are far more influential on the chosen v than price relationships.

stagnation. The interesting conclusion which emerges from these equations is that this may be the result of several distinct causes. "Investment opportunities" may be low because G' is low relatively to G, i.e., the entrepreneurs' expectations are involatile, and/or they are pessimistic; hence they expect a lower level of demand for the future than corresponds to potential demand, governed by G. On the other hand, "liquidity preference" may be too high, or the risks associated with investment too great, leading to an excessive r. (This is perhaps the factor on which Keynes himself set greatest store as a cause of unemployment and stagnation.) Finally, lack of competition may cause "over-saving" through excessive profit margins; this again will cause stagnation, unless there is sufficient compensating increase in v (through the generation of "excess capacity" under conditions of rigid profit margins but relatively free entry) to push up Gv, and hence $\frac{I}{Y}$.

If, however, equations (23.2)–(23.6) are all satisfied there will be an inherent tendency to growth and an inherent tendency to full employment. Indeed the two are closely linked to each other. Apart from the case of a developing economy in the immature stage of capitalism (where equation (23.4) does not hold, but where $\gamma < G$), a tendency to continued economic growth will only exist when the system is only stable at full employment equilibrium—i.e. when $G' \geqslant G$.

This is a possible interpretation of the long-term situation in the "successful" capitalist economies of Western Europe and North America. If G' exceeds G, the investment/output ratio $\frac{I}{Y}$ will not be steady in time, even if the *trend* level of this ratio is constant. There will be periodic breakdowns in the investment process, due to the growth in output capacity outrunning the possible growth in output; when that happens, not only investment, but total out-

put will fall, and output will be (temporarily) limited by effective demand, and not by the scarcity of resources. This is contrary to the mechanics of our model, but several reasons can be adduced to show why the system will not be flexible enough to ensure full employment in the short period.

(1) First, even if "profit margins" are assumed to be fully flexible, in a downward, as well as an upward, direction the very fact that investment goods and consumer goods are produced by different industries, with limited mobility between them, will mean that profit margins in the consumption goods industries will not fall below the level that ensures full utilization of resources in the consumption goods industries. A *compensating* increase in consumption goods production (following upon a fall in the production of investment goods) can only occur as a result of a transfer of resources from the other industries, lured by the profit opportunities there.

(2) Second, and more important, profit-margins are likely to be inflexible in a downward direction in the short period (Marshall's "fear of spoiling the market") even if they are flexible in the long period, or even if they possess short period flexibility in an upward direction.[46]

This applies of course not only to profit margins but to real wages as well, which in the short period may be equally inflexible in a downward direction at the *attained* level, thus compressing $\frac{I}{Y}$, or rather preventing an *increase* in $\frac{I}{Y}$ following upon a rise in the entrepreneurs' desired rate of expansion G'. Hence in the short period the shares of profits and wages tend to be inflexible for two different reasons—the downward inflexibility of $\frac{P}{Y}$ and the downward inflexibility of $\frac{W}{L}$—which thus tend to reinforce the long-period stability of these shares, due to constancy of $\frac{I}{Y}$, resulting from the long period constancy of Gv and $G'v$.[47]

[47] This operates through the wage-price spiral that would follow on a reduction in real wages; the prevention of such a wage-price spiral by means of investment rationing of some kind, or a "credit squeeze," is thus a manifestation of downward inflexibility of $\frac{W}{Y}$.

We have seen how the various "models" of distribution, the Ricardian-Marxian, the Keynesian and the Kaleckian are related to each other. I am not sure where "marginal productivity" comes in in all this—except that in so far as it has any importance it does through an extreme sensivity of v to changes in $\frac{P}{Y}$.

24   Economists
and the History of Ideas[*]

PAUL A. SAMUELSON

The concern of the economic theorist is the generation of technical knowledge about the satisfaction of the material wants of individuals and society. His efforts are embodied in the hypotheses, concepts, and analytical tools which he fashions to explain economic phenomena. While the history of economics includes the sum total of these efforts, relatively few have proven to be the kind of seminal contribution to pure theory on which future generations have been able to build. Contributions of this magnitude are no less rare in economics than they are in the natural sciences. In the article which follows, "Economists and the History of Ideas," Paul Samuelson suggests that the names of Quesnay, Cournot, and Walras head the list of those who have contributed to pure theory. Perhaps not all historians of economic thought would agree with his choices (which he shares with the late Professor Joseph A. Schumpeter), but there would probably be agreement that the contributions of these three have generally had less impact on the course of human events than did the ideas of those whom we classify as political economists.

"For there are, in the present times, two opinions: not, as in former ages the true and the false; but the outside and the inside."

J. M. Keynes (1921)

"The proper study of Mankind is man." So said the infallible poet. And past experience at these annual gatherings of the sons and daughters of Adam Smith suggests that the popular subject of discussion among economists is not so much economics as economists. Usually the annual presidential address is an exception—an exception that does not always improve upon the rule.

According to our annals, an expiring president of this occult body begins with

Reprinted from Paul A. Samuelson, "Economists and the History of Ideas," *The American Economic Review*, Vol. 52, March 1962, pp. 1–18. Dr. Samuelson is Professor of Economics, Massachusetts Institute of Technology, Cambridge.

[*] Presidential address delivered at the Seventy-Fourth Annual Meeting of the American Economic Association, New York, December 27, 1961.

two choices. He may, on the one hand, give an address that summarizes his lifework or his basic contribution to some important field of scholarship. Thus, my old teacher, Paul H. Douglas, just as he was about to come out of his academic cocoon and emerge as a senatorial butterfly, gave his 1947 address on the Laws of Production, summarizing his decades of work measuring statistical production functions.

I am afraid this choice is not open to me. My own scholarship has covered a great variety of fields. And many of them involve questions like welfare economics and factor-price equalization; turnpike theorems and osculating envelopes; non-substitutability relations in Minkowski-Ricardo-Leontief-Metzler matrices of Mosak-Hicks type; or balanced-budget multipliers under conditions of balanced uncertainty in locally impacted topological spaces and molar equivalences. My friends warn me that such topics are suitable merely for captive audiences in search of a degree—and even then not after dark.

This leaves me still with several possible choices. For one thing, I can always talk about methodology. But although my children think of me as a remnant of "the olden days," to myself I seem just recently to have become emeritus from the category of *enfant terrible;* and the only thing more terrible than the sight of an immature youth is the sight of a half-baked elder statesman. So, that part of methodology which consists of passing on good advice concerning the scholarly pitfalls to avoid and the proper paths to climb, I had better avoid.

But there is another possibility: I could give a sermon tonight on the use and misuse of mathematics in economics. This subject is the only commodity in the world that seems not subject to Gossen's law of diminishing marginal utility. It was only yesterday that three successive presidential addresses touched upon this delicious topic;

and the strongest of those attacks on mathematics led to so resonant a response with this annual audience as to give rise to a standing ovation for the speaker.

Thomas Hardy remarked, "If the Archbishop of Canterbury says that God exists, that is all in the day's business; but if he says God does not exist, there you have something really significant." What a Daniel-come-to-Judgment I would be, if I, the lamb that strayed fustus' and mustus' from the fold, were to testify before God and this company that mathematics had all been a horrible mistake; that right along, it has all been there in Marshall, Books III and V; and that the most one needs for life as an economist is a strong voice, and a compass and ruler.

I wish I could be obliging. Yet even if my lips could be brought to utter the comforting words, like Galileo I would hear myself whispering inside, "But mathematics does indeed help."

I am left then finally with one choice. This evening I shall talk less about technical economics than about economists. Where do we members "of the most agreeable of the moral sciences" fit in the great stream of ideas and ideologies? On this solemn occasion I shall eschew gossip, leaving that to the corridors and lobbies. But I shall unavoidably have to deal with personalities and names if I am to explore the interrelations between professional economic thought and the general history of ideas.

WITHIN THE LOOKING GLASS

As my old teacher Schumpeter used to say, "We are all girls here together." Hence, mine can be the view of an insider looking in, and an insider looking out.

I begin with two books. One is a work of scholarship; the other is, and you will excuse the distinction, merely a textbook. Compare *The History of Economic Anal-*

ysis by Joseph Schumpeter with *The History of Economic Doctrines* of Gide and Rist, which students used to study in my day when preparing for general examinations. I dare say that all the names mentioned by the latter authors can be found in Schumpeter's index. But how different is the emphasis: reading Gide and Rist you would be forgiven for thinking that Robert Owen was almost as important as Robert Malthus; that Fourier and Saint-Simon were much more important than Walras and Pareto. The A. Young in their index is, of course, Arthur Young, not Allyn Young.

Now turn to Schumpeter. Everything is there; no name left out. But now it is Marshall, Walras, Wicksell and such people who steal the stage. Of course Adam Smith is given his due. But what a due! He is rather patronizingly dismissed as a synthesizer who happened to write the right book at the right time: his analytic contributions are certainly minimized.

How can we account for these differences? By the fact that Schumpeter is writing some 40 years after Gide and Rist? Only in the smallest part, I think. By 1913 Wicksell, Wicksteed, and Wieser had done their great work, but only Wieser gets a mention from Gide and Rist—one mention. The treatment of Walras is even more indicative. Walras is indeed mentioned by them; but yet not primarily for his work as a theorist so much as for his views on nationalization of land, free trade, and the State—views which Pareto and Schumpeter thought of as simply silly, like Irving Fisher's food fads and teetotalism. To verify that I am not having sport by picking on a particular set of authors, turn from Gide and Rist to Alexander Gray's brief book, the busy student's friend, to see how Walras fares there. In Gray, Leon Walras is "crowded out" by his father Auguste and is referred to as the "younger Walras," which is a little like referring to Maynard Keynes as the "younger Keynes."

No one can really deny that we have two different sets of standards here. When I began graduate study at Harvard in 1935, Schumpeter rather shocked me by saying in a lecture that of the four greatest economists in the world, three were French. (I had thought the non-Frenchman was English, probably Adam Smith; but after looking into Schumpeter's later book for the purpose of checking, I think my inference must have been incorrect and that he then meant Alfred Marshall rather than Smith.) And who were the Frenchmen?

Of course, one was Leon Walras, whom Schumpeter had no hesitation in calling the greatest economist of all time, by virtue of his first formulation of general equilibrium. Today there can be little doubt that most of the literary and mathematical economic theory appearing in our professional journals is more an offspring of Walras than of anyone else (and I stress the adjective *literary*). The comparison that Lagrange made of Newton is worth repeating in this connection: Assuredly Newton was the greatest man of science, but also the luckiest. For there is but one system of the world and Newton was the one who found it. Similarly, there is but one grand concept of general equilibrium and it was Walras who had the insight (and luck) to find it.

I ought to add that this rating by Schumpeter deserves more credit, coming in 1935, than it would coming today. For it had predictive value as to what was to happen to our professional writings. Back in 1935, Marshall was still propped up on his throne and in large parts of the world even the zealots of the mathematical method tended to look upon Walras merely as the predecessor of the great Pareto. The bourse for professional reputations shows changing price fluctuations: if at one time Alfred Marshall was overpraised and quoted at an inflated price which left little of consumer's surplus to the buyer, he had to pay for this by later being sold at an overdiscount—as will become evident.

Since I ought not to leave you waiting for the other shoes to drop, I hasten to name the other Frenchmen. One is Cournot, a choice that will not seem too surprising. Certainly there is a professional competence about the 1838 Cournot, in the field of partial equilibrium, monopoly and oligopoly, that the modern literature only reattained by 1930. (Think only of the *rediscovery* in *this* century of the concept of marginal revenue!) I do not know that the name of Schumpeter's final giant will seem so obvious a choice. It is François Quesnay, who is deemed to be great on account of his cryptic *Tableau* and anticipation of the circular flow of economic life. Back in the days before Leontief and the resurrection of Karl Marx's Volume 2 model of circular reproduction, I thought this last choice even more far-fetched than I do today.

THE PECKING-ORDER OF ANALYSTS

I need not labor the point farther. Within economics, we economists rate writers of the past in a quite different order than does the outside world. And, as far as economic analysis itself is concerned, the present generation of economists gives a quite different ranking than did earlier generations of economists.[1]

Now I am not really concerned here with the history of pure theory and the changing fortunes of different writers. A critic can rightly argue that Gide and Rist were writing a history of economic *doctrines,* while

Schumpeter was writing a history of economic *analysis;* and hence I ought not to be surprised if there turns out to be a considerable difference in emphasis. Who would want to deny that Cournot, writing in 1838, had an analytical power and freshness that is breathtaking? But who in his right mind could argue that Cournot had been a great force on the history of ideas: what Paris *salon* preoccupied itself with sellers of mineral water? Except through possible indirect influences of his teachings, Cournot's impact on ideology must surely have been negligible.

I quite agree. In many ways the history of a subject's technical analysis is easier to write precisely because it need not involve the determination of social influencings.[2] Tonight we do not want to linger on analytics, except perhaps to draw the obvious moral that, if economists spend more and more of their time on highly technical

[1] There is a great deal of evidence that this is more than the view of the *avant garde* and more than a passing fad. One straw in the wind would be to examine the successive revisions since 1939 of a book that did not begin with any prejudice in favor of economic analytics, Eric Roll, *A History of Economic Thought,* 3d ed., Englewood Cliffs, N.J., 1956.

[2] If the history of science is still generally in a crude form, that is primarily because scholars have just recently begun to take it seriously. In the case of mathematics, there is a most ludicrous ignorance of the true sequence of contributions: if a formula, such as Lagrange's interpolation formula, is attributed by name to a person, the betting is good that small research will show it appeared in earlier writings. What I have in mind here is not the statement that there is nothing new under the sun and all knowledge is a repetition of previously known knowledge: on the contrary, such a statement is the reverse of the truth; mathematical knowledge has been cumulative and, with enough research and luck, we might hope to clean up the false history of the subject. The situation in mathematics is especially simple if one takes the view that the objects of mathematical research are theorems and that most importance attaches to the date of their first rigorous *proof.* Thus, it is meaningful to say that the "strong ergodic theorem" goes back to G. D. Birkhoff in 1931, and that J. v. Neumann deserves the credit for two-person zero-sum game theory. (But if one is also interested in conjecture, heuristics and partial insight, the matter is not so simple. Some modern mathematicians, one feels, will rename Fermat's Last Theorem to Schwartz's Theorem if the first man to prove it happens to be named Schwartz.) In economics, datings are harder: thus I cannot tell you who first disproved "the labor theory of value," much less who originated it.

mathematics and statistics, they must not be surprised if the intelligent man of affairs comes to ignore this part of their activities. It is true that Voltaire and Madame du Châtelet, his great and good friend, wrote profusely on Newton's universal law of gravitation; but this really amounted to vulgarization of that subject, gross vulgarization on the part of Voltaire and neat vulgarization on the part of that gifted lady. While we should not minimize the importance of vulgarization—I mean communication—we must not blink the fact that this is an area where Gresham's Law operates in its most remorseless fashion: vulgar vulgarization drives out subtle, just as strong ideology outsells weak.

The split, between "the inside look" of a subject in terms of the logic and experience of its professional development and its implications for the man-in-the-street or the academician down the campus, is well recognized. No one gets a Nobel Prize for an essay on the relationship of quantum mechanics to free will and God; but one who has already received such a prize will get a better hearing for his random or systematic thoughts on the topic. Nor, these days, do you get appointed to chairs of economics by virtue of your social eloquence; indeed, until academic tenure has come, you are best advised not to write for *Harpers* or the *Manchester Guardian* (to say nothing of the *National Review* or the *New Republic*) lest you be indicted for superficiality.

Good writing itself can be suspect. (I interject that if good literary style is indeed a sin, it is not a sin that is very widespread among our economics brotherhood.) John Stuart Mill tells us in his remarkable autobiography that his father, James Mill, thought poetry was overrated; but that since poetry *was* overrated, young John ought to try his hand at it. I believe it was Yale's Tjalling Koopmans, himself a creative economist blessed with clarity of style, who advanced the austere argument that exceptionally fine writing is a biasing factor which might bring to an argument more attention and credence than it really deserved. There is something to this: but no one should be taken in by the false corollary that the *intrinsic* worth of an argument is enhanced by virtue of its being phrased obscurely. Having said this, one must add grudgingly that, while obscurity may not add to the intrinsic worth of an argument, it has often been a contributory ingredient to fame. How many Marxians have read *Das Kapital*—I mean read it through? Bernard Shaw once claimed that he was the only man in England, including H. M. Hyndman and contemporary Marxian leaders, who had read the book. Shaw himself was observed at the British Museum by Harcourt[3] in the act of reading Marx (in the French translation, of course); so at least part of Shaw's claim may be true. But Shaw was sitting in the British Museum with a copy of *Capital* stretched before him and beside it a copy of the score of *Lohengrin*; one can guess on which he could have earned the higher exam grade.

This brings me to mention one of our members who is far away tonight toiling on a distant shore. I refer of course to J. Kenneth Galbraith and have in mind *The Affluent Society*. To compare this book with *The Theory of the Leisure Class* would be in some of our common rooms, to damn it; in some, to praise it. Gibbon tells us how he found his *Decline and Fall* on every boudoir table soon after its publication. When we economists think how often in recent years people have been asking us, "What do you think of *The Affluent Society*?"—and how embarrassing the question has been to so many of us busy beavers —we can appreciate that this work stands as good a chance as any of being read and remembered twenty years from now.

[3] This gives Sir William Harcourt a second claim to fame, beyond that of his famous one-tenth truth: "We are all socialists now."

Yet always members of a guild have their defenses against the man who ventures away from home. "It was all in Keynes's 1930 *Saturday Evening Post* article, 'Economic Possibilities for Our Grandchildren.'" "Two-thirds of the title came from Tawney's *The Acquisitive Society*." "The point about the need to spend more these days on public rather than private wants was already made eloquently by Alvin Hansen and others; in any case it involves a value judgment not a scientific finding." "Harvard professors may have incomes high enough to satiate them, but most people do not." "So what's the matter with big auto fins? Didn't you ever hear of Freud? And how about Jeremy Bentham's dictum concerning the equality of pleasures, 'Pushpin is as good as poetry?'" "Are commercially created wants different, or less satisfying, or less worthy than natural wants, whatever those may be?" "The book's style is superficially attractive but its message is not profound."

I am afraid people in the boudoir, today or twenty years from now, will not seek the benefit of our professional reactions. Within the body of economics itself, *The Affluent Society* will find a place that is proportionate to the new predictions about economic regularities it may suggest. But whatever the later verdict about the operational meaning of its propositions, we can no more recall it or wipe out half a line of it than we can—by professional exegesis— expunge Henry George's *Progress and Poverty* from the historical record.

POLITICAL ECONOMISTS: OURSELVES TO KNOW

Leaving aside how our own profession rates and ranks the craftsmen of its trade, I now want to close in on the differences between our view of ideologies and *Weltanschauungen* and that of the intelligent man of affairs. Who do *we* think were the great *political* economists as against just great economists?

Adam Smith

Going back no earlier than Adam Smith, we can let Smith stand for the classical tradition. And, in my telescope, he stands on a pinnacle. While I think Smith is underrated as an economic theorist, it must be admitted that his impact as a political economist does not rest upon his having improved upon theories of his friend David Hume; nor upon his having anticipated the various refinements of Malthus, West, Ricardo, Torrens, and John Stuart Mill.

Here is a case where the inside view and the outside view are one. The intelligent man of affairs, and even Macaulay's schoolboy, were profoundly influenced by Smith's attacks on mercantilism and state interference and by his spirited championing of *laissez faire*. To be sure, the amateur never appreciates the nuances of Smith's position: *e.g.*, his skepticism about the businessman's passion for tough competition; his definite role for limited government; his general pragmatism rather than dogmatism.

Still, it is significant that the great critics of the classical tradition generally chose to controvert the *Wealth of Nations* rather than the writings of later members of his school.

David Ricardo

In time Ricardo came to be the whipping boy for continental romantics and historicists. Yet there is not much evidence that they had to read him closely in order to find fault with his abstract methodology. I must confess that I find Ricardo hard to give semester-type grades to. He is par excellence an economist's economist. A sweet man, Ricardo is certainly one of the luckiest that ever lived. And here I have not so much in mind his success in speculating; although he was no slouch in that department, as some facts from his biography illustrate.[4]

Ricardo was lucky in being on the spot when the Napoleonic Wars were causing the value of money to misbehave in the most interesting fashion. He was lucky to

[4] Cut off for marrying outside his faith with a few thousand dollars, within twenty years Ricardo had become a millionaire a few times over, the equivalent in this present day of taxes, higher prices and higher general real incomes, to tens of millions of dollars. The Duke of Wellington may have regarded the battle of Waterloo as "a damned near close-run thing," but David Ricardo urged before the battle that his friend Robert Malthus go the limit in holding British government bonds; and Malthus, a parson with small means and a convex-from-above utility function, lived to reproach himself for not having followed that advice. Retiring young from business to devote himself to leisure, study, politics, and being a gentleman, Ricardo astutely realized that his numerous children were not chips off the old block in financial acumen; so, and this is purely my conjecture, being convinced by his studies that land rent tends to rise as capital and labor progressively grow, Ricardo arranged to buy self-sufficient gentry estates for his offspring, succeeding so well in his purpose as to keep his descendants out of shirtsleeves until the end of the century and, at the same time, conferring upon them the bonus of being absorbed into county society. At the urging of his friends, Ricardo indulged in conspicuous consumption by buying his way into Parliament. (He did this by invoking the later doctrine of "opportunity cost": *i.e.*, he lent £20,000 interest-free to an Irish holder of a rotten borough, one which Ricardo never bothered to visit.)

Ricardo's parliamentary career was something of an anticlimax. He was not a gripping speaker, and the build-up of his reputation was a grave handicap. It is interesting that Ricardo was a genuinely disinterested man and generally favored measures that were against the interest of landlords. When once accused of having a special interest in some proposal, he candidly replied that his interests were so diverse that he himself could not tell on which side the balance of his Hicksian income effects would fall, thus showing himself to be a master of *quadratic* programming of the type needed for optimal Markowitz portfolio balancing; and little wonder, since in 1817 Ricardo's comparative cost theory had involved him in linear programming. One feels he was a natural at trading in, and arbitraging, Lagrangean multipliers and other dual-price variables. See Volume 10 of the Sraffa edition of Ricardo's work for most of the facts from which this account has been fabricated.

have James Mill as taskmaster and press agent. He was lucky in having been deprived of higher education, so that his resulting written expositions had the clumsiness necessary to give that ingredient of obscurity so conducive to a reputation for great profundity. Finally, and I hope it comes as no anticlimax, Ricardo was lucky in being profound.

Still, when I once heard George J. Stigler say that Malthus was the most overrated of economists, I heard myself replying: "That's funny. I think David Ricardo is the most overrated of economists." Probably this conversation tells more about Stigler and me than about Ricardo and Malthus. What I had in mind was this: Ricardo was a keen reasoner and almost always comes out to be logical in the end, if you accept his implicit and explicit definitions and assumptions. But he makes unnecessarily rough weather of the matters he deals with, and the reader is inclined to think him miraculous for being able to get out of the holes he has dug for himself by his mode of attack and exposition. Analytically, his theory of rent is excellent but not clearly better than or earlier than the contemporaneous theories of rent of Sir Edward West and Malthus. Ricardo did have a rigorously handled general equilibrium model of primitive type; but its dynamics merely elaborate on what is already in the population theory of Malthus and Smith, and ought not today to be regarded as very "magnificent."

His greatest tour de force was the theory of comparative advantage; and though it would be simply irrelevant to point out that Isaac Gervaise had developed similar notions in the preceding century, one has to take into account that Colonel Torrens, a mere mortal, had also developed pretty much the same analysis at pretty much the same time. Moreover, in most of the debates that Ricardo's work gave rise to, the points of his critics were well taken, not so much in proving that Ricardo's reasoning was wrong in terms of its assumptions, as in pointing out that his conclusions were apt to be misunderstood and were of limited significance. Instead of regarding it as a scandal that so much ink has had to be spilt over Ricardo's flirtations and retreats from a labor theory of value, his admirers think this makes him a seminal thinker.[5] In short, the notion of Keynes that "Ricardo's mind was the greatest that ever addressed itself to economics" does not agree with my assessment of his high I.Q. or creativeness in relation to that of other economists.

Ricardo's name was certainly used as a rallying cry for the school that favored freer trade in England. But Smith had already made the needed points; if exaggeration is what was needed, Herbert Spencers and Bastiats can usually be found who are unencumbered by the subtleties of refined economic analysis. Moreover, detailed researchers will more and more reveal that the Ricardian School provided the background for early Victorian thinking but did not, in a detailed fashion satisfactory to the historian of direct political development, have important influences upon such legislative events as the repeal of the Corn Laws. Indeed, Ricardo was subtle enough to muck up the simple-minded case for harmonious free trade.

Jeremy Bentham, a friend of James Mill and Ricardo, was a character who would have been unbelievable if he had appeared in a book. (He once seriously asked James Mill for his eldest son. James thought that an excessive demand on friendship, but did lease him John to help clean out the Augean stables of Bentham manuscripts; this was but one of the feats of Hercules that John accomplished with distinction and at incredibly early ages.)

Bentham's influence on modern law and institutions has always been recognized by historians as having been great: the nineteenth century where legislation is concerned is truly Bentham's shadow writ large, as Dicey has said. Crane Brinton once quipped: "The New Deal had a good deal of old Bentham in it."[6] And I have dared to suggest that the logic of Bentham's position would in later times have gone beyond his fortuitous individualism, so that his thought is really congenial to that of Fabians like Sidney Webb. Bentham, though not an economist's economist nor even primarily an economist, had I am sure an influence far greater than that of Ricardo.

Have I now not proved too much? Why then has Ricardo had the good press with posterity if my strictures are at all near the mark? I think the answer depends upon a different kind of luck. David Ricardo happens to be the darling both of the liberal economists who followed in his direct line and of the Marxian critics of capitalism. Like me, you may not agree with Ricardo's famous letter to Trower which says, "Political economy . . . should rather be called an enquiry into the laws which determine the division of the produce of industry amongst the classes who concur in its formation." But you can perceive how Ricardo's laconic and unsparing remarks about distribution would stimulate the so-called Ricardian socialists who regarded property incomes as exploitation of labor. And once Karl Marx took him up as an object of worthy study, Ricardo was, so to

---

[5] Soo my two papers on Ricardian systems, which elaborate on my views and give a physiocratic interpretation, "A Modern Treatment of the Ricardian Economy," *Quart. Jour. Econ.*, I, Feb. 1959, *73*, 1–55, II, May 1959, *73*, 217–31; also my paper on related Marxian models, "Wages and Interest: A Modern Dissection of Marxian Economic Models," *Am. Econ. Rev.*, Dec. 1961, *47*, 884–912.

[6] C. C. Brinton, *Ideas of Men: The Story of Western Thought*, London 1951, p. 392. Incidentally, Brinton's index has between Rhodes, Cecil and Richards, I. A. no Ricardo, David.

speak, in on both sides of the street. Having Piero Sraffa as an editor merely capped Ricardo's good luck.

John Stuart Mill

I pass by Nassau Senior and the other classical writers to mention Mill briefly. Mill was modest; Marshall was not. The world takes people too much at their word. The result is that Marshall's claims to analytical originality are received too seriously; and Mill's forging of the general-equilibrium concept of demand and supply schedules, even before the 1838 date of Cournot's definitive partial-equilibrium formulation, is ignored by all but the true gourmets of economic theory, who recognize it as an analytical contribution of the first magnitude.

John Stuart Mill, son of a dogmatic father, was himself eclectic and had an engaging ability to change his mind when new facts or arguments became available or merely from rethinking old attitudes.[7] It

[7] Sweden's Gustav Cassel, whom the public regarded as about the world's leading economist in the 1920's and who might have become a truly outstanding scholar if his temperament had been different, is shown by the following story to be a good opposite to Mill. H. C. Sonne, the distinguished merchant banker and chairman of the National Planning Association, has told how Cassel visited at Sonne's family home in Denmark in the days around the First World War. A guest happened to mention that some scholar had just made a fresh study of the relationship between the price level and gold supply and had come up with conclusions strongly at variance with the famous Cassel thesis. When asked what he intended to do about it, Cassel replied as follows. "I have a son-in-law whom I have put through Divinity School at some considerable expense. Now that he has graduated and qualified for his diploma, he comes to me and says that he has lost his faith and asks what to do. My advice to him was simple: 'Just carry on as if nothing had happened.'"

Relevant too is a conversation I had last month in London after I had given the Stamp Memorial Lecture in the University of London for 1961. In that lecture I discussed, among other things, some of the problems of economic forecasting and stressed the need for scientific validation and the desirability of each forecaster's going back ruthlessly to review *ex post* his *ex ante* predic-

is almost fatal to be flexible, eclectic, and prolific if you want your name to go down in the history books: get known for one idea, however farfetched it may be—such as that the rate of interest has to be zero in the stationary state or that land is the source of all value—and you are sure to get at least a paragraph in the history books for it. Also, Mill had what Nietzsche once referred to as an offensively clear style.

Yet so great was Mill as a thinker and reflector that he was able to overcome these handicaps. His views on liberty will, even in the post-Freud world, never go out of date and can perhaps be summarized in the words of Mrs. Pat Campbell, Bernard Shaw's pen-mistress: People should be allowed to do anything they like—provided only they don't scare the horses in the street.

Mill is truly a transitional figure. Shaw shows this in one of his wittiest plays, *You Never Can Tell.* A typical Shavian New Woman returns from the West Indies after an absence of some 20 years to find that all her revolutionary Millian notions have become old-hat, superseded by new Fabian notions. The same conflict between the eighteenth and twentieth century went on in Mill's own mind: it was father James against friend Harriet with John advancing two steps and going back one. It is ironical that evolutionary socialism in England and elsewhere finds itself today backing up from its post-Benthamite insistence on nationalization of the means of production to something like the society dimly envisaged by Mill. No wonder Karl Marx hated Mill and denounced him as a vulgar bourgeois economist. Marx could recognize the enemy when he saw him. (Curiously, the well-read Mill either never heard of

tions. "A great mistake," I was told by one of the best forecasters in English academic life. "It is fatal ever to read what you have earlier written. It breaks your nerve as a forecaster." His lips were smiling but his eyes looked serious.

Marx or never thought him worth mentioning—this despite Mill's interest in the Revolution of 1848, the *Communist Manifesto* by Marx and Engels of that date, and Mill's survival beyond the 1867 date of *Capital* Vol. 1.)[8]

Karl Marx

From the viewpoint of pure economic theory, Karl Marx can be regarded as a minor post-Ricardian. Unknowingly I once delighted a southern university audience: my description of Marx as a not uninteresting precursor (in Volume 2 of *Capital*) of Leontief's input-output analysis of circular interdependence apparently had infuriated the local village Marxist. Also, a case can be made out that Marx independently developed certain vague apprehensions of underconsumptionist arguments like those of the *General Theory*; but on my report card no one earns too high a grade for such a performance, since almost everyone who is born into this world alive experiences at some time vague intimations that there is a hole somewhere in the circular flow of purchasing power and production. This seems to come on the same chromosome as the gene that makes people believe in Say's Law; and Marx's bitter criticisms of Rodbertus for being an underconsumptionist shows us that he is no exception.

As long as I am being big about admitting small merits in Marx, I might mention a couple of technical suggestions he made about business cycles that are not without some interest: Marx did formulate a vague notion of 10-year replacement cycles in textile equipment as the determinant of cyclical periodicity—which is an anticipation of various modern "echo" theories. He also somewhere mentioned the possibility of some kind of harmonic analysis of economic cycles by mathematics, which with much charity can be construed as pointing

toward modern periodogram analysis and Yule-Frisch stochastic dynamics. A much more important insight involved the tying up of technological change and capital accumulation with business cycles, which pointed ahead to the work of Tugan-Baranowsky (himself a Marxian), Spiethoff, Schumpeter, Robertson, Cassel, Wicksell, and Hansen.

What can be gold in the field of fluctuations can be dirt in the context of pure economic theory. Marx claimed in Volume 1 that there was some interesting economics involved in a labor theory of value and some believe his greatest fame in pure economics lies in his attempted analysis of "surplus value." Although he promised to clear up the contradiction between "price" and "value" in later volumes, neither he nor Engels ever made good this claim. On this topic the goodhumored and fair criticisms of Wicksteed and Böhm-Bawerk have never been successfully rebutted: the contradictions and muddles in Marx's mind must not be confused with the contradictions and muddles in the real world.

Marx, like any man of keen intellect, liked a good problem; but he did not labor over a labor theory of value in order to give us moderns scope to use matrix theory on the "transformation" problem. He wanted to have a theory of exploitation, and a basis for his prediction that capitalism would in some sense impoverish the workers and pave the way for revolution into a new stage of society. As the optimism of the American economist Henry Carey shows, a labor theory of value when combined with technological change is, on all but the most extreme assumptions, going to lead to a great increase in real wages and standards of living. So the element of exploitation had to be worked hard. Here Marx might have emphasized the monopoly elements of distribution: how wicked capitalists, possessed of the nonlabor tools *that are essential* to high production, allegedly gang up on the workers and make

---

[8] *Cf.* A. L. Harris, *Economics and Social Reforms,* New York 1958.

them work for a minimum. Or, were it not for his amazing hatred toward Malthus and his theory of population, Marx might have kept wages dismal by virtue of biological conditions of labor supply. The monopoly explanation he did not use, perhaps because he wanted to let capitalism choose its own weapons and assume ruthless competition, and still be able to show it up. Marx tried to demonstrate the same dramatic minimum character of real wages by means of his concept of the "reserve army of the unemployed."

Here is the real Achilles' heel of the Marxian theory of distribution and its implied prophecies of immiserization of the working classes. Under perfect competition, technical change will raise real wages unless the changes are so labor-saving as to raise the rate of maintainable profit immensely; Joan Robinson and others have pointed out how contradictory is Marx's notion that both profit rates and real wages can fall once Marx jettisons Ricardo's emphasis on the scarcity of land and the law of diminishing returns. Marx simply has no *statical* theory of the reserve army. If an appeal is made to a vague dynamic theory of technological displacement or recruitment from the country, close analysis will suggest that Marx (like Mill) was a very bad econometrician of his times, not realizing how much real wages in Western Europe had been raised by new techniques and equipment; and he was a bad theorist because his kind of model would almost certainly lead to shifts in schedules that would raise labor's wages tremendously, in a way more consistent with the 1848 *Communist Manifesto's* paeans of praise for the capitalistic system than with his elaborated writings.[9]

In brief, technical change was gold in

[9] If migration from the country kept wages down to a city minimum, then the average wage and living standard of country-*cum*-city would be raised in accordance with the optimization desired by a technocrat—unless, again, Malthusianism is admitted back into the rural hovel.

giving Marx cyclical insights, and dirt in giving him secular insights or an understanding of evolving equilibrium states. I should warn you that this is my opinion, and that I have always been surprised that I should be a virtual monopolist with respect to this vital analysis.

So far I have been talking about Marx as an economist. And I have been doing my best, subject to truth, to find some merit in him. (You may recall Emerson's neighbor in Concord: when he died the minister tried to find something to say at the funeral eulogy and ended up with, "Well, he was good at laying fires.") Even this represents a resurrection of Marx's reputation. Keynes, for example, was much more typical of our professional attitudes toward Marxism when he dismissed it all as "turbid" nonsense. (In view of the tendency of the radical right—for whom all Chinese look alike —to equate Keynesianism with Marxism, this ironical fact is worth nothing; and also its converse, since there is nothing communists deplore more than the notion that capitalism can be kept breathing healthily by the Keynesian palliatives of fiscal and monetary policy.)

Technical economics has little to do with Karl Marx's important role in the history of human thought. It is true that he and his followers felt that their brand of socialism differed from the sentimental brands of the past in that Marxist socialism was scientifically based and, therefore, had about it an inevitability and a special correctness. I need not labor the point before this group that the "science" involved was not that body of information about commercial and productive activity and those methods of analyzing the behavior relations which *we* would call economics. Political economy in our sense of the word was the mere cap of Karl Marx's iceberg. *Marx's bold economic or materialistic theory of history, his political theories of the class struggle, his transmutations of Hegelian philosophy* have an importance for the historian of "ideas" that far transcends his façade of economics.

Finally, one must never make the fatal mistake in the history of ideas of requiring of a notion that it be "true." For that discipline, the slogan must be, "The customer is always right." Its objects are what men have *believed;* and if truth has been left out, so much the worse for truth, except for the curiously-undifficult task of explaining why truth does not sell more successfully than anything else. Marx has certainly had more customers than any other one aspiring economist. A billion people think his ideas are important; and for the historian of thought that fact makes them important, in the same way that he would have to regard as diminished in importance the subject of Christianity, were it conceivable that it had been the region merely of a transitory small group who once occupied the present country of Jordan or the state of New Mexico.

Alfred Marshall

What killed Mill for economists was not the socialism that killed it for Shaw's no-longer-New Woman. The marginalist school of Jevons-Walras-Menger perpetrated the murder. The roster of neoclassical economists would include the names of Böhm-Bawerk from Austria, J. B. Clark from the United States, Pareto from Italy, Wicksteed from England, and Wicksell from Sweden. But, for all that I have said earlier about his overvaluation in the market for reputations, few will doubt that Alfred Marshall of Cambridge is the prototype as *political economist* for this group. Marshall may now be old hat, but in his day he was some headpiece.

Marshall had strong social sympathies. At the same time he realized the harms that precipitate reform may bring. He was the prophet of moderation. If you graft Keynesian models of income determination on his thought and update his Victorianisms, you come close to the median member of this Association. His pupils filled, Foxwell could say by 1888, half the chairs of political economy in the United Kingdom; his influence permeated the other half and, methodologically speaking, today we are all Marshallians in the same sense that we are all higher primates.

But what has been Marshall's role in the history of ideas, the panorama of human thought? Never has he had one-hundredth the notice of, say, Henry George. I remember talking to the aged Frank Taussig at a Harvard Society of Fellows dinner before the war. Taussig quoted in despair a recent remark of John Dewey that Henry George was the greatest economist America had ever produced. George was the whipping boy for the economists just before my time; but within my time as a high school student in the Middle West, you could still find vestigial single-taxers, the old principal of my high school being one and my civics teacher another. George was not original in attacking incomes that come from land; as Foxwell said long ago, nationalizers of land we have always with us. This is understandable from the Hume-Ricardo recognition of rent as a price-determined (rather than price-determining) surplus to a factor in inelastic supply; but, as I have recorded elsewhere, my implicit belief that George gave a good statement of Ricardian rent theory will not stand up after a search through *Progress and Poverty* for suitable quotations to put in an anthology. While the single-tax movement is recognizable today as being adverse to socialism, Henry George's attack on the inequality of property ownership in land was influential in turning many people toward socialism: thus Shaw tells us he became a socialist after hearing Henry George speak in London.[10]

[10] Later Shaw went successively from Marxism to Jevonsism with a Fabian twist. Philip Wicksteed's conversion of Shaw away from Marxism is one of the most amusing and incredible incidents in the history of thought: for once a ra-

Let us leave aside impact on the *hoi polloi*. What was Marshall's influence over his long life on the educated man of affairs? For years I looked for every trace I could find in books to show that someone other than a professional economist or student had read Marshall. I realize Marshall himself thought he was writing for the businessman; but anyone who looks at the *Principles* will realize that no businessmen in good Queen Victoria's time or since would be likely to find it attractive. (Actually Marshall's literary style is excellent, his graphs are in footnotes, and his rather awkward mathematics is buried in special notes at the end; but all this was to no avail.) I was able to come up essentially with only two bits of evidence, one negative and one positive. Pollock in his letters to Justice Holmes urged him to read Marshall; Holmes, who was a man of the most catholic interests, replied that he had tried it and it was not the dish for him. On the positive side, C.C.N.Y.'s great philosopher, Morris Cohen, reported somewhere that his inclination to be an eclectic in philosophy had received inspiration from Alfred Marshall's eclecticism in economics.

To be sure, Marshall taught at a leading world institution where half the English upper classes received their instruction. But actually he taught at Cambridge little more than 20 years, not very much longer say, than, I have taught at M.I.T. Sixty was a generous number for those who attended his popular lectures, and that was

tional argument changed, or seemed to change, someone's mind.

It must have been on that same trip to England that Henry George debated Alfred Marshall in Oxford: little David beat Goliath, if we can believe the record; in part perhaps because Marshall was a home-boy, and the well-to-do undergraduates of those days started out hostile to George; there is also the fact gleaned from Henry George's biography that he slept miserably on that trip and the night before the debate. Playing the parlor game of Charles Lamb and William Hazlitt as to which characters in history one would like to meet, I would plunk for being present when Alfred Marshall debated Henry George.

the beginning attendance not the final. As I know from personal conversations with Alfred North Whitehead, Marshall's contemporaries at Cambridge did not like him as a man ("He was a popish man who treated Mary Marshall very badly." "A second class mind?"); and one gets the impression from autobiographies of such contemporaries as J. J. Thomson, the discoverer of the electron and Nobel Prize winner, that they had no great opinion of the economics being offered at that time in Cambridge.

WE HAPPY FEW

If then Marshall and neoclassical writers have had influence upon the affairs of men, and I think they have had pronounced influence, we must regard these influencings as being indirect rather than direct.

For a long time John Maynard Keynes was known for one famous quotation, the casual remark: "In the long run we are all dead." Now that Keynes himself is dead, he is best known for a different quotation:

> . . . the ideas of economists and political philosophers, both when they are right and when they are wrong, are more powerful than is commonly understood. Indeed the world is ruled by little else. Practical men, who believe themselves to be quite exempt from any intellectual influences, are usually the slaves of some defunct economist. Madmen in authority, who hear voices in the air, are distilling their frenzy from some academic scribbler of a few years back. I am sure that the power of vested interests is vastly exaggerated compared with the gradual encroachment of ideas. Not, indeed, immediately, but after a certain interval; for in the field of economic and political philosophy there are not many who are influenced by new theories after they are twenty-five or thirty years of age, so that the ideas which civil servants and politicians and even agitators apply to current events are not likely to be the newest. But, soon or late, it is ideas, not vested interests, which are dangerous for good or evil.

This is fine writing. And no doubt it is flattering to our egos. But is it really true?

Keynes did not specify what academic scribblers he had in mind, and I am not sure how easy it would have been for him to do so. (Thus, when we see a politician ·favoring protective tariffs or a balanced budget, do we have to look for any profound analysis from some earlier thinker or can we not simply reflect that most people generate such notions almost unthinkingly? Yet, even if that is so, what are we to conclude in the case where we observe a politician favoring free trade or deficit-financing? The issue is certainly not a simple one.)

The leaders of this world may seem to be led around through the nose by their economist advisers. But who is pulling and who is pushing? And note this: he who picks his doctor from an array of competing doctors is in a real sense his own doctor. The Prince often gets to hear what he wants to hear.

Where does that leave us then as economists? It leaves us where we ought to be. Our map of the world differs from that of the layman. Perhaps our map will never be a best seller. But a discipline like economics has a logic and validity of its own. We believe in our map because we cannot help doing so. In Frank Ramsey's beautiful quotation from William Blake:

> "Truth can never be told so as to be understood and not be believed."

Ours is an uncertain truth and economic scholars are humble about its precision—but our humbleness is bluilt out of knowledge, not out of ignorance.

Not for us is the limelight and the applause. But that doesn't mean the game is not worth the candle or that we do not in the end win the game. In the long run, the economic scholar works for the only coin worth having—our own applause.[11]

---

[11] Lest I be misunderstood, I elaborate. This is not a plea for "Art for its own sake," "Logical elegance for the sake of elegance." It is not a plea for leaving the real-world problems of political economy to noneconomists. It is not a plea for short-run popularity with members of a narrow in-group. Rather it is a plea for calling shots as they really appear to be (on reflection and after weighing all evidences), even when this means losing popularity with the great audience of men and running against "the spirit of the times."

25   The Influence
of Events and Policies
on Economic Theory
GEORGE J. STIGLER

What hypotheses can be constructed to explain the nature and content of the economic theories of the past and present? Many scholars are impressed with the merits of the "environmental theory." Broadly interpreted, the "environment" of a theory may be conceived of as including the events that preceded or occurred contemporaneously with its formulation, the *Weltanschauung* or philosophical outlook embodied in its methodology, the political framework which nurtured it, and even the developments which took place in related disciplines. The evidence supporting the environmental theory is, however, less than convincing to George Stigler, who has undertaken, in "The Influence of Events and Policies on Economic Theory" to review and evaluate the claims which have been advanced for it.

The full range of subjects and problems which have attracted economists' attention throughout our history has been both extraordinarily wide and tolerably stable. The great multitude of modern economists do not work on a broader terrain than did Adam Smith and his sprinkling of contemporaries. True, some minor areas have been yielded up to younger sciences; for example, the economics of primitive peoples is now handled or mishandled by anthropologists. True, some minor additions have been made to our present-day agenda; for example, certain types of statistical problems are generally treated only by economists. But in the broad, the boundaries of the discipline have not varied much.

Within these wide-flung boundaries, however, the problems which arouse active interest and the variables which are deemed most significant have fluctuated greatly over time. In 1830, no general work in economics would omit a discussion of population, and in 1930, hardly any gen-

Reprinted from George J. Stigler, "The Influence of Events and Policies on Economic Theory," from *The American Economic Review,* May 1960, pp. 36–45. Dr. Stigler is Professor of Economics at the School of Business, University of Chicago.

eral work said anything about population. The problem of economic growth was at the forefront of discussion in 1825, it was almost ignored in 1900, and today it is again *haute mode*. And the question which has been posed to me is: To what extent have the areas of active work and the lines of attack been influenced by contemporary economic events and economic policies?

To be sane one must recognize at least a portion of the physical and social world in which he lives; so the sane economic theories have always had at least a possible connection with the world in which they were written. It is not surprising, therefore, that many historians have explained and even justified past economic theories by the special circumstances of the time and place in which they were written.

An example both contemporary and extreme is afforded by W. Stark, who has said that "modern economics immediately appears as a simple product of historical development, as a mirroring of the socio-economic reality within which it took its origin, not unlike the various theories which have preceded it." [1] Literally read, Stark seems to assert even that the growth of mechanization between 1817 and 1820 forced Ricardo to qualify the labor theory of value published in the former year. [2]

No such detailed reconciliation of economic theories with their environments, however, is even remotely tenable. When two Englishmen, named Mill and Cairnes, found themselves on opposite sides with respect to the validity of the wages-fund doctrine, both theories could not be mirroring the same reality. If their mirrors were turned to different realities, the environmental explanation of economic theories becomes too flexible to be useful.

Wesley C. Mitchell presented the same general viewpoint in a much more qualified version:

> The passing on of ideas from one to another and the development of these ideas by successive generations as an intellectual stunt has been in economics a secondary rather than a primary factor. The thing which has most of all stimulated the minds of successive generations of economists has been to endeavor to contribute to the understanding of the problems with which their generation as a whole was concerned. . . .

> These economic problems were caused primarily by changes in the economic life of the people, changes that were coming about through a cumulative process. [3]

Thus Mitchell finds the leitmotiv of Smith in the emergence of individualism, of Ricardo in the problems raised by the Napoleonic Wars, of Marx in the growth of an urban proletariat, etc.

That major economic problems sometimes become matters of paramount interest to economists is not debatable. But this is not enough to make the environmental theory useful; i.e., to make it more than a platitude. To be useful in explaining the subject matter of economics, the environmental theory must be given a more specific content. The theory could be developed in various directions. Let me discuss three.

First, it could be asserted that every truly major economic development leaves its imprint on economic theory, at least in the choice of subject matter of the theory and possibly in its major empirical hypotheses. Although some historians approach this view (e.g., Leo Rogin in a special policy oriented version), it seems to me clearly untenable. At the height of the industrial revolution, when great technological advances were crowding hard upon one another, the main tradition of classical economics treated the state of the arts as a datum. The arts were held to be subject to sporadic improvements, but not of a magni-

[1] *The History of Economics* (New York, 1944), p. 2.
[2] *Ibid.*, p. 37. Actually Ricardo had the same value theory at both dates and also in 1819.
[3] *Lecture Notes on Types of Economic Theory* (New York, 1949), pp. 45–46.

tude comparable to the force of diminishing returns in agriculture. Here, then, the almost overwhelming characteristic of economic life was excluded from economic theory. Again, perhaps the second most influential development (or a special form of the first) in economic life in the nineteenth century was the improvement of transportation, which never played a strategic and usually not even an explicit, role in economic theory.

Second, it could be maintained that even though not all major social and economic developments left their imprint on economic theory, every important element of economic theory sprang from this source. And this, too, would be untenable. The prolific analyses of utility theory from 1870 to 1915 and from 1932 on reflect no detectable environmental influence. The doctrine of noncompeting groups emerged centuries after it would have been most realistic. The economic system did not become linear about 1946. Of course, after the event one can always find something in the environment—especially if we include the intellectual environment—that may be related to the development in economic theory, but this is an exercise in erudition, not in explanation.

At this point we may pause to observe that a basic distinction must be drawn between the period in which a field of study is dominated by controversies over policy (applications) and the period in which it is a discipline pursued by professional scholars. In the age of mercantilism, all economics was oriented toward contemporary problems and institutions. Some of the writers analyzed problems more deeply than the immediate policy needs dictated, but their work was highly personal and mostly noncumulative. Beginning with the Physiocrats, economics began to be cultivated increasingly by scholars, and scholarly values such as consistency, generality, precision, and elegance began to be introduced.

In the period of the classical economics, this disciplinary aspect of economic study became increasingly more prominent. Hume, Smith, Malthus, Senior, Whately, Longfield, and Cournot all had scholarly, and usually academic, orientations towards economics, and after 1870 this orientation became, not merely dominant, but well-nigh exclusive.

Thus it is a sign of the maturity of a discipline that its main problems are not drawn from immediate, changing events. A genuine and persistent separation of scientific study from the real world leads to sterility, but an immediate and sensitive response to current events stultifies the deepening and widening of analytical principles and techniques. The leading theoretical chemists are not working on detergents or headache remedies and the leading economic theorists need not be concerned with urban renewal or oil embargoes.

There remains a third interpretation of the environmental theory: that economic problems and developments can be classified into groups which impinge very differently upon economics. This seems to me both correct and potentially fruitful, and I shall attempt a tentative classification of economic problems from this viewpoint.

The vast majority of all current—I shall call them popular—social economic problems are routine from the viewpoint of economic theory. This excise or that central banking policy, this farm subsidy or that housing program, this stock pile or that form of wage bargain—all are essentially routine in their demands on the theory. The facts of the case may vary, or the juxtaposition of two policies may offer complications, but fundamentally no new demands are put on the theory.

This is not to say that the theory is necessarily adequate to the demands one would like to put on it. The theory may have deficiencies in logic, or be ambiguous with respect to significantly different outcomes, or its predictions may even be contradicted in certain respects by events. But imperfection is as inevitable in theory as it is in man, and one does not need new incidents to document it.

A second class consists of events of major economic significance: the colonization of a continent; major wars; basic technological advances such as the railroad; and great depressions. It is more remarkable that most of these events leave economic theory essentially unaffected. Since Ricardo's time, wars have had little effect upon the basic theory, although many illustrious economists (among them Edgeworth, Pigou, and Wicksell) have been stimulated to write about the economics of war. The current popularity of the economic theory of development has not yielded important theoretical results. It may be (though I somewhat doubt it) that Keynes's *General Theory* was the product of the Great Depression, but if so it is one of the very few great events that have affected the basic theory.

One reason for the impotence of great events is that from the viewpoint of economic theory they are also usually routine. A war may ravage a continent or destroy a generation without posing new theoretical questions. And even the theoretically challenging catastrophes are not likely to be influential, for a simple reason: the great event is a poor stimulus to anything except a basic reconstruction of the science. Minor changes in a theory hardly seem appropriate—let alone adequate—to great new problems, and extensive reconstructions of economic theory are usually the result, not of a frontal assault on the traditional theory, but of the systematic elaboration of a single basic and pervasive idea which previously had been ignored or given only *ad hoc* recognition.

And this suggests the third and theoretically influential type of economic problem: that which is pervasive. It is not enough that a problem be of vast importance, if that importance is momentary; it is not

enough that the problem be persistent, if it is local to a particular market. A theory is a statement of general relationships: a theory of unique events is a contradiction in terms, and a theory of local events is simply uninteresting from the scientific viewpoint. The most pervasive problem of economic life is of course that of value, and this is why the routine and undramatic problem of value has elicited the supreme efforts of the greatest theorists.

On this view, one can predict that certain problems will affect economic theory and others will not. The problem of personal income distribution will eventually receive much theoretical attention, since it is a problem of all economies and all times. On the other hand, the economic problems of cold wars will not influence economic theory unless such wars become general and persistent—and this will probably not happen because cold wars seem intrinsically unstable situations.

Since neither popular economic problems nor heroic events influence much the development of economic theory—and please notice that I distinguish economic theory from discussion by economists, and deal only with the former—do theoretical changes come only from, as Mitchell puts it, "the development of these ideas by successive generations"?

My answer is, proximately, yes. The dominant influence upon the working range of economic theorists is the set of internal values and pressures of the discipline. The subjects for study are posed by the unfolding course of scientific developments. With the introduction of mathematical technique it became inevitable that there be a theory of general equilibrium. The marginal utility theory must sooner or later—the great surprise is that it took two decades—lead to the general marginal productivity theory. The untidiness in the theory of the firm was bound to attract a Sraffa and a Viner.

This is not to say that the environment

is without influence, for every great economist injects some portion of it into the developing theoretical corpus. This element of realism, however, need have no simple or direct connection with the contemporary scene. Menger, Jevons and Walras took the most pedestrian, even vulgar, "fact" of diminishing marginal utility of objects to man as their element of realism, and what it reconstructed a large part of the theory of value. Marshall took an equally pedestrian fact—that it takes time to do things thoroughly—and constructed his theory of short- and long-run normal prices.

Whether a fact or development is significant depends primarily on its relevance to current economic theory. There is no intrinsic basis for saying that the fact (1) people spend a lesser fraction of their income on food as they become richer is less important than the fact (2) people save about the same share of their income as they become richer. Yet Engel's law (now a century old) had no effects on economic theory for a long time, and no direct influence to this day, but Kuznets' finding has contributed substantially to the excitement and controversy over the consumption function. Kuznets' fact was an ostensible contradiction of the ruling theory whereas Engel's fact was and is outside the domain of the ruling theory.

Every major development in economic theory in the last hundred years, I believe, could have come much earlier if appropriate environmental conditions were all that was needed. Even Keynes's *General Theory* could have found an evident empirical basis in the post-Napoleonic period or the 1870's or the 1890's. Perhaps this amounts only to saying—what is surely true and almost tautological—that the elements of an economic system which economists believe to be basic have been present for a long time. The nature of economic systems has changed relatively little since Smith's time.

Thus I assign a minor, and even an accidental, role to the contemporary economic environment in the development of economic theory since it has become a professional discipline. Even where the original environmental stimulus to a particular analytical development is fairly clear, as in Ricardo's theory of rent, the profession soon appropriates the problem and reformulates it in a manner that becomes increasingly remote from current events, until finally its origin bears no recognizable relationship to its nature or uses.

The channel through which economic events are reaching economic theorists is undergoing change. Specialization has created the empirical research economist, who collects and systematizes the (some) facts of economic life. He is becoming substantially the only source of information for the specialized theorists: the only things the theoretical economist knows about economic life are those things the empirical economist tells him. All other sources (the theorist must increasingly assume) are unreliable or unrepresentative—in short, unscientific.

It does not follow that the theorist is the slave of the empirical economist, for the latter usually collects data recommended by the ruling theories. The national income accounts, for example, are a creature of economic theory. But the empirical economist also collects many facts not dictated by the theory, some because of his own intuitions (be they theoretical, propagandistic, or what), some because policy enforcement makes the data available.

Whether this specialization will increase the sensitivity of theory to events is an open question. The statistical work of Gardiner Means on administered prices has had an extensive effect on theoretical literature,[4] but it can hardly be said (and in-

---

[4] Much of this work was also done earlier by Frederick Mills, however, without a comparable effect—partly because Mills did not use it as a springboard for extreme policy insinuations.

deed Means expressly desires) that the phenomena he found were new phenomena. The work of John Kendrick and others will undoubtedly influence the theorizing on technical progress, but again the underlying phenomena are not new. My guess is that most empirical research economists will possess the professional values, and hence will seek pervasive and stable empirical uniformities rather than seek to detect quickly any new economic phenomena. If so, the specialization will not affect greatly the relationship between theory and contemporary events.

Public policy is no doubt a part of the environment broadly construed, but it is a separable part. Policies and policy proposals are not closely geared to events. Policies designed to lessen income inequality emerged during a period when market forces were making substantial contributions to this end, and a similar relationship between policy and events is found in hours of labor, provision of education, the development of domestic manufacturing, etc. Here policy rides on the wave of events, although often it makes impudent claims to leadership. Often, too, policies are initiated in one country to deal with problems which are more serious in other countries: American antitrust policy is an example.

Nor should we forget that few policies, even successful policies, change the basic nature of the economy. The fact that our country had a protective tariff before 1932, but England did not, was not enough to make the basic theories of economics less applicable to one of the countries. Reformers and deformers of economic life dare not take the Olympian stance of economic theory, but neither dare economic theory become academic journalism with its excitement over fundamentally unimportant changes.

The classical problems of public policy have always provided much of the standard fare of economic theory: tariffs and monetary standards; monopoly; control of business fluctuations; the role of government and unions in labor markets; the incidence of taxes; banking structure; the treatment of the indigent—these have been persistent problems of policy and therefore of economic theory. The efforts of economists to understand these problems have led to advances in every branch of theory, including the most abstract branches.

It should not be necessary to retrace in detail the argument of the previous section, which is fully applicable: only general and persistent policy questions are likely to call forth permanent advances in the theory. The unending train of ephemeral or local policy questions is of no more significance for economic theory than the corresponding types of economic developments.

But continuity and pervasiveness of policy are not enough to command influence on theory. We have been regulating railroads for seventy-two years, but neither this instance nor a hundred others of governmental regulations have brought forth even the rudiments of a theory of regulation. Nor has a century of protectionism called forth a substantive theory of the content and level of tariffs. On the other hand, our antitrust policy has been a main source of continued interest in monopoly, and it may be more than coincidence that the interest of English economists in industrial organization has been reviving since a monopoly policy was adopted in England. Like empirical facts, policies must be directly relevant to the main topics of traditional theory if they are to achieve easy influence.

Policies have better press agents than events; so a commanding policy controversy—such as that on full employment in the thirties or the rapid attainment of terrestrial prosperity today—captures the interest of a large number of economists. This tendency is now reinforced by the foundations, which are headed by men who (like all sensible people) find a headline more comprehensible and persuasive than a vague prospectus for a scientific expedition. But important, basic theory is not very responsive to explicit demands. A great many facts will be found or fabricated, and a literature will be amassed and then tidied up, but a basic development awaits a man of vision. He, likely as not, is wholly preoccupied with something which only he will make important. The marginal utility theory owed nothing to immediate policy problems, nor did the marginal productivity theory, the theory of capital, the theory of imperfect competition, game theory, etc. Conversely, all the disinterested and avaricious attention lavished upon business cycles has not yielded a useful short-run theory, and the ratio of cliché to analytical creativity in the literature of economic development is awesome to contemplate.

Often, of course, the explicit policy desires of economists have had a deleterious effect upon the theory itself. The bending of theories to views of tax justice popular with economists as well as the public has been chronic. Ever since Mill recanted the wages-fund doctrine ostensibly for unimportant analytical reasons, much of labor economics has had a flavor easier to explain by economists' policy preferences than elaboration of their general economic analysis. Almost always, I conjecture, the effect of policy views on the general theory (and not merely one man's version) has stemmed from a feeling that the theory must adapt to widely held humanitarian impulses.

Yet economic theory often takes a hostile stance toward policies of great political popularity. For long periods the tradition of economic theory has been opposed to protectionism, minimum wage legislation, price and production controls, and "just" (nonrational) prices. When I say that the policies are hostile to the theory, I mean of course only that the traditional use of the theory led to policy views contrary to those adopted.[5]

This audience does not need to be told that under these conditions the economists have not simply altered the theory to suit the policy. The policy views of the ruling theory have generally not catered to popularity. The general theory still says that these policies are inefficient and hence undesirable. There are many defenses of these policies by economists, but they are almost invariably antitheoretical: the main theoretical results are repudiated as "unrealistic." The chief effect of continued adversity of policy has been resignation, and it is fair to say that indignation and outrage have disappeared from economics. This is no doubt the reason economics is at the moment highly respectable and—if I may transgress on Professor Wilcox' subject—lacking in promise of basic influence on policy in the future. I do not know whether it is an occasion for pride or for regret that the economist is using Marquis of Queensbury arguments in an arena where emotional brass knuckles continue in fashion.

On a broad interpretation, the development of related disciplines is also a part of the environment within which economic theory evolves. The influence upon economics of other disciplines is a large subject on which only a few tentative observations can be offered here.

If one were to seek a major economic theory whose existence depended directly and essentially upon prior work in another field, he would find few likely candidates. Putting aside for a moment the methodological fields of statistics and mathematics, there is in fact no important candidate. A theory of behavior, such as our profit maximizing assumption implies, could have

[5] For some remarks on this point, see "The Politics of Political Economists," *Q.J.E.*, Nov., 1959.

come from psychology, but of course it did not. In fact Smith's professional work on psychology (in the *Theory of Moral Sentiments*) bears scarcely any relationship to his economics, and this tradition of independence of economics from psychology has persisted despite continued efforts from Jennings (1855) to Herbert Simon and George Katona to destroy it. Again, the theory of production could be the economist's summary of the technological sciences, but of course it has never been. Economists have produced whatever laws of production they have.

The methodological disciplines are in a different relationship to economics: obviously we use mathematics and statistics with all our might. The effects of methodology, in this instrumental sense, are pervasive: it affects our choice of problems, our methods of analyzing them, and—since a good theory is at least as reliable as a report of facts—our view of the nature of the economic system. It may well be that a superlative algebraist could make better predictions of the future directions of economic theory than any economist. But it may also be that the algebraist could not: the branches of mathematics seem to have their turns at popularity in economics, and in a longer run may really be servants of the discipline. For surely statistics has had this role: it has had immense influence on the nature of economic investigation but (as yet) almost none on the nature of economic theory. The extensive use of these disciplines in economics, however, still covers too short a period to disentangle relationships from wishes.

The developments in other substantive fields have had a general effect upon what Schumpeter called our "scientific vision." Although we have made frequent verbal use of Darwin's theory, for example, in our economics, we have made almost no substantive use of it, but by analogy it has increased our awareness of the malleability of economic institutions and men (as has Marx's theory of history). The ascendancy of positivism in the natural sciences has had a large effect upon the methodology, and a minor one upon the content, of economics. Most of the effects of these other fields, however, have been subtle and indirect; so it is virtually impossible to point to a single important theory in economics that is plausibly the direct consequence of developments in neighboring fields.

There are many voices that tell us that this is a deplorable state of affairs: that our insularity has kept us from solving many problems (or even seeing them). We are told that political science is obviously important to a study of political economy, that organization and learning theory are essential to (e.g.) a successful theory of oligopoly, that only a sociology of groups can illuminate fully the behavior of labor unions, etc. And how chemistry was revivified by modern physics.

Many of the claims in this direction rest on deep conviction, and the promises of large success support professional position and hopes; so no cavalier comment upon any one would be appropriate. Yet I would emphasize here, as I have with respect to events and policies, the immense degree of autonomy that any successful science must apparently possess. A theory whose continual progress demands the association of very different specialists is outside the historical experience of economics, and—I conjecture—that of other sciences as well.

This autonomy of a science is surely essential to its existence. A discipline which was in intimate and continuous dependence upon the current output of events or other disciplines would simply not be a discipline; it would be a temporary collection of subjects. It could have no specialists—who would be pathetically obsolete in a few years—nor any accumulated theoretical corpus, for its theory would change with each new liaison or external development. It would be, not a science, but an edition of the encyclopedia of knowledge. Why, even its professors could not have tenure!